W9-DCU-765

UNDERSTANDING PARENTING

2nd EDITION

Michael L. Jaffe
Kean College of New Jersey

Allyn and Bacon

Boston London Toronto Sydney Tokyo Singapore

Vice President, Education: Nancy Forsyth
Series Editor: Frances Helland
Editorial Assistant: Cheryl Ouellette
Marketing Manager: Kathy Hunter
Editorial Production Service: Chestnut Hill Enterprises, Inc.
Manufacturing Buyer: Megan Cochran
Cover Administrator: Linda Knowles

Library of Congress Cataloging-in-Publication Data

Jaffe, Michael L.
    Understanding parenting / Michael L. Jaffe.
      p.   cm.
    Includes bibliographical references and index.
    ISBN 0–205–18997–0 (paper)
    1. Parenthood. 2. Parent and child. 3. Family. I. Title.
HQ755.8.J329 1997
649'.1—dc20   96–4185
                                                    CIP

Printed in the United States of America

10 9 8 7 6 5 4 3 2   01 00 99 98

CONTENTS

PREFACE   v

1 PARENTING IN PERSPECTIVE   1

2 THE TRANSITION TO PARENTHOOD   29

3 THE PROCESS OF PARENTING   67

4 MARRIAGE, DIVORCE, AND NEW FAMILY CONFIGURATIONS   99

5 PARENTAL AUTHORITY, CHILD COMPLIANCE, AND PARENTING STYLES   139

6 CHANGING CHILDRENS' BEHAVIOR   169

7 COMMUNICATION AND RELATIONSHIPS IN FAMILIES   201

8 SELF-CONCEPT, SELF-ESTEEM, AND GENDER IDENTITY   235

9 ADJUSTMENT, STRESS, AND COPING   263

10 PARENTING AND ACHIEVEMENT   295

11 PARENTING ADOLESCENTS   327

12 SPECIAL CHILDREN, SPECIAL PARENTS   353

13 FAMILY VIOLENCE, CHILD ABUSE, AND NEGLECT   375

14 SELECTED TOPICS   401

EPILOGUE   419

APPENDIX A   FAMILY SYSTEMS THEORY   421

APPENDIX B   FREUD'S PSYCHODYNAMIC MODEL   425

APPENDIX C   ERIKSON'S PSYCHOSOCIAL THEORY   429

GLOSSARY   432

REFERENCES   434

SUBJECT INDEX   489

AUTHOR INDEX   494

PREFACE

My first goal in writing a second edition of *Understanding Parenting* is to give students, especially those who are not parents, a real sense of what parenting is like. I know of no responsibility in life that is more "awesome" than bringing a new being into this world and raising that being to be a decent, competent, loving individual. What other role requires such commitment, sacrifice, and emotional vulnerability?

A second goal in writing this book is to offer students a rigorous, stimulating, and comprehensive overview of the parenting process. Parents, prospective parents, and those who work with families require and deserve the best information about child rearing that is currently available.

In this thoroughly reorganized and updated version of *Understanding Parenting*, I attempt to provide a blend of parenting research, theory, and practical information that is accessible to students at all levels of higher education. Rigor and accessibility are not incompatible. Readers should not have difficulty connecting much of what they are reading in this book to what they already know about families from their own life experiences. Having a sense of humor is an essential factor in maintaining parental sanity. Thus, when appropriate, I like to acknowledge the lighter side of family dynamics.

The list of new topics is extensive, reflecting the everchanging nature of the modern family and new perspectives in parenting theory and research. New topics include poverty and parenting, why study parenting, delayed first-time child rearing, adoption, foster families, parental competence, grandparenting,

children of gay and lesbian parents, new reproductive technologies, and parenting biracial children. Cultural perspectives and gender issues in parenting are discussed throughout this text, I hope in a sensitive yet forthright manner.

Some of the developmental research and theory presented in the first edition has been deleted because it can easily be found in child psychology textbooks. Three influential theories with important implications for parenting (family systems, and the developmental theories of Sigmund Freud and Erik Erikson) are presented in the appendixes, to be assigned at the instructor's discretion. Four selected topics (parent training, dual-career parenting, day-care programs, and children in self-care) that were included in the first chapter of the earlier edition have been updated and now comprise the final chapter.

Special topics are highlighted as Spotlights, two or more of which appear in most chapters. Study questions precede many sections of text. Their function is to help students anticipate and think about the key points being made. Each chapter ends with a glossary and a set of thought questions that take the student a little further into the chapter material. Throughout the second half of the book, we gain access to the everyday realities of the parenting process through the eyes of "Mark's Mom," a single mother who kept a journal of her parenting experiences while a student in my undergraduate parenting course. Her gradual "enlightenment" regarding her desire to parent thoughtfully and sensitively may very well inspire other students to do the same.

In addition to reviewing the very extensive parenting literature, I include in this text clinical material from my own experiences in private practice as a family therapist specializing in parenting-related problems. Working with and studying distressed families helps us understand the complexities and vulnerabilities of the family system. Many of the child-rearing problems and issues discussed in this text are gleaned from the parenting workshops I have had the pleasure of conducting over the past 20 years. Raising two sons has provided my wife and me with a realistic view of the ups and downs of parenting. For the second edition of this book, I gatefully acknowledge the support of Frances Helland, my editor at Allyn and Bacon, and the following colleagues who thoughtfully reviewed the manuscript: Virginia Erion, Central Washington University; Beulah Hirschlein, Oklahoma State University; and Roger Wise, Utah Valley State College.

PLAN OF THIS BOOK

Chapter 1, Parenting in Perspective, provides an overview of the parenting process: the decision to parent, reasons for having or not having children, four goals of parenting, and a brief history of childhood. The serious problems facing many children in today's world are then acknowledged. To help students appreciate the crucial role that research plays in the study of parenting, two interesting research studies are analyzed. Chapter 2, The Transition to Parenthood, describes what it is like to become a parent and provides useful information about pregnancy, birth, parent-infant bonding, and the incredible life changes that occur whenever a family acquires a new member.

Chapter 3, The Process of Parenting, explores the many personal qualities and abilities that comprise competent parenting. In this chapter, we pursue the question, why are some parents more effective than others? Chapter 4, Marriage, Divorce, and New Family Configurations, reviews the possible effects of parental conflict, separation, and divorce on children. This chapter also examines several nontraditional family configurations, including single mothering and fathering, stepparenting, foster parenting, and grandparenting.

Chapters 5, 6, and 7 provide a detailed examination of discipline, communication, and relationships in families. Taken together, the three chapters provide a broad context for understanding the relationship between parental authority, parenting styles, and children's compliance or lack thereof. Chapter 8 examines parental influences on children's self-concept, self-esteem, and gender identity. Chapter 9 explores children's emotional development in families, emphasizing the role of stress and coping resources. Chapter 10 discusses home and family factors in the development of competence and achievement motivation. Chapter 11 addresses the special pleasures and problems of parenting adolescents. Chapter 12 discusses parenting children with special needs. Chapter 13 considers the effects on children of family violence, child abuse, and neglect. Chapter 14 contains in-depth treatment of four selected topics: parent training, dual-career parenting, day care, and children in self-care. The epilogue reviews the key points made in this text.

CHAPTER

1

PARENTING IN PERSPECTIVE

OBJECTIVES 2
Meeting Mark's Mom 2
THE DECISION TO PARENT 2
FAMILY LIFE: CONTENTMENT AND CHAOS 3
WHY HAVE CHILDREN? 4
All Kinds of Reasons for Having Children 6
Box 1-1 Parental Rights, Parental Responsibilities 6
FOUR GOALS OF PARENTING 8
Box 1-2 Why Do Men Become Fathers? 9
GOAL #1—GOOD BEHAVIOR 10
GOAL #2—COMPETENCE 10
GOAL #3—GOOD PARENT-CHILD RELATIONSHIPS 11
GOAL #4—SELF-ESTEEM AND SELF-CONFIDENCE 11
THE HISTORY OF CHILDHOOD 11
CHILDREN IN TODAY'S WORLD 15
Spotlight: Poverty and Parenting 17
RESEARCH ON PARENTING 18
Why Study Parenting? 18
Parenting Research 19
Research Example 1 20
Research Example 2 21
WHO INFLUENCES WHOM IN FAMILIES? 23
Box 1-3 Parenting Across Cultures 24
Combined Influences 25
SUMMARY 27
GLOSSARY 27
THOUGHT QUESTIONS 28
RESOURCES 28

OBJECTIVES

After studying Chapter 1, students should be able to:

1. Explain what is meant by the "fulfillment-struggle" polarity of parenting
2. Describe at least five reasons for having children
3. Describe the four goals of parenting and the rationale for each one
4. Describe how families have become more child-centered over the past few centuries
5. List five current problems facing large numbers of children and adolescents in the United States
6. Describe how we benefit from the study of the parenting process
7. Describe how researchers study the parenting process using objective methods of observation
8. Distinguish unidirectional from bidirectional models of family influence

Meeting Mark's Mom

"Closing in on the next due date for his book report, I could feel the tension mounting. My mood was 'edgy' and demanding—bad start. When I realized I was cursing under my breath, I decided it was high time to change the course of things. So we worked at it as much as we could with the time that was left. This new book was less comprehensible to him. Two days after it was due, he's still not finished reading it.

"I'm taking a more laid-back approach to Mark and, also, his room. At this point, there are clothes, refuse, toys, blankets, drawings, everywhere. We can't move through the room without stepping on something. I've told him if he doesn't find the dirty clothes for me they won't get done with the laundry. Do you think it's possible to be a discouraged parent? I feel like we're going

nowhere and I want to give up! I know it won't do anyone any good if I do, though. I've thought about your stance of no punishment . . . how does one work up the courage and where does one begin?" (Mark's mother).

Throughout this text, we will have several opportunities to follow the progress of Mark and his mother, a single woman attending my undergraduate parenting class. This particular journal entry captures the occasional frustration, confusion, and discouragement of parenting.

THE DECISION TO PARENT

When deciding whether to have children, we may envision the joyful, tender moments that we associate with parenting. And such moments are plentiful. However, most parents discover that child rearing is more difficult than they anticipated. One father of three reported that parenting "changed our lives in a lot of ways. We don't have a lot of freedom; we don't have much time for each other. Every free minute we have, somebody needs something." But he added, "When they smile, it makes it all worthwhile."

Ideally, the decision to become a parent should be based on realistic expectations about living with children, the burdens of providing child care, and our own willingness and ability to place someone else's needs before our own. Deciding whether or not to parent raises many fascinating questions. Why have children in the first place? Will I be a good parent? In what ways will becoming a parent change my life? How will it affect my relationship with my partner? What will my children be like?

Upon further reflection, additional considerations arise. What are the financial implications of raising children? Who will care for my children during their infancy and toddlerhood? How will I discipline them? Though we may decide to have children to enrich our own lives, these questions remind us of the profound responsibilities associated with bringing a child into the world. The above questions suggest a polarity: the potential fulfillment of parenting versus the daily challenge (and occasional struggle) to do it well.

FAMILY LIFE: CONTENTMENT AND CHAOS

Informal polls clarify this polarity. A parent survey conducted by the magazine *Better Homes and Gardens* (October, 1986; results summarized by Collins, 1986a) elicited responses from 30,000 readers (Note: This was not a scientific survey, and the opinions expressed, although interesting, should not be considered representative of parents in general.) A majority reported believing that, compared to their own parents, they are better parents, they spank their children less, and they express more affection. In describing their family life, 70 percent depicted it as loving, 65 percent said it is fun, and only 4 percent characterized it as hostile.

Fifty-one percent of the respondents depicted family life as "chaotic," which the researchers did not interpret negatively. Sixty-one percent of the parents reported believing that communication among family members is better and more open today and 88 percent said they feel that they are good parents. Most significantly, 90 percent said they believed that having children is worth all the sacrifices, and 80 percent reported that, if they could start the parenting process over, they would have the same number of children.

On the other side of the polarity, 75 percent of respondents claimed that it is much harder to parent today than in the past, and 51 percent reported that they sometimes feel overwhelmed by their responsibilities. The

TABLE 1.1   Common Concerns of Parents

Financial problems, including the cost of raising children

Feeling overwhelmed by responsibilities

Child disobedience and disciplining children

Sibling rivalry and conflict

Crime and other threats to children's safety

Balancing employment with home life

Finding quality day care

Not enough time to spend with children

Division of labor with partner

most frequently cited problem was financial, even in middle-class families. Almost half reported having difficulty balancing work with home responsibilities. A third reported difficulties in disciplining their children. Parents complained about disobedience and were disturbed by conflicts between their children. Though most respondents felt that they were good parents, almost three-quarters were critical of *other* parents for not spending enough time with their children!

Two more recent studies, conducted and published in the early 1990s, reveal a similar discrepancy between how parents view their own parenting and how they perceive other families. The National Opinion Research Center of the University of Chicago (1991) conducted face-to-face interviews with 1400 adults, including parents and non-parents. The Princeton Survey Research Associates (1991) conducted a phone study of 1700 parents and 900 children ages 10 to 17 years. While 76 percent of adults responded that parents often do not know where their children are, 88 percent of the parents said they did know where their own children were all or most of the time. They also claimed that they knew what their children were doing when the children were away from home.

Both surveys reported that parents are very concerned about money and crime. In one out of ten families, parents worry "a lot" that their children will be shot. Sixty percent of Hispanic (Latino) parents, 23 percent of African-American parents, and 6 percent of white parents expressed this fear. About 60 percent of the parents wished they could spend more time with their children. Their children contracting AIDS was a major concern of Hispanic and African-American respondents.

These findings reinforce one of the themes of this textbook: parenting can be both fulfilling and overwhelming, sometimes on the same day! The more realistic our expectations about children and ourselves and the more informed we are about child development and the parenting process, the more likely that we will fall closer to the fulfillment end of the continuum.

In this chapter, we examine good and not so good reasons for having children. We consider parenting goals that can provide direc-

tion to parents regarding how they want their children to "turn out." We review the history of childhood and some of the serious problems facing children and adolescents today. Finally, we will examine the nature of parenting research and the multifaceted nature of the parenting process.

WHY HAVE CHILDREN?

One of the ironies of human reproduction is that conceiving and bearing children need not be planned. A mother of a 6-year-old girl disclosed, "We didn't plan on having a baby, but we didn't practice any birth control. We just let nature take its course." Planned or not, society considers the parenting role to be normal behavior for adults, especially for women. About half of the 68 million families in the United States have children under the age of 18 (U.S. Census Bureau, 1994). Many people view the decision to not have children as unnatural, selfish, or even neurotic—it violates the "motherhood mandate" (Russo, 1979).

There are at least three organizations of childless adults, the Childfree Network, Childless by Choice, and No Kidding. They are not against people having children; rather, they want their right to not have children to be respected. They do not want to have to defend their decision (Lafayette, 1995). A forty-one-year-old woman who belongs to the Childfree Network put it this way, "It's unspoken, but if you don't have children, you are kind of stigmatized. I don't know of anything that gets the same reaction as when I say I don't have kids" (quoted by Nemy, 1995). Even having one child raises eyebrows. Some people believe that childfree women either do not like children or are afraid of them. However, women and men who are childfree by choice often work with and enjoy the company of children, for example, as teachers or child care workers (Schwartz, 1995b).

Justin Jaffe

Childfree couples typically report greater marital satisfaction than those with children, perhaps because couples who are unhappily married often decide to stay together for the sake of their children. It is possible that the presence of children intensifies either marital happiness or marital dissatisfaction. According to psychologist Jay Belsky, some couples decide to not have children because "they strongly value their marital relationship and their independent lifestyle, and are concerned about the effects of children on that relationship and lifestyle" (quoted by Kutner, 1991).

Other adults cite financial considerations and personal and social restrictions as deterrents to having children (Campbell, Townes, & Beach, 1982; Gerson, Berman, & Morris, 1991). It is estimated that it will cost about $137,000 to raise a child born in 1990 to the age of 18 years and an additional $120,000 to cover the cost of a private college education (Family Economics Research Group, U.S. Dept. of Agriculture). But the frustrations of parenting are not primarily economic. We expect parents to sacrifice their own needs and comforts when they conflict with those of their children.

Potential stresses of parenthood include the coordination of infant and child care, the division of household labor between parents, handling misbehavior, and meeting the demands of employment (Ventura, 1987). Most adults receive almost no preparation for the daily challenges of living with children. Nevertheless, when children misbehave, their parents are held responsible. Parents are legally responsible for their children's conduct until children reach the age of 18 years. Some communities fine parents or send them to parenting classes when their children violate community laws and standards (Egan, 1995). Parents of an out-of-control Michigan teenager were convicted by a jury of failing to exercise "reasonable parental control" (Meredith, 1996).

Despite high birth rates, many adults are cautious about bringing children into this complex and imperiled world. People are remaining single for longer periods, and an increasing number of single adults report that they expect to remain childfree (Lafayette, 1995). An organization known as NON (National Organization of Nonparents) maintains that parenthood is glamorized and commercialized in our culture. Divorce rates intimidate young couples engaged in family planning as marriage comes to be seen as a less-than-permanent arrangement (Neal, Groat, & Wicks, 1989).

Single women who prefer to remain childfree say they anticipate greater personal and financial freedom, more satisfying marriages, and fewer obstacles in pursuing careers (Houseknecht, 1979). Women who are voluntarily childfree, whether single or married, "recognize fewer benefits and greater costs in having children than do similarly educated women who want to become parents or are already mothers" (Callan, 1986, p. 269). A few have had unhappy childhoods or come from troubled families and do not want to risk repeating that painful experience (Kutner, 1991).

Based on their study of 96 expectant and non-parent couples, Cowan and Cowan (1992) identified four patterns of decision-making regarding having children. The *planners* (about half of their study sample) made a deliberate decision to have or to not have children. *Acceptance-of-fate couples*, about 14 percent of their sample, were pleasantly surprised by their pregnancies and readily accepted their fate. *Ambivalent couples* expressed positive and negative feelings about parenthood. *Yes-No couples* expressed strong, unresolved conflict about family life. Given that this latter group contained lots of men who were very reluctant to have children, it is not surprising that of the four groups, the Yes-No couples showed the most dramatic drop in marital satisfaction following the birth of their child. Sadly, many of these marriages did not last very long.

B o x   1 - 1

Parental Rights, Parental Responsibilities

What does it take to be a responsible parent in the eyes of society? In the mid 1990s, there is heated debate about two apparently contradictory legislative trends—parents' rights to raise their children as they see fit and parental responsibility for their children's conduct. Larger issues include who is responsible for raising children and whether children are being adequately socialized within their families (Applebome, 1996; Berger, 1996).

Half of the states in the United States have laws that make parents liable for their children's antisocial behavior. Parents in a town in Oregon were cited in Municipal Court because their children were caught smoking or shoplifting (Egan, 1995). Two parents in Michigan were prosecuted, convicted, and fined for not exercising "reasonable parental control" over their teenaged son (Meredith, 1996). On the other hand, we hear about parents who have run-ins with the law because they discipline their children too harshly (Berger, 1996).

Since the middle of this century, non-family institutions such as schools, religious institutions, and government have been playing an increasing role in family life. Those who advocate sex education in the schools, curfew laws for adolescents, and computer chips in TV sets to censor violent programming argue that non-family social institutions need to play an even greater role in regulating children's behavior. The implication is that parents are not getting the job done. At the same time, conservative groups promote parental rights laws that would make it harder for municipalities to pass laws that restrict parents' authority in areas such as counseling, discipline, and sex education. Daniel Katz, counsel for the American Civil Liberties Union, notes that if both types of laws are enacted, parental rights laws could be used to overturn parental responsibility laws (Applebome, 1996).

All Kinds of Reasons for Having Children

Study Question   *What would be your reasons for deciding to have or to not have children? Try to list at least three reasons for and against your having children.*

The traditional reason for bearing children (and still the case in many developing countries) is *labor*. Parents viewed having children as a necessity—as "helping hands" for the family's economic benefit. Since the welcome introduction of child labor laws early in this century, the major economic benefit of having

children has been as a tax deduction. It is hard enough to get today's children to wash the dishes or clean their rooms, let alone plow the fields or plant the crops. Our ancestors also counted on their children to provide *financial security* and care in old age. Unfortunately, this need still exists today for many of our older citizens. Some of our ancestors depended on their children to *pass on the family name*. (A mother being interviewed by one of my students said that she wanted to have children "to gain a sense of my own mortality. I wanted a part of me to go on").

Some people enjoy *exercising authority*. Since other adults may resist "being pushed around," these individuals may decide to have children. Although I am exaggerating the point, exercising authority is a motive that can be satisfied in parenting. Unfortunately, power is a motive that is often abused, most sadly at the expense of a dependent child.

Many adults seek to *gain prestige* from the accomplishments of their children. This may not always be to a child's advantage, particularly when parents pressure their children to perform at unrealistically high standards. If you attend competitive athletic events and listen to some of the more vocal parents, you know what I mean. There is nothing wrong with being proud of our children's achievements, but when we derive satisfaction from comparing favorably our children to other children, we ignore what is special about them in their own right.

A fifth possible reason for having children (if you're counting), is to *please someone else*—perhaps one's partner or one's own parents. Parents put pressure on their adult children (particularly daughters) to reproduce. Our parents, when they subtly hint about the patter of little feet, are not just acting as agents of society. They want their grandchildren. Without reproduction, society dwindles into oblivion. Many religions, for similar reasons, encourage us to "be fruitful and multiply." Having children to accommodate other people's wishes is not a sign of maturity or independence.

A variation on this theme is that *childbearing is women's destiny*. Each culture has its own myths and ideology concerning motherhood. Women cannot be completely fulfilled unless they bear and raise a child. Women who cannot successfully juggle the roles of housewife, homemaker, mother, and employee are maladjusted. Good mothers always are patient, nurturing, self-sacrificing, and willing to devote their lives to their children. Mothers are responsible for how their children turn out (Hoffnung, 1989). Interestingly, no equivalent claims are made about men.

Some adults who have had unhappy childhoods view having children as an *opportunity to compensate* for their own misfortune. These parents may "live through their children." Adults who have suffered material deprivations may wish for their children a life that is better than theirs. There are adults who view child rearing as a *lifelong project*, with unlimited opportunities for creative expression. These parents enjoy planning, arranging, and designing their children's futures (Campbell, Townes, & Beach, 1982). They have a clear image of how they want their child to be. They invest their child-rearing years with strategies designed to fulfill their visions. For most parents, child rearing is a lifelong project, but much of it does not go according to plan. As we will see in Chapter 5, unforeseeable events can play a significant role in the shaping of children's character.

A seventh reason for having children (are the reasons improving?) is *personal growth*. Before I had young children, I could stay out as late as I wanted and then sleep until 10

TABLE 1.2 All Kinds of Reasons for Having Children

Their ability to provide assistance

Financial security in old age

Exercising authority

Gain prestige from their accomplishments

To please someone else, for example, one's own parents

Childbearing is a woman's destiny

Opportunity to compensate for parent's sad childhood

As a lifelong project

Personal growth

Like children

To enjoy raising them

a.m. or later the next morning. I could go to the movies on the spur of the moment and travel to distant lands unencumbered by diapers and bottles (I hope this doesn't sound too nostalgic). As a parent of the male persuasion, I had a lot to learn about putting another person's needs before my own. (Many of us get a little bit of practice doing this in close relationships before we have children.)

Imagine waking up at 4 a.m. on a cold, wintry morning, to the fervent cries of your hungry little angel. Imagine stumbling downstairs to the refrigerator, searching for the milk, and pouring it through a tiny opening without spilling any (at 4 a.m.). Imagine warming the milk (without melting the bottle) and feeding the baby, who signals its gratitude by belching and immediately falling back to sleep. Imagine changing the baby's splendidly soiled diaper and then stumbling back to bed. Out of such experiences does personal growth arise. The transition to parenthood brings unlimited opportunities to grow, to expand, and to fulfill our potential as complete, nurturing, caring individuals.

Perhaps the most common reason parents give for having children is *"because I like children."* Companionship is a very sensible reason for having children. Children are great companions—warm, affectionate, funny. I have spent some of my best moments in their company, driving them to nursery school or to visit a college, waiting with them at bus stops or train stations, riding bicycles, reading, or singing with them. They are so safe to be with and very "in the moment." Great conversation, strange jokes, astute observations, intense sadness, warm hugs—companionship.

Perhaps the best reason for having children is to enjoy raising them. It is sad that so many parents forget this reason. Many come to see parenting as a struggle, as one frustration after another (see "Meeting Mark's Mom" at the beginning of this chapter). And sometimes they blame the child! Children cannot help

being children. If we can't appreciate their "perfection," that's not their problem. Or it shouldn't be. I am not saying that child rearing is easy. That would be absurd. But the challenge of raising children can become an enormous source of fulfillment if we understand, accept, and enjoy them as they are and as they change.

FOUR GOALS OF PARENTING

Study Question *If you were a parent, what values or priorities would guide your child-rearing strategies?*

All societies hold parents responsible for raising their children. Recent debates in the political arena about "family values" have given rise to the notion that out-of-control families are largely responsible for all of the problems of young people today (Shucksmith, Hendry, & Glendinning, 1995). Parents are accountable for their children's health, safety, and socialization until the time that young people can live without adult supervision and support. However, parents compete with other potentially powerful sources of influence, including their children's friends, siblings, TV, and all of the temptations of modern youth culture.

Parenting does not occur in a vacuum. Most parents are preoccupied with the stresses and strains of their own hectic lives. Unfortunately, adults are vulnerable to multiple stressors, including job dissatisfaction, illness, marital conflict, drug problems, and financial pressures. The psychological effects of these stressors often spill over into parenting (Larson & Richards, 1994). Amidst the dramas of their daily lives, some parents lose direction. Many are relieved just to make it through another day. Parents who have one bad day after another, and who find that they

B o x   1 - 2

Why Do Men Become Fathers?

Mackey, White, and Day (1992) asked 90 men who were students at a community college to indicate the order of importance of 10 reasons for becoming a father. They also asked 136 women students to predict the men's answers. The men indicated that they believe that men in the United States become fathers for emotional reasons based on psychological and social rewards. The reasons that men most agreed with included: (1) children bring love and emotional satisfaction, (2) children carry on one's name or bloodline, and (3) children are fun. Most men downplayed economic advantages and social expectations. Interestingly, the women accurately predicted the men's responses.

Weiss (1990) summarized the "meaning" of fatherhood as follows:

1. Fatherhood helps men make sense of their lives.
2. Fatherhood gives additional meaning to marriage.
3. Fatherhood adds new linkages between parents, grandparents, and siblings (who become aunts and uncles).
4. Fatherhood changes men's friendships.
5. Fatherhood turns men into "family men," more stable and with more responsibilities and burdens (pp. 166–168).

are not enjoying raising their children, begin to wonder why they had children in the first place (and then feel guilty for having such selfish thoughts).

To parent effectively, we need considerable support, but we also need direction. We need to know what we're doing, but first we have to decide where we want to go. Many parents eagerly seek child-rearing techniques and strategies that they believe will help their children become well-behaved and self-sufficient. However, before we can make decisions about methods of child rearing, we have to be clear about our priorities. What types of outcomes are we seeking?

This book suggests four parenting goals. They are not the only parenting goals one could propose. LeVine (1974) studied child-rearing practices across cultures. He concluded that parents in all cultures share the following three goals: (1) physical survival, (2) teaching the child economic self-sufficiency, and (3) helping children fulfill their potential

to be fully functioning human beings. Maccoby (1992) defines "adequate functioning" as consisting of the habits, skills, values, and motives that allow individuals to (1) avoid acting in ways that disrupt or annoy other people, (2) support themselves and their families, (3) form and maintain close relationships, and (4) be able to rear their children. A father of three young children expressed his parenting goals this way: "I want my kids to be self-sufficient, independent, free-thinking people with a lot of self-esteem and empathy for other people. I want them to be good and decent human beings."

The following goals are not based upon any particular theoretical model. They are meant to focus our attention on important and desirable outcomes of parenting. They probably reflect a middle-class bias. Most studies in the child development literature have investigated white, middle-class children. As will be discussed in Chapter 5, parents in different socioeconomic classes, ethnic groups, and cultures have somewhat different goals and different approaches to child rearing (Harkness, 1992; Maccoby, 1980). What we consider to be a favorable outcome of parenting must take into account the environment in which the child will eventually function (Harrison, Wilson, Pine, Chan, & Buriel, 1990). The parenting styles advocated in this text are consistent with and support the following parenting goals.

Goal #1—Good Behavior

Parents of well-behaved children enjoy caregiving more than do parents of poorly-behaved children (Kochanska, Kuczynski, & Radke-Yarrow, 1989). Child rearing is more satisfying when children cooperate with their parents and siblings instead of behaving defiantly. Hence, it is no surprise that most parents indicate that good behavior is a high priority. But how do we define good behavior? Just as there is no one correct way to raise children, there is no agreed upon set of rules about how children should act. It is not uncommon for mothers and fathers to disagree about what constitutes appropriate behavior. They might disagree about their children's bedtime, snacking, or choice of college. Though children can learn to accommodate the different rules or standards of each parent, it is preferable for the parents to arrive at one set of standards that is agreeable to both. Consistency in parental standards reduces children's confusion about what is expected of them.

In defining good behavior, it is tempting to cite the Boy or Girl Scout pledge and suggest that children should be helpful, friendly, courteous, kind, reverent, and so on. However, parents must decide for themselves what constitutes good behavior for their child. Keep in mind that children benefit when they can please other people too, not just their family members. It is not to a child's advantage to be

accepted at home but be perceived as obnoxious by a friend's parents or the kids in the schoolyard. Once parents decide what personal qualities they value, they can act in ways that foster those qualities in their children.

Goal #2—Competence

Parents are expected to teach their children useful behavior, that is, behavior that accomplishes something of value. Infants cannot be expected to solve any but the simplest problems. Toddlers are capable of exercising a wide range of self-help and other useful skills, such as cleaning, dressing, and toileting themselves. One of the major accomplishments of childhood is mastering the physical environment. This often takes the form of problem-solving skills that allow a child to identify a problem, generate a possible solution, and test it. If their attempt fails, competent children have learned to persist until they succeed.

Parents can contribute extensively to their children's cognitive development. They evaluate their children's intellectual skills as reflected in their record of academic achievement. Most parents highly value achievement in school and convey to their children that they take their schoolwork very seriously. Self-reliance is an important component of competence. Young children usually are closely supervised by parents and teachers. As they develop, they become more independent in their judgments, decisions, and actions. Adolescents are better at delaying gratification than younger children. They have more adult-like intellectual abilities and prefer to handle their problems themselves rather than seek assistance. Again, there is much that parents can do to promote good judgment, achievement, and independence in their children. Thus, our second parenting goal is competence, comprising cognitive and intellectual abilities, achievement motivation, and self-reliance.

Goal #3—Good Parent-Child Relationships

We inhabit a world of people. Close relationships provide us with much of the satisfaction that life has to offer. One of the challenges of parenting is teaching children to get along with each other and with adults. This is particularly challenging because children are self-centered. Occasionally, children are selfish, impulsive, insensitive, and demanding. These qualities set the stage for parent-child conflict. Good parental judgment often stands in opposition to a child's demands for immediate gratification.

The family is a "training ground" for having relationships. What children learn about relationships from their family life will be reflected in their outside relationships. Children observe their parents and siblings closely, and learn. The relationship skills or deficits that result may influence their relationships during adolescence and adulthood. Of the dozens of factors that affect a child's development and personality, *the quality of moment-to-moment parent-child interactions stands out as potentially the most important.*

Thus, we socialize our children within the context of our relationship with them. The parent-child relationship, cultivated throughout childhood, becomes the major source of our influence with our children when they become adolescents. A warm, supportive, parent-child relationship is our third parenting goal.

Goal #4—Self-Esteem and Self-Confidence

To some observers, such as the late psychologist Carl Rogers (1961), the nucleus of personality is self-esteem, that is, how we evaluate and feel about ourselves. People who don't like themselves are prone to anxiety, depression, and self-destructive behavior pat-

TABLE 1.3 Four Goals of Parenting

Good behavior
Competence and achievement
Good parent-child relationships
Positive self-esteem and self-confidence

terns. People who like and accept themselves usually have more satisfying and productive lives and better relationships.

The ability to accept and like ourselves depends partly on how we interpret the feedback we get from other people early in life, especially our caregivers. It also derives from how we interpret our ongoing record of successes and failures, especially in domains of our lives that we consider important, for example, relationships and academics (Harter, 1987). Because self-esteem and self-confidence play such a central role in personality, we include them as our fourth parenting goal.

Our four parenting goals are (1) good behavior, (2) competence, (3) good relationships, and (4) self-esteem and self-confidence. When interacting with their children, parents can make all four goals priorities. It does not make sense, for example, to raise children to be obedient at the expense of having low self-esteem. Why pressure our children to achieve in school at the cost of a poor parent-child relationship? Throughout this text, we will examine ways of spending time with children and ways of raising them that are consistent with these four parenting goals.

THE HISTORY OF CHILDHOOD

Study Question *How has the concept of childhood changed over the ages?*

Our contemporary view of children and childhood is strikingly different from that held by our ancestors (Cleverley & Phillips, 1986) and somewhat different from that held by people in many non-Western societies (Ambert, 1994). Families in most industrialized societies view children as innocent, vulnerable, young beings requiring loving care and protection. Children have "emotional value" for their parents rather than, as in the past, a bond based on family honor, heritage, parental authority, or religious affiliation (Ambert, 1994).

A review of the history of childhood reveals that ignorance about children and prevailing economic conditions were key factors influencing their status in society. Archeological evidence suggests, for example, that **infanticide** (killing infants or allowing them to die) and ritual slayings of children were common in ancient, crowded Carthage. Child sacrifice controlled population growth and allowed families to maintain their fortunes over generations. It is estimated that about 20,000 children were sacrificed between 800 B.C. and 146 B.C., when Roman invaders destroyed Carthage (Browne, 1987).

Greek philosophers advocated that children be raised to be responsible and productive citizens and that children with special talents be groomed for public service. Plato suggested separating young children from their parents and having them be raised instead by the state. Presumably, these children would be free of the corruption that plagued Greek government. Aristotle contended that only those children with special abilities should be raised to become leaders. Aristotle also was one of the first to suggest that parents adjust their childrearing strategies to accommodate children's individual natures.

Advantaged children in ancient Rome fared well. Mother-infant bonding at birth was the norm. Boys and girls played with toys and learned how to read and write, although only boys attended school. Roman views of child-hood and family apparently resembled those of modern times and were relatively enlightened compared to those that ensued during the Middle Ages (Luepnitz, 1988).

Scholars disagree about how ancestral children were viewed and treated by their parents. Based on historical records and paintings, French historian Phillipe Aries (1962) concluded that before the 17th century, childhood was not recognized as a separate stage of life. According to Aries, children were seen as smaller and weaker versions of adults, but not as intelligent. Aries concluded that parents were not very attached to their children and often treated them harshly. David Elkind (1988), however, identified references to children's distinctive nature in the Bible and in the works of Greek and Roman philosophers. Linda Pollack (1983), based on her analysis of literature and personal memoirs of historical figures, also concluded that throughout history, children have been perceived by their parents as being different from adults. According to Pollack, most parents loved their children, provided appropriate care and protection, and viewed child rearing as a great responsibility. Given the limited evidence available, it is hard to tell whether children of the past were treated as humanely as most children are today.

As important to parents as survival in this world was salvation in the next. Calvinist and Puritan parents believed that children are inherently sinful. Faith in God and firm discipline were considered to be necessary for healthy development (Kagan, 1978). "Good habits were developed under a strict regime of controlled sleeping, fasting between meals, whispered requests for food at the table, regular family prayers, and the judicious application of corporal punishment" (Cleverley & Phillips, 1986, p. 29).

Today, many parents view independence and assertiveness as desirable personality

S p o t l i g h t

Poverty and Parenting

Study Question   How does economic hardship hinder parents' ability to provide care to their children?

The rich get richer and the poor have children. Unfortunately, this tired cliché has a grain of truth. The economic gap between poor and affluent families continues to increase (Holmes, 1996). About twenty-two percent of children in the United States grow up in poverty (U.S. Bureau of the Census, 1993), about twice the number reported in other industrialized nations. A disproportionate number of these children are African-American and Hispanic. Most live in single-parent households led by unemployed mothers (Garbarino & Kostelny, 1993). Homeless families represent a growing segment of the homeless population (Hausman & Hammen, 1993). Poor children need their fathers the most but usually have the least contact with them (Mosley & Thomson, 1995). Enduring economic hardship during childhood foretells difficult peer relationships, problems in school, and low self-esteem, especially for boys (Bolger, Patterson, & Thompson, 1995; Brooks-Gunn, Klebanov, & Duncan, 1996). These negative outcomes usually persist into adolescence and adulthood.

Poverty and deprivation make parenting more difficult (Brody, Stoneman, Flor, McCrary, Hastings, & Conyers, 1994; Duncan, Brooks-Gunn, & Klebanov, 1994; Elder, Conger, Foster, & Ardelt, 1992; Garbarino & Kostelny, 1993). Parents adapt to hostile environments and deprivation but sometimes in ways that are detrimental to their children. They are forced to keep their children at home because the streets are too dangerous. Even at home, young children are not allowed to play on the floor because they might be bitten by rats. Dubrow and Garbarino (1989) interviewed ten mothers who live in a high-rise public housing development about the dangers that their children face. The mothers agreed that shooting was the most serious threat. All their children had experienced first-hand encounters with shooting by the time they were 5 years old. Most mothers coped by trying to stay physically close to their children. Parents manifested their fear of crime by becoming very restrictive and punitive when disciplining their children. Their children, in turn, became aggressive, antisocial, and underachieving.

Poverty affects children indirectly, mainly by stressing and distracting parents (Huston, McLoyd, & Garcia Coll, 1994; McLoyd, 1990). Poor parents lack the educational, emotional, and economic resources needed to parent well. They struggle against all odds to provide consistent daily care, nurturance, and a stable family environment (Halpern, 1990). Economic strain undermines parental involvement in children's lives (Simons, Lorenz, Conger, & Wu, 1992). Depressed and demoralized parents often resort to harsh, overly controlling measures (Conger, Conger, Elder, Lorenz, Simons, & Whitbeck, 1993; Dodge, Pettit, & Bates, 1994; Elder, Eccles, Ardelt, & Lord, 1995; Hashima & Amato, 1994).

Financial pressure also leads to parents' cutting back expenditures for food and medical services, increased indebtedness, and feelings of anger. Parents who are breadwinners become more abrasive, irritable, and hostile. When parents reach their "stress-absorption capacity," marital harmony deteriorates and children's development suffers (Conger, et al., 1993). "Reservoirs of resilience become depleted, infant mortality rates soar, day-to-day care breaks down, and rates of exploitation and victimization increase. Moral development itself may be compromised" (Garbarino & Kostelny, 1993, p. 215).

out of school each year. One-third to one-half of preschool children are not properly immunized against childhood diseases. Qualities that children need to be successful in school, including confidence, curiosity, cooperation, and self-control, are lacking in large numbers of children (Mitchell-Meadows, 1992).

All is not well as far as the treatment of children is concerned. This is especially true of disadvantaged children living in the inner cities where homicide, crime, drug addiction, AIDS, welfare dependency, bitterness, and resentment toward society exist at epidemic proportions. Ninety-one percent of the children born with AIDS in New York City are African-American or Hispanic. Three times as many African-Americans as whites live below the poverty level (Bernstein, 1988). Asian-American, Mexican-American, and American-Indian children disproportionately face the obstacles of poverty and discrimination.

Few if any of these problems have simple solutions. However, cost-effective prevention and treatment programs exist (Dryfoos, 1990; Kazdin, 1993). If these programs were widely available they could save thousands of lives and billions of dollars. A one-dollar investment in prenatal care saves three dollars in short-term hospital costs. One dollar spent on childhood immunizations saves ten dollars in later medical costs. One dollar spent on preschool education saves six dollars in later social remediation. Parent training programs (discussed in chapter 14) can lead to dramatic improvements in child care and lessen the likelihood of abuse and neglect. Most of the problems cited above are preventable but, unfortunately, are getting worse.

RESEARCH ON PARENTING

Why Study Parenting?

No two families are alike and no two parents raise their children in exactly the same way (Fine, 1993). The study of the parenting process reveals remarkable diversity in caregiving among different ethnic and cultural groups (Bornstein, 1991). Although such differences are fascinating, we study parenting mainly because we are interested in and concerned about, children's development. We are particularly curious about, the relationship between how we raise and educate children and how they "turn out."

Our ancestors speculated about the origins of children's character, wondering whether character is innate or acquired (Crain, 1992). Today, we take it for granted that both biology and rearing guide children's development and adjustment (Kagan, 1994). There is not much that we can do about a child's biological packaging, but there is considerable room for improvement in how we nurture and socialize young people. Perhaps the most practical reason for studying parenting is to gain information that helps us create healthy, nurturant, supportive family and community environments in which children can achieve their full potential.

Who benefits from the study of parenting? Parents and those who plan to become parents benefit by having good information about prenatal development and different methods of preparing for childbirth and raising children. Many parents express an almost desperate need for useful information about child care and effective discipline methods. Given the importance of the parenting role, it is ironic that most parents receive virtually no formal training that would enable them to perform confidently and competently.

Teachers benefit from having knowledge about parenting because they work with children and parents. Teachers are more aware than most people of the key role that parents play in their children's education. Because of this awareness, teachers are in an excellent position to support parents in helping their children learn and achieve. Knowledge about children's development also encourages teachers to provide emotional support to children who are undergoing family stresses such as parental separation and divorce.

Knowledge that results from the study of parenting is of potential use to anyone who works with children and parents, including social workers, psychologists, coaches, guidance counselors, and pediatricians. The main group that benefits from the study of parenting is children. The quality of the parent-child relationship appears to be the critical factor that determines children's development and adjustment. Parents and children enjoy family life more when parents know what they are doing.

Parenting Research

What reasons do people give for deciding to have children? What is the best stage of life for bearing children? What motivates some individuals to want to raise children to whom they are not biologically related? Do older parents raise their children differently than younger parents? What is it like to become a parent? How does living with an infant affect the marital relationship? Is reward or punishment a more effective discipline tool? Do high-achieving parents usually have high-achieving children? Do parents raise their children using the same methods practiced by their own parents? How do parenting practices vary from one culture to another? How do parents feel when their children leave home for good?

These questions are just a tiny sample of the kinds of questions that researchers ask and answer using objective methods of observation. If you look through the table of contents of research journals such as *Child Development, Developmental Psychology, Adolescence, Journal of Marriage and the Family, Journal of Family Psychology,* and many others, you will find a wealth of articles addressing different facets of parenting and child development. Some

TABLE 1.4 Who Benefits from the Study of Parenting?

Parents

Grandparents

Teachers

Guidance counselors

Coaches

Child care providers

Psychologists and social workers

Pediatricians

Judges

Children

sample titles are: "Parent-adolescent conflict: An empirical review"; "Satisfaction With Child Care Arrangements: Effects on Adaptation to Parenthood"; "Prediction of Infant-Father and Infant-Mother Attachment"; and the enigmatic title of a study described below, "Parturient Women Can Recognize Their Infants by Touch." The method sections found in research articles like these demonstrate the careful, logical planning necessary to draw meaningful conclusions from observations of behavior and development.

You might think that researchers answer questions about parenting mainly by observing how parents interact with their children. Although many investigators do observe parents and their children interacting in natural settings or laboratories, most researchers gather information by asking questions. Information gathered from surveys and questionnaires is useful as long as the purpose of the research is clear and the results are not generalized beyond the individuals who participated.

Reread the research questions cited above and think about how you would go about answering some of them. You'll see that some of the questions can be answered only by observing behavior and that other questions can be answered only by interviewing people. As children grow older, they keep inner feelings and questionable behaviors increasingly to themselves. Although very young children are not capable of providing researchers with reliable verbal information about their behavior, older children and adolescents are indispensable informants regarding inner feelings and problems that may be hidden from their parents (Verhulst & van der Ende, 1992).

There is no question that for researchers, mothers and fathers are potentially rich sources of information about child rearing (Phares, 1995). Over an extended period of time, they observe and participate in private encounters that are inaccessible to even the most curious and innovative observers. This admittedly subjective information only can be tapped by interviewing family members. Much of what we learn about family life by questioning family members appears to be valid (Cook & Goldstein, 1993), despite the fact that parents and children often disagree with each other about what parents actually do (Tein, Roosa, & Michaels, 1994).

Investigators use systematic observation, questionnaires, surveys, census data, and many other research approaches, often in combination, to study the parenting process. Some research methods are unusual and creative. Atkinson and Blackwelder (1993) investigated changing views of fatherhood during this century by analyzing popular magazine articles published between 1900 and 1989. How would you go about finding out whether children, when they become parents themselves, use discipline methods similar to ones their parents used?

Research Example 1

A considerable amount of knowledge about parenting is obtained by asking parents and children questions. For example, one group of investigators wanted to know whether discipline practices are passed from one generation to the next (Simons, Whitbeck, Conger, & Wu, 1991). We often observe similarities between parents and children in their behavior, emotional expressions, and cultural patterns (Deveaux, 1995). Do children learn to parent by watching their own parents? In a study entitled "Intergenerational Transmission of Harsh Parenting," published in the journal *Developmental Psychology* (Volume 27, pp. 159–171), Simons and his colleagues hypothesized that children of aggressive parents treat their own children harshly if and when they become parents.

Think for a moment about how you would go about testing this hypothesis. How would you define a harsh discipline style? How would you determine whether children eventually adopt their parents' style? Clearly, at least two generations of parents have to be studied. Since young children are not parents, the first generation we would investigate would be their parents. The second generation would then have to consist of these children's grandparents. In other words, we would want to compare the parenting styles of these children's grandparents to that of their parents to see whether or not the parenting styles are similar. Since we can no longer observe the grandparents raising the parents, this information must be obtained by asking questions.

The participants were members of 451 two-parent families with at least one child in the seventh grade. The seventh graders were attending public or private schools in Iowa in 1989. Each seventh grader had a sibling who was relatively close in age. All the families were white (which limits the generalizability of the findings) and had a wide variety of income levels (which increases the generalizability of the findings). Each family was paid $250 for participating in the research project. Each of the four family members (mother, father, seventh-grader, sibling) completed questionnaires addressing such topics as parenting, psychological adjustment, self-concept, and economic status. Each family member spent about 6 hours completing the questionnaires, explaining the hefty monetary payment for family participation.

Parents reported their parenting practices, harsh or otherwise. What if the parents were reluctant to describe their parenting in unfavorable terms? To control for parental truthfulness, their children also reported how frequently their parents engaged in harsh parenting practices. Thus, to insure reliability of the data, the investigators used two sources of information to measure the harshness of parenting. But how do we assess the grandparents' parenting practices? Each mother and father completed a four-item Harsh Discipline Scale rating each of *their* parents. For example, one item asked, "When you did something wrong, how often did your mom (dad) spank or slap you"?

The results supported the hypothesis. Grandparents who (as parents) had used harsh punishment practices typically produced next generation parents who also practiced punitive parenting. The generational resemblance was stronger for mothers than for fathers, perhaps because mothers usually are more involved than fathers in regulating their children's behavior. The investigators tentatively concluded that "repeated exposure to aggressive parenting provides individuals with a model of the parent role that they use with their own children in a reflexive way, with little awareness of alternatives or concern with rationalization" (p. 168).

Thus, through repeated exposure, children learn and eventually imitate their parents' discipline style. However, the study revealed that the present-day parents were far less abusive toward their children than their parents were to them. This finding suggests that current parents are somewhat more enlightened than their own parents concerning the use of positive discipline practices.

Research Example 2

Based on the findings of the aforementioned study, we might wonder how coercive parenting practices affect children's immediate behavior. For example, do children respond to parental anger and criticism with compliance or with defiance? Crockenberg and Litman (1992) published an article entitled, "Autonomy as Competence in 2-Year-Olds: Maternal Correlates of Child Defiance, Compliance, and Self-Assertion" (*Developmental Psychology*, Volume 26, pp. 961–971). The investigators wanted to see whether or not there is a relationship between how aggressive a mother is when disciplining her toddler and the likelihood that the child will comply with or defy her instructions.

The participants were ninety-five mothers and their 2-year-old children. Each mother was paid $20 to participate. The mothers' ages ranged from 18 to 41 years. Most were white, with a small number of African-American, Hispanic, and Asian mothers. Unlike the previous study, where family members were asked questions only about parenting style, in this study, interactions between mothers and children were actually observed both in a laboratory setting and at home.

Mothers brought their children to the laboratory at their convenience. After a 6-minute free play period and a 35-minute maternal interview during which many toys were available to the child, the mother was instructed to tell her child to pick up all the toys and place them in a basket. The mother and child were left alone in the room and their interactions were videotaped through a one-way mirror. About a month later, the same mothers and children were observed interacting in their home at about dinnertime. This interaction was audiotaped.

Using the videotape and audiotape, the behaviors of the mother and child were coded using a coding system for describing mother-toddler interactions, specifically maternal control strategies and children's defiance, compliance, and self-assertion. The definition of maternal negative control included maternal displays of anger, annoyance, criticism, threats, and punishment. Child compliance was defined as children putting the toys in the basket. Self-assertion was defined as the child saying "no" to the mother's requests. Defiance was defined as the child doing the opposite of what the mother asked or expressing anger or aggression to the mother's request.

The investigators found that when mothers used mainly negative control—threats, criticism, and anger—to get their children to clean up toys, the children responded with more defiance. This occurred both in the laboratory and at home. Child defiance was even more likely when mothers followed a child's self-assertion—for example, saying "no"—with negative control. In a correlational study like this one, we face the old chicken and the egg problem. Which came first, harsh parenting or a defiant child?

We do not want to conclude prematurely that it is the mother's behavior that is causing the child's response. It is possible that difficult children "create" harsh parents. Crockenberg and Litman argue against this explanation in the present study. When mothers used positive control (instruction, reward) plus guidance (suggestions, offers to help), children were more compliant. The researchers concluded that harsh parenting styles are "ineffective in achieving a resolution that most parents would consider satisfactory." They suggest that "strategies that combine a clear statement of what the parent wants with an acknowledgement of the child's perspective are quite effective in both gaining compliance and avoiding defiance" (pp. 970–971).

Although most parenting studies require that participants be interviewed, direct observation of behavior, or some combination of observation and interview, there are many other research strategies that investigators use to illuminate the parenting process. One interesting experiment, for example, demonstrated that mothers and fathers can identify their newborn infants just by touching them (Kaitz, Lapidot, Bronner, & Eidelman, 1992; Kaitz, Meirov, Landman, & Eidelman, 1993; Kaitz, Shiri, Danziger, Hershko et al., 1994).

In the first study, within hours after they had given birth, forty-six Israeli women were instructed to stroke the hands of three sleeping infants, one of which was their own child. They were then asked to guess which child was theirs, solely on the basis of touch. All other cues (e.g. sight, sound, smell) were eliminated. Two-thirds to three-quarters of the mothers who had had more than one hour of contact with their child since birth were able to identify their child! Only one-third of correct selections would be expected by chance alone. Mothers with less than one hour of contact were unable to identify their infant by touch. Most mothers who were successful claimed that they recognized their child on the basis of the texture or temperature of the infant's hand. The authors speculate that new mothers possess "an exceptional ability to recognize their newborns by tactile cues" (p. 38).

The one element that runs through virtually all research studies is **objective observation**. Researchers commit to observing and measuring behavior in an unbiased fashion as carefully and systematically as possible. This is not easily accomplished. For example, when some parents (particularly fathers) know that they are being "watched," their behavior changes, usually in ways meant to enhance their image as parents (Russell, Russell, & Midwinter, 1992). Researchers take such "observer effects" into account when interpreting their findings (Tein, Roosa, & Michaels, 1994).

Most of the information presented in this text is based upon research studies like the ones described above. Because all research studies have limitations or flaws, their findings are always tentative. At some point in the distant future, readers of this text who are parenting experts may very well howl with laughter and derision at some of our current beliefs. This is OK—interpretations and conclusions should be questioned and challenged when new information becomes available.

We also must acknowledge cultural, ethnic, racial, and gender bias in the developmental and family research literatures and in our own perceptions of events. For example, most developmental researchers are white, educated, and middle-class and they study mainly white, middle-class families. Parents of ethnic minority children are somewhat less likely to participate in research than parents of non-minority children (la Greca & Silverman, 1993). We try to be careful and not generalize our findings beyond the groups being studied. Because I cannot remind the reader about this limitation of research every time I cite a particular study, I emphasize it now.

Aware of cultural biases and the tendency of social scientists to view the world ethnocentrically, researchers study and compare families of different racial, ethnic, and cultural groups. For example, Fernald and Morikawa (1993), in a study entitled "Common Themes and Cultural Variations in Japanese and American Mothers' Speech to Infants" (*Developmental Psychology*, Volume 64, pp. 637–656), observed Japanese and American mothers playing with their infants at home. The study reveals both common characteristics of and differences between mother-infant speech in Japan and the United States. Mothers in both cultures simplify language to infants and repeat phrases frequently. Mothers in the United States label objects more frequently and consistently than do Japanese mothers, whereas Japanese mothers use objects to engage infants in social routines more often than mothers in the United States.

An important finding is that mother-child interactions reflect beliefs and practices concerning child rearing specific to each culture. Mothers in the United States emphasized objects and their names ("That's a car. See the car?") whereas Japanese mothers reinforced mutual dependence and verbal politeness ("I give it [a toy car] to you. Now give this to me"). By studying diverse populations, we learn what is distinctive about child rearing in each culture and what is universal (see Box 1-3, "Parenting Across Cultures").

Incidentally, why all this attention to mothers rather than fathers? Until recently (Phares, 1995), mothers were more available than fathers to participate in parenting studies. "Mothers are often in a unique position to sample their children's behavior more frequently, across a greater variety of situations, and over more extended periods than other informants" (Richters, 1992, p. 485).

Despite our considerations about the limitations of objective research, we can be confident that gradually we are gaining greater insight into the parenting process. Although the research literature is our most reliable source of knowledge about parenting, we can also learn about the parenting process in other ways—through informal observations of parents and children, by reading parents' and childrens' accounts of their family lives, and from our own experiences as family members. Our knowledge of the research process helps us to not draw general conclusions based solely on our personal observations or interpretations. The one conclusion that we can draw without fear of contradiction is that family life and the parenting process are far more complex (and interesting) than we can imagine at the present time.

WHO INFLUENCES WHOM IN FAMILIES?

The earliest theoretical models of development were **unidirectional** in nature. That is, they emphasized one possible direction of family influence—parents influence (mold, shape) children's character. For example, Freud suggested that the manner in which parents toilet train their children (harshly or patiently) could have a profound influence on children's personalities. Similarly, behaviorist

John Watson cautioned that if parents display too much attention or affection to their children, they will spoil them.

Sociobiologists recognize the importance of biology and heredity in human development but they play down the fact that how genes express themselves partly depends on environ-

B o x 1 - 3

Parenting Across Cultures

One of the most daunting tasks facing parents is to **enculturate** their children, to prepare them for the variety of physical, social, and economic situations that they will encounter in their community and culture. Successful parenting strategies promote the development of "culturally appropriate" ways of thinking, feeling, and behaving (Morelli & Tronick, 1991; Patel, Power, & Bhavnagri, 1996).

Are ethnic and cultural differences in parenting significant? Do they lead to differences in how children turn out? Are they related to differences in the "national characters" of people from different countries? Evidence suggests affirmative answers to these questions (Bornstein, 1991; Rohner, 1994). Because there is considerable cultural variation in how parents think about and treat their children (Ambert, 1994; Fine, 1993), we can view culture as an "independent variable" that has diverse and unpredictable effects on children's development.

Most studies of parenting are culture-bound, as are our ideas about what constitutes proper mothering and fathering. Psychologists, sociologists, and anthropologists who engage in costly, time-consuming cross-cultural investigations do so because they are curious about child-rearing practices in societies other than their own. Collaborating with colleagues who live in the society being studied lessens the risk of **ethnocentric**

bias (Bornstein, 1991), the assumption that our Western, middle-class rearing practices are universal and desirable for all children (Ambert, 1994; Fowers & Richardson, 1996).

For example, Mayan parents in Guatemala think it shocking that most parents in the United States sleep separately from their infants (Morelli, Rogoff, Oppenheim, & Goldsmith, 1992). Mayan infants sleep with their mothers, fathers, or older siblings until the birth of a new sibling. How would parents in the United States feel about the Mayan arrangement?

Cultural comparisons provide a "natural experiment" for testing scientific hypotheses about what is universal in parenting and what is culture-specific (Bornstein, 1991; Camras, Oster, Campos, Miyake, & Bradshaw, 1992; Harkness, 1992). Having babies spend the night in a different bed or room from parents is culture-specific because it is common in the United States but not elsewhere. Comforting a distressed infant is culture-universal because we observe this practice in all societies. Should we assume that because a particular parenting behavior is universal or near-universal, it must be biologically rooted? Comforting a crying infant could very well be an innate reaction to a child's distress, but it could also reflect shared economic, ecological, or other factors that encourage parents in different cultures to think or act alike.

mental factors, such as diet and stressors. Like many behaviorists, feminists downplay biological differences between males and females. They emphasize instead the role of power and opportunity in socialization. In sum, most current models of development are not prepared to address the complexity of real life events where everything potentially affects everything else.

Unidirectional models emphasize that various elements of parenting, including parental personality, behavior, and beliefs, directly or indirectly guide a child's development (Peterson & Rollins, 1987; Stafford & Bayer, 1993). It took time for researchers to notice how profoundly children affect their parents. Yes, parents have a lot to say about how their children turn out, but parents do not remain unaffected by the ebb and flow of parent-child interactions (Belsky, 1981). Unidirectional theorists, including early Freudians, behaviorists, and sociobiologists were not obtuse. They knew that child qualities such as temperament influence parents. However, their models were not yet flexible enough to handle a more complex, bidirectional analysis.

Bidirectional models, emphasizing mutual influence, recognize that children are active participants in family relationships as well as selectors and creators of their own environments (Peterson & Rollins, 1987; Stafford & Bayer, 1993). New parents confirm that the arrival and presence of an infant changes almost every aspect of family life. The arrival into a family of a new member (child, adult, or pet) requires adjustment by all family members. It changes existing relationships and lifestyles, making life more interesting (and hectic) for everyone (Hooker, Fiese, Jenkins, Morfei, & Schwagler, 1996).

The reciprocal nature of influence in parent-child relationships is now well-documented (Bell & Harper, 1977; Lewis & Rosenblum, 1974). Infants provide cues to their caregivers (for example, frowns and cries) that reflect their momentary needs and they

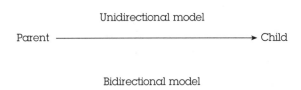

Figure 1.1 Who influences whom in families? The unidirectional and bidirectional models of parenting.

reinforce appropriate parental responses by smiling and cooing. If you observe a parent with a young infant, you will notice that the infant continually initiates and responds to social signals (the latter is called **social referencing**). Responsive parents use such signals to establish an "interactional synchrony" or goodness of fit between their own behavior and that of the child (Isabella, Belsky, & von Eye, 1989). Another example of how children affect their parents is the observation that preschool children, especially sons, "protect" their parents from divorce. Divorce rates for families with young children are about half of what we observe for childfree couples (Cherlin, 1981), suggesting that many unhappy couples remain in unsatisfactory marriages for the sake of the child. Infants who are difficult to raise probably exert greater influence on their caregivers than the other way around. By gradually changing their parents' behavior and personality and by altering the moment-by-moment flow of parent-child interactions, children help determine the course of their own development! (Bell, 1968; 1979; Mohar, 1988).

Combined Influences

We can learn about human development by studying one variable at a time or by studying the combined influence of several variables. The so-called **ecological model of development** takes into account factors (activities, roles, interpersonal relations) within families and within other social systems and society as a whole. It also allows the testing for **interactions** among the various social systems and settings through which a person moves (Bronfenbrenner, 1986). That is, a change in one component of a system affects the entire system. For example, a child's stressful encounter with a bully in school might lead to a hostile encounter with a younger sibling at home later in the day. A parent who receives notice of a promotion at work may be more available to her children when she arrives home. Bronfenbrenner emphasized that it is an individual's interpretation of life events rather than the events themselves that affect behavior and development. Tapping personal meanings is a challenge for the researcher.

Studying several types of influence at one time allows us to understand how the personal and psychological characteristics of parents and children interact with situational factors like work experiences and cultural factors such as beliefs and customs (Tronick, Morelli, & Ivey, 1992). Adopting this strategy,

we can better understand how **contextual** (situational and cultural) factors in family members' lives influence parenting behavior (Luster & Okagaki, 1993).

Studying several factors at a time allows us to make more accurate predictions about how parents will respond in a given situation. According to Luster and Okagaki (1993), "Knowing that a parent has an explosive temper, that a child is temperamentally difficult, and that the family is experiencing an economic crisis would lead us to believe that the child is at risk for receiving poor parenting; knowing only one of these three facts would make any prediction more tenuous" (p. 228). To understand the parenting process, "we need to consider the life course of the parent, and the way in which the life course of the parent is related to the parent's characteristics and the current circumstances in which the parent-child relationship is developing" (p. 229).

The factors that influence parenting behavior change over time. Living with an infant is very different from living with an adolescent.

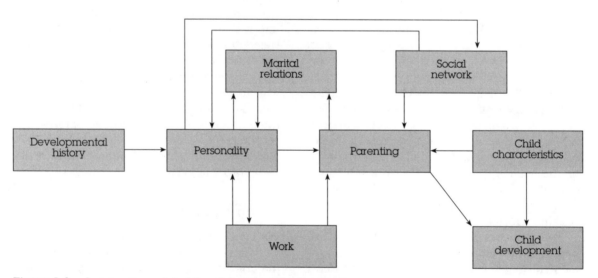

Figure 1.2   A process model of the determinants of parenting

(J. Belsky, "The Determinants of Parenting: A Process Model" in *Child Development*, 55, page 84, 1984. © The Society for Research in Child Development, Inc. Reprinted by permission of the publisher and author.)

Over time, parents change and their life circumstances change. Families move, parents change jobs, take courses, some get divorced. Parents create and change life situations which in turn change them in ways that affect their children. Experiences that we have early in life continue to influence us (and therefore our children) later in life.

SUMMARY

1. The process of parenting suggests a polarity: the potential fulfillment of child rearing versus the challenge (and struggle) to do it well.

2. There are many reasons (good and bad) for deciding to have children. Among the best reasons are personal growth, companionship, and the enjoyment of raising children. Unfortunately, many parents, with their hectic, stressful lifestyles, forget why they wanted children in the first place.

3. Four parenting goals are stated that indicate desirable outcomes of parenting. They include (1) good behavior, (2) competence, (3) good parent-child relationships, and (4) positive self-esteem and self-confidence. The parenting styles advocated in this book support these four goals.

4. The history of childhood reveals that economics and ignorance about children were major factors influencing children's status in society. Given the high mortality rate for infants and children, our ancestors may have been reluctant to form the strong emotional attachments to their children that we take for granted today. Brutal treatment of children, infanticide, and abandonment were not rare occurrences. Since the sixteenth century, more enlightened views of children and childhood have gradually emerged. Children are now seen as innocent and vulnerable. Childhood and adolescence are considered to be separate and unique stages of life.

5. Despite overall progress in children's status, many children in the United States are raised under extreme conditions. Millions live in poverty, surrounded daily by violent crime and drug abuse. Large numbers experience physical, emotional, or sexual abuse. Too many receive inadequate health care and inferior education.

6. Researchers study parenting mainly because it is an important and interesting topic. We are concerned especially about the relationship between how parents raise their children and how children "turn out." We hope that the knowledge we acquire about the parenting process will help create optimal family environments in which children are able to achieve their full potential.

7. There are many approaches to the study of parenting. Researchers use objective methods of observation to obtain information about how parents and children "raise each other." The major obstacle to the study of the parenting process is its complexity.

8. Parenting behavior is influenced by biological, personal, social, ethnic, cultural, and situational factors of such variety that they almost defy analysis. Investigators applying the ecological model of development study several different levels of influence at one time, allowing the discovery of interactions among the different levels. With great persistence, we continue to search for general principles that will help us understand the parenting process.

GLOSSARY

bidirectional model   A model of influence that suggests that there is a reciprocal (mutual) influence between individuals and their environment

contextual factors   Situational factors that affect behavior and development

ecological model of development   A model of influence that views children as developing within a complex system of relationships that are influenced by multiple levels of the physical and social environment, including family, school, peer group, and culture

enculturation   The process of preparing children for the variety of physical, social, and cultural situations that they will encounter in their community and culture

ethnocentricity   The belief that one's own culture or race is superior to all others

experiment   A powerful research method that uses manipulation of variables and controlled observation to prove that one variable is influencing another

infanticide   The intentional murder of an infant

interaction   When the effects of a variable on behavior depend upon the specific value of another variable. For example, the effects of divorce on children may depend upon a child's age and gender

objective observation   In psychology, the attempt to observe and describe behavior in an unbiased fashion

social referencing   Relying on a trusted person's emotional expressions to infer the meaning of or to decide how to act in an ambiguous situation

unidirectional model   A model of influence that suggests that environmental factors directly or indirectly determine behavior and development

THOUGHT QUESTIONS

1. Why are some parents more influential than others regarding how their children turn out?

2. Should parents be prosecuted for the criminal behavior of their children?

3. Some people have children for the wrong reasons. What are some dubious reasons for having children?

4. Chapter 1 offers several parenting goals. What additional goals do you or would you set for yourself as a parent?

5. What, if anything, does a society's treatment of its children tell us about that society?

6. How might you benefit from your study of the parenting process?

RESOURCES

The following journals contain articles on child development and the parenting process:

Adolescence

American Journal of Orthopsychiatry

Child Care Quarterly

Child Development

Children

Developmental Psychology

Exceptional Children

Family Process

Family Relations

Journal of Family Issues

Journal of Family Psychology

Journal of Marriage and the Family

Journal of Youth and Adolescence

Youth and Society

THE TRANSITION TO PARENTHOOD

OBJECTIVES 30
THE TRANSITION TO PARENTING 30
Mothering and Fathering 31
MARITAL TRANSITIONS 32
Changes in Marital Satisfaction 34
Marital Transitions and the Quality of Parenting 36
STAGES OF PARENTHOOD 36
Evaluation 39
ASSISTED REPRODUCTION TECHNOLOGIES: WHERE DO
   BABIES COME FROM? 39
Effects on Children? 40
Spotlight: Gender Selection 41
REALISTIC EXPECTATIONS ABOUT PARENTING 42
REALISTIC EXPECTATIONS ABOUT OURSELVES 44
PREGNANCY 44
Physical Discomfort and Psychological Stress 44
Expectant Fathers 45
Prepared Childbirth 46
Gentle Birth 47
PARENT-INFANT BONDING 48
Other Factors That Influence Bonding 51
Spotlight: Breast-feeding 52
Box 2-1 Multiple Births 54
POSTPARTUM ADJUSTMENT AND DEPRESSION 53
PREGNANCY LOSS 55
SUDDEN INFANT DEATH SYNDROME 55

The childbirth itself was very hard, long, and painful. It was a vaginal delivery and ended nineteen hours of suffering. During the birth, my husband felt very uncomfortable and stressed out, but when the child's head started showing a lot of dark hair, he was so excited that he started crying. So did I. My pretty little girl was born on November 15, 1992, at about 11 a.m. She weighed 7 1/2 pounds and was 20 inches long (Mother of a three-year-old girl).

It's a wonderful experience. There's nothing like the feeling of that little person who loves you so much and depends on you. It's a full-time job—it's very exhausting. It's much more tiring than work. You're mentally tied up all day long. But it's worth it when she kisses you goodnight and gives you a hug and gives you back that love (Mother of a 4-year-old girl).

Spotlight: Latecomers—Delayed First Time Childbearing 57
ADOPTION 59
Box 2-2 Adoption Considerations 62
FOSTER FAMILIES: WHOSE CHILD AM I? 63
SUMMARY 63
GLOSSARY 65
THOUGHT QUESTIONS 65

OBJECTIVES

After studying Chapter 2, students should be able to:

1. Compare the life changes and adjustments of new mothers and fathers
2. Describe how the challenges of parenting change as children grow
3. Describe how new reproductive technologies have changed the traditional meanings of terms like mother, father, and parent
4. Describe some of the common sources of stress and discomfort during pregnancy
5. Discuss the conflicts that some expectant fathers experience
6. Present the key features of prepared childbirth and Leboyer's gentle birthing procedure
7. Describe how circumstances of birth and the characteristics of an infant can influence parent-child bonding
8. Describe several factors that are associated with the "maternal blues"
9. List the primary risk factors for Sudden Infant Death Syndrome.
10. Describe the advantages and disadvantages of raising young children later in life
11. Discuss some of the special issues and problems facing adoptive and foster families

THE TRANSITION TO PARENTING

The Monty Python comedy group often began their offbeat sketches with the phrase, "And now for something completely different." Perhaps obstetricians should echo this sentiment to parents upon delivering a first-born infant. It is hard to imagine a more profound life change than becoming a parent. For first time parents, pregnancy signals the beginning of a life and lifestyle that is "completely different" from what came before.

In this chapter, we explore the transition to parenthood, a period of life that usually begins with the awareness of pregnancy, spans the prenatal period, birth, and the early years of child rearing, and ends, on the average, by the first child's second birthday (Cowan, Cowan, Heming, & Miller, 1991). The birth or adoption of a child provides new parents with opportunities to grow as individuals and to grow as a couple. The introduction of a new family member redefines the marriage relationship, usually in the direction of less romance and a greater sense of partnership and responsibility.

The family systems model (described in Appendix A) portrays the family as a complex, dynamic social system. The structure and organization of a family changes dramatically when a new member arrives. "My life changed when I became a parent. I slowly came to see my wife differently, as mother to my child. I began to view myself differently. Like so many men, the almost obsessive thought, 'I'm a father' continually echoed in my consciousness. But what does it mean to be a father? I was committed to full, equitable participation in the raising of my children, not out of obligation, but really for the joy I anticipated in spending time with 'little kids.'"

"I observed that my wife and I both became more nurturant, more caring, and mainly, more tired. When we had been childless, our marital relationship allowed for greater spontaneity and independence in time and place. As parents, our new responsibilities were clearly defined, and our dependence on each other was more clear cut. Someone always had to be there as caregiver. Our infant son was difficult, issues arose daily on how to handle him, and our confidence wavered from day to day. Thirteen years later, we still waver a bit, but we are still enjoying" (Father of two boys).

As this quote suggests, parenthood brings not only joy, but also a change in one's identity, changing roles and relationships, heightened responsibilities, and new patterns of interaction among family members (Cowan & Cowan, 1992). Some parents report changes in their personalities following their child's birth (Antonucci & Mikus, 1988; Cowan, 1988). Whether these changes are positive or negative depends upon many factors, but especially the quality of the marital relationship and the infant's temperament (Sirignano & Lachman, 1985). As we shall see, the life changes that accompany the transition to parenthood affect the marital relationship in ways that new parents cannot anticipate (Belsky, 1990; Sollie & Miller, 1980). (In this Chap-

ter, we consider the transition to parenting for couples. We recognize that individuals without partners also can take on the role of parent. We address the topic of single parenting in Chapter 4).

Mothering and Fathering

Study Question *How does becoming a mother differ from becoming a father?*

Childbirth is "an extraordinary phenomenon which is infrequent in the life of any one woman and much more dangerous than more 'normal' life events" (Colman & Colman, 1991, p. 102). The reality of reproduction is that women have a greater biological investment in their children than men do. Women carry their fetuses for the better part of a year. Babies come out of women's bodies, not men's, and they drink their mother's milk. It is the mother's body that must recover from birth, a process that can take weeks or months. According to Unicef, about 585,000 women die each year in pregnancy and childbirth and millions more suffer debilitating illnesses or injuries (Crosette, 1996). Given the much greater biological and caregiving investment of mothers, it is understandable that mothers quickly develop an intense emotional commitment to their offspring (Hawkins, Christiansen, Sargent, & Jill, 1995; Hooker et al., 1996).

For most fathers, however, the transition to parenthood is quite different. Children gravitate to people who are warm, nurturant, affectionate, and patient. Although men and women are equally capable of displaying these qualities, children observe them more frequently in females. Becoming a mother differs from becoming a father in several ways, but mainly in that the average woman is better prepared and more motivated than the average man to cater to the needs of a dependent child (Daly, 1995; Hawkins, et al., 1995). In the light of cultural assumptions and reproductive realities, it is easy to see why so many people assume that mothers are primary caregivers and that fathers (at best) are mothers' helpers. It is this type of reasoning that leads some fathers to expect appreciation or gratitude from their partners when they provide care for their own children.

That women can be fulfilled only through motherhood is a myth that we disputed in chapter 1. Nevertheless, becoming a mother for most (but not all) women fulfills both their cultural conditioning and their need to care for and nurture the next generation (Erikson, 1982). It would be hard to defend the idea that parenting is inherently more fulfilling for women than it is for men, but females more than males are socialized to enjoy and nurture children. There is considerable evidence that sex role training encourages nurturant qualities more in daughters than in sons (Unger & Crawford, 1992). Girls are encouraged to play with dolls and to babysit. Most boys are not given comparable opportunities to spend time with babies or to develop nurturant qualities in other ways.

Most women take on and attempt to fulfill the role of devoted mother, but not without a price (Chira, 1994a). "A woman who accepts this traditional definition [of devoted mother] may (a) experience guilt and anxiety when she is separated from her child, (b) believe that separations are harmful for the child, and (c) reject the use of alternative caregivers, believing she alone is capable. This perspective of motherhood has viewed mothers as generic entities and has overlooked individual needs and characteristics inherent in the unique identities of women who choose to have children" (Hock & DeMeis, 1990, p. 286).

That biological, emotional, and behavioral differences exist between males and females no longer is debated by reasonable people. The nature and source of these differences re-

main controversial topics. We can assume that differences between men and women in how they relate to children are rooted partly in their biological investment in childbearing, but perhaps more deeply rooted in cultural expectations and practices (Unger & Crawford, 1992). I make these points to help distinguish becoming a mother from becoming a father. In all industrialized societies, the two roles are far from identical. "Once a woman becomes a mother, the role is hers for life, and she will be defined by society largely through that role, much more than men are defined through their role as fathers" (Unger & Crawford, 1992, p. 405).

For most of this century, women looked forward to and eagerly accepted the role of primary caregiver for their children. The role of father is less straightforward than the role of mother in that fathers usually have a choice regarding how involved they want to be in caregiving. Daniels and Weingarten (1988) interviewed 72 couples who had their first child at different times in their life cycles. Regardless of age, all of the women in the study had to readjust their lifestyles for motherhood. Most reported drastically reducing their nonfamily workloads. Only one of the 72 fathers, however, had to make extensive readjustments in educational plans, professional ambitions, or personal goals. Fathers of all ages reported that their work commitments were "insulated from the daily cares of hands-on parenting" (p. 39).

MARITAL TRANSITIONS

The ecological-interactional model of development described in Chapter 1 implies that a host of personal and situational factors influence marital transitions, including individual characteristics of spouses (e.g. their maturity and sensitivity), qualities of the infant (especially its temperament), and the larger sociocultural context in which the marriage and family is embedded (Levy-Shiff, 1994).

A strong marital relationship facilitates the transition to parenthood. We hope that the couple has been together long enough to bond with each other so that a close, trusting relationship exists by the time the child is born. Marriage partners must negotiate new ways of interacting with and treating each other as each develops a special relationship with the infant (Emery & Tuer, 1993).

Parenting is more satisfying when the new parents can balance their own individual needs with those of their infant and spouse (Belsky & Rovine, 1990; Levy-Shiff, 1994). The presence of children in a family typically gives rise to a **parenting alliance**, but it can also intensify existing marital problems. A parenting alliance, reflecting shared pride in child rearing, compensates (to some extent) for the lessening romance and intimacy in the marriage (Emery & Tuer, 1993).

Parents are busy people, yet the infant's needs (and one's partner's needs) must be met. Where will the time come from? How will the new parents cope with their new and everchanging priorities? How will physically exhausted parents find the time and energy to

satisfy each other's needs for romance, intimacy, and companionship (Sollie & Miller, 1980). New parents also wonder, Are we good parents? They realize that their attachment to this new family member is deep and lifelong.

First-time parents become acutely aware of their loss of freedom. "Even though you think you are ready for a child, you don't realize how drastically your life changes. You don't have time for yourself anymore. I never really had a family to help me out with my babies. My husband and I simply stopped socializing with other couples for many months after the delivery" (Mother of three).

New parents also must adjust to the physical demands of caring for a newborn. "Having a baby launches a couple into the responsibilities of continuous coverage for that baby: someone, either the couple themselves or their representative must always be on call . . . It is the loss of free time accompanying parenthood that surprises and bothers new parents more than anything else" (Larossa & Larossa, 1989, p. 139).

Children give their parents lots to think about and discuss. Regardless of the state of their relationship, couples inevitably must address (1) how to discipline their children, (2)

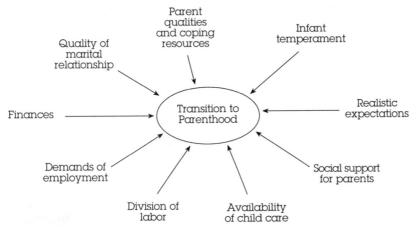

Figure 2.1 Factors influencing the transition to parenthood

escalating financial pressures, (3) feeling unappreciated by their partner, and (4) how to achieve a fair division of labor. Partners can enjoy watching each other practice new roles and responsibilities. When we become parents, our parents become grandparents, increasing the opportunities for meaningful multigenerational encounters. New aunts, uncles, and cousins also enter the family fold. Stories that parents tell their toddlers revolve around themes such as feeling close to each other and belonging to the family (Fiese, Hooker, Kotary, Schwagler, & Rimmer, 1995). With each new family member, there are new relationships and a growing sense of family (Weiss, 1990).

Changes in Marital Satisfaction

Marriage is a rich and meaningful experience in its own right, but parenthood adds even greater significance to this venerable institution. Marital satisfaction before and during pregnancy usually foretells how well couples will adjust to the stresses and strains of living with an infant. Satisfying relationships usually remain satisfying after the birth of a child, especially when couples share child care and household responsibilities and negotiate solutions to their problems even-temperedly. Relationships that are poor before birth are likely to deteriorate even further (Lewis, 1988b; Snowden, Schott, Awalt, & Gillis-Knox, 1988). Distracted by marital problems, distressed parents may compromise their children's development (Cowan & Cowan, 1995).

Although there are marked individual differences in how spouses adjust to the transition to parenting, many new parents (especially mothers) report a moderate decline in marital satisfaction, displays of affection, and feelings of closeness throughout the early child-rearing years and an increase in marital conflict (Belsky & Rovine, 1990;

Hock, Schirtzinger, Lutz, & Widaman, 1995; Levy-Shiff, 1994). The increased workload and resultant scarcity of leisure time usually increases tensions between new mothers and fathers. As parents become preoccupied with providing child care, they have considerably less time to devote to each other (Hackel & Ruble, 1992). They have fewer discussions that are not child-related.

After the birth, most men and women gravitate toward traditional gender roles, with mothers becoming primary caregivers and fathers continuing as breadwinners and assistants to their partners (Cowan & Cowan, 1992; Starrels, 1994a). Following childbirth, most new fathers continue to perceive themselves as workers and husbands; most women view themselves as caregivers first (Hawkins, Christiansen, Sargent, & Hill, 1995). It is usually the mother, for example, who wakes up several times a night to feed the infant, even if she is employed. Some new mothers feel overwhelmed by the demands of providing child care and resent what they interpret as their partner's lack of sensitivity and cooperation. Many fathers resist an equitable distribution of household labor, even when their wives work. Yet they still protest the lessening availability of sex, affection, and companionship provided by their exhausted spouses. They may resent what they see as their wives' "overinvolvement" with the baby. These and other issues test the marital relationship (Belsky, Lerner, & Spanier, 1984; Belsky, Lang, & Huston, 1986; Cowan & Cowan, 1995; Levy-Shiff, 1994; Rubenstein, 1989).

At birth, like new mothers, new fathers hold their child and have strong feelings of caring and protectiveness. Like their partners, fathers' feelings of pride and joy are tempered by disappointments and frustrations. They begin to have experiences for which they are unprepared and that they cannot easily assimilate into their world view (Hawkins, et al., 1995).

Perhaps the hardest feeling for a new father to deal with is his jealousy for the baby, who always demands and gets his partner's attention—and her body. What could be worse than a two-week-old rival? If he succeeds in establishing as close a relationship with the baby as his partner has, he risks evoking her jealousy. Now that there are three, someone always feels left out (Colman & Colman, 1991, p. 191).

Babysitters dominate new parents' social lives. Travel is encumbered by diapers, bottles, and changes of clothing. Money usually is in short supply. Most couples weigh the financial advantages of having both spouses work against the potential benefits to the child of having one parent remain home to provide full-time care (Leventhal-Belfer, Cowan, & Cowan, 1992). The toll taken on the marital relationship by the demands of child rearing is reflected in a boost in reported marital satisfaction when the last child leaves the family nest (Belsky, 1990; Belsky & Rovine, 1990; Klinnert, Gavin, Wamboldt, & Mrazek, 1992).

Does the decline in marital satisfaction among new parents reflect the transition to parenthood or is it a reflection of a more general disenchantment with marriage? The decline in marital satisfaction early in marriage is typical of spouses *whether or not* they have children. In other words, many young couples report having difficulty adjusting to marriage regardless of their parenting status. Using the survey method, Kurdek (1993b) compared changes in marital quality over a 4-year-period for 49 couples who had their first child and 68 couples who did not become parents during this time. Parents and nonparents showed an *equivalent* decrease in amount of agreement, satisfaction, and expression of affection over the 4 years of the study. Confirming the results of similar studies, Kurdek found no evidence that parents and nonparents differed in these measures of marital

quality. Understandably, parent couples did show a steeper decline in joint activities compared to nonparent couples.

Belsky and Pensky (1988) suggest that nonparent couples may have less stable relationships to begin with, accounting for their higher divorce rate. Longer term studies indicate that couples with children are less likely to divorce, suggesting that the presence of a child helps keep a marriage intact, if not happy (Bumpass & Rindfuss, 1979). Cowan and Cowan (1995) maintain that it doesn't matter whether or not it is the transition to parenthood that increases marital tensions in young couples. In their opinion, the fact that marital distress is so common among young parents threatens children's development and requires attention and perhaps professional intervention regardless of the cause.

When men do not fulfill their wives' expectations about what constitutes a fair division of labor, women report more negative feelings about their marriages (Belsky & Rovine, 1990; Levy-Shiff, 1994). This is especially true when husbands, prior to birth, lead their wives to believe that they will share the burdens of child care (Leifer, 1980). "When Adrienne was an infant, it was a chore for my husband to take care of her needs. I don't think he enjoyed giving her a bottle or changing her diaper. As she grew and developed a personality, he enjoyed her a lot more. But we never shared the responsibilities. My contributions compared to his were always 80:20 or 90:10" (mother of two).

The shift toward gender-typed behaviors following birth leads to a redistribution of marital power. "Rather than sharing family tasks equally, women and men each gain and lose influence according to the roles they assume . . . the normative shifts in the boundaries of power result in women assuming increased authority in parenting and family relationships, whereas men take on greater influence in the family's interaction with the outside world" (Emery & Tuer, 1993, p. 130).

Gender-typed behaviors are not usually a source of marital conflict unless they contradict one or both partners' expectations about what constitutes appropriate mothering and fathering. Couples who view their relationship as a partnership and who have "easier" babies usually are more content as parents regardless of whether their relationship is traditional or modern. Women who hold traditional views of marriage usually are less bothered by having to perform a disproportionate amount of child care (Belsky, Lang, & Huston, 1986; Hackel & Ruble, 1992).

Apparently, women are willing to do more than their share of domestic work when they believe that they have a say regarding division of labor and when they feel that their efforts are appreciated (Hawkins, Marshall, & Meiners, 1995). Most women, however, do view partner involvement as an indication of love and caring (Levy-Shiff, 1994).

Couples with children are less likely than child-free couples to divorce. The presence of children, especially boys, appears to delay (but doesn't ultimately prevent) divorce in unhappy couples. Financial considerations convince many troubled couples that they are "stuck with each other." The most unhappy couples usually divorce (Belsky, Lerner, & Spanier, 1984).

Marital Transitions and the Quality of Parenting

The effects of marital transitions on the quality of parenting are not well understood. Marital closeness and good communication skills foretell better parenting, perhaps because the mother's emotional needs are being met (Cox, Owen, Lewis, & Henderson, 1989). Parents in stable marriages usually are more invested in the parenting role than are parents in troubled marriages. They display greater sensitivity and warmth toward their children (Lewis, 1988c). Some parents (especially mothers) compensate for their unhappy marriages by becoming more involved with their children (Brody, Pillegrini, & Sigel, 1986). Fathers who feel neglected by their wives often become increasingly jealous and resentful of their children. If mothers become much more emotionally invested in their children than fathers do, there is a danger that Mom and Dad will grow apart (Hawkins et al., 1995). Maritally unhappy men frequently withdraw from their wives and children (Dickstein & Parke, 1988).

Children who are temperamentally difficult can become a source of irritation and marital conflict (Sheeber & Johnson, 1992). The arrow of causality flies in both directions. Marital conflict, leaving Mom and Dad more irritable and less emotionally available, brings out the worst in temperamental children. The strength of the marital relationship and everyday life stressors involving money, health, and work influence parent's ability to cope with difficult children (Belsky, 1990; Klinnert et al., 1992).

For the most part, however, parenthood brings considerable satisfaction and happiness to parents. Typically, the presence of children increases **family cohesiveness** (a sense of belonging to a family). Children become active participants in a family's ongoing activities, lifestyle patterns, and emotional exchanges (Lewis, 1988c). Most parents feel needed and loved by their children when they remember to "stop and smell the roses."

STAGES OF PARENTHOOD

Study Question   *How do the issues and challenges of parenting change as children grow?*

As Erik Erikson noted, we continue to change and grow throughout life. We spend considerably more life time as adults than we do as children. Adulthood provides us with endless opportunities to contribute, expand, and to see things differently. Life experiences, especially challenging ones, provide most of the fuel for this growth. Erikson (1982) declared that the primary developmental challenge of adulthood is learning to care for others and future generations, a process he called *generativity*. The middle-age life task that Erikson labelled **generativity versus stagnation** emphasizes the opportunities for growth inherent in the parenting or mentor role. Generativity reflects an adult's interest in establishing and guiding the next generation. Having children (or working with children) provides adults with countless opportunities to nurture and care for someone, to put a child's needs ahead of their own (Schwartz, 1995b). Failure to achieve generativity, which Erikson called *stagnation*, results in self-indulgence and interpersonal impoverishment.

Erikson's model, however, provides little detailed information about specific changes in the parenting role over time and the challenges that accompany these changes. Pregnancy and the birth of a child are tremendously exciting, yet these events bring up issues from one's own childhood that may not have been resolved, issues concerning authority, responsibility, the meaning of family, the role of parents, and expectations about parenthood (Simkin, Whalley, & Keppler, 1991).

Ellen Galinsky (1981), Co-president of the Families and Work Institute in New York, described several challenges for each of six stages of parenting. During the first, or **image-making stage**, expectant couples encounter several tasks. According to Galinsky, the major task of pregnancy is preparing for birth and parenthood. "This includes preparing for a changing sense of self and changing relationships with one's partner and one's own parents. Parents-to-be begin to get attached to the unborn baby, begin to understand that the baby will be a separate person, and they ready themselves for the actual birth" (p. 14). Emotionally, this stage contains many highs and lows. Most expectant parents are both excited about the birth and concerned about their ability to parent well. Before birth, however, all they have to go on are "images," hence, the image-making stage.

Do adults really construct specific images of what it will be like to be a parent? Silverman and Dubow (1991) administered questionnaires to 216 unmarried and child-free college students who were taking an introductory psychology course. The students were questioned about their expectations of parenthood. The study's results confirmed Galinsky's prediction. These young adults were able to construct "well-formed images both of their future children's behavior and of their behavior as parents" (Silverman & Dubow, 1991, p. 248). Whether the images are accurate or not, it is clear that young people fantasize about what it would be like to raise children of their own. Even grandparents-to-be go through this stage.

I waited so long for a grandchild. I often thought about the child. What would we do together if it was a little girl, or a grandson? Would we have such a wonderful time together, like I did with my grandparents? Could I relive those days with my new grandchild? Those thoughts made me happy. Now it's real (Kornhaber, 1996, p. 77).

Like many expectant parents, the students in the study imagined that their future infants would have difficult temperaments. This was particularly true for those who had younger siblings. Is this because they had vivid memories of conflicts with their younger siblings or did they stereotype all babies as cranky and irritable? Students who babysat had a more positive view of young children. Nurturant child-rearing attitudes were associated with babysitting experience in males and with positive self-esteem in females. Why might this be the case?

The second or **nurturing stage** in Galinsky's model corresponds to infancy. During this stage, "parents compare their images of birth, of their child, and of themselves as parents with their actual experience" (p. 9). In this stage, the major challenge facing parents is to become attached to the infant. This requires adjusting to the difference between the imagined and the real infant and accepting that this flesh-and-blood infant is theirs. "Pregnancy, particularly my first, was one of the most special times in my life. I was 32 years old when I had my first child and since having children was something I wanted all of my life, it was a thrilling, super experience. My first pregnancy was extremely easy, with no complications or illness, and the delivery was equally exciting and easy. My second pregnancy also went very well, but was a little more tiring with a toddler in tow" (Mother of two).

One potential problem during this stage is that the infant may have qualities that irritate or disappoint the parents. For example, most expectant parents express a gender preference. For some parents, a preference for a male or female child affects their subsequent parenting behavior (Abbott & Brody, 1985; Lewis, 1988c). A study of Swedish families showed that children whose gender did not match their parents' prenatal preference had poorer relationships with their parents throughout childhood and adolescence. This was particularly true for girls whose fathers wanted a boy (Stattin & Klackenberg-Larsson, 1991).

The third or **authority stage** spans the preschool years. During this stage, parents must learn how to assert their authority and how to establish and enforce rules. They also must learn how to communicate with their children and how to communicate with each other about their children. "In the authority stage, parents are grappling with fundamental issues of power. Out of the welter of these issues, self-concepts are beginning to be shaped—both for the parent and the child" (Galinsky, 1981, p. 177).

The fourth or **interpretive stage** corresponds to the elementary school years. The major challenge for parents during this stage is interpreting the world to their children. In the process of explaining, parents teach their children skills and values and help shape their self-concept. When trying to answer their children's questions (e.g. "Why do people fight?"), parents are clarifying their own views and values while revising their theories of child rearing. According to Galinsky, parents are confused about how involved they want and need to be in their children's lives. When does one intervene? When does one ask helpful questions? When does one say nothing?

The fifth or **interdependent stage** spans adolescence. Authority and communication issues arise again. "The same questions are asked because the child's growth often renders the old solutions obsolete" (Galinsky, 1981, p. 237). Ironically, as the problems grow larger, parents' authority declines. During early adolescence, parents must acknowledge and accept their children's desire for independence and their budding sexuality. "While teenagers are pursuing questions of identity, so are parents. Many are sizing themselves up, seeing how they have measured up to their dreams, how close or how far they are from the marks they set for themselves" (p. 273).

The final or **departure stage** occurs when grown children leave home. Parents are wise to prepare for a child's departure. It is a good time to take stock of their successes and failures. The major challenge of this stage is "accepting one's grown child's separateness and individuality, while maintaining the connections" (p. 307). When the last child leaves, parents have to redefine their individual identities ("I have grown children") and their identity as a couple.

Evaluation

Galinsky's stage model of parenting reminds us that raising children changes parents and children. Each day provides new challenges, conflicts, and potential crises. Sometimes we rise to the occasion, other times we throw in the towel. The stakes are high for our children and for ourselves. Erikson highlights the challenges that children face as they move from stage to stage. Galinsky's model does the same for parents, giving us perspective and courage to accept the challenge and, on good days, to welcome it. I was both excited and apprehensive when each of my sons entered puberty. As the difference in our sizes diminished, we shared an identity crisis. Could we learn to relate to each other in ways that allowed us to be comfortable with our new roles and evolving relationships?

Assisted Reproduction Technologies: Where Do Babies Come From?

The specific meaning of terms like mother, father, and parent is difficult to capture, partly because there are so many different ways that one can become a parent and be a parent. Until recently, the answer to the question, "Where do babies come from?" was fairly simple. Mothers contributed their eggs and fathers contributed their sperm. Thus, each child received half of its genetic structure from each parent.

New, expensive reproductive technologies are changing the rules about who can have children and what kind of children they can have. For example, consider a child who was conceived in the reproductive tract of a "surrogate mother" using an egg donated by a single woman and the sperm of an anonymous male donor and who at birth is adopted by the single woman who eventually marries. Who is the child's biological mother?

TABLE 2.1 Galinsky's Six Stages of Parenting

Image-making stage	What will it be like to be a parent?
Nurturing stage	Becoming attached to the infant
Authority stage	Parents assert their authority and enforce rules
Interpretive stage	Parents interpret the world to their children
Interdependent stage	Accepting the child's desire for self-regulation
Departure stage	Remaining connected to a grown child who has left home

For practical purposes, we will define a parent as someone who raises and nurtures a child regardless of whether there is a legal or genetic relationship between the caregiver and child and regardless of the caregiver's marital status. Most children, however, can say that their parents contributed their genes, gave birth to them, are their legal guardians, live with them, and raise them (Lakoff, 1987). Couples who are having difficulty conceiving a fetus the old-fashioned way or who have a family history of genetic disease and who decide not to adopt can choose among several assisted conception alternatives (Meyers, Diamond, Kezur, Scharf, Weinshel, & Rait, 1995). The techniques are very expensive, not usually covered by insurance, and success is not guaranteed. A couple might spend $15,000 for one month of infertility treatments and still have negative results (Lee, 1996).

Artificial (or donor) insemination consists of using a syringe to place donated semen into a woman's cervix or uterus. Donated semen is used because a woman's partner is infertile or impotent or a woman does not have a male partner. (**Infertility** is defined as the inability to conceive after a year of unprotected sexual intercourse. About 5 million couples in the United States have fertility problems.) As a result of artificial insemination, a child is genetically related to its mother but not to its father. In the case of **egg donation**, a donor egg is fertilized (by the father's sperm) in the laboratory or in the uterus. This method allows a child to be genetically related to its father but not to its mother. If egg and sperm are donated, the child is genetically related to neither parent. This is similar to adoption except that the parents experience pregnancy and their relationship with the child begins at birth (Golombok, Cook, Bish, & Murray, 1995).

The procedure known as **in vitro fertilization** (first accomplished in 1978) allows the conception of an embryo outside of its mother's uterus. A woman's egg is withdrawn from her ovary and fertilization takes place in a laboratory, usually because her fallopian tubes are blocked. Several fertilized eggs are placed in the woman's uterus (sometimes resulting in a multiple pregnancy) by inserting a catheter through her vagina. When the sperm and eggs come from the couple who are trying to conceive, the embryo is genetically related to both of its parents. Eggs and sperm also can be purchased from donors for hundreds or thousands of dollars. Several attempts usually are necessary to achieve a successful pregnancy (Golombok, Cook, Bish, & Murray, 1995; Simkin, Whalley, & Keppler, 1991). By early 1996, there were about 300 in vitro fertilization clinics in the United States attempting 40,000 fertilizations a year (Gabriel, 1996).

For **surrogate motherhood**, a woman who usually is paid for her participation is impregnated with the father's sperm (usually by artificial insemination), carries the baby to term, and gives the baby to the father and his partner. The man is the biological father and his wife must formally adopt the child. With surrogacy, the child could be genetically related to both, one, or neither parent, depending on who donated the sperm and egg (Golombok, Cook, Bish, & Murray, 1995). What problems can you foresee from use of this technique?

Reproductive science clearly has benefited infertile couples but also has generated much controversy. Terms like biological mother and biological father are not as clear-cut as they used to be. By selecting one sperm or egg donor over another, parents have a say in the size, appearance, race, and even IQ of the new baby [See **Spotlight**, "Gender Selection"].

Pregnancy after menopause also has become reality, allowing women in their fifties and sixties to conceive. In December 1993, a 59-year-old London woman gave birth to twins. The eggs were donated by a younger woman and fertilized by the older woman's husband. Critics wonder, Is this woman too old to raise young children? I wonder, Can pregnant men be far behind?

Effects on Children?

Study Question   *What are the possible psychological consequences for a child in being genetically unrelated to one or both social parents?*

How might assisted conception procedures affect the resultant child? Since most children are never told about the circumstances of their conception (Cook, Golombok, Bish, & Murray, 1995), negative consequences of assisted conception procedures would most likely reflect an "impaired" parent-child relationship. In other words, parents who lack a genetic relationship to their child might express less warmth and sensitivity or be less responsive to their child's needs. However, most parents who conceived through the new technology are deeply appreciative of their children and careful in their child rearing (Colpin, Demyttenaere, & Vandemeule-broecke, 1995; Rosenthal, 1996).

Golombok and her colleagues (1995) studied 41 families with a child conceived by in vitro fertilization and 45 families with a child conceived through donor insemination. These families were compared to 43 families with a naturally conceived child and 55 families with a child adopted at birth. All the families were from the United Kingdom and all the children were 4 to 8 years old at the time of the study.

The investigation revealed that the quality of parenting in families with a child conceived by assisted conception was *superior* to that of families with a naturally conceived child, even when the sperm or egg was donated by a non-parent. Mothers were warmer and more emotionally involved with their children. Fathers had close relationships with their children. How did the children fare? There were no group differences among the children in their emotions, behaviors, or relationships with

Spotlight

Gender Selection

Study Question Should parents be allowed to select the gender (or height, hair color, or eye color) of their child?

"We really wanted a girl and I was secretly hoping we'd have one, so I have to admit I was kind of disappointed. The box of girlish clothes I've been collecting is going into the attic" (pregnant mother of two boys after being told that she is carrying another male, quoted by Frenkiel, 1993).

At birth, nature produces roughly an equal number of male and female babies. Nowadays, most parents want at least one boy and one girl, preferably in that order. Researchers have reported that a majority of college students (both men and women) express a preference for bearing a male first child. Many people and many ethnic traditions prize firstborn males as a means of carrying on the family name.

Reproductive technology can reveal early in pregnancy a fetus's gender. Geneticists are able to provide prenatal diagnoses to couples, some of whom might choose to abort the fetus solely on the basis of its gender (few will publicize the fact). This practice is widespread in China, where parents have a strong preference for male children. Some

geneticists approve of the use of prenatal diagnosis for the purpose of selecting a child's gender but many others are disturbed by this practice.

Sperm sorting, identifying semen samples rich in X or Y sex chromosomes that can be artificially inseminated into a woman, is also an option. If society permits couples or single individuals to exercise such preferences, we might experience a preponderance of first-born males and laterborn females. It is difficult to predict how this gender pattern would affect society (Frenkiel, 1993).

Most parents who have a gender preference accept and love whatever child nature delivers. Some parents truly are disappointed if they are not able to raise a male or female child. One mother of two boys said, "When I heard it would be a boy, I felt sad because I realized again how much I truly wanted a girl. Of course I was happy that we were having a healthy child, but the disappointment didn't go away." The father said he "couldn't have been more pleased to have another son" but agreed that if the technology were available to have a daughter, he and his wife would have used it (both parents quoted by Frenkiel, 1993, p. C6).

parents. Almost all the children were doing fine. The investigators noted that parents who required assisted conception had a higher commitment to parenting. Perhaps they were more grateful for having children, given the fertility problems they had to overcome. They also were somewhat older than parents of the naturally conceived children, which could partly explain their greater ability to appreciate their children. The investigators concluded that "genetic ties are less important for family functioning than a strong desire for parenthood" (p. 296).

REALISTIC EXPECTATIONS ABOUT PARENTING

Study Question   *What is the job of a parent?*

Parenting is not only a full-time job, it is a permanent job. Even when our children are grown, we are still their parents. Although less involved in the lives of our adult children, we remain deeply attached to them and concerned about their welfare. We realize that most of our parenting work is accomplished during the first twenty or so years of parenthood, in the form of **socialization**. Socialization has two worthy goals: discouraging unacceptable behavior and teaching desirable behavior, values, and beliefs. As far as society is concerned, if you choose to parent, this is your job. Given the complexity of the adult roles that our children will eventually take on, successful socialization requires 20 years or more of persistent parental effort. The gradual nature of child rearing is not always appreciated. Parents of young children, in particular, sometimes become frustrated or annoyed when their children misbehave. Parental impatience during discipline encounters is likely to interfere with effective socialization, not enhance it.

That parents have unrealistic expectations about children and child rearing is understandable. Few have studied child development, undergone parent training, or had extensive experience raising children before they had their own. New parents may be surprised (and dismayed) when they discover that infants do not sleep through the night until they are about 7 months old. Even then, they awake very early and demand attention and servicing.

Some parents become frustrated when they are unable to comfort a crying or cranky infant. Children's "misbehaviors" do not lessen with age. My "grown" children still lose new sweatshirts and forget to give us phone messages. But how can I complain? I frequently misplace my possessions and forget almost everything.

Parents also may have unrealistic expectations about the influence they can exert on their children's character. As Galinsky (1981) notes, "Before they had children, many parents have built their images of themselves in opposition to [incompetent] parenting in favor of a humane, respectful, peaceful relationship . . . Now they have the role of parent—they have the child whining at the circus, demanding crackers, cookies, candy, gum at the supermarket, jumping off the curb into the street, interrupting when they are in conversation. And almost by surprise, some hear themselves speak their own parents' words or act the part of the resentful, angry, or complaining parent" (p. 123).

Galinsky cites several unrealistic parental expectations that parents may hold. Good parents never get angry at their children. Good parents always feel unconditional love toward their children. We must be better parents than our parents were. My children must always be obedient and nice. My little baby will remain my little baby forever. Each of these unreasonable beliefs can sabotage the parent-child relationship by promoting parental guilt, disappointment, and discouragement.

TABLE 2.2   Unrealistic Expectations About Parenting

Good parents never get angry at their children

Good parents always feel unconditional love

We must be better parents than our parents

My children always must be obedient and nice

My little baby will remain my baby forever

Perhaps the biggest surprise for new parents is the amount of work required to care for an infant. One mother of three volunteered: "Having a third child, I soon found out there is no more time for self. I became more organized. Wash days were Monday and Friday, with towels in between. Children must be fed at routine times or they become crabby and the baby will scream. Children were all on nap and bedtime schedules. Nap time became and still is my favorite time of day so I could catch up with chores and try to have a cup of tea in peace."

Beyond the daily routine, the unanticipated daily hassles associated with child care are stressful. Feelings of irritation and frustration toward young children are common and for some parents, provide the fuel for abusive behavior. The combination of interrupted sleep (for the parent) and seemingly endless crying (by the infant) can produce angry, hostile, and then guilty feelings that make many parents uncomfortable.

All parents have some experience with being nagged or whined at, settling arguments between siblings, repeatedly cleaning up their children's messes, as well as a myriad of other possible everyday events of a similar nature. Although any one of these events may have little significance in and of itself, their cumulative impact over a day, several days, or longer may represent a meaningful stressor for a parent (Crnic & Greenberg, 1990, p. 1628).

Fortunately, most children comply with their parent's requests most of the time. However, parents who expect immediate compliance or unquestioning obedience may, through their unrealistic expectations or demands, expose their children (and themselves) to unnecessary stress. *At least our children are enormously grateful for all of our parental sacrifices and efforts on their behalf.* Back to earth. Most parents are fortunate to receive the occasional hug or a scribbled card on mother's or father's day.

Some parents expect perfection. Children who learn that they can never satisfy their parents become discouraged and eventually stop trying. Overprotective parents, by treating their children as incompetent, may weaken their self-esteem and self-confidence. Inadvertently, they discourage accomplishment and encourage a lack of responsibility (Zimbardo & Radl, 1981). As Piaget taught, having realistic expectations about children requires our remembering that they do not perceive the world as we do. Good parenting requires that we accommodate our children's needs as well as our own (Bettelheim, 1987).

If this depiction of living with children sounds a bit cynical, it is only because our expectations of parenthood are so hopeful. Children have much to offer us. I cannot think of a potentially more satisfying or meaningful role in life than that of parent. Why else would parents like me say about our early child-rearing years, "They went too fast." But don't expect from your children expressions of gratitude, glowing reports from teachers, brotherly or sisterly love, tidy rooms, unquestioning obedience, instant toilet training, meaningful phone messages, or a pleasant disposition. Just accept and appreciate these blessings when they occur. Parental mental health is best served when we expect only one thing—change.

REALISTIC EXPECTATIONS ABOUT OURSELVES

Guilt is not an uncommon parental emotion. Parents sometimes feel guilt (or shame) when their children behave poorly. Perhaps they feel inadequate in their handling of discipline encounters. Raising children is an enormous undertaking. Child-rearing problems are inevitable. "If you feel that you constantly have to be the perfect parent and love your child totally, it complicates your job as a parent. If there's one thing we know about parenting, it's a humbling experience. There are no perfect parents, only real parents" (Yogman, quoted by Kutner, 1988v).

Enjoying child rearing requires not only a good grasp of the nature of children, but also an accurate assessment of our own strengths and weaknesses. Parents are human. We have emotions, we make mistakes, and we have been known to be unreasonable. My favorite parental admonition is the oft-shouted, "STOP YELLING!" Acknowledging our limitations makes us less susceptible to guilt. It also demonstrates to our children that they do not have to be perfect either.

PREGNANCY

Physical Discomfort and Psychological Stress

Study Question *What are some common sources of physical discomfort and psychological stress during pregnancy?*

Complex hormonal and metabolic changes occur inside a woman's body during pregnancy. These changes require both physical and psychological adjustments by the expectant mother. As the fetus grows, a woman's internal organs become increasingly crowded.

This may be reflected in gastrointestinal distress and, as bladder capacity is intruded upon, more frequent visits to the bathroom. Because the growing fetus changes a woman's center of gravity, she finds herself making postural adjustments, another possible source of tiredness. The added weight of the fetus and difficulty sleeping also contribute to fatigue. About three-quarters of pregnant women report experiencing nausea and vomiting ("morning sickness"), usually early in pregnancy. High levels of estrogen are responsible. In late pregnancy, the breasts swell in preparation for milk production and become increasingly sensitive (Simkin, Whalley, & Keppler, 1991).

Events associated with pregnancy sometimes lead to heightened sensitivity, mood swings, crying, and other forms of emotional distress. Persistent, intense stress is problematical. Both mother-to-be *and* the fetus suffer when the mother's body creates excessive amounts of the stress hormone epinephrin (adrenaline). The hormone arouses the mother's body, irritates the fetus, and reduces its oxygen supply. Psychological stress results from the physical discomforts already noted and a woman's concern about her appearance and her relationship with her partner. As preg-

TABLE 2.3 Sources of Discomfort During Pregnancy

Gastrointestinal distress, nausea, and vomiting

Fatigue due to postural adjustments and weight gain

Sensitive breasts

Mood swings and emotional distress

Concerns about appearance and relationship with partner

Loss of mobility and independence

Concern about the health of the fetus and about birth

nancy progresses, some women become apprehensive about losing their mobility and independence. Most of all, they are concerned about the health of the fetus and its eventual birth. "We were both worried that she wouldn't be healthy because my nephew is very sick. I was also concerned that we wouldn't be able to give her everything she needed" (Mother of a 6-year-old girl). During this time of heightened vulnerability, pregnant women depend on the support of relatives and friends, but especially on their partners. Sharing their fears and concerns usually helps (Colman & Colman, 1991; Simkin, Whalley, & Keppler, 1991).

Despite these changes and concerns, many women report that they never felt happier than when they were pregnant. The mother quoted above said this about her pregnancy: "It was an amazing experience and no words can do it justice. It was the happiest time of my life. I couldn't believe a person was growing inside of me. I had some bad morning sickness and was uncomfortable at the end—I was so fat." How did her husband react to her appearance? "He was a typical man, always making jokes. But he always told me that he loved me and that I was beautiful."

Expectant Fathers

Pregnant women occupy a special status in our society. Given their heightened vulnerability and the contribution they are making by perpetuating our species, they certainly deserve the support and consideration that they usually receive. What about "expectant" fathers? It is not unusual for expectant fathers to feel both excited and threatened by some aspects of pregnancy. "Many have never felt so important yet so ignored, so married yet so abandoned, so deeply in love and sexual yet so afraid of sex, and so creative yet so drained of energy" (Simkin, Whalley, & Keppler, 1991, p. 39).

In the past, husbands were expected to get their partners to the hospital on time for the delivery and then anxiously pace back and forth while puffing on a smelly cigar. Fathers rarely participated in the delivery. Partly because of changing conceptions about fatherhood, men today experience increasing pressure to be more involved in their partner's pregnancies (Shapiro, 1987b).

He shows no physical signs of pregnancy, but in some ways, emotionally and psychologically, he is as pregnant as she is. This is particularly true in America today, where society expects fathers to play an increasingly large role during pregnancy and birth . . . From the moment he knows of the pregnancy, a man is thrust into an alien world. He is encouraged, instructed and cajoled to be part of the pregnancy and birth process, something he knows little about. He is expected to become the coach or supporter for his wife, who has the leading role in the drama. He has no role model, since his own father almost certainly didn't do what he is expected to do (Shapiro, 1987a, pp. 36–38).

Shapiro (1987a) interviewed 227 expectant and recent fathers. They ranged in age from 18 to 60 years and were from a wide variety of backgrounds. Shapiro observed a "cultural double bind." We encourage men to be fully involved during pregnancy and birth. At the same time, they are told that they are outsiders. Any negative feelings that they have, such as fear, anger, or sadness, should be kept to themselves, lest their mates become upset. The process of pregnancy caters to the needs of the expectant mother. The "father-to-be has neither the support systems nor the cultural sanctions for what he experiences" (p. 38).

The men in Shapiro's study voiced several concerns. They feared feeling queasy during the birth and were apprehensive about anticipated financial pressure. Many were uncomfortable accompanying their wives to obstetrical examinations. Some men said they feared losing their spouse or child during the delivery. Some expressed fear of being replaced by the infant in their wives' affections. A few men even wondered if they were the child's father. Some said they felt greater responsibility to remain alive and healthy to take care of their families.

Most of the fathers felt they could not share these concerns with their partners out of fear of upsetting them. Most kept their worries to themselves (an unfortunate male trait). The intensity of the fears increased when partners were unavailable emotionally, physically, and sexually. These men had no substitute support system to compensate for the reduction in partner support. They wondered whether they would be strong enough to deal with their concerns on their own. Men who feel neglected before or after birth sometimes act in ways that destabilize their marriages. They may not provide their partners with needed support or they may express their resentment in other ways. Some expectant fathers report physical and psychological changes (e.g. weight gain, nausea, anxiety) that resemble those of pregnancy, a malady known as **couvade syndrome** (Colman & Colman, 1991; Simkin, Whalley, & Keppler, 1991).

Like their partners, expectant fathers adjust better when they express their concerns. Men who are able to disclose their concerns to their partners benefit from the closer and deeper relationship that results. Childbirth preparation classes also provide a forum for both partners to obtain good information and gain perspective. Pregnancy brings most partners closer. Men usually behave in an increasingly protective and caring fashion (Colman & Colman, 1991; Simkin, Whalley, & Keppler, 1991).

Prepared Childbirth

For thousands of years, women have borne children under unsterile, often terrifying conditions, reflecting our ancestors' ignorance of the birth process. Enlightened attitudes about birth developed in this century largely due to the pioneering efforts of British physician Grantly Dick-Read (1933) and French physician Fernand Lamaze (1972). Both men, appreciating the importance of involving expectant parents in the birth process, emphasized education and relaxation. In the past, pregnant woman were treated as obstacles to be overcome during the delivery of their children. Today, there are many birth options available to parents. Prepared childbirth is one of the most popular.

Because my older son experienced an unanticipated forceps delivery, I was not allowed to observe and participate in his delivery. My wife and I had completed a course in Lamaze training and were very disappointed. Five years later, I was present for and participated in the birth of my second child. With all due credit to my wife's efforts, I never worked so hard in my life!

I was massaging, comforting, watching the fetal monitor, reminding my wife to use the proper breathing or relaxation routine, and (yes, I admit it) taking pictures. Being present for the birth of one's child and the opportunity to participate in the delivery is "totally awesome." In Galinsky's terms, a real baby replaces an imagined baby. Holding your real baby moments after its birth is an incredibly moving and memorable experience.

Prepared childbirth is based on the premise that a birth should not be a mysterious and threatening process (Lamaze, 1972). Prospective parents attend six weekly classes beginning during the seventh month of pregnancy. They are given information about the anatomy and physiology of pregnancy and birth. The questions and concerns of pregnant parents are addressed in an informal and supportive manner. Fathers-to-be learn how to monitor and coach their partners during the delivery. (Bringing fathers into the parenting process at this early point has potential benefits that we will examine in a later section of this chapter.)

Pregnant women are taught how to conserve energy and reduce fatigue and pain during birth by relaxing their bodies. They learn various muscle relaxation exercises and breathing techniques that they can apply during the different stages of labor. Because she will be participating in her delivery, it is important that a pregnant woman exercise the muscles she will be using to expel the infant. Without this preparation, these muscles might become strained during labor (which can last up to 20 hours or more) (Simkin, Whalley, & Keppler, 1991).

Exercising and being physically fit help during the delivery. A study published in the Journal of the American Medical Association in May, 1988 found that moderate physical activity, including jogging, swimming, cycling, and playing tennis, does not endanger the fetus of a healthy woman who has a normal pregnancy, as long as she does not push herself to her limits.

Thus, prepared childbirth training encourages father involvement, provides good information about the birth process, and allows minimal dependence on drugs that could harm the fetus during delivery. (Local and regional anesthetics that provide pain relief without side effects to mother or fetus are available if needed.) A mother's ultimate "reward" for her efforts is seeing the birth of her child and holding her precious newborn moments later.

Studies comparing women who have had successful Lamaze deliveries to those who preferred medicated deliveries are difficult to interpret. Both groups are "self-selected" rather than randomly assigned to the method of birthing. Therefore, they might differ in significant ways that could affect their parenting. Nevertheless, women who feel in control of their labor and who have their partners present during the delivery usually report more positive experiences (Entwisle & Doering, 1981; Sosa, Kennell, Klaus, Robertson, & Urrutia, 1980).

Gentle Birth

Frederick Leboyer, a French obstetrician influenced by the works of Lamaze and Dick-Read, suggested that increasing the comfort of the mother during the birth process is addressing only half the problem (Leboyer, 1975). What about the comfort of the newborn? The fetus leaves a relatively dark, quiet, and warm fluid-filled uterus to enter a relatively bright, noisy, cool, hospital delivery room. Adding insult to injury, the newborn is turned upside down and slapped on the behind. Welcome to Earth.

In an effort to minimize the "transition shock" from uterus to delivery room, Leboyer urged that the conditions of the delivery room (which could be in a hospital, birthing center, or the parents' home) be adjusted to approximate those of the uterus. He recommended that there be dim light, low noise (whispers), and gentle handling of the newborn. The infant is placed in a warm bath that not only cleans its body but is reminiscent of the warm, amniotic fluid that recently surrounded it.

Research has not demonstrated that gentle handling produces measureable long-term benefits, but several of Leboyer's procedures have become part of mainstream obstetrical care (Evans, 1989). Some critics worry about the potential danger of obstetricians or midwives working in dim light and the possibility of infection in non-sterile settings. However, many believe that LeBoyer's procedures, in their gentleness and sensitivity, are more humane than the traditional hospital delivery. What do you think?

PARENT-INFANT BONDING

Study Question *Is there a critical period soon after birth during which parents become strongly bonded to their newborn?*

"Although I could intellectually relate to my wife's pregnancy and see that she was bonding with this unborn child, I had very little emotional attachment. I was getting anxious and excited about the birth—but I had no emotional attachment to the baby. I was curious about why I felt none. It didn't really bother me that much. But there was a striking change the minute she was born. I underwent such a change. All of a sudden, I was emotionally attached to this 'thing'" (Father of two).

Almost all parents develop powerful nurturant and affectionate feelings toward their children. We use the term **bonding** to describe the process by which these feelings arise and intensify following a child's birth. The nature of the bonding process is not completely understood, although we can assume that both biology and learning are involved. The father quoted above suggests that his attachment to his newborn daughter was immediate. It is important to remember that bonding is a gradual process (Smolak, 1986).

Parents who have nurturant feelings toward their children will be concerned about their welfare and treat them well. The bonding process therefore increases the likelihood that the infant will survive and prosper (Bowlby, 1969). Affectionate feelings also help parents cope with the occasional frustrations that accompany child rearing. Parents who have ambivalent or negative feelings about their children, or no feelings at all, are not as likely to take good care of them. Parents who at first have mixed feelings about a child usually become strongly attached. Children of parents who are weakly bonded are at greater risk for child abuse or neglect (Egeland & Sroufe, 1981).

Circumstances surrounding the birth may enhance or weaken the bonding process. Bonding may be inhibited when a child is not wanted. Some parents have ambivalent feelings when a newborn is the "wrong" gender. Some bond more slowly to children who are hard to care for, including cranky, premature, and handicapped infants. Bonding proceeds more smoothly when there is "goodness of fit" between a child's temperament and parental expectations and beliefs about how infants and toddlers should behave (Lerner, 1993).

Other conditions of birth may influence bonding. When couples attend prepared childbirth classes, the father is permitted to be present during the delivery to coach his partner and share the moment of birth. In a home delivery, other family members, including children, may be present for the birth. Anesthetics that induce drowsiness during delivery prevent women from actively participating in the birth and from holding the newborn moments later. Infants born to anesthetized mothers are also less alert and active. Many women decide to not use general anesthetics during their deliveries. The combination of alert mother and responsive infant makes it more likely that there will be early, successful mother-infant interactions, probably enhancing the bonding process. (Murray, Dolby, Nation, & Thomas, 1981). Women who have cesarean or premature deliveries are not likely to have early contact with their infants. This could temporarily inhibit bonding (Simkin, Whalley, & Keppler, 1991).

The most dramatic moment in the bonding process occurs when proud parents first hold their newborn. "The first time that parents do, in fact, hold their child can be a powerful experience. Perhaps they feel the baby's skin on theirs, nestle the baby against them, cover the baby's tiny fingers with their hand, rub their mouths over the fuzz of the baby's hair, and look into the baby's eyes. Perhaps the mother offers the newborn her breast and the baby licks the nipple. Or perhaps the mother or father gives the baby a bottle" (Galinsky, 1981, p. 59).

How important is early parental contact with the newborn to the development of parent-infant attachment? Do humans, like many other species, have a critical period for bonding soon after birth? In the absence of sufficient early contact, will affectionate feelings fail to develop? These are important questions because knowledge about bonding partly determines our cultural practices concerning birth and child care.

Klaus and Kennel (1976) wondered whether different amounts of mother-infant contact soon after birth influence the bonding process. Two groups of low-income, first-time mothers were given different amounts of time with their newborns. The two groups were matched on several demographic and cultural variables so that they could be considered comparable. They were treated alike in all re-

spects, except that one group of mothers received five hours a day of extra "cuddling" time with their newborns. The extra contact began within three hours of birth and lasted throughout the three days until mother and child left the hospital. Both groups of mothers had a glimpse of the newborn at birth, a short visit 6 to 12 hours after the birth, and fed their infants every 4 hours.

The researchers interviewed the mothers and filmed them feeding their infants one month and twelve months after the birth. They found that the extra-cuddling mothers appeared to be more strongly attached to their infants than the control mothers, both one month and one year later. Mothers held their infants closer while feeding them and stayed closer during an examination by a pediatrician. They also responded more quickly if the infant cried. The extra-cuddling mothers displayed greater concern and interest in their babies than did the mothers in the control group.

Justin Jaffe

Studies like this one raised questions about traditional hospital practices that separated newborns from their mothers immediately after birth. They led to innovative procedures such as allowing the infant to room-in with its mother during the hospital stay. Studies like Klaus and Kennel's imply that early contact and interaction between parent and infant foster the bonding process.

Klaus and Kennel went even further in their analysis. They concluded that there is a **critical period** soon after birth during which parents establish an initial relationship with the newborn. If this were true, it would have serious implications regarding how we bear children. Parents would be quite nervous if circumstances prevented them from having early contact with their newborns. Goldberg (1983) and others criticized the methodology of the Klaus and Kennel study and disagreed with the conclusion that there is a critical period soon after birth or ever. One criticism was that Klaus and Kennel studied only poor, ethnic minority women; most previous studies of bonding had studied middle-class women. Perhaps the bonding process differs for these two groups.

At the present time, there is no convincing evidence of a critical period in the formation of parent-infant bonds. Parents who are temporarily separated from their infants usually do not display weaker emotional bonds. Adoptive parents will be quick to point out that they are strongly bonded to their children, some of whom they first met many years after their children's births (Hodges & Tizard, 1989). The bonding process can tolerate less than perfect conditions of birth or early contact.

"We need to emphasize that we are talking about a **sensitive period** here rather than a critical period. A sensitive period means that conditions for the mother-to-infant attachment are optimal. In other words, the attachment can be formed more easily now than during some other period of development" (Smolak, 1986, p. 56).

There may be mild short-term effects of early contact. Mothers with early or extra contact report more tender feelings toward their

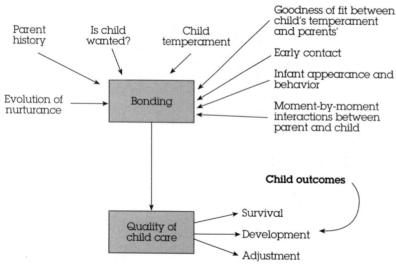

Figure 2.2   The bonding process

TABLE 2.4 Factors That Could Influence Parent-Child Bonding

Desire to have a child

Support from partner and others

Type of delivery and use of anesthetics

Early or delayed contact with infant

Infant's appearance and behavior

Is the child the desired gender?

Goodness of fit between parent and child temperament

Amount of work necessary to care for infant

Frequency of pleasing interactions with the infant

young and may breast-feed them for longer periods. It is not likely that these differences have a noticeable impact on children's development. Mothers who are at heightened risk for becoming abusive or neglecting, however, probably benefit from early and extra contact (Lamb, Campos, Hwang, Leiderman, Sagi, & Svejda, 1983). Certainly, we should encourage the bonding process for high-risk parents in as many ways as possible.

Other Factors That Influence Bonding

Study Question *What characteristics of the infant might influence the bonding process?*

An infant's appearance may enhance bonding. One study reported that mothers of attractive firstborn infants were more affectionate and playful with their children than mothers of less attractive infants (Langlois, Ritter, Casey, & Sawin, 1995). They also had a more positive attitude toward their babies. Fortunately, most parents find their newborns to be phys-

ically appealing. The infant's "cute" features, reproduced in teddy bears and stuffed animals, include a relatively large head with a protruding forehead and a small face, large dark eyes, chubby cheeks, and a small mouth. These features elicit an almost instinctive attraction (Lorenz, 1943).

In addition to their appearance, infant behaviors such as smiling, laughing, and cooing also promote bonding by eliciting positive feelings and reactions in parents. The most potent factor in bonding could very well be the pattern of frequent, positive, reciprocal parent-infant interactions that emerges during the first year of life. During play and affectionate moments, parents and infants enjoy countless opportunities for mutually satisfying encounters. One broad smile and an innocent gurgle from an infant apparently compensates for about six hours of parental weariness, fatigue, and frustration.

Watch parents exchange smiles and vocalizations with their infants. Note the mutually reinforcing nature of such interactions. As already noted, parents of children who are difficult to care for may have fewer enjoyable interactions with their children. However, parents of premature or sick infants should not fear that their lack of early contact with the infant soon after birth will impair their relationship (Galinsky, 1981). The ongoing, mutually satisfying interactions between parent and child can compensate for less than optimal conditions soon after birth.

Studies on father-to-infant bonding have produced inconsistent findings. Early father-infant contact does not seem necessary for quality fathering. It seems likely, however, that early father participation in child care improves the mother-father relationship which, in turn, promotes greater father involvement in child rearing (Palkovitz, 1985). Maternal characteristics, especially a woman's adjustment to her status as a new mother, also influence the course of bonding.

Spotlight

Breast-feeding

Study Question In what ways is mother's milk superior to formula?

"The closeness you feel with that baby is unbelievable. But you have to be willing to feed on demand. Some mothers say to me, 'Are you nuts?' It depends upon the type of mother you are. You really have to want to do it, or forget it" (Mother who nursed all three of her children).

Healthy mothers who eat well and who avoid drugs promote good health in their children by breast-feeding. During the early part of this century, most babies were breast-fed or fed cow's milk. From the early 1920s through the middle of the century, most parents chose to bottle-feed their infants. By the late 1960s, less than a quarter of infants were breast-fed (Martinez & Krieger, 1985; Simkin, Whalley, & Keppler, 1991). In the 1970s, the benefits of breast-feeding were widely publicized. Yet in 1992, only about 54 percent of mothers in the United States nursed their infants while in the hospital, down from 62 percent in 1982 The rate began to rise again in the early 1990s (Ross Products Division of Abbott Laboratories, 1994). Women who are employed part-time are more likely to breast-feed (and for longer durations) than women who are employed full-time (Lindberg, 1996).

The advantages to the young child are many (Eiger & Olds, 1987). Breast milk is the ideal food for human infants. It is easier to digest than formula. It is high in good cholesterol, which stimulates metabolism, and in lactose, which stimulates the growth of "good" bacteria in the child's intestinal tract. Breast-feeding confers on the child the mother's immunological protection against colds, allergies, and minor infections, at least during the first three months of life. Mother's milk can be fortified with minerals, proteins, and calories for premature infants, increasing the likelihood of their survival.

Infants who are nursed are less likely to be overfed compared to infants who are bottle-fed. However, they are not at lower risk for obesity, as previously believed. They consume fewer calories than bottle-fed infants but their metabolism is slower. Breast-fed infants have healthier, straighter teeth, and are less likely to suffer from diarrhea than bottle-fed infants (Brody, 1989). The intimate skin-on-skin contact that occurs during nursing probably enhances maternal bonding. Breast-feeding also is linked to lower rates of ovarian and breast cancer for the mother.

Breast milk is not perfect. It has less vitamin D than formula. Some mother's milk may be deficient in zinc, the lack of which can cause skin disorders and delayed infant growth (Brody, 1989). Bottle-feeding frees mothers to be elsewhere at baby's mealtime and encourages fathers to participate in caregiving. (Mothers do not have to be present to breast-feed. They can "express" breast milk when they are home and refrigerate it until feeding time.) A small percentage of women cannot nurse for physical reasons. Women who smoke cigarettes and who use alcohol and other drugs should not breast-feed. Their infants would ingest substantial amounts of these harmful chemicals. Women who choose to breast-feed also must accept bland diets to avoid passing nutrients that are not easily digestible to their infants.

Jones (1987) surveyed 1,525 mothers regarding their decision to breast- or bottle-feed. Breast-feeding was associated with a woman's age, social class, and parity (number of previous children). Women were strongly influenced by their partner's preferences. They were also influenced by the feeding method used by their mothers. The most frequent reasons given for preferring breast-feeding were that it "was better for the baby" and that it was "natural."

One mother reported that she chose breast-feeding after speaking to her doctor. "I learned that breast milk is sterile and easier for babies to digest. It certainly was cheaper. Even though it was somewhat inconvenient and a bit tiring, I found that overall it was not so bad." Effective breast-feeding is a learned skill for both the mother and infant. First time mothers need assistance in learning how to feed and hold their child. First attempts can be frustrating; patience is the key. Bottle-feeding is often chosen by women who consider breast-feeding inconvenient or embarrassing, or by those who previously have been unable to nurse. Women who are uncomfortable about nursing should understand that bottle-feeding is an acceptable substitute. Ultimately, a woman should select the manner of feeding with which she is most comfortable.

POSTPARTUM ADJUSTMENT AND DEPRESSION

Study Question   *Why do so many new mothers feel depressed?*

"I was transformed from a competent lawyer into a new mother crippled with doubt, confusion and unshakable sadness. Too terrified to hold my baby, I cried even more than she did. My nightmarish postpartum depression lasted for months" (Mother quoted by Brody, 1994).

Birth, the transition from pregnancy to parenthood, brings both positive and negative changes. Most parents are joyful and relieved following the long-anticipated birth of a healthy child. Like the mother quoted above, a significant number of new mothers suffer from a variety of depressive syndromes. The so-called *maternity blues syndrome* is the most common alteration in mood following pregnancy. Lasting only a few days, it is characterized by frequent episodes of irritability, tearfulness, and crying. Although moodiness is a normal part of postpartum adjustment (**postpartum** means "after birth"), for a relatively small number of women it signals the beginning of severe depression (Hopkins, Marcus, & Campbell, 1984).

Postpartum psychosis has received considerable media attention. New mothers, apparently suffering from hallucinations and delusions, have killed their young infants. Some employ a legal defense based on postpartum mental illness. Fortunately, instances of mothers actually harming their babies are rare.

Mild to moderate postpartum depression is fairly common, affecting from 10 to 20 percent of new mothers. Depressed mothers may report the following symptoms: tearfulness; feeling sad, irritable, and lethargic; a loss of appetite; various sleep disturbances; and lessened sexual interest. They feel unable to provide infant care. Some report having ambivalent feelings about the baby. Such depressive episodes last an average of 6 to 8 weeks. Some women report feeling depressed as much as one year after giving birth, but usually there is an improvement in mood over the first few months following birth. Positive feelings about the baby also increase over the first 16 months postpartum (Fleming, Klein, & Corter, 1992; Fleming, Ruble, Flett, & Van Wagner, 1990; Hopkins, Marcus, & Campbell, 1984).

The causes of postpartum depression are not known. Suspected factors include the physical discomforts and stress associated with pregnancy, labor, and delivery, the hormonal changes associated with pregnancy and lactation (milk production), unhappiness about one's appearance, and medications that are administered throughout this period. Some women are depressed during pregnancy and their symptoms carry over or intensify after birth. Six weeks usually is allotted for recovery from childbirth, but many women continue to have physical discomfort considerably longer. During the post-

Box 2-1

Multiple Births

About one out of every forty deliveries is a multiple birth—two or more infants born together. Multiple births have become increasingly common, largely due to increasing maternal age, the use of fertility drugs, and high-quality prenatal care, which allows prematurely born infants to survive (Behrman, 1992). It is not known why women over the age of 35 are more likely to bear twins or supertwins (three or more infants). About 98 percent of multiple births produce twins (Martin, 1996).

There is a higher risk of premature birth for multiples, which not only increases the expense of the delivery but also increases the risk of delivering low-birth-weight babies who suffer from cerebral palsy and other serious diseases. Twins and supertwins can be genetically identical or in the case of fraternal twins, as genetically different as any other non-twin siblings. Fraternal twins can be same or opposite gender.

partum period, women may experience fatigue, breast soreness, vaginal discomfort, constipation, and poor appetite. Other symptoms, including pain during sexual intercourse, may first appear months after birth (Simkin, Whalley, & Keppler, 1991).

With pregnancy and birth come the significant life changes that accompany the transition to parenthood. These may include financial pressures, marital tensions, and a loss of freedom. Working women feel pressured to return to their jobs. And, of course, caring for a new infant, particularly one with a

TABLE 2.5 Suspected Causes of Postpartum Depression

Physical discomforts of pregnancy, delivery, and recovery

Psychological stress during pregnancy, delivery, and recovery

Hormonal changes related to pregnancy

Unhappiness about one's appearance and lack of mobility

Medication

Lack of support from one's partner or others

difficult temperament, is a tremendous challenge (Gelfand, Teti, & Fox, 1992). How many men would become depressed if they gave up as much freedom (and sleep) and took on as many responsibilities as the average new mother? (In fact, how many new fathers are depressed? We don't know because reproduction usually is treated as a women's issue.)

The link between infant temperament and depression may be mediated by the woman's feelings of inadequacy as a mother (Cutrona & Troutman, 1986). Women may feel pressured "to do all this childbearing perfectly; have a truly 'natural' birth, breast-feed (with no supplements), get a flat stomach, bond with the baby (without ambivalence) and prove that the baby won't have an adverse impact on her career and marriage" (Henshaw, 1988).

Positive postnatal adjustment is predicted by positive prenatal adjustment, the quality of the marital relationship, positive attitudes about pregnancy, the infant's health and behavior, and the mother's social support system (Gelfand, Teti, & Fox, 1992). Women in unhappy marriages who are experiencing daily life stresses and who lack social support are at greatest risk (Cutrona & Troutman,

1986; Gelfand, Teti, & Fox, 1992; Hopkins, Marcus, & Campbell, 1984; Stemp, Turner, & Noh, 1986).

We need to learn more about the effects of a mother's postpartum depression on a child's development. Postpartum depression distorts the normal patterns of mother-infant interaction (Cohn, Campbell, Matias, & Hopkins, 1990; Field, 1995; Leadbeater, Bishop, & Raver, 1996). "As a group, depressed mothers look away from their infants more, are angrier and more intrusive, and display less positive affect than normal mothers" (Tronick, 1989, p. 116). Although mothers' moods influence their evaluations of their children, it is not clear whether depressed mothers exaggerate their children's behavior problems (Jouriles & Thompson, 1993; Richters, 1992).

Children of chronically distressed mothers do seem to have more than their share of problems (Campbell, Cohn, & Meyers, 1995; Hay & Kumar, 1995; Lee & Gotlib, 1989; Nolen-Hoeksema, Wolfson, Mumme, & Guskin, 1995). It is possible that many of these children are insecurely attached to their mothers and learn maladaptive ways of interacting with other people (Dodge, 1990; Murray, 1992; Rutter, 1990; Teti, Gelfand, Messinger, & Isabella, 1995).

PREGNANCY LOSS

It is difficult to imagine a greater source of pain than the loss of a child. Couples who experience pregnancy loss experience many emotions, including shock, disbelief, anger, and guilt (Simkin, Whalley, & Keppler, 1991). They also grieve deeply for the child that should have lived. Our understanding of this process is very limited. Studies suggest that social support and particularly the quality of the marital relationship are key factors in how couples cope with loss (Smart, 1992).

Lasker and Toedter (1991) conducted a lon-gitudinal study of couples who experienced spontaneous abortion, stillbirth, neonatal death, or ectopic pregnancy (the fetus develops outside of the uterus). They found that the ability to cope with pregnancy loss depends on emotional and social coping resources. For example, women who suffered from depression prior to pregnancy were suffering the most two years following the pregnancy. Those who felt that they had the support of their friends and partners showed the best adjustment. "The evidence for both chronic and delayed grief directs attention particularly to those groups—men and people with early losses—who are the least likely to receive support and understanding, either from the hospital staff or from friends and family members" (p. 520). The investigators caution that individuals who are at high-risk for chronic grieving are not necessarily the ones who cry the most. They may very well be the ones who are withdrawn and quietly despairing.

Females grieve more deeply than their male partners, or at least show their pain more readily. Men tend to hide their grief or deny it (sometimes to themselves). Women may interpret their partner's lack of expressiveness as a lack of caring. Men often try to help their partners end their grieving and get on with their lives, a strategy that probably is better suited for males. Women urge their partners to express their grief. Men and women support each other by talking, listening, holding, and crying. Mutual support appears to be the key factor in successful coping (Smart, 1992).

SUDDEN INFANT DEATH SYNDROME

About 6000 times a year, an apparently healthy infant stops breathing, usually late at night, without warning (Brody, 1995). Parents awake in the morning to find that their precious child is dead in its crib. This still mysterious phenomenon used to be called crib death. It is now known as Sudden Infant Death Syndrome, or SIDS (Sears, 1995). SIDS is the most common type of infant death during the first year, not including the first week after birth. SIDS is not really a cause of death, but a diagnosis given when all other known or suspected causes have been ruled out (Cantor, 1988).

SIDS is most likely to occur between 2 and 4 months following birth, but can occur up to 9 months of age (Sears, 1995). Three quarters of the babies who die suddenly have had good prenatal care and have well-to-do parents. Infants of smoking mothers are at greater risk. Researchers speculate that a subtle brain abnormality or allergic reaction may cause the disorder. Naturally, parents are devastated by the loss and often feel guilty about not having

prevented the death (Ostfeld, Ryan, Hiatt, & Hegyi, 1993). (Coping with the death of a child is discussed in Chapter 9.)

Infants identified as being at high risk for SIDS can be connected to portable, battery-operated monitors that record heart rate and breathing. These devices mainly are for home use. They sound an alarm if the infant does not breath for a designated amount of time, alerting parents to the danger. False alarms, which are common, almost scare the parents to death (Sears, 1995).

Research has not yet proven the effectiveness of these monitors. The SIDS mortality rate has not improved with their use. However, a New Jersey poll revealed that 15 percent of the parents of high-risk infants believed their infants would have died with-

More and more parents are having their first-born children in their thirties and forties.

S p o t l i g h t

Latecomers—Delayed First Time Childbearing

Study Question What are some advantages and disadvantages of raising children later in life?

According to the Bible, Abraham was 100 years old when his son Isaac was born, and his wife Sarah was 90 (menopause hadn't been invented yet). We know little else about this blessed event other than that God played a major role. Due to the paucity of developmental researchers during ancient times, we know next to nothing about what it was like for Isaac to have parents who were a century old. Perhaps they were given parent training by Methuselah, who begat a son when he was 187. Abraham, Sarah, and Methuselah serve as our first example of "latecomers," adults who delay childbearing until middle, or in their case, very, very late adulthood (Yarrow, 1991).

The average age at which women bear their first child has varied considerably during the modern era. As this century draws to a close, the trend is toward older parenting. The median age for first motherhood is about 24 years and for fatherhood about 26 years. About 7 percent of children in the United States are born to mothers over the age of 35 years. In the past, most of these children would be last-borns. But more and more parents are having their first-born children in their mid- to late thirties, or later (Clay, 1996a, 1996b).

Factors contributing to this trend include birth control technology, infertility, a large increase in the number of working mothers, relatively high rates of divorce and remarriage, and adoption. Some latecomers to parenting report that their own parents inspired them to postpone childbearing or describe life situations or careers that dissuaded them from having children earlier.

Some were caring for their own aged parents during their twenties and thirties (Yarrow, 1991).

The advantages of delayed parenting include more flexible occupational choices for women, greater financial security, less likelihood of divorce, and greater emotional stability. The greater maturity of older adults enables them to enjoy parenting more than younger parents do (Clay, 1996a). They have lived longer, perhaps they know more. Certainly they have more "life experience" to share with their children (Dion, 1995). Older parents usually have been married longer, perhaps long enough to overcome the obstacles to marital satisfaction we noted earlier. Men especially have more time and energy to devote to parenting and provide for their family after their career goals are met (Clay, 1996b; Heath, 1994). However, some educated men who are latecomers to parenting still feel torn between career aspirations and involvement in child care (Coltrane, 1990; Cooney, Pedersen, Indelicato, & Palkovitz, 1993).

Possible disadvantages of later childbearing include the "biological clock" that predicts a higher risk of complications during pregnancy and birth defects for older mothers, negative attitudes in society about "delayed" childbearing, being out of synch with one's peers, and the likelihood that there is more of a "generation gap" between older parent and child. However, age is not a disease. Most older parents are highly motivated to have and raise children and need not be dissuaded by the calendar (Simkin, Whalley, & Keppler, 1991).

Surprisingly little research exists concerning older first-time parents. A study of 105 mother-infant pairs, with mothers ranging in age from 16 to 38 years, reported that increased maternal age is associated with greater satisfaction with parenting, a greater time commitment, and more optimal parental behavior (Ragozin, Basham, Crnic, Greenberg, & Robinson, 1982). Heath (1994) reports that a group of men who fathered their first child after their 35th birthday spent more time with their children and were more nurturant than a comparable group of on-time fathers.

Andrew Yarrow (1991), a reporter for *The New York Times* and himself a child of older parents, surveyed 180 people and interviewed 70 of them at length about their experiences as children of older parents. Many reported being struck by how much older their parents looked compared to the parents of their friends or parents on TV sitcoms. The most common complaint about having older parents was embarrassment, particularly during adolescence. Older parents typically had "old-fashioned" or conservative values, particularly regarding sex, that led to conflict during their children's adolescence. Some respondents reported that for some reason, it was harder to rebel against older parents (who don't hear as well). A majority of respondents, however, felt that their parents influenced their beliefs positively. Sixty-three percent accepted their parent's values compared to 8 percent who didn't.

"I thought having older parents was wonderful. Parents in their twenties are growing up with their kids. My parents were more grown-up and had more time to share their lives. People who are older are also more financially set. I think I was closer to my parents because they were more patient and gave me more encouragement than other kids got. They instilled a sense of responsibility, love, and hope. That ghost of fear—that skeleton in the closet of old age, that fear of death—was there but there wasn't a loss of love" (Bonnie, a nurse from Philadelphia, p. 103).

Some of Yarrow's respondents reported that their parents lied about their ages and tried to hide their age cosmetically. Their parents' embarrassment about their age probably increased the children's embarrassment. Many regretted that their parents were not vigorous enough to participate in sporting events or camping trips. Not everyone agreed. Many described older parents who hiked, looked fit, and were healthy and involved. And those who didn't participate in physical activities offered their children theater or other cultural-type events instead. Some studies confirm that children of older parents are intellectually and socially advantaged (e.g. Zajonc & Marcus, 1975) and have better relationships with their parents (Umberson, 1989).

Roger, one of those interviewed by Shapiro, was born in 1948 when his father was 47 years old and his mother was 20. He reports feeling "self-conscious about being seen in public with my parents because they seemed old. It was embarrassing that they were older than other parents. I didn't want my friends to see me with these old codgers . . . when I was ten, my father was nearly sixty and was balding. And you're so conscious as a kid of things that make you stick out in any way" (p. 10).

out them. There are few preventative steps that parents can take. "Babies with no apparent symptoms have died in their mother's arms while nursing and on doctor's examining tables. Death is apparently instantaneous and painless and cannot be reversed . . ." (Cantor, 1988). As of late 1995, parents were being urged to put their infants to sleep on their backs and to avoid soft bedding (Brody, 1995).

ADOPTION

Interview with an Adoptive Mother

Q. Why did you choose adoption?

A. Because Jim and I could not have children on our own.

Q. How did your family and friends feel about your decision to adopt?

A. Basically, they were very supportive. When Sam finally came along I think it was harder for some of them to accept him and adjust to it. They kept expecting him to be different somehow. Now Sam is two years old and he's just part of the family. Everyone has a different way of dealing with it.

Q. How do you think they feel now?

A. Oh, I think they love him because he's adorable and special. He's got a lot of personality, you know.

Q. Once you made the decision to adopt, how long did you have to wait to find out about Sam?

A. About ten months. It was a good agency.

Q. How old was Sam the day you picked him up?

A. Five weeks old.

Q. Describe the day you first saw him.

A. We flew down to Arkansas. We flew all day and were exhausted.

The agency told us that no matter what time we arrived the baby would be waiting. It was 9:30 at night, raining, and we were lost. We finally found the place. It was behind a shopping mall with a little sign that said adoption agency. Sam was sitting on the floor in a little car seat sound asleep. He was just so beautiful. His eyes were so beautiful. We kept saying, "Is that him?" and the man said "Yeh, come on now and sign the papers." Sam never made a sound until we got to the hotel. I put him down and went into the other room for a minute. I said, "Jim, there's a funny noise in the other room" and he said, "Hon, it's the baby" and I said, "Oh yeah, we have a baby now." It was so exciting.

Q. What were your feelings holding Sam for the first time?

A. I think I was mostly scared. I thought he was amazing but what if he breaks. What if I don't know what to do with him or what if he cries. I guess I was afraid because I only had two weeks to get ready to be a mother when most women get nine months.

Q. How will you tell Sam about the adoption?

A. We actually talk about it now. This morning, he came running into the kitchen and said, "I adopted, ma." I said "That's good Sam" and he said, "Yeah." We talk about how he's special and that he's adopted so he knows the word. We'll just tell him the truth when he asks, that's really all you can do.

Obviously, bearing a child is not the only way to become a parent. Millions of children are raised by people who are not their biological parents. About half of adopted children are raised by relatives such as uncles, aunts, and grandparents (National Committee for Adoption, 1989). By late 1995, three states (New York, Vermont, and Massachusetts) recognized the right of unmarried couples to adopt a child (*The New York Times*, November 3, 1995).

Approximately 2 percent of children in the United States under the age of 18 years are adopted. Fewer children are available for adoption today compared to twenty years ago because of the greater use of contraceptives and a higher rate of legal abortions. Unmarried mothers also are more likely to keep their infants (Hersov, 1990). Thus, the demand for adoptive children is somewhat greater than the supply (Bachrach, London, & Maza, 1991).

Why do people adopt? Most adoptive parents are infertile couples with a long history of disappointment regarding their inability to bear children (Levy-Shiff, Bar, & Har-Even, 1990). Some individuals change their minds about having children after they have had their fallopian tubes tied or have had vasectomies. However, not all people who want to adopt are infertile. Some seek to adopt after pregnancy loss or the death of a child. Nevertheless, fertility problems coupled with the desire to have children are the major reasons couples offer for their desire to adopt (Bachrach, London, & Maza, 1991).

Adoption refers to a judicial process wherein biological parents give up their rights to a child and new rights and obligations are acquired by adoptive parents. In other words, a new parent-child relationship is created and recognized as such by the legal system. An adopted child gains all the rights, privileges, and obligations of a biological child including the right of inheritance.

The key factor influencing a judge's decision to grant an adoption should be a determination of what is in the best interests of the child. When possible, agencies attempt to place a child with a family that is of the same race, religion, and socioeconomic level as the child's biological parents. The consent of the biological parents to allow adoption is required unless the parents are deemed not fit or if they have abandoned, rejected, or abused the child.

A detailed investigation of prospective parents, often stressful and intrusive for the couple, is conducted over an extended period of time. Following placement, there is a probation period. Prospective parents understand that if they are found to be unsuitable, they will not be allowed to keep the child. This discourages some couples from giving themselves completely and unconditionally to a child until the probationary period is over (Levy-Shiff, Goldschmidt, & Har-Even, 1991).

Study Question *Should biological parents have the right to have a relationship with a child after they give it up for adoption?*

Adoption records are sealed to protect adopted children from the stigma of "illegitimacy." Even the names on the original birth certificate are changed. Recently, social agencies have been under pressure from adoptees, parents who have given up their children for adoption, and concerned professionals, to make adoption proceedings and information more "open." Adoptive children usually become interested in their "roots." Many desire information about and even contact with their biological parents. Increasing numbers of birth parents express a desire to participate in the selection of adoptive parents and a desire to maintain contact with their child after placement (Gilman, 1992). In a three-year study of adoptees, adoptive parents, birth parents, and adoption agency workers, almost all of those interviewed agreed that adoption information should be available to all of the parties involved in the adoption (Sachdev, 1991). However, some adopted children want no contact with their biological parents and some biological parents want no contact with the children they gave up. Courts have ruled that adopted children are not obligated to have contact with biological parents if they don't want to.

Even though 75 to 80 percent of adopted children are well-adjusted, adoptees, particularly during early adolescence, suffer from a disproportionate number of emotional, social, and academic problems compared to nonadopted children (Brodzinsky, Schechter, Braff, & Singer, 1984; Cohen, Coyne, & Duvall, 1993; Dickson, Heffron, & Parker, 1990; Fergusson, Lynskey, & Horwood, 1995). Many possible causes have been suggested, including genetic history, adverse prenatal circumstances, early life disruption, psychological problems in adoptive parents, mismatch between child and adoptive family, inadequate coping skills in adoptees, and identity problems in adopted adolescents (Brodzinsky & Schechter, 1990; Hajal & Rosenberg, 1991).

Although most adoptive parents are as psychologically well-adjusted (and better adjusted on some measures) than biological parents, adoptive families do encounter life and adjustment problems that differ from those of non-adoptive families (Levy-Shiff, Bar, & Har-Even, 1990; Levy-Shiff, Goldschmidt, & Har-Even, 1991; Smith & Brodzinsky, 1994). Whereas biological parents have nine months of pregnancy to prepare for an impending birth, adoptive parents face a more abrupt transition, including a long period of uncertainty about whether or not the adoption will even occur. While expectant biological parents are enjoying baby showers and other social rituals, prospective adoptive parents face "a frustrating, sometimes agonizing, waiting period, a time of expectations raised and often dashed" (Hajal & Rosenberg, 1991, p. 80).

There are several possible reasons for the cultural stigma that surrounds adoption (March, 1995). Most adopted children are born out of wedlock. There is an absence of "blood" (genetic) kinship between adoptive parent and child. One adoptee put it this way: "I was treated like any child would be treated by their parents. But, outside the family, it's different. They never believe that your adoptive parents love you like their parents love them. Because you aren't biological" (quoted by March, 1995).

Adoptive parents miss the pregnancy and childbirth experiences. Some fear getting a less than perfect child, since adopted children's genetic dispositions are essentially invisible. Prospective parents also worry about how a child will cope with the knowledge that he or she is adopted (Bachrach, London, & Maza, 1991). Some of the stigma reflects the "secrecy clause" that seals children's original birth records and restricts the release of background information (March, 1995).

There are fewer role models for parents who adopt and much less social support than that received by biological parents. The bonding that occurs at birth and soon after usually is not possible (Levy-Shiff, Bar, & Har-Even, 1990). On the other hand, adoptive parents have several of the characteristics of the "late-comers" described earlier—they are older, married longer, and more financially secure than most parents expecting their first child (Brodzinsky & Huffman, 1988). These qualities foretell healthy parental coping resources.

The fact that most adoptive parents have long been denied what they want so much leads not only to positive expectations about parenthood but also to positive parenting experiences (Levy-Shiff, Goldschmidt, & Har-Even, 1991). The key point is that both expecting adoptive and expecting biological parents experience unique adjustment problems that require coping and problem-solving skills (Cohen, Coyne, & Duvall, 1993). Although individual couples vary considerably in these skills, there is little reason to believe that either path to parenting is inherently more or less difficult than the other.

A difficult question that adoptive families grapple with is whether or not children should be told that they are adopted and if so, how they should be told and at what age. If children discover on their own that they are adopted or that their parents have not been honest with them, their trust might be shaken (Hersov, 1990). "If you lied to me about this, what else have you lied about?" Once children realize that they are adopted and understand what the term means (for most children, between 5 to 7 years of age), they ask countless questions about who their biological parents are and why their parents gave them up. It helps for adoptive parents to be open and accepting of their children's curiosity.

Gilman (1992) suggests that parents provide simple explanations to young children, for example, "You grew inside a woman, just like all babies do, but not inside me" and "Sometimes people can't take care of the children they give birth to, so other parents raise them. That's how you came into our family" (p. 284). As children mature and their conception of adoption broadens, parents might offer additional information. Parents should keep in mind that disclosure often raises concerns in children about the permanency of their relationship.

Like almost all adolescents, adopted adolescents struggle to construct an adult identity. They express curiosity about their biological parents and may want to meet them. This request raises issues of attachment and loyalty to their adoptive families. "Tensions between the adolescent and the adoptive parents often give rise to threats of desertion or ejection. The adolescent's wish to achieve autonomy is at times read as rejection or abandonment by adoptive parents" (Hajal & Rosenberg, 1991, p. 83). Surveys of adopted adolescents usually reveal that they adjust well but are curious about their biological parents. They would like to see what their parents look like and find out why they had been placed for adoption (Lewin, 1994).

Clearly, family relationships, parental attitudes, and parent-child communication play an important role in how adopted children resolve their identity issues. In most adoptive families, there are frequent opportunities for family members to reaffirm the psychological and emotional bonds between child and parent. Family therapy can be very helpful for adoptive families that become overwhelmed by issues of origins, secrecy, loyalty, and identity. As adults, adoptees still face decisions about what they will tell their mates, friends, and importantly, their own children,

---

B o x   2 - 2

Adoption Considerations

Lois Gilman, author of *The Adoption Resource Book* (HarperCollins, 1992, pp. 6–7), recommends that individuals considering adopting a child consider the following questions:

How important is it for you to be a parent?

How important is it for you to have a baby?

How important is it for you to experience a pregnancy?

Are you satisfied that you can provide a healthy family life for a child?

Have you adequately explored avenues other than adoption for parenting?

If you have a fertility problem, how have you dealt with it? Are you still grieving?

How do you feel about parenting a child who is not biologically related to you?

Can you love a child for what he or she is, rather than what you hoped he or she would be?

Do you have the ability to accept a child different from yourself?

What are your fears about adoption? Are you worried that you will never be seen as your child's real parent? What else concerns you?

about their special status (Hajal & Rosenberg, 1991).

FOSTER FAMILIES: WHOSE CHILD AM I?

To whom do children belong? Ask them. In biological and adopted families they will tell you they "belong" to their parents or to their families. Children in foster care, confused by their contacts with social agencies, courts, hospitals, foster parents, and therapists, sometimes wonder, "Whose child am I?" (Kates, Johnson, Rader, & Strieder, 1991).

Children usually arrive in foster care after being mistreated by their biological parents. These children bring to their foster families histories of abuse or neglect that shape their behavior and emotional needs (Azar, 1995a). Although foster care is supposed to be temporary, sometimes too little is done to rehabilitate children's biological parents so that the family can be reunited. Sadly, about one-third of foster children, many of them with severe physical or emotional disabilities, find themselves being shifted from one foster family to another. Nevertheless, children are better off in foster care than they are living in a chaotic home environment or in an institution (Fein, 1991).

States require that "reasonable efforts" be made to reunite children with their biological parents when possible, discouraging foster parents from getting too attached. Reunification is most likely when children continue to have rewarding contacts with their biological parents while in foster care. Even if children never reunite with their biological parents, continued contact usually is desirable.

The key to successful foster placement is "goodness of fit" in lifestyle and personality between the child and the parents. For example, inflexible mothers and defiant children are not likely to hit it off (Doelling & Johnson, 1990). Some foster children are physically or mentally disabled; many are below grade level academically. Children who are female, African-American, nondisabled, and those who have positive feelings toward their biological parents usually function better (Fein, Maluccio, & Kluger, 1990). It is difficult to separate out the effects of foster care on children from the stressful family circumstances and traumatic separation from biological parents that usually precede foster care.

Although most foster children adjust adequately, many are confused about their family identities and have difficulty forming relationships. Those who are moved around from family to family may become angry. "Crying, tantrums, verbal aggression, and school difficulties are behavioral manifestations of the depression and anxiety that may result from the unresolving mourning of separations. The destruction of property, physical violence, and threats of suicide are at the more extreme end of the behavioral spectrum that we have observed" (Kates et al., 1991).

The good news about foster care is that there are large numbers of warm, generous individuals who are willing to provide nurturance and care to children who might be difficult to raise. Permanent foster care is a good arrangement for some children. "Many children are in stable homes and appear to be functioning adequately . . . [The] initially negative effects of separation and placement in foster care can be counteracted through the influence of stable foster placements and strong services to the children and their biological and foster families" (Fein, 1991, p. 582).

SUMMARY

1. The birth of a child, especially a first child, is a major life transition that is accompanied by significant personal, family, and professional changes.

2. The transition to parenthood begins with the awareness of pregnancy. Pregnancy is an exciting and challenging time in life with opportunities and problems that require adjustment by all family members.

3. Becoming a mother is different from becoming a father. The average woman is better prepared than the average man to meet the needs of a child. More than males, females are raised to enjoy and nurture children. The fact that women are more invested in child rearing usually means that they end up providing more than their share of child care. Men, however, also must adjust to parenthood, a demanding role for which most men are unprepared. Some new fathers feel neglected by their partners and competitive with their offspring for their partner's attention.

4. Marital satisfaction is an important factor in caregiving because satisfied spouses usually do a better job of parenting. Good marital relationships become better after the transition to parenting and poor relationships often deteriorate. The presence of children usually increases family cohesiveness and gives parents a new sense of belongingness and meaning.

5. The presence of young children encourages marital stability by discouraging divorce or separation. However, most parents report a moderate decline in marital satisfaction after birth. Spouses report fewer displays of affection and more conflict. There is less time for leisure and romance and more opportunities for conflict and disagreement. Tension is especially likely when fathers do not satisfy mother's expectations about equitable division of labor.

6. The nine-month period of pregnancy provides expectant couples with opportunities to prepare for parenthood by obtaining adequate prenatal care, cultivating a social support system for child care after birth, obtaining information about birth and child care, and adjusting their lifestyle so that the fetus is properly nourished and protected from harmful substances.

7. Most, though not all, pregnant women report physical discomforts and psychological distress. Good information about pregnancy and birth, together with social support, usually make pregnancy a positive experience. Couples who choose prepared childbirth receive information and training for birth. Parents-to-be also can select a gentle birth delivery.

8. Parent-infant bonding is strengthened by approaches to birth that encourage the father's participation, that allow the infant to "room-in" with its mother during her recovery, and that give parents plenty of early contact with the newborn. However, early contact with the infant is not necessary for bonding.

9. Many women report feeling depressed after bearing a child. The causes of postpartum depression are not clear. Stress, hormonal changes, fatigue, physical discomfort, marital tension, feelings of inadequacy, and the burdens of child care are likely factors. Sudden Infant Death Syndrome (SIDS) claims about 6,000 young infants each year. Children at risk can be attached to monitors that signal the parent if the infant's breathing is disrupted.

10. The greater emotional maturity and stability of those who become parents later in life allows them to enjoy parenting somewhat more than their youthful counterparts. Their children, however, may be self-conscious about having parents who look like grandparents and who are out of touch with youth culture.

11. About 2 percent of children in the United States are adopted. It is misguided to believe that most adopted children are maladjusted; however, a disproportionate number do suffer from emotional, social, and academic problems, especially during adolescence. Adoptive parents face special problems and issues, including what to tell a child about being adopted.

12. Foster care is intended to provide temporary shelter to children who cannot live with their biological parents. Ideally, the goal is to rehabilitate the biological family so that foster children can return, but many unfortunate children are moved from family to family.

GLOSSARY

adoption   A judicial process wherein biological parents give up their rights to a child and new rights and obligations are acquired by adoptive parents

artificial (donor) insemination   Placing donated semen into a woman's cervix or uterus

authority stage   Parents learn how to assert their authority

bonding   The process by which parents become emotionally attached to their children

couvade syndrome   The symptoms of pregnancy as experienced by expectant fathers

critical period   A relatively brief period in development during which young members of a species are susceptible to certain environmental influences

departure stage   Grown children leave home

family cohesiveness   A feeling of belonging to one's family

generativity versus stagnation   The life task that Erik Erikson associated with middle age. The positive outcome is generativity, establishing and guiding the next generation. The negative outcome is stagnation, or personal impoverishment

image-making stage of parenting   Preparing for birth and parenthood

infertility   The inability to conceive

interdependent stage   Parents acknowledge and accept their child's desire for independence

interpretive stage   Parents interpret the world to their children

in vitro fertilization   The conception of an embryo outside of a mother's uterus

nurturing stage   Becoming attached to the infant

parenting alliance   Parents working cooperatively in raising their child, based on their shared pride in child rearing

postpartum   Following birth

sensitive period   A period of heightened sensitivity to environmental influences

socialization   The process by which children acquire the values, beliefs, and behaviors that are considered desirable by their parents and society

surrogate motherhood   A way to become parents in which a woman (not the potential father's wife) is paid to be impregnated by a father's sperm, carry the fetus to term, and give the infant to the father and his partner

THOUGHT QUESTIONS

1. What kind of life experiences prepare people for becoming parents?

2. Would you prefer to have a male or female child first? If so, why?

3. Why do expectant fathers receive so much less support than expectant mothers?

4. What steps can hospitals take to optimize the bonding process?

5. Why would middle-aged people want to become parents?

6. You are informed that you are adopted. How would this discovery change your self-concept and your feelings about your adoptive family members? Would you be curious about your biological parents?

THE PROCESS OF PARENTING

OBJECTIVES 68
THE PROCESS OF PARENTING 68
DO PARENTS MAKE A DIFFERENCE? 70
SPOTLIGHT: SMALL MOMENTS MODEL OF
   DEVELOPMENT 71
PARENTAL COMPETENCE 73
Box 3-1 Psychohistory? 74
Parental Psychological Functioning 75
Parental Emotional State and Expression 76
Parental Interaction Style 77
Parental Discipline Style 79
How Parents Think and Reason About Parenting 80
Parental Consistency and Flexibility 82
Parental Self-Efficacy 83
FACTORS ASSOCIATED WITH PARENTAL
   COMPETENCE 84
Experiences in Family of Origin 85
Parent Education 86
Stress and Parenting 86
FATHERING 87
Fathers and Daughters 91
Fathers as Primary Caregivers 92
COMPARISONS OF FATHERS' AND MOTHERS' PARENTING
   STYLES 92
Attachment 93
Play 93

"After I had the baby, I had this feeling of motherhood. I knew that I had someone to care for, who needed me as much as I needed her. Even though I had more responsibility, it was not a burden. Just the opposite. My husband was very loving of both of us, and still is. Being parents changed us for the better. We show more respect to each other" (Mother of a 3-year-old girl).

"Children, for men, are a commitment, an investment, an obligation, a hope. They are men's chief contribution to the world and justification for their lives. The children are loved for themselves, yes, but they are also loved as carriers of their father's efforts and hopes and selves. Indeed, the two kinds of love cannot be disentangled" (Weiss, 1990, p. 193)

Interest and Interaction 94
Discipline 95
SUMMARY 96
GLOSSARY 97
THOUGHT QUESTIONS 97

OBJECTIVES

After studying Chapter 3, students should be able to:

1. Describe how evolutionary models of parenting attempt to explain parental investment in child rearing
2. Contrast socialization and genetic models in the debate about whether parents make a difference in how their children turn out.
3. Describe the small moments model of development
4. Define parental competence
5. Relate parental competence to the following parental attributes:
   a. psychological functioning
   b. emotional state and expression
   c. interactional style
   d. discipline style
   e. beliefs and reasoning ability
   f. consistency and change
   g. self-efficacy
6. Describe recent trends regarding father involvement in child care and factors that have promoted these changes
7. Analyze the obstacles that discourage father involvement in child care
8. Compare fathers who are primary caregivers to fathers who are not
9. Compare the parenting styles of mothers and fathers regarding:
   a. attachment
   b. play
   c. interest and interaction
   d. discipline
10. Describe how parents raise their sons and daughters differently

THE PROCESS OF PARENTING

Study Question *What purpose do parents serve?*

Who are we and why are we here? These two profound questions have occupied philosophers and other thoughtful people for at least 2000 years. Although there may be "higher" reasons for our presence on earth, most scientists seek explanations of human nature that are rooted in biology and in our understanding of the evolution of life. To the scientist, humans are a complex form of animal life on earth, here to reproduce our genes.

Although we are aware of occasional romantic feelings, it is never our **conscious** intention to reproduce or proliferate our genes. Instead, we experience a desire to "have children" (who, of course, happen to carry large numbers of our genes). Reproductive behavior in humans differs from that of other species in that we are aware that sexual intercourse can lead to pregnancy, birth, and a very dependent child. Reproductive behavior in other species is hormonally and instinctively controlled. Mr. and Ms. Squirrel have no awareness or understanding of the con-

68

nection between their passionate behaviors, Ms. Squirrel's pregnancy, and the pitter-patter of little paws up and down the tree.

Like all species, humans are subject to evolutionary-genetic pressure to reproduce. It is almost as though my genes want to reproduce themselves and the only way they can accomplish this is by getting their vessel (me) to have children. Through the mechanism of heredity, evolution has programmed animals to reproduce. Unlike other species, humans are aware of this fact and are subject to complex cultural and social pressures that can promote or inhibit sexual desire or sexual behavior.

What does all of this have to do with parenting? Evolutionary pressure to reproduce is not "satisfied" merely by sexual activity, pregnancy, or even birth. For my genes to proliferate, my children must survive long enough to reproduce my (and my wife's) genes and then produce and raise my grandchildren so that they can continue our ancient genetic line. I can ensure my own genetic proliferation by having large numbers of children or (my preference) by maximizing the likelihood that my limited number of children (and hypothetical grandchildren) live long and prosper. In other words, the key to successful reproduction of genes is having a large family or practicing high-quality parenting (or both). Because there is such a long period of dependence of human children on their parents before reaching maturity, the quality of parental care becomes the critical factor in a child's survival and growth (Goodyer, 1990; Maccoby, 1992).

If someone asked me why I try to be a good father, I would not respond, "So that my genes will proliferate." If my house were on fire, I would not shout to the fire personnel, "Hurry please, my DNA is asleep in the second-floor bedroom." My conscious motive for trying to be a good parent is valuing my children, not my genes. The evolutionary pressure to bear, nurture, and protect my children is real (and powerfully reinforced by social con-

ventions) but it is not something that I am ordinarily aware of.

In this vein, many aspects of mate selection, bonding, attachment, parenting and grandparenting behavior, and child rearing are thought by some to be guided by evolutionary pressures (Azar, 1996b; Feingold, 1992; Low, 1989; Scarr, 1993; Singh, 1993; Tiger & Fox, 1989). Evolutionary theory, for example, suggests that men who are attracted to women are attracted primarily on the basis of visual cues that indicate a woman's ability to reproduce. These include youth and physical features that indicate fertility. According to this model, women are attracted to men largely on the basis of nonphysical attributes (such as socioeconomic level, ambition, and intelligence) that give a competitive survival advantage to their prospective children (Feingold, 1992). Low (1989) suggests that the different strategies parents use to raise boys and girls correlate with optimal male and female reproductive patterns.

The greater nurturance we usually observe in women compared to men is addressed by another evolutionary theory, the **parental investment model** (e.g., Bjorklund & Kipp, 1996). Since women can bear only a limited number of infants but men can (theoretically) impregnate large numbers of women, evolutionary theory predicts that women should be more invested than men in any particular offspring (Feingold, 1992). Another way of contemplating differential male and female investment in our "seeds" is that females are born with only a few thousand eggs whereas each male ejaculation contains about half a billion sperm. In other words, the relative "scarcity" of egg cells compared to sperm makes them more valuable to their carrier.

Note how the parental investment model suggests two different, gender-related ways of proliferating one's genes—high-quality parenting (mothers are more involved in child care than are fathers) and having lots of children (traditionally, men have been more

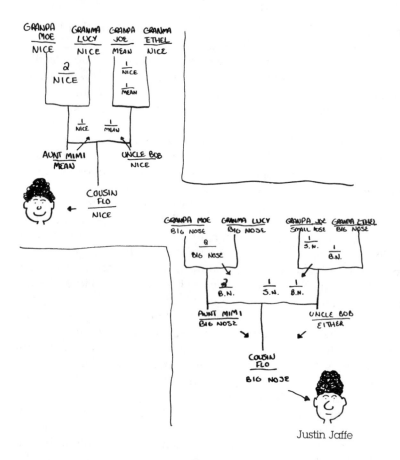

Justin Jaffe

promiscuous than women). Although these theories about evolutionary pressure on reproductive and parenting behavior are interesting and provocative, they are only theories. By no means are they universally accepted by researchers and theorists. In fact, some people find these ideas sexist and offensive. Although it is clear that biology disposes us to reproduce and to provide care for our offspring, we must be careful not to minimize the important role that personal history and social factors play in courtship, mating, and parenting behavior (Baumrind, 1993). Why is this chapter called The Parenting Process? The term *process* refers to the way in which something develops (changes gradually) in a more or less predictable fashion. Over time, most parents get better at what they do. The skills and even the personal qualities of competent parents emerge gradually. In this chapter, we consider what these skills and qualities are and where they come from.

DO PARENTS MAKE A DIFFERENCE?

This is an odd question to raise in the third chapter of a parenting text. Yet, there is an ongoing debate in the parenting literature about whether who a child's parents are makes much of a difference in how the child turns out (Harris, 1995). Psychologist Sandra Scarr (1992, 1993) contends that children raised in families that provide "a good enough

Small Moments Model of Development

Study Question   What effect do everyday parent-child encounters have on children's behavior and personality?

Most traditional theories of development (e.g. Freud, Erikson, Piaget) portray change in terms of critical life events or stages. It is as though children are a certain way for a while and then something (biology, learning) happens that makes them noticeably different. Children who initially sit or lie where we left them eventually crawl, creep, and then walk. Children who make cooing and babbling sounds eventually speak words and then sentences. Stage models suggest that we view these events in terms of a "pre-locomotion" stage that sets the occasion for a "locomotion stage" and a "pre-language stage" followed by a "language stage." A corollary of most **stage models of development** is that children of a given age or developmental level share common cognitive structures that support the development of new abilities (Bandura, 1986; Piaget, 1954).

Behavioral learning theories, such as B.F. Skinner's (1953) operant conditioning model, reject the major premise of stage theories of development (that development occurs in leaps and bounds). They claim that personality develops in small increments rather than in large steps. The **small moments model** is in the tradition of the cumulative learning theories. It attributes a child's development over time mainly to the daily, moment-by-moment interactions between children and their caregivers.

Proponents of this model contend that "there are no critical phases in a child's life—the oral and anal periods of psychoanalysis, for example—but rather a long continuum of important moments" (Goleman, 1986a).

Virtually every time parents and children interact, both parties are changing each other slightly, almost imperceptibly. *In the small-moments model, no period of life is attributed greater or less importance for development than any other period.*

Researchers have carefully analyzed videotaped parent-child interactions. They observe distinctive ways in which mothers, for example, through their "countless small exchanges" with their children, shape "the child's pattern of interaction in later relationships in life" (Goleman, 1986a). In one instance, all of the interactions between a mother and her twin sons were videotaped in periodic 3-hour sessions until the children were 15 months old. "At three-and-a-half months there were repeated exchanges in which the mother and Fred would gaze at each other. Fred would avert his face, his mother would respond by trying to engage eye contact again and Fred would respond with a more exaggerated aversion of his face. As soon as the mother looked away, though, Fred would look back at her, and the cycle would begin all over, until Fred was in tears. With Mark, the other twin, the mother virtually never tried to force continued eye contact. Mark could end contact with his mother when he wanted" (Goleman, 1986a). When the infants were observed at later dates, Fred appeared more fearful and dependent than Mark. Fred continued to use gaze aversion to break off contact with other people. Mark looked people straight in the eye, usually with a smile.

This type of micro-analysis of a parent-child interaction reveals subtle patterns in parental behavior that encourage or discourage specific behavior patterns in children, including self-regulation (Raver, 1996). Infants become more securely attached and children are more compliant when their parent's response is "attuned" to their actions. Reciprocal, mutually rewarding contact lets an infant know that he or she is affecting another person and is being understood (Isabella, Belsky, & von Eye, 1989; Westerman, 1990).

One of the implications of the small moments model is that early experiences, as influential as they may be, do not necessarily have a greater impact on development than later experiences. In fact, in the case of early abuse or deprivation, experiences later in life (such as therapy or a supportive relationship) sometimes can alleviate prior emotional harm. "An imbalance at one point can be corrected later; there is no crucial period early in life—it's an ongoing, life-long process" (Stern, quoted by Goleman, 1986a).

The small moments model encourages a fine-grained analysis of the parent-child relationship. In the next section, we will study how distinctive patterns of parental sensitivity and responsiveness influence children's behavior patterns and dispositions (Dadds, 1987). The child's momentary actions and reactions, in turn, guide parental behavior. Subtle, gradual changes in daily parent-child interactions during infancy and early childhood lead to changes in children's behavior and the parent-child relationship over the course of childhood and adolescence. A related model in physics, **chaos theory** (Gleick, 1987), describes how, over time, small events can have large effects. One spark can lead to the destruction of an entire forest. A seemingly insignificant experience (small moment) during childhood such as a visit to a library or a new kid moving in next door can have unanticipated large effects over time.

The small-moments perspective challenges traditional, global stage theories of development (like Freud's) that attribute greater influence to maturation than to the accumulated effects of reciprocal, daily encounters. Stage theorists criticize the small moments model for ignoring the powerful role that maturation plays in development. Do not feel compelled to choose between these two models. Both bring our attention to important patterns of change.

environment" usually turn out fine. In her words, "Ordinary differences between families have little effect on children's development, unless the family is outside of a normal, developmental range. Good enough, ordinary parents probably have the same effects on their children's development as culturally defined super-parents" (Scarr, 1992, p. 15).

Scarr claims that virtually all nonabusive family environments above the poverty line are equally likely to produce children who are within the normal range of development. She reasons that most parents provide their children with a "good enough environment," that is, the basics children need to thrive—nurturance, affection, instruction, adequate care, and so on.

If not parenting style, what does account for differences among children? Scarr (1993) contends that individual differences in personality among children raised in ordinary families are due mainly to genetic variations and how these genetic variations lead children to "construct" their experiences. Scarr plays down the "details of socialization" (p. 1341) in explaining differences among children. Instead, she emphasizes the role of heredity.

Another accomplished researcher, Diana Baumrind (1993), vehemently disagrees with Scarr's contention that a "good enough environment" is all that children need to be "normal." To support her view that different families affect children differently, Baumrind makes the following points: (1) parents in different cultures raise their children somewhat differently and their children's personalities usually reflect their "national character" (e.g., Asians are less likely to express their emotions publicly than are Europeans or Americans); (2) the environment that many children experience today, including frequent exposure to crime, drug abuse, high dropout rates, and sexually transmitted diseases, is not "good enough" for the average child; (3) parents who are very involved in their children's lives have much more influence on their children's development than uninvolved parents; and most importantly, (4) there are countless studies (many cited in this chapter) that demonstrate the important role that parental competence plays in determining children's social and cognitive development. Baumrind maintains that parents make a big difference in their children's development through their use of discipline, supervision, family problem solving, and encouragement. Judith Harris (1995) suggests that the most important socialization experiences occur not at home, but in peer groups and other groups outside of the home.

Scarr (1993) doesn't deny the importance of socialization but suggests that variations in parenting style do not produce significant differences among children. What does? Again, Scarr believes that children's genetic makeup is the key to understanding individual differences. Baumrind worries that if parents accept this premise, they will be less motivated to provide high-quality parenting. If parents believe that their efforts do not make much of a difference in how their children turn out, why bother?

PARENTAL COMPETENCE

Study Question *What does it mean to say that one person is a more competent parent than another person?*

It is always informative to watch parents and children interact in a public setting such as a library, supermarket, or park. A typical first impression is that parents are remarkably different in how they speak to and interact with their children. We notice that some parents are more vigilant and more involved in their children's activities, more sensitive to their child's current emotional state than other parents. Some parents respond quickly and effectively when a child is distressed or in danger; others seem to hardly notice. Although we observe just a small sample of parental behavior (which may or may not be representative of the parent we are observing), it is difficult not to conclude that some people are better at parenting than others.

We can define **parental competence** on the basis of how parents interact with their children or on the basis of child outcomes, that is, how children "turn out." Regarding the latter, our premise is that parents must be doing something right if their children are caring, well-behaved, good problem solvers, self-confident, and are fun to be with (Maccoby & Martin, 1983).

This premise is shaky in one respect. Parenting is hardly the only factor that determines how children turn out. Some children who enjoy high-quality parenting have serious adjustment problems. Other, so-called **resilient children** (discussed in Chapter 9), are surprisingly well-adjusted despite being abused or neglected (see Box 3-1). One more qualification—although I use the terms competent and incompetent parenting, parental competence is better understood as a continuum than as an all-or-none phenomenon. And, almost all parents have good and bad days.

We study parental competence mainly by focusing on parent-child interactions. We try to relate specific parenting qualities, behaviors, and beliefs to desirable child outcomes such as those cited above. We do not yet have a simple, clear-cut model of parental competence. As the ecological model of development

Box 3-1

Psychohistory?

Is it possible to attribute particular adult behaviors or personal qualities directly to documentable childhood experiences? Wanda Kaczynski's son Theodore allegedly is the Unabomber, the man accused of constructing and mailing bombs that killed three people and injured 23 across the United States. Mrs. Kaczynski is haunted by traumatic incidents in Theodore's early life.

When he was nine months old, for example, he was restrained on a hospital bed—wild fright in his eyes—while doctors photographed an unusual case of hives that kept him isolated in the hospital away from his mother for a week. She remembers that he would not look at her when she arrived for a visit or when she returned to take him home. When he was four years old, he would not look at a picture of himself pinned to the bed. "He refused to look at it anymore. And I thought, "Oh my God, he's having the

same feelings that he had when he was held down that way" (Star-Ledger, June 17, 1996, p. 6).

"I ponder endlessly over it," says Ted's tormented mother. "What could I have done to keep him out of the wilderness? What could I have done to give him a happier life?" Ultimately, it is futile to try to relate specific adult behaviors or problems to specific early childhood experiences, traumatic or otherwise. Many children who had childhoods much worse than Ted's turned out alright and many of those who enjoyed relatively contented childhoods suffer major adjustment problems later in life. Even when we can document intense experiences during childhood, it is impossible to know the meaning of the event to the child or to know what coping resources might have been available to soften the impact of the disturbing episode.

suggests, the parent-child relationship is embedded in a broad array of biological, family, community, and cultural influences. An encounter between a parent and child usually reflects several different types of influence, some present in the immediate situation, some found in the personalities and the life histories of each party.

Influences include, but are not limited to, the following: personal qualities of each party (such as parental psychological functioning, education, and beliefs and the child's age, gender, and temperament); the type of activity in which they are engaged (play, feeding, discipline encounter); the immediately preceding activity; and the emotional state and coping resources of each participant (Dowdney & Pickles, 1991; Vondra & Belsky, 1993) (see Table 3-1).

As noted in Chapter 1, parents who live in different cultures display predictable similarities and differences in how they raise their children (Bornstein, 1991; Bornstein, Tamis-LeMonda, Pecheux, & Rahn, 1991; Bronstein, 1994; Rohner, 1994). For example, Indian parents, when holding their infants, display brief periods of intense affection. In the United States, however, parents rarely display affection to infants while holding them. Rather, when holding their infants, fathers play with them and mothers provide either caregiving or discipline. Unlike parents in the United States, Indian parents rarely engage in rough play with their infants (Roopnarine, Talukder, Jain, Joshi, & Srivastav, 1990). Even within a particular society, different socioeconomic and ethnic groups display somewhat different

TABLE 3.1 Factors Associated With Competent Parenting

Parent psychological functioning

Quality of the marital relationship

Personal qualities of each parent

Parental emotional and coping resources

Parenting style

Parent discipline style

Parental beliefs and expectations about parenting and children

Life stress

Experiences in family of origin

styles of parenting (Kelley, Power, & Wimbush, 1992).

Ultimately, we who study parenting must accept a difficult fact of life—every parent-child relationship is unique. The complexity of even a single parent-child encounter can be so formidable that we should not expect to discover simple relationships between specific parental actions and child outcomes. Further, parenting is a very gradual process. Over time, parents change, children change, relationships change.

Parental Psychological Functioning

Adults who have serious psychological or emotional problems usually bring these problems with them into their marriages and family life. People who are chronically depressed, angry, or anxious must make a special effort to have a successful close relationship. An individual's psychological functioning also influences his or her choice of mate and the quality of the marital relationship. How two partners function as individuals and how they perform as a couple will affect their experience of pregnancy and the birth of their child (Emery, 1988).

The parents' relationship also affects the quality of the relationships that each parent has with each child (see Fig. 3-1). For example, as noted in Chapter 2, a chronically depressed mother may create or participate in an unhealthy marriage relationship which in turn leads to a less than optimal parent-child relationship. The key point is that there is a link between one's psychological functioning, one's ability to create close, caring relationships, and one's competence as a parent (Brook, Whiteman, Balka, & Cohen, 1995; Demo & Acock, 1996; Fisher & Fagot, 1993; Leadbeater, Bishop, & Raver, 1996; Vondra & Belsky, 1993; Woodworth, Belsky, & Crnic, 1996).

Competent parenting is linked to certain desirable personal qualities of parents, including psychological maturity, warmth, the ability to empathize, and a secure self-image (Benn, 1986). "It is unlikely that an individual who is caught up with his or her own psychological concerns will have the ability to decenter and take the perspective of a dependent infant. Without the psychological resources to understand, and consequently tolerate, the daily demands and frustrations of an infant or young child (let alone a teenager), a parent will be hard-pressed to demonstrate the patience, sensitivity, and responsiveness that effective parenting requires" (Vondra & Belsky, 1993, p. 5).

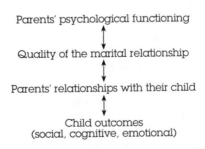

Figure 3.1 Links between parents' psychological functioning, family relationships, and child outcomes

Parental Emotional State and Expression

We seem to be a particularly emotional species. As responsible individuals, we try to act rationally most of the time. However, when push comes to shove, strong emotions often prevail. Parenting induces a lot of strong feelings. "Along with contentment and joy, parenting brings anger, dejection, and anxiety at levels matched by few other endeavors" (Dix, Reinhold, & Zambarano, 1990, p. 465). Even casual observation reveals a high rate of positive and negative emotional expression as parents and children interact (Dix, 1991).

One important goal of most parents is to promote healthy social-emotional development in their children. We want our children to feel good about themselves and about other people. The ability to experience and express emotions, including feelings of attachment and affection, plays a crucial role in having close relationships (Izard, Haynes, Chisholm, & Baak, 1991). Although parents in different cultures express affection and rejection differently, children in all cultures sense whether or not they are loved (Rohner, 1994).

Think back to your own childhood. How would you rate your parents on a warmth-hostility continuum? How often were you kissed, hugged, complimented, and caressed? Did you feel loved and accepted by your parents or did you feel disliked and rejected? Many investigators confirm that displays of parental warmth play an important role in healthy parent-child relationships (Bronstein, 1994; MacDonald, 1992; Rohner, 1994).

Adults who as children had warm and affectionate parents typically "sustain long and relatively happy marriages, raise children, and [are] involved with friends outside their marriage at midlife" (Franz, McClelland, & Weinberger, 1991, p. 592). Children of cold or distant parents often report feeling depressed and unworthy and do not feel successful as adults (Lasko, et al., 1996). Can you sense a connection between the feelings your parents conveyed about you during your childhood and how you feel about yourself today?

Children's desire to communicate and to comply with parents' requests depend partly on their parent's ability to provide a warm, emotionally expressive environment (Gottman, Katz, & Hooven, 1996; Herman & McHale, 1993). Mothers who are warm and sympathetic often have children (particularly daughters) who are empathic, helpful, and emotionally supportive of others (Fabes, Eisenberg, & Miller, 1990). Children of mothers who are facially expressive are better able to recognize and produce a variety of emotional facial expressions than children of cold or hostile mothers (Camras, Ribordy, Hill, Martino, Sachs, Spaccarelli, & Stefani, 1990).

It does not follow that displays of negative emotions by parents always are inappropriate. Occasional, mild expressions of parental anger, disappointment, and disapproval teach children an important lesson—their actions affect other people's feelings. Frequent or intense displays of anger or hostility by parents toward their children are counterproductive and render children less susceptible to effective socialization (Camras et al., 1990; Maccoby, 1992).

As we will discuss further in Chapter 9, most children can cope with occasional parental displays of anger and annoyance. It is chronic, excessive parental anger that taxes the coping abilities of most children. Many of us remember how humiliated we felt as children when an adult shouted at us. Harsh reprimands rarely made us feel like pleasing anyone. Distressed parents often have a hard time motivating compliance in their children. Not surprisingly, they frequently report feeling inadequate as parents. They feel helpless, have negative feelings about their children, and sometimes blame their children for the unhappy state of the family (Dix, 1991).

Although parents try to adjust their facial and emotional expressions according to their child's emotional tendencies (Fabes, Eisenberg, Karbon, Bernzweig, Speer, & Carlo, 1994), children's emotional responses do not usually match those of their parents. During parent-child play, positive emotions are expressed by both parties. During conflict, there are displays of negative emotions by both participants, although children's emotional reactions are more a product of a parent's interactional style and the situation than of the parent's displayed emotion. Even affirmative parental behaviors sometimes induce distress in children, as when upset children become enraged when their parents try to make them laugh (Dowdney & Pickles, 1991). Competent parents know how and when to elicit laughter. For example, they use humor or distraction to defuse a tense situation such as going to the doctor. Children are more likely to comply with parental requests when they are in a good mood.

Parental mood, everchanging, affects how parents interpret and react to their children's misbehaviors. For example, angry mothers expect their children to behave more negatively. They have a more pessimistic view of their children's problems (Fox, Platz, & Bentley, 1995). Depressed mothers and fathers often are overly critical of their children's behavior (Dix, Reinhold, & Zambarano, 1990; Simons, Beaman, Conger, & Chao, 1993b).

Does being in a positive mood help parents respond better when their children are disobedient? Apparently not. Positive parental moods intensify parents' negative reactions to disobedience, partly because parents will interpret a child's behavior more negatively. Children's disobedience appears more negative to parents in a good mood because it contrasts with their positive outlook and expectations. Also, we resent when people, even children, "bring us down" from our good feelings (Dix & Reinhold, 1991).

TABLE 3.2 Role of Emotions in the Parent-Child Relationship

Expressing affection helps children feel loved and lovable

Warm, sympathetic parents often have children who are empathic, helpful, and emotionally supportive

Children of facially expressive mothers have a larger emotional "vocabulary"

Humor and affection can defuse tense situations

Parental moods can affect parental interpretations of children's behavior

Dix (1991) draws several conclusions concerning the role of emotions in parent-child relationships (see Table 3.2): (1) strong feelings, positive and negative, are almost continually experienced and expressed by parents and their young children; (2) parental emotions, such as warmth and hostility, predict the quality of the caregiving environment; (3) parental emotions are partly determined by life events such as marital and job stress and by parental coping resources; and (4) chronic and intense negative parental emotions predict family dysfunction, child abuse, and maternal depression. "Thus, perhaps more than any other single variable, parents' emotions reflect the health of parent-child relationships. They are barometers for the quality of parenting, the developmental outcomes that are likely for children, and the impact that environmental stresses and supports are having on the family" (p. 4).

Parental Interaction Style

Picture if you will a father and daughter building a play house with blocks. How well do they work as a team? Are Dad's actions coordinated with his daughter's or do the two work independently? How in tune is dad with his child's emotional state, attention, and desires? Current views of parenting emphasize the importance of **active partnership**, that is, appropriate, contingent responding during parent-child interactions (revisit **Spotlight**, "Small-Moments Model"). Play and instructional encounters proceed more smoothly when parents focus on the object or activity that the child is interested in (joint attention), ask the child relevant and interesting questions, and respond to the child's remarks positively, contingently, and appropriately (Moore & Dunham, 1995; Raver, 1996; Roberts & Barnes, 1992; van den Boom, 1994).

Other examples include topic maintenance (parents continue the thread of their children's comments); social routines (parents arrange situations where the topic or activity is familiar and predictable to the child); and

modeling (parents provide examples of appropriate language responses) (Kaiser, interviewed by Azar, 1995b). This all takes practice. Most children perform better when their parents provide an optimal level of stimulation and guidance, not too much or too little (Belsky, Lerner, & Spanier, 1984).

This is not to suggest that there are hard and fast rules about how to interact successfully with children during instruction and play. However, most children are more compliant and learn better when parent's actions are supportive of and coordinated with the child's (Bronstein, 1994; Dumas & LaFreniere, 1993; Hauser-Cram, 1996). Not only should a parent's actions be guided by what the child is doing, parents also should provide guidance only when it is needed. When the child is able to continue successfully on his or

Competent parents bring to their child's attention the critical features of a task.

her own, parental support should temporarily be withdrawn. Other times, taking turns would better support children's active participation and learning (Fiese, 1990).

Alert parents provide a structure for learning that is age-appropriate. This process is called **scaffolding**, in that parents provide a temporary support for a child's emerging abilities (e.g., Choi, 1993; Denham, Mason, & Couchoud, 1995; Kirchner, 1991; Plumert & Nichols-Whitehead, 1996). They take a task like getting dressed or writing a report and break it up into manageable units that enable a child to be successful. They bring a child's attention to each critical feature of the problem as it becomes relevant to finding a solution. Such parent-child interactions become routines which the child can apply at a later time and in other problem situations (Rogoff, 1990). Parents of younger and disabled children need to be more directive in their interactions with their children, and more responsive to their children's efforts (Landry, Garner, Pirie, & Swank, 1994; Plumert & Nichols-Whitehead, 1996).

Children's speech, vocabulary skills, and cognitive development benefit from a responsive, conversational style through which parents encourage a child's expression and communication (Olson, Bates, & Kaskie, 1992; Roberts & Barnes, 1992). Such exchanges are most helpful when they are frequent and occur in a variety of contexts (Hoff-Ginsberg, 1991; Pratt, Kerig, Cowan, & Cowan, 1988). Infants and toddlers learn that their parents are available, responsive, and trustworthy when parental responding is in synchrony (coordinated) with a child's distinctive emotional and behavioral style (Fabes, Eisenberg, Karbon, Bernzweig, Speer, & Carlo, 1994; Isabella & Belsky, 1991; Isabella, Belsky, & von Eye, 1989).

Westerman (1990) observed 16 mothers interact with their toddlers on block-building tasks. Prior to the study, half of the mothers reported having serious compliance problems

and half reported having mostly cooperative encounters with their children. The mothers with cooperative children adjusted their behaviors so that their instructions were more specific when their child was failing and less specific when the child was succeeding. The mothers who were more alert provided guidance when it was needed and withdrew guidance when the child was on track.

It takes time for new parents to learn how to regulate their behaviors according to the signals their children provide. They learn gradually how to match or accommodate their infant's gaze, vocalizations, and emotional responses (Barratt, Roach, & Leavitt, 1992; Bornstein et al., 1992). To help them learn interactional skills, new parents should observe how experienced parents and teachers create an active partnership in learning and play with young children.

Parental Discipline Style

Competent parents try to guide their children's behavior without being overly controlling (Baumrind, 1975). They understand the importance of structuring household environments so that children can explore areas and manipulate interesting objects safely (Maccoby, 1992). When their children are defiant, responsive parents avoid coercive tactics such as threats and criticism. Instead, they adjust their behaviors in ways that promote cooperation and harmony (Pettit & Bates, 1989).

Alert parents notice the difficulty that young children have in disengaging from current activities. Their engrossment in pleasurable activities prevents youngsters from noticing or responding to their parent's instructions or requests. Awareness of their child's current state allows parents to judge whether instructional or power-assertion strategies are more appropriate (Dix & Reinhold, 1991).

When their children refuse to comply,

thoughtful parents "negotiate, compromise, convince, and frame events in ways that make cooperative courses of action acceptable to children" (Dix, 1991, p. 7). The net result is that parent and child both have positive feelings about the activity and about each other. "Parents experience less negative and more positive emotion if they coordinate interactions with children such that mutually satisfactory behaviors and outcomes occur" (p. 6).

There is less resistance to parental requests when parents are sensitive to children's concerns. Further, parents who anticipate misbehavior and direct their young children's attention toward acceptable objects or activities avoid the development of behavior problems and gain greater compliance and cooperation (Holden & West, 1989; Pettit & Bates, 1989).

For example, parents who use conversation to distract their toddlers in a supermarket or who give their children even minimal explanations for denying their requests in a toy store have less conflict with their children than parents who simply refuse such requests (Bates, Lounsbury, & Klein, 1976; Holden, 1983). In Chapters 5 and 6, we will examine effective discipline strategies in much greater detail.

How Parents Think and Reason about Parenting

Powell (1993) points out that parenting is "an active, cognitive process" (p. 87). Most of the time we do not react impulsively to a child's actions. How we respond depends partly upon how we feel about what the child is doing. In turn, how we feel about a child's behavior depends partly upon how we interpret both the behavior and the specific context in which it occurs.

Compared to children's thinking and reasoning, parents' beliefs, expectations, and interpretations have received minimal research attention. This is odd because parental cogni-

tions guide much parenting behavior and problem solving (Baden & Howe, 1992; Boddy & Skuse, 1994; DeBaryshe, 1995; Pridham, Denney, Pascoe, Chiu, & Creasey, 1995). A given child behavior, such as splashing water, may elicit a favorable reaction in one situation (a swimming pool) and a negative reaction in another (a bathtub). As previously noted, a parent's mood influences how he or she interprets a behavior or encounter. Thus, parental beliefs, interpretations, and mood states all mediate between what a child does and how a parent feels about and responds to the behavior (Bugental, Blue, & Lewis, 1990; Dix & Reinhold, 1991; Mills & Rubin, 1990; Strassberg, 1995).

Where do parenting beliefs come from? This is not a simple question. Many new parents actively seek out information and ideas about parenting and child development from friends, neighbors, and from "experts" who appear in TV panel discussions or who write books. A visit to a large bookstore's parenting or family section will reveal dozens of books that provide parenting advice and information of varying quality (Young, 1990).

Presumably, our childhood experiences in our family of origin shape some of our beliefs about how to raise children. Cultural stereotypes about boys, girls, parents, and families also influence parental beliefs (Okagaki & Divecha, 1993). The workplace is another setting where parents can acquire information that influences their model of parenting (Crouter & McHale, 1993b). The media, including TV depictions of harried parents and sassy children, often provide a distorted view of family life that is somewhat discouraging.

Parental beliefs and expectations also derive from daily parent-child interactions. "As parents and children accumulate a long history of interacting with one another, each acquires a set of expectations concerning the other's behavior and stereotyped ways of interpreting the other's reactions. Probably,

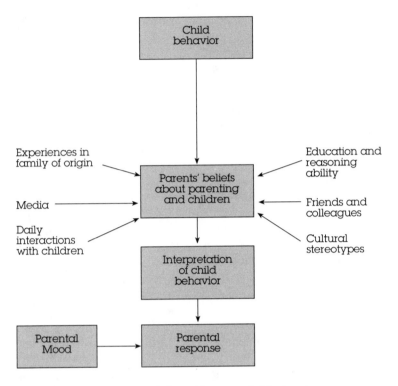

Figure 3.2 Parental beliefs guide parental behavior.

each progressively reacts to the other more in terms of these stereotypes than in terms of the other's actual moment-to-moment behavior" (Maccoby, 1992, p. 1014).

When parents interact with their children, they usually have specific concerns or plans in mind. They may want a child to eat breakfast or to clean her room. Parental annoyance occurs when a child's actions frustrate these concerns or plans. Alert parents usually interpret the situation accurately so that they have sufficient understanding and control to promote their agenda (Dix, 1991). For example, if a child refuses to do her homework, before expressing disapproval a parent might attempt to understand the source of the resistance (Parent: Why don't you want to do your homework? Child: I don't know. I just don't want to. Parent: Is it because the work is too hard?)

We also expect that a parent's ability to reason about child rearing will be related to his or her ability to reason in general. Parents with limited reasoning skills and those who are not knowledgeable about child development frequently have naive, overly simplistic beliefs about their ability to influence their children's behavior (Baden & Howe, 1992). At the extremes, they assume that they have either total control or no control over their children's actions. Competent parents arrive at a middle ground understanding that they can either improve the situation or deteriorate it further (Dix & Reinhold, 1991; Goodnow, 1988a; Kochanska, 1990; Miller, 1988; Pratt, Hunsberger, Pancer, Roth, & Santolupo, 1993).

As noted above, we are concerned about parental cognitions because their beliefs about why children act the way that they do guide parents' responses to their children's behavior. If a parent convinces himself that his child's misbehavior is innate or dispositional, he will blame himself less and thus avoid feeling guilty or incompetent (Baden & Howe, 1992). However, he may also downplay any potential influence that he might have in correcting his child's behavior. Thus, parental beliefs, because they guide parenting behavior, can have a significant impact on children's long-term development (Baumrind, 1993; Himelstein, Graham, & Weiner, 1991; Hyson, Hirsh-Pasek, Rescorla, & Cone, et al., 1991; Murphey, 1992).

Like psychologists, parents usually attribute children's behavior to one of three categories of influence—heredity (disposition), rearing, or situational factors. Naturally, parents like to take some credit for their children's accomplishments ("My daughter, the genius."). They also can let themselves off the parenting hook by attributing misbehavior to their children's dispositions ("He's a difficult child.") or by blaming the situation ("She didn't get enough sleep last night.").

According to the present analysis, parents enhance their effectiveness when they hold realistic beliefs about their potential influence on their children's behavior and development. Realistic beliefs are those that lead to constructive action (Himelstein, Graham, & Weiner, 1991; Pridham, et al., 1995). For example, if a child is doing poorly in school, blaming the teacher ("He's not patient enough with the children.") or blaming the child ("She's not good in math.") lets the parent off the hook but suggests no helpful course of action. Rather than placing blame, competent parents define the problem ("Why is she having difficulty?") and then seek practical solutions ("How can we help?"). Compared to less thoughtful parents, parents who are capable of more complex reasoning about the parent-child relationship also are more accepting,

warm, and stimulating (Dekovic, Gerris, & Janssens, 1991).

Parental Consistency and Flexibility

Study Question *How can parents balance consistency with flexibility?*

Consistency and flexibility are two additional elements of skillful parenting. Being consistent is important in that children function better in a stable, predictable environment. Parents who set limits but who do not follow through confuse their children and undermine their own credibility. Within a given developmental period, whether it be infancy or adolescence, consistency in parenting values and style is desirable.

Flexibility and change are just as important as consistency. As children mature, most parents adjust their parenting style accordingly. As children get older, they require less control and supervision. They benefit from greater autonomy (self-regulation). Whereas younger children sometimes require physical forms of control (e.g., restraining, lifting), older children (especially teenagers) respond better to reasoning, persuasion, negotiation, and yes, compromise. Although parental values (e.g., lying is bad) usually remain consistent over time, the manner in which specific values are taught should reflect the situation and the child's maturity.

McNally, Eisenberg, and Harris (1991) examined maternal consistency and change from childhood to adolescence. Using a longitudinal, repeated-measures design, the investigators interviewed 32 mothers five different times over a period of eight years. Their children (16 boys and 16 girls) were about 8 years old at the beginning of the study and about 16 years old when the study was completed. The investigators hypothesized that maternal control would gradually decrease with age until children reached adolescence and then would either level off or increase because of maternal concerns about dating, sex, and drug usage. The mothers were questioned about their displays of affection, their attitudes about parental control, child independence, and disciplinary practices.

The study revealed a relatively high degree of consistency in the mothers' reported child-rearing practices over the 8-year period, confirming that "individual differences in mothers' child-rearing attitudes and values, as reflected in practices, sometimes are quite stable over time and are based on deep-seated beliefs and goals" (p. 196). There were some age-related changes in maternal practices, however. As predicted, maternal control *increased* with child age during mid-adolescence. Mothers reported that they expressed fewer positive feelings and more negative feelings when their children (especially their sons) were older. Although maternal values are fairly stable over time, the way in which mothers express these values changes as children mature.

Parental flexibility is seen in other ways. Parents vary their involvement in different areas of their children's lives according to the importance they attribute to a particular domain (Costanzo & Woody, 1985). There are times when children need their parents' help and there are times when parental involvement discourages self-reliance. The specific way that parents respond to their children's behavior reflects several factors, especially their interpretation of their child's behavior and abilities. Depending upon circumstances (and parental mood), parents may be competitive or cooperative, strict or permissive, affectionate or annoyed. From observing their parents, children learn that although personality traits and parenting styles are fairly stable, everyday behavior is situation-specific.

Parental Self-Efficacy

Study Question   *What role does self-confidence play in competent parenting?*

Bandura (1982, 1986) introduced the concept of **self-efficacy** to describe one's sense of being capable of solving a given problem or succeeding at a task. Clearly, some people display greater confidence in their problem-solving abilities than do others. A successful track record in a specific domain (popularity, academics, sports) usually increases one's expectations of future success, whereas perceptions of failure usually weaken self-efficacy. Bandura contends that our beliefs about our competence play a central role in our behavior and personality, particularly regarding our willingness to take risks, accept challenges, and persist toward elusive goals.

Parents who believe that they are capable caregivers usually do a better job. In turn, successful parenting strengthens parental self-confidence. "A mother's ability to attend to and integrate cues and signals from her infant is dependent upon how effective she perceives herself to be, which in turn influences her ability to respond in a sensitive, contingent manner" (Donovan, Leavitt, & Walsh, 1990, p. 1638).

Believing that one is inadequate as a caregiver is self-fulfilling in that this belief discourages actions that might disprove the premise. For example, a father who believes that he is not capable of comforting his young son may not even try. On the other hand, believing that one has control over events that are not easily controllable (such as an infant's distress or an adolescent's mood) also can impair parental self-confidence (Donovan, Leavitt, & Walsh, 1990).

Teti and Gelfand (1991) investigated the role of self-efficacy in young mothers' interactions with their infants. They hypothesized that the effects of depression, social support, and maternal perceptions of infant temperament on caregiving behavior depend on how confident mothers feel about their efforts. We noted in Chapter 2 that depressed mothers typically offer less than optimal care to their children. But why?

Teti and Gelfand observed 48 clinically depressed and 38 nondepressed mothers as they interacted with their infants. They also questioned the mothers regarding their self-confidence and their children's temperaments. They found that maternal self-efficacy (self-confidence) is significantly related to maternal competence. Mothers who are confident in their parenting ability behave more competently and are less prone to depression. They also are less likely to perceive their children as difficult.

Mothers who feel capable apparently marshal their resources and rise to the occasion when dealing with difficult babies. Mothers who doubt themselves are more likely to withdraw and are less creative and resourceful. Since experience is a great teacher, we can predict that parents of older children and parents who have several children would feel more self-confident about their parenting than less experienced parents (Fish & Stifter, 1993).

FACTORS ASSOCIATED WITH PARENTAL COMPETENCE

Study Question   *What personal qualities and life experiences distinguish competent from less competent parents?*

Although there is evolutionary pressure on individuals to reproduce and to experience nurturant feelings toward children, parenting skills are not innate. Differences in parenting ability are rooted mainly in family and life histories and in current life circumstances (Goodyer, 1990). Recent research findings repeatedly bring our attention to what is called the **ecology of parenting**, "the interplay of individual and environmental factors that together shape parental behavior" (Vondra & Belsky, 1993, p. 25).

Personal qualities that are related to parenting, such as self-esteem, self-confidence, level of education, and coping resources, reflect earlier life experiences. In addition, parental behavior reflects current situational factors such as life stress, the quality of the marital relationship (for parents who are married), and the availability of social support (see Fig. 3.3). We consider some of these factors below.

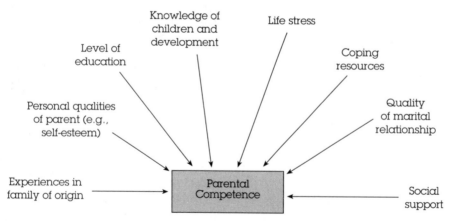

Figure 3.3   Factors associated with parental competence.

Experiences in Family of Origin

"What was experienced in the family of origin shapes what an individual expects from other close relationships including, presumably, both one's partners and one's children" (Vondra & Belsky, 1993, p. 13). It doesn't surprise us that much of what we know about relationships and caring is learned during childhood in our own family of origin (Lewis & Owen, 1995). For better or for worse, the people who raised us become the primary role models for how we raise our own children. Over the course of childhood and adolescence we develop interpersonal skills (and deficits) that determine our ability to have close relationships with friends, partners, and, if we become parents, with our own children (Miller, 1993).

This is not to say that we treat our children exactly as our parents treated us. In the absence of extensive training, we tend to recreate with our own children the basic relationship patterns we observed and practiced in our family of origin (Benson, Arditti, De Atiles, & Smith, 1992; Biringen, 1990; Martin, 1990; Simons, Beaman, Conger, & Chao, 1993a; Sroufe & Fleeson, 1986). For example, in Chapter 1 we discussed a study of the "generational transmission" of harsh parenting behaviors. Children exposed to harsh parenting practices often repeat these practices when they become parents. On the other hand, people who as children enjoyed warm, supportive parenting learn that parenting is "a pleasant, gratifying endeavor, and this message increases the probability that their children will grow up to experience interaction with [their] offspring as rewarding" (Simons, Beaman, Conger, & Chao, 1993a).

What we learn about having relationships in our family of origin depends partly on what we see happening between other family members and partly on how individual family members treat us. Watching our parents argue or hurt each other teaches us about the use of verbal and physical aggression in close relationships. Frequent, harsh treatment at the hand of mom or dad (our primary authority figures) teaches us that when someone does something you don't like, get even. When we begin to form close relationships during adolescence, we will probably practice what we know, that is, what we have learned while growing up (Martin, 1990).

A dramatic and unfortunate example of how children's experiences in their family of origin can influence their own parenting competence involves sexual abuse. Boundaries regarding sexual behavior exist between parents and children to protect children from adult exploitation. About one-third of the parents who maltreat their children were themselves abused by their own parents. Some women who as children had their sexual boundaries violated by their parents display seductive behaviors toward their sons and reject their daughters (Sroufe, Jacobvitz, Mangelsdorf, DeAngelo, & Ward, 1985; Sroufe & Ward, 1980).

Burkett (1991) videotaped families with mothers who had been sexually abused as children and families with nonabused mothers. On a variety of tasks, compared to nonabused mothers, the sexually-abused mothers were more self-focused than child-focused. They also relied more upon their children for emotional support. "The findings of both the videotaped observations and the interviews with mothers strongly suggest blurred boundaries between parent and child subsystems in families in which mothers experienced childhood sexual abuse" (p. 432). Of the twenty abused mothers observed, five parented well, nine "appeared to be caught up in a smothering, overcontrolling kind of pseudonurturing," and six "functioned marginally as parents, having little energy or emotional resources available for raising children" (p. 432).

These data demonstrate that a history of sexual abuse does not necessarily impair maternal competence. However, some abused mothers require counseling and extra social support to help them maintain proper boundaries between them and their children. Again, we do not mean to imply that people automatically raise their children the way that they were raised. As usual, the story is more complicated. Although sons who lack nurturant male role models will be somewhat hindered in their efforts to create a meaningful fathering role, intervening life experiences and instruction can "deflect" faulty patterns learned during childhood and replace them with nurturant and competent parenting practices (Vondra & Belsky, 1993).

Parent Education

Study Question   *What advantages in child rearing do educated parents have?*

Education is an extremely valuable life resource. Knowledge helps us to solve everyday problems and it helps us to understand and appreciate the world and ourselves. Cross-cultural research confirms that educated parents are advantaged in the domain of child rearing, especially regarding their ability to communicate verbally with their children (Hortaçsu, 1995; Richman, Miller, & LeVine, 1992).

Educated mothers view their children as being more cooperative and more sensitive than mothers with less education (Bronfenbrenner, Alvarez, & Henderson, 1984; Greenberger & O'Neil, 1992). Educated parents understand children better and are more informed about effective child-rearing strategies (Benasich & Brooks-Gunn, 1996; Fox, Platz, & Bentley, 1995). They are better able to find or create resources and social support networks that enhance their parenting and coping skills (Cochran, 1993). Educated parents also serve as role models for their children regarding achievement, re-

sponsibility, good work habits, and occupational aspirations (Amato, 1989; Haveman, Wolfe, & Spaulding, 1991; Hess & Holloway, 1984).

Stress and Parenting

Stress is unavoidable in life, especially for parents (Crnic & Greenberg, 1990; Deater-Deckard & Scarr, 1996). Partly because parenting requires postponing one's immediate desires and needs in order to provide care for another person, it is an inherently frustrating role. Raising children with special needs or with difficult temperaments is particularly challenging (Hauenstein, 1990; van den Boom, 1994). Parents also face economic and work pressures that can increase marital tension, lessen spouse support, and lead to harsh parenting, discouragement, and depression (Lavee, Sharlin, & Katz, 1996; Simons, Beaman, Conger, & Chao, 1993b; Simons, Lorenz, Wu, & Conger, 1993).

The question at hand, however, is not whether child rearing is stressful. We are more concerned about whether or not a given parent possesses the personal resources and social support necessary to function competently in this role. Whether we view chronic stress as a personality trait or as situationally induced, it affects how parents treat their children. Anxious parents are preoccupied with their elevated tension levels and therefore are less attentive to their children's needs and actions, compared to parents who are more relaxed (Lipsky, 1985).

Koeske and Koeske (1990) use the term *strain* to refer to the emotional consequences of chronic parenting stress. Strain includes "a sense of being overburdened, exhausted, inadequate, or pressed beyond what is comfortable or possible. Over the long run, mothers who continue to function under strain may experience negative outcomes such as physical or psychological symptoms, lowering of self-esteem, and dissatisfaction with parenting" (p. 441).

Coping with stress is an important component of competent parenting. Knowing how to relax, how to enjoy one's family life, and knowing where to find social support all help parents cope. Young parents in particular and those who are single, divorced, or separated, function better when they have access to reliable child care, emotional support, and good advice about discipline. The more help parents receive, the greater their emotional well-being and thus, the better the parenting (Cochran, 1993; Crockenberg, 1981; Jacobson & Frye, 1991; Parks, Lenz, & Jenkins, 1992; Simons, Beaman, Conger, & Chao, 1993b; Tessier, Piche, Tarabulsy, & Muckle, 1992). Mothers typically seek assistance from relatives and when they are not available, from non-relatives. Riley (1990) identified several types of support sought by harried fathers, including financial assistance, someone to talk to about marital problems, and enjoyable social activities.

In their study of 125 mothers, Koeske and Koeske (1990) observed that educated mothers and those who enjoyed high levels of so-cial support showed almost no negative effects of stress. Fathers who felt less stressed and more in control of their interactions with their infants reported more positive feelings about parenting and were more likely to participate in child care. Spouse support is a particularly important buffer for financial and other pressures (Goldstein, Diener, & Mangelsdorf, 1996; Greenberger & O'Neil, 1993; Noppe, Noppe, & Hughes, 1991; Simons, Lorenz, Wu, & Conger, 1993).

FATHERING

Study Question *Why do so many fathers have so little daily contact with their own children?*

Before industrialization, fathers and mothers worked together to survive economically and to raise their children. With the advent of industrialization, child care became exclusively women's work. Fathers took on the role of sole breadwinner and continued to be role models for their sons (Lamb, 1986). As the dominant parent and head of the family, fa-

Fathers who feel less stress have more positive feelings about parenting and are more willing to provide child care.

thers were expected to teach their sons how to be rugged and independent. Because mothers stayed home to care for their children, fathers' minimal participation in child rearing became the norm (Atkinson & Blackwelder, 1993). Influential psychologists like Sigmund Freud came to equate parenthood with motherhood and to see development as "unfolding primarily within the mother-child dyad, with fathers essentially peripheral to child development" (Silverstein, 1993, p. 267).

Today, we read and hear about the "new father," a family-oriented man who is eager to participate in a parenting alliance with his partner. In films like *Kramer vs. Kramer* and *Mrs. Doubtfire*, men rebuffed by their wives go to great lengths to maintain custody of their children (Coltrane, 1995). Is the new father a reality or a creature of TV sitcoms and films? Theorists do not agree. Some claim that each year we are seeing more good fathers and more bad fathers (Furstenburg, Jr., 1995).

Griswold (1993) contends that the image of the new father is essentially a "strategy of survival" that allows middle-class men to accommodate their wives' careers and financial contributions. Today, most mothers work (see Chapter 14, Selection 2, "Dual Career Families"). After work, they come home to their "second shift," taking responsibility for home and child care. As more women become providers, men increasingly become caregivers. Middle-class fathers who do not carry their caregiving weight risk criticism and condemnation from liberal quarters while neoconservatives argue that it is not man's nature to change diapers and sing lullabies (Silverstein, 1993). Although gender roles are becoming more flexible, fathers with working spouses still provide considerably less attention and care to their young than their partners do (Hossain & Roopnarine, 1994; Marsiglio, 1991; Paulson & Sputa, 1996).

Relatively few poor African-American children live with their biological father, at least for an extended period. Father-child contact is infrequent or nonexistent (Furstenburg, Jr., 1995). Limited father contact is disturbing, given evidence that links father involvement to social, emotional, and cognitive gains in children and greater intimacy with their partners (Barnett, Marshall, & Pleck, 1992; Belsky, Youngblade, Rovine, & Volling, 1991; East, 1991; Forehand & Nousiainen, 1993; Franz, McClelland, & Weinberger, 1991; Hawkins et al., 1995; Parke, 1995; Phares & Compas, 1992). For example, through the processes of modeling and identification, nurturant fathers appear to have an inordinate amount of influence on their children's (boys and girls) interactional style (Turner & Gervai, 1995).

It is tempting to assume that most fathers would spend more time with their children (as caregivers, playmates, and teachers) if not for rigid gender-role attitudes, long working hours, and unsympathetic employers. We would like to believe that fathers value time alone with their children, that they want to provide their mates with the co-parenting that they so desire and deserve. The reality, alas, is more complicated (Bryant & Zick, 1996; Gable, Belsky, & Crnic, 1995; Minton & Pasley, 1996; Silverstein, 1993; Sperling, 1993).

Socialized to achieve and to earn a living, it is not unusual to hear men declare that they show their interest in and fulfill their obligation to their children through their role as breadwinner (Doherty, 1991). More than anything else, it is men's commitment to their work (and lack of preparation for nurturing) that lies behind their limited contact with their children (Griswold, 1993; Weiss, 1990). Compared to employed women, it seems harder for men to tear themselves away from work, partly due to employer attitudes and partly due to self-imposed constraints. During industrialization, employment came to offer men more potential satisfaction and fulfillment than caring for children. "Active parenting is expected only of men whose jobs allow it. This conditional feature of the role . . . provides a legitimate rationale for men to escape heavy parenting duties" (Harris & Morgan, 1991, p. 532).

Another obstacle to increased father involvement in child care is the persistent cultural belief that women are more nurturant and sensitive than men. Few people perceive child care as a masculine enterprise. Social institutions like schools often ignore the existence of fathers or discourage them from taking an active role in child care (Power, 1984). Even some mothers are ambivalent about father participation in child care (Cowan & Cowan, 1992). The cultural message is clear—women are better with children ("mother love"). Men are reputed to be too rough, too insensitive, too distracted, or too ignorant to provide decent child care. While it is true that lots of men are not very enthusiastic about providing child care, parents of both genders can be heard moaning about the monotony of changing diapers, preparing meals, and giving baths.

Another obstacle for men who want to "do it right" is the paucity of male role models who teach that being nurturant is compatible with being masculine (Palkovitz, 1984). Since most sons are cared for mainly by their mothers and other female caregivers, they have few opportunities to view males being sensitive and caring. Lacking their own "father figures," well-intentioned fathers find their initial attempts to provide care stressful (McBride, 1989). Although many fathers claim that, unlike their own fathers, they want to be active participants in their children's lives, they aren't clear about how to accomplish this goal (Daly, 1995; DeAngelis, 1996b).

The least painful type of child care involvement for many men is time spent with children while mothers are present. "When alone with their children, fathers, not surprisingly, are vulnerable to the boredom, fatigue, and tension so familiar to mothers" (Baruch &

Barnett, 1986a, p. 991). To a considerable extent, father participation in child care depends on men's relationship with their partners. "The mother seems to function much as a gatekeeper, regulating the father's involvement with the infant, and she continues to influence his relationship with the infant even when he is not at home, in the way she refers to him in his absence" (Yogman, Cooley, & Kindlon, 1988, p. 61).

A father's commitment to his children often depends upon his current feelings about his wife (Marsiglio, 1995). Given the incidence of marital conflict and divorce, this is risky business. Fathers who are strongly bonded to their children are less likely to "abandon" them during marital conflict and other hard times. Less invested fathers see child care as drudge work which can be easily delegated to a more willing mother. Some women find that it is easier to provide care than to plead for help or argue constantly about equitable division of labor (Hawkins, et al., 1995). These mothers pick up the slack, in effect conspiring with their husbands to treat child care as women's work. A mother of a three-year-old describes her husband: "He's never changed a diaper in his life. He's even afraid to change her clothes. He's a big man—he's afraid he's going to hurt her. He will feed her, now that she's older."

A father comments, "Annie is really a lot of work. I would not want to spend a tremendous amount of time with her. Lisa [his wife] is just much more tolerant of that than I am . . . A one-year-old has no fear of anything. They have to be watched constantly. That's very tiring . . . I sort of feel guilty about how much time I spend with Annie versus how much time Lisa spends. Lisa is the woman—she always gets the responsibility of Annie. I think it's like thirty percent of the time it's me. Lisa said that she has no problem with that" (quoted by Weiss, 1990, p. 172). This father compensated for his lesser participation in child care by helping out his wife in other ways, such as doing errands. A woman's gender-role attitudes and her feelings about her own father's availability influence her expectations about partner involvement (Baruch & Barnett, 1981; de Luccie, 1995; Willoughby & Glidden, 1995).

Optimally, paternal commitment reaches a critical point where it leads to greater participation in what becomes a self-perpetuating cycle of increasing involvement. Men who participate in prepared childbirth classes and the delivery of their infant and then provide early care are likely to want to continue their involvement. A father gets "hooked" into child care when he cares too much about his children not to be (Levine, Murphy, & Wilson, 1993; Palkovitz, 1985).

Phares (1993) suggests that the "dad-cad" dichotomy is false; there is a continuum of involvement from the most involved to the least involved fathers. It is a continuum of financial, physical, and emotional sustenance reflecting many influences, including the parents' gender-role attitudes, employment status, and the gender, age, and number of children. Regarding gender, fathers spend more time with sons than with daughters, partly because of similar interests ("male bonding") (Bryant & Zick, 1996). Having sons brings fathers further into the parenting fold for sons and daughters (Katzev, Warner, & Acock, 1994). Fathers are least involved in families with only female children (Harris & Morgan, 1991).

Although men gradually are increasing their involvement in child care, the best fathers do not necessarily spend the most time with their families. Several investigators (Easterbrooks & Goldberg, 1984; Grossman, Pollack, & Golding, 1988) report that the quality and quantity of fathering are not necessarily related. Fathers who like their jobs and who are the most satisfied feel better about themselves and have good relationships with their children. Although satisfying, their jobs also are demanding, leaving them with relatively little time to spend with their families.

How does fathering change as children age? de Luccie and Davis (1991) interviewed fathers with firstborn children in four age groups: 3–5 years, 7–9 years, 11–13 years, and 15–17 years. The fathers were questioned about their child-rearing practices and attitudes and about their satisfaction with the fathering role. Fathers viewed themselves as more nurturant, affectionate, and supportive when their children were preschoolers. They reported being less involved with school-aged children, probably because older children require less attention and supervision. Fathers said that they displayed less affection to older children and spent less time with them.

Based on a study of 39 father-son dyads, Salt (1991) reported agreement between fathers and sons that affectionate touch is important in their relationship. However, fathers displayed less affectionate touching as their sons got older. Is this because fathers become less comfortable expressing affection to older children? Probably not. Older sons were less accepting of touch than were their fathers. Many parents notice that when their sons and daughters approach adolescence, they become uncomfortable about parental displays of affection, especially hugs and kisses. This seems to be an inevitable part of the separation process so evident during early adolescence, so parents should try not to have their feelings hurt when rebuffed.

In de Luccie and Davis's study, fathers of adolescents conceded that they are neither as accepting nor as involved in the daily lives of their teenaged children as they were when their children were younger. Nevertheless, reported father satisfaction was highest during adolescence! Why would fathers be least satisfied when they were most involved with their children (during the preschool years) and most satisfied when they were least involved (during adolescence)? The labor and pressure of caring for firstborn infants and toddlers seems to take its toll on paternal role satisfaction. Parents of older children spend less time providing child care and given their experience, they parent with greater confidence (de Luccie & Davis, 1991).

Despite their limited involvement in child care, we should not conclude that fathers are little more than playmates to their children or assistants to their mates. To their sons especially, involved, caring fathers are role models in (1) how to view the world, (2) how to act toward females, (3) how to manage crises and provide protection of the family, and (4) how to approach and solve problems. The best fathers find many ways to encourage their sons and daughters to be independent, goal-oriented, and persistent, and to teach them the value of being productive. "Fathers, in essence, teach their children how to 'get along' with friends and strangers outside of the family" (Bridges, Connell, & Belsky, 1988, p. 99).

Fathers and Daughters

"My father treated us as he would have treated boys. He encouraged the same education, the same aspirations for career. What he taught us was that working hard was a good thing and I interpreted working as working outside the home. I never thought about being a mom. In the back of my mind, I figured one day eventually, it would come with the territory of being female" (daughter of an accountant, mother of 3 girls, quoted by Richardson, 1992).

Although many fathers encourage these qualities in their daughters, often there is a discrepancy between what daughters need and what fathers provide. Daughters seeking intimacy with and connectedness to their fathers often are disappointed. Some men believe that having feelings of closeness, let

alone displaying them, is not manly. During adolescence many girls (and some boys) report feeling distant from their fathers (Youniss & Smollar, 1985). This is unfortunate because the key element of effective fathering may well be a man's ability to convey acceptance and love to his children (Forehand & Nousiainen, 1993).

"Father may feel ill-equipped to relate to his daughter, to understand her needs, and to cope with her physically maturing body. As a consequence, he may withdraw or become rejecting. . . . A father who is distant, rejecting, or inappropriate can have a profound, negative impact on his daughter's self-esteem and sexuality. . . . Whether father was available and accepting, cruel and hateful, or something in between, each woman is faced with the challenge of making peace with this very important figure in her life" (Cifrese, 1993, pp. 2–3).

Fathers As Primary Caregivers

Study Question   *Can fathers be as nurturant and sensitive as mothers?*

Most men who adopt the role of primary caregiver do so for relatively short durations. Single fathers aside, there are very few fathers in nuclear families who provide long-term primary care for their children. Radin (1988) and her colleagues studied primary caregiving fathers in families with at least one preschool child who live in Ann Arbor, Michigan, a university community. A follow-up study was performed 4 years later, allowing them to compare families that persisted in primary father care with families that reverted to primary mother care.

They found that men who become primary caregivers are somewhat older, better educated individuals with flexible working hours. They have small families and are satisfied with their wives' employment status and the child-care arrangements. Many have negative views of their own father's lack of involvement in child rearing. Some of their wives were raised in homes with working mothers and had positive views of their fathers.

When these parents were asked why they prefer father care, they gave several reasons. Many felt that children should be left with a parent, not with a baby-sitter. One wife commented, "It's a comfortable arrangement that we fall into naturally, and my husband won't quit child care even if there is a change in his job status." Radin suggests that there are so few men who provide primary care because "it is difficult to find the combination of conditions which may be necessary for a family to withstand the powerful societal pressures on those who try to create new parental patterns of behavior" (Radin, 1988, p. 140).

Boys and girls benefited cognitively from high father involvement. This probably is attributable to the special way fathers interact with their children. "They tend to be more physical, more provocative, and less stereotyped in their play than mothers . . . primary caregiving fathers spend more time than do traditional fathers in cognitively stimulating activities with children, particularly with daughters" (Radin, 1988, p. 140).

COMPARISON OF FATHERS' AND MOTHERS' PARENTING STYLES

Study Question   *Are there differences in how mothers and fathers interact with their children?*

"The father, as socializer and playmate, provides the infant with cognitive and social stimulation that is qualitatively distinct from that provided by the mother" (Bridges, Connell, & Belsky, 1988, pp. 92–93).

One theme of this chapter is that although there is considerable overlap between the roles of mother and father, the two roles are not equivalent (Averill & Power, 1995; DeAngelis, 1996a; Starrels, 1994b; Walker & Armstrong, 1995). Specialization between the two roles is traditional and a normative fact of life in most or all cultures (Collins & Russell, 1991; Emery & Tuer, 1993; Mboya, 1995). In most two-parent families, when a child is in the presence of both parents, the mother's primary function is to provide care or nurturance and the father's job is to maintain order and assist the mother (Power, McGrath, Hughes, & Manire, 1994). Usually, when alone with a child, either parent is capable of providing both services. Thus, we usually observe gender role specialization, but occasionally we observe gender flexibility in parenting (Bryant & Zick, 1996).

The fact that fathers who are primary caregivers (such as single fathers) act like traditional mothers suggests that in parenting, role and situation usually are stronger than gender (Martin, 1994; Walker & Armstrong, 1995). In other words, as primary caregiver, a male parent is more parent than male (Starrels, 1994b). Parents of both genders monitor their children, provide transportation, and urge their children to study and clean up after themselves. Nevertheless, we bring our gender to the roles we play. Thus, mothers and fathers perform these "genderless" activities differently (Coltrane, 1995; Weiss, 1990). And, as noted previously, men must make a more concerted, conscious effort to invest themselves in daily family work (Hawkins, et al., 1995).

Researchers study and compare the parenting styles of mothers and fathers (Parke & Suomi, 1983; Pratt, Kerig, Cowan, & Cowan, 1992). The most important finding is that fathers and mothers are equally capable of caregiving (Collins & Russell, 1991; Easterbrooks & Goldberg, 1984). Perhaps because as a group fathers are less interested in providing care, mothers spend far more time tending to young children (Baruch & Barnett, 1986b) and are more involved with older children (Paulson & Sputa, 1996). Mothers provide nurturance, comfort, and care to infants and toddlers. They are more involved in their children's daily lives and more responsible for promoting harmony in family relationships. As a result of their greater involvement, mothers have more conflict with their children than fathers do, especially during adolescence. It is not unusual to hear adolescents complain that their mothers are overinvolved in their lives and their fathers are underinvolved (Shek, 1995; Steinberg, 1990).

Fathers stimulate and play with their young children and provide assistance to their partners when asked. They usually are more concerned about their children's education and values than their momentary emotional state. "Fathers tend to be specialists in the world outside the home. Men feel they are acting most as fathers when they can interpret the world for their children, train the children to deal with it, protect the children from its dangers, and sponsor the children— the boys especially—into a place in the world" (Weiss, 1990, p. 170).

Mothers usually are less focused than fathers on achievement in the wider world and more concerned about their behavior at home. They specialize more in caring for children in the present. As a result, mothers usually become the preferred attachment figure to children and fathers become the preferred coach or playmate (Berk & Berk, 1979; Bretherton, 1985; Robinson, 1977; Weiss, 1990). To the extent that fathers are invested in their children's achievement, they experience pride when their children perform well. Pleasing one's father seems to be a particularly important factor in children's academic performance (Cooksey & Fondell, 1996; Forehand & Nousiainen, 1993).

Attachment

A father enters a room, his baby daughter smiles, says "Dada," and raises her arms to be held. A mother leaves her infant son with a new babysitter, the boy moans and cries for several minutes. Children show their attachment to their parents by hugging and smiling, by clinging and crying. Strong emotions are likely to be displayed upon separating from or rejoining parents. Psychologists consider the attachment bond to be the emotional core of parent-child relationships (Ainsworth, 1989; Bowlby, 1951)

We can identify similarities and differences in how children become attached to their mothers and fathers (Cox, Owen, Henderson, & Margand, 1992). For mothers and fathers, positive, affectionate interactions with infants enhance security of attachment (e.g., Belsky, 1996). For mothers but not for fathers, the amount of time spent with a child is a very good predictor of security of attachment.

Why would the amount of time a father spends with a child not be a good predictor of attachment? It is likely that when mothers work, fathers spend more time with their children (whether they want to or not). More than mothers, fathers' attitude toward the infant and toward parenting is an important predictor of secure attachment in infants. Because fathers usually are not primary caregivers and because they spend much less time with their children than mothers, their attitudes about the child and their satisfaction with the parenting role become key factors in the father-child relationship. In any case, most children are equally attached to both parents and feel affection for both parents throughout life (Barnett, Marshall, & Pleck, 1992).

Play

"Emotionally, the bond between me and Angela is stronger because she spends more quality time with me. When she is sick or hurt, she comes to me. However, Angela is 'Daddy's girl' when it comes to playing and fun" (Angela's mother).

Play behavior is an important modality of father influence in western cultures, particularly with sons (MacDonald, 1993). Many studies have compared father and mother play. Almost all have found that father play is less conventional and less verbal than mother play (particularly with preschoolers). Whereas mother play is more reserved and visual, father play is more unpredictable and exciting. Because father play often is rough-and-tumble, it elicits stronger positive and negative reactions from children (and mothers) (Belsky & Volling, 1987).

Through competitive activities such as sports, fathers cultivate in their children determination, resilience, the ability to function under pressure, and (usually) good sportsmanship. Fathers feel more confident coaching their sons than coaching their daughters, especially during adolescence (Weiss, 1990). "I would do more physical things with Dan than with his sister—be a little rougher in our play. We had a pool with our first house. We have photographs of me tossing Dan way up into the sky, and he'd fall back into the water. We also liked to wrestle on the floor" (father of 2).

Larossa and Larossa (1989) note that play, father's preferred activity, is "cleaner" than the forms of baby care provided by mothers (e.g., changing diapers, feeding). It is also less demanding and requires less parental attention. "Fathers, in other words, may choose play over work because play 'eats' less into their own free time" (p. 141).

Interest and Interaction

There is a remarkable similarity between the feelings expressed by mothers and fathers following birth. A father's interest in his children is reflected partly in his presence and partici-

TABLE 3.3 Comparison of Fathers' and Mothers' Parenting Styles

In most families, we observe both gender role specialization and gender flexibility in parenting.

Fathers and mothers are equally capable of competent caregiving. Most children are equally attached to both parents.

Typically, a mother's main function is to provide care and nurturance whereas a father's main job is to maintain order and assist the mother.

Because mothers usually are more involved in providing child care, they have greater involvement in discipline than fathers and have more conflict with their children (especially during adolescence).

Mothers spend more time providing nurturance, comfort, and care. Fathers spend more time playing with children and teaching them about "the world" outside the home.

Father play is more "rough-and-tumble" than mother play and elicits stronger reactions in children.

pation during birth and in his desire to hold and gaze at the newborn. It is also evident in his descriptions of elated feelings and pride following birth. Mothers who have extended contact with their infants at birth demonstrate greater bonding, even a year later. Similarly, fathers who have extended contact at birth interact more with their infants and become more involved in caregiving responsibilities (Keller, Hildebrandt, & Richards, 1985).

Yogman and his colleagues videotaped mothers and fathers interacting with their young infants. They concluded that fathers are "capable of skilled and sensitive social interaction with young infants" (Yogman, Cooley, & Kindlon, 1988, p. 56). They observed that "by three months of age, infants successfully interacted with both mothers and fathers with a similar, mutually regulated, reciprocal pattern, in which both partners rhythmically cycled to a peak of affective involvement and then withdrew . . . Mothers and fathers were equally able to involve the infant in games" (p. 56).

New fathers bottle-feed their infants about the same amount of milk as mothers. They are equally sensitive to such cues as mouth movements, coughs, spitting up, and sneezes. They adjust their speech to infants almost as well as mothers do and report feeling as attached to their infants as mothers are (Parke & Suomi, 1983; Pratt, Kerig, Cowan, & Cowan, 1992). Although distressed infants usually are more comforted and soothed by contact with their mothers, they are emotionally and behaviorally responsive to both parents (Hirshberg & Svedja, 1990).

Study Question *How do fathers' interactions with their sons change when their wives are present?*

As predicted by family systems theory (see Appendix A), how a parent interacts with a child is partly a function of the presence or absence of his or her spouse. A father's presence changes the pattern of mother-child interactions and a mother's presence changes the nature of father-child interactions. Gjerde (1986) studied family interaction patterns in 44 intact, mainly white, middle-class families, each with an early adolescent child. Each adolescent was observed interacting alone with a father, alone with a mother, and with both parents together. Trained observers independently rated the three types of interactions.

Based on previous observations of a relatively high rate of conflict between mothers and their adolescent sons, Gjerde hypothesized that the father's presence during an interaction would enhance the quality of the mother-son relationship. He also hypothesized that the mother's presence would lessen the father's involvement during the interaction. The data supported both hypotheses.

When fathers were present, mothers were more engaged and consistent with their sons than when mothers were alone with their sons. Thus, the quality of mother-son interactions improved when fathers were present. Presumably, fathers assume some responsibility for controlling their sons, lessening pressure on the mother to adopt a controlling stance. The father's presence apparently increases the son's responsiveness to the mother, freeing her to act more nurturantly.

The quality of father-son interactions deteriorated when mothers were present. Fathers were rated as being less involved and more critical and antagonistic compared to when they were alone with their sons. Why would the presence of a mother reduce a father's involvement with his adolescent son? Apparently fathers, who usually are quite willing to engage their sons directly when mothers are absent, defer parenting control to mothers when they are present (Gjerde, 1986). The study did not reveal similar dynamics for the presence of the father on mother-daughter interactions. Thus, we remain cautious about generalizing between parent-son and parent-daughter relationship patterns or assuming that mother-adolescent and father-adolescent patterns are equivalent.

Discipline

To compare mothers and fathers as disciplinarians, Yogman and his colleagues (1988) provided slightly frustrating tasks to toddlers and observed parent-child interactions. One task was a two-minute prohibition episode, during which two attractive objects (a toy frog and a tape recorder) were presented, one of which was designated "off limits." The researchers videotaped the parents' attempts to promote compliance with their instructions that the child not touch the tape recorder.

They found that the fathers' and mothers' interactions with the toddlers were much more similar than different. They were alike in who gave the first directive, the number of directives given, and the compliance elicited from the child. Mothers did verbalize more often than fathers. The investigators concluded that the stereotype of fathers as family disciplinarian was not supported by their observations.

Power and Parke (1986), observing families at home, noted that mothers attempt to enforce more rules than fathers do. Many studies confirm that mothers are more demanding and more emotionally expressive than fathers (e.g., Buhrmester, Camparo, Christensen, Gonzalez, & Hinshaw, 1992). This probably reflects the greater involvement of mothers in disciplining their children. In most ways, however, mothers and fathers adopt comparable discipline strategies (McHale, Crouter, McGuire, & Updegraff, 1995). It is interesting, however, that boys often show more compliance to their fathers than to their mothers whereas girls seem to be equally compliant to both parents (Power, McGrath, Hughes, & Manire, 1994).

Russell and Russell (1987) interviewed parents of school-age children and observed them interacting with their children at home. They observed that mothers interacted more with their children, and were more directive and involved in caregiving. Fathers interacted primarily in the context of play. The investigators did not find differences between fathers and mothers in parental sensitivity or reactions to misbehavior. Fathers were not found to be more negative or restrictive. In fact, fathers were observed engaging in more physical affection, warmth, and playful joking with children than were mothers! Brachfeld-Child (1986) observed parents teach their infants to place a cube in a cup. She found that mothers and fathers spent the same amount of time and used the same types of strategies directing the infants' activities. Fathers talked more to the infants and, unlike

those in the three previously cited studies, did set more limits.

McLaughlin (1983) videotaped parents attempting to achieve compliance verbally in their preschool children during free play at home. He observed that mothers and fathers behaved similarly, but fathers used more commands. Children complied equally with mothers' and fathers' suggestions and questions. These studies reveal basic similarities in discipline strategies practiced by mothers and fathers.

SUMMARY

1. There is evolutionary pressure for human beings to reproduce. Successful reproduction requires more than childbearing. Parents can maximize the likelihood of continuing their genetic line by having a large number of children or by practicing high-quality parenting (or both).

2. Parental competence can be defined in terms of the quality of child care parents provide or by child outcomes (how children "turn out"). Since child outcomes reflect more than just parenting influences, our treatment of parental competence in this chapter is based mainly on caregiver behavior.

3. Factors associated with parental competence include parental psychological functioning, emotional state, and expression of emotions; style of interacting with children; discipline style; beliefs and reasoning ability; consistency and flexibility; and self-confidence. Other predictive factors include a parent's experiences in family of origin, educational level, life stress, social support system, and personal coping resources.

4. Role specialization in providing child care made sense when fathers went to work and mothers were full-time homemakers and

caregivers. Because most mothers work, there is increasing pressure on fathers to become more involved in child care. Fathers consider work to be a higher priority than child care, but they are willing to help their partners when asked.

5. Most fathers spend relatively little time alone with their children. When they do, they view themselves as helping out their partners rather than taking primary responsibility for caregiving. Mothers usually plan and supervise fathers' child care activities.

6. It is becoming more acceptable for males to be nurturant, sensitive, and affectionate, and for females to be assertive, independent, and achieving. These changes encourage men to seek closer and more satisfying relationships with their children. Caring, involved fathers are role models to their children, especially their sons, regarding how to live in the world beyond the family. Fathers who are primary caregivers act more like traditional mothers than like traditional fathers.

7. Although mothers and fathers have somewhat different, gender-related styles of parenting, their parenting behaviors and philosophies are more similar than different.

GLOSSARY

active partnership Parents' ability to respond appropriately and contingently during interactions with their children

chaos theory A model that physicists use to describe how small events, over time, can have large, unanticipated effects

ecology of parenting The interplay of individual and environmental factors that shape parental behavior

parental competence Parents' ability to achieve their child-rearing goals

parental investment model The evolutionary model that suggests that females are more genetically invested in offspring than are males

resilient children Children who adjust well despite extreme family or life experiences such as neglect or abuse

scaffolding Parents' ability to provide a temporary structure for learning that is appropriate to a child's current level of performance

self-efficacy The belief that one is capable of solving or coping with a problem or succeeding at a task

small moments model A model that attributes children's development mainly to the daily, moment-by-moment interactions between children and their caregivers

stage models of development Models of development, such as Freud's and Erikson's, that view developmental change as occurring in discrete, universal stages

THOUGHT QUESTIONS

1. From an evolutionary perspective, what function do parents serve?
2. Should people who want to become parents be required to obtain a parenting license that confirms their competence in this role?
3. Should people who have displayed gross incompetence in parenting be barred from having more children?
4. How would you go about providing an emotionally supportive home environment for your children?
5. What have you learned about parenting by being raised by your parents?
6. What do fathers miss by not being more involved in raising their children?
7. In what ways do the roles of mother and father differ?

4
CHAPTER

MARRIAGE, DIVORCE, AND NEW FAMILY CONFIGURATIONS

OBJECTIVES 100
PARENTS WITH PARTNERS 101
MARITAL AND FAMILY CONFLICT 103
Spotlight: Two Styles of Marriage: Male and Female 106
SEPARATION AND DIVORCE 107
Custody Arrangements: "Bests Interests of the Child" 109
Joint Custody 110
Stages of the Divorce Process 111
Noncustodial Parents 112
Visitation: Parenting from a Distance 113
Effects of Divorce on Children 114
    Parental Absence 116
    Adjustment of Custodial Parent 116
    Economic Disadvantage 116
    Parental Conflict 116
    Stressful Life Changes 117
Children's Age and the Divorce Process 118
    Adolescents 119
    Young Adults 119
Gender Differences In Adjustment 121
Interventions for Children of Divorce 121
SINGLE MOTHERING 122
Children of Single Parents 124
Evaluation 125
SINGLE CUSTODIAL FATHERS 126
STEPPARENTING 127

"Angry confrontations between parents, which go on for many years, create a negative emotional climate that can undermine a child's psychological development. It can spill over into problems the child has with playmates, which can be among the early signs of trouble" (Radke-Yarrow, quoted by Goleman, 1985a).

"I know she doesn't like it when we argue, because she cries and gets extremely upset when I'm upset. The worst thing is when she pushes him [her father] away. She thinks he's upsetting me. She can't help it. She has to realize people do fight. It doesn't mean they don't love each other" (mother of a 3-year-old girl).

Stepfathering 128
Stepmothering 129
Stepfamily Research 129
Parenting Stepchildren 130
Evaluation 131
GRANDPARENTING 131
Grandparents as Disciplinarians 134
Spotlight: Children of Gay and Lesbian Parents 135
SUMMARY 137
GLOSSARY 138
THOUGHT QUESTIONS 138

OBJECTIVES

After studying Chapter 4, students should be able to:

1. Describe the key ingredients of a successful marriage
2. Describe how marital conflict affects children
3. Compare the experience of marriage for men and for women
4. Discuss why so many couples have difficulty maintaining their relationship
5. Analyze the "divorce process" as a sequence of stressors for children
6. Describe the special problems faced by parents in single-parent families and stepfamilies
7. Describe the special role that grandparents play in children's lives
8. Describe the relationship between parent's sexual orientation and children's adjustment

Virtually all parents are heterosexual couples who discuss and consent to a pregnancy, have sexual intercourse, become pregnant, carry the child to term, and spend the next 20 or so years providing child care. Or are they? This familiar scenario ignores increasingly common situations that deviate from the stereotype of the traditional family, including unplanned pregnancies, parents who are not married to each other or at all, father absence and abandonment, divorce, custody battles, single-parent families, stepfamilies, adoption, grandparents raising grandchildren, and pregnancies resulting from artificial insemination, adultery, rape, or incest (Chaffin & Winston, 1991; Siegel, 1995).

A related cultural stereotype is that the optimal home environment for producing well-adjusted, healthy children can be provided only by middle-class, heterosexual, married, harmonious, two-parent families in which the father works and the mother stays at home with her children. Presumably, these generic parents are of the same culture, race, and religion. Although there really are such families, they are in the minority and their numbers are diminishing. The more we study parenting, the more we recognize "the multiplicity of pathways through which healthy psychological development can take place and the diversity of home environments that can support such development" (Patterson, 1992, p. 1025).

TABLE 4.1 Types of Family Configurations

Nuclear family

Single-parent family

Stepfamily

Adoptive family

Foster family

Grandparent-headed families

Families headed by gay parents

Families headed by unmarried adolescent parents

Families headed by cohabitating heterosexual couples

"Can stepfamilies ever really blend? Before my husband and I got married sixteen months ago I thought, definitely yes—we will easily blend—no problem. However, we are still working on blending and I am confident that we will be for some time to come. At first, I felt guilty about the minor difficulties we were experiencing—where was the 'perfect blend' we expected? But I have come to realize that it is going to take a lot of perseverance, love, communication, and time."

"Our problems, to name a few, are: one child resenting attempts by the stepparent to impose discipline; having to deal with my feelings of not having been the first (but the third, after his first wife and child) to share my husband's life; having to raise my husband's child, of whom he has joint custody; and something we are both guilty of, favoring our own children over our spouse's. We suppress it at every opportunity, but it is difficult not to favor your own flesh and blood. We may never feel the same kind of love for the stepchild, but

as long as we keep that hidden deep inside of our hearts, that is the best we can do. As far as they are concerned, we love them both" (a new stepmother).

In this chapter, we examine how marital conflict and family configuration affect children's development. Current concern about marital conflict stems from the common belief at midcentury that juvenile delinquents come from broken homes. It was soon realized that more than parental divorce, it is excessive family conflict and poor parenting that lie at the core of most children's behavior problems. Children who come from harmonious families usually adjust well during childhood, adolescence, and adulthood (Rutter, 1994).

We also will explore the topic of nontraditional family configurations, many of which, in one way or another, reflect the decline of the nuclear family. **Family configuration** refers to the structure of relationships within a family—whether children are raised by one or both biological parents, a single parent, cohabitating parents (two unmarried people who live together), adoptive parents, stepparents, grandparents, or by other caregivers. As we shall see throughout this text, it is not so much family structure as family process that determines the well-being of family members (Henry & Lovelace, 1995).

PARENTS WITH PARTNERS

In the United States and many other Western societies, we are witnessing an increasing separation of marriage and childbearing (Siegel, 1995). Today, fewer than half of all families in the United States have children and of those that do, one-third are headed by single parents (U.S. Census Bureau, 1994). Only one out of four households consists of married couples with children, the traditional **nuclear family**. From the 1950s to the 1990s, the number of single-parent families increased from 13 to 30 percent of all families with children. The U.S. Census Bureau defines a **family** as two or more persons related by birth, marriage, or adoption and living together. A **household** consists of all of the individuals who live together, whether they are related or not.

Each year in the United States, more than two million couples marry. About 40 percent of these unions are remarriages (Wilson & Clarke, 1992). Many parents **cohabitate**, that is, they live with but are not married to their partners. Some parents who remarry do not live with their biological children but live with and help raise stepchildren. In this section, we consider parents with partners who are raising at least one child.

A marriage is many things. It is a legal contract, a social institution, an intimate relationship, and to many, a lifelong commitment. For our present purposes, we can view marriage as an intimate relationship with distinctive stages and fairly predictable problems. For example, as discussed in Chapter 2, the transition to parenthood is stressful for most new parents and is accompanied by decreased marital satisfaction.

Children usually arrive early in a marriage, although sometimes before or outside of marriage. About 40 percent of women conceive their first child premaritally and about 30 percent give birth premaritally (U.S. Census Bureau, 1991). Although there is less disapproval nowadays for unmarried childbearing, most social institutions and traditions strongly encourage marital childbearing. Cohabitation is a precursor to marriage for white women in their twenties and is an alternative form of singlehood for African-American mothers and white adolescent mothers (Manning, 1993; Nock, 1995; Wu, 1995).

Typically, spouses hardly have time to get to know each other before a new family member arrives. With the advent of pregnancy, there are problems to be solved and decisions to be made. Difficult issues arise that require negotiation and compromise. Couples with similar expectations about marriage and family life usually have more satisfying relationships (Deal, Wampler, & Halverson, Jr., 1992).

As discussed in Chapter 2, following the birth of a child, marital relationships require extra attention and consideration (Lavee et al., 1996). Weary parents have limited amounts of time to devote to each other's needs. As children and their parents grow, the marital relationship presents new opportunities and issues regarding identity, intimacy, autonomy, dependency, emotional support, sex, control, and power (Kovacs, 1983; Wallerstein, 1994).

Marriages vary enormously in how well the spouses get along, their emotional investment in the relationship, sexual fulfillment, the allocation of time and financial resources, the distribution of power, and in the division of labor practiced by the partners. The key ingredients of stable marriages include not only love and commitment, but also autonomy, good communication skills, conflict resolution skills, intimacy, cooperation, and of course, a sense of humor (Robinson & Blanton, 1993; Weiss & Heyman, 1990). Intimacy in most marriages is enhanced by honest self-disclosure, acceptance of one's partner's self-disclosures, affection, cooperation, and trust (Levinger & Huston, 1990).

Getting married is risky business. It has become less likely over the past 30 years that couples who marry will achieve marital success (Glenn, 1991). Members of distressed couples are not very skillful at avoiding confrontations. Unhappy wives attempt to coerce unavailable husbands into compliance with their requests or demands. Unhappy husbands complain about lack of attention and affection. Everyday problems and issues remain unresolved and sometimes escalate into hurtful power struggles. Distressed partners feel increasingly helpless and angry. Many eventually decide to end the relationship.

TABLE 4.2 Characteristics of Successful Marriages

commitment

interdependence

reciprocity (desire to please)

good communication

integrity, credibility, and trust

intimacy and self-disclosure

emotional support and validation

good conflict resolution skills, especially flexibility, negotiation, and compromise

patience, sensitivity, and tolerance

congruent perceptions of the relationship

This chapter's focus on marital conflict and divorce should not detract from the accomplishments of the "lucky" half, couples who despite the odds manage to remain close and supportive until death do they part. The fact that most adults marry and that most divorced adults remarry confirms that there is something about the institution of marriage that works for most people. Marital satisfaction sometimes "spills over" into competent parenting *and* healthy psychological functioning in spouses (Demo & Acock, 1996; Erel & Burman, 1995; Vondra & Belsky, 1993). The fact that so many marriages fall apart is a tragedy for those involved and a challenge to those of us who try to understand close relationships.

MARITAL AND FAMILY CONFLICT

Study Question *How does marital conflict affect children?*

The family systems model (see Appendix A) stresses that each relationship in a family affects every other family relationship. The marital relationship is especially influential. Children in two-parent families learn about adult relationships mainly by watching how their parents speak to and treat each other. Children benefit emotionally and socially when their parents and other family members treat each other kindly and respectfully (Erel & Burman, 1995). Children suffer emotionally and socially when they are subject to frequent displays of negativity, anger, hostility, and especially physical aggression (Bretherton, 1985; Cummings & Davies, 1994; Emery & O'Leary, 1984; Fincham, 1994; Jenkins & Smith, 1991; Jouriles, Murphy, & O'Leary, 1989)

Boys sometimes react to conflict with hostile and aggressive behavior. Some studies suggest that girls exposed to intense family conflict have poor self-images and become withdrawn and anxious (Emery, 1982, 1988; Fergusson, Horwood, & Lynskey, 1992; Holden & Ritchie, 1991; Jaycox & Repetti, 1993; Jouriles, Murphy, Farris, Smith, Richters, & Waters, 1991; Kline, Johnston, & Tschann, 1991; Reid & Crisafulli, 1990; Smith & Jenkins, 1991). Marital conflict and family conflict often co-occur, making it difficult to distinguish their effects.

Family conflict refers to behaviors between family members that range from verbal disagreements and criticism to acts of physical violence (Jaycox & Repetti, 1993). Parental harmony and agreement about child rearing are related to positive outcomes for children (Vaughn, Block, & Block, 1988; Vuchinich, Vuchinich, & Wood, 1993), but exposure to parental arguments does not necessarily damage children. Although all families have occasional disagreements and confrontations, most children in these families do not display adjustment problems (Grych & Fincham, 1990; Jouriles, Murphy, & O'Leary, 1989). Those who witness occasional displays of marital discord are momentarily agitated, but most cope well, especially those who enjoy good relationships with their parents.

It may even be beneficial for children to witness *constructive* family disagreements, for example, observing their parents resolve disputes in good faith with minimal displays of hostility and aggression (Cummings & Davies, 1994; Easterbrooks, Cummings, & Emde, 1994). In this way, they can learn useful conflict resolution skills (Grych & Fincham, 1993; Grych, Seid, & Fincham, 1992).

Parental strife creates a climate of tension and other background emotions (Cummings, 1987). Jaycox and Repetti's (1993) study of families with preadolescents suggests that family discord is a much better predictor of children's maladjustment than is marital discord. Perhaps this is because most parents try to prevent their children from becoming aware of marital tensions. Although some maritally distressed couples can hide their angry feelings from their children and coparent successfully, it is more likely that partners who cannot get along with each other will not be able to support each other in their respective parenting roles (McHale, 1995).

Children who witness the angry exchanges and recriminations that accompany parental conflict usually are not present when their parents make up. They do not see apologies, expressions of remorse, and subsequent attempts to reestablish closeness. This is unfortunate because these children not only fail to observe adult coping and problem-solving skills, they are left with distorted views about how their parents feel about each other.

The amount of distress children report when their parents argue depends partly on how they interpret the meaning of the conflict (Cummings, Davies, & Simpson, 1994). Grych and Fincham (1993) describe three types of cognitions used by children to appraise their parent's conflict: (1) the degree of perceived threat, (2) their interpretation of cause or blame for the dispute, and (3) their belief that they can cope with the intensity of the encounter. Boys in particular feel threatened when they believe that a heated argument might escalate into violence and that they may be drawn into the conflict (Cummings, Davies, & Simpson, 1994). Children may fear that their embattled parents will divorce. Children (especially boys) sometimes blame themselves when parents argue about topics related to child rearing (Grych & Fincham, 1993). When they attribute their parents' argument to their own misbehavior, they become even more upset.

Sometimes boys and girls intervene when their parents quarrel, especially if they believe that their parents are arguing about them. Even infants and toddlers sense their parents' distress during arguments (Cummings & Davies, 1994; Easterbrooks, Cummings, & Emde, 1994). Self-blame and shame is one link between parental fighting and children's adjustment problems, at least for girls (Cummings, Davies, & Simpson, 1994). Children risk additional harm when they become enmeshed in the marital relationship or involved in heated encounters (Grych & Fincham, 1990; Grych & Fincham, 1993; Grych, Seid, & Fincham, 1992; Jouriles et al., 1991).

It is more the intensity and type of marital conflict that children observe than its frequency that predict antisocial behavior in children (Hanson, McLanahan, & Thomson, 1996). Angry, hostile marital encounters seem to be most damaging. The greater the number of heated exchanges that children witness, the more sensitized and vulnerable they become to subsequent expressions of anger and hostility (Cummings & Davies, 1994). Witnessing supportive and affectionate exchanges between parents desensitizes children to subsequent hostile episodes (Rutter, 1994).

Investigators are trying to relate specific types of marital conflict to specific adjustment problems in children (Emery, 1982; Fincham, 1994; Katz & Gottman, 1993; Jouriles et al., 1991). Since researchers would not intentionally expose children to parental conflict, studies in this area are usually correlational. Regarding the direction of influence, it is possible that difficult children create marital disharmony by giving their parents more to argue about (Emery & Tuer, 1993; Grych & Fincham, 1990). Most theorists reject this interpretation, contending that parental conflict aggravates child behavior problems (Gottman & Katz, 1989). The use of longitudinal studies will help clarify this issue (Fincham, Grych, & Osborne, 1994).

Marital conflict affects children's adjustment directly and indirectly (Forehand, 1992). The stress of constant marital strife can lead to inconsistent and ineffective parenting (Fauber & Long, 1991; McHale, 1995). ((Kurdek (1996) maintains, however, that parenting satisfaction and marital satisfaction are distinct and unrelated)). Parents who feel alienated from their partners may devote less time and attention to their children and feel less close to them (Brody, Pillegrini, & Sigel, 1986; Emery, 1982), jeopardizing the security of parent-child attachment (Bowlby, 1973). It is also possible that: (1) children imitate their parents' hostile actions and emotional manipulation; (2) children "act out" to distract their parents from marital problems and to bring attention to themselves; (3) children blame themselves for their parents' problems and become fearful and self-hating; and (4) maritally frustrated parents use inconsistent, rejecting, or punitive child-rearing strategies or are emotionally unavailable to their children. Available data do not consistently support one of these explanations over the others (Camara & Resnick, 1988; Emery, 1982; Fauber & Long, 1991; Fincham, Grych, & Osborne, 1994; Holden & Ritchie, 1991; Jenkins & Smith, 1991; Kline, Johnston, & Tschann, 1991).

Some mothers who are dissatisfied with their marriage become overinvolved with their children. Although this compensatory reaction is rooted in marital unhappiness, it further alienates the father both from the mother and the child (Brody, Pillegrini, & Sigel, 1986). I once counseled such a couple. The mother had been emotionally and sexually unavailable to her husband for many months. According to him, she had no other interests in her life besides her young daughter. The neglected husband often thought of leaving his wife. He fantasized that if he did, his daughter would play no role in his life. When he was angry, rejecting his daughter (whom he clearly loves) was just another way of showing his wife his unhappiness.

It is possible that distressed wives who become overinvolved with their children are compensating for what they consider to be "bad fathering." Belsky, Youngblade, Rovine, and Volling (1991) studied patterns of marital change in 100 families participating in the Pennsylvania Infant and Family Development Project. They found that the father-child relationship mainly reflects fathers' marital satisfaction. As noted in Chapter 3, unhappy husbands behave toward their children in a more negative and intrusive manner than husbands who are maritally content.

The marital relationship usually exerts more influence on the quality of fathering than on the quality of mothering. Fathers who are unhappy in their marriages often withdraw from their children, especially from their daughters (Howes & Markman, 1989; Kerig, Cowan, & Cowan, 1993; Stoneman, Brody, & Burke, 1989). Mothers fulfill their parental role to the best of their ability regardless of their marital satisfaction. Fathers are more emotionally invested in their children when their marital expectations are satisfied. Some men simply are ineffectual in any relationship, whether with their wives or with their children.

The ecological model reminds us that marital conflict and children's adjustment are complex phenomena, both embedded in the larger context of the family system and the community at large (Rutter, 1994). At this

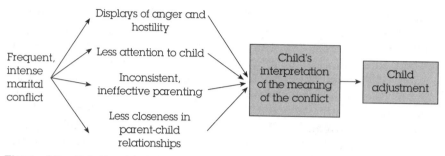

Figure 4.1 Relationship between marital conflict, parenting quality, and child adjustment

Two Styles of Marriage: Male and Female

Despite high divorce rates, marriage continues to be the popular choice for romantically committed couples. A happy marriage is one of the life goals that most adults mention (Glenn, 1993). It is also telling that most divorced people want to remarry and do remarry. The core quality of stable marriages is interdependence: sexual, economic, emotional, and communicational (Levinger & Huston, 1990). However, there remains a basic destabilizing force in every marriage: one partner is male and one is female. Research and everyday observation reveal that men and women bring somewhat different needs to marriage and different expectations about what marriage entails (Barich & Bielby, 1996).

Melinda Blau (1994) cites the following issues: "Communication (she wants more talk; he wants more action). Intimacy (she needs to relax to have sex; he needs sex to relax). Division of household labor and child care (she says she does more; he talks about how much he does). Money and careers (she says he doesn't value her job as much as his; he notes that he makes more money)" (p. 87).

Gender differences in power, relationship skills, and emotional investment in relationships can be observed as early as childhood (e.g., Davis, 1995). Women desire and expect greater intimacy in relationships than men do. "Men are much more likely to be either satisfied with the status quo or seeking changes that would provide them with greater distance and autonomy" (Jacobson, 1989, p. 30). Whereas men often complain about their sexual advances being spurned, women complain that men are too demanding sexually. Men often portray women as moody and self-absorbed and women view men as condescending and inconsiderate. Not surprisingly, the poorer the relationship, the longer the list of complaints (Buss, 1989).

Ted Huston, a psychologist at the University of Texas at Austin, interviewed 130 couples concerning their view of the marital relationship. The men and women differed regarding their interpretations of what constitutes emotional intimacy in a close relationship. "For the wives, intimacy means talking things over, especially talking about the relationship itself. The men, by and large, don't understand what the wives want from them. They say, 'I want to do things with her, and all she wants to do is talk'" (Huston, quoted by Goleman, 1986b).

Dr. Huston found that men are much more likely to accommodate their partners' desire for intimacy during courtship than during marriage. As marriage proceeds, men come to prefer spending more time at work or with their friends. When there is a large discrepancy between their partner's behavior during courtship and then after marriage, women become disappointed or angry. Marital conflict may ensue, particularly if differing intimacy expectations result in miscommunications and sexual anger (Jacobson, 1989).

Many women do not know how to convey to their partners that they look to them for emotional support. Unfortunately, most men have difficulty recognizing this need and become defensive or angry when confronted with their alleged inadequacies. Dr. Huston counsels, "You can't force intimacy. It has to arise spontaneously from shared activities." Many wives eventually resign themselves to getting emotional support from their female friends or from their mothers. Husbands who are capable of satisfying their wives' needs for intimacy and emotional support have more stable romantic relationships (Jacobson, 1989).

Ironically, men seem to need marriage more than women do. Their physical and social needs are more likely to be satisfied in marriage than are their partner's. Men and women agree that men get "a better deal" in marriage (Felmlee, 1994). Men report greater satisfaction with marriage than women. It is not surprising, therefore, that men evaluate almost all aspects of marriage more positively than do their wives. They are more satisfied regarding sex, money, power, relationship with parents, romance, and communication. Women are less satisfied with their marriages, complain more about them, and suffer more within them. Perhaps this helps us understand why women are twice as likely as men to file for divorce. Women's psychological health, more than men's, seems to depend upon the quality of the marital relationship (Lewis, 1988a).

Clearly, men and women have a lot to offer each other in intimate relationships. However, women usually have a stronger relationship orientation than men, including high expectations about emotional support that many men find difficult to fulfill. Women usually are more giving (DeAngelis, 1989). In marriage, this sometimes is at their own expense. Parents who appreciate the importance of intimacy and caring in close relationships make a special effort to instill these qualities in their sons and daughters.

point, we can be certain of one thing—there is a dynamic, reciprocal relationship between how well parents get along with each other, the quality of their parenting (especially for fathers), and their children's adjustment (Belsky et al., 1991).

SEPARATION AND DIVORCE

"Being the sole custodian of my daughter, I can honestly say that I do think a custody arrangement like mine can be in the best interests of the child. For example, Laurie's (my five-year-old daughter) father didn't want joint custody. It wasn't even considered. He did not share much in the responsibilities of raising her when we lived together and he was not interested in taking on any additional responsibility when we separated.

"I had always taken care of Laurie and continued to do so after we separated. It takes a lot of patience and effort (and love) to raise a child successfully on your own, but I was willing to do it and worked hard at it, reaping the obvious rewards such as her deep, unconditional love. My daughter is relatively well-adjusted and a happy child in spite of the mountains we have scaled" (Laurie's mother).

Perhaps no family-related change has a more devastating and enduring impact on children than parental divorce. Children experience high levels of family tension, a marked reduction in contact with the non-custodial parent, and a changing relationship with the custodial parent. When parents separate and divorce, children lose what should be the most stabilizing force in their lives—daily contact with both parents.

About one out of three schoolchildren in the United States has experienced parental divorce. Thirty percent of these children eventually become members of stepfamilies. The rest, like Laurie, live in a single-parent household. From the mid-nineteenth century to the mid-twentieth century, the nuclear family was considered to be the basic unit of society. It was usually headed by a working father and a caregiving mother. When their father was away at work, young children could count on their mother's presence and her active participation in their daily lives. Other relatives, including grandparents, usually lived nearby and had frequent contact with young family members.

Societal changes since the middle of this century have led to a proliferation of nontraditional family configurations and lifestyles that, compared to the nuclear family, make it more challenging for parents to provide guidance, support, and stability for their children. Despite their commitment to parenting, working mothers are not as available to their children as the stay-at-home mothers of the past. Grandparents often retire to places far away from their grandchildren. And large numbers of parents have difficulty remaining in love with their partners.

Ironically, it would never occur to young children that one of their parents could, or would even want to, permanently leave home. This realization makes parental separation that much more jolting. Children experience a double loss when their single mother seeks full-time employment to compensate for the economic slide that usually follows separation. It takes approximately 2 to 3 years for most families to reorganize following the disruption and turmoil of divorce (Gray & Coleman, 1985).

Parental separation becomes just the first of a series of transitions that challenge the coping resources of parents and children alike (Abelsohn & Saayman, 1991; Bray & Hetherington, 1993; Hetherington, 1989; Wallerstein & Blakeslee, 1989). Even the extramarital affairs that sometimes precede parental separation take their toll on children, whose welfare becomes a lower priority to the preoccupied parent (Brooks, 1989; Lawson, 1988).

Study Question *Why is the divorce rate so high?*

It is well-known (yet still quite disturbing) that the divorce rate in the United States and other industrialized countries has stabilized at about 50 percent. That means that half of the marriages that occur each year will not endure. Most divorces occur within 10 years of the marriage. Second marriages have an even higher divorce rate (Wilson & Clarke, 1992). About 2 million children experience their parents' divorce each year (U.S. Bureau of the Census, 1994). About one-fifth of them will experience a second parental divorce, and some a third (Brody, Neubaum, & Forehand, 1988). Family disruptions are more common than these statistics imply because divorce statistics don't include the breakups of cohabiting (unmarried) couples with children (Coleman & Ganong, 1993). Half of all children in the United States live with a single parent for at least part of their childhood.

Why is divorce so common? Are people today unhappier in their relationships? Have relationships become more difficult to maintain? These questions are not easy to answer (Hopper, 1993). The divorce rate reflects the stability of marriages, not their quality. There are bad marriages in which individuals will not even consider divorce (Heaton & Albrecht, 1991). There are successful marriages in which couples separate for reasons having nothing to do with their feelings about each other (Belsky, Lerner, & Spanier, 1984).

Some married couples are afraid to commit emotionally to their partners because they are not confident that their marriages will last. For some, "Till death do us part" has been replaced by a different vow—"as long as no one better comes along" (Glenn, 1991, p. 268). The dilemma is that high divorce rates intimidate the newly married. Some spouses are reluctant to fully commit emotionally to the marriage. Low commitment predicts low satisfaction with the relationship (Kurdek, 1993a).

To our ancestors, divorce was a shameful act. Unhappy spouses were expected to stay together for the "sake of the child." During this century, there has been an easing of the constraints that in the past discouraged unhappy spouses from separating. Even today, many unhappy couples stay together either because they have young children or because they cannot afford the costs of divorce, including lawyer's fees and supporting two households (Schwartz, 1995a). However, most of those in hopelessly unsatisfying relationships realize that they are not doing anyone a favor by staying together. This is particularly true when their children witness hostile, sometimes violent, exchanges between their parents. Until the late 1960s, to gain a divorce, an individual would have to prove adultery, cruelty, or desertion on the part of one's spouse. No-fault divorce laws instituted in 1970 represent society's acknowledgment that individuals must retain "freedom of relationship," despite the hardships and suffering that often result. Some suggest that society makes it too easy for unhappy couples with children to separate (Galston, 1995). Conservative legislators, blaming no-fault divorces for the rise in divorce rates, are trying to pass legislation that would make it more difficult for couples to file for divorce. Psychologists generally oppose such efforts, reasoning that it is children who suffer the most from chronic exposure to marital strife (Seppa, 1996).

Women are twice as likely as men to initiate divorce proceedings. In the past, women who left their husbands returned to their parents, often with children in hand. Today, most women would not consider such a fate. Valuing their independence, they would rather seek or increase the amount of their employment and work toward self-sufficiency. Leaving their unhappy marriages behind, many divorced mothers are less anxious, less depressed, and feel more fulfilled and happier than while married (Hetherington, 1993).

Custody Arrangements: "Best Interests of the Child"

Until the mid-nineteenth century, fathers almost always were awarded sole custody of their children and home when their marriages dissolved. This was due to men's superior financial status and power. Most women had no independent means of support and the judges were all men. In those days, children were considered the property of their fathers. Single fatherhood is not new. Many men became single parents following desertion or the death of their wives during childbirth (Griswold, 1993).

Subsequently, courts decided that mothers and children have rights too and moved to the other extreme—almost always awarding sole custody to mothers. Such rulings were based on the assumption that women are more nurturant than men and are more willing and able to care for young children. Fathers could gain custody only by proving the mother unfit. A mother would have to be mentally ill or a drug addict to be denied custody. Recent changes in the legal system have made it easier for fathers to win custody, and more fathers want custody. Some claim that an anti-feminist backlash leads male judges to deny custody to women who work late hours and depend heavily on day care (Hoffman, 1995). Women who have been their children's primary caregivers are emotionally devastated when they lose custody to ex-partners who had minimal involvement with their children (Clay, 1995b). The joint custody arrangement has been proposed as a way of avoiding bias against either gender (Greif, 1985). Disabled parents also have struggled to be treated fairly during custody evaluations (DeAngelis, 1995).

Joint Custody

Study Question   *What type of custody arrangement serves the best interests of children of divorce?*

There are a variety of custody arrangements. When **sole custody** is granted, one parent is given sole legal responsibility and the other parent usually is given visitation rights. **Split custody** occurs when each parent is given sole custody of one or more children. **Joint legal custody** gives both parents legal custody of a child, requiring shared parenting responsibilities and decision making (Hanson, 1988). Joint legal custody does not necessarily mean

that both parents will share physical custody of the child. **Joint physical custody** does require that a child reside with both parents some of the time. Unfortunately, it often is granted when feuding parents cannot find a custody arrangement that meets their needs, as opposed to their child's needs (Maccoby & Mnookin, 1992).

Joint custody ensures noncustodial parents' visitation rights. It also assures their right to participate in decision making and other significant parenting activities. However, many nonresident parents with joint custody do not take advantage of the rights granted them. There are many variations regarding how joint custody is carried out (Arditti, 1992).

The joint custody arrangement initially was considered an ideal way of providing children with continuing access to both parents, therefore avoiding the anguish associated with father nonvisitation. Noncustodial mothers usually remain in close contact with their children following divorce (Clay, 1995). Most states have mandated joint legal *and* physical custody if both parents agree, unless the court decides that the arrangement is not in the best interests of the child (Hanson, 1988).

Joint custody is favored by many judges and parents. Compared to noncustodial fathers, fathers with joint custody see their children more frequently and are more satisfied with the custody arrangement. Whether their greater involvement and satisfaction helps their children is not yet known (Arditti, 1992).

Following divorce, three styles of coparenting predominate (Maccoby, Buchanan, Mnookin, & Dornbusch, 1993):

1. *Cooperative parents* talk frequently and seldom argue. They attempt to coordinate households and try not to undermine each other's authority.
2. *Hostile parents* argue frequently, challenge each other's competence, and try to sabo-

tage the other parent's relationship with their children

3. *Disengaged parents* have minimal contact with their ex-spouses.

Wallerstein (1987) and others report that children of parents who maintain an amicable relationship following their divorce are not affected by the custody arrangement. However, when parents bitterly contest the divorce, children are psychologically disadvantaged when joint physical custody is imposed. Exposure to parents who constantly bicker and denigrate each other may harm a child (Johnston, Kline, & Tschann, 1989).

Furstenberg and Nord (1985) sampled representative households across the United States to study relationships among parents, stepparents, and children following separation and divorce. They found that "coparenting among formerly married couples is more of a myth than a reality . . . marital disruption effectively destroys the ongoing relationship between children and the biological parents living outside the home in a majority of families. Nearly half of all children have not seen their nonresident fathers in the past year" (p. 902).

For joint custody to work, a degree of cooperation between parents is required that usually is not present in post-divorce relationships (Camara & Resnick, 1989; Felner, 1985; Maccoby, Buchanan, Mnookin, & Dornbusch, 1993). Wallerstein cautions that these findings do not suggest that joint custody is harmful, but neither should it be viewed as the ideal arrangement for all children of divorce.

Wolchik, Braver, and Sandler (1985) compared children in maternal and joint custody and found no differences in psychological status between the two groups. However, children living in joint custody reported more positive family experiences than children in maternal custody. They also displayed higher levels of self-esteem and had more frequent

contact with the noncustodial parent. Many studies confirm that continuing participation of both parents in the lives of children of divorce is important to their eventual adjustment, especially when the parents get along with each other. Nonadversarial forms of mediation help parents arrive at custody arrangements that are best suited to their family (Coller, 1988; Kitzman & Emery, 1994).

Stages of the Divorce Process

Wallerstein (1988) distinguishes three stages in the divorce process, although they are not inevitable. The *acute phase* begins with the formal separation of the marital partners (filing for divorce) and a parent's (usually the father's) departure from the household. Most children recall vividly, some for the rest of their lives, both being told about the divorce and the day one of their parents left home. Much of the stress of this period reflects the fact that the decision to separate usually is not mutual.

The acute phase lasts from several months to over a year. Disruptive parental behaviors include "verbal accusations, threats, and rage accompanied by violence, and depression which may include a preoccupation with suicide (p. 276) . . . Children are rarely protected from witnessing the angry scenes and, in fact, in some families the fighting only occurs when the children are present" (p. 279).

Perhaps out of guilt and distraction, custodial parents soften their discipline. Their children are exposed to inconsistent, even contradictory, standards from day to day. During the year following the separation, "the custodial parent tends to be less competent as a parent, less able to maintain the structure of the household, and less available to the children. The youngsters are irritable, edgy, and often accusatory and rebellious" (Wallerstein, 1988, pp. 277–278).

The second or *transitional phase* "spans a

period of several years, during which adults and children embark on unfamiliar roles and relationships within the new family structure" (p. 275). This may involve a change in residence and lifestyle, new responsibilities in the home, and a reduced standard of living. The third or *stabilizing phase* finds the family reorganized and functioning well. The custodial parent usually remarries and the family continues to face new challenges.

Noncustodial Parents

Study Question *Why do so many noncustodial fathers have minimal contact with their children?*

Divorce places fathers at greater risk than mothers for problematic relationships with their children (Cooney, Hutchinson, & Leatler, 1995). Following divorce, about half of all children almost never see their fathers. This is unfortunate because noncustodial parents continue to have a psychological, emotional, and financial impact on the family members they left behind. Visitation, letters, phone calls, and child support decline in the years following the divorce. Many children feel rejected and unlovable (Furstenburg & Nord, 1985; Loewen, 1988; Seltzer, Schaeffer, & Charng, 1989).

Bitter mothers cite father absence and lack of child support as evidence that the absent parent is uncaring. "It really makes me angry. I cannot understand, for the life of me, how these guys can walk out the door and never look back. I mean, it makes my blood boil. Every night when I go to bed, I wonder how my ex-husband can turn his back on Brian and Chris. I told him, 'I don't know how you can look at yourself in the mirror' (mother of two boys, quoted by Frerking, 1992, p. 21). Naturally, children suffer when they hear one parent denigrate the other. How can they

maintain close ties to two people who can't stand each other?

Most children miss their absent father and desire contact with him, although diminished contact helps some children reconcile themselves to the fact of parental divorce. Nonvisitation fathers suffer too. Divorced men are prone to medical and psychological problems, including depression. Many cite the emotional strains of visitation, particularly uncooperative and hostile ex-spouses, as the major reason for their absence (Ahrons & Miller, 1993; Alvarez, 1995; Teyber & Hoffman, 1987).

When noncustodial parents do visit their children, it is more of a social ritual than an opportunity for closeness. Parent and child spend time together, but it is not a conventional parent-child interaction as when a parent is assisting or nurturing a child. Noncustodial parents "typically give up decision-making authority, and exercise little direct influence over their children's upbringing" (Furstenburg & Nord, 1985, p. 903).

Custodial parents complain about the lack of involvement and support they receive from the noncustodial parent. In Furstenburg and Nord's (1985) study, more than half of the custodial parents claimed that to avoid conflict they did not discuss their child rearing with their ex-spouse. Over time, communication between parents becomes less frequent, but so do arguments. Noncustodial parents complain about the care their children receive from the custodial parent—they don't like the "junk food" their children are eating, the unsuitable videos they are watching, or their lack of supervision.

A common complaint is that the other parent is too lax in discipline (Maccoby, Buchanan, Mnookin, & Dornbusch, 1993). Given the bitterness of divorce, one must be wary about the claims made by custodial and noncustodial parents about each other. Data from studies that ask custodial parents to comment on the conduct, visitation, or child support of their ex-spouses are always suspect (Braver, Wolchik, Sandler, Sheets, Fogas, & Bay, 1993).

Nonresident fathers offer several reasons for why they lessen their involvement with their children following divorce: (1) they are unwilling or unable to provide child support, (2) they are reluctant to interact with their ex-spouse, (3) they cease to feel obligated to support children they do not see, and (4) eventually, many fathers assume parenting responsibilities with new families (Coleman & Ganong, 1992; Furstenburg & Nord, 1985; Stephens, 1996).

However, noncustodial fathers who live nearby and who feel that they have some control over their child's upbringing usually remain emotionally and financially supportive (Braver et al., 1993). Perceived control seems to be the key. Rather than coercing "deadbeat dads" to provide child support, courts could do a better job of helping fathers work cooperatively with their ex-spouses to stay emotionally connected to their children.

Of course, many nonresident parents (especially mothers) want to and do remain very involved with their children, but they are the exception. To be fair, it is difficult (though far from impossible) for parents to remain close to their children when they do not live together, even if they share legal custody and visit every weekend. Young children come to prefer the company of the parent or stepparent with whom they live. Adolescents usually prefer to be with their friends.

It is desirable for nonresident parents to "keep in touch" by phoning their child at least once or twice a week, writing letters or sending tapes, and by participating in school-related and other activities that are meaningful to the child (Kutner, 1992a). If relations between ex-spouses are hostile, children feel awkward during visitation. Parents make their children feel uncomfortable when they "cross-examine" them in order to gain unflattering information about an ex-spouse.

Visitation: Parenting from a Distance

What is the best visitation arrangement following divorce? One group of investigators, based on a longitudinal study of 121 children in the custody of their divorced mothers, concluded that no one arrangement suits all families. Sons who were close to their fathers showed more positive self-esteem with frequent visitation from fathers but mothers reported more behavior problems in these boys. Why would there be mixed effects? The investigators note that "every contact [with dad] also brings a new loss" (Healy, Malley, & Stewart, 1990, p. 540).

Girls who experienced frequent father visitation displayed lower self-esteem. They may have felt alienated from their fathers because of their loyalty to their mothers. Father visits are most beneficial when they do not elicit emotional conflicts in children. This usually requires that the father and mother be civil (at least in the children's presence) and that the father have a good relationship with the child. Even occasional visits from noncustodial fathers allow them to maintain a meaningful relationship with their child, one that is relatively independent of the residential parent's attitudes about the former spouse (Maccoby, Buchanan, Mnookin, & Dornbusch, 1993).

Fathers who relinquish custody are not subject to the same intensity of blame and guilt as mothers who voluntarily or involuntarily give up their role of primary caregiver. Noncustodial mothers are subject to hostility and disapproval from their families and from the community (Clay, 1995). Sometimes they are seen as unfit ("What kind of mother could leave her children?"). Living apart from one's children is a difficult pill to swallow for almost anyone. Noncustodial parents grapple with issues involving loss, guilt, loneliness, and blame and sometimes merit professional attention (Kissman & Allen, 1993).

Effects of Divorce on Children

Study Question *Should unhappy spouses stay together for the sake of their children?*

Coleman and Ganong (1992) detect deep-seated feelings against members of nonnuclear families. They sense "an undercurrent of moral outrage directed toward those who divorce . . ." (p. 448), a belief that those who do not conform to the nuclear family ideal should be punished. Divorce is punishment enough for all family members. Yet sometimes it is the only reasonable solution to a hopeless marital situation.

The intended effect of divorce is to relieve marital distress and reduce the suffering resulting from continuing animosity between the parents (Wallerstein, 1988). "The decision to divorce or remarry may be made on the basis of the possibility for improved well-being of the parent, in many instances with little or no consideration for the concerns of the child. Few children wish for their parents' divorce, and many children resent their parents' remarriages" (Hetherington, Stanley-Hagan, & Anderson, 1989, p. 303). Wallerstein and Blakeslee (1989) note that divorce is the price that children pay for their parent's inability to get along. Family members eventually accept the breakup of the marriage but related issues and stressors persist. The specialization in parenting roles we noted in the last chapter breaks down following divorce. Mothers may have difficulty taking on responsibilities that fathers had performed, such as finances and discipline. Fathers often have a hard time cleaning house and maintaining affectional bonds with their children, services that probably were provided by their ex-partners (Emery & Tuer, 1993).

"The children are often neglected. In the first couple of years after the divorce, children have less regular bedtimes and mealtimes, eat together as a family less, hear fewer bedtime stories, and are more often late for school. Discipline is less consistent, positive, and affectionate. And perhaps most salient of all,

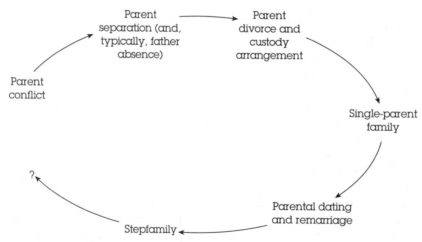

Figure 4.2 The divorce process

the aftermath of divorce brings economic disaster for most mothers and children" (Clarke-Stewart, 1989b, p. 61).

Many children of divorce experience the following sequence of events, a multistage process of family change known as the *"divorce process"* (see Fig. 4.2): (1) parental conflict, (2) parental extramarital affairs, (3) parental separation, (4) acrimonious divorce and custody proceedings, (5) single-parent family, (6) moving to a new community and school, (7) increased maternal employment, (8) parental remarriage into a stepfamily with a new stepparent and stepsiblings, and (9) stepfamily conflict possibly leading to another divorce. Events that follow parental divorce, for example, the amount of conflict between ex-spouses and downward economic mobility, seem to affect children's adjustment more than the divorce itself (Forehand, 1992; Hetherington, 1989; Kaslow & Schwartz, 1987; Morrison & Cherlin, 1995).

Study Question *Does parental divorce inevitably harm children?*

Each couple handles its divorce differently. Thus, each child of divorce is exposed to a different constellation of parental dynamics (Ahrons & Miller, 1993; Ahrons & Rodgers, 1987; Forehand, 1992). Keep in mind that children in intact families also experience extremely diverse parental situations (Martinson & Wu, 1992). It is not divorce per se, but rather the frequency and intensity of displays of hostility between parents before and after divorce that jeopardizes children's well-being (Kline, Johnston, & Tschann, 1991).

Long and Forehand (1987) questioned teachers about the academic performance and social behavior of 40 adolescents. Half of the students had parents who recently divorced and half belonged to intact families. Teachers could not distinguish between those students from disrupted families and those from intact families on the basis of their behavior in school. However, they could distinguish between those children whose parents displayed high levels of conflict and those children whose parents got along. This finding suggests that parental conflict is a better predictor of adjustment in children than parental separation.

"Divorce is a different experience for children and adults because the children lose something that is fundamental to their development—the family structure. The family comprises the scaffolding upon which children mount successive developmental stages, from infancy into adolescence. It supports their psychological, physical, and emotional ascent into maturity. When that structure collapses, the children's world is temporarily without supports" (Wallerstein & Blakeslee, 1989, p. 11).

Their parents' divorce and the conflicts leading up to and following it can have long-term effects on children (Amato & Keith, 1991b; Wallerstein & Blakeslee, 1989; Zill, Morrison, & Coiro, 1993). A significant number of children, but still a minority, develop serious emotional disorders and antisocial behaviors that may require professional attention (Brady, Bray, & Zeeb, 1986; Grych & Fincham, 1992; Kalter, 1987).

Less extreme problems involving peer relationships, performance in school, noncompliance, and psychological distress, are quite common in children following parental divorce. Because children of divorce adjust so differently, as a group they are not easily distinguishable from children who live in intact families (Allison & Furstenberg, 1989; Amato, 1993a; Bisnaire, Firestone, & Rynard, 1990; Brodzinsky, Hitt, & Smith, 1993; Chipuer, Plomin, Pedersen, McClearn, et al., 1993; Long & Forehand, 1987; Stevenson & Black, 1995).

Some studies report that children are not adversely affected by their parents' separation and divorce, at least in the short term (Forehand, 1992). Amato and Keith (1991b) performed a meta-analysis of 92 studies that compared the well-being of children living with divorced single parents to the well-being of children from intact families. Although they found that divorce and related events lowered the well-being of children, the effects were weak. Recent studies reveal weaker short-term effects than earlier studies. The long-term consequences of divorce for quality of life during young adulthood may be more serious than the short-term emotional and social consequences that most researchers look for (Amato & Keith, 1991a; Cain, 1989; Cooney, Hutchinson, & Leatler, 1995; Zill, Morrison, & Coiro, 1993).

A few children adjust quite well following the breakup of their parents' marriage. They probably benefit from less exposure to parental bickering and hostility. Some custodial parents provide more attention to their children after separation. So-called resilient children do well despite their exposure to the full spectrum stressors described above (Werner, 1989b). We still have a lot to learn about the personal resources and social supports that buffer or protect children from family dysfunction and breakdown (Sim & Vuchinich, 1996).

How might the divorce process lead to behavior problems in children? Investigators have emphasized five likely factors: (1) parental absence, (2) adjustment of the custodial parent, (3) economic disadvantages, (4) conflict between parents, and (5) stressful life changes (Amato, 1993a).

Parental Absence

If two parents are needed to provide an optimal family environment for children's development, then the family environment provided by one parent presumably is not as good. Due to father absence and maternal employment, most children of divorce re-

ceive less parental attention and supervision than do children in intact families. It is possible that children's social skills suffer from the paucity of parent role models at home (Amato & Keith, 1991b). When noncustodial fathers maintain good relationships with their ex-spouses and children, their children (especially sons) do better (Beaty, 1995; Thomas & Forehand, 1993; Westerman & Schonholtz, 1993).

Adjustment of Custodial Parent

Following divorce, children are pretty much in the hands of the custodial parent. The main premise of this third hypothesis is that when the custodial parent adjusts well, the children adjust well (Amato, 1993a).

Economic Disadvantage

A family's standard of living usually decreases following divorce. Older children from middle-class families voice their resentment about living in smaller quarters or having to sacrifice some of the pleasures or necessities of life, including cable TV and college plans. In working class families, economic deprivations sometimes affect children's nutrition and health and reduce opportunities for activities that promote academic accomplishment, including books, educational toys, and private lessons. Children who live in poverty suffer the greatest deprivations (Coleman & Ganong, 1992). According to the **economic disadvantage hypothesis**, children will not suffer because of their parents' divorce when there is no decrease in their standard of living. This usually occurs when the custodial mother maintains her standard of living through remarriage or when an affluent father gains custody (Amato & Keith, 1991b).

Parental Conflict

A fourth hypothesis suggests that conflict between estranged parents stresses children. As we discussed in an earlier section, children suffer emotionally from excessive exposure to hostility and aggression between their parents. Conflict preoccupies and stresses parents and distracts them from their child care responsibilities. According to the **family conflict hypothesis**, it is not a change in family structure that threatens children's well-being as much as the friction and strife that accompany the structural change (Stevenson & Black, 1995).

Stressful Life Changes

Many studies confirm that the greater the number of stressors children face, the poorer their adjustment (Rutter, 1988). Parental divorce brings many stressful life changes, such as moving and changing schools, having to adjust to parental dating, and possibly one or both parent's remarriage.

In reviewing the research related to these five factors, Amato (1993a; Amato & Keith, 1991b) concludes that the parental conflict hypothesis has the most support. Marital conflict is responsible both for the divorce and children's adjustment problems. This model implies that parental separation increases the well-being of children who, as a result of the separation, are exposed to fewer displays of hostility. Amato (1993a, 1993b) notes that there is some research support for all five hypotheses. Kurdek (1993c) wonders whether the relative influence of each of the five factors varies according to children's age and gender.

Other investigators note that the short-term effects of the divorce process on children depend on (1) the quality (closeness) of each parent-child relationship, (2) parental psychological functioning, especially of the custodial parent, (3) the ability of the parents to work together, (4) monitoring by the residential parent, (5) the organization of the custodial household, and importantly (6) the

coping resources of each child (Buie, 1988; Fishel, 1987; Forehand, 1992; Hetherington, 1989; Isaacs, Leon & Kline, 1987; Kalter, Kloner, Schreier, & Okla, 1989; Kline, Tschann, Johnston, & Wallerstein, 1989; Maccoby, Buchanan, Mnookin, & Dornbusch, 1993; Wallerstein, 1988).

Study Question   *How do children respond emotionally when their parents divorce?*

Children of divorce report a wide range of intense feelings (Wallerstein & Blakeslee, 1989). These include fear and insecurity about their future; a fear of being abandoned by the custodial parent; anger toward the parent that they hold responsible for the separation; depression and helplessness about their plight; loneliness; and guilt regarding their perceived role in the marital break-up. "In the period immediately following divorce, children may grieve for the absent parent, may respond with noncompliance and aggression to parental conflict and family disorganization, and may become confused by and apprehensive of changing relationships with parents" (Hetherington, Stanley-Hagan & Anderson, 1989, p. 304). Keep in mind that children's immediate reactions to parental divorce do not necessarily predict their long-term adjustment (Sim & Vuichinich, 1996).

Some children believe that their nonresident parent left because of their misbehavior or because the parent no longer cares about them. Therefore, it is crucial that separating parents reassure their children that the divorce had nothing to do with their feelings about the child, whom they both will always love. It is not helpful for children to hear that their parents no longer like or love each other, even though it is usually the case. Young children do not know what the term "divorce" means. Everything about the new arrangement should be explained to them sensitively so that they do not imagine that things are worse than they really are. On the other hand, there is information that upsets some children that is not necessary or helpful for them to know, perhaps concerning parent's romantic affairs or financial arrangements.

Few children of divorce report that a sympathetic parent or adult spoke to them caringly during their times of distress (Wallerstein & Blakeslee, 1989). McCoy (1984) describes how a mother and father told their young child about their decision to separate. "They told her Mommy and Daddy couldn't get along anymore and had trouble living together, so they had decided, after a lot of thought and trying, to get a divorce. This meant, they said, that Mommy and Daddy would live in different houses. She would live with Mommy most of the time, but Daddy wouldn't live far away, and she would visit him at his new house soon. They explained that this divorce was something between Mommy and Daddy and that they would always love her and be her parents. She would still go to the same school and see her friends" (p. 112). The fact that parents are together when they provide this information reassures children that both parents will continue to care for them.

During normal times, when children suffer intense and threatening feelings, their parents provide comfort and reassurance. When the parents themselves are preoccupied with their own needs and problems, children require additional support from friends, relatives, and other concerned adults (Cowen, Pedro-Carroll, & Alpert-Gillis, 1990; Kurdeck & Fine, 1993; Marks, 1995).

During separation some adults unwisely seek emotional support from their children. Following divorce, most parents eventually become involved with new partners. Some are distracted from their child care responsibilities. Their children may remind them of their failed relationship (Brooks, 1986). Children who have the most difficulty adjusting come from homes that are characterized by con-

flict, punitive parenting, and poor conflict-resolution skills. The fathers or stepfathers of maladjusted boys often are unavailable or rejecting (Hetherington, 1989).

Children's Age and the Divorce Process

Study Question   *Do older or younger children have more difficulty adjusting to the divorce process?*

It has been suggested that the younger children are when their parents divorce, the greater its eventual impact on their development (Allison & Furstenberg, 1989; Emery, 1988; Zill, Morrison, & Coiro, 1993). After all, younger children are more dependent upon their parents than are older children. They also lack coping mechanisms that would help them to adjust to the prolonged disruption of their lives.

Wallerstein's 15-year longitudinal study (1987; 1988; 1991) of 60 predominantly white California families of divorce found, however, that preschool children, although initially the most frightened, eventually showed the *best* long-term adjustment. Children who were very young at the time of separation had limited understanding and recall of the predivorce drama that often traumatizes older children. However, if the custodial parent was very anxious or distracted, the child suffered.

After 18 months had passed, young children's distress worsened. Boys in particular were disruptive at school and home. Even 5 years after the separation, the younger children were showing signs of maladjustment. However, by 10 years after the separation, the youngest children seemed to have adjusted, many claiming that they could no longer remember their lives before the divorce. Other studies (e.g., Zill, Morrison, & Coiro, 1993) report that children who are 6 years old or younger when their parents separate show slightly more adjustment problems during young adulthood, especially if they had a poor relationship with their fathers.

When Wallerstein (1987) performed the 10-year follow-up study, most of the children were finishing high school or starting college. About three-quarters were in the custody of their mothers and the rest lived with their fathers. "Feelings of sadness, of neediness, of a sense of their own vulnerability, were expressed by a majority of these young people. Although two thirds of their lives have been spent in the divorced or remarried family, they spoke sorrowfully of their loss of the intact family and the consequent lack of opportunity for a close relationship with the father . . . Anxieties about relationships with the opposite sex, marriage, and personal commitments ran very high" (p. 210).

Ten years following the divorce, some of the younger children still were fantasizing that their parents would get back together. The children who lived with their mothers revealed a strong desire to contact their natural fathers as they approached adolescence. Some wrote to these men, even when their letters were not answered. Most of the younger children were optimistic about their future relationships. Older siblings anticipated continued loss and betrayal in their lives. Adolescent girls in particular showed a delayed or sleeper effect, displaying lower self-esteem and increased anxiety about having relationships with men (Wallerstein & Corbin, 1989).

Adjustment to divorce comes slowly and sometimes not at all. "We found that although some divorces work well—some adults are happier in the long run, and some children do better than they would have been expected to in an unhappy intact family—more often than not divorce is a wrenching, long-lasting experience for at least one of the former partners. Perhaps more important, we found that for virtually all the children, it exerts powerful and wholly unanticipated effects" (Wallerstein, 1989, p. 19).

Adolescents

Reflecting their more sophisticated thinking skills, adolescents are in a better position than younger children to understand the causes of divorce. They understand concepts like incompatibility and compromise. They are less parent-dependent and more capable of finding support outside of the family when necessary. Adolescents in divorced families usually are granted more autonomy and argue less with their parents (Smetana, Yau, Restrepo, & Braeges, 1991), perhaps because they have less contact. Adolescents usually do well when they have a close relationship with the residential parent and when they are not pressured to choose sides (Buchanan, Maccoby, & Dornbusch, 1991; Forehand, 1992; Maccoby, Buchanan, Mnookin, & Dornbusch, 1993; Thomas & Forehand, 1993).

Some adolescents whose parents recently divorced display a variety of academic and emotional problems and antisocial behaviors that interfere with normal adolescent transitions (Frost & Pakiz, 1990). Adolescents are less likely to have academic problems when their mothers are adjusting to their marital separation and when family members get along (McCombs & Forehand, 1989). Some adolescents (especially girls) who have experienced parental divorce become wary of entering new relationships (Amato, 1996; Wallerstein & Corbin, 1989). Some resent either parent attempting a social life of his or her own. Raising adolescent sons appears to be more difficult in divorced families than in intact families (Borduin & Henggeler, 1987).

Young Adults

About a fifth of all divorces end marriages that have endured for over 15 years. Usually the children are grown. If they are 18 years old or older, custody and support issues are less pressing. While it had been assumed that young adults are less vulnerable to their parent's divorce than children and adolescents, recent evidence suggests otherwise (Cooney, Hutchinson, & Leatler, 1995; Hetherington, 1993).

Cooney, Smyer, Hagestad, and Klock (1986) interviewed undergraduates between the ages of 18 and 23 years whose parents had divorced within the past 3 years. Sixty-two percent of the women and forty-two percent of the men reported emotional problems early in the divorce proceedings, with about one-third reporting subsequent relief. More than half of their 39 subjects reported that their emotional health had suffered.

These students so identified with their parents that they felt as though they were undergoing the divorce themselves. Many of the students reported that their relationships with their parents (particularly mothers) improved following the divorce, perhaps reflecting the students' investment in the emotional crisis. There was least relationship improvement between fathers and daughters, with daughters expressing considerable anger toward their fathers. Those who were already having difficulty with their own physical separation from their parents became the most distressed by the parental divorce. However, it makes little sense for parents to postpone their divorce until their children are grown. Adult children are not pleased to learn that their parents remained unhappily married because of them (Cain, 1989; Cooney, et al., 1995).

Most young adults have difficulty adjusting to their parent's divorce, even when they are relieved. Whether they feel closer or more distant from each parent depends on whom they blame and the specific circumstances. In any case, adult children of divorce get less support (child care, advice, loans) from single and remarried parents than do adult children from intact families (Bonkowski, 1989; Cain, 1989; Marks, 1995; White, 1992).

Wallerstein's (1991) pessimistic conclusion that almost half of the children of divorce are "scarred" for life has been challenged by the findings of some studies and confirmed by others. Weaknesses in Wallerstein's study include (1) a small sample size, (2) the sample was overrepresentative of families that sought clinical help, and (3) the absence of a control group of intact families with which to compare the families undergoing divorce. Some of the reported "effects of divorce" may be characteristic of intact families too. Additionally, many children who are identified as "troubled" following parental separation had problems beforehand (Cherlin & Furstenberg, 1989; Demo & Acock, 1988).

However, support for Wallerstein's main conclusion is not hard to find. Longitudinal data from the National Survey of Children were examined for long-term effects of parental divorce (Zill, Morrison, & Coiro, 1993). The survey allowed comparison of adult children from divorced families to adult children from intact families (a total sample of 1,147 youths). Young adults from disrupted families were twice as likely as those from nondisrupted families to have poor relationships with their fathers (65 versus 29 percent) and mothers (30 versus 16 percent). Twenty-seven percent had dropped out of high school (compared to 13 percent for those from nondisrupted families) and 41 percent received psychological help (compared to 22 percent from nondisrupted families). The investigators emphasize, however, that most of the children exposed to the divorce process were in the normal range on most of the indicators of well-being they monitored.

Divorce is wrenching for people of all ages. Each age group is busy working on different developmental tasks. Children respond to the divorce according to their current level of understanding and with the coping resources that are available. Within age groups, children differ considerably in their ability to adjust. "Many children eventually emerge from the divorce or remarriage of their parents as competent or even enhanced individuals" (Hetherington, Stanley-Hagan & Anderson, 1989, p. 310).

Gender Differences in Adjustment

Study Question *Do children suffer more from parental divorce when they "lose" the same-gender parent?*

Early studies, most based on clinical samples, suggested that divorce is more traumatic for boys than for girls, presumably because boys usually are losing regular contact with their same gender parent. Later studies (e.g., Allison & Furstenberg, 1989) challenged this assumption. In fact, there appears to be a mild "sleeper effect" wherein girls show some effects of their exposure to the divorce process during early adulthood (Wallerstein, 1991; Zill, Morrison, & Coiro, 1993).

How boys and girls adjust to parental di-

TABLE 4.3 How Divorce Affects Children

Disrupted lifestyles, including having to move and change schools

Increased feelings of sadness, distress, fear, and insecurity about the future

Feeling different from one's peers

Less consistent discipline from both parents

Decline in one's standard of living

Less contact with noncustodial parent

School performance declines

Problematical peer relationships, including difficulty trusting people

Less exposure to parental bickering

vorce depends more on their personal characteristics and their postdivorce circumstances than on their gender. For example, temperamentally difficult boys usually have the most serious adjustment problems (Hetherington, 1989). When the absent parent is the father, boys are more vulnerable (Warshak, 1992). This is particularly true for boys who live with an unmarried mother and have limited contact with their fathers after the separation. Boys generally do better when their mothers remarry and the boys regain a male role model in their daily lives.

The fact that fathers are more involved in the rearing of their sons has been used to explain the observation that parents of sons have a somewhat lower risk of separation or divorce, compared to parents of daughters. Mothers and fathers usually agree that sons need their fathers more than daughters do. This belief sometimes serves as a deterrent to divorce. On the other hand, if unhappy parents with sons stay married longer, they expose these boys to longer periods of marital strife (Shaw, Emery, & Tuer, 1993). Gender is a relatively weak factor in adjustment compared to other personal and situational factors. We will revisit this issue in the section on single-parent families.

Interventions for Children of Divorce

Most children eventually adjust to their parents' divorce but a significant number do not adjust well (Hetherington, Stanley-Hagan, & Anderson, 1989). Children from divorced families are more likely to be referred for mental health services than children from intact families. Given their exposure to intense parental conflict, parental separation, parent absence, economic strains, and much more, it is surprising that so many children apparently remain relatively unscathed by their painful experiences.

Grych and Fincham (1992) evaluated three types of interventions intended to help families adjust: (1) psychoeducational groups that provide social support and that attempt to teach coping skills to parents and children; (2) divorce mediation, offered as an alternative to hostile, courtroom proceedings; and (3) child custody and support laws intended to improve children's postdivorce adjustment. The investigators conclude that most current interventions do not reflect what we know about the problems and needs of children of divorce.

Group interventions seem helpful for children but there is little empirical support for their effectiveness (Lee, Picard, & Blain, 1994). Since parental behavior is the best predictor of children's adjustment, interventions probably should focus on adult behavior. For example, a family court judge in New Jersey orders all parents who file for divorce to attend mandatory parent education workshops (Friedland, 1993). Divorcing parents must attend two sessions covering how children respond to divorce and offering strategies for coping with family breakups. To avoid arguments between ex-spouses, the judge assigns parents to different sessions. The goal of the program is to minimize the trauma of divorce for children. During sessions, parents learn how to help their children cope with the pain of divorce and how to take care of their own emotional needs. Parents are encouraged to protect their children from parental arguments and to avoid pressuring them to take sides (Lewin, 1995c).

SINGLE MOTHERING

Study Question   *What special problems are faced by parents without partners?*

"As a single mother, I made financial sacrifices. I assumed full responsibility for my children's growth and development. I had no one to depend on for emotional support. I made all decisions alone. I had sole responsibility for providing home, security, love, discipline, and religious training" (single mother of three children).

Child care is a full-time job. The duties usually shared by two parents include providing nurturance and affection, earning a living, making good decisions about child care, and solving everyday problems. Parents also must purchase goods and services, prepare meals, clean house, and launder clothing. Parents transport children, participate in and supervise play activities, help with school work, teach life skills, and much, much more.

When these responsibilities are shared by two adults, even if both are employed, they usually are manageable. Of course, this depends upon how well the parents work together, their ability to afford child care assistance, how many children they have, and so on. What happens when these "chores" must be performed by one parent with limited financial resources? What if the parent is employed in a relatively low-paying job? What if the parent is coping with the stress of recent separation or divorce, a hostile or uncooperative ex-spouse, and distressed children? "One parent can model only one gender role, give only so many hugs, offer so much discipline, and earn so much money" (Clarke-Stewart, 1989b, p. 61). Welcome to the plight of the single parent.

Technically, the term *single-parent family* is a misnomer. Most children in this particular family configuration have two parents, but they live with only one. The term **binuclear family** is preferable because it helps normalize the participation of the absent parents in their children's lives (Ahron & Rodgers, 1987; Kissman & Allen, 1993), but I will stick with the common term.

Single parents head about a third of families with children in the United States, 86 percent of them being mothers. This means that there are 9.3 million women raising children without the assistance of a partner. Two-thirds of these single-mother families resulted from divorce, separation, or abandonment. Never-married women, about half of them adolescents, women over 30 having children on their own, and widows also belong to the single-parent category (U.S. Bureau of the Census, 1994).

In the United States, approximately one-quarter of children under the age of 18 years (15 million children) are living with single parents. In 1991, women headed 58 percent of all African-American families with children, compared to 19 percent among whites. More than half of all African-American children and almost one-third of Hispanic children live with a single parent. The median income of these families is about one-third the national average (Census Bureau Statistics).

In the United States, single, never married mothers comprise the fastest-growing category of new family configurations. (Only 1.1 percent of births in Japan were to unwed mothers in 1994, compared to 30.1 percent in the United States (Wu Dunn, 1996).) Some women accidentally become pregnant by men they do not choose as partners. Some get tired of waiting for Mr. Right or are ambivalent about getting married. They want to be mothers but do not want to be wives (Siegel, 1995). Others hope that the right partner (right for mother and child) will eventually come along. Most do not care to be called unwed mothers. These mothers explain to their young children that not all families have daddies, but the children may still feel somewhat different (Lawson, 1993b).

To make ends meet, over two-thirds of single mothers seek employment. Lacking work experience or higher education, most settle for unskilled or semi-skilled low-paying jobs with little opportunity for advancement. Those with preschool children either work part-time or spend a significant part of their salary for child care. Many struggle to provide adequate supervision. Recently, there have been dramatic stories in the media of young children left at home or in cars by themselves while their mothers engage in hard-to-find, low-pay work. The mothers claimed that they could not afford child care and had no alternative.

One of the biggest obstacles faced by single parents is negative attitudes and beliefs about their ability to parent well. Many family advocates criticize the **family deficit model**, the idea that the single-parent family (or any non-nuclear family) is inherently dysfunctional. As previously noted, there is a widespread belief that the two-parent family is better for children than alternative family forms. This assumption has unfortunate consequences for members of nontraditional families who feel stigmatized (Coleman & Ganong, 1992). Compared to economic factors, social support, and the quality of parent-child relationships, family configuration is a relatively weak variable (Kissman & Allen, 1993). This is not to suggest that family configuration plays no role in children's development. Parenting research helps us understand the advantages and disadvantages of each family form for the particular individuals and circumstances at hand.

It is not too hard to think of advantages of raising children as single parents: lack of conflict in making child-rearing decisions, children not being exposed to marital tensions, extra social support from family and friends, and more opportunities to become independent for children and parents (Shore, 1986). Kissman and Allen (1993) remind us that "contrary to popular opinion, mother-headed families can be competent and successful in nurturing, socializing, and supporting children" (p. 5). Although as a group single and remarried mothers report being less happy and more distressed than first-marriage mothers (Marks, 1995), the majority of single-mother families are as successful as two-parent families on measures of emotional adjustment and children's academic achievement (Cashion, 1982; Kissman & Allen, 1993).

Children of Single Parents

"Sometimes I fantasize about the white picket fence, the marriage where the wife stays home with the kids. In a way I feel that this is something I did to myself, but my daughter's paying the price too" (unmarried mother quoted by Lewin, 1992, p. B6).

About one-quarter of white families and two-thirds of African-American families in the United States are headed by a single parent, usually a mother (U.S. Census Bureau, 1994). Most parents worry about their children, but single mothers who are divorced have at least one extra worry—how will father absence affect their children? Researchers have difficulty answering this question because it is hard to separate the effects of living with a single parent and father absence from all the other factors that go along with the divorce process. For most children, living in a single-parent family is a "package deal." As Wallerstein notes, children experience more stress in the joint custody of two hostile parents than they do living in the sole custody of one composed parent. In a two-parent family, even if one parent is psychologically impaired, living with a second parent who is well-adjusted usually leads to favorable child outcomes. Being raised by two parents, each of whom has serious psychological problems, is bad news for children (e.g. Goodman, Brogan, Lynch, & Fielding, 1993).

Children in single-parent families have special concerns. Many have mixed feelings about their parent dating. Some worry that the new man in mom's life will replace them in her affections. Adolescent boys may have ambivalent feelings about their mothers' dating, wanting their mothers to be happy but also wanting to protect them from being exploited or hurt. Daughters in single-mother families who are not close to their fathers may see men as unreliable or manipulative. They may worry about their own ability to have romantic relationships (Kissman & Allen, 1993).

Children who feel threatened by their parent's friendships sometimes attempt to sabotage them, one way or another. Other children, having become attached to a parent's new "friend," are devastated when the relationship ends. Most children eventually recognize and accept their parent's need for companionship and a social life. It is important that parents be sensitive to their children's needs and concerns when they introduce them to new romantic partners (Kissman & Allen, 1993).

Do children in single-parent households do better if they live with the same-gender parent? Santrock and Warshak (1986) concluded that children living with a parent of the same gender usually do better. "Children living with opposite-sexed parents tend to be more immature and dependent, and to show higher levels of anxiety and lower levels of self-esteem. . . ." Downey and Powell (1993) disagree. They examined data from a study of 3,483 eighth graders living in mother-only families and 409 eighth graders living only with their fathers. Of the 35 social psychological and educational outcomes studied, they could not find one in which boys or girls significantly benefited from living with the same-gender parent. The mix of parent-child gender seems to be a relatively weak factor in adjustment compared to other process variables like relationship quality and nurturance. "While I think boys do need their fathers and girls their mothers, I also think boys need their mothers and girls their fathers . . . it's important for a child to maintain a relationship with both parents" (Warshak, quoted by Meredith, 1985).

Study Question *Is the best parent a happy parent?*

Mullis, Mullis, and Markstrom (1987) questioned single and married mothers about their children's behavior. Married mothers reported having better relationships with their children than did single mothers, who rated their sons less favorably in independence and obedience. Better-educated mothers reported having better behaved children, reminding us that parental education is a valuable resource in single parenting.

Wadsworth, Burnell, Taylor, and Butler (1985) compared British children from single-parent, step- and nuclear families on a variety of measures. They found that, on the average, children from single-parent families scored worst and children from nuclear families scored best on tests of behavior, vocabulary, and visuomotor coordination. Children from single-parent families were also perceived as more antisocial and as slightly more neurotic than children from two-parent families.

Webster-Stratton (1989) confirmed that single mothers are more critical and demanding than married mothers and that their children are more deviant and noncompliant. One naturally wonders whether single mothers who have trouble parenting do so because their lives are so stressful or because of personal qualities they bring into parenting. Evidence supports both possibilities (Fox, Platz, & Bentley, 1995; Gringlas & Weinraub, 1995; Simons, Beaman, Conger, & Chao, 1993b).

A national survey (Gelles, 1989) revealed that poor single mothers are more likely to behave violently toward their children than mothers who live with partners. Mothers with antisocial qualities are more prone to divorce and generally do not parent well. Their children suffer on both accounts (Bank, Forgatch, Patterson, & Fetrow, 1993). Given the number of children being raised by single parents, these findings are disturbing. Fortunately, most single parents do a good job under difficult circumstances.

TABLE 4.4 Characteristics of Single-Parent Families

Having to deal with the social stigma of living in a "broken home"

Eighty-six percent of single custodial parents are female

Both parents may be less available to children compared to nuclear families

Custodial parent requires greater cooperation and independent behavior from children

Children must cope with parental dating and romance

Children have limited contact with the noncustodial parent

Children have less exposure to parental bickering

Children in single-parent families have more school-related and relationship problems

Evaluation

Stereotyping all single-parent families as dysfunctional is unfortunate and undeserved (Kissman & Allen, 1993). To adjust well, children need to be raised by at least one healthy, concerned caregiver. However, partly due to the multiple stressors they face, some single mothers report feeling especially depressed and helpless. Unless they take steps to improve their well-being, their children (especially adolescent boys) are at risk for socio-emotional and academic problems (Gringlas & Weinraub, 1995). Divorced single parents function better when they can (1) enlist the support of their ex-spouse, (2) provide authoritative discipline to their children, (3) develop coping skills for the heightened stress of single-parenting, and (4) enlarge their social support system of family members and friends (Kissman & Allen, 1993).

SINGLE CUSTODIAL FATHERS

Study Question *How well do men perform in the role of single parent?*

Fathers head 14 percent of all single-parent families. About 8 percent of these fathers are widowers and about 25 percent never have been married. The rest are divorced. Most fathers (59 percent) who have custody of their children are unmarried. Forty-one percent of fathers with custody (592,000) have remarried. The upshot of all these numbers is that close to a million unmarried fathers are raising over a million children in the United States today (Meyer & Garasky, 1993).

Single custodial fathers are better educated, make more money, have a higher-status job than fathers in nuclear families, and are better off financially than single mothers. Most enter single parenthood in a better position than most women to support their children and maintain their predivorce standard of living. Recent trends suggest that increasing numbers of working-class men will be joining their ranks (Eggebeen, Snyder, & Manning, 1996; Hanson, 1988; Meyer & Garasky, 1993).

"The single father's financial resources probably allow him easier access to day care, baby sitters, and other substitute parenting arrangements. Usually, he is better able to pay for help with housework when needed . . ." (Kissman & Allen, 1993, p. 111). Given their relatively comfortable financial situation (compared to single mothers), custodial fathers usually do not have to move to another home or community. Thus, they can maintain stability in their children's daily life (Hanson, 1988). Even though they are not as poor as mother-headed families, a significant number (about one-fifth) of father-headed families are poor (Meyer & Garasky, 1993).

Many single fathers sought neither divorce nor custody, but accepted both reluctantly because the situation required it. They do not adjust as quickly to the fathering role or parent as skillfully as fathers who actively seek custody. "Most men were not socialized to develop the nurturing, interdependent side of themselves in relationships. Most did not think of themselves as the parents primarily responsible for child care prior to their becoming primary custodial parents" (Kissman & Allen, 1993, p. 114).

Fathers who have been involved in their children's care since their children were infants are more likely to seek custody and are better prepared to serve as primary caregivers. They also report feeling closer to their children and believe that they are doing a good job. Most single-custodial parents consider themselves to be the better parent and love their child. Some fathers assume this role because the mother refuses to accept custody (Greif, 1985; Hanson, 1988).

Children living with single fathers are a little older than children living with single mothers, but fathers sometimes raise young children. About one-third of father-led families have a preschool child. Single fathers are more likely to be raising sons than daughters (56 percent sons, 44 percent daughters) (Meyer & Garasky, 1993). Hanson (1988) reported that compared to children from nuclear families, children raised by single fathers rated them as more nurturing.

Most single fathers share homemaking chores with their children. The latter seem to benefit from the responsibility. Children in single-father homes appear to be happier and better behaved than children in single-mother homes (Ambert, 1982). Many custodial fathers report that they do not have enough time to spend with their children or to create a satisfying social life for themselves.

Studies of single fathers confirm that highly-motivated men can provide their children with high-quality parenting (Risman,

1989). This is reassuring because their ranks are growing (Meyer & Garasky, 1993). "Most fathers were happy with their decision to have sought or consented to custody, and they felt that they were clearly the better choice of parent. Children reported happiness with this arrangement, and there did not appear to be much yearning to live with the noncustodial parent" (Hanson, 1988, p. 185).

STEPPARENTING

Study Question *What type of family history do most children have before they become members of stepfamilies?*

For most adults, the divorce process leads to remarriage. When children are involved, we have a stepfamily. Also known as remarried, reconstituted, or blended families, stepfamilies are becoming increasingly common. About one out of three children will live in a stepfamily before age 18. Some estimate that by the year 2000, stepfamilies will be the most common type of family unit (Kutner, 1989a).

There are many stepfamily variations. A single mother or father may marry another single father or mother or they may marry a childfree adult who may or may not have been previously married. New partners may bring children into the stepfamily. One partner or both may also have biological children who are living with an ex-partner. Most often, a man (who, if he has children, may or may not have sole or joint custody of them) marries a women with custody of her children. "In these instances, while the mother and her children share common background, history, and cultural values, the new stepfather has a different background and history, and his values may differ considerably from those of his new stepfamily. Thus, the new stepfather is often in the position of trying to break into a unit of mother and children, whose bonds predate the association between the spouses" (Santrock, Sitterle, & Warshak, 1988, p. 145).

People who are not familiar with stepfamilies are amazed at the degree of adjustment and organization required just to allow routine family functioning (Henry & Lovelace, 1995). To get a taste of the problems and concerns of stepparents, reread the second quote on page 101, column 1. Note that the newly married couple, first and foremost, must adjust to their new relationship. Stepfamilies, like single-parent families, are viewed less positively than nuclear families—the family deficit model strikes again! (Claxton-Oldfield, 1992).

Sadly, remarriages are even more likely than first marriages to end in divorce. It takes less deterioration in the quality of a marriage to get previously divorced individuals to divorce again (Booth & Edwards, 1992; Brody, Neubaum, & Forehand, 1988). "Researchers believe that partners drag into the new marriage all of the insecurities and personality problems that disrupted the old one. And with one divorce under their belt, they feel less hesitant about obtaining a second one when trouble appears" (Turkington, 1984d).

The marital relationship in stepfamilies plays a big role in how children get along with their stepparents (particularly their stepfathers) (Fine & Kurdek, 1995; Ganong & Coleman, 1987). When parents clash, children usually remain loyal to their biological parent and line up against their stepparent or stepsiblings. Relationships in stepfamilies usually are more fragile than those in nuclear families. Because stepparenting is more challenging, it is not surprising that stepparents are somewhat less satisfied with parenting than biological parents (Fine, Voydanoff, & Donnelly, 1993; Ishii-Kuntz & Ihinger-Tallman, 1991).

As in nuclear families, stepfathers' relationships with children reflect the state of the marital relationship. Low levels of marital conflict encourage positive feelings among all family members. Newlywed parents in step-families should be aware that their children probably do not yet share their optimism and good will. Having children participate in the wedding may lessen some children's resistance to a new stepparent, but they should not be taken on the honeymoon. Lest we forget, the marital relationship is the key factor in any two-parent family's functioning (Marsiglio, 1992).

Stepfathering

Stepfathering results when a man marries and lives with a divorced, widowed, or never-married woman who has custody of her children. Santrock and his colleagues (1988) reviewed the literature on stepfathering. The stepfather-stepchild relationship depends partly on a child's age when the stepfather marries into the family. Children younger than nine years are more likely than older children to accept and form a warm relationship with a stepfather.

Most stepfathers report that they are unprepared for the challenges and conflicts that arise when they remarry into an established family. "He is expected to master many roles in a hurry. He is expected to quickly win the respect and caring of the stepchildren. He must meet the needs and expectations of his new wife and himself as a loving husband. And he must come across as an affectionate parent to her children even though they may resent him" (E. Visher, quoted by Brooks, 1988).

Common problems for new stepfathers include communicating with their stepchildren, deciding how much authority to assume in their role as father (especially when they hear, "You're not my real father"), and coping with guilt feelings regarding their biological children living with their ex-spouses. They also may be unhappy about how their ex-spouses discipline their children (especially their

sons). Hanson, McLanahan, and Thomson (1996) report that stepfather households have more parental conflict than other types of households.

Some new stepfathers are wary of their stepchildren's ongoing relationship with their biological father. Children in remarried households may experience a conflict of loyalty between their biological parents and their stepparents. Clingempeel and Segal (1986) observed that the more frequently girls visited their nonresident biological mothers, the poorer their relationship was with their resident stepmother.

Gaining the acceptance and respect of their stepchildren is a key factor in stepfathers' adjustment to their new family. Children usually resent being disciplined by anyone but their biological parent. The parental role should not be assumed too quickly. Those with experience advise new stepparents to "move slowly and be patient, emphasizing that developing a relationship with the stepchild takes time. It seems gradual participation in the parenting process by the stepfather may often be the best answer" (Santrock et al., 1988, p. 155).

The early months of remarriage usually are the most difficult (Bray & Berger, 1993). People who have not previously raised children naturally feel awkward about joining an established family. Most have unrealistic expectations about how quickly they will be accepted by their acquired family. When hostile children treat them as intruders, they take it personally. They do not know how to react. Stepfathers usually have more difficulty with daughters, particularly adolescent girls who might view the stepfather as competing with them for their mother's companionship. Many stepfathers compensate by being "polite strangers," that is, acting sensitively and nonintruding toward their stepchildren. Early adolescent children (especially girls) are likely to ignore these overtures (Vuchinich, Hetherington, Vuchinich, & Clingempeel, 1991). Some children reject their stepparent's initiatives regardless of the latter's sensitivity or friendliness (Brown, Green, & Druckman, 1990).

Stepmothering

Contradicting the "wicked stepmother" stereotype of children's fables and fairy tales, stepmothers usually are accepted by children more quickly than are stepfathers. They have a closer, warmer relationship, and are more involved in their stepchildren's daily lives. In fact, stepmothers have been found to be as involved with their children as mothers in intact families (e.g. Fine, Voydanoff, & Donnelly, 1993).

"It seems that remarriage may have a positive and stabilizing effect on custodial mothers, which is then reflected in their relationship with their children. More money is available for child support and other aspects of running a household than was likely the case as a single parent. Also, stepfathers are available to help with family work, and perhaps more important, to offer nurturance and support to their wives. . . ." (Santrock et al., 1988, p. 161). Stepmothering resentful children frustrates most women, particularly when they receive minimal support from their husbands (MacDonald & DeMaris, 1996). When communication is poor between children and their stepparents, some children run away or ask to live with their noncustodial parent.

Stepfamily Research

An early study by Bowerman and Irish (1962) found that relationships in stepfamilies were characterized by more stress and ambivalence than those in nonstepfamilies. Ganong and Coleman (1987) wondered whether these differences continue to exist given the demographic changes of the past 30 years. They used the same questions as Bowerman and Irish to examine the attitudes of 126 adolescent stepchildren about their stepmothers or stepfathers, depending upon the family configuration.

The stepchildren reported feeling at least moderately close to their stepparents. They did not report feeling more distant from stepfathers than from stepmothers. Stepsons and stepdaughters perceived their stepparents similarly. The stepdaughter-stepfather relationship usually is the least emotionally close of the stepparent-child relationships, perhaps reflecting daughters' resentment of an "intruder" replacing their role as their mother's main confidant. Some adolescent girls, adjusting to the heightened sexuality that accompanies puberty, withdraw from stepfathers because they feel threatened by the presence of a nonbiologically related adult male (Fischman, 1988b; Vuchinich, Hetherington, Vuchinich, & Clingempeel, 1991).

Sexuality is a visible element in new stepfamilies in several ways. The newlywed parents are in the honeymoon phase of their relationship. Many adolescents are uncomfortable about expressions of affection and sexuality between their biological parent and stepparent. Opposite-gender adolescent stepsiblings sometimes find that they are sexually attracted to each other or to their opposite-gender stepparent. Young girls in stepfamilies are at greater risk for sexual abuse by their stepfathers than girls in nuclear families are by their biological fathers. The situation is complicated by occasional false accusations of abuse (Visher & Visher, 1988). Verbal affection usually is preferred over physical displays, especially by girls. Biological mothers should be properly vigilant (without being unduly suspicious) about inappropriate displays of affection between family members.

Relationships in stepfamilies are reasonably good (Ganong & Coleman, 1987). Mothers and children in most stepfamilies report being as happy as their counterparts in nondivorced families. Stepchildren perceive themselves as happy, successful, and achiev-

TABLE 4.5 Common Issues in Stepfamilies

Social stigma surrounding "broken" or reconstituted families

Children's lack of trust of new stepparent reflecting feelings of loyalty to noncustodial biological parent

Children's desire for biological parents to reconcile

Lack of preparation for parenting by new stepparent

Stepparents' wariness of stepchildren's continued relationship with noncustodial biological parent

Sexuality issues surrounding children's lack of "blood" relationship to stepparents or stepsiblings

Territorial disputes with people "intruding" into an established family or family setting

---

ing as do most children from nuclear families. For large numbers of children, living in stepfamilies compensates for many of the negative effects of divorce and father absence (Visher & Visher, 1988).

Does it help for the remarried couple to have a child together? How do stepchildren feel about the birth of a sibling? Younger children seem to be more accepting of new siblings in a blended family, but the addition of a new family member can also destabilize the fragile stepfamily system (MacDonald & DeMaris, 1996). Remarried couples in blended families who give birth to "mutual" children do not appear to differ in the strength or quality of their relationships from remarried couples who choose not to have additional children (Ganong & Coleman, 1988). Yet fathers who live with their biological children and stepchildren report that they feel more "fatherlike" (Marsiglio, 1992).

Parenting Stepchildren

If you find stepfamilies complicated and confusing, imagine how stepchildren must feel.

"The children have a strong loyalty to their father and want to protect him. Divorce was their biggest nightmare. Now, on top of that, they have another parent and two homes where there are no similarities in discipline and rules. The children are very confused" (mother of two, quoted by Lawson, 1991).

The first challenge of the remarried family is for the new marriage partners to strengthen their relationship, which is the backbone of the remarried family. According to one mother, "You feel so torn. You feel loyalty to your new husband, yet you have to help your children with their new reality. It is a constant balancing act" (quoted by Lawson, 1991).

New stepparents should proceed slowly and sensitively when interacting with stepchildren without becoming disengaged. They should support, but not replace, the biological parent as primary family authority. This may be more difficult for men, as the traditional role of father is to lead rather than to support one's spouse. It is desirable that adolescents residing with their biological mothers be in good communication both with their biological father and their stepfather (Collins, Newman, & McKenry, 1995).

Young children will accept stepparents more readily than will older children or adolescents. Young adolescents, trying to separate from their parents and establish an adult identity, have the most difficulty adjusting to stepfamily life. Adolescents do best when parents are flexible, household routines are stable, and communication is open (Collins, Newman, & McKenry, 1995; Henry & Lovelace, 1995). The discipline and communication methods we consider in the next few chapters are particularly useful in stepfamilies (Dinkmeyer, McKay, & McKay, 1987).

Following their parents' divorce, most children hope for and fantasize about their reconciliation. When either parent remarries, it becomes clearer that the divorce is irrevocable. Children may direct their anger to the person they perceive as being responsible for the breakup, often the intruding stepparent. Like children in single-parent families, children in remarried families have more problems in school and with peer relationships, and have more emotional problems compared to children from intact families (Amato & Keith, 1991b).

"After several complaints from Laurie's preschool teacher, I began to realize that she was going through a difficult time in her development. She had lived with me (and slept in the same bedroom) for 2 1/2 years after her father and I separated. She didn't have to compete with anyone else for my attention. All at once I got married and acquired a husband and stepdaughter, and Laurie acquired a stepfather and stepsister. Her stepfather slept in the same room with Mommy, she didn't. She was attending a new school and was living in a new house. All of this change was too much for her. Her way of getting my attention was to misbehave in school. Once we figured out the problems and communicated our support and concern for her, she got over her problems in school and with time, she has adjusted remarkably well to her new life" (Laurie's mother). It helps children to see both of their biological parents together occasionally, especially if they can treat each other civilly. If family life becomes unmanageable, professional help may be needed (Visher & Visher, 1988).

Evaluation

There is more conflict in stepfamilies, especially those with adolescent children. It is possible that some of the problems we see in older children in stepfamilies are the delayed, "sleeper effects" we discussed in the section on divorce. It is also likely that adolescent issues involving identity and individuation interact with unresolved issues about their parent's divorce (Bray & Berger, 1993).

Members of stepfamilies have minimal conflict when parents support each other and parents and children have good communication, realistic expectations about each other, and sensible ways of handling discipline and nurturance issues. Mutual respect is the key. There is no question but that a harmonious stepfamily is a vast improvement over a conflictual nuclear family (Bray & Hetherington, 1993).

GRANDPARENTING

"When my grandmother died, my parents had a public mourning with our big family, but mine was a private mourning, because no one paid attention to what the children were feeling. None of the grown-ups had any idea that my grandmother was the center of the magic in my life. She was my partner in fantasy" (young woman interviewed by Kornhaber, 1996, p. 101).

During interviews, children confirm that their emotional bond with their grandparents is second only to their bond with their parents. Children report that relationships with their grandparents are special, with most children becoming especially attached to their grandmothers (Creasey & Koblewski, 1991). Consistent with Erikson's suggestion that contributing to the next generation (generativity) is the key developmental task of middle adulthood, grandparents acknowledge that their love for their grandchildren provides considerable meaning and joy to their lives (Kornhaber & Woodward, 1981).

The role that grandparents (and stepgrandparents) play in the lives of their children has changed considerably during the twentieth century (Bengston & Robertson, 1985). Because the average lifespan was relatively short before this century, few people lived long enough to become grandparents. Today, for the first time in history, children get to know most or all of their grandparents (Kennedy &

In addition to providing nurturance and affection to their grandchildren, grandparents teach skills, values, and important lessons about life.

Keeney, 1988). The vast majority (94 percent) of older Americans with children are grandparents (Kornhaber, 1996). Forty percent of those over age 65 are *great*-grandparents (Doka & Mertz, 1988). Most adults of grandparent age (late 40s and beyond) are healthy, relatively well off economically, and live with a spouse (Aldous, 1995).

Partly due to their increasing numbers, grandparents are getting more attention. The U.S. Congress designated 1995 to be the Year of the Grandparent. Yet compared to parents, grandparents hold relatively low social status. Unlike Mother's day and Father's Day, Grandparent's Day receives minimal attention and celebration.

Grandparents contribute to their grandchildren directly through their genes and through nurturant interactions during visits, and indirectly, by supporting their grandchildren's parents (their own adult children) emotionally and financially (Clingempeel, Colyar, Brand, & Hetherington, 1992). African-American grandparents tend to be much more involved with their grandchildren than white grandparents (Cherlin & Furstenberg, 1986; Kivett, 1993), although when they live with their children and grandchildren, relationships often become strained (Chase-Lansdale, Brooks-Gunn, & Zamsky, 1994). Because they have more time than most parents to share their extensive life experience, grandparents teach everyday survival skills, values, and lessons of life that may have a lifelong influence. Through their roles as mentors, role models, wizards, heroes, and playmates, grandparents inspire and motivate their grandchildren (Kornhaber, 1996).

Like expectant parents, grandparents-to-be fantasize about what it will be like to become a grandparent (Kornhaber, 1996). The first grandchild usually occupies a special place in the hearts of grandparents, sometimes causing other grandchildren to feel neglected. "For grandfathers who were unable to spend much time with their own children, favoring a particular grandchild may give them a chance to relive and change some of the things they regret about their past. It offers them an opportunity to relate to children in ways that may have felt uncomfortable 25 years before" (Kutner, 1990).

Only about 20 percent of grandparents become very involved in their grandchildren's daily lives. Most have variable contact and about 15 percent have little or no relationship (Kornhaber & Woodward, 1981). Of this latter group, some assert that they have already "served their time" as parents and have little nurturance left to give. Some grandparents have difficulty relating to adopted or step-grandchildren or children with emotional or behavioral problems. Others live too far away to establish a close bond. Older grandparents lack the vigor necessary to keep up with young children (Kornhaber, 1996).

Like parents, grandparents grapple with distinctive issues regarding their role (Kornhaber, 1996). Is it OK to have a favorite grandchild? What does it mean to spoil a grandchild? How involved should grandparents be in providing child care? What happens to their right to see their grandchild if their adult child loses custody following divorce? And, if they do not approve of the way their child parents, do they keep their opinions to themselves or risk putting in their "two cents."

The quality of the parent-grandparent relationship sets the tone for the grandparent-grandchild relationship (Mathews & Sprey, 1985). Tension between parents and grandparents about how to raise a child can lead to less contact between grandparent and child (Whitbeck, Hoyt, & Huck, 1993). Some grandparents feel rebuffed when their child-rearing advice is not solicited or worse, rejected. Adult children who are parents resent their parent's criticism. "Arguments about the grandchildren may be symbolic ways for par-

ents and grandparents to argue about their own relationships" (Dr. Helen Kivnick, quoted by Kutner, 1992c). It is crucial for family harmony that grandparents be supportive, yet not undermine their children's parental efforts. Aldous (1995) notes that many grandparents are torn between two contradictory norms—the norm of noninterference (boundary maintenance) and the norm of obligation. The situation is complicated when grandparents provide child care or financial support or live with the family.

Does the onset of puberty increase the distance between adolescents and their grandparents the way that it increases parent-child distance? Or do grandparents provide an emotional buffer for their grandchildren during their teenage years? In a longitudinal study designed to answer these questions, children, their mothers, and grandmothers from 186 Caucasian, middle-class families completed questionnaires about the adolescents' perceived closeness to their grandparents (Clingempeel, Colyar, Brand, & Hetherington, 1992). Seventy-three of the families were intact, 64 were mother-custody, single-parent families, and 49 were stepfamilies. Grandparents, especially grandfathers, reported being more involved with adolescent children from single-parent families. Puberty appeared to increase the distance between grandfathers and granddaughters, but grandsons reported greater involvement with and feeling closer to their grandparents. Creasy and Koblewski (1991), on the other hand, noted that during adolescence, granddaughters reported better relationships with grandparents than did grandsons. In any case, because adolescents are not dependent on their grandparents or under their authority, they probably do not feel that they have to separate from their grandparents they way that they do with their parents (Kornhaber, 1996).

Due to destructive effects on families of drug abuse, alcoholism, child abuse, AIDS, divorce, and parental death, increasing numbers of grandparents are gaining custody of their grandchildren (de Toledo & Brown, 1995; Kennedy & Keeney, 1988). The U.S. Census Bureau estimated in 1991 that 3.3 million children in the United States lived with their grandparents, a 44 percent increase from 1980. Grandparents sometimes choose to parent rather than surrender their grandchildren to a foster family. Their primary goal is to provide their grandchildren with a stable family environment (Jendrek, 1993a; O'Reilly & Morrison, 1993).

Not all grandparents who "rescue" their grandchildren feel that they had a choice. Older couples who had been contemplating peaceful retirements find themselves being drained, financially and emotionally, by unanticipated child-rearing obligations. Their senior citizen friends usually are not very willing to accommodate their parenting lifestyle. Because most states refuse to consider grandparents as foster parents (didn't they fail with their own children?), some swallow their pride and apply for welfare (Jendrek, 1993b). Many cope with grandchildren who have been emotionally scarred by their parents' divorces, drug problems, and custody disputes (de Toledo & Brown, 1995). Grandparents complain that taking in grandchildren causes them to alter their lifestyles, have less time for themselves, and to feel more tired, but about two-thirds of custodial grandparents acknowledge that child rearing makes their lives more meaningful and keeps them "in shape" (Jendrek, 1993b; Kornhaber, 1996; Malcolm, 1991; Saltzman, 1992).

Many of these grandparents need help, group or professional support, so that they can resolve their anger toward their own adult children and help their grandchildren not feel abandoned by their parents (de Toledo & Brown, 1995; Kennedy & Keeney, 1988; O'Reilly & Morrison, 1993). A 61-year-old woman raising her 6-year-old grand-

daughter because of her own daughter's substance abuse problem disclosed, "I'm a lot older and a lot wiser parent this time. More patient, too. But with the Brownies, the gymnastics, the parents' nights and the sudden earaches, we've lost our entire circle of friends. Our lives are on hold, indefinitely" (quoted by Malcolm, 1991).

Note that the motives of grandparents who have parenting foisted upon them differ from those of "latecomer" parents who want to bear and raise children despite their advancing age. The fact that so many grandparents do an excellent job of parenting should lessen social prejudice against older first-time parents. Day-care grandparents have the best deal. They love their time with their grandchildren, they're least affected by their caregiving role, and the kids go home at the end of the day (Jendrek, 1993a). Advice for grandparents raising their grandchildren? Join a support group, get professional advice regarding their legal relationship to their grandchild, talk to the children about their parents, and don't forget their own needs (de Toledo & Brown, 1995). Grandparents who are not raising their grandchildren can try to spend time with them individually, stay in touch with what's going on in their everyday lives, and if regular visits are not feasible, write or phone often.

Grandparents as Disciplinarians

It is a truism that in their encounters with their grandchildren, grandparents vow to not make the same mistakes that they made in raising their own children. In a sense, they have "the better of the bargain" because they get more joy and less hassle than the parents do (Kornhaber, 1996). Each involved grandparent creates a unique style in an attempt to balance closeness, nurturance, and authority (Cherlin & Furstenberg, 1986). Grandparents usually are more nurturant than parents (e.g.,

Martin, Halverson, Wampler, & Hollett-Wright, 1991), more permissive in setting and enforcing limits, and more indulgent regarding children's requests. However, in the presence of a stranger, children still prefer their mother to their grandmother (Myers, Jarvis, & Creasey, 1987).

Some grandparents, particularly maternal grandmothers, exercise considerable responsibility in caring for and disciplining their grandchildren. Blackwelder and Passman (1986) compared 24 mothers' and 24 maternal grandmothers' disciplinary interventions under identical circumstances. The investigators were able to manipulate the number of correct responses that the children scored on a task. As the children's performance worsened, both mothers and grandmothers increased the amount of reward and punishment.

With further decrements in performance, mothers continued to increase the intensities of reward and punishment, but grandmothers leveled off. The investigators found that the disciplinary styles of mothers and grandmothers were more similar than different. Maternal grandmothers "act as role models

and advisors," to their daughters. Both mothers and grandmothers were somewhat likely to overlook errors, but rarely overlooked opportunities to dispense rewards.

There were some differences in discipline style between the two groups. When the children were performing well, grandmothers dispensed significantly more rewards than mothers did. By the end of the session, when the children were performing poorly, grandmothers were less punitive than mothers. Three grandmothers refused to punish at all. No mother chose to withhold punishment. The differences support the common perception that grandmothers "are more giving, less punitive, and more forgiving than are mothers" (p. 80). However, the more responsibility that the grandmothers felt that they had for teaching, socializing, raising, and disciplining the children, the more intensely they punished. "Grandmothers who more closely approximated the conventional maternal role were found to discipline more intensely than did less involved grandmothers" (p. 86). Thus, role superceded personal style.

Spotlight

Children of Gay and Lesbian Parents

For reasons that are deeply ingrained in western culture, the topics of homosexuality and children do not easily mix (Crosbie-Burnett & Helmbrecht, 1993). Individuals with homosexual orientations often are portrayed in media such as movies and newspapers as child molesters. In reality, the vast majority of children who are sexually abused are assaulted by *heterosexual* members of their own families. Many parents incorrectly interpret pleas for sexual tolerance as condoning nontraditional sexual

lifestyles. The fact of the matter is that from 6 to 14 million children in the United States are being raised by parents who are not heterosexual (Crosbie-Burnett & Helmbrecht, 1993; Patterson, 1992).

How do gay men and lesbians become parents? Many have children in heterosexual relationships before they realize or acknowledge their homosexuality or bisexuality. Many children living with gay parents are children of divorce. They may have as a stepparent a same-sexed partner of their gay biological parent. Many gay women, single or in lesbian relationships, decide to have children through adoption or via donor insemination. Gay men become parents through adoption or foster care. Because the legal system still is somewhat hostile toward the concept of gay parenting, gay men and women usually pursue parenthood without telling others about their true sexual orientation (Patterson, 1992; Unger & Crawford, 1992). As of 1995, eight state supreme courts have ruled that sexual orientation should not be a factor in adoption cases. Five had ruled the opposite (Cavaliere, 1995a).

The main problems facing gay parents include misgivings about their parenthood from their own parents and from society, social isolation, and ambivalence about their ability to raise children in a "straight" world. Many gay parents hide their sexual orientation from society (and sometimes from their children) because they are afraid of losing custody of their children. Such fears make it difficult for researchers to locate and study families with gay parents.

Patterson (1992) reviewed evidence concerning the personal and social development of children raised by gay and lesbian parents. Because many of these children have undergone parental divorce, the most common type of study compares children with custodial lesbian mothers to children with custodial heterosexual mothers. Thus, the factors of parental divorce and living with a custodial mother are controlled for. However, more divorced lesbian mothers than divorced heterosexual mothers live with partners, presenting a potentially confounding factor.

What can we say about children who are raised by gay parents? Are they maladjusted? Are they more likely than children of heterosexual parents to develop homosexual preferences? Do they have difficulty in their relationships with peers? Are they more toler-ant of different viewpoints? Studies of children of gay and lesbian parents reveal that these children are not noticeably different from children in families with heterosexual parents regarding their sexual orientation, their personality development, and their social relationships (Golombok & Tasker, 1996; Hoeffer, 1981; Javaid, 1993; Kirkpatrick, Roy, & Smith, 1978; Kirkpatrick, Smith, & Roy, 1981; Patterson, 1992; Tasker & Golombok, 1995).

"Despite long-standing legal presumptions against gay and lesbian parents in many states, despite dire predictions about their children based on well-known theories of psychosocial development, and despite the accumulation of a substantial body of research investigating these issues, not a single study has found children of gay and lesbian parents to be disadvantaged in any significant respect relative to children of heterosexual parents. Indeed, the evidence to date suggests that home environments provided by gay and lesbian parents are as likely as those provided by heterosexual parents to support and enable children's psychosocial growth" (Patterson, 1992, p. 1036).

"I remember men being in the house at some point after my mom died. But I don't remember knowing that they were my dad's partners. And I don't think we ever had a conversation like, "Dad are you gay?" But when I realized the truth, I was angry at him, because everybody else was different and because I had to lie to everybody" (Bill, 17-year-old son of a gay father, quoted by Minton, 1994, p. 14).

Children's adjustment is better when, as early as possible, they can accept and acknowledge their parent's homosexuality and have minimum exposure to homophobic attitudes and values. As Bill implies in the quote above, depending on how it is handled, being teased by peers about their parent's sexual orientation, especially during adolescence, can be a blow to children's self-esteem or a lesson in the importance of tolerance.

The research to date has not revealed any reason to suspect that the quality of parenting is related to a parent's sexual orientation. As we have emphasized throughout this chapter, the circumstances of birth and the quality of family relationships are much more influential in family dynamics than family structure or parent's sexual orientation (Hare & Richards, 1993; Patterson, 1992; 1995; Tasker & Golombok, 1995).

SUMMARY

1. Demographic, social, and economic changes in the late 20th century have given rise to a wide variety of family configurations. They differ from both the traditional extended family and the modern nuclear family.

2. Large numbers of children experience a long, stressful sequence of transitions: parental conflict, parental divorce, single-parent family, father absence, parent remarriage, and stepfamily.

3. Children are adversely affected more by frequent exposure to overt parental conflict than by parental separation or divorce. Frequent parental conflict that is intense, unresolved, and child-related upsets children the most.

4. Parental conflict, separation, and divorce overwhelm many children's coping ability while some children take it in stride. It takes at least two to three years for most children (and parents) to recover from the impact of family disintegration. However, it is misguided to believe that the divorce process inevitably leads to psychological disturbance. Most children and parents from divorced families eventually are as well-adjusted as individuals from intact families.

5. Unhappy parents in poor marital relationships are not doing their children a favor by staying together "for the sake of the child." Custody battles usually increase childrens'

suffering. This is particularly true when parents continue to bicker after custody is decided. Typically, a mother is granted sole custody and a father receives visitation rights and support obligations.

6. Divorce mediation and joint custody are becoming more common. Both attempt to minimize the pain of divorce for children and their parents. Joint custody usually increases father's participation in children's lives following divorce. Joint custody works best when ex-spouses maintain a good working relationship.

7. As a result of divorce, the nature of children's relationship with each parent changes. Many children feel compelled to be loyal to one parent or the other. Economic hardship leads to a series of stressful transitions for children, including moving to a new neighborhood and school. Children in the sole custody of their mothers usually have little contact with their fathers. More important than custody arrangements are the ongoing relationships children maintain with both parents.

8. Almost one out of three households with children are headed by single parents. About 86 percent of single parents are mothers. Their median income is about one-third the national average. About one million fathers have sole custody of their children and they usually perform well as parents.

9. Stepfamilies are varied and complex family configurations. Adults entering step-

families usually are ill-prepared for the step-parent role. Stepchildren often resent their authority and resist their "intrusion" into the family. Gaining their acceptance takes time and patience. Stepmothers usually are accepted more quickly than stepfathers, possibly because they become much more involved in their stepchildren's lives. Generally, children in stepfamilies report being as happy as children in other family configurations.

10. Today's grandparents are younger, better educated, healthier, and most want to be involved in their grandchildren's lives. Sometimes when parents no longer are willing or able to take care of their children, grandparents reluctantly step in and become substitute parents. This usually is at a considerable cost to their lifestyles and emotional well-being.

11. Although social bias against gay and lesbian parents remains, their children are not recognizably different from children in traditional families.

GLOSSARY

binuclear family   A family where children have two parents but live with one (usually following parental divorce)

cohabitation   Living together as adult partners who are not married

family   Two or more persons related by birth, marriage, or adoption, or unmarried partners living together

family configuration   Type of family structure, including parents' relationship to each other (e.g., married or not) and whether they are biologically related to their children

family deficit model   The belief that any particular family configuration is inherently superior to another

household   All of the individuals who live together, related or not

joint legal custody   Legal custody of a child shared by both parents

joint physical custody   Physical custody of a child shared by both parents so that the child lives with each parent part of the time

nuclear family   Married parents living with one or more biological children

sole custody   Custody of a child granted only to one parent

split custody   Custody of a child shared by both parents

THOUGHT QUESTIONS

1. Why do people assume that the nuclear family is the optimal family configuration for raising children?

2. Why do so many married people have difficulty getting along?

3. In what sense is divorce as stressful for children as it is for their parents?

4. How might children interpret the absence of the noncustodial parent?

5. How does society express its biases against nontraditional families?

6. Defend the premise that grandparenting has a genetic basis.

7. What are the advantages and disadvantages for a child being raised by

    a. a single parent
    b. a gay parent

PARENTAL AUTHORITY, CHILD COMPLIANCE, AND PARENTING STYLES

OBJECTIVES 140
HOW DO PARENTS PERCEIVE THEIR CHILDREN? 140
ROOTS OF PARENT-CHILD CONFLICT 144
Understanding Noncompliance 145
Analysis of Misbehavior 148
Parental Requests and Compliance 149
CULTURAL PERSPECTIVE: HOW CHINESE AND
    JAPANESE PARENTS RAISE THEIR WELL-BEHAVED
    CHILDREN 150
INTERNALIZATION OF PARENTAL STANDARDS 152
CHILDREN'S CONCEPTIONS OF ADULT AUTHORITY 153
ADOLESCENTS' CONCEPTIONS OF PARENTAL
    AUTHORITY 154
NO SIMPLE FORMULA FOR HANDLING DISCIPLINE
    ENCOUNTERS 155
The Discipline Dance 155
DIMENSIONS OF DISCIPLINE 156
Spotlight: Chance Encounters 157
BAUMRIND'S MODEL OF PARENTING STYLES 158
Spotlight: A Team Approach to Discipline 161
PARENTING STYLE AND PARENTING PRACTICES 163
POWER AND PUNISHMENT IN PARENTING 164
Hoffman's Model of Parental Power Assertion 165
Punishment 166
SUMMARY 167
GLOSSARY 168
THOUGHT QUESTIONS 168

"Parents who understand the subtext of a toddler's defiance do not take her negative behavior personally. They realize it is not a rejection of their love or authority. It is simply a way the child prepares herself for independence . . . the child is developing an awareness of herself as an individual. She is also trying to figure out the difference between what she can do and what she should do" (Kutner, 1988t).

"My Carla can be so sweet and affectionate at home. She'll do anything to please me. But she has a mind of her own. She can be very stubborn and strong-willed when she doesn't get her way. She tests you all the time. Even as a baby she was demanding. At preschool she has a lot of trouble getting along with the other children. And she'll be fresh to the teachers. What am I going to do with her?"

OBJECTIVES

After studying Chapter 5, students should be able to:

1. Describe the biases that influence parents' perceptions of their children's character and behavior
2. Describe unrealistic expectations that parents might have about raising and living with children
3. Explain the advantages of parents having realistic expectations about their children and about the parenting role
4. Discuss the role that gratification and responsibility play in parent-child conflicts
5. Describe how children's views of adult authority change as they mature
6. Identify the distinctions that adolescents make regarding parental jurisdiction and authority
7. Distinguish between different types of noncompliance, and describe how parents adjust their discipline strategies as children mature
8. Explain the assertion, "Parents and children raise each other"
9. Identify the influences with which parents compete in raising their children
10. List the various dimensions of discipline that investigators have suggested and studied
11. Outline Baumrind's model of discipline styles, and describe the characteristics of children that tend to be associated with each parenting style
12. Describe the characteristics of punitive parents and the role that power plays in their discipline strategies

Teaching children to behave well may be the most challenging part of the parenting role. Child-rearing strategies evolve gradually, almost on a trial-and-error basis. Flexible parents seek new ways of relating to and communicating with their children. They value good information about children and good ideas about handling misbehavior. Rigid parents have fixed ideas about how children should behave and about how to handle misbehavior. They depend heavily on criticism and coercion, rather than seeking constructive ways of gaining compliance.

Look up the term *discipline* in a dictionary. You will probably note several meanings that relate to child rearing: correcting misbehavior, teaching self-control, submission to authority, and punishment. This chapter explores the topic known as **discipline**: the process by which parents attempt to change their children's behavior. It presents the groundwork for the following two chapters on child behavior change techniques and communication. There are many approaches to discipline, some more effective than others. In this text, an approach to discipline is considered effective if it supports our four parenting goals.

HOW DO PARENTS PERCEIVE THEIR CHILDREN?

Over time, parents formulate a model of their child's personality. These models are important because they guide parents' interactions with their children (Strassberg, 1995). Chances are, if you instruct a parent, "Tell me about your little girl," you will hear something like the preceding description of Carla. Parental models are remarkably stable over time (McNally, Eisenberg, & Harris, 1991).

A mother of an eight-year-old girl reports, "During a single day, Grace's attitude and temperament change by the minute. She will be mean, rude, obnoxious, and lewd toward one of us and then, without an apology or

Much of what parents know about children and child rearing comes from everyday observation and interaction.

even blinking her eyes, will turn around and start talking about something else in a totally different state of mind."

Based on her observations, Grace's mother offers her mini-theory of their relationship. "Grace and I have a love/hate relationship. She's very special to me because I understand all of her problems. But because of her total defiance toward me, we always seem to be fighting. Of course, I give in and Grace wins. All our harsh words and threats are forgotten until our next battle." (Grace's mother's analysis contains several clues about why their relationship is so bumpy. Can you identify them?)

Like Grace's mother, what most parents know about children and child rearing comes mainly from observation and interaction.

George Holden (1988) asked 192 adults—mothers, fathers, and nonparents—to figure out why an infant was crying, based on clues that they were given. "Women were more efficient and accurate than men in solving the problem, and nonparents, particularly males, had more difficulty in solving the problem than parents" (p. 1623). It is reassuring that practical experience with infants leads to better problem solving. To a large extent, in solving child care problems, parents learn to do what seems to work.

Do parents view their children's behavior objectively? Apparently not. The Rev. Consuela York, a Baptist minister, quoted family members of inmates in a Chicago prison. "They'll say, 'He's in there for rape, Mother

York, but he's a good boy. Or 'He killed four or five people, but he didn't mean to'" (*The New York Times*, January 30, 1989). Parents have very strong feelings about their children. We would be surprised, even disturbed, to meet parents who viewed their child with complete objectivity.

We expect parents to express a positive bias toward their children. (Parents of different children often complain to each other about their children's conduct, but complaining about one's children is more socially acceptable than bragging). We expect most parents to credit their children for their achievements,

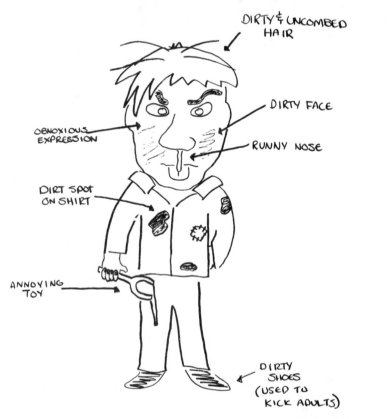

Justin Jaffe

to rationalize their failings, and, occasionally, to overestimate their children's abilities (e.g., Miller, 1986).

The existence of such parental biases is supported by research. Gretarsson and Gelfand (1988) interviewed 60 mothers regarding their perceptions of their children's social behavior. "Mothers will see their children's praiseworthy social behavior as innate, stable, and dispositional, and their negative behavior as temporary and situationally caused" (p. 264). Thus, good behavior is credited to the child (and indirectly to the parent's childrearing ability). Misbehavior is blamed on the situation (Himelstein, Graham, & Weiner, 1991). The parent's model of the child's personality can therefore be based mostly on good behavior. Bad behavior can be dismissed as temporary and atypical.

This perceptual bias serves at least two useful functions for parents. First, it reassures them that they are good parents. After all, they have good children. Second, it promotes more harmonious parent-child relationships. Parents of generally well-behaved children can view them as "basically good," even when they misbehave. Gretarsson and Gelfand (1988) suggest that this positive bias may reflect parents' perceiving their children as dispositionally similar to themselves. Parents make this assumption because their children "are similar genetically, are reared by the parents, and are viewed by others as extensions of their parents" (Gretarsson & Gelfand, 1988, p. 267).

Parents of difficult children like Carla see them as dispositionally difficult. (A less palatable alternative would be to view themselves as inept). Viewing the oppositional child this way "relieves parents of responsibility for the child's condition and for improving it" (p. 268). Such a view protects parental self-esteem. It also justifies spending more time with their better-behaved children. With difficult children, this type of bias may discourage parents from taking corrective actions. They

may believe that such attempts are bound to fail (Gretarsson & Gelfand, 1988).

Study Question *Should young children be held responsible for their misbehavior?*

How parents evaluate their children's behavior is also affected by their judgment of the behavior's desirability (Dix & Reinhold, 1991; Dix, Ruble, Grusec & Nixon, 1986; Strassberg, 1995). Mothers may attribute children's helpful behavior to good intentions and dispositions. They may attribute misconduct to situational factors (e.g., temptation or peer pressure) or to developmental limitations (e.g., short attention span). As children get older, their parents become more likely to attribute their behavior to personal dispositions and intentions.

Parents are more likely to hold a child responsible for misconduct, and possibly punish, if the parent believes that the child understood the violated rule and could have acted more appropriately (Dix, Ruble, & Zambarano, 1989). Parents assume that when their older children misbehave, they understand that what they are doing is wrong (Goodnow, Knight, & Cashmore, 1983). Therefore, the parents become increasingly annoyed by misbehavior ("At your age, you should know better"). If a younger child is perceived as not intending to break a rule or not able to inhibit the misbehavior, parents are less upset and less likely to punish (Dix & Grusec, 1985). Parents' child-rearing philosophies, their temporary mood states, and situational factors also influence their judgments about why their children disobey their requests and thus how they should handle noncompliance (Arnold & O'Leary, 1995; Dix & Reinhold, 1991).

Parents also attribute, often erroneously, particular significance to certain traits or behaviors that they consider important; at the same time, they may overlook other traits and behaviors that they deem insignificant (Sansbury & Wahler, 1992). I have counseled parents who were very worried about their young children's toileting problems, thumb-sucking, crying, or their child's resistance to going to sleep. More often than not, the behavior perceived as a problem is quite normal for a child of that age.

Sibling conflict, another source of worry to parents, is very common and even healthy. Some parents find any form of family friction unacceptable. If they are unduly worried about it, they might pressure the child (or children) to change. Children usually resist direct attempts to change their behavior, and unnecessary parent-child conflict may arise. In this example, if parents could appreciate how sibling conflict contributes to their children's development, they might be able to inhibit their premature interventions.

Parents revise their models as their children grow. They look for "predictive signs" of their children's progress. Because they usually lack an objective basis for evaluation, they compare their children to other children they know. Thus children may be compared to their siblings or friends. Parents will also assess a child's progress over time (in effect, comparing the child to herself—"She's a lot calmer than she used to be"). I have always looked forward to conferences with my children's teachers. Teachers naturally spend a lot of time observing and interacting with children. I enjoy comparing their opinions about my children to mine. They are usually quite similar.

Why are we so interested in how parents view their children? Parents do not view their children objectively, nor do they react to their children objectively. Parenting behavior is guided by parents' perceptions of their children, their values, and by what they consider to be positive outcomes. Parental beliefs about gender differences or other child qualities also guide their parenting behaviors (Dekovic, Gerris, & Janssens, 1991; Luster, Rhoades, & Haas, 1989; Stern & Karraker, 1988).

In formulating and revising their models, parents are a little like scientists, "actively observing, framing sometimes far-reaching hypotheses, acting so as to foster some outcomes and thwart others, and continually revising their internal models of their children" (Costanzo & Woody, 1985, pp. 429–430).

ROOTS OF PARENT-CHILD CONFLICT

Study Question *Why is there usually so much conflict among family members?*

Parents sometimes wonder, "What do children want?" Young children are motivated by what Freud called the **pleasure principle**, the immediate gratification obtained when their senses are stimulated or their desires are satisfied (see Appendix B). Pleasure is a powerful (though invisible) reinforcer. What parents consider to be misbehavior usually produces gratification for children. They have a name for it—"fun." Children are not usually intentionally bad. They are disposed to do whatever produces positive (or avoids negative) outcomes.

Thomas Gordon (1970), the originator of parent effectiveness training, suggested that we strike the word *misbehavior* from parents' vocabularies. Misbehavior usually refers to behavior that is inappropriate, harmful, or offensive to others. He contends that children don't misbehave—they simply behave—to get their needs met or to have fun. Along the way, their behaviors, such as shouting, interrupting, and chasing, annoy grownups and get them into trouble. Some theorists contend that children's noncompliance is more a reflection of unskillful parenting than of children's desire to annoy (Patterson, 1982; Sansbury & Wahler, 1992).

Parental behavior is usually guided not by gratification but by responsibility for a child's welfare. Society holds parents responsible for their children's health, safety, socialization, and general development. Responsibility begins with pregnancy, when a woman shares her body with the developing fetus. In fact, parental responsibility begins well before pregnancy when a woman acts in ways to promote the health of her reproductive system.

Legal responsibility is assigned to parents until their child is 18 years old. Society gives us about 20 years to attain our parenting goals. We have 20 years to raise children who will be responsible, honest, sensitive, productive, and loving. Personally, I feel I will need every minute.

Parents hold children accountable for their actions after the first year. They begin placing limits on their infant's behavior. And children will test these limits, from simple refusal to bold defiance (Kochanska & Aksan, 1995; Kuczynski & Kochanska, 1990). We have noted the importance of having realistic expectations about children. We should not be surprised when children hit, lie, take what is not theirs, plead for a cookie, beg to stay up late, or seek gratification in other ways. These behaviors are quite common in young children. It is not the behavior but the parental response to it that shapes the course of development.

Gaining compliance from children is a first step on the road to self-regulation (Kochanska & Aksan, 1995). Parents regulate children's behavior because children cannot regulate their own behavior. The early stages of socialization involve several processes, including the transmission of parental standards of behavior, inhibiting undesirable behavior, and children's learning how to engage in family-approved and socially-approved behaviors. Parents decide what standards to teach, how to teach these standards, and how to monitor children's progress toward **internalization of standards** (conscience) and wholehearted compliance (Gralinski & Kopp, 1993; Kochanska & Aksan, 1995).

Understanding Noncompliance

Study Question   *What is usually the source of parent-child conflict?*

Helping children learn to behave well requires considerable effort and persistence over an extended period of time. To parent effectively, parents need good information about why children act as they do. Such information helps parents understand why their children are acting or feeling a certain way. For example, parents who are familiar with Erikson's theory of psychosocial development (Appendix C) can view toddlers' "mischievous" behavior in a positive light. They will interpret the toddler's independent behavior as a striving for autonomy (self-determination). Lacking this insight, parents could easily view this crucial period of development as "the terrible two's" and push their own agenda (compliance and socialization) without consideration of their child's agenda (autonomy and gratification) (Belsky, Woodworth, & Crnic, 1996).

"As children progress from infancy to toddlerhood, they display an increase in self-assertiveness and a desire for autonomy. Consequently, parents are required to divert a variety of negative and oppositional behaviors into acceptable channels while fostering growth in the child's self-control" (Dowdney & Pickles, 1991, p. 606).

Effective parenting requires a multilevel perspective on parent-child interactions. Defiant behavior is best understood in the context of biological factors (such as an infant's temperament), the personal and marital resources of the parents, and the style of discipline adopted by each parent. Difficult children who have coercive parents in an unhappy marriage are at greatest risk for developing behavior problems (Dadds, 1987; Fisher & Fagot, 1993).

For parents, discipline encounters are best guided by long-term perspectives. These include respecting the child's legitimate striving for autonomy, preserving one's ongoing relationship with the child (parent goal #3), and fostering the child's self-esteem (parenting goal #4). For these reasons, our attention is directed to the interactive nature of the child's resistance style and the parent's discipline style .

When we make a request or give an instruction to a child, we desire compliance. Most of the time, children do comply (Zern, 1991). As children mature, the consequences of their actions and parental standards of conduct temper the power of immediate gratification. Freud used the terms *ego* and *superego* to represent these two processes. Behaviorists cite reinforcement and observational learning.

Children's compliance may be wholehearted or reluctant (Kochanska & Aksan, 1995). Noncompliance and rule-breaking behaviors are very common during early childhood and therefore should not be considered abnormal (Forehand, 1977; Holden & West, 1989; Kuczynski & Kochanska, 1990). *Skillful* noncompliance by children is not associated with behavior problems. Unskillful and excessive noncompliance, however, are indicative of behavior problems in childhood (Kuczynski & Kochanska, 1990).

Parents benefit from understanding both the causes and consequences of their children's moment-to-moment emotions and behaviors (Dix & Reinhold, 1991). This is not a simple task. For example, you firmly request that a toddler stop pounding her fist on the door of her bedroom. She keeps pounding. How you interpret her motives partly determines your response. If you believe that she is intentionally challenging your authority, your response may be power-assertive. If you infer that her behavior is not willful but rather is spontaneous and unintentional, your reaction may be more measured. "Parents must monitor changing conditions and behaviors; infer the motives, limitations, and situational pressures that may control children's responses;

and decide what immediate consequences should be sought or avoided" (Dix & Reinhold, 1991, p. 251).

Occasional protest and defiance on the part of children is understandable. After all, mothers are more noncompliant to their children than their children are to them (Eisenberg, 1992). As a parent, would you want your children to be passive, subservient, or unquestioningly obedient? If so, how would they respond to deviant peer influence or to manipulative adults? Parents who demand blind obedience frequently end up with children who lack autonomy, spontaneity, and positive self-esteem (Baumrind, 1971). Infants of abusive mothers sometimes are compulsively compliant, not a desirable quality (Crittenden & DiLalla, 1988).

Thoughtful parents provide boys and girls with opportunities to learn to think for themselves and to speak up for themselves, to have a voice (Brown & Gilligan, 1992). This includes the freedom to disagree with and challenge other people's viewpoints, including their parents. Although parents resent "back-talk" from children, children's ability to express themselves reflects newfound cognitive and social abilities, including abstract thinking, language skills, and the ability to defend what they see as their own interests. Most parents strike a "delicate balance" between validating their children's self-expression and achieving their own socialization goals (Kochanska & Aksan, 1995). Most children eventually learn to balance their needs and desires with those of their caregivers and nonfamily members (Gralinski & Kopp, 1993).

Challenging parental views, verbally or nonverbally, is a way of testing parental authority. Further, many children occasionally witness rude behavior from their family members or on wacky TV sitcoms that portray smart-alecky, impudent dialog between parents and children as normal family behavior. Why should cheeky behaviors from children on TV amuse parents but raise hackles when they are displayed by their own children? (Kutner, 1992b).

Most parents are not distressed by occasional noncompliance. They are willing to repeat requests and offer reasons for complying until a child is directly or rudely defiant. Conflicts between parents and young children are brief and usually do not lead to negative feelings. Most conflicts end in a standoff. It is not unusual for parents to concede a point in a discussion, even when a child is clearly mistaken. Mothers usually do not demand that their children submit as long as they, the mother, have the last word. When parents say no in a way that indicates that they mean it or when they give good reasons for refusing a request, their children almost always comply (Eisenberg, 1992; Lytton, 1979; Vuchinich, 1985).

As children mature, parental standards of conduct and the cumulative consequences of children's actions temper the power of immediate gratification. Parents who instruct their children while maintaining shared positive emotions with them are most successful at gaining wholehearted compliance (Kochanska & Aksan, 1995; Kuczynski & Kochanska, 1995). Forceful strategies that suppress children's desires elicit greater resistance, especially when children highly value what their parents are denying them. Children's resistance usually elicits negative feelings in parents and encourages inconsistent and coercive parenting (Arnold & O'Leary, 1995). Punitive parents gain temporary (situational) compliance, but perhaps at the cost of a child's internal regulation (Kochanska & Aksan, 1995). If this pattern occurs often enough, it becomes habitual and prevents the learning by parents and children of the cooperative strategies described in Chapter 3 (Campbell, 1995; Dix, 1991; Sansbury & Wahler, 1992).

How do children test parental authority? At least four distinct forms of resistance, or noncompliance, have been identified (Kuczynski & Kochanska, 1990; Kuczynski, Kochanska, Radke-Yarrow, & Girnius-Brown, 1987). Each elicits a different parental reaction.

1. *Passive noncompliance*, ignoring a parental request, decreases between the ages of 2 to 3 years. It usually elicits another (often louder) parental request or demand.
2. *Direct defiance* by children, often expressed angrily, also decreases with age. It usually elicits coercion and punitive responding from parents.
3. *Simple refusal* increases with age and is less aversive to parents than is direct defiance.
4. *Negotiation, bargaining,* and *persuasion* comprise the fourth type of resistance. This is the most advanced form of resistance. It increases with age and is the least objectionable to parents. Parents may interpret these attempts as a display of autonomy and assertion, which many parents value.

Mothers tend to increase their use of verbal-persuasive control strategies—commands, explanations, bargaining, reprimands, suggesting alternatives—as children mature and such parental strategies become more effective. Parents gradually abandon physical strategies—touching, distraction, or physically guiding desirable behavior—as children become more skillful in resisting (Kuczynski et al., 1987).

As a child's style of resistance changes, so does parental control. Both parties usually prefer persuasive strategies over power struggles. Parents also lessen control as their children display more autonomy. Parents influence their children's interactive styles by negotiating with them (e.g. "What do *you* think we should do?"). Both parental modeling and reinforcement of negotiation strategies encourage this process (Kuczynski et al., 1987).

With infants and toddlers, occasional use of commands and power-assertive methods to gain compliance makes sense. With older children and adolescents, gradually introducing reasoning, negotiation, and compromise promotes the development of internal attributions for behavior. We see a shift from external to internal regulation. That is, children learn that there are good reasons for behaving well (Kuczynski & Kochanska, 1990). Parents of older children who depend upon power-assertive discipline methods often have the least compliant children. Not surprisingly, these children are the least skillful in the use of negotiation strategies (Kuczynski & Kochanska, 1990; Patterson, 1982).

Understanding their children's behaviors and misbehaviors allows parents, even during conflict, to experience positive emotions that "motivate attunement to children, facilitate responsiveness to children's wants and needs, and enable parents and children to coordinate their interactions to the benefit of both" (Dix, 1991, p. 19). This is not easy to accomplish, but in the long run this strategy minimizes unnecessary conflict and power struggles.

Analysis of Misbehavior

Instead of asking why a particular behavior occurs, behavioral psychologists prefer to perform what is known as a **functional analysis** of behavior (see Table 5.1). Rather than asking why a particular behavior such as nagging occurs, behavioral psychologists ask "under what conditions does nagging occur?" This question stresses the **situational context** of a behavior, which is observable, rather than a child's history, inner feelings, or intentions, which are not observable.

Some parents and psychologists, when considering why a particular behavior occurs, are drawn to historical analyses. When I am working with parents who are upset about a child behavior problem, I surely will ask them at some point to describe its first occurrence. A historical assessment may indeed improve one's understanding of a behavior's origins. However, parents' perception, memory, and interpretation of events are fallible. We can almost never know with certainty how or why a particular behavior pattern arose.

Children basically do what they have learned to do. They generally learn to do what pleases them. Terms like "pleasure" and "gratification" refer to subjective states that are not accessible to observation. Therefore, behavioral psychologists depend upon the **law of effect** or **reinforcement principle** to characterize lawful relationships between the situation, the child's behavior, and observable consequences.

TABLE 5.1   Functional Analysis of a Discipline Encounter

What exactly did the child do?

What was the situation (setting, circumstances, people present)?

How did the parent respond?

What other consequences occur following the behavior?

When did such behavior first occur?

What were the circumstances of its first occurrence?

How often does it occur?

How have the parents tried to correct the behavior?

What has worked and what has not worked?

If children learn, for example, that they can provoke us by saying a "bad" word or talking freshly, then our angry reaction itself (verbal and nonverbal) may reinforce the child's remark. Why would a child *want* to provoke us? Why would they find our display of anger reinforcing? Rudolf Dreikurs noted children's desire to exercise power over their parents and others (Dreikurs & Grey, 1970). It also seems to be part of the nature of human interaction that when we feel hurt or mistreated by someone, we return the suffering "in kind." The basic, unverbalized philosophy is something like, "If you hurt me, I'll hurt you back," or "I'll teach you a lesson." Because parents know that they are physically more powerful than their children, they might assume a pose of "I can hurt you more than you can hurt me." Even if true, this attitude is likely to engender resentment and further provoke the child.

When we either provide an aversive stimulus to a child (e.g. criticism) or remove a positive reinforcer (e.g., take away TV for the day), the child, in her frustrated state, may become disposed to retaliate. She may use any provocative tactic that "worked" in the past (e.g., "I hate you, Mommy"). Parents inadvertently teach their children the best ways of "hurting them back" through the intensity of their reactions to their children's provocations (e.g., "Don't you ever say that to me again"). Escalating power struggles often follow. Once a child had developed a repertoire of defiant or oppositional behaviors, it is that much more difficult to teach prosocial behaviors (Dadds, 1987; Sansbury & Wahler, 1992).

Although children's behavior problems are often attributed to negative parental strategies such as punishment, coercion, criticism, and inconsistent discipline, it is plausible that the *absence of positive parenting* may also be a contributing factor. As discussed in Chapter 3, effective parenting strategies include guiding and monitoring children's behavior; expressing affection; and modeling cooperative be-

havior (Dix, 1991). Pettit and Bates (1989) observed family interaction patterns of 29 4-year olds and their mothers and concluded that positive maternal behaviors predict fewer behavior problems in children. Negative parental behaviors, such as coercion, predicted behavior problems in these children, but not as strongly as the absence of positive parenting strategies.

Parental Requests and Compliance

Study Question   *What are the first rules that parents teach their children?*

Gralinski and Kopp (1993) were interested in how mothers help their children become self-regulating. In a longitudinal study, they instructed mothers of toddlers and preschoolers to keep track of the rules for everyday behaviors that they cited to their children and to record whether their children complied with these rules. The investigators wanted to see whether the requests and prohibitions parents cited changed as their children developed from toddlers to preschoolers.

Previous research (e.g., Dunn & Munn, 1987; Power & Chapieski, 1986) had suggested that maternal standards center around property issues, such as playing with dangerous or breakable objects, and household rules, such as children's doing things they are not supposed to do. By the time they are 3 or 4 years old, the rules that parents cite mainly concern protecting children from harm, preventing damage to people's property, following daily routines, and doing their chores.

Gralinski and Kopp found that the first rules that mothers teach are meant to ensure a child's safety, preserve the families' possessions, and discourage unkind behavior (e.g., "No kicking"). The researchers were surprised by the dominant role that safety concerns played in mothers' overall rule systems. The parents in this study were relatively affluent and lived under relatively safe circumstances. How much weight to safety issues is given by parents who live in high-risk, violent neighborhoods (Garbarino, 1995)?

At about 18 months of age, there was a noticeable increase in both the number of rules and the kinds of prohibitions mothers communicated to their children. As children grew, mothers' rules expanded from child protection and interpersonal issues to family routines, self-care, and other forms of self-regulation. Throughout the course of the study, mothers' rules always took into account and were appropriate to children's cognitive and language abilities.

When children were about 3 1/2 years old, a third level of rule organization emerged. Mothers' rules increasingly addressed safety, interpersonal behaviors, and self care. Mothers elaborated rules associated with family and social norms and social conventions: "Do not scream in a restaurant, appear naked in front of company, pretend to kill, hang up the phone when someone is using it, fight with children in school, play with guns, pick your nose, or go to a neighbor's house too early in the morning" (Gralinksy & Kopp, 1993, p. 581). Not surprisingly, as children grew from toddlers to preschoolers, there was a substantial increase in compliance to mothers' rules.

CULTURAL PERSPECTIVE: HOW CHINESE AND JAPANESE PARENTS RAISE THEIR WELL-BEHAVED CHILDREN

Western visitors to China and Japan are often impressed by the good behavior of Asian infants and children. They wonder whether the differences that they observe between Asian and Western children reflect in-nate dispositions or different rearing practices (Kessen, 1975).

One observer (Butterfield, 1981) reported that Chinese children are "quiet, obedient, quick to follow their teacher's instructions, and they seldom exhibit the boisterous aggressiveness or selfishness of American children . . . The Chinese children do not cry, whine, throw tantrums or suck their thumbs." To those of us who are intimately familiar with children in the United States, this description strains our credibility. How do Asian parents and teachers manage (if indeed their socialization practices are responsible) to achieve these results? And, is there a trade-off between Asian children's good behavior and other personal attributes that people in the United States value?

Butterfield cites several differences in how Chinese and Western parents and teachers approach caregiving. Chinese parents strive to promote intense closeness between themselves and their children. They swaddle their infants, binding their legs tightly in cloth. Chinese infants sleep in the same bed with their parents or grandparents.

"Part of the explanation for Chinese children's good behavior, some American psychologists who have visited China feel, is that Chinese parents and the teachers in nurseries and kindergartens tend to be warm, kind and attentive. During a day in the factory nursery school, this correspondent did not witness a single incident of physical punishment or harsh verbal rebuke by a teacher" (Butterfield, 1981). The school's director insisted that they never spank a naughty child. Rather, they use persuasion to correct misbehavior. If one child pushes another down, he is asked to help the child up and then apologize.

Some Chinese parents expressed concern that the regimentation their children face in nursery school and kindergarten makes them too placid and uncreative. "For the Chinese,

Asian mothers are much more involved in their children's daily lives than are mothers in the United States.

the first twelve years of life are not a time to raise questions about autonomy, fairness, or the right of choice. They concentrate on learning, playing, and living, and think it strange that anyone should ask them whether they are happy or bored. Life is straightforward and plain. There are simple rules to obey, but compliance does not mean that they are obedient. It is the way things are, and they are only children" (Chin, 1988).

Japanese children are raised similarly. As infants, they sleep at their mothers' breasts, and are carried during the day on their mothers' backs. "American mothers stimulate their infants and encourage them to be active. Most infant vocalizations are greeted with further encouragement. Japanese mothers tend to pacify and soothe their children" (Dworetzsky, 1984, p. 494). Japanese children are strongly encouraged to develop a dependency on their families, and eventually on their peers, teachers, and employers.

Surprisingly, compared to parents in the United States, Japanese parents are less demanding of their children, less nurturant, and more punitive, especially when their children are disrespectful (Power, Kobayashi-Winata, & Kelley, 1992). Asian mothers are more involved in their children's daily lives than U.S. mothers, especially in regard to their children's education and achievement (Chao, 1994; Shek, 1995).

Asian children develop a much stronger group orientation than Western children. Children in the United States learn to value autonomy more than do Asian children. They value group participation, but not as much as they value individual achievement. There appear to be substantial differences in rearing practices between Western and Asian children. We also observe different parental values and behaviors in the two cultures (Tamura & Lau, 1992). The relationship between rearing and behavior remains unclear.

INTERNALIZATION OF PARENTAL STANDARDS

Study Question   *How do children develop a "conscience"?*

Earlier in the chapter we noted that as children mature, their behavior becomes increasingly guided by their own internal standards rather than by parental command (Lewis, 1981). Without internalization, parents or other socialization agents would have to constantly monitor children's behavior (Kochanska, 1994). How does internalization occur? Early psychoanalytic formulations suggested that upon being frustrated by parental prohibitions, children feel anger toward their parents and then feel guilty for feeling angry. Children adopt parental rules and standards as a way to avoid these uncomfortable feelings and to avoid losing their parent's love. Current psychoanalytic models view internalization of parental standards more positively, through identification with a parent and as a way of achieving parental love.

As we shall see in a later section, Diana Baumrind (1975) and others maintain that internalization of parental values is supported by firm parental control, reasoning, and discussing with children how their actions affect others. **Attribution theory** (Lepper, 1981), on the other hand, implies that the acceptance of parental standards is best served by minimizing external pressure.

In other words, the least conspicuous ways of gaining compliance foster the greatest acceptance of parental values. "The child who obeys under only mild adult pressure cannot as easily attribute his or her own compliance to external pressure and must draw another conclusion, such as the following: 'I am obeying, so I must be the kind of person who obeys rules' or 'I am obeying, so it must be because I believe in this rule'" (Lewis, 1981, p. 548). The key point is that giving children the impression that they are choosing to behave well rather than being forced to behave well, increases their acceptance of parental standards and values. The more controlling the parent, the less invested a child becomes in parental standards (Deci, Driver, Hotchkiss et al., 1993).

Social cognition models of internalization hypothesize links between a parent's style of discipline, a child's specific misbehavior, personal qualities of the parent and child, and especially the way in which parents and children interpret misbehaviors. According to social cognitive models, for internalization to occur, children must accurately perceive their parent's message, be willing to accept the message (believe it to be self-generated), and allow it to guide their behavior. "The reformulation requires that parents be flexible in

TABLE 5.2   Comparing Models of How Children Internalize Parental Standards

Psychoanalysis	Children feel anger toward their parents and then feel guilty about their hostile feelings. They adopt parental rules and standards to avoid losing parental love
Psychoanalysis (modified)	Children internalize parental standards by identifying with parents as a way of gaining their love
Attribution theory	Parents give children the impression that they (children) are choosing to behave well. Thus, they own their parents' standards and values
Social cognition model	Children perceive their parents' standards, accept them as their own, and use them to guide their behavior

their disciplinary reactions, matching them to the child's perceptions of and reactions to the conflict situation. Effective parenting involves sensitivity to the child's emotional state and cognitions" (Grusec & Goodnow, 1994, p. 17).

Social cognitive models emphasize children's interpretations and understanding of caregiver messages. Thus, they are not applicable to internalization during infancy and toddlerhood. With their limited understanding of their own behavior and their parents' expectations, young children's emotions, temperament, and parental power play a greater role in guiding their behavior (Hoffman, 1994; Kochanska, 1994). The role played by emotions, motivation, attributions, and situational factors in the internalization process of older children continues to be hotly debated (Hoffman, 1994). Specific discipline strategies that promote internalization are discussed in Chapter 6.

CHILDREN'S CONCEPTIONS OF ADULT AUTHORITY

Study Question *In what ways must parents adjust their discipline styles as their children mature?*

Younger children usually accept the legitimacy of adult authority without question, partly because they lack the cognitive abilities to challenge it. When young children say "No, I don't want to," they are not challenging the *legitimacy* of the parent's authority. Rather, their noncompliance reflects their unwillingness or inability to delay gratification. The noncompliant child is not saying, "You have no right to tell me what to do." Rather, she is saying, "I don't want to do it now (or ever)."

Adolescents who ask indignantly, "Why should I?" may indeed be challenging power-based authority as practiced by most parents.

This is often seen, for example, in stepfamilies, when an adolescent declares to a stepparent, "I don't have to listen to you. You're not my real father." We will see shortly how parents adjust their discipline styles as children mature and assert their autonomy.

Infants and toddlers, however, are guided largely by gratification. Many parental requests and demands delay or prevent pleasurable outcomes for a child. A good example of this is the parental request that a child prepare for bed. Typically, the child is playing or watching TV. The request interferes with her immediate enjoyment. In addition, it requires effort (washing, brushing teeth, undressing) toward an unwanted outcome (sleep). The resistance we encounter in this situation is predictable and understandable. Asking "Do I have to do it now," saying "I don't want to," or simply ignoring the parental request are common reactions.

Adults set limits, which children test. Parents establish rules, which children occasionally violate. In effect, children are testing parents' willingness to enforce standards of behavior. This is normal. Even adults occasionally challenge society's ability to enforce its rules (called laws). For example, do all drivers come to a full stop at a stop sign when no officer is in sight? When parental authority is challenged by a child, there is no one correct way of responding. Parents should encourage compliance with the "least controlling means." (Specific discipline methods that support our parenting goals are described in the next two chapters.)

As children develop, we notice changes in how they view their obligations to obey requests and commands, to report violations of rules, or to make their own decisions about their conduct. These changes reflect changes in how they interpret their own behavior and its possible consequences.

Tisak (1986) interviewed 120 children from ages 6 to 10 years to assess their perceptions of the boundaries of adult authority. She found that children feel justified in reporting a rule violation by another child if someone is harmed. This would not be considered "tattling." Children felt that their parents have the right to establish rules that prohibit stealing and that require them to report observed violations. Children also reported feeling obligated to obey such rules, though less so for rules whose violation would not harm others. This would include rules involving household chores and choice of friendship. Reporting other children's rule violations for these less serious acts would be considered "tattling."

Thus, children set boundaries on adult authority that are related to the content of the violation. The children's rationales were based on their perception of how the rule violations affect the welfare of others. Older children granted themselves, not their parents, the right to make choices about actions that primarily affect themselves, such as their choice of friends. If the violation was not serious, children preferred to remind the violator about the consequences of his actions rather than report it to an adult.

Children are usually encouraged to respect authority. However, it is not always clear to children what constitutes a legitimate authority. In children's eyes, authority usually is derived from the legitimacy of the rule being invoked; from the role and status of the individual invoking the rule (e.g., parent, teacher); and from a fear of negative consequences for noncompliance (Braine, Pomerantz, Lorber, & Krantz, 1991; Laupa & Turiel, 1986). Laupa and Turiel (1986) found that children consider the age and social position of the person as well as the type of instruction given. Children gave priority to adult authority over peer authority and to peer authority over adult nonauthority. In the "old days" parents may have felt comfortable urging their children to respect and obey "all grown-ups." Today, cautious parents teach their children how to say no to certain inappropriate behaviors in others regardless of their age.

ADOLESCENTS' CONCEPTIONS OF PARENTAL AUTHORITY

Study Question   *How do adolescents view parental authority differently from young children?*

One of the major sources of conflict between parents and adolescents involves the degree of control that parents retain over their children's activities (Smetana & Asquith, 1994). At this writing, my older son is 20 and attends college out-of-state (and next semester, out-of-country). My wife and I accept that when he lives away from home, we have little say in his everyday decisions and activities. Like noncustodial parents, we wonder, how does one parent from a distance? The three of us frequently are aware of the awkwardness of this transition of control from parent to child.

Parents usually grant greater autonomy as their children mature, but younger adolescents in particular report dissatisfaction with parental control in certain domains. "Adolescents appear to view an increasing range of issues that were once viewed as legitimately subject to parental control as now under personal jurisdiction" (Smetana, 1988, p. 321). Such issues include their eating habits, the movies or TV shows they watch, social activities, how they dress, their appearance, and their choice of friends.

Smetana (1988) studied how adolescents and their parents view the domains of parental authority. She interviewed 102 adolescents, ranging in age from 10 to 18 years, and their parents. She found that parents of preadolescents and early adolescents view all events in their children's lives as being under their jurisdiction. As their children matured, however, parents became more willing to lessen their control regarding *personal* issues (e.g., friends, clothes, music) but not over *moral* issues (acts that are wrong because they harm others), or *conventional* issues (accepted ground rules about how people should act).

Children and adolescents agreed that parents should maintain jurisdiction over moral and conventional issues throughout adolescence. However, adolescents often differed from parents regarding whether an issue, for example friendship, is personal or conventional (Smetana & Asquith, 1994). Smetana also found that whereas mothers are more likely to reason about justice (or fairness) than fathers, fathers are more likely to reason about responsibility. Who do you think adolescents will approach for such negotiations, mothers or fathers? And why?

NO SIMPLE FORMULA FOR HANDLING DISCIPLINE ENCOUNTERS

I usually begin my parenting workshops by taking questions. The most frequent questions are of the "How do I deal with . . ." variety. Parents ask about crying, bedtime, fears, feeding, dressing, sibling conflicts, school-related problems, bed-wetting, and shyness. Parents of older children and adolescents inquire about moodiness, chores, homework, peer pressure, drugs, and sexual activity. Such questions imply that there are formulas for dealing effectively with childhood problems. "All you have to do when she wets her bed is . . ." Such miracle cures are presumably independent of the particular child's history, temperament, family circumstances, situational factors, and so on.

Although there are predictable patterns in each of these situations, there is no simple, guaranteed formulation that applies to all children in all situations. "In parenthood, there are no such systems, no easy step one,

step two plan to follow. Not only that, the child will probably test any strictures to see how steadfast they are, if they'll sway. The child wants and needs to know what the real ground rules are and how his or her parents react to pressure" (Galinsky, 1981, p. 120).

Will we ever discover universal "laws of parenting" that apply to all children, all parents, all families, and all situations? Don't count on it. Children are so different from each other. A discipline encounter must be tailored to the particular child and to the specific circumstances. Thoughtful parents, when motivating children, take into account their child's age, special needs, and personal qualities. For example, children who are competitive will dress quickly when having a fast-dressing contest. Children who are picky about food might be more willing to try something they have helped to prepare themselves.

Rather than seeking formulaic solutions to behavior problems, parents need to understand why their child is acting a certain way in a given situation and then, with *creative thinking*, find a way to help the child act differently. "The best way to intervene may be to help parents achieve an understanding of the child as a developing individual, rather than teaching parents specific behaviors of how they should (or should not) act. The parent who is able to understand more fully the nature of the parent-child relationship and to comprehend and coordinate different points of view within a situation, should be able to cope more successfully with the requirements of parenthood" (Dekovic, Gerris, & Janssens, 1991, p. 538).

The Discipline Dance

A discipline encounter between parent and child resembles a dance. The parent and child as "dance" partners anticipate and adjust to each other's sudden moves and motions. Much of the interplay, involving facial expressions, gestures, and body language, is nonverbal. Like good dancers, parents need to be *proactive* rather than *reactive* to their children's actions. *Anticipating and avoiding opportunities for misbehavior has been shown to be a more effective discipline strategy than reacting to misbehavior* (Holden & West, 1989).

Anderson, Lytton, and Romney (1986) had mothers of either sociable or conduct-disordered boys (boys who are defiant and aggressive) supervise both types of children on a simple computational task. Whether they were working with their own sons or not, mothers were more demanding and coercive when they worked with the difficult boys than when they worked with the sociable boys. The conduct-disordered boys, through their noncompliance and lack of cooperation, provoked punitive responses from every mother with whom they interacted.

This study helps us appreciate how parents adjust their style of discipline to a child's behavior and temperament. It is becoming increasingly apparent that a punitive parenting style makes difficult children even more difficult. The present study demonstrates that difficult children elicit punitive, coercive behavior, even in people who are not their parents. It is important that we recognize how these two processes may generate an escalating cycle of coercive parenting and defiant reactions in children.

Most children quickly learn to identify their parent's vulnerabilities and exploit them when possible. "In the course of their interaction, children, randomly at first, hit upon something sooner or later that is their mother's and/or father's Achilles' heel, a kind of behavior that especially upsets, offends, irritates, or embarrasses them. One parent dislikes name-calling, another teasing, another food eaten sloppily, or smeared on the face, another bathroom jokes" (Galinsky, 1981, p. 122). Parents who are easily provoked by such actions give their children enormous

manipulative power over them, a serious error (Dreikurs & Grey, 1970).

The ultimate feedback parents receive regarding the effectiveness of their discipline style is their child's behavior. The child's responses to specific discipline encounters gradually modifies the parent's discipline style (Mulhern & Passman, 1981). A feedback loop emerges that, under optimal conditions, encourages flexible and experimental parenting strategies. Competent parents continually adjust their strategies according to their effectiveness. Parents, not children, will ultimately decide whether the discipline cycle that develops is coercive or flexible.

DIMENSIONS OF DISCIPLINE

In Chapter 3, we discussed what constitutes competent parenting. Our premise was that some parents are better able to accomplish their parenting goals than others. But how do they accomplish this? Can we identify different parenting patterns or styles that are associated with different outcomes in children's behavior and adjustment? To answer these questions, researchers interview parents about their parenting strategies, administer standardized tests, observe parent-children interactions, and try to identify relationships between rearing style and a variety of child outcomes.

A number of presumably independent dimensions of discipline style have been proposed and investigated. Examples of such dimensions are: (1) acceptance-rejection or warmth-hostility (Becker, 1964; Maccoby, 1980); (2) restrictive-permissive or parental control (Sears, Maccoby, & Levin, 1957); (3) competence-incompetence (B.L. White, 1971); and (4) high involvement–low involvement (Maccoby & Martin, 1983).

Erikson (1963), in his psychosocial theory of development, emphasized two of these di-

S p o t l i g h t

Chance Encounters

Study Question   What role does "fate" play over the course of one's life?

Social scientists face serious challenges when they try to predict the course of human personality over the life span. One major challenge is anticipating the effects of chance encounters (Bandura, 1986). Each day we make many decisions. We may decide to buy a lottery ticket, go to a movie, or have a physical checkup. Such ordinary actions can have consequences that drastically alter our life paths. Consider how you met your current life partner or best friend, or decided which college to attend. What unforeseen factors led you to choose your present major or career path?

People's lives have been significantly altered by a book, a blind date, a car accident, a phone call, or a college course taken because others were not available. A few years ago, a student in my child psychology class inquired about a parenting course that was being offered the following semester. I wasn't aware that my school offered such a course. I thought I would enjoy teaching a parenting course, and I was right. While teaching the course, I decided to write a

parenting textbook. If not for that student's chance inquiry, I would not have spent literally hundreds of hours over the past few years composing and revising this text.

People are not equally susceptible to chance encounters, and not all such encounters have the same effects. Individuals who are successfully recruited by religious cults, for example, are typically lonely, isolated, and have low self-esteem. When they are exposed to a "closed system" of rigid beliefs, they might accept what they are being taught without question.

Parents naturally are concerned about how their children will turn out. Most try to satisfy their children's physical and emotional needs. They hope that their children will be happy, well adjusted, and productive. In reality, parental influence competes with countless other influences. Many are known; some cannot be anticipated. It is therefore reassuring that we can lessen children's susceptibility to potentially harmful chance encounters. We do so by encouraging the good judgment, positive self-esteem, autonomy, evaluative skills, and emotional resources encompassed by our parenting goals.

mensions, parental warmth and parental control. Parental warmth is usually defined as the expression of affection and approval toward one's children. Maccoby (1980) defined warmth as the parent's commitment to children's welfare and sensitivity and responsivity to their needs. Warmth is also expressed as willingness to spend time with children and showing enthusiasm for their accomplishments.

Hostile or rejecting parents are generally

punitive, using coercion rather than approval to motivate compliance (Campbell, 1995; Sansbury & Wahler, 1992). They are likely to ridicule and criticize misbehavior. A student of mine mentioned that she knows a parent who makes her son dress up "like a girl" when he misbehaves. Such humiliation does not bode well for this child's mental health. Fortunately, the vast majority of parents are generally affectionate rather than hostile. Nevertheless, most parents occasionally are

TABLE 5.3   Dimensions of Discipline and Discipline Styles

Acceptance—rejection (warmth—hostility)

Restrictive—permissive

High control—low control (demanding—undemanding)

Responsive—unresponsive (affectionate—aloof)

hostile ("What's wrong with you?"). Few parents are either always warm or always hostile.

Let's look more closely at the restrictive-permissive continuum. Parents are considered restrictive if they discourage independence, establish narrow rules, and punish children vigorously. Restrictive parents are demanding and impose strict limits on their children's autonomy. Most parents become less restrictive as their children mature. Permissive parents make few demands on their children and are lax in stating or enforcing rules. They encourage their children to express their opinions ("What do you think?") and to make decisions (Sears et al., 1957).

After distinguishing a variety of parental discipline styles, researchers assess children's behavior and personality. Global behavioral and adjustment measures are obtained such as assertiveness, aggressiveness, achievement, self-esteem, and dependency. These measures are based mainly on structured interviews, standardized testing, and observation of children in varied settings (e.g., Belsky, Woodworth, & Crnic, 1996; Steinberg, Lamborn, Darling, Mounts, & Dornbusch, 1994).

Do different parenting styles predict different personality characteristics in children? Research confirms that they do (Steinberg, Lamborn, Darling, Mounts, & Dornbusch, 1994). For example, parental warmth is associated with children's secure attachment, good behavior, academic achievement, and positive self-esteem (Coopersmith, 1967; Estrada, Arsenio, Hess, & Holloway, 1987). Parental hostility and rejection during childhood predict depression during adolescence (Lefkowitz & Tesiny, 1984). Is warmth by itself enough to promote optimal development? It's not likely. Permissive parents are warm, but as we will see, their children may be less competent socially and cognitively.

Weisz (1980) analyzed 244 letters that children submitted to a newspaper contest entitled, "Why Mom is the Greatest." Note that only children who like their mothers would respond to such a contest. Weisz concluded that children evaluate their parents largely on the basis of warmth and affection. Children and adolescents both viewed parental control as a sign of caring. Children of excessively permissive parents might feel uncared for.

BAUMRIND'S MODEL OF PARENTING STYLES

Diana Baumrind (1966; 1967; 1968; 1971; 1975; 1991) distinguishes four styles of parenting that vary on the dimensions of parental acceptance and control. She contends that each parenting style predicts distinctive behavioral patterns in children. She labeled the four styles authoritative, authoritarian, indulgent, and neglectful (see Table 5.4). (The similar spelling of the terms **authoritative** and **authoritarian** require that you read these terms carefully. The first part of each word, derived from the word **authority**, conveys that these parents are willing to "take charge" of their children. However, authoritative and authoritarian parents take charge in quite different ways).

Authoritative parents are warm (accepting) and firm (controlling). They use reason

TABLE 5.4   Parenting Styles and Children's Behavior

Parental Type	Children's Behavior
Permissive-indulgent parent	*Impulsive-aggressive children*
Rules not enforced	Resistive, noncompliant to adults
Rules not clearly communicated	Low in self-reliance
Yields to coercion, whining, nagging, crying by the child	Low in achievement orientation
Inconsistent discipline	Lacking in self-control
Few demands or expectations for mature, independent behavior	Aggressive
Ignores or accepts bad behavior	Quick to anger but fast to recover cheerful mood
Hides impatience, anger, and annoyance	Impulsive
Moderate warmth	Aimless, low in goal-directed activities
Glorification of importance of free expression of impulses and desires	Domineering
Authoritarian parent	*Conflicted-irritable children*
Rigid enforcement of rules	Fearful, apprehensive
Confronts and punishes bad behavior	Moody, unhappy
Shows anger and displeasure	Easily annoyed
Rules not clearly explained	Passively hostile and guileful
View of child as dominated by uncontrolled antisocial impulses	Vulnerable to stress
Child's desires and opinions not considered or solicited	Alternates between aggressive unfriendly behavior and sulky withdrawal
Persistent in enforcement of rules in the face of opposition and coercion	Aimless
Harsh, punitive discipline	
Low in warmth and positive involvement	
No cultural events or mutual activities planned	
No educational demands or standards	
Authoritative parent	*Energetic-friendly children*
Firm enforcement of rules	Self-reliant
Does not yield to child coercion	Self-controlled
Confronts disobedient child	High-energy level
Shows displeasure and annoyance in response to child's bad behavior	Cheerful
Shows pleasure and support of child's constructive behavior	Friendly relations with peers
Rules clearly communicated	Copes well with stress
Considers child's wishes and solicits child's opinions	Interest and curiosity in novel situations
Alternatives offered	Cooperative with adults
Warm, involved, responsive	Tractable
Expects mature, independent behavior appropriate for the child's age	Purposive
Cultural events and joint activities planned	Achievement-oriented
Educational standards set and enforced	

From Baumrind, 1967, pp. 43–88.

and persuasion to gain compliance. They explain rules and encourage verbal give-and-take with their children. They are flexible in setting limits and are responsive to their children's needs. They encourage independent thinking in their children and are accepting of opposing points of view. During a disagreement, authoritative parents might ask a child, "What do you think we should do?" or "How can we both get what we want?" Note that during a discipline encounter, authoritative parents cultivate the child's understanding of the situation rather than relying on parental power. They are not permissive; when reason does not prevail, they are willing to use power to gain compliance.

Authoritarian, or punitive, parents value obedience above all. They limit their child's freedom by imposing many rules, which they strictly enforce. They favor punitive, forceful measures and mainly use power to gain compliance. They value preservation of order and tradition and are uncompromising. They do not encourage verbal give-and-take with their children. The authoritarian stance is exemplified by the power-assertive phrase, "Because I said so."

Whereas authoritative parents assume that misbehavior reflects a deficit in children's attention, memory, or self-regulatory ability, authoritarian parents assume that their children are being willful. They view disciplinary encounters in terms of obedience and blame (Dix & Reinhold, 1991). Their rigid, restrictive parenting style reflects inflexible thinking, a preoccupation with their own point of view (Dekovic, Gerris, & Janssens, 1991).

There are two types of **permissive** parenting: indulgent and neglectful. **Indulgent** parents are accepting but not controlling. They consult with their children, explain family rules, encourage autonomy, and use reasoning. They differ from authoritative parents primarily in their avoidance of supervision and control. They indulge their children

rather than enforcing standards of conduct. Sometimes they set standards that are way below what their children could meet.

Neglectful parents (not depicted in Table 5.4) combine low control with low acceptance. They throw up their hands and exclaim, "I give up" or "I don't care what you do." Maccoby and Martin (1983) investigated the neglectful parent, who they called "uninvolved." Such parents expend minimal effort toward the care and socialization of their children. They seem to have little interest in their children's development. They might respond to a child's request for a cookie with, "Do what you want." Neglectful parents usually satisfy the basic needs of a child for food and shelter, but they remain emotionally distant. They disregard their children's social and emotional needs. (A more extreme version of this style is displayed by neglecting parents, discussed in Chapter 13).

Baumrind concluded that observed differences in children's self-reliance, self-control, achievement, mood, and aggressiveness are related to differences in parenting styles. Authoritative parents, combining warmth with firmness, usually have children who are the most competent, self-reliant, self-controlled, socially responsible, achievement-oriented (particularly girls), friendly (particularly boys), and happy.

Authoritarian (punitive) parents have children (particularly sons) who are the most unhappy, unfriendly, fearful, and moody of the four groups (Baumrind, 1968). Children of authoritarian parents usually are more aggressive and withdrawn than children of authoritative parents. Indulgent parents, reluctant to take charge, frequently have children (particularly sons) who are well-adjusted but very peer-oriented and not very invested in school or achievement. As we might expect, children of neglectful parents show the poorest social, cognitive, and emotional outcomes, sometimes even by the age of 2 years (Egeland & Sroufe, 1981).

A Team Approach to Discipline

Although it is not unusual for two parents to treat their children differently, it is desirable for parents to act as a unit during discipline encounters. Parental agreement about child rearing supports healthy family functioning. After all, children learn how to resolve interpersonal problems by watching their parents. Yet, one of the most frequent sources of marital conflict is disagreement about how and when to discipline (Deal, Halverson, & Wampler, 1989; Grych & Fincham, 1990; Vuchinich, Vuchinich, & Wood, 1993). Parental disagreements about how to handle discipline encounters sometimes indicate a more fundamental problem in the relationship (Deal, Halverson, & Wampler, 1989).

Why would parents disagree about how to manage a discipline encounter? They may have different parenting styles or different standards of acceptable behavior (Belsky, Crnic, & Gable, 1995). Typically, one parent is more lenient than the other. They may differ regarding their beliefs about what constitutes normal development or effective discipline. Perhaps they interpret the situation differently (Blechman, 1985).

The more incongruent two parents' styles, the more confused children become during discipline encounters. Children suffer the most when parents argue with, denigrate, or undermine each other in their children's presence. As noted in Chapter 4, observing their parents argue about them makes children feel anxious and responsible for the altercation. It is preferable that children observe their parents discuss or debate an issue calmly and achieve some resolution through negotiation and compromise (Cummings & Davies, 1994).

A team approach discourages children from using a "divide and conquer" strategy for getting what they want by playing one parent against the other (Vaughn, Block, & Block, 1988). Some children learn to get what they want by approaching the more lenient parent. If one parent refuses a request, they approach the other parent. Such tactics undermine parental authority and could precipitate marital conflict.

In marriage counseling, I sometimes hear spouses complain, "She always makes me the bad guy" or "He's worse than the kids." Learning to use marital conflict to their advantage is not healthy for children's development. Nor do they benefit when their mothers avoid parental responsibility by adopting the "Wait till your father comes home" strategy. This ploy encourages children to fear their father's arrival home as well as suggesting that females cannot take charge in difficult situations.

Most discipline situations are predictable. Parents who relate well to each other can formulate a parenting alliance, a commitment to acknowledge, respect, and value each other's point of view (Frank et al., 1991). Parents can attempt to discuss alternatives and then agree upon an acceptable strategy for handling specific discipline problems. It helps if they work on one problem or issue at a time.

Ideally, parents will negotiate a tentative strategy or plan, try it out, and then evaluate its success at a later time. With older children, parents can develop strategies for handling conflict during regularly scheduled family meetings. At such times, the child's point of view should be solicited and discussed (Silberman & Wheelan, 1980). Suggesting that parents form an alliance is not to say that parents should "gang up" on a child. Adolescents in particular will resist what they perceive as a rigid parental coalition (Vuchinich, Vuchinich, & Wood, 1993).

Children see parental control as a sign of caring.

Many studies confirm these findings, at least for white, middle-class families (e.g., Hart, DeWolf, Wozniak, & Burts, 1992; Maccoby & Martin, 1983; Shucksmith, Hendry, & Glendinning, 1995; Steinberg, Lamborn, Darling, Mounts, & Dornbusch, 1994; Steinberg, Lamborn, Dornbusch, & Darling, 1992). The link between disciplinary styles and child outcomes that Baumrind (1978) observed in intact, white, middle-class families may or may not be observed in other ethnic or economic groups or in other family configurations (Kelley, Sanchez-Hucles, & Walker, 1993; Shucksmith, Hendry, & Glendinning, 1995). For example, African-American mothers who take their child's perspective seriously during a discipline encounter often use power assertive techniques (Kelley, Power, & Wimbush, 1992). We will return to this point in the next section.

Based on these findings, Baumrind and other investigators endorse the authoritative

style of parenting. Notice that both authoritative and authoritarian parents are more controlling than permissive parents. They differ, however, in how they exercise control. Authoritative parents are firm, but they prefer to control through discussion, reason, and persuasion. Authoritarian parents are strict and punitive. They demand obedience and discourage verbal expression from their children.

Because most studies of parenting style are correlational, we should not automatically infer causality between parenting style and child characteristics. That is, we can conclude that parenting style *is related to* patterns of children's behavior, but we should not *attribute* children's behavior patterns to a specific parenting style. As previously noted, parenting style partly reflects a child's behavior and temperament. The Anderson et al. (1986) study demonstrated that difficult children can create coercive parents. The reciprocal influences between parent and child (discussed in Chapter 1) make it difficult to distinguish cause from effect in family life.

Parents who practice different rearing styles probably differ in other ways that could affect their children. Parents from lower socioeconomic classes, for example, may value different traits and may have more punitive and restrictive parenting styles than middle-class parents. They also may differ in their level of education, marital satisfaction, and life stress. It might be these moderator variables that are influencing children's personalities and behavior rather than (or in addition to) parenting style.

Lewis (1981) maintains that the authoritative parenting style is a reaction to children's personality rather than a cause of it. Diane Baumrind disagrees. She contends that authoritative parents model caring and assertiveness, which their children eventually imitate. Such parents are more adept at reinforcing prosocial and competent behaviors in their children than punitive or permissive parents. Their children perceive them as fair and understanding and therefore internalize their values. Although research generally supports Baumrind's view, further research is needed to shed light on the direction of causality (and interaction) between parenting style and children's behavior.

PARENTING STYLE AND PARENTING PRACTICES

Although the construct of parenting style is useful for investigating how constellations of parent attributes *are related to* specific child outcomes, it is not likely that a given parenting style works the same way in all populations, family configurations, or for children of all ages. In other words, the effects of a particular parenting style depend partly upon the par-

ent's goals, the specific methods of child rearing they use, the age of the child, and so on.

For example, the authoritative parenting style foretells academic achievement in white, middle-class adolescents but seems to be least effective in promoting achievement in Asian, Hispanic, or African-American adolescents. It is possible that Asian or African-American parents who practice the authoritative parenting style have different goals or use different rearing strategies than white, middle-class parents regarding their children's achievement behavior (Harrison et al., 1990; Julian, McKenry, & McKelvey, 1994; Kelley, Power, & Wimbush, 1992).

Further, parents who practice different rearing styles differ in other ways that could affect their children. Younger, single parents from poorer socioeconomic classes who have more punitive and restrictive parenting styles may cultivate different traits in their children and have somewhat different goals than older, middle-class married parents (Fox, Platz, & Bentley, 1995; Kelley, Sanchez-Hucles, & Walker, 1993; Kelley, Power, & Wimbush, 1992; Maccoby, 1980). They also may differ in their level of education, marital satisfaction, and life stress. It might be these moderator variables that are influencing children's personalities and behavior, rather than (or in addition to) parenting style. We should also expect to find considerable diversity of parenting styles *within* a given ethnic or socioeconomic group (Abell et al., 1996).

To help clarify the conditions under which specific parenting styles influence children, Darling and Steinberg (1993) distinguish between parenting style and parenting practices. **Parenting style** is "a constellation of attitudes toward the child that are communicated to the child, and that, taken together, create an emotional climate in which the parent's behaviors are expressed" (p. 488). Elements of parenting style that communicate parental attitudes toward a child include a parent's tone of voice when speaking to the child, a parent's body language, and expressions of affection or hostility toward the child.

Parenting practices, on the other hand, refer to specific parental duties such as attending school functions, showing interest in a child's activities, or spanking a child. Parenting practices always operate within a particular domain of child rearing, such as achievement, independence, or relationships and usually are oriented toward specific goals. Parenting style includes parenting practices, but also includes all other aspects of parent-child interaction that convey to children how their parents feel about them.

Darling and Steinberg contend that the four parenting styles described by Baumrind are independent of the content of parenting behavior. As parents provide daily child care, they communicate to their children how they feel about them. Children of authoritative parents, perhaps feeling more cared for than children of authoritarian parents, become more susceptible to parental influence. Children of punitive or permissive parents, feeling angry and uncared for, may become less susceptible to parental influence. A key point of Darling and Steinberg's model is that parenting style "alters the parent's capacity to socialize their children by changing the effectiveness of their parenting practices" (p. 493).

Imagine two sets of parents who want to become more involved in their child's schooling. One set of parents practices the authoritative style and the other set practices the authoritarian style. Because the authoritative parents use reasoning and persuasion to help their child complete assignments, choose courses, and make decisions about school, the child becomes increasingly receptive to their assistance. The authoritarian parents also want to be involved, but they resort to coercive methods that inadvertently alienate their child. In this case, the two sets of parents have the same goals (increasing their involvement to improve their child's education), but their parenting styles have different outcomes—one child actively seeks their help and the other resists it.

At this point, we know relatively little about how individual parents come to adopt a particular parenting style or how child characteristics induce changes in parenting style, especially as children age. We do know that parenting styles vary somewhat according to ethnic group membership and have varied from one historical period to another (Harrison et al., 1990; Julian et al., 1994; Marshall, 1995). We also know that mothers and fathers tend to have parenting styles that differ in degree of involvement and conflict with children (Collins & Russell, 1991; Forehand & Nousiainen, 1993). Darling and Steinberg (1993) hope that the distinction between parenting style and parenting practices will shed further light on these topics.

POWER AND PUNISHMENT IN PARENTING

Unlike children in the past, children today have rights, including the right to be protected from their own parents, if necessary. Nevertheless, society gives parents wide latitude regarding the choice of childrearing practices. Straus and Donnelly (1993) define **corporal punishment** as the "use of physical force with the intention of causing a child to experience pain but not injury, for purposes of correction or control of the child's behavior." Cultural practices regarding the use of corporal punishment vary widely (Giles-Sims, Straus, & Sugarman, 1995).

Most parents and many school systems in the United States use corporal punishment at least occasionally to discipline children and adolescents (Sears, Maccoby, & Levin, 1957; Straus & Donnelly, 1993). Some cultural traditions encourage parents to be controlling and punitive (Deyoung & Zigler, 1994; Seppa, 1996). In other cultures, for example, Sweden, parents can be arrested for striking their children.

I once counseled a single mother and her two young teenagers. The mother regularly slapped or spanked her son and daughter. She sometimes used switches on their ankles when they were disrespectful or defiant. Since the switches left marks on her daughter's legs and ankles, the mother was reported anonymously to a state agency that investigated the complaint.

Although concern was expressed by a social worker about the mother's harsh treatment of her children, no charges were filed. The daughter began to threaten that she would report her mother to the police if her mother hit her again. The daughter did, in fact, call the police once. The lieutenant who handled the case told the girl that her mother had the right to spank her. In fact, he spanked his own children!

It is not always easy to distinguish between harsh parenting and abuse. Both usually are administered in a state of anger. Although our society condemns child abuse, most parents see corporal punishment as a necessary discipline tool (Holden, Coleman, & Schmidt, 1995). Even children view spankings as justifiable for serious rule violations (Catron & Masters, 1993). We will return to the topic of corporal punishment in the next chapter.

Hoffman's Model of Parental Power Assertion

Hoffman (1967) investigated the effects of excessive parental power assertion on children. He defined power as the "potential an individual has for compelling another person to act in ways contrary to his own desires" (p. 128). He defined **power assertion** techniques as those that "put direct coercive pressure on the child to change his entire ongoing pattern of behav-

ior immediately" (p. 129). Children, because of their dependency and low power status, cannot avoid power-assertion by adults.

"The parent possesses and controls the material and emotional supplies needed by the child. As the controller of these supplies, and with his greater physical strength, he is in the position to punish the child at will, either physically or through deprivation . . . Furthermore, the parent's treatment of the child—outside of extreme neglect and cruelty—is subject to little, if any, legal restraint. Probably in no other relationship does a person in our society have such complete power over another" (Hoffman, 1967, p. 129).

According to Hoffman, when parents use power assertion or love withdrawal to gain compliance, they are imposing their parental will on the child. They do so without any explanation or compensation to the child for their compliance. Gerald Patterson (1982) has noted that parents of aggressive children punish according to their mood, rather than a child's actions. Hoffman suggests that excessive use of power-assertive techniques frustrates children. It also weakens their sense of autonomy. Heavily punished children report feeling distressed and depressed (Turner & Finkelhor, 1996) and frequently treat other people abusively (Straus, 1991; Weiss, Dodge, Bates, & Pettit, 1992). These antisocial qualities are most dramatically observed in the behavior of bullies (discussed in Chapter 13).

Hoffman tested his model using a sample of 12 middle-class and 10 working-class families with a child attending a half-day nursery school. He found that working-class fathers use more power-assertions than middle-class fathers. Working-class mothers show more frequent initial power-assertions than middle-class mothers. Hoffman concluded that the frequent use of power-assertions by mothers leads to the development of hostile feelings which children then direct toward their peers.

Ronald Simons and his colleagues note

that parents who are harsh usually are also uninvolved and inconsistent (Simons, Johnson, & Conger, 1994). They maintain that it is these parents' lack of involvement in their children's lives and their inconsistency in discipline that produces negative outcomes in adolescents, not their harsh parenting.

Punishment

Study Question   *Why do so many parents resort to punishment before trying more positive means of gaining compliance?*

Parents are in a position of authority. Authority implies power. The traditional model of parental discipline has been punitive, that is, based on the power to punish. Traditionally, it was assumed that punishment was necessary to save a child's soul ("Spare the rod, spoil the child"). As described in Chapter 1, our ancestors assumed children to be innately mischievous, if not downright wicked. It was believed that if parents spared the rod, their children would be unmanageable.

Parents who hit usually hit often (Holden, Coleman, & Schmidt, 1995). Boys are hit more frequently than girls. Mothers are more likely than fathers to hit adolescent girls (Straus & Donnelly, 1993). Nevertheless, over the course of human history, and particularly in the present century, there has been a gradual shift away from punishment and coercion to motivate behavior change. This shift from aversive control has been accompanied by a trend toward greater individual freedom (Skinner, 1971). Parents are becoming wary about using punitive authority, although at times they attempt to rationalize it. A Harris Poll conducted in 1995 reported that 80 percent of the 1,250 parents surveyed admitted to spanking their children. But younger parents are less likely to use corporal punishment (Collins, 1995).

Parents who spank claim that they are most likely to hit when a child has behaved aggressively, violated someone's rights, or has engaged in dangerous misbehavior (Holden et al., 1995). Parents still rationalize, "This will hurt me more than it hurts you" or "I do it for your own good." Thus, punishment can be depicted as a reflection of parental concern and even affection.

Today, thanks to people like Darwin and Freud, we are more aware of the relationship between frustration and aggressive behavior. Parents are more likely to punish when they are frustrated by their children's misbehavior or by their own life problems. It is well-documented that abusive parents strike in anger. Oldershaw, Walters, and Hall (1986), for example, found that, compared to nonabusive mothers, abusive mothers "use more commands, and more power assertive and less positively oriented control strategies . . ." (p. 722).

Some parents punish strategically. (Using punishment effectively is discussed in the next chapter). They remain calm and thoughtful and punish to accomplish specific discipline goals. Most parents appear to punish non-strategically, when they are frustrated and angry. Sadly, their own aggressive impulses are satisfied by striking out at their children (Holden et al., 1995).

Excessive punishment does not support our four parenting goals. Rather, it thwarts our attempts to promote compliance and competent behavior (Turner & Finkelhor, 1996). When children's failures are criticized, they may develop a fear of failure. Harsh punishment also threatens the parent-child relationship ("Wait till your father comes home"). It encourages children to develop negative feelings about themselves and about their parents. Harsh discipline also appears to distort the process by which children process social information (Weiss, Dodge, Bates, & Pettit, 1992).

"Children who struggle for power are defiant and rebellious. They may argue about all requests from their parents, they may ignore them, or they may comply in a way other than the parent wanted . . . If the struggle for power continues and children feel they cannot defeat the parents, they may seek retaliation and revenge. Children who pursue revenge feel they are not lovable; that they are significant only when they can hurt others as they believe they were hurt" (Berns, 1985, pp. 133, 135).

Children who are obedient may also be fearful. Some learn antisocial ways of avoiding detection, such as lying. Ironically, parents who use physical punishment are more likely than non-punitive parents to have children who misbehave and violate rules (Hoffman, 1970; Power & Chapieski, 1986). Adams and Tidwell (1988), for example, questioned parents of hearing-impaired children about how they handled their children's misbehavior. Parents who felt that they were successful in correcting misbehavior said they used mainly discussion and explanation, whereas parents who felt that they were unsuccessful in discipline relied mainly on scolding.

Let's remember that rule-breaking children may put pressure on their parents to punish (Bell, 1968). Thus, the direction of causality is not clear. Nevertheless, parental use of punishment is to some extent determined by its effectiveness in changing children's misbehavior (Mulhern & Passman, 1981).

Silberman and Wheelan (1980) observe that children can profit from adult reasoning and still challenge adult authority (p. 17). Adults have authority over children and should exercise it judiciously. Most parents continue to punish. If punishment is used at all, it should be used as a last resort, when all else fails (Birnbrauer, 1994; Mulick, 1994).

SUMMARY

1. Childrearing strategies are guided by parents' everyday encounters with their chil-

dren but also by parental biases and beliefs. Parents who consider their children to be well behaved attribute their good behavior to the child's disposition. They blame misbehavior on situational factors. Parents who perceive their children to be difficult or oppositional view such behavior as dispositional. This discourages attempts to improve their behavior.

2. Much parent-child conflict is rooted in children's desire for immediate gratification. When their desires are not satisfied, children become frustrated and learn to repeat whatever actions gain satisfaction. Parents often inadvertently reward the very behaviors they complain about.

3. As children mature, they desire greater autonomy over personal decisions. Adolescents accept parental control in moral and conventional matters but desire more say in personal matters like clothes, friends, and music.

4. Baumrind distinguishes four discipline styles, authoritative, authoritarian (punitive), indulgent, and neglectful. She contends that children's behavior and adjustment reflect their parents' style of parenting, but the direction of causality is not always clear. Coercive parenting does not support our four parenting goals.

5. Children benefit when parents adopt a "team approach" to discipline. Most parents learn to adjust their discipline strategies to a child's age and stage of development. As their children mature, parents become more willing to negotiate and reason.

6. There is no simple formula for handling a discipline encounter. Parental strategy should reflect a good understanding of the particular child and the specific circumstances at hand.

7. Some parents use excessive force in disciplining their children. Punitive parents often punish when they are upset. Heavily punished children often become angry and resistant and may learn to treat other people abusively. Excessive punishment is inconsistent with our four parenting goals. Parents who choose to punish should use punishment sparingly, in combination with positive discipline methods.

parenting practices   How parents actually treat and provide care for a child

parenting style   Parental attitudes about a child that convey how a parent feels about a child and the emotional climate that surrounds the parent-child relationship

power assertion   Parental use of threats and coercion to change a child's behavior

GLOSSARY

authoritarian parenting style   Authoritarian parents are controlling, but not very accepting of their children

authoritative parenting style   Authoritative parents are warm and firm, accepting their children while setting and enforcing limits on their behavior

corporal punishment   The use of physical force with the intention of causing pain to correct or control a child's behavior

indulgent parenting style   Indulgent parents are accepting and overly permissive of their children

internalization of parental standards   The process by which children adopt their parents' values and standards of acceptable behavior

neglectful parenting style   Neglectful parents are neither accepting nor controlling. They have little interest and involvement in their children's lives

THOUGHT QUESTIONS

1. How do you think your parents interpret your personality (what is their mini-theory)?

2. How does Freud's "pleasure principle" help parents understand children's "misbehavior?"

3. How do parents adjust their discipline strategy as children mature?

4. Based on the chapter's presentation of different parenting styles, describe the parenting style your parents used in raising you and how it might have affected how you "turned out."

5. What role should a parent's emotional state play during a discipline encounter?

6. How does frequent punishment affect children's self-concept and their behavior?

CHANGING CHILDREN'S BEHAVIOR

OBJECTIVES 170
Mark #1 (Continued) 171
INFANT DISTRESS 171
**SETTING LIMITS FOR OLDER INFANTS AND
    TODDLERS** 172
Standards of Acceptable Behavior 172
Promoting Rule-Following Behavior 173
Discipline Strategies 174
PARENTING INFANTS 175
Sleep 175
Crying 177
Toilet Training 178
THE ROLE OF OPERANT CONDITIONING 179
Carol and the Cookie 180
Mark #2 181
Strategic Use of Reinforcers 181
Differential Reinforcement of Other Behavior (DRO) 182
Reservations About the Use of Operant Conditioning 183
Spotlight: Anatomy of a Tantrum 185
TYPES OF REINFORCERS 186
Using Social Reinforcement 186
        Mark #3 186
        Mark #4 187
Activity Reinforcers 188
Tangible (Token) Reinforcers 188

"My parenting definitely needs more structure. In the area of motivation, for instance, I erroneously approached this from the negative angle. I'd set high standards and tell Mark how I knew he could do better than he was doing. B's and C's had to become A's in schoolwork. I realize now that I must reinforce all positive efforts rather than complaining about half-measures. At times though, I feel *blinded* by my first perceptions. I'm hasty and harsh in my judgments. Then it is too late for me to renege. (Mark #1)

USING REINFORCERS JUDICIOUSLY 188
NATURAL AND LOGICAL CONSEQUENCES 189
Eric's "Sick Day" 190
Discouraging Self-Reliance 190
Mark #5 191
OBSERVATIONAL LEARNING 191
PUNISHMENT 193
Mark #6 193
Defining Punishment 193
Using Punishment Effectively 194
Side Effects of Punishment 195
Learning to Avoid Detection 196
Overcorrection 196
Spotlight: Time Out from Reinforcement 197
Should Parents Use Corporal Punishment? 198
SUMMARY 198
GLOSSARY 200
THOUGHT QUESTIONS 200

OBJECTIVES

After studying Chapter 6, students should be able to:

1. Explain why rules are useful and what parents can do to encourage rule-following behavior

2. Describe discipline strategies that are appropriate for infants and toddlers

3. Describe how parents sometimes unintentionally encourage such undesirable behaviors as temper tantrums

4. Describe how operant conditioning principles can be used to change children's behavior

5. Evaluate the reservations that have been expressed about the use of rewards in discipline

6. Distinguish between intrinsic and extrinsic reinforcers and describe their role in teaching new behavior

7. Distinguish between social, activity, and token reinforcers, and give examples of each

8. Define natural and logical consequences and how their use helps parents avoid power struggles

9. Describe how some parents inadvertently discourage self-reliance

10. Define observational learning, and explain why it is a powerful learning process

11. Distinguish between two types of punishment and describe how to use each effectively

12. List and explain the possible side effects of punishment

13. Describe how overcorrection may be applied in child rearing

14. Evaluate the advantages and disadvantages of the time-out procedure

Mark #1 (Continued)

"When Mark seems completely indifferent about sports, culture, grades, and achievements, I get so frustrated! He seems to be self-centered and 'one-track-minded'. Play and his friends seem to be the only things that matter. I've been trying to acknowledge all of his efforts lately, at homework and being responsible. It looks as though he senses more encouragement from me and likes it. I'm trying to be less domineering and meddling. I can't help myself, though, when it comes to homework. Everyday without fail, I go through his book bag checking for homework assignments, memos, etc. Somehow I don't feel it's invading his privacy, but rather keeping tabs on him. Uninvolved and unconcerned parents end up with unpleasant surprises, don't they?"

Mark's mother is a single-parent who was attending my undergraduate parenting class. We will have the opportunity to share additional entries in her journal and trace her efforts to improve her communication and relationship with Mark, her 9-year-old son. Mark's mother is expressing a common parental dilemma—how involved should parents be in regulating their child's behavior? On the one hand, children provide numerous instances of irresponsible and selfish behavior that are difficult to overlook. Unconcerned parents end up with unpleasant surprises, don't they? On the other hand, becoming upset about misbehavior rarely improves things. Most parents seek a middle-ground position that combines a reasonable amount of vigilance with thoughtful interventions when appropriate.

Of the four parenting goals emphasized in this book, parenting goal #1, good behavior, seems to be of greatest immediate concern to parents. It is helpful, however, to view good behavior in a broader context that includes the other three parenting goals described in Chapter 1. The proper focus of a discipline encounter is not a child's misconduct, but rather parents' response to it.

Effective discipline requires that parents be responsive, not reactive, to their children's misbehavior. This means that, during discipline encounters, parents should try to act in ways that support all four parenting goals, rather than respond impulsively to the child's misconduct. Reactive parents take the child's behavior at face value—they are annoyed and they criticize. As Mark's mother noted, they are blinded by their first impressions. But their disapproval has minimal effect ("I've told you a hundred times . . ."). Responsive parents view a discipline encounter as an opportunity to teach the child something rather than as an opportunity to vent their anger. This chapter examines the strategic use of learning principles to change children's behavior.

INFANT DISTRESS

Study Question *Can infants be spoiled?*

Parents of infants wonder when effective discipline strategies can and should be applied. Practical questions arise about feeding or holding distressed infants, whether infants should be allowed to cry themselves to sleep, and how to respond when infants solicit attention and care. Because infants cry or fret reflexively for most of the first year, it does not make sense to ignore their distress. Parents should follow their natural impulse and comfort a crying infant (Barr, 1993). Failing to respond to a distressed infant may have an unintended outcome—a child with a heightened need for attention and reassurance.

"Put yourself in the baby's position. If you were unable for whatever reason to correct a situation you were in, and the best you could

Taking children's distress seriously lets them know that they can trust their caregivers.

do was scream in the hope that something would happen to improve your condition, how would you feel if no one came to help you? . . . If you're ignored and left alone to cry, you're always going to feel deprived and you'll probably be *more* likely to turn out a brat" (Balter, quoted by Winn, 1989).

Responsive parents allow their children to learn that they can have an effect on their environment. They respond promptly and appropriately to their infant's actions. They are careful not to "spoil" their child—that is, not to lavish the infant with unwanted or unneeded attention. Infants of responsive parents learn that they can "trust" their parents to care for them when they are truly in need (Erikson, 1964).

SETTING LIMITS FOR OLDER INFANTS AND TODDLERS

Study Question *How does one "discipline" older infants and toddlers?*

Since the older infant and young toddler are not yet able to grasp abstract concepts such as "good behavior" and "bad behavior," parents define limits by consistently responding to specific acts under specific conditions. Silberman and Wheelan (1980) suggest "brief, firm statements and physical restraint. If the child is doing something that we want to discourage, it is best to say 'no' and name the object involved and the possible consequences of the child's action (such as 'no—dishes break') and, if that does not suffice, to remove the child from the situation" (p. 117). Because many months or years may be necessary for children to learn to inhibit unacceptable behaviors, consistency and patience become necessary ingredients of competent parenting.

Standards of Acceptable Behavior

What is "unacceptable behavior?" That is for parents, other caregivers, and the community to decide. They should take into account a child's ability to understand and follow rules. We try to provide our children with skills that will gain them both personal satisfaction and acceptance from the community-at-large. We try to discourage behaviors that are considered obnoxious or annoying and that might lead to social rejection.

Parents residing in most middle-class communities have fairly similar values regarding child rearing. Most encourage their children to be friendly, cooperative, helpful, and so on. Similarly, most parents discourage hitting, teasing, bullying, stealing, lying, and cheating. Such behaviors are not uncommon among young children. To some extent, they reflect limitations in children's understanding of rules and insensitivity to other people's feelings.

Nevertheless, parents must set and enforce limits on these behaviors beginning in infancy. During the second year, children become more sensitive to the emotional state of other family members and begin to modify their behavior accordingly. Kagan (1981) has demonstrated that, during the second year, children become interested in discrepancies between what is expected and what actually occurs. They show distress when they cannot satisfy goals set by adults. Kagan interprets these observations to mean that children are beginning to understand and become concerned about adult standards.

Promoting Rule-Following Behavior

Sometimes parents express desired behavior patterns or performance standards as rules. Rules specify what behaviors are expected, in what situations, and what will happen if a rule is satisfied or violated (Baldwin & Baldwin, 1986, ch. 11). For example, consider the rule: "As soon as your hands are clean, you can sit down at the table for dinner." The rule states a positive outcome, but implies a negative consequence (no dinner) if the desired behavior does not occur. Children eventually learn to appreciate the need for rules. They

help guide our behavior, and adherence to rules minimizes social conflict.

Children resist rules that they consider unfair. Such rules seem to serve other people's interests at their expense. Children benefit when parents offer a reason for obeying the rule that the child can understand. Parents should remind children about rules ("What is the rule about washing your hands before dinner?") and reinforce rule-following behavior rather than criticize transgressions. Verbal reminders should gradually by replaced by situational cues. For example, instead of telling children to put on their seatbelts, a parent can sit silently in the driver's seat until all seatbelts are fastened.

Parke (1969; 1973) advocated the use of cognitive structuring procedures in discipline, such as providing reasons for not breaking rules. Children may not automatically understand a rule, its value, or the consequences of disobeying it. Parke found that providing children with a simple reason for following a rule combined with a punishing buzzer resulted in more rule-following than punishment alone. Parke suggested that providing verbal prompts to children makes more sense than a display of parental power. Rule-following behavior is also encouraged by giving children responsibility for enforcing the rule, by encouraging them to see themselves as honest, and by teaching specific self-instructions for resisting temptation (Toner, 1986).

One way to help children learn a rule is to have them repeat it in an applicable situation ("What is the rule about holding scissors?"). One of the earliest rules that parents teach (the so-called Golden Rule) is, "Treat other people the way you want them to treat you." To a young child, this might be expressed, "If you are nice to other people, they will be nice to you." The converse should also be noted. "If you are mean to other people, how will they treat you?" This simple rule is very useful because it is a generally valid description of human interaction. However, it requires years of interpersonal experience and cognitive maturation before children can grasp its full meaning and implications.

An obstacle to rule learning is that exceptions to rules may impede one's ability to appreciate their usefulness. For example, even when 2-year-old Brian is mean to Grandma, she may still be nice to him. In any case, we remind children about these relationships, when appropriate, so that they eventually become internalized rules (self-statements) that will guide their behavior.

"The rules we have, however, need to be stated and restated until they are internalized. Beginning statements over and over again with the simple phrase, 'The rule is . . .' helps a child focus on what we are saying. It is also important to show young children what we expect, not just tell them. And this is a good time to start accompanying directives with brief, understandable reasons, such as, 'Push your cup away from the edge of the table. The juice won't spill if you do that.' By doing this a child begins to sense that our authority is more rational than arbitrary" (Silberman & Wheelan, 1980, p. 121).

Whenever a family rule (e.g., "No running in the house") is broken, a parent can take the child aside and calmly ask the following four questions: (1) What are you doing? (2) What is the rule? (3) Why do we have this rule? and (4) What happens if you break the rule? The first question brings the child's attention to her be-

havior. The second question obligates the child to verbalize the rule, helping her remember it. The third question helps the child internalize the rationale for the rule. The fourth question reminds the child about the consequences for violating the rule (see Table 6.1).

It makes sense for parents to provide a warning before applying a consequence. When a new rule is introduced to young children, such as "When we are finished playing, we clean up our toys," parents should break the task down into simple steps and help the child accomplish the chore. Gradually, the child should be given more responsibility for completing the task, and of course, praise for successful performance ("I knew you could do it").

Discipline Strategies

Parental attempts to gain compliance from children begin during infancy (Dunn & Munn, 1985), usually in the form of directive questions ("Where is the spoon?") and contextual cues. Parents also learn crucial verbal and nonverbal strategies for bringing infants' attention to the task at hand and then encouraging their involvement in it. "By successfully manipulating [the infant's state], the parent can avoid the clash-of-wills that is so often portrayed as typical of all socialization efforts, whereby compliance is supposedly extracted from an invariably reluctant child" (Schaffer & Crook, 1980, p. 60). The key point is that re-

TABLE 6.1   Steps in Rule Enforcement

Question	Function
What are you doing?	Brings child's attention to his/her behavior
What is the rule?	Helps child learn to remember and articulate the rule
Why do we have this rule?	Helps child remember the rationale for the rule
What is the consequence of breaking the rule?	Helps child remember that his/her behavior has consequences

sponsive parenting can usually avoid child noncompliance (see Table 6.2).

Power and Chapieski (1986) found that infants complied with their mother's initial attempts to restrict their handling of objects about half the time. When infants did not comply, the mothers usually repeated the rule, and the infants eventually did obey. Infants of physically punishing mothers showed the *least* amount of compliance and were the most likely to grab breakable objects! Physically punitive mothers also had the fewest number of objects available at home for infant play.

This study, like many others, implies that punishment is an ineffective long-term discipline strategy. Infants and young children respond to gentle strategies that bring their attention to the task and that use directive questions and nonverbal cues to motivate compliance. Reactive, punitive parenting styles seem to provoke defiant, limit-testing behaviors.

Occasionally, parents must physically prevent a child from biting the dog, grabbing a knife, or leaning out of a window. This gentle restraint should be accompanied by an authoritative, "No—you'll hurt yourself." Physical restraint also should be accompanied by an explanation, even if the reasoning cannot yet be grasped by the young child. Distracting young children from dangerous situations or objects often works.

Perhaps the most efficient long-term "discipline" strategy for very young children is to arrange a safe and stimulating environment with minimal opportunities for mischief and mayhem. "Babyproofing" rooms and homes typically occurs by the age of 6 months, when infants begin to crawl and then creep from room to room. Play areas should be arranged to encourage desirable play activity with attractive, age-appropriate toys or play materials that challenge and entertain. Caregivers always should be present or nearby, not only for

TABLE 6.2 Gentle Discipline Strategies For Infants and Toddlers

Directive questions (e.g., "Can you sit on your chair?")

Use of contextual cues (e.g., "What do we do when we finish our bath?")

Stating rules (e.g., "Keep your hands to yourself")

Gentle restraint with explanation (e.g., "We might cut ourselves if we grab the knife")

Arrange a safe and stimulating environment with minimal opportunities for misbehavior

Read or make up stories that pertain to child's misbehaviors (e.g., "The girl who wouldn't share her toys")

Use praise, charts, or stickers to reward improvement in behavior

the child's safety. Vigilant caregivers provide positive reinforcement and arrange natural consequences that are interesting and stimulating outcomes for an infant's behavior.

PARENTING INFANTS

Sleep

Study Question *How should parents respond when their children resist going to sleep?*

Infants, on the average, spend about 16 hours a day asleep, an additional 2 hours in a drowsy state, and almost 2 hours a day crying. They spend about 2 hours in a state called alert inactivity, which is the optimal time to play or interact with an infant, and about 2 hours a day awake and active (Wolff, 1966). By the time infants are a year old, they are sleeping "only" about 12 hours a day. Sleep time gradually decreases over childhood, stabilizing at about 8 hours by the teenage years.

Newborns do not sleep for 16 hours in a row, but rather divide their sleep into 7 or 8 shorter naps, about once every 2 hours. By 7 months of age, to their parents' delight, most infants sleep through the night. One of nature's cruel tricks is that during the preschool years, children are early risers (like 6 A.M.!). However, as soon as they sense a school bus is on its way, you cannot awaken them with a cannon. Newborns apparently dream about half the time they are asleep. By the age of 1 year, like their parents, they spend only about a quarter of their sleep time dreaming.

Between 20 and 30 percent of infants have problems sleeping, and as many as one-third of children between the ages of 1 and 5 years awaken during the night (Brody, 1986c). So-called **sleep-resistant children** either refuse to go to bed or awaken in the middle of the night calling for attention. Infants who awaken at night usually have been trained to "expect" to be held or rocked back to sleep. It is helpful for parents to understand that sleeping alone in one's bed is a skill that some children learn faster than others. This should not be confused with an occasional request by a child to sleep with a parent following a nightmare, a scary TV program or movie, or in a new setting such as being on a family vacation.

Most children's sleep difficulties are related to how their parents put them to sleep. Most parents in the United States believe that taking an infant or child into their bed is unhealthy (Morelli, Rogoff, Oppenheim, & Goldsmith, 1992).

So-called cosleeping is associated with child and parent anxiety and issues of separation and sleep management (but not with inappropriate sexual contact) (Rath & Okum, 1995). Put to bed in their own room, children will learn to do anything that keeps their parents close by at bedtime. Who would want to be alone in the dark when everyone else is downstairs having a great time? Ignoring children's pleas to delay bedtime ("Just one more story") works well but distresses parents (Edwards & Christophersen, 1994).

Dr. Richard Ferber (1985), a major figure in the study and treatment of children's sleep problems, recommends that parents let children cry for a designated amount of time before they comfort the child. In effect, children have to learn how to fall asleep on their own and how to stay asleep when a parent is not present (Edwards & Christophersen, 1994; Kerr & Jowett, 1994). This is one reason why medication and strategies such as cosleeping or rocking an infant to sleep often are counter-productive. At bedtime, infants who are rocked or held become dependent upon the presence of a parent (Lawson, 1993a).

"The treatment for trained night crying is to let the baby cry. Otherwise, children will demand attention nightly until age 3 or 4" (Brody, 1986c). Parents can respond to the infant's cries after 5 minutes the first time, then wait 10 and 15 minutes before responding the second and third time. When parents do respond, they should stay only for a minute, touch the child or make a brief reassuring comment, and then leave. The more curt the parental response, the less "payoff" the child receives for all of her efforts (Chadez & Nurius, 1987).

It is difficult for parents to withhold responding when an infant or toddler is distressed, but if the technique is applied consistently, the crying episodes should become less frequent over the next few days. Dr. Ferber cautions that the method should be used only if the family is comfortable with it. It is not appropriate for all children. "If a child is frightened at night or has separation anxiety, leaving him alone to cry is the worst thing you can do" (Ferber, quoted by Lawson, 1993a). Infants also can be helped to sleep through the night by increasing the time between daytime feedings. By gradually giving the infant fewer meals, he or she learns to tol-

TABLE 6.3 Steps in Putting a Child to Bed

Start a predictable sleep preparation routine at the same time each night

Quiet presleep activities like reading or listening to music induce drowsiness

Child always sleeps in his or her bed, with occasional exceptions for illness or night fears

Let infants cry for increasingly long periods of time before parental intervention

When parent does respond, it is only for a brief comment or kiss

Use bedtime story to reinforce child's cooperation in preparing for bed

With older children, parents might consider letting children turn out the light when they feel sleepy, as long as they stay in bed

Let child get a drink of water or use the bathroom as needed but without parental participation

Child should be responsible for as much presleep activity (brushing teeth, putting on pajamas) as his or her age allows

erate longer delays between feeding periods. During nighttime feedings, infants can be given diminishing amounts of food. They do not need to eat at night.

Children who sleep separately from their parents are less resistant to bedtime when they have a consistent sleep time, a predictable bedtime ritual, quiet presleep activities, and security objects such as stuffed animals (Edwards & Christophersen, 1994; Kerr & Jowett, 1994). It is not realistic to expect children to fall asleep when they are not tired. Although occasionally allowing children to sleep in their parent's beds is not linked to any behavioral problems, toddlers who sleep with their parents more than once a week become very resistant to sleeping alone (Fackelmann, 1990). Children with bedtime-related fears should be given a sense of control over

the situation (for example, a flashlight). Older children who complain that they cannot fall asleep can be encouraged to read or listen to quiet music until they feel drowsy, a technique that works for many adults.

Crying

Birth is followed by testing, cleaning, and draining the breathing passages, and, for the first time, states of deprivation and discomfort. These presumably stressful events elicit innate reactions in infants—most noticeably, crying. The young infant's cry is an involuntary response to pain or deprivation. It is usually, though not always, a signal that some need is not being met (Barr, 1993). Infants cry when they are tired or hungry. The primary function of this loud, irritating noise is to elicit caregiving behaviors that will eliminate the source of their distress. Skinner would characterize crying as a negative reinforcer (to the parent) because it motivates nurturant behavior that leads to its removal.

When an infant cries, a caregiver usually approaches and picks up the infant, puts it on his or her shoulder, talks to and strokes the infant, and rocks it back and forth, or moves in a swaying pattern. Thus, initial reactions to crying are nonspecific attempts to comfort the distressed infant. Further responses are more specific and aimed at relieving the source of the infant's distress—for example, checking its diaper or offering a bottle (Gustafson & Harris, 1990).

Those who provide care for infants claim that they eventually come to distinguish among different types of cries, reflecting different levels of distress (Lester, Boukydis, Garcia-Coll, & Hole, 1992). Some parents may overinterpret the different cries when they label them as the hunger cry, the mad cry, the attention cry, or the sick cry. Parents learn to interpret the causes of infants' crying partly on the basis of situational cues, such as food or sleep deprivation (Reich, 1986), and behavioral cues, such as eye rubbing ("he's tired") or sucking movements ("she's hungry") (Gustafson & Harris, 1990).

For example, if an infant hasn't eaten for several hours and cries, the parent interprets the behavior as a hunger cry. If the infant has recently eaten but hasn't slept for several hours, the distressed reaction is considered a "tired" cry. Others believe that there really are distinctive cries and that parents eventually learn to recognize them. Thompson analyzed recordings of infant cries for their acoustic properties. He found that the cries of very young infants resulting from different needs do sound different. When situational cues were eliminated, both experienced and naive adults accurately judged cries for *levels* of anger, fear, and distress (Hostetler, 1988b).

Zeskind (1980) found that as the pitch of the infant's cry increases, so does the urgency of the parent's need to respond. "If a baby is just a little distressed, say by being a bit hungry, he gives a regular, rhythmic, lower-pitched cry. Parents, we find, are not very bothered by that cry. But as the baby gets more distressed, his crying becomes higher pitched, the rhythm becomes faster paced, and the 'wah wah' segments get shorter. Parents get more distressed themselves as this happens" (Zeskind, quoted by Goleman, 1988f).

Frequent or prolonged crying disturbs parents. In their frustration and confusion, they may argue with each other about how to handle the situation. Worse, they may direct their anger at the already distressed infant. Since crying occurs reflexively for much of the first year, it makes little sense either to blame the infant or to ignore the crying (Barr, 1993). Psychologists usually suggest that parents hold and comfort crying infants. Toward the end of the first year, crying comes under voluntary control, and language skills begin to emerge. At this point, parents should respond according to their interpretation of why the infant is

crying, sometimes comforting it, sometimes ignoring it (St. James-Roberts, 1989). Ultimately, parents must trust their own judgment about how to respond when a child cries.

Toilet Training

Toilet training can begin whenever the infant or toddler is ready. When is an infant ready to be toilet trained? Chinese parents believe that infants can be trained at about 12 months of age. They seem to be successful in their efforts. Western parents believe that children are not developmentally ready to be trained until they are 2 or 3 years old, so this is when most Western children are toilet trained. Maturationally speaking, the longer that parents wait to train, the more successful their efforts will be (Luxem & Christophersen, 1994).

Children who can dress and undress themselves, who can label the parts of their body, and who are highly motivated usually are ready (Azrin & Foxx, 1976). Some children are ready before their parents. Some toddlers are prepared to give up their diapers before their parents think they are. In any case, parents who have realistic expectations about their children's abilities, who know how to teach toileting skills, and who are patient will be successful (eventually).

"Children need to experience the natural consequences of poor toileting habits, and parents need to interfere less in what should be a self-managed body function. Most children learn toileting without any intervention, or with minimal intervention, by their parents" (Blechman, 1985, p. 76). Blechman suggests the following steps in toilet training:

1. Let children be responsible for cleaning up after an accident, teaching them the skills they will need to change their clothes, change the sheets, wash them, and so on. Self-reliance is promoted when children

are given responsibility for toileting themselves, within their capabilities.

2. Increase the likelihood of bowel movements in the toilet, making the toileting situation as comfortable and private as possible.
3. Reward the child for bowel movements in the toilet, making sure you explain that you are using the rewards to help the child learn this skill. Many forms of positive reinforcement are available: praise, charts, stickers, prizes.
4. Make dry days and nights more likely by using these steps, by purchasing a conditioning device if necessary, and by frequently rewarding the child for being dry.

TABLE 6.4 Steps in Toilet Training

Make sure the child is developmentally ready to learn

Can child dress and undress self and label the parts of the body?

Devote one or two days to intensive training

Supply the child with ample amounts of favorite drinks and snacks to induce toileting behavior

Ask child frequently (about once every half hour) if he/she has to use the toilet

Have realistic expectations about how long training may take—be patient and supportive

Have child clean up after an accident, whether clothing or bed clothes

Make toileting situation as comfortable and convenient as possible

Use strong reinforcers (social, activity, token) to motivate compliance and for successful toileting

For nighttime training, during the day have the child rehearse "waking up," and getting out of bed to go to the bathroom or potty seat

THE ROLE OF OPERANT CONDITIONING

Study Question *What role do rewards and punishments play in changing children's behavior?*

B.F. Skinner (1904-1990) was one of the towering figures of twentieth-century psychology. He was best known for studying environmental factors that shape behavior and personality. Most psychological theories, in explaining behavior, speculate about events inside of the person, such as feelings, the mind, the self, conflicts, instincts, and motives. Skinner argued that environmental events shape and control our behavior. We are products of our learning histories (Skinner, 1953; 1971; 1987).

Skinner assumed that behavior is controlled by environmental factors that, for the most part, are observable. Scientists cannot gain direct access to events inside our skin, such as feelings or ideas. Skinner looked to the environment to find controlling variables. **Operant conditioning** refers to a type of learning in which the consequences of a behavior lead to changes in its frequency. Certain consequences make a particular behavior more likely to occur. Parents usually call these consequences rewards, but behavioral scientists call them **reinforcers** (to reinforce is to strengthen). Other types of consequences lessen the frequency of the behavior they follow. The processes involved are called punishment and extinction. **Punishment** is said to occur when a behavior is weakened by the presentation of an aversive stimulus (something "bad") or the removal of a positive reinforcer (something "good"). **Extinction** refers to the weakening of a behavior when the reinforcer that motivated the behavior is withheld. Extinction and punishment contingencies can be used to discourage inappropriate or annoying behavior. All these consequences are defined by their effects on behavior.

Behavior modification refers to the use of operant conditioning principles in practical situations, including education and child rearing. Using positive reinforcers to encourage desirable behavior not only is more effective but also more practical and more humane than using coercion, threat, or punishment (Baldwin & Baldwin, 1986; Kazdin, 1984).

Behavior modification approaches usually advocate the following strategy: think behavior, think small steps, think positive, think flexible, and think future (Kanfer & Schefft, 1988). Parents are encouraged to view discipline in terms of changing children's behavior rather than trying to change personality traits or dispositions. Solutions usually require changing the consequences of children's behavior. This usually means that parents must change their own way of responding to the misbehavior. Positive outcomes are preferred to criticism or punishment.

Parents are encouraged to notice and reinforce improvement in behavior, no matter how slight. Setting realistic goals enhances the likelihood of success, building both the parent's and the child's self-confidence. Flexibility means that there are many ways to achieve a positive change. If one strategy doesn't succeed, plan another. Thinking about the future allows parents to concentrate on how they want their child to be, rather than on how he or she has been in the past.

Parents occasionally violate basic principles of learning in their attempts to reward and punish their children's behavior. For example, they may ignore good behavior and instead, "catch the child being bad." Ironically, even negative attention to misbehavior may encourage future occurrences. Parents can learn to analyze their children's behavior in everyday situations such as bedtime, dinnertime, or sibling relations. They can learn how to use positive means to motivate compliance.

Understanding how children's behavior is influenced by situational factors and behavioral outcomes dramatically enhances parents' ability to encourage good behavior while avoiding unnecessary family conflict.

One of the most useful skills for parents to learn is ignoring misbehavior. Parental attention is a subtle but powerful reinforcer for children's behavior. Misbehavior is inherently "attention-getting." Most parents understand the power of attention. They teach their children to ignore another child's teasing behavior because "if he sees it upsets you, he'll continue to do it." The problem is that misbehavior often is provocative. Parents react impulsively rather than strategically. Sometimes, the best response is selective ignoring.

Carol and the Cookie

Let's examine a common parent-child interaction. Right before dinner, Carol asks her father for a cookie. Her father naturally refuses, and for good reasons. He has invested a considerable amount of time preparing dinner, and, like most parents, he will find it reinforcing to see Carol eat healthy food. Father knows that if Carol eats a cookie now, she will be less interested in eating dinner. Therefore, Father gently refuses Carol's request.

But Carol really wants this cookie! She pleads, she whines, she begs, she *demands* a cookie. Notice that Carol has already learned that when initial requests are not granted, try, try again. Many children, like Carol, have learned to impose upon Mom and Dad an annoying situation (nagging) from which they can easily escape by giving in. Very clever, these children. All Dad has to do to escape from Carol's harangue is to give her the cookie.

Because Dad has previously been (negatively) reinforced for relenting, he gives Carol the cookie. (Negative reinforcement involves escaping from or avoiding something bad.

Dad is escaping from Carol's nagging). He adds a brief warning about how Carol had better eat her dinner when it is ready. Dad's strategic error, of course, is reinforcing Carol's nagging behavior by giving her the cookie. Next time Dad refuses a request, Carol will be more likely to nag.

What has Dad learned? Giving in "works" for Dad in the short run. Carol's nagging stops, but, because Dad's giving in has been reinforced, he becomes more likely to relent in the future. If Carol doesn't eat her dinner, Dad may hold out longer next time before giving in, or perhaps Dad may not give in at all. It is exactly Dad's unpredictable behavior, either waiting longer before giving in or sometimes not giving in, that encourages persistence in Carol's nagging. Nagging is like gambling; sometimes it pays off, and sometimes it doesn't. Since Carol never knows the outcome ahead of time, she makes the effort. In the long run, giving in to Carol doesn't work for Dad, because, periodically, he will have to put up with her nagging.

It is almost certain that if Dad strategically withheld these payoffs, Carol's nagging would eventually cease. Withholding reinforcement from an established behavior is called extinction. When it is clear that our parental attention is reinforcing the annoying response, withholding our attention will discourage further occurrences. Notice that in extinction, nothing is being taken away from the child. Rather, the usual reinforcer, in this case attention or a cookie, is being withheld. It is easy to see how parents who are not aware of behavior principles often encourage the very behaviors they disdain.

Dad should also know that extinction often elicits increased or exaggerated arousal before the gradual reduction in nagging begins. Initially, Carol may escalate her efforts to get her cookie; she may even have a tantrum. Dad also should anticipate "spontaneous recovery" of nagging behavior in the future and remember how to respond accordingly. ("Carol, what is the rule about snacks before dinner?").

Mark #2

"About a week ago, the counselors from Mark's after-school program told me that he had to leave the activities because he was misbehaving. He was singing silly songs or making unpleasant noises and would not stop when asked to. On these occasions, I apologized to the counselors and talked to Mark. I explained to him that his behavior is rude and how difficult it must be for the counselors. Then I asked him to please try to behave himself. The other day, there was another incident.

"He was disrupting art lessons by making animal-type noises. When the counselor told me, I told Mark to apologize and promise to try to not misbehave again. He said 'I'm sorry' softly and quickly, leaving it at that. All three of us knew it meant nothing at all. In the car, he proceeded to be loud and unruly and continued making noises. I asked him to calm down and told him to stop. He still kept it up. I tried to get him to stop again, but he couldn't even hear me. As I realized how he must be enjoying this power, I dropped out. I simply ignored his behavior; shortly after, he lost interest, and stopped."

Strategic Use of Reinforcers

Reinforcers are most effective in teaching new behavior when they immediately follow the desirable response. Sometimes, caregivers assume that a stimulus is a positive reinforcer when actually it is a neutral or even an aversive stimulus. We can only be sure that the stimulus is a reinforcer if it encourages the specific response it follows. Keep in mind that repeated presentations of the reinforcer may lead to satiation. That is, the stimulus may eventually lose its reinforcing properties ("too much of a good thing").

The ways in which parents schedule reinforcers may encourage persistent, objectionable behavior in their children. Tantrum behavior (see Spotlight: Anatomy of a Tantrum) is encouraged by parents' waiting longer and longer before giving in to their children's demands. As we have seen, parents encourage children to escalate their efforts by occasionally giving in. (Dramatic displays of temper and tantrums are more likely to "succeed" in public settings, when parents submit rather than endure public humiliation.)

Let's revisit Carol's home two nights later. Before dinner, Carol asks Dad for a chocolate cupcake. Dad remembers that Carol did not finish her dinner two nights ago and turns down Carol's request. Because of Carol's previous "success," her nagging behavior is even more persistent than it was before. And Dad is confronted with an even more unpleasant situation. All he has to do to escape from Carol's outburst is give in. If Dad waits a little longer tonight before he submits, Carol's nagging may escalate into a tantrum. Get the picture?

Study Question   *How can parents get their children to take their "No" seriously?*

What's a father to do? By stating a rule, such as "No snacks before dinner," and explaining the reason for the rule, "If you eat sweets before dinner, you won't feel like eating the healthy stuff," Dad finally takes control of the situation. When Dad firmly enforces the rule, Carol learns two things: why there are no snacks before dinner and that Dad means what he says. Parental responsibility, not Carol's desire for sweets or her nagging, should guide Dad's behavior in this situation.

How should Dad respond to Carol's inevitable nagging? He should apply the extinction procedure. If, after explaining the "no snacks before dinner" rule to Carol, she still continues to whine, another rule is stated: "I will not listen to you when you whine." If Dad's attention and arguing are reinforcing Carol's nagging and they now are consistently withheld, we can expect a gradual lessening of this behavior over time.

Punitive parents often respond to a child's "why should I?" with the famous angry retort, "because I said so." This thoughtless response is the clearest invitation to a power struggle I can imagine. Children deserve to be reminded of the relevant rule, and they deserve a decent explanation of the rule's rationale. If, in the above example, Carol were open to a discussion of the nutritional facts of life, Dad should welcome such an exchange of information. Once we are confident that Carol finally understands both the rule and its rationale, we are no longer obligated to debate the issue further.

It is more helpful to ask, "Carol, what is the rule?" Children will argue indefinitely if we let them, and this wears parents down. "But why . . . but why?" Parental responsibility requires clearly stating the rule, explaining it once at a level a child can understand, and firmly refusing to participate in a coercive, nagging ritual. Although children resist the logic of "I'm doing it for your own good," they ultimately gain from hearing the sensible reasons behind our decisions.

Differential Reinforcement of Other Behavior (DRO)

Attempting to weaken a behavior, through extinction or punishment, can be tedious. We should first consider replacing the unwanted behavior with one that is more desirable. Remember, strategies that weaken behavior do not teach children what to do. Rather, they teach what not to do in that situation.

A schedule of reinforcement that encourages any response other than the undesirable one is called differential reinforcement of other behavior, or DRO. For example, we can discourage thumb-sucking behavior by reinforcing "hand-out-of-mouth" behavior. Contingent praise, or using material incentives, can increase the frequency of out-of-mouth behavior, thereby reducing hand-in-mouth behavior. "Linda, I'm so proud of you when your fingers are not in your mouth, and you look so grown-up."

Parents and teachers can also learn to identify "competing" responses, that is, behaviors that are incompatible with the offensive behavior. For example, when my children were younger, I offered them sliced apples or other fruit several minutes before their anticipated visit to the kitchen for a sweet snack. The "Law of Least Effort" suggests that an apple in hand is worth a cookie in the kitchen.

I also tried to catch the rare instances when they were being nice to each other to express my appreciation. "Thank you for being patient with Eric. I know he asks a lot of questions." Increasing the frequency of more desirable responses automatically reduces the occurrence of the misbehaviors we are trying to discourage. "Catching the child being good" is preferable to the perpetual critical stance of some parents.

"... When a loud unruly child plays quietly, that is the perfect time for parents to use praise, rewards and privileges, or suggestive praise. At first, some parents find it difficult to give this attention. When their children behave well, they are relieved that there are no problems and hope the quiet, desirable behavior continues. They may even stay away from the well-behaved children, afraid their presence will upset the pleasant behavior. If parents do not use their positive skills when their children behave well and, instead, respond to their children for misbehaving, they create an escalating cycle of punishment and misbehavior that is sustained by parental attention" (Dangel & Polster, 1988, p. 24).

Reservations About the Use of Operant Conditioning

Behavior change strategies based on the thoughtful application of positive outcomes can be powerful parenting tools. Nevertheless, there are critics who question the wisdom, the usefulness, and even the ethics of rewarding children's behavior (Kohn, 1993). Criticisms include asserting that parents who use rewards are "bribing" their children to behave well, that special incentives deprive children of the opportunity to take responsibility for their duties and make the parent responsible instead, and that children will become "spoiled" in that they will always expect or demand to be rewarded for their good behavior.

Some have claimed that children can become "dependent" on rewards. A desirable behavior may cease when the reward is withdrawn or might occur only in the presence of those with the power to reward or punish (Dinkmeyer & McKay, 1982; Kazdin, 1984). There is increasing evidence that rewards can undermine prosocial behavior in that such behavior may cease when the rewards are terminated (Fabes, Fultz, Eisenberg, May-Plumlee, & Christopher, 1989). This seems especially true for children whose parents depend heavily on the use of incentives. Such children may offer help when rewards are available and refuse to help otherwise. Schwartz (1986) contends that the use of incentives may be at the expense of rule finding, hypothesis testing, and other cognitive operations.

Part of the problem in using rewards as incentives is that the "payoff," rather than the desired behavior, becomes the focus of the child's attention and motivation and therefore undermines intrinsic motivation. Children should not be offered a reward for doing their homework. The suggestion that a reward is necessary suggests that the activity is disagreeable or that the child is doing the parent a favor. It might be difficult getting the child to perform the activity in the future without an incentive. Further, the child's performance may suffer as a result of trying to obtain the incentive as soon as possible.

It is misguided, however, to equate the use of rewards with bribery. Bribery is usually defined as offering someone an incentive to act illegally or immorally. Offering children in-centives for good behavior hardly fits such a definition. I agree, however, that the "if-then" approach ("If you brush your teeth, then you can read for 5 minutes"), which does motivate children (Boggiano & Main, 1986), encourages cooperation for the "wrong" reason (Ginott, 1965).

Rewards can be a powerful child-rearing tool when used judiciously. Appreciating the strategic use of incentives requires a distinc-

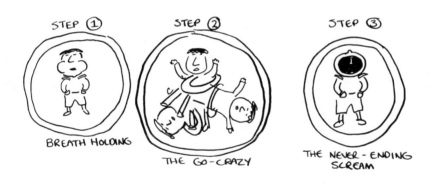

THE TANTRUM

THE THREE STEPS TO A TANTRUM

STEP ① — BREATH HOLDING

STEP ② — THE GO-CRAZY

STEP ③ — THE NEVER-ENDING SCREAM

STEP ④

DO NOT FEED THE KID

LOCKED-UP IN THE ROOM

Justin Jaffe

S p o t l i g h t

Anatomy of a Tantrum

My older son threw his one and only temper tantrum, when he was about 3 years old, on our living room floor. I do not recall the details, but I was sitting on the couch, *The New York Times* in hand, probably turning down a request to visit the toy store.

Since I had never witnessed a tantrum at close range, I was enormously curious and would have liked to scrutinize his every action and perhaps videotape his performance for posterity. The drama of the event was impressive. Heart-rending sounds of screaming, crying, and floor pounding filled our home. I realized that paying even the slightest attention to his behavior might encourage a repetition. I continued reading my newspaper, with barely a glance in his direction. Fortunately, I have not yet had another opportunity to observe this fascinating phenomenon.

According to Blechman (1985), "A temper tantrum takes place when a child, who has not been mistreated, is out-of-control for at least 1 minute, screaming, crying, throwing things, or hitting . . . Usually tantrums occur when a child has been told no or when a child is very tired" (p. 89). The dramatic display of frustration and anger is the ultimate expression of Freud's concept of the id— "Give me what I want immediately or I will make your life miserable." Ironically, toy stores and birthday parties are common settings for tantrums. Placing children near toys or ice cream that they cannot have immediately is as sensible as striking a match on a can of gasoline.

Unlike psychologists, most parents do not find tantrum behavior exotic and fascinating. They find tantrums extremely annoying and, when they occur in public, very embarrassing. "At first I felt angry. I felt that the people in the store would think I'm a horrible mother, that I can't control my child. I knew it was going to be a real battle . . . Those people in the store are strangers. You have to take care of your child first" (Sternberg, quoted by Kutner, 1987b).

Because the tantrum is aversive to parents, they are tempted to give in to the child. This usually stops the excitement. As you supposed, this is a poor way of handling a tantrum. Children have tantrums to get what they want. By reinforcing the outburst, a parent almost guarantees a repeat performance.

Many parents have found that gently removing the child from the immediate setting in which the tantrum is occurring alleviates the child's distress. It also demonstrates the parent's control of the situation. Responding in a matter-of-fact way rather than "losing it" also prevents the incident from escalating into a power struggle. At home, responding to the child's frustration, but not reacting to the tantrum, may comfort the child without encouraging an inappropriate display of temper. For persistent tantrum behavior, the time out procedure, discussed at the end of the chapter, is useful.

Parents should encourage their children to express their disappointment or anger verbally rather than through out-of-control behavior. Caspi, Elder, and Bem (1987) studied adults who had had temper tantrums in late childhood (ages 8 to 10 years). They found that men who had tantrums during childhood were likely to display adjustment and relationship problems as adults. Women who had childhood histories of tantrum behavior were ill-tempered mothers and were prone to divorce.

The researchers suggested that individuals who as children adopt explosive interpersonal styles come to evoke responses in other people that perpetuate this maladaptive pattern. This is all the more reason to discourage such high-arousal states in children.

tion between intrinsic and extrinsic reinforcers. Extrinsic reinforcers, such as toys, money, and grades, are arbitrarily related to the activity being encouraged. Gold stars or "happy faces" can be used to reward cooperative behavior in kindergarten, but the payoff has no obvious connection to the behavior that produced it. Money is a highly valued, extrinsic reinforcer that governs much of our working lives.

Intrinsic reinforcers are inherent in the activity itself. Consider the enjoyment we get from hearing ourselves play the piano well or seeing our well-hit tennis ball return over the net. Nobody has to offer us an incentive for eating, reading, kissing, taking a bath, or brushing our teeth. These activities are intrinsically reinforcing—they are reinforcing in their own right. In education, unfortunately, the use of extrinsic reinforcers, particularly grades, has undermined the traditional intrinsic reinforcers that motivated scholars of the past, particularly knowledge for "its own sake" (Glasser, 1990; Rabow, Radcliffe-Vasile, Newcomb, & Hernandez, 1992).

When teaching children new behaviors, we initially rely on extrinsic reinforcers such as toys, stickers, or preferably, social reinforcers (discussion follows) such as praise and approval, because without these incentives the desired behavior would probably not occur. Children say, often with good reason, "I don't want to," or ask, justifiably, "Why should I?" Punitive parents might respond, less justifiably, "Because I said so."

Parents can ease the transition into new habit patterns, such as toileting skills, by offering children extrinsic reinforcers for new behaviors. However, once the new behavior is occurring at some strength, the extrinsic reinforcers should be gradually faded out so that the intrinsic (natural) reinforcers can assume control. We avoid the risk of extinguishing the new response pattern by not withdrawing the external incentives prematurely.

It is usually a mistake to offer a reward for an established behavior pattern that is intrinsically reinforcing. If a child enjoys dressing herself, and this ability enhances her self-esteem, it would be misguided to offer her an incentive for the same activity. Occasionally acknowledging or appreciating achievement and self-reliance is appropriate, but offering someone a reward for something that they are doing for a more natural outcome is counterproductive.

TYPES OF REINFORCERS

It is useful to distinguish between different categories of reinforcers. **Primary (unconditioned) reinforcers** such as food, water, and sleep acquired reinforcing properties over the course of evolution because of their role in survival. These stimuli are reinforcers at birth; no learning is required.

Secondary (conditioned) reinforcers acquire their reinforcing properties by becoming signals for subsequent reinforcement. The odor of food cooking acquires its reinforcing properties by signaling that that food is near. Seeing Dad's car pull into the driveway becomes reinforcing because it signals that soon we will be bouncing on his lap. Our employer's scowl becomes a negative reinforcer because it predicts a "chewing out" or worse. We will consider three categories of conditioned reinforcers: **social**, **activity**, and **tangible (token) reinforcers**.

Using Social Reinforcement

Mark #3

"Well, he finished the book and book report, not exactly on time. Left to his own devices on my school night, he chose to ride his bike instead of starting his report. My unsuspecting

landlady reminded him (once he was in for the night) that he should do his homework. At 10:30 PM when I came home, he was just beginning his second draft. When I realized his ploy to 'have it his way,' I was very annoyed. I rapidly began reading over his first draft and criticized how it 'told too much for a summary.' Many words and minutes later, I saw my poor parenting in motion. I finished reading it, told him more fairly that it really was a good book report and that he could finish tomorrow. (He ended up finishing it at lunchtime the next day). I asked him whether he felt good and proud that he finished the book. I told him I was proud of him. Mark immediately seemed relieved that I had let up on the pressure, and admitted he was happy and proud too."

For most of us, negative reactions from others can be very discouraging. Positive feedback has become a major incentive for us to behave well. Mark's mother caught herself in mid-lecture and decided to praise what he had accomplished rather than criticize what he had not. Social reinforcers, such as attention, praise, approval, hugs, kisses, and smiles acquire their reinforcing properties when they become signals for additional reinforcement.

At birth, infants are oblivious to these stimuli, but whenever anything "good" happens to them, such as being fed, held, or played with, a caregiver is present. The caregiver's presence, characteristics, and behaviors are repeatedly paired with, and therefore become signals for, the gratification that follows. Eventually, the caregivers themselves become powerful reinforcers, whose presence, attention, and approval can motivate new learning.

Children learn many "attention-getting" responses because they can't get the "good stuff" (primary reinforcers) until they first get our attention. Approval becomes a particularly powerful social reinforcer because people who approve of us are very likely to reinforce us in

other ways. It is important, however, that our praise of children be sincere and appropriate rather than excessive or manipulative. Too much praise causes children to focus on an outcome such as a grade rather than on the task at hand. Excessive or inappropriate praise (flattery) undermines the credibility of the caregiver. Earning praise for mediocre performance implies that children have little ability or that their caregivers have low expectations. Sincere, selective praise for competent performance or improvement provides a comfortable middle ground for parent and child.

Stimuli such as criticism, frowns, and sarcastic tones of voice acquire their negatively reinforcing properties by setting the occasion either for punishment or for the loss of positive reinforcers. In other words, people who signal their disapproval (e.g., dirty looks, unfriendly behavior) are less likely to give us what we want (reinforcers). Children gradually learn to behave in ways that avoid such disapproval. Most parents (myself included) could do better in accentuating the positive, as when we greet a report card with 2 A's, 2 B's and a C with, "What's with the C?"

Mark #4

"Daily, I've been trying to show Mark that I notice his efforts but my attempts seem feeble. Sometimes it's because I can't think of any positive feedback to give him. 'You got an A– on your safety test for Industrial Arts—ALL-RIGHT!'; 'Only one wrong—that's excellent.' 'I knew that if you listened in class, you'd do well.' 'I bet you feel good about that . . .' He'd answer affirmatively, saying, 'It was easy.' "

Notice that Mark's mother's approval was directed at Mark's behavior rather than at Mark. That's good, because we want to encourage competent behavior, not make Mark dependent on other people's approval. The use of social reinforcement is more desirable than that of tangible, extrinsic reinforcers because social reinforcers are more natural. It makes more sense to teach children that good behavior pleases other people than to teach them to behave well to get a cookie or a toy. Of course, there usually are better reasons for behaving well than just pleasing others, but for children, this is a useful place to begin.

In motivating responsible behavior in children, we move hierarchically. We go from tangible, extrinsic reinforcers such as gold stars, food, and toys, to social and other conditioned reinforcers, such as smiles, "thank you's," and grades. Eventually, children's behavior will be guided by intrinsic and natural consequences inherent in the activity itself.

Activity Reinforcers

Activities such as rocking and sucking are innately reinforcing to the infant. Most activities acquire reinforcing properties by being paired with already existing reinforcers. Children's activities and play behavior result in interesting sensory stimulation (e.g., drawing), gratification of some need (e.g., achievement), a desirable social consequence (e.g., winning a game), or some combination of the three. As a result, the activities themselves become reinforcing (fun).

David Premack (1962) pointed out in his famous "Premack Principle" that highly preferred activities can be used to reinforce less preferred activities ("After you room is clean, you can ride your bicycle"). The principle is most applicable when a child is, in this example, highly motivated to ride a bicycle. Reversing the contingency ("OK, you can ride your bicycle first, but make sure you clean your room afterwards") lessens or eliminates its motivational impact. Most parents have learned that their children will work hard to gain valued reinforcers. Parents who are aware of the activities that their children

enjoy can use these activities to reinforce less desired ones.

Tangible (Token) Reinforcers

Token reinforcers are "things" that have acquired reinforcing properties, such as money, toys, grades, or gold stars. Most 2-year-olds, if offered a choice of a fifty dollar bill or five shiny new pennies, would probably choose the coins. It doesn't take long for children to learn, however, that the green paper can be exchanged for other reinforcers, such as candy, toys, game cartridges, baseball cards, sneakers, and comic books. In this way, the funny green paper acquires reinforcing properties and children will ask (and work) for it. Tangibles are low-level reinforcers and should be used sparingly, or when higher-level, social or natural reinforcers are not available or effective. Food, a powerful primary reinforcer, generally is not appropriate for motivating new learning. If food is misused as an incentive, faulty eating patterns may be learned.

USING REINFORCERS JUDICIOUSLY

Natural consequences (discussion follows) are preferred to those that are ordinarily contrived by parents and teachers. In many situations, however, social and activity reinforcers are the natural consequences of appropriate behavior. In any case, thoughtfully arranged consequences are a powerful teaching tool. Hundreds of studies and everyday observation demonstrate that primary and secondary reinforcers can be used to motivate the learning of new behavior and to motivate the performance of established behavior patterns in children of all ages.

Optimal use of reinforcement requires knowledge of several learning principles. Importantly, reinforcement is most effective when it is delivered immediately following the desired response, particularly during new learning. Similarly, reinforcement is more effective when it occurs after every correct response. Once the new response is established, reinforcers can be administered more occasionally and with some delay. It is during this period that contrived reinforcers can be replaced with natural outcomes. Even after the behavior is quite ingrained, occasional reinforcement such as appreciation encourages its persistence.

NATURAL AND LOGICAL CONSEQUENCES

Study Question *What natural consequences might follow if*

1. *Tom refuses to brush his teeth?*
2. *Adriana's room is a mess and she refuses to straighten it up?*
3. *Tracy doesn't come to dinner after the first call?*

As children mature, parental regulation of their behavior becomes less necessary. Most adolescents do not need and, in fact, resent the regulation of their behavior through parental rewards and punishments. Adults take showers, brush their teeth, go to bed at a reasonable hour, and dress appropriately on cold days because of the natural consequences of these actions. That is, we feel fresh, clean, alert and comfortable as we move around the community.

The concepts of **natural** and **logical consequences** is associated with Rudolf Dreikurs (Dreikurs & Grey, 1970). Dreikurs encouraged parents to give their children the opportunity to experience the effects of their choices, good or bad (Berns, 1989). Rather than rewarding or punishing behavior, which makes the parents responsible for the child's actions, children should be allowed to make their own decisions. When their judgment is good, they reap the benefits. If their judgment is poor, they will suffer the consequences. In this way, children's behavior and judgment become more adult-like, guided by their natural outcomes rather than by parental rewards and punishments.

For example, if Carlos is late for dinner, his meal will be cold or not there at all. If he is hungry, he will prepare his own food and perhaps have to eat alone. This should not be conceived of as punishment. Carlos is suffering from the natural consequences of his tardiness, not from some contrived parental penalty. If Susan chooses not to wear a hat or gloves when the windchill factor is minus 12, why not let her experience the consequences of this decision. This is done not to punish or hurt her but to provide her with the opportunity to learn how to dress sensibly.

With the best intentions, parents often try to protect their children from such negative outcomes. Pointing out such consequences before they occur and helping a child to consider alternatives is good parenting. Arguing, shouting, and using coercion make little sense when natural outcomes, though unpleasant, lead to faster learning and a better appreciation of how the world works.

Obviously, we would never allow a child to put herself into a dangerous situation just to "teach her a lesson." For example, if Danielle runs into the street to get her ball, we will not wait for a trip to the emergency room for her to learn greater caution during play. When a natural consequence is inappropriate, we use what Dreikurs called a logical consequence, one that "fits" the situation (Dinkmeyer & McKay, 1982). If we cannot trust Sam to be careful when he plays outside, he will have to play inside. This should not be construed or communicated as a punishment, because it is not an arbitrary penalty. Rather, it is connected in a logical way to Sam's careless behavior.

Natural and logical consequences are generally preferable to rewards and punishments. They allow parents to avoid power struggles while giving children the opportunity to learn the real-life consequences of good and bad choices.

Eric's "Sick Day"

When my younger son was 4 years old, in an angry moment he refused to go to nursery school. I was not willing to force him to go to school. That would be a power struggle. Since I had no obligation to be elsewhere, I said "Fine, but remember you only stay home when you are sick." This is a logical consequence. He put on his pajamas and stayed in bed all day (because he was "sick"). There was no TV in his room in those days, and I couldn't play with him because I didn't want to catch what he had (attitudinitis). For lunch, he had toast and jelly. You get the point. He had an extremely boring day being sick, and he learned something about making threats.

"The purpose of allowing natural consequences to occur and of designing logical consequences is to encourage children to make responsible decisions, not to force their submission. This mode of discipline permits a child to choose and then to be accountable for the decision, whether it turns out well or not. Most children, when permitted to make poor decisions, learn from the consequences" (Dinkmeyer & McKay, 1982, p. 73).

Discouraging Self-Reliance

Study Question   *How do some parents inadvertently undermine their children's self-confidence?*

Parents often do things for children that children could do for themselves. This is not necessarily bad, but such episodes represent lost learning opportunities for the child. Children who are able to should dress themselves, prepare their own meals, do their own homework, and solve their own social problems. If guidance or support is needed, children should learn to ask for it. Sometimes the parent's motive is to "save the child from himself." Should parents step in and save a child from the unfortunate consequences of his own actions?

Fischer (1985) quotes one parent as saying, "You have mixed reactions because you don't want your children relying on you all the time, but you don't want them to fail either. Against my better judgment, I've typed term papers for my children, saved their jobs by making deliveries, made phone calls to cancel appointments when they forgot." Such parental rescue missions, by preventing children from experiencing the aversive consequences of their irresponsibility, may encourage further thoughtless behavior. Of course, if the child is "in over his head," abandoning him to catastrophe would not constitute good parenting.

When staring in the frightening face of failure, children gain more by having their parents help them clarify how they "messed up" and what they can do about it. "If your child claims to be incapable of the work, it's much more helpful to look for the reasons why. Giving a child advice on time management or making an appointment together to see a teacher is a far cry from sitting at a child's side and supplying half the sentences for a term paper" (Lopez, quoted by A. Fischer, 1985).

According to Dr. Lopez, if the child is capable of doing a job, but procrastinates to the point of failure, "let him fail. This is difficult for parents to swallow. But if Tommy's grade gets lowered, or he's fired from his part-time job, there's a better chance the next time he'll do his own homework assignment or keep his personal life from interfering with his working hours. It's part of a child's training to take on responsibilities, to deal with the conflicts and to experience what happens if the job doesn't get done . . . By rushing to the rescue they're not giving their children the motivation or the inner resources to succeed independently."

Mark #5

"With my busy schedule of full-time work and part-time schooling, I found it 'easier' to do things for Mark rather than explain to him how and why. Very often, especially while he was small, I'd dress him before I woke him. Rather than argue with him about chores, I'd keep his room neat, pick up after him, make his bed and exempt him from regular chores. Now and then over the years, I'd establish some mild expectations and request his cooperation. But as my attention wandered, I let things drop.

[2 weeks later] "One interesting observation Mark made this week is 'Why don't you ever do things for me anymore?' I was refreshed to see that he noticed and that he didn't seem angry about it. At the time he had asked me to tie his sneakers, because his shirt would come out of his pants, if he did it. I had teased him by whistling and then said, 'Well, I guess you can just put your shirt back in again.' I explained that it was 'good' for him to learn to do things for himself; that he was old enough now to be responsible for himself; and that our lives are very busy now and I need all the help he can give me.

"P.S. He's still not making his bed nor feeding his fish (without 3 reminders), nor flushing the toilet in the morning. On that last one, I stopped nagging him, so yesterday for once he did it. So I was able to praise him instead for a change (today he didn't flush again)."

Study Question *Analyze Mark's mother's initial motivation to do things for him that he could do for himself. Describe the factors that seem to discourage her efforts to modify Mark's behavior.*

OBSERVATIONAL LEARNING

Like most parents, I would have little difficulty describing many ways in which my children resemble my wife and me and many ways in which each is his own person. It is not difficult to "explain," at least after the fact, similarities or differences between parents and children. Regarding similarities, we can assume that parents teach their children to act like them through instruction or by rewarding their children for doing things the way their parents do them.

It is also likely that children come to resemble their parents simply by watching and interacting with them. For example, as part of a term project, one of my students was playing monopoly with a 7-year-old boy. She reports, "When the game ended and he clearly was the winner, I told him that he did a good job. He looked up and said to me, 'If you did your best, then you still won because you tried.' When I asked him who told him that he said, 'My mama always tells me that when I get mad because I lose. She says that as long as I had fun, it doesn't matter if I lose.' " By soaking up his mother's wisdom, he was able to pass it on to another person under similar circumstances.

Albert Bandura (born 1925) has proposed a comprehensive and influential theory of human personality that analyzes how we learn from watching other people's behavior (Bandura, 1986). Children observe a parent's behavior and mentally represent (in words or images) what the parent did or said. At some future time, the child can use these mental representations to guide her behavior. Bandura calls this process **observational learning**.

Observational learning refers to an often unintentional mode of learning in which someone learns a new behavior by watching another person (a model) engage in that behavior. Parents and teachers take advantage of this ability when they say to a child, "Watch

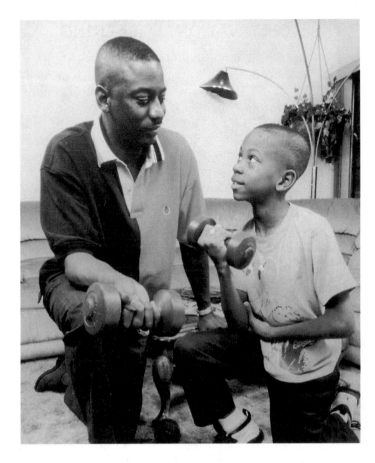

Much of what children learn from their parents, including their values, opinions, and beliefs, comes from watching their parents behave and listening to what they say.

what I do and then you try." Bandura suggests that by observing other people behave and noticing the consequences of their actions, we form beliefs about the possible outcomes of our own behaviors. The term observational learning encompasses other processes, notably imitation and identification.

Although new learning may occur simply from observing the model's behavior, the likelihood that the behavior will be *performed* depends upon many factors. These include the model's prestige, status, perceived similarity to the observer, the number of models, the child's age and intelligence, the activity being observed, and the consequences of the model's behavior (Berns, 1989). Parents usu-

ally are high-status models and have many opportunities to reward children for "matching" their behaviors.

It seems likely that much of what children learn from their parents is learned *not* through formal instruction or through the use of incentives, but rather by watching and listening to what their parents do and say. This knowledge scares ill-behaved parents ("Do as I say, not as I do"). Sometimes we hear young children make comments that they could not possibly understand, only to find out they were repeating ideas expressed by their parents. Children also are likely to observe and then imitate the behaviors of their siblings, peers, teachers, and popular culture heroes.

It is fortunate that children can learn through observation. It usually is easier to teach by example than to have to explain or instruct. Parents can say, "Watch what I do and then you try it." Children's moral reasoning and rule-following behavior also are very susceptible to the influence of models (Toner, Moore, & Ashley, 1978; Toner & Potts, 1981).

PUNISHMENT

Study Question *Why must parents be careful to avoid the excessive use of punishment?*

Observe parents in the company of their young children. What do you hear them say? "No!," "Stop that," "Don't you do that again," "Keep your hands to yourself," "That's not nice to say," and "Sit still." Parents often expend greater effort discouraging misbehavior than they do promoting good behavior. What we call socialization largely refers to the inhibition of undesirable behaviors.

Parents are frustrated by their children's misbehaviors. Frustration may be accompanied by aggressive feelings and behaviors. It is not surprising that parents, when annoyed, raise their voices and show threatening facial expressions and gestures. Many parents strike their children when they are in this agitated emotional state (Holden et al., 1995). Young children are weak and not likely to retaliate. (In my early days of parenting, my unnecessarily harsh or loud rebukes were punished when they inadvertently elicited sadness or crying in my children. I found myself in the awkward but necessary position of having to apologize for my over-reaction to their misconduct.)

The frequency of misbehavior can be so high that some parents conclude that their children are being deliberately provocative ("looking for trouble"). This increases their frustration and anger. We can easily under-stand why frustrated parents adopt punitive strategies to "correct" their children's behavior. Punitive methods are intended to discourage unacceptable behaviors by following them with unpleasant or painful outcomes.

Mark #6

"All was going as well as could be expected until I decided to look at his homework. Then I exploded. 'What kind of crap-writing is this? You're supposed to be an artist and your circles look like they were done by someone who's retarded!' I was terrible. I angrily told him he had better clean up his act.

"Okay, so I lost it. Now I'm sorry and realize how damaging that type of response can be. It's overwhelming how frustrating parenting can be. If I am not constantly vigilant in my attempts to parent my son lovingly and firmly, my chances of success are unlikely. So I will try again . . . relentlessly, because I love him."

Parental "hurting" responses can escalate into conflicts of major proportions. Giving young children this type of power over our emotional reactions is counterproductive. It encourages "power struggles" between parents and children. Parental responsiveness to children's behaviors can encourage either new patterns of interpersonal skills or patterns of spiteful defiance.

Defining Punishment

Behavioral psychologists consider a stimulus to be a **punisher** if its presentation following a response suppresses the response; that is, a stimulus is only considered to be a punisher if its presentation weakens the response. If a child continues to tell lies after a spanking, the spanking does not satisfy this definition of punishment.

Parents sometimes wonder why punishment "doesn't work." According to the present definition, if it doesn't work, it's not punishment. Many factors influence children's behavior in addition to rewards and punishments. Children sometimes continue to misbehave following a spanking because the incentives for misbehaving are stronger than the punishment. Continuing to misbehave may also constitute "retaliation" for the punishment.

Psychologists have distinguished two types of punishment. **Positive punishment** describes the presentation of an aversive stimulus following a specific response and the subsequent weakening of that response. (A stimulus is considered "aversive" if we try to avoid or escape from it). If Mom's frown following Pete's fresh answer leads to a reduction in freshness, then Mom's frown is a punisher (in that instance). If her frown has no effect, or indeed, encourages "an attitude," it is not a punisher.

Negative punishment is defined by the removal of a positive reinforcer (usually some privilege) following a misbehavior, leading to a reduction in its occurrence. After grabbing and pulling his sister's hair, Raymond is penalized by having to leave the dinner table and go without dinner. Raymond no longer mistreats his sister. Thus, his banishment constitutes negative punishment. A frequently used negative punishment technique is time out from reinforcement (see Spotlight: Time Out From Reinforcement).

Punishers can be verbal statements (threats, warnings, reprimands, criticisms), a loud or angry voice, facial expressions (frowns, glaring looks), physical or corporal punishment (spanking, slapping), or poor grades. If the occurrence of any of these outcomes discourages a behavior, the definition of punishment is satisfied. Note that a stimulus, such as a laugh or a reprimand, can serve as a reinforcer or a punisher, depending upon its effect on behavior.

Negative punishers involve the removal of opportunities for positive reinforcement, such as losing the chance to visit friends, to use the family car, or being "grounded." The latter eliminates opportunities for out-of-house reinforcers, including interactions with friends and outdoor play activities.

It can be seen from the definitions of positive and negative punishment that punishment does not teach children good behaviors. It only teaches children what not to do. The use of punishment (particularly corporal punishment) in discipline is controversial, and it should be. Most psychologists discourage its use, preferring positive methods instead (Straus, 1994a; Turner & Finkelhor, 1996). Removing reinforcers is more desirable than presenting aversive stimuli. Aversive stimuli, such as spanking or criticism, generally increase a child's arousal (seen as crying, sadness, fear, or anger) and might produce "side effects" (see "Side Effects of Punishment").

Now let us discuss how to punish effectively. I do not advocate or condone the use of harsh punishment because excessively used, punishment does not support our four parenting goals. However, its use is widespread, and when used sparingly it can be effective. Parents who choose to punish should be aware of the principles as well as the risks of punishment (Hergenhahn & Olson, 1993; Straus, 1994b).

Using Punishment Effectively

Punishers are most effective when they immediately follow a misbehavior. Like reinforcers, punishers are weakened by delayed presentation. Children who are exposed to frequent punishments seem to adapt to the aversive stimuli ("Hit me, I don't care"). They become less susceptible to its effects. Some children learn that after they are punished, their parents feel guilty and offer reinforcers. This "mixed message" is likely to encourage rather than discourage subsequent misbehavior (Kazdin, 1984).

Frequent and predictable punishment of the offending behavior is more effective than occasional punishment. Parents should encourage an acceptable alternative to the punished behavior that produces equal or greater reinforcement. For example, instead of drawing on the wall, children could be encouraged to draw on a board or easel.

Punishers should routinely be preceded by warnings and statements of relevant rules. Noncompliance should be followed by the designated punishment. In this way, warnings acquire aversive properties and may discourage misbehavior in their own right. "If you treat the baby roughly again, you will have to sit in the time-out chair for 5 minutes." It is crucial that parents follow through. Idle threats will be ignored and weaken parental credibility. State rules that help children learn the relationship between their misbehavior and subsequent penalties.

TABLE 6.5 Side Effects of Punishment

Physical punishment could injure a child.

Punishment elicits strong emotional arousal in a child and might alienate the child from the punishing agent. It is hard to feel close to or trust someone who hurts you.

Punishment may lead to an increase in aggressive behavior toward the punishing agent or someone else. Power struggles may ensue.

Punishment may lead to avoidance of the punishing agent or deception (lying) about one's behavior.

The effects of punishment may generalize to the setting in which punishment occurs.

Punishment may interfere with the learning of more desirable behavior.

Parents might become "dependent" on punishment rather than seek more positive strategies.

Side Effects of Punishment

Study Question *What "side effects" might discourage parents from using punishment?*

Both research and conventional wisdom suggest that using punishment indiscriminately can lead to undesirable or harmful side effects (Hergenhahn & Olson, 1993; Toner, 1986; Turner & Finkelhor, 1996). Intense physical punishment can lead to serious physical injury or emotional disturbance. Even if the punishment is not extreme, it may upset children enough to interfere with the learning of more adaptive behavior. If children are intimidated, the parent-child relationship suffers.

Physical punishment also models a "might makes right" philosophy of social influence (Kazdin, 1984). There is a famous cartoon of a father spanking his son, and the caption reads, "This will teach you to hit your sister." It probably will! The parent who often punishes also runs the risk of becoming an aversive stimulus. The child may come to fear, hate, or at least resent the indiscriminately punitive parent, rendering him or her less effective in that role (Toner, 1986). So many close family relationships are of the "love-hate" variety, partly because excessive punishment makes it difficult to feel safe with or close to the punisher.

The setting in which excessive punishment occurs, home or classroom for example, also acquires aversive properties leading to avoidance through disruptive behavior, truancy, or running away. Because the misbehavior may momentarily cease following punishment, parents are misled into believing that the temporary change is permanent. Finally, parents may become "dependent" on punishment as a way of achieving immediate compliance instead of using more thoughtful methods that support our parenting goals.

"Parents who use punishment a lot often complain that their children trap them into using more and more punishment by acting indifferent about mild punishment and provoking them into making punishment tougher. For example, a boy who is spanked holds back his tears, rather than letting his father see how much pain he feels" (Blechman, 1985, p. 15). Many children learn, when they feel that they are being unfairly treated, to not give the punisher the "satisfaction" of seeing their pain. And parents then increase the intensity of their punishments in an escalating power struggle with an enraged child.

Learning to Avoid Detection

Study Question *If a child admits to misbehaving and is then punished, for what is the child being punished?*

Children may learn to reduce the likelihood of punishment by not getting caught. In other words, they become more deceptive, and some learn to lie. If a child admits to having knocked over and broken a lamp and then is punished, what behavior is being punished? A strategic approach would have us say, "Thank you for being truthful. We'll talk about the lamp later." Because we do not want to punish truth telling, we immediately reinforce the admission and address the misbehavior at a later time. Some children put more energy into "not getting caught" than into practicing socially acceptable behavior.

Hoffman (1967) observed that children of parents who use a power-assertive discipline style demonstrate higher levels of rule-breaking behavior when they are away from home. This suggests that these children may be learning to discriminate between situations on the basis of the probability of punishment. In other words, such children may become more likely to break rules in situations where punishment of rule-breaking behavior is improbable.

Overcorrection

Kazdin (1984) considers overcorrection to be punishment by compulsory effort. **Overcorrection** is a type of logical consequence wherein restitution must be made for the unacceptable behavior. This is followed by extensive positive practice of a more appropriate response. Restitution means correcting the consequences of one's actions. For example, Lynne has to help the boy she pushed down stand up and then she must apologize to him.

A variation requires that the child restore the environment to a "better-than-original state" (Jensen, Sloane, & Young, 1988). A child who throws his clothes on the floor might be required not only to pick up his clothes but to vacuum the carpet and dust the furniture. Positive practice requires the repeated performance of behaviors that are preferred alternatives to the misbehavior. A recent application of this principle is the creation of "boot camps" for wayward juveniles. Rather than going to jail, they "voluntarily" attend military-type training camps where they practice prosocial behavior discipline and acquire practical job skills. The effectiveness of these programs remains to be demonstrated.

"Although overcorrection consists of restitution and positive practice, the constituent procedures sometimes are combined and other times used alone, depending upon the behaviors that are to be surpressed" (Kazdin, 1984, p. 136). If, for example, a situation cannot be corrected, positive practice is used alone. Repeating a pattern of correct behavior presumably has aversive properties that can be avoided by behaving well.

In the past, teachers may have had children write, "I will not be late again" a hundred times, certainly an aversive task, but writing it is not the same as doing it. Unlike most punitive methods, positive practice teaches desirable behavior, an important advantage

Spotlight

Time Out from Reinforcement

There are two types of punishment. The more common consists of following a misbehavior with a punisher, such as a reprimand or criticism. One can also punish by withholding opportunities for reinforcement following misbehavior. Children may forfeit their dessert or the opportunity to go outside to play. This latter practice is called "grounding." Strictly speaking, grounding a child by sending her to her room does not eliminate access to all positive reinforcers. Most children have an abundant supply of reinforcers in their rooms.

Kazdin (1984) defines **time out from reinforcement** as "the removal of all positive reinforcers for a certain period of time . . . The crucial ingredient of time out is delineating a time period in which reinforcement is unavailable" (p. 131). Like other punishers, time out is most effective when it is applied during or immediately following a transgression.

The punishing stimulus is the child's removal from a reinforcing activity. Short time out intervals (3 to 5 minutes) seem to work as well as longer intervals. If children resist by shouting or kicking, we tell them that the time out does not begin until they are quiet. We should praise children for the first appropriate response after time out (Dangel & Polster, 1988).

Many schools have time out rooms or booths that isolate misbehaving children from social and other reinforcers in the classroom. Brief isolation is appropriate when a child behaves aggressively toward another, or engages in a response that a parent will not tolerate.

As a punishment procedure, time out from reinforcement is effective, brief, and it does not involve pain. Therefore it is less controlling than spanking. Like other punitive methods and extinction, time out does not teach appropriate behavior. Hence, it should be used in combination with positive reinforcement for acceptable behavior. In addition, isolating or removing a child from a given setting requires preparation, as the child might resist. Time out can be a powerful way of discouraging misbehavior but it should not be used excessively.

TABLE 6.6 Steps in the Use of the Time-Out Procedure

Time out consists of brief removal from a reinforcing activity or setting.

Use the four questions cited in Table 6-1.

Prepare a time-out location (away from all reinforcers, such as TV) and chair.

Upon misbehavior, immediately remove the child from ongoing activity and assign to the time-out chair.

The time out interval does not begin until the child is sitting quietly.

Use time-out in combination with positive reinforcement for acceptable behavior.

The length of the time-out interval should be roughly one minute for each year of a child's age.

(Kazdin, 1984). Learning when and how to use overcorrection, while avoiding physical confrontation with the child, requires practice. Other less restrictive procedures should be tried first (Jenson, Sloane, & Young, 1988).

Should Parents Use Corporal Punishment?

The more we learn about punishment, the more aware we become of how it can be misused. According to recent polls (Collins, 1995), most parents use physical force (spanking, slapping, grabbing, shoving) with the purpose of causing pain but not injury. Presumably, the parent's intention is to demonstrate to a child that misbehavior will lead to pain. Parents are most likely to use corporal punishment when a child hits someone, especially if the child hits a parent (Straus, 1994a; 1994b). What is the logic of hitting somebody for hitting somebody? What does it teach children?

Because there is a risk of injury, some observers consider corporal punishment to be abusive (Straus, 1994a; 1994b). I avoided using punishment when disciplining my children when they were little, and I know that I would never strike them. Many parents use punishment prematurely, without understanding its possible side effects. There are too many positive alternatives for encouraging good behavior and discouraging misbehavior. Parents who do punish usually don't punish well. The misbehavior continues and the parent-child relationship may be damaged.

There are times when judiciously administered punishers can be used to discourage persistent, annoying, self-destructive, or dangerous actions. Swift punishment may be appropriate when children run into traffic, play with matches, or hang out a window. Larzelere (1994) maintains that corporal punishment is beneficial to children when (1) spanking is limited to a maximum of two slaps to the buttocks with an open hand, (2)

the child is between 2 and 6 years of age, (3) spanking is used to supplement positive parenting, and (4) spanking is used to back up more positive discipline strategies. What do you think?

The occasional use of brief reprimands has been found to be effective when the child's name is spoken with eye contact, neutral facial expression, and neutral tone of voice. If the reprimand is not effective, time out follows. If the reprimand is effective, more acceptable behavior is praised (Jensen et. al., 1988). Toner (1986) suggests as alternatives to punishment "appeals to reason tailored to children's cognitive levels, exposure to rule-following models, provision of rewards for rule-following behavior, and provision of guidelines for resisting temptation" (p. 27).

"Used judiciously, punishment can be quite effective in suppressing unwanted behavior, without adversely affecting desirable behaviors. This excludes extremely severe punishment, and that which is administered by a hostile and rejecting caregiver. What we are referring to is punishment used by a responsible and concerned person in teaching acceptable behavior" (Walters & Grusec, 1977, pp. 176-177).

SUMMARY

1. New parents are often unsure about how to comfort a distressed infant without "spoiling" it. For most of the first year, infants cry reflexively. Parents should provide comfort by feeding or holding infants or through other appropriate actions. Toward the end of the first year, parents should become more discriminating about how and when to respond.

2. When infants misbehave, brief, firm statements and physical restraint are appropriate. Arranging a safe and stimulating envi-

ronment with minimal opportunity for mischief is an excellent precaution. As always, patience is the key to good parenting.

3. Responsive parents place limits on children's behavior. Children naturally test these limits. By the age of 2 years, most children can learn to inhibit actions that elicit disapproval. Having a few, simple, clearly stated rules fosters internalization of parental standards. Parental inconsistency and permissiveness encourage defiance. Parental coercion may lead children to take parents seriously but possibly at the expense of other parenting goals.

4. Human behavior is very much influenced by its consequences. Parents gain from understanding how to use positive reinforcers to encourage desirable behavior. Stating rules and applying appropriate reinforcement contingencies is a powerful combination of strategies.

5. Some critics question the strategic use of rewards, because there usually are better reasons for behaving well than "getting something." Nevertheless, incentives provide a powerful means of teaching and motivating new behaviors until more natural or intrinsic outcomes can exert their influence.

6. In changing children's behavior, parents should address one problem at a time in small steps. They should create a flexible plan that will motivate a positive change in behavior. They should also arrange immediate positive outcomes (particularly social reinforcement) for improvement. Parents should ignore misbehavior when possible. A gradual shift from contrived to natural consequences is helpful.

7. When parents perform tasks or solve problems for their children, they are doing them a disservice. They are depriving them of the opportunity to learn self-management and other skills that increase their autonomy and enhance their self-esteem. Although it is sometimes difficult to watch our children falter, experience is an excellent teacher. We should avoid interfering with natural outcomes unless a child's health or safety is at stake.

8. Extinction consists of withholding consequences that may be reinforcing misbehavior. Very often, parental attention to a misbehavior encourages its repetition. Children will learn to nag, whine, or complain when such behaviors get them what they want. Parents may inadvertently shape obnoxious behaviors such as tantrums by making the child nag or cry for longer and longer periods before giving in.

9. Some parents adopt a punitive discipline style. Parents who become agitated when their children misbehave may fall into a power struggle of escalating, provocative interactions with their children.

10. Parents who punish excessively may encourage unwanted behavioral and emotional patterns in their children, including resentment and anger toward the parent. Such children may behave aggressively toward other children. Parents who decide to use punishment should learn to punish strategically. Removing privileges is preferable to presenting aversive stimuli. The latter provokes intense emotional reactions, including anger and hostility. Punishment should always be preceded by a warning.

11. Overcorrection requires that a child make restitution for his misbehavior and that he practice more desirable behavior. Time out from reinforcement consists of removing a child from reinforcing activities for a brief time. Punishment suppresses unwanted behavior but it does not teach a child correct behavior. The possible side effects of excessive punishment should motivate parents to learn more thoughtful discipline strategies.

GLOSSARY

activity reinforcer   An activity such as play that, due to biology or learning, has reinforcing properties

behavior modification   The use of operant conditioning principles in practical situations such as child rearing

extinction   Weakening a behavior by removing the reinforcer that typically follows it

logical consequence   A consequence that logically follows a behavior, for example, an adolescent's losing a privilege such as driving a car for driving irresponsibly

natural consequence   A consequence that ordinarily follows a behavior, such as feeling uncomfortable when one is not properly dressed in very cold or hot weather

negative punishment   Inhibiting a behavior by following it with the removal of something "good"

observational learning   Learning a new behavior by carefully observing a model engage in the behavior

operant conditioning   Changing the frequency of a behavior by altering its consequences or by changing the situation in which it typically occurs

overcorrection   A type of logical consequence wherein exaggerated restitution is made for an unacceptable behavior, for example, by having to remove graffiti from an entire wall when a child only spray painted a single word

positive punishment   Inhibiting a behavior by following it with something "bad"

primary (unconditioned) reinforcer   A stimulus such as food or touch that has reinforcing properties without learning

punisher   A stimulus whose presentation leads to a decrease in a behavior's frequency

punishment   Discouraging the occurrence of a behavior by following it with a negative consequence or by removing a positive reinforcer

secondary (conditioned) reinforcer   A stimulus such as money or a good grade that acquires its reinforcing properties through conditioning

sleep-resistant children   Children who refuse to go to sleep or who awaken in the middle of the night calling for attention

social reinforcer   A reinforcer such as praise or attention that takes the form of someone else's behavior

tangible (token) reinforcer   An object such as a toy or money that has reinforcing properties

time out from reinforcement   A punishment strategy wherein children are temporarily removed from ongoing enjoyable activities as a means of discouraging misbehavior

THOUGHT QUESTIONS

1. Reprimands sometimes are positive reinforcers. Explain.

2. How would you teach a child to follow the rule, "Hang up your jacket whenever you come home."

3. What role, if any, should rewards and punishments play in teaching children self-help behaviors such as toileting and bathing?

4. Why is the use of natural and logical consequences preferable to the use of rewards and punishments?

5. What reservations would you have about using punishment to discourage antisocial behaviors in your child?

COMMUNICATION AND RELATIONSHIPS IN FAMILIES

OBJECTIVES 202
Mark #7 202
RELATIONSHIPS 204
ATTACHMENT 204
PARENTAL SENSITIVITY AND RESPONSIVENESS 206
**PARENTAL UNDERSTANDING, ACCEPTANCE, AND
   PATIENCE 207**
Mark #8 207
Mark #8 Addendum 209
COMMUNICATION SKILLS 209
Mark #9 209
Attention 210
Mark #10 210
Sympathetic (Active, Reflective) Listening 210
Mark #11 211
Acknowledging Feelings 211
Encouraging Emotional Expressiveness 211
Nonverbal Communication 213
Descriptive Praise 214
Constructive Feedback 214
Exploring Alternatives and Owning Problems 214
I Messages 215
Apologizing 215
COMMUNICATION PITFALLS 216
Criticism 216

"When a child has misbehaved, the father or mother moves physically close to him, to offer him support. This will help the offending child to overcome his fear and guilty feelings, and make the best use of the teaching the parent is about to offer" (Satir, 1972, p. 16).

Spotlight: Parental Support and Expressions of Physical
   Affection 217
FAMILY ARGUMENTS, FAMILY MEETINGS 218
CHILDREN IN FAMILIES 219
Family Size 220
Birth Order 220
Single-Child Families 221
Sibling Status Effects 223
BOX 7-1 AND BABY MAKES FOUR 223
SIBLINGS 224
Sibling Ambivalence/Conflict 225
Parents and Sibling Conflict 226
Differential Treatment and Perceived Favoritism 227
PARENTS AND FRIENDS 228
Spotlight: Nonshared Family Environments 229
SUMMARY 232
GLOSSARY 233
THOUGHT QUESTIONS 233

OBJECTIVES

After studying Chapter 7, students should be able to:

1. Describe the role that attachments play in family relationships
2. Analyze the importance of the following in child rearing:
   a. Parental alertness and sensitivity
   b. Parental responsiveness
   c. Parental understanding
   d. Parental acceptance
   e. Parental patience
3. Discuss several common pitfalls in parent-child communication
4. Describe the role of each of the following parental communication skills, and give one original example:
   a. Attention
   b. Sympathetic listening
   c. Acknowledging feelings
   d. Nonverbal communication skills
   e. Descriptive praise
   f. Giving constructive feedback
   g. Exploring alternatives
   h. Problem ownership
   i. I Messages
   j. Apologizing
5. Explain what is meant by "sibling ambivalence"
6. Describe how children react to perceived differential parental treatment
7. Explain why children in the same family are so different from each other
8. Describe how family relationships affect children's friendships

Mark #7

"It was close to dinnertime so I called down to my 9-year-old son. He answered me back sharply, stating 'not now.' He and his friends were in pursuit of a mouse. The boys were

very excited, trying to corner it on our front lawn. I yelled for them to keep their voices down. Within moments, the tension and excitement climaxed. One boy all along had been arguing to 'leave the mouse be.' Other boys were enjoying the terrorism. My son, torn between peer approval and good judgment, got so wound up that in an attempt to restrain the mouse by stepping on its tail ended up crushing it.

"In the flood of mixed reactions, I spied what I perceived as a smirk of self-satisfaction on Mark's face. Immediately I went down to 'set him straight.' I scolded him in front of his friends, explaining that he should be ashamed of himself, that it was a very cruel and heartless thing to do, etc., etc., etc. I added that his behavior made me ashamed of him and that he'd be punished the rest of the week!

"During dinner, Mark had to leave the table because he could not restrain himself. (He had gone to his room, closed the door and hid his crying until dinner. Once at the table a few moments he began crying again). I asked him to tell me what was bothering him because I wasn't sure whether he was angry about the punishment, embarrassed in front of his friends by the scolding, or sorry for his actions. He went into his room again, crying very hard. I tried to hold him, comfort him and encourage him to talk to me about it. Eventually, he explained that he was very upset about the 'poor mouse' and how 'he must be suffering' and how this was the first time he had ever killed anything.

"I continued to try to hug and hold him, wipe his tears and explain to him that the mouse was dead and out of pain. I told him that we're all human and all make mistakes and that with all the excitement 'things just got out of hand,' that God would understand and forgive him if he was truly sorry. We talked for a long time and he was upset for hours, but I think we both learned something from the experience. I learned not to be so rash

but rather to remove him from the situation, calmly, and privately ask him to explain his behavior before I unjustly blurt out a punishment. (By the way, I revoked the punishment after all, when I realized how sorry he was). Mark learned (I hope) to have more respect for living creatures."

This journal entry brings to our attention several likely phases of parent-child communication during conflict: a crisis; a "flood of mixed reactions" from the parent and child; confusion and misinterpretation; a scolding or lecture that provokes strong reactions in the child, including crying and guilt; perhaps an attempt to communicate with caring; the expression of strong feelings; acknowledgement of the child's feelings; and some type of resolution.

In her journal, Mark's mother wondered whether Mark, the "new kid on the block," may have been trying to be the "tough guy by standing up to me and talking back" and by being the one who captured the mouse. By trying to understand his motivations and actions, she was taking an important step in improving her parenting skills. She was learning to withhold, or temper, her immediate, angry reactions in favor of more thoughtful and caring communications.

In this chapter, we examine parent-child communication and the nature of relationships in families. The material we cover applies to all four parenting goals, but particularly goal #3, good parent-child relationships. Poor communication is almost always a factor in poor family relationships and interpersonal conflict. Successful, caring relationships require effective, direct communication. This chapter also describes several parental communication skills that encourage children not only to express themselves freely but to behave well. The communication skills include descriptive praise, constructive feedback, sympathetic (active) listening, I messages, and how to "own" a problem. Communication skills give children access to the different perspectives and life views of family members and non-family members (Dunn, 1993). Keeping the channels of communication open always is a factor in healthy, supportive family relationships and interpersonal harmony (Masselam, Marcus, & Stunkard, 1990; Vuchinich, Vuchinich, & Coughlin, 1992).

"Once a human being has arrived on this earth, communication is the largest single factor determining what kinds of relationships he makes with others and what happens to him in the world about him. How he manages his survival, how he develops intimacy, how productive he is, how he makes sense, how he connects with his own divinity—all are largely dependent on his communication skills" (Satir, 1972, p. 30).

RELATIONSHIPS

Study Question *In what ways might our early family relationships influence our relationships outside of our immediate family?*

Most people derive considerable satisfaction from their relationships. Parents are particularly concerned about their relationships with their children for at least three reasons. First, parents love their children and enjoy affectionate interactions with them. Second, parents' psychological well-being reflects the quality of the parent-child relationship (Umberson, 1989; Umberson & Gove, 1989). Third, parents feel responsible for teaching their children how to have satisfying relationships.

"The person I admire most is my oldest brother Ronnie. Ever since I was allowed to go outside, I would always follow him around because I thought he was the greatest, and he still is in my eyes. I used to

dress like him, listen to the same music, and I always tried to talk like him. In fact, I still use certain phrases that I learned from him many years ago. I admired him so much because he understood everything I was going through. I've always wanted to be just like him when I grew up, and I think I am" (freshman college student).

As the preceding quote suggests, families are "training grounds," particularly for having relationships. Whatever we learn (or fail to learn) about getting along with and caring for our own family members will probably be evident in our "working model" of relationships outside the family (Hazan & Shaver, 1987; Miller, 1993; Parish & Necessary, 1994). Relationship patterns, once established, are fairly resistant to change and are usually repeated, with some variation, over one's lifetime.

Sroufe and Fleeson (1986) suggest three ways in which early relationships influence later relationships: (1) early relationships, particularly those between infants and caregivers, influence personality formation; (2) early relationships, such as those with siblings, shape our expectations about how relationships work, how available other people will be to us, and what is considered acceptable behavior; and (3) early relationships leave us with basic relationship skills or deficits (Miller, 1993; Raver, 1996; Volling & Belsky, 1992).

ATTACHMENT

Most of us would not select as a companion someone who cries, burps, drools, lacks toileting skills, and sleeps most of the day. And yet, many of us not only enjoy the company of such individuals, we experience intense love and caring for them. As discussed in earlier chapters, intense emotional ties bind parents to their children. These powerful feelings of affection and devotion are at the heart of the parenting process. They motivate parents to be close to and care for their children. Hence, they are of great interest to psychologists. The term **attachment** is used to describe the strong feelings that bind children to their parents and other caregivers and the behaviors that accompany these feelings (Goldberg, Muir, & Kerr, 1995; Rutter, 1994).

With the cutting of the umbilical cord, we observe the end of a child's physical attachment to its mother and the beginning of its emotional attachment. We have all observed young children use their parents as a secure base from which to explore a new environment and the way that they depend on their parents for comfort and reassurance, especially when they (the children) are upset.

Because attachment is the emotional cornerstone of development during infancy, we would expect the quality of an infant's attachment to its primary caregivers to predict significant aspects of the child's development (Rutter, 1994). For example, we assume that a child's attachment to caregivers is related to his or her ability to form and maintain relationships with non-family members, perform successfully in school, cope with everyday life stressors, and become self-reliant (Hetherington, 1994; Kerns, Klepac, & Cole, 1996; Teti & Abbard, 1989).

The essence of **attachment theory** is that parental behavior, especially a parent's ability to adjust to and accommodate his or her child's behavioral style, is the key determinant of a child's attachment to a parent (Bowlby, 1982). Attachment theory postulates that high quality parenting helps children to become securely attached to their caregivers. Mary Ainsworth and her colleagues (Ainsworth, 1989; Ainsworth, Blehar, Waters, & Wall, 1978) distinguished three ways in which infants can be attached to their parents, reflecting three distinct patterns of parental treatment (see Table 7.1). According to Ainsworth, infants become *securely attached* to parents who are warm and responsive. About 70 percent of Ainsworth's infant sample were designated securely attached.

Securely attached infants used their caregiver as a base for exploration and for coping with unpredictable or stressful events. They became upset when their mothers separated and greeted them affectionately when they returned. They were friendly to strangers when their mothers were present. Mothers of securely attached infants typically responded appropriately and caringly to them. These mothers were more loving, more helpful, and more playful.

About 20 percent of Ainsworth's infant

TABLE 7.1 Relationship Between Parenting Style and Security of Attachment

Parenting style	Child qualities and behaviors
Warm and responsive	Securely attached: Babies cry or protest when mother separates and greets her happily upon her return. Use mother as secure base for exploration
Parents are not sensitive or responsive to child's needs	Anxious avoidant: Babies rarely fret when mother leaves and avoid her when she returns. They are angry and do not like being held or being put down
Inconsistent parenting— sometimes responsive, sometimes not	Anxious resistant (ambivalent): Babies fret before mother leaves and when she actually separates. Upon her return, babies seek contact but also resist contact by pushing away or kicking

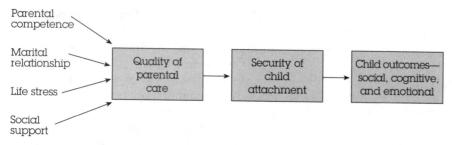

Figure 7.1   Quality of parental care, security of child attachment, and child outcomes.

sample were categorized as *anxious avoidant*. Anxious avoidant attachment occurs, according to Ainsworth, when parents are not sufficiently sensitive or responsive to their infant's needs. These infants did not get upset when their mothers separated, but they avoided contact with them when they returned. About 10 percent of Ainsworth's sample were categorized as *anxious resistant*. These infants also became upset when their mothers left but when mothers returned, the infants resisted contact with them and were difficult to console. This form of attachment is believed to occur when parents are inconsistent—sometimes responsive, sometimes not. Parents of securely attached infants seemed to enjoy their children more than did mothers of infants designated as insecurely attached.

It is difficult to draw firm conclusions about the relationship between parental treatment of a child and the child's attachment to the parent because parents of securely attached infants differ from parents of insecurely attached infants in several ways (personal resources, stress, social support) that could directly or indirectly affect a child's attachment (Belsky et al., 1995). For example, parents who abuse drugs have difficulty providing responsible and effective care (Brook, Whiteman, Balka, & Cohen, 1995). It is also likely that child characteristics such as temperament that influence caregiving be-

havior indirectly affect attachment security (Crockenberg, 1981) (see Fig. 7.1).

Although caregiver sensitivity, warmth, responsivity, and involvement all have been linked to children's security of attachment (Belsky et al., 1995), the relationship between parental behavior and infants' security of attachment is still hotly debated (Belsky et al., 1995; Lamb, 1987; Rutter, 1994; Schneider-Rosen & Rothbaum, 1993). It seems likely that contextual factors in parents' lives (e.g., stress, support) affect the quality of parent-child interactions, which in turn affect attachment security (Belsky, 1996; Belsky et al., 1995).

There is considerable support for the existence of a relationship between security of attachment and children's social and cognitive development (e.g., Bus & van Ijzendoorn, 1988; Jacobson & Wille, 1986; van Ijzendoorn & van Vliet-Visser, 1988). Children who are securely attached to their parents generally are more sociable, more compliant, and more competent than less securely attached children (Cohn, 1990; Kerns et al., 1996).

PARENTAL SENSITIVITY AND RESPONSIVENESS

Study Question   *Why are most parents so sensitive to signs of distress in their children?*

Over the course of human evolution, children of watchful and wary parents have had a distinct survival advantage (Bowlby, 1969). As a result, genes that encourage parental sensitivity and responsiveness have proliferated over the ages. At one extreme of parental concern, "overprotective" parents are preoccupied with their children's comfort and safety. At the other extreme, neglecting parents do not notice or care about their children's distress and discomfort. Occupying the middle ground, alert parents pay attention to and notice their children's facial expressions, sounds, and actions and respond quickly and appropriately when their child is distressed or in harm's way.

As noted in Chapter 3, parental sensitivity includes consistent monitoring and accurate interpretations of a child's behavioral and emotional "signals." Responsiveness refers to appropriate (contingent) responding to a child's behavior. As discussed in the previous section, parental responsiveness promotes healthy emotional development in children, including secure attachment to a parent. The security of a child's attachment to a parent is maximized when parents are attentive to a child and their responses are well-timed, reciprocal, and mutually rewarding (Ainsworth, 1973; Isabella & Belsky, 1991; Isabella, Belsky, & von Eye, 1989).

The security of a child's attachment is fostered by an optimal amount (for a given child) of interpersonal stimulation and by a predictable partner. Parents risk insecure attachments to their children if their interactions are non-responsive, intrusive, or poorly coordinated. Children of such parents "shut down" because their attempts to interact are not successful (Isabella & Belsky, 1991; Isabella, Belsky, & von Eye, 1989).

Both sensitivity and responsiveness can be observed when a father, while preparing dinner, glances toward his seated infant. With eye contact and a smile, he asks the child a question. If the infant drops her bottle, is fretting, or is about to tip over in her seat, dad's watchfulness allows him to assess the situation quickly and respond appropriately. Such contingent responding teaches infants that their sounds and actions have effects (Symons & Moran, 1987). It also encourages reciprocal response patterns. This basic sequence of parental alertness and appropriate responding exemplifies a fundamental component of good parenting.

Immediate, appropriate responding encourages sustained interactions between parent and child. Face-to-face interactions with positive emotional tone seem to be especially critical to children's emotional growth. These face-to-face, affective interactions, in turn, provide the basis for initial socialization (Raver, 1996; Watson, 1981). Infrequent positive emotional expressions, in particular, may increase the risk status of children in multiproblem families (Cohn & Tronick, 1989).

A parent's ability to adjust his or her attentional and emotional reactions to an infant's rhythms contributes to the quality of their relationship (Kaye, 1982). Children exhibit more distress when their mothers fail to adjust their responses to the child's patterns (Cohn & Tronick, 1989). We recall that infants of depressed mothers are less responsive and express fewer positive emotions than infants of healthy mothers. Mothers who are distressed often miss important signals in their children's behavior (Wahler & Dumas, 1989).

PARENTAL UNDERSTANDING, ACCEPTANCE, AND PATIENCE

Mark #8

"Mark was given a mimeographed sheet of questions and multiple-choice problems as science homework. All week long he has been

proudly relating what he was learning about photosynthesis. Now when it came time to put it in writing, he decided to 'display inadequacy.' Mark sat and stared into space. When I impatiently prodded him to "get started!" he heaved a sigh of resignation and began to read over the paper. Repeatedly, he'd complain that he didn't understand the question, couldn't read a word, had no idea of the answer, was too tired, etc. This complaining and whining went on and on.

"As I was doing the dishes, I started to sense that he was purposely 'playing dumb.' I made some suggestions that he re-read the pages and start 'using his head.' As time went on, I got angrier and angrier and began to threaten him. I told him that I was getting angry enough to 'beat him' (although he's never experienced a 'beating' from me yet—only smacks now and then), that he'd better re-read all of it if necessary. I threatened that we'd stay in, and stay up late every night, until he developed good study habits in school and at home.

"He continued to whine, slouch, moan, fake cry and stutter over words he'd normally never have trouble with. I finally got my emotions so out of control that I smacked him, once over the head and three times on his back and shoulders. He immediately went off crying to his room, closing the door. Right away I felt frightened that I had gotten so angry and sorry that I'd lost my good sense. I still felt that in some way I had to convey to him that I would not fall prey to his manipulations, that I wouldn't give him the answers or let him 'skip it.' My reaction was completely out of line, but my pride got in the way so I told him that he had 5 minutes to finish his homework.

"His next reaction was positive. When he did come out, he was more willing and attentive. I, in turn, was more patient, loving, instructional, and encouraging. I hinted on how to decide what sections needed to be re-read in the book, looking for key words in the paragraphs and using the glossary. By the time we

were through, he had even done additional work."

Study Question   *In this encounter, what assumptions did Mark's mom make about his behavior?*

Needless confrontations between frustrated parents and discouraged children occur all too frequently. As we follow the sequence of "communications," we notice that something is wrong. Parental expectations are being frustrated at every turn. Impatience gives rise to anger and even violence. Mark's mom assumed that he was "playing dumb." One suspects that if she had interpreted the situation differently (as she eventually did), she would have responded more sympathetically.

What information about children do we need to help us interpret such encounters more constructively? It helps to remember that children are different from adults physically, emotionally, and cognitively. Their thinking is less logical and more intuitive and they are less informed. They have shorter attention spans and are more easily frustrated. They also have relatively few coping mechanisms, which leaves them emotionally vulnerable. As we have seen, children are very much controlled by immediate gratification. Despite the beliefs of our ancestors, they are anything but miniature adults!

What children say and do usually makes sense to them, if not always to us. As Piaget emphasized, they have difficulty grasping our adult perspective. As parents, we have the opportunity to appreciate their unique, if limited, perspectives, to try to see (and feel) things as they do, and respond accordingly. This willingness to consider their perspective rather than to impose our own can make a big difference in discipline encounters.

I do not advocate that parents yield to a child's point of view. Rather, children need help clarifying their issues, understanding our adult perspective, and finding a resolution between the two. The alternative to problem solving usually is conflict and anger. Negative emotional expressions disrupt the problem-solving process (Forgatch, 1989).

The better we understand children, the easier it becomes to accept them as they are. Understanding is a prerequisite to patience and, therefore, to subsequent change. In the incident cited above, Mark's mother initially did not know how to handle him as a stubborn student, and she reacted punitively. Eventually she changed her perspective, understood his plight, and helped him through it. Good parenting.

Mark #8 Addendum

"Both incidents ended with us both pleased to have the task behind us. I tucked him in, said his prayers with him and snuggled a little and teased him by tickling him to make him laugh. I'm sure I did these things to reaffirm my love and to regain an equilibrium in our relationship." (See Spotlight: Parental Support and Expressions of Physical Affection on page 217.)

COMMUNICATION SKILLS

It is ironic that many adults treat their friends more kindly than they treat their children. If a child spills her drink, she may hear, "What's wrong with you. Why can't you be more careful. Now clean this mess up right now!" If an adult friend of the same parent spills a drink, she might hear, "Oh, don't worry about it. It's O.K., really, I'll clean it up in a second." How would the adult friend have responded to the first parental reaction? Why don't adults adopt at least the same standards of sensitivity, kindness, and respect in communicating with their children as they do with each other? (The Nobel Prize for Parenting awaits the genius who can answer that one).

Children learn and display listening and communication skills similar to the ones that their parents model (e.g., McDevitt, Ewers, & Oreskovich, 1991). Further, all four parenting goals are supported by good communication. When we speak kindly to our children, they feel cared for and understood. They learn to value our concern and participation in their lives. As Carl Rogers (1961) taught, when we communicate acceptance to children they learn to accept themselves more and like themselves more.

The communication skills that are described in the following sections are not easy to learn. Good communication requires thoughtfulness and patience, scarce parental resources. Parents who improve their communication skills find that over time, their relationships with their children become richer and more satisfying (Dinkmeyer & McKay, 1982). As the next entry in Mark's mother's log illustrates, children are not always receptive to parental feedback, especially when they feel that they are being criticized.

Mark #9

"More often than not, at school and in the after-school program, Mark seems to be vying for attention. Teachers have stated on his report card that he 'interrupts a lot.' Counselors have told me again and again that he has to be reprimanded for talking and misbehaving. Usually the accounts that are told to me are ones in which he's playing the 'class clown.' The past few days or so he's begun mimicking and mocking me and others. First, I'd tell him how that 'isn't very nice' and that 'it's rude,' but then I'd just drop it because he'd continue or make a joke of it.

"When I try to discuss with him how he might feel if he was the one being mocked, he squirms and says untruths such as he'd feel okay, it wouldn't bother him. At that point, I feel frustrated and drop the subject."

Attention

Good communication begins with careful attention to the signals a child conveys, verbally and nonverbally. Young children wear their emotions on their sleeves. They have not yet learned to disguise their real feelings. By adolescence, many children have learned to mask their true feelings. Perhaps this is because these feelings were not understood or respected by their parents or peers. Many children learn that it is not safe to express powerful emotions, such as anger, fear, or sexual feelings. People's reactions to frank disclosures are unpredictable and often unsupportive.

Sensitive parents show interest when their children are upset, disappointed, frightened, or angry. They may set aside a special time to discuss these feelings. Observant parents, despite their busy schedules, notice facial expressions, tone of voice, body postures, and gestures that convey uncomfortable feelings. They attempt to discover what is "behind" them (Ginott, 1965). By observing, by listening, and by encouraging their children to clarify their feelings and seek solutions to their problems, parents model good communication skills and stay emotionally in touch with their children.

Mark #10

"At least twice this week I lost my cool (confession time). When he admitted for the umpteenth time that he forgot to write down his homework assignment, I said, "Can I ask you a question? Not to be mean, but how far do you think you can push your teachers before they decide to keep you back?" I asked him, did he want to stay back? After some sarcasm, he admitted he did not. I told him, if any teachers approach me and suggest keeping him back, that I wouldn't put up a fight. I told him his life could be so much easier if he'd stop being so stubborn.

"The other incident was when he was fumbling through his math homework. I had already explained it calmly three times and showed him that the examples in the book also explained it. He said he still didn't understand and I went 'off.' 'If you're going to continue to play dumb, you'd better plan on being a garbage man. The only art you'll be able to do is that on the side of your truck—for free!' (Remember, he's gifted in art.) Well, he answered back in sarcasm, 'Good! I'll be a garbage man and my truck'll look great.' Later, when I calmed down, I explained the math to him again, and kept telling him, 'I knew you could do it.' The long way around. . . . geez!"

Sympathetic (Active, Reflective) Listening

Study Question   *In communicating with their children, how are parents like detectives?*

It is not helpful to tell our children how they should or should not feel. It is helpful to gently solicit their actual feelings. How do we do it? By asking good questions and *listening* to their answers. Active listening means really trying to hear what children are saying (McDevitt, Ewers, & Oreskovich, 1991). When parents listen sympathetically, they listen for the often hidden or disguised messages conveyed by their children's verbal and nonverbal behaviors (Ginott, 1965).

Parents often take their children's comments or complaints at face value. Discovering their actual meanings often requires a little digging. When a young girl says, "I hate boys; they're so mean," she is summarizing an entire episode in one short sentence. The average parent might say, "Oh, boys aren't so bad." A more sensitive parent will combine good questions with attentive and thoughtful listening. "What happened at Judy's party? . . . How did it make you feel?"

"How can we help a child to know his feelings? We can do so by serving as a mirror to his emotions. A child learns about his physical likeness by seeing his image in a mirror. He learns about his emotional likeness by hearing his feelings reflected by us" (Ginott, 1965, p. 40). By reflecting (or repeating) the key ideas and feelings being expressed by the child, parents serve as a "sounding board." At the same time, they show that they care and that they really are interested and concerned. When they are listening sympathetically, parents are trying to find out what happened, how the child really feels about what happened, and how they can help her clarify her options. However, sympathetic listening is not always appropriate or desirable. A child who asks a direct question should get a direct answer. If children do not want to talk, we should respect their right not to have to.

Mark #11

"I tried reflective listening the other night but ended up lecturing. Mark had commented that 'the counselors stink like they just fell into some fish water' and that he hates them. I said he sounded angry because he felt embarrassed at having been scolded and punished. He said 'no,' that he really did hate them because 'talking once is no reason to pull me off an activity for a week.'

"I should have reflected that he was feeling the 'unfairness' of it all and draw him out from there. But instead I reminded him that three times already I have been told of his misbehaving and subsequent punishment, that didn't he think three warnings was enough? I went on to explain how responsible and difficult a job it must be for the counselors as it was, without any added trouble. Anyway, as you can assume, the subject was dropped, probably the moment I began my spiel. So I learned that that type of half-hearted attempt at reflective listening is as good as none."

Acknowledging Feelings

Young children initially express their positive and negative feelings freely unless they are taught not to do so. If a child asserts, "I look ugly," the immediate parental reaction is often, "You're not ugly, don't say that." Dismissing such negative feelings does not help a child resolve them. A more helpful response might be, "You're unhappy about the way you look." Notice that this acknowledgment of the child's utterance and the feeling behind it conveys caring and respect. It invites the child to continue expressing himself. The first parental reaction, "Don't say that," accomplishes the opposite result. The child sees that there is no point in continuing to express himself because what he is saying is upsetting his parent.

Study Question *Identify the feelings behind the following children's assertions and specify a helpful parental response:*

1. "Nobody at school likes me."
2. "I'm dumb at spelling."
3. "I'm going to kill Paul if he teases me again."

Encouraging Emotional Expressiveness

Parents can exert considerable influence over how children view and express their "private" feelings (Zeman & Shipman, 1996). Although children's feelings often motivate their behavior, they usually have minimal awareness of, or at least interest in, their internal states (unless they "hurt").

Parents can support the development of such awareness by noticing the child's facial expressions, verbal and nonverbal responses, and the child's interpretation of a situation. They can then label the child's probable feeling state. "Katie, are you disappointed that Grandma's not coming?" Using the correct emotional label in an appropriate situation helps the child to not only learn the label but also to apply it to her current feeling state. Mothers encourage their daughters, more than their sons, to communicate their feelings, perhaps setting the stage for the greater emotional expressiveness we observe in females later in life (Dunn, Bretherton, & Munn, 1987; Zeman & Shipman, 1996).

Some parents do not take their children's feelings seriously. This may reflect the fact that children occasionally express their emotions manipulatively (as in "fake" crying) to get what they want. By dismissing true expressions of fear, anger, or disappointment, parents can discourage the expression of these feelings and even the child's awareness of them.

Many psychologists contend that human behavior can be influenced by motives and feelings that are outside of our awareness and that this is not always to our advantage. Parents can help their children be in touch with their internal states and motives by acknowledging and labeling these events appropriately. They also provide the child with a useful emotional vocabulary.

Parents occasionally ignore, dismiss, or discourage children's behavior that makes them uncomfortable. Sometimes we advise people who are distressed, "Don't be upset." Is this really helpful? We probably are communicating, "When you're upset, I become uncomfortable." By placing our needs ahead of theirs and not taking their distress seriously, we risk further discouraging them, and we convey a lack of caring.

Three-year-old Tony falls and scratches his knee. He cries, but Father proclaims, "Oh Tony, that doesn't hurt." How is Tony to interpret that pain in his knee that he thought did hurt? By contradicting his son's immediate experience, Tony's father confuses him and impedes the development of his self-awareness. Many parents shy away from their children's expressions of sexual curiosity. By the time children are four years old, their parents should be prepared to answer their questions about sex openly and honestly (at a level appropriate to the child's understanding) and properly label the sexual parts of the body. Speaking about sex in a relaxed manner and providing accurate information help the child to realize that her curiosity is normal and acceptable (Cavaliere, 1995b).

Parents may also displace their frustrations and hostilities onto their children, who cannot suspect the real causes of their parents' upset. Young children may perceive themselves as responsible for their parents' strong feelings, particularly parental anger. They also believe that they can help change their parents' feelings (Covell & Abramovitch, 1987). As noted in Chapter 4, parental conflict upsets children; as they get older, they may attempt to intervene in increasingly sophisticated ways (McCoy & Masters, 1985). Children appear to be very sensitive to anger, particularly chronic anger, which E.M. Cummings (1987) calls "background anger." He hypothesizes that such anger distresses children and is distinguished from other background emotions.

Sensitive parents take their children's (and their own) emotional expression seriously. They encourage the honest expression of strong positive *and* negative, even embarrassing, feelings. When they are apparent, feelings can be addressed. Mothers who take the time to discuss feeling states with their children usually have children who do the same (Dunn et al., 1987).

When children are troubled, we support our parenting goals through active, sympathetic listening to their view of the problem, helping them clarify how they feel, why they feel that way, and what they can do about it. Similarly, when parents are upset, they can model sensitive ways of expressing strong feelings honestly and directly. Children gain not only by seeing how adults express their sadness, frustration, and anger, but also by seeing them express affection and concern.

Such parental modeling gives children the opportunity to view the facial expressions and hear the words that accompany strong positive and negative emotions. Modeling empathic behavior motivates them to express caring and concern to someone they perceive as distressed (Zahn-Waxler, Radke-Yarrow, & King, 1979). Abused toddlers, on the other hand, lacking these experiences, become distressed when they are with peers who are upset. They may even attack them verbally and physically (Main & George, 1985).

Although parents often attempt to shield their children from strong emotional arousal and upset, hiding strong feelings from them is counterproductive. "A child who sees strong emotions openly acknowledged is less likely to misinterpret those emotions than one whose parents try to cover things up. By admitting that you are angry or frustrated or sad, you are providing a context for your child to understand what you are doing and saying. Perhaps more important, you are showing your child that it is O.K. for him to express emotions, too" (Kutner, 1988b). A healthy emotional climate in the home is supported by taking children's emotional expressions seriously, by sympathetic listening, asking good questions, appropriately labeling emotions for the young child, and modeling supportive and caring interpersonal skills.

Not only do these parental actions support healthy emotional development, they also play an important role in children's cognitive and social development. Interesting and supportive verbal exchanges provide a key opportunity for parents to broaden their children's understanding of human relationships, human motivation, and social understanding (Dunn, 1993; McDevitt, Ewers, & Oreskovich, 1991).

Nonverbal Communication

"It is not so much what you say, it's how you say it." This cliché suggests the importance of nonverbal signals in communication. Nonverbal messages can be so powerful that they can contradict the accompanying words. For example, if we say to someone, "you're wonderful," in a sarcastic tone of voice, we are really expressing the opposite sentiment. Rolling one's eyes with a shake of the head requires no further comment. When we communicate, our facial expressions, eye contact, gestures, body contact, affectionate touching (touch, hug, and smile), body stance, distance from the child, vocal loudness, silences, and general emotional tone speak volumes and should be consistent with what we are saying in words.

Study Question *A parent is comforting a child with a splinter in her finger. For each of the nonverbal behaviors mentioned in the preceding paragraph, describe how parents can provide optimum reassurance (e.g., reassuring tone of voice).*

Another cliché, "actions speak louder than words," suggests that what we express verbally should be consistent with our subsequent behavior. Our credibility as parents partially depends on our willingness to keep our word and to follow through on promises and warnings. Since there is considerable variation in how people express themselves nonverbally, the meaning of nonverbal behavior is difficult to interpret, especially for children. Like adults, children eventually come to depend on nonverbal cues to understand and convey information (Silberman & Wheelan, 1980).

Some children suffer socially because they are insensitive to the nonverbal feedback they receive from other children. They may not be aware that they are annoying or hurting others. Such children often require special help in learning how to interpret other children's facial expressions, gestures, and other nonverbal behaviors (Nowicki & Oxenford, 1989).

Descriptive Praise

Study Question   *Give examples of descriptive praise that can be offered when a child:*

1. Shares a valued toy
2. Finishes her homework
3. Answers the phone politely

One of the discipline practices implied by the operant conditioning model is "catching the child being good." Rather than falling into the all too common "criticism trap," parents can better support a child's efforts through the use of clear, contingent descriptions of desirable behaviors (Dangel & Polster, 1988).

Criticism (e.g., "Your room is a mess") usually does not specify what the child should be doing. Descriptive praise (e.g., "It is a pleasure to visit your room when it is so neat") emphasizes positive behavior. Because there is no criticism, the child does not have to adopt a defensive ("I didn't do it") or offensive ("You're worse than I am") posture (Faber & Mazlish, 1995). Descriptive praise is delivered in a sincere, pleasant voice. It specifies what the child did that the parent liked in a way that does not embarrass the child (Wagonseller & McDowell, 1979). "Thank you for helping your sister. It makes me feel good to know that you take care of her when I'm away." "I really liked the way you read that poem at assembly. I feel proud when you make an effort to do a good job." Keep in mind the distinction between common praise, which usually is judgmental ("You're a very smart girl") and descriptive praise, which specifies what the child is doing and how we feel about it.

Constructive Feedback

Nobody likes being criticized, yet everyday life dictates that we must sometimes give negative feedback. It is possible to provide feedback without threatening or humiliating the recipient. At the beginning of this chapter, we read how Mark's mother scolded him in front of his friends. She later realized that she had just made matters worse. Among other things, her timing lacked sensitivity. Because parents give their children so much feedback, it is important that the seriousness of the communication be proportional to the seriousness of the transgression. Some parents respond to spilled milk as though it were nuclear war. This dilutes the effectiveness of more serious communications.

Silberman and Wheelan (1980) suggest that we refrain from giving children negative feedback when they are in a "weak" position, that is, when they are feeling bad about themselves. They also suggest that we postpone talking until the strong feelings pass. Parents should avoid interpreting children's behavior ("You're just saying that to get attention"). Rather, describe what it is that they did or didn't do that we object to. Feedback usually can be given in positive terms ("I really appreciate your help when I'm preparing dinner"). It should describe what we would like to happen rather than what it was that disappointed or annoyed us. Poorly given feedback, at best, is a waste of time. Parents would be better off saying nothing than criticizing or humiliating their child.

Exploring Alternatives and Owning Problems

Dinkmeyer and McKay (1982) discourage parents from giving advice. They believe that giving advice is not helpful in teaching children problem-solving skills. They encourage exploring alternatives, which means assisting children in "identifying and considering the options available to solve a problem" (p. 57). In helping children come up with specific courses of action, they suggest using sympathetic listening to help children understand what is really upsetting them.

They advocate exploring alternatives through the technique of **brainstorming** (generating many possible solutions without judging them). Helping children select a possible solution to a problem, discussing the likely effects of the decision, obtaining a commitment, and agreeing to evaluate a plan after trying it out are good problem-solving strategies.

Helping children solve their problems this way is predicated on the decision of problem ownership. In his best-selling book, *Parent Effectiveness Training*, Thomas Gordon (1970) defined problem ownership the following way. If the child's needs are not being satisfied, and he or she is upset or unhappy, then it is the child's problem. If the child is satisfying his or her own need, but is also annoying his or her parent, then it is the parent's problem.

When a child owns the problem, the parent can use **sympathetic listening**. The parent does not "solve" the child's problems, but supports the child's problem-solving skills by helping him or her explore alternatives. If the parent owns the problem, I messages are appropriate (Dinkmeyer & McKay, 1982).

I Messages

Yes, parents have feelings too, and we know what happens if we ignore them or if we let them build up. How can we communicate our adult feelings to children without overwhelming them? An **I message**, naturally, begins with the word "I," and expresses how the parent feels about the child's actions. "I am getting annoyed because I cannot rest when you make so much noise." A less helpful message

might be a shouted, "You are so inconsiderate. You never give me a minute's peace." Notice that I messages can convey strong feelings but in a nonaccusatory way.

A you message, on the other hand, "lays blame and conveys criticism of the child. It suggests that the child is at fault. It is simply a verbal attack . . . An I message delivered in anger becomes a you message conveying hostility" (Dinkmeyer & McKay, 1982, p. 59). Usually, when we begin a sentence with the word "you," particularly if we are communicating displeasure, the person we are addressing becomes defensive and may counterattack. I messages defuse the situation by asserting *my* annoyance or disappointment rather than *your* "nastiness" or "badness."

I messages usually have three components: (1) the child's behavior ("When you . . .), (2) how the parent feels about the behavior ("I feel . . ."), and (3) the consequence of the behavior ("because . . ."). "*When you* don't call or come home after school, *I worry* that something might have happened to you, *because* I don't know where you are" (Dinkmeyer & McKay, 1982, p. 60). Notice how I messages convey caring by explaining why the parent is feeling upset and what the child can do to correct the situation. Thomas Gordon (1970) also describes appreciative I messages (earlier referred to as descriptive praise). They balance the occasional criticisms and preventative I messages that anticipate and attempt to avoid problems. "I would appreciate your having showered before you go to bed, so that I don't have to wait for the bathroom in the morning."

Apologizing

People in authority have as many interpersonal "lapses" as anyone else, but some may not feel comfortable acknowledging their mistakes. Employers and parents sometimes fall into this category. Rationalizing or denying our errors rather than admitting them not only gives children an inaccurate view of our fallibility, but it also prevents them from learning how to apologize. Children who bellow, "It's not my fault" when they are (at least partly) responsible for an incident are revealing an important lesson they may have learned from their parents: "Don't get caught messing up."

"Parents who have the most difficulty admitting they've been wrong come from families where their own parents were authoritarian. They're afraid they will lose control and that their children will think they're weak" (Cleminshaw, quoted by Kutner, 1988d). In fact, the opposite seems to be true. We tend to admire, or at least forgive, those who "own up" to their mistakes.

Children benefit from having realistic expectations about themselves and their parents and by understanding human frailty. Acknowledging rather than denying our fallibility facilitates the development of a realistic

self-concept. By accepting our imperfection, we do not have to go through life pretending to be perfect.

COMMUNICATION PITFALLS

Parents who have not developed effective communication skills generally talk too much to their children. They nag, whine, lecture, suggest, advise, explain, re-explain, plead, criticize, blame, remind, threaten, ridicule, preach, judge, analyze, and speak sarcastically (Dinkmeyer & McKay, 1982). Some parents act as though they always "know better" than their children. They convey impatience, even hostility, and a lack of respect for the child's thoughts and feelings. Most adults would never communicate this way to their friends. If they did, they wouldn't have friends.

Criticism

Children who are repeatedly criticized or who are not heard at all become discouraged. As a family therapist, I often get to meet such children. They have little to say, it seems, and have learned that it is pointless to seek their parents' counsel when they have problems or feel troubled. Such children often have low self-esteem. They have learned to anticipate disapproval from their parents (and others) and they feel rejected. (Some children receive so much criticism and disapproval that they become desensitized to it, though their self-esteem will probably suffer.)

One 14-year-old high school freshman, an agreeable, bright boy, told me that his mother hated him and thought he was crazy. His mother didn't really hate him, but acted as if she did when he wasn't doing well in school. She seemed to have absolutely no understanding of or sympathy for his predicament. Though she was an intelligent woman, she lacked the insight or personal resources to

TABLE 7.2   Communication Pitfalls

Nagging

Whining

Shouting

Lecturing

Blaming

Pleading

Threatening

Sarcasm

Criticism

Reminding

Ridiculing

Preaching

From Dinkmeyer & McKay, 1982.

Parental Support and Expressions of Physical Affection

"There is a deep hunger on the part of men to feel that they're valued and appreciated and beloved by their fathers. They long to hear that they're loved. Instead, many come away confused . . . Their fathers work very hard, they sacrifice, but they're not present . . . Men find it hard to put things into words" (Osherson, quoted by Keyes, 1993, p. 4).

Throughout this book, we emphasize the importance of parental encouragement and support. Supportive parental behavior conveys acceptance and caring. Support can be operationally defined by such behaviors as "praising, approving, encouraging, helping, cooperating, expressing terms of endearment, and physical affection" (Barber & Thomas, 1986, p. 783). Of all these behaviors, expressions of physical affection (appropriate touching, holding, hugging, kissing, picking up) most powerfully communicate acceptance and caring.

Do mothers express physical affection to children more frequently than do fathers? Are fathers more affectionate with their daughters than with their sons? Barber and Thomas (1986) surveyed male and female college students at Brigham Young University regarding demographic characteristics, their parent's support behaviors, and their self-perceptions, including self-esteem. Four separate dimensions of parental support were identified: (1) general support, (2) physical affection, (3) companionship, and (4) sustained contact.

According to the students, their fathers expressed much less affection to sons than to daughters. Mothers were equally affectionate to sons and daughters. Mothers and fathers expressed more companionship support to the same-sexed child. Analysis revealed that "daughters' self-esteem is best predicted by mothers' general support and fathers' physical affection. Sons' self-esteem is best predicted by mothers' companionship and fathers' sustained contact" (p. 783). Daughters'

self-esteem seems to be positively related to parental (particularly paternal) expressions of affection.

Parents, especially fathers, differ considerably in their ability to convey love, caring, and acceptance, verbally and physically. Ralph Keyes (1993) interviewed dozens of men about their fathers. One son told him that following a divorce he had returned home for assurance. His father turned on a football game and said nothing. Years later he asked his father about his silence. "I knew you were hurting. But I didn't know what to say. So I put on the game, because that was something we'd always done together" (p. 5). This discomfort about expressing feelings seems to be transmitted from one generation of males to the next. Let us hope that the "new father" will reconsider not only issues of role and division of labor, but also the importance of expressing verbal and physical affection to his children.

Expressing affection has not traditionally been considered a masculine trait. Children of all ages report that they have better relationships with their mothers than with their fathers (Thornton, Orbuch, & Axinn, 1995). Keyes (1993) suggests that men take the initiative in talking to their fathers about their feelings. Asking about their fathers' childhoods and what their grandfathers were like as parents might present an opening. "Take the initiative. Sons are in a better position to do this than fathers. If sons don't begin talking to their dads, that conversation may never take place . . . Keep in mind that your father is a son too" (p. 5).

Fortunately, children can be made to feel cared for in a variety of ways. Many of us have heard people say, "My father didn't show me much affection, but I knew he loved me." As children get older, they probably receive fewer overt expressions of physical affection. However, people of all ages seem to find affectionate encounters meaningful and among the most satisfying life experiences.

During family meetings or informal family gatherings, parents have the opportunity to express affection and model communication and conflict-resolution skills.

help her son. In her frustration, she became a punitive parent.

"Everything a parent says and does for the child communicates an attitude toward her. Hopefully, all parental communication has at base one central message: the parent loves the child and cares about her world . . . Unfortunately, most children hear more negative than positive comments about themselves" (Wagonseller & McDowell, 1979, p. 28).

FAMILY ARGUMENTS, FAMILY MEETINGS

Verbal conflict is likely in groups such as families where there is frequent contact and intense emotional bonds (Vuchinich, 1985). Occasional conflict between family members is common, inevitable, even healthy. Vuchinich, Emery, and Cassidy (1988) videotaped 140 families at dinnertime. They observed that mothers talk more to children than fathers do and ask children more questions. When conflict arises, it is usually between siblings, unless parents are busy correcting their children's manners (or each other's). The investigators observed that fathers, frequently the more powerful parental figure, are least likely to be attacked by other family members and that mothers often play the role of peacemaker.

Family arguments usually begin when a parent's expectations are not fulfilled. Perhaps children do not perform their chores, eat their dinner, brush their teeth, or complete their schoolwork. Occasionally during verbal conflict, family members express "true feelings" that previously had been suppressed. This may "clear the air" or provoke further strong feelings. Conversely, during conflict, we may express thoughts or feelings that, while felt in the moment of anger, are not representative of our real feelings.

Verbal attacks usually elicit counterattacks, both often taking the form of "disagreements, insults, corrections and challenges. They are often characterized by negative remarks . . . shouting or exaggerated ways of speaking and gestures" (Vuchinich, 1985, p. 42). Conflicts become more heated and personal as they progress. Vuchinich found that family arguments usually end in one of four ways: (1) withdrawal (leave the room, stop talking); (2) submission (giving in); most frequently, (3) standoff (dispute ends without resolution); or preferably, (4) compromise (individual or mutual concessions).

Third-party involvement in conflicts between two family members can make things better or worse. Vuchinich, Emery, and Cassidy (1988) observed routine family arguments during dinnertime. They found that when two family members were in conflict, additional family members "butted in" about one-third of the time. When they did, "they were equally likely to attempt to end or to continue the conflict, they formed alliances about half the time, and their intervention strategies were related to the outcome of the conflict as well as its patterning" (p. 1293).

Girls were more likely than boys to intervene (particularly as peacekeepers) unless it was a marital dispute. Mothers and fathers supported each other when either intervened in an ongoing dispute. Parents rarely took sides against each other. This is fortunate given the importance of a "unified parental front" in child rearing. Fathers used authority strategies and mothers preferred a mediational approach. Reflecting their lower power status, children used distraction to end disputes. Standoffs were the most frequent outcome, compromises the least frequent. Parents should not overlook misbehavior or unsatisfactory performance just to avoid conflict. But escalating feelings, verbal attacks, sarcasm, shouting matches, threats, and instilling guilt rarely improve a bad situation.

Some parents adopt authoritarian discipline strategies during conflict. They issue commands or use coercion. They overreact when their children challenge their authority. This, in turn, provokes defiance in their children. Frequent, intense arguing and conflict "can disrupt social interaction, erode family bonds and leave painful emotional residues" (Vuchinich, 1985, p. 40).

The communication skills described in this chapter offer an alternative to shouting matches and hurt feelings. Discussion, negotiation, and problem solving are more promising methods of resolving conflict than fighting or giving in. "Parents who use direct commands or force, are more likely to have children who are openly defiant. Parents who use suggestions and explanations have children who learn to negotiate" (Kuczynski, quoted by Kutner, 1988b).

Family meetings provide an excellent forum for such discussions. At a time that is mutually convenient, parents and children get together to express their individual concerns, assign chores, resolve disputes, plan family events, and exchange information of general interest (Dinkmeyer & McKay, 1982). All family members, regardless of age, have the right to speak their mind. All points of view are respected and the leader (a rotated position) keeps family members focused on one issue at a time. Minutes are kept, as are records of negotiated agreements. During family meetings, parents have the opportunity to model the communication skills described in this chapter.

CHILDREN IN FAMILIES

Unfortunately for researchers, family life is complex and varied (Minuchin, 1988). It is not easy performing studies that isolate one factor at a time, such as family size or amount of parental education, to determine its effect on children's behavior and development. In families, many factors covary, including socioeconomic status, parental employment, the quality of marital and parent-child relationships, and genetic makeup (Rende, Slomkowski, Stocker, Fulker, & Plomin, 1992). The diversity of families precludes simple generalizations about the effects of these variables. In this section, we examine research findings on family size, birth order, only-child status, spacing of siblings, and sibling conflict.

Family Size

Study Question *In what ways might the size of a family influence the nature of relationships between family members?*

To some extent, deciding how many children to have reflects parents' own family histories. Some parents who were only children regret their lack of a sibling and choose to avoid that status for their children. There may also be constraints such as infertility, financial pressures, and dual-career issues that discourage parents from having more than one child. Families in the United States are getting smaller, with an average in the 1990s of not quite 3 children per family (U.S. Bureau of the Census, 1994).

There are potential advantages and disadvantages for both large and small families. These will be mediated by many other important family characteristics. Let's consider some differences between large (i.e., more than 4 children) and small (1 or 2 children) families. The larger a family, the greater the number of relationships. There are 3 relationships with 3 family members (mother-father, mother-child, father-child), 6 relationships with 4 family members, and 10 relationships with 5 family members. As family size increases, children participate in more relationships and have the opportunity to observe more relationships. Whether this is beneficial, of course, depends upon the quality of the interactions they participate in and observe.

In larger families, older siblings, particularly females, will spend more time caring for their younger siblings. The total amount of attention each child receives increases with family size. However, the average amount of parental attention per child decreases with each additional child (Zajonc & Markus, 1975). Depending upon the age spacing, older children may benefit from the greater amount of attention they received when they entered the initially smaller family unit. Thus, children in small families participate in and observe fewer family relationships than children in large families, but may "enjoy" more parental attention.

Research reveals that children from small families perform slightly better on intelligence and other standardized tests, get more schooling, and achieve more academically and occupationally than children from large families (Blake, 1989; Hauser & Sewell, 1985). "In larger families, child rearing becomes more rule ridden, less individualized, with corporal punishment and less investment of resources" (Wagner, Schubert, & Schubert, 1985, p. 65). A balanced view recognizes several advantages and disadvantages for children in both types of family configurations.

Birth Order

The relationship between birth order and personality has been hotly debated for most of this century, fueled mainly by the intriguing writings of Alfred Adler (1928). Adler described the distinct socialization processes associated with each birth position. Firstborns have the most privileged position, because parental attention does not have to be shared, at least initially. The special attention parents bestow on their firstborns is evidenced by the "diminishing snapshot effect." Parents accumulate hundreds of photographs of firstborns, dozens of secondborns, and about twelve each of laterborns.

The major hazard confronting the firstborn, according to Adler, is "dethronement," or the loss of privilege and the sharing of parental attention with the arrival of a younger sibling. This can engender hostility and resentment toward the parents, who are perceived as favoring the newborn. Adler allowed that if parents handle the birth of a new sibling sensitively, the firstborn will probably adjust well and become caring and protective of the baby. Research supports Adler's conjecture (Teti, Sakin, Kucera, Corns, & Eiden, 1996).

Firstborns have been depicted as high achievers, leaders, verbally aggressive, obedient, responsible, and more self-confident than their younger siblings. Children in the middleborn position were characterized by Adler as ambitious, rebellious, and envious, but better adjusted than the older or younger sibling. The lower self-esteem often associated with middleborn children was attributed to this birth position being the "least special." Though Adler characterized the youngest child as spoiled, the contemporary depiction of the lastborn child is likable, sociable, cuddly, friendly, popular, disobedient, physically aggressive, and having low self-esteem.

Is there any truth to these generalizations? Is Adler's basic premise correct, that the different birth positions are associated with different socialization patterns? Firstborns (and children without siblings, who are similar to firstborns in some ways) are overrepresented in high achieving groups, such as those listed in *Who's Who*, presidents of the United States, astronauts, and in the graduate school population (Goleman, 1985b). Parents probably do have higher expectations and set higher standards for their older children. As a result, firstborns also receive more criticism.

Laterborns almost certainly receive less parental attention and have to cope with occupying the least powerful position in the family (Hart & Risley, 1992). "The status tactics, bossiness, and dominance of firstborns are typical of the powerful members of any social system—those who are larger and have greater ability; the appeals of laterborn children to their parents for support are typical of the weak members of social groups and are encouraged by the greater indulgence and comfort offered to laterborn children by their parents" (Dunn, 1985, p. 71).

Steelman and Powell (1985), in a relatively well-controlled study of birth order, analyzed data from two nationally representative samples of U.S. children and found no correlation between birth order and academic achievement. They did report a significant relationship between birth order and social success (favoring laterborns), defined by "such social skills as outgoingness, getting along with others, popularity, and ease in making friends . . ." (p. 117). Birth order predicted leadership skills for males (favoring laterborns, not firstborns!), but not for females. Research suggests that the influence of birth order on development probably is exaggerated, at least when compared to other parent-child, sibling, and family-related characteristics (Hart & Risley, 1992).

Single-Child Families

About 22 percent of U.S. families with children under the age of 18 years have one child. The situation of so-called only children resembles that of firstborns except for the experience of dethronement. Only children resemble lastborns in that they will never get the opportunity to help (or torment) younger siblings. As onlyborns, they are automatically special and may be raised more permissively than children with siblings. Falbo and Polit (1986) confirm that only children are very similar to firstborns. Both groups are very susceptible to adult influence. They are as popular, and as adults are as happy and satisfied as peers with siblings.

Importantly, they are born into an adult intellectual environment that will not be "diluted" by the presence of younger siblings. Therefore, it is not surprising that, compared to children with siblings, only children score higher on intelligence tests, show more developed abstract reasoning and problem-solving skills, and have higher academic aspirations. They also get about 3 years more schooling and achieve higher occupational prestige and higher income than children with siblings (Blake, 1989; Falbo, 1984; Falbo & Polit, 1986).

Compared to children with siblings, only children are stereotyped as being more lonely, selfish, spoiled, and maladjusted. Baskett (1985) found that adults expect children without siblings to be more academically oriented and higher achievers. They also stereotype them as self-centered and not very likeable. Despite negative stereotypes directed toward this family configuration, the single-child family is becoming more common and more acceptable (Collins, 1984b). Some parents decide to have a second child to avoid "stigmatizing" their firstborn (Kutner, 1988q).

It is clear that negative stereotypes associated with only children (and their parents) are false. Rosenberg and Hyde (1993) note that only children do not comprise a homoge-

Justin Jaffe

neous category. These investigators distinguish three types of only children: normal, well-adjusted children; impulsive, acting out children; and those they refer to as "firstbornish" in that they resemble the stereotypes cited above. In terms of intellectual and social development only-child status is, if anything, an advantage. This is due mainly to the special relationship only children have with their only parents.

Sibling Status Effects

What is the optimal spacing between children's births? Most children are born within 2 or 3 years of a sibling's birth (Dunn, 1995). Research suggests that this is the least optimal spacing pattern, although family planning should not be overly influenced by this

finding. Working mothers, for example, might not want to prolong their child-rearing years by spacing children several years apart.

There do seem to be benefits in spacing intervals of either less than 2 years or more than 5 years (Dunn, 1995). Short intervals between births minimize the dethronement factor because infants cannot really appreciate the possible threat of a new sibling to their special position. Resentment and rivalrous feelings are more likely after 2 years of age when a child might miss the undivided parental attention to which she has become accustomed. Five- and six-year-olds usually are sufficiently self-reliant to cope with or avoid these feelings (Dunn, 1995) (see Box 7-1).

Another advantage of longer spacing intervals (more than 4 years) is that parents will treat a newborn as specially as they treated

B o x 7 - 1

And Baby Makes Four

In Chapter 2, we considered the transition to parenthood. Raising two children is different from raising one, so let's consider briefly the transition from a one-child to two-child family. Although most parents expecting a second child can look forward to an easier pregnancy and faster delivery, parents are concerned about how the firstborn will react to Mom's pregnancy and the entry of a new member into the family system.

There is much that parents can do to prepare the firstborn for the arrival of a sibling. Although the presentation should reflect the firstborn's age and understanding, psychologist Judy Dunn (1995) suggests that parents explain to the child that the family is going to have a new baby and that the child's baby sister or brother is growing inside Mom, from a very tiny egg. After answering any questions, the parents can explain that when the baby is big enough, the parents will go to a hospital where the baby will be born. Parents can also describe what the child can expect to happen when he or she visits the hospital to meet the baby.

Dunn suggests keeping answers short and truthful. Some children will be more interested in these events than others, but for those who are, there are many appropriate books in the library for parents to read with children about birth and having siblings. It is important to reassure children that both parents have enough love for both children (or more, if twins show up). Once the baby is born, parents should provide the older child with extra attention, but not overindulge the child or tolerate manipulative behavior (Dunn, 1995).

the firstborn. Middleborns, too, seem to feel more special when there are longer intervals between them and their siblings. "A spacing of about five years is apparently optimal. It frees the parent from having to meet the demands and pressures of two children close together in age, thus allowing parents and children more time in one-to-one interactions for a more supportive and relaxed relationship," (Kidwell, quoted by Goleman, 1985b). Parents who finance their children's college education will experience less crunch when there is only one child in college at a time.

There is a trend toward greater spacing between siblings, partly due to the increasing rate of remarriage following divorce. Fertility problems also contribute to longer spacing intervals. A disadvantage of very long spacing is that the siblings may have few if any interests in common. For parents, this is almost like having two only children. It is not likely that spacing influences children's personalities. It is a weak factor compared to other family variables. Spacing apparently interacts with other factors, including birth order, family size, and parental beliefs about sibling status (Musun-Miller, 1993). The quality of the individual parent-child relationship is more powerful than these other factors, even in combination.

SIBLINGS

"Though they clearly love each other, my children are constantly bickering. The younger provokes the older, the older overreacts, the younger one comes crying to me. The older one loves teasing his little brother. In fact, they seem to enjoy tormenting each other. Usually, the little one gets hurt. When I try to figure out what happened, I always hear the same thing from both, 'He started it.' When they are fighting and I get angry, I usually make things worse" (Father of two sons).

Adults choose their partners and together decide whether or not to have children. Children do not choose their parents ("I didn't ask to be born") or their siblings ("Can't we take her back to the hospital?"). Ironically, the involuntary sibling relationship, experienced by 80 percent of all children, is probably the most enduring in life. As the father quoted above makes clear, siblings expose each other to an incessant stream of positive and negative stimulation which, in the long run, will sharpen their social skills and expand their coping resources.

Young siblings, particularly those spaced closely in age, spend more time with each other than they do with anyone else including their parents. This often encourages a closeness, even intimacy, not often found in other types of relationships. Given the frequency of daily sibling interactions, it would be naive to wonder whether siblings influence each other.

There are few easy generalizations to be made about *how* siblings influence each other—every sibling relationship is unique. Age, spacing, birth order, gender of each sibling, type of sibling relationship (biological, adopted, step-sibling), temperamental and personality differences, the emotional climate of the family, parent-child relationships, the marital relationship, and heredity all play some role in how siblings relate (Boer & Dunn, 1992; Dunn, 1985, 1988, 1993, 1995; Dunn & McGuire, 1992; Rende, Slomkowski, Stocker, Fulker, & Plomin, 1992; Stocker, Dunn, & Plomin, 1989). Because siblings spend so much time together during childhood, they develop a unique understanding of each other. They become better able to predict what will please and what will annoy. Gradually, they learn to adjust their behavior accordingly.

Children learn all kinds of neat stuff from their older siblings by watching them, listening to them, and by asking them questions (Azmitia & Hesser, 1993; Dunn, 1983). The sibling relationship also serves as a stress buffer for children who live in households with marital strife (Jenkins, Smith, & Graham, 1989).

Siblings are good for each other. They encourage strong feelings and give children the opportunity to learn to cope with such feelings. Siblings provide each other with countless opportunities to practice relationship skills such as sharing, comforting, cooperating, and helping (Dunn, 1983, 1995). Children's adjustment during middle childhood and early adolescence is partly related to the quality of the sibling relationship (Dunn, Slomkowski, Beardsall, & Rende, 1994).

The birth of a sibling, with the accompanying reduction of parental attention, was considered by Freud to be threatening to a child. However, studies reveal three possible outcomes: distress and misbehavior, no change, or improvements in behavior. Some children temporarily become upset by the "intruder," particularly when parental attention is less available. Most children display considerable interest in and caring for the newborn.

Sibling Ambivalence/Conflict

Study Question *What are the roots of "sibling ambivalence"?*

The term "sibling rivalry" is too one-sided. **Sibling ambivalence** is a more appropriate characterization of an older child's mixed feelings about the birth (and existence) of a brother or sister (Newman, 1994). When overt hostility occurs, it can be directed toward the mother or the infant. When a mother is preoccupied with her infant, the older sibling is likely to display such "naughty" behaviors as crying, clinging, throwing things, and other attention-getting behaviors. More disturbing changes, such as difficulties involving sleep, toileting, and aggression toward the mother, usually disappear by about 8 months after the

birth. The development of intense fears and the tendency to withdraw may persist much longer, and are indicative of a more serious problem (Dunn, 1985; 1995).

Stewart, Mobley, Van Tuyl, and Salvador (1987) interviewed 41 middle-class families at five intervals, from one month preceding birth to 12 months following birth. They found "more problems with toilet habits, demands for bottles, clinginess and other anxiety displays, and increased confrontations and aggression" following the birth of a sibling. Such "regressive" acts may be imitative of the infants' behavior or reflections of increased anxiety in general. One month following birth, children's reactions to the new sibling were either imitations of the infant or confrontations with either the mother or the infant. At 4 months after birth, there were more anxiety reactions but fewer imitations or confrontations.

Same-sexed siblings had more problems than opposite-sexed siblings, partly due to competition for gender-related reinforcers. Mothers spent much less time with the firstborn child after birth, but fathers' interactions remained stable over time. Fathers also became more involved in child-care activities (Stewart et al., 1987). Decreased maternal attention and sensitivity to the older child's interests following the birth of a sibling were also reported by Dunn and Kendrick (1980).

Poor adjustment to the birth of a new sibling can be minimized by providing extra (but not excessive) attention to the older child. Fathers can increase their involvement with the older sibling; parents can emphasize how much the infant will enjoy his older sister or brother and give the older sibling "grown-up" responsibilities in caring for and feeding the infant.

By bringing the older sibling into transactions with the infant ("Look, he's smiling at you, he really likes it when you help me dress him"), parents can cultivate feelings of friendliness, affection, and pride (Dunn, 1995; Dunn & McGuire, 1992; Howe & Ross, 1990).

Sibling relationships often are stereotyped as conflict-ridden. There is more than a grain of truth to this generalization, especially when siblings have contrasting temperaments (Dunn, 1995). If the older sibling is more easy-going, her temperament may buffer interactions with a temperamental younger sibling. When the older sibling has the more difficult temperament, there will be more bickering. Parents complain that managing conflict between siblings is a major family problem; it is one of the most common family problems leading parents to seek professional help. Virtually all sibling relationships are characterized by conflict and caring. The balance between these two varies widely from family to family (Dunn, 1993). Despite parent's complaints about perpetual sibling conflict, peaceful coexistence with occasional rivalry is the norm in most families (Newman, 1994).

Parents and Sibling Conflict

Parents play an important role in how their children treat each other. Not surprisingly, children's treatment of their siblings partly depends on how their parents treat them and each other (Brody, Stoneman, & McCoy, 1994; Volling & Belsky, 1992). Family cohesion and positive parent-child relationships contribute to the development of prosocial behavior in children. On the other hand, mothers and fathers who are overly controlling often have children who are nasty and obnoxious to each other (Brody, Stoneman, & McCoy, 1992, 1994; Dunn, 1993; Dunn & Kendrick, 1980; Dunn & Plomin, 1990; Dunn, Slomkowski, Beardsall, & Rende, 1994; Volling & Belsky, 1992).

Parents often intercede prematurely when their children are fighting, partly because sibling conflict is so noisy (Brody & Stoneman, 1987; Dreikurs, 1964). Hasty intervention weakens siblings' incentive to work things out for themselves. Obviously, if a child is in danger or cannot cope with a sibling's verbal or physical attack, swift intervention is appropriate. For most conflicts, however, children benefit from the opportunity to sharpen their social (and coping) skills. Tattling on a sibling provides a good example. Children tattle when they want to get a sibling (or playmate) in trouble. Although it is appropriate for children to confer with an adult when certain rules have been violated or when someone is in danger, tattling reflects a child's inability to resolve conflict. Tattling usually is not an adaptive response to sibling conflict. Parents should help their children understand what tattling is, why it is undesirable, and teach other more effective ways of handling interpersonal strife.

Ross and her colleagues observed parental interventions in sibling conflicts for 40 Canadian families with 2- and 4-year-olds (Ross, Filyer, Lollis, Perlman, & Martin, 1994). There was an equal number of all possible brother and sister combinations in the sample. How parents reacted to sibling conflict depended on the content and quality of children's disputes. In this study, parents did not display a bias in favor of younger siblings. Parents supported younger siblings more frequently, but only because younger siblings' rights were violated more frequently than the reverse. Parents supported children not according to age, but according to whether a child's rights had been violated. Older children were more likely to tattle and parents frequently solicited tattling rather than punishing it. When children settled disputes on their own, they were not very likely to apply the rules that their parents would have imposed to resolve the conflict. Under these circumstances, older siblings took advantage of their younger siblings. Thus, parental intervention makes it more likely that justice will be served, but reduces children's motivation to work things out themselves.

When parents decide that intervention is necessary, it makes sense to acknowledge the conflict, halt the hostilities, and when calmness is restored, review the events impartially. Remember, both siblings believe that they are in the right and the parent usually does not know what really happened. If there clearly is an aggressor, the aggressive child can be helped to empathize with his or her sibling ("How do you think she felt when you grabbed her crayon?"). Sibling disputes are likely to center around possessions. Parents can anticipate and possibly minimize unrest by establishing rules regarding possessions. They should encourage such prosocial behaviors as sharing and requesting objects rather than taking them. Such skills develop quite gradually over childhood and adolescence.

The mere occurrence of conflict should not discourage parents. In fact, Kramer and Baron (1995) report that sibling hostility does not bother parents as much as the *absence of warmth* between siblings. In any case, conflict between siblings is normal, even beneficial (Dunn, 1995). It gives children the opportunity to learn how to express and cope with intense feelings such as anger. They also learn how to negotiate and compromise, in other words, how to resolve differences. It is not the occurrence of conflict between siblings that determines the interpersonal competencies that children eventually achieve. Rather, children's conflict resolution skills reflect how parents manage the conflict, including strategic nonintervention and the modeling of empathy and concern (Ross et al., 1994).

Differential Treatment and Perceived Favoritism

"Most of the time, I try not to show favoritism. But there have been times when one will say, 'Oh look what she did and she got away with it.' I can't treat them the same all the time" (mother of three).

Children pay close attention to how their parents treat their siblings (Dunn & Munn, 1985). True or not, most children come to believe that their parents have a favorite child (Zervas & Sherman, 1994). Perceived parental favoritism can affect the sibling relationship even more than actual parent-child interactions (Brody, Stoneman, & Burke, 1987; Brody, Stoneman, & McCoy, 1992).

Older children do not necessarily resent differential treatment as much as they resent perceived favoritism (McHale & Pawletko, 1992). Older children reluctantly accept the developmental fact of life that parents provide more attention and care to younger, sick, or disabled siblings (Quittner & Opipari, 1994). However, some forget that when they were the same age as a younger sibling, they also received "preferential treatment."

Understandably, adults (parents and nonparents) have higher expectations for older than for younger children ("You should know better, you're older") (Baskett, 1985). Parents should be wary of automatically holding the older sibling responsible for sibling conflict. Older children who feel mistreated may take out their resentment on a younger sibling rather than expressing it directly to the parents.

Strategic nonintervention dictates that parents avoid premature involvement during conflicts when possible, particularly if they find themselves always siding with one child (Dunn & Plomin, 1990). Parents also should discourage sibling competition by treating each child as an individual, not fostering resentment through comparison, and mostly by modeling appropriate ways of getting along and resolving conflict (Faber & Mazlish, 1987; Volling & Belsky, 1992). "Talking to each child about the other, explaining feelings and actions, emphasizing in a consistent way the importance of not hurting the other—all these appear to be linked to the development of a more harmonious relationship" (Dunn, 1985, p. 167).

Harsh treatment of an older sibling during parental intercession may increase sibling rivalries. This is particularly true if the older sibling perceives the younger sibling as receiving preferential treatment ("You always take her side"). Believing that their parents have favorites takes its toll on children's self-esteem (Zervas & Sherman, 1994). Self-esteem sometimes is enhanced when children believe that their mother or father favors them. On the other hand, children feel guilty, embarrassed, or unworthy of their special treatment, especially if the preferential treatment is blatant.

Harris and Howard (1985) questioned adolescents from intact families with at least one sibling about perceived parental favoritism. About half the subjects, girls more often than boys, reported that one or both parents demonstrated favoritism. The teenagers perceived the youngest child in the family as being the favorite of the mother, and perceived the middle child as being least likely to be a parental favorite. "Subjects who perceived a sibling as being favored evidenced increased anger and depressive feelings as well as identity confusion. This latter effect was most pronounced when a parent of the same sex favored a sibling of the same sex as the subject" (p. 45).

Treating children as individuals is good parenting. Children of varied ages, temperaments, and abilities have diverse needs that require different parental responses. The point is that we assume that sharing the same parents would make siblings more similar. In fact, differential parental treatment increases the somewhat different dispositions that already exist among siblings (Dunn & Plomin, 1990). (See Spotlight: Nonshared Family Environments.)

The sibling relationship is another important source of differential experience, especially when sibling temperaments clash. During their childhood, one of my sons had an easy brother and one had a "temperamental" brother. One had a younger brother, the other had an older brother, and so on. As a result, their reactions to and perceptions of the relationship are quite different (Dunn & Plomin, 1991).

The number of diverse "mini-environments" that siblings inhabit is extremely large, in and outside of the family. They have different friends, different teachers, and watch different TV programs. They also are likely to differ regarding accidents and illnesses. Thus, it is misguided to assume that children, simply because they belong to the same family, have similar life experiences (Plomin, 1989).

TABLE 7.3 *Handling Sibling Conflict*

Avoid premature intervention

Avoid automatically blaming older sibling

Encourage siblings to work out problems on their own (and reinforce this behavior when it occurs)

If necessary, use the natural consequence of separating siblings when they are too noisy or aggressive

Discourage tattling behavior

After dispute, review events to encourage empathy

Talk to each child about the other, explaining feelings and actions

Avoid comparing one sibling to another as this engenders resentment

PARENTS AND FRIENDS

Study Question   *How can parents help their children maintain close friendships?*

Nonshared Family Environments

Study Question   Why do siblings, who share half of their genes and who seem to share common family experiences, usually turn out so different from each other?

Parents who have only one child might assume that all children are more or less like theirs. Having a second child cures them of this misconception (Dunn, 1995). Second children often are described by parents as the "complete opposite" of the first. Children in the same family are only slightly more alike in personality than are children from different families! Knowing one child in a family tells you almost nothing about what the other children in the family are like. A study of brothers attending the same school revealed that their personalities were hardly more similar to each other than they were to boys whose backgrounds were completely different (Scarr & Grajek, 1982).

"This low sibling resemblance is unsettling when one reflects that, on the average, siblings share 50 percent of the same genes, they are part of the same family, they are brought up by the same parents, and they grow up in the same community environments" (Daniels, 1986, p. 339). The slight similarities that we do observe in sibling personality appear to be due to their shared genes, not to their common experiences. The differences in sibling personalities, however, which are far greater than the similarities, mainly seem to reflect aspects of the environment that are not shared (Anderson, Hetherington, & Howe, 1994; Dunn & Plomin, 1990, 1991; Loehlin, 1992; Loehlin, Willerman, & Horn, 1987; Rowe & Plomin, 1981).

What do we mean by **nonshared family influences**? Family, adoption, and twin studies indicate that children in the same family experience "subtle disparities" in their home and community environments that make them increasingly different from each other (Dunn & Plomin, 1990; Goleman, 1987b; Rowe & Plomin, 1981). This is not to say that siblings are exposed to entirely different family experiences or that they are complete opposites of each other (Anderson, et al., 1994). They do share many features of their environment, including parents, relatives, school system, diet, neighborhood, housing, and vacations. Surprisingly, these common experiences do not make them more alike (McGuire, Neiderhiser, Reiss, Hetherington, & Plomin, 1994). "Environmental factors make siblings in a family different from, not similar to, one another" (Daniels, Dunn, Furstenberg, & Plomin, 1985, p. 764).

One reason for this is that common experiences are not necessarily shared experiences (Plomin, Reiss, Hetherington, & Howe, 1994; Wachs, 1996). Siblings have the same parents, but this does not mean that their parents treat them alike (Anderson, Hetherington, & Howe, 1994; Conger & Conger, 1994). Parents usually feel closer to, spend more time with, or talk more to one child than to another. They may be more lenient with a younger child and more strict with the older. Daughters may be treated differently than sons. Children are more sensitive to differential parental treatment than parents are. At least half of all siblings report differential parental treatment. Mothers who have been interviewed on this topic agree with them (Dunn & Plomin, 1990, 1991).

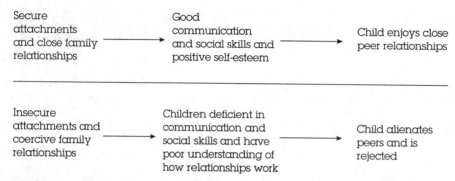

Figure 7.2 Children recreate in friendships the relationship patterns that they observe and practice at home

Psychologists and parents alike are interested in the topic of children's friendships. Psychologists' interest partly reflects the fact that children use their friends as cognitive and social resources on a daily basis (Hartup, 1996). Social isolation and peer rejection are associated with psychological and behavioral problems during childhood and adolescence (Asher & Coie, 1989; Dunn & McGuire, 1992; Parker & Asher, 1987; Sameroff & Emde, 1989; Smith, Bowers, Binney, & Cowie, 1993).

Having close friends and feeling accepted by a peer group are crucial ingredients of a healthy childhood. Like sibling relationships, close friendships provide children with countless opportunities to learn coping, interpersonal, conflict resolution skills and moral values. Laughing, sticking up for each other, walking to school together, sharing secrets, and providing companionship cement close relationships during childhood (Furman, 1982).

Gaining the acceptance of one's peers requires a variety of social skills. Friendly children with a sense of humor are likely to be more popular and have better relationships than shy or anxious children. Their relationship successes, in turn, boost their self-esteem and encourage further socializing (Dodge, 1983; Hartup, 1989, 1996; Ladd, 1990).

Parents want their children to be popular. They are tempted to manage their children's friendships, probably a good idea when children are very young. They do so by designing social environments for their children, arranging play opportunities with specific children, regulating and overseeing children's ongoing interactions with peers, and consulting with children about their peer relationships (Ladd, Le Sieur, & Profilet, 1993). Parents differ considerably regarding how involved they are in each of these facilitator roles and in how they go about teaching their children how to have satisfying relationships (Pettit & Mize, 1993).

Parents are concerned when they notice that their children have difficulty making friends, keeping friends, or just getting along with other children. Monitoring their children's interactions is an important source of information for parents. Bullying, selfish and antagonistic behaviors, and calling attention to themselves are signs of children's social immaturity. These behaviors usually alienate other children (Newcomb, Bukowski, & Pattee, 1993). Well-behaved and cooperative children are preferred as playmates by their peers. Children who lack good communication skills and who are disliked by peers usually act in ways that perpetuate their low status in a peer group (Black & Hazen, 1990). Children with serious social skill deficits benefit from social skill coaching by professionals (Mize & Ladd, 1990).

Although there is nothing wrong with being popular, having one or two close friends is usually a better predictor of adjustment than children's popularity (Hartup, 1996). Some children are satisfied spending time by themselves much of the time. As long as they seem content this should not in itself be a cause of parental concern. Parents should also be aware that most shy children become less shy over time. Arranging for them to participate in supervised activities with other children provides opportunities to learn and practice group and interpersonal skills (Bierman & Furman, 1984).

Close relationships outside of the family are influenced by children's attachment to their family members, the nature of relationships within the family, and by what parents teach children about social relationships (Baumrind, 1975; Dunn, 1993; Dunn & McGuire, 1992; Hart, DeWolf, Wozniak, & Burts, 1992; Hartup, 1986; Kerns, Klepac, & Cole, 1996; Kochanska, 1992; Kuczynski & Kochanska, 1990; Miller, 1993; Pettit & Mize, 1993; Sroufe & Fleeson, 1986; Strassberg, Dodge, Bates, & Pettit, 1992).

How mothers speak to their children appears to be a particularly important determinant of how children speak to their peers (Putallaz, 1987). For example, mothers who use coercive, punitive speech commonly have children who display similar behaviors. The risk is that these children will be rejected by their peers. Children of power-assertive parents often resort to hostile and disruptive actions, such as arguing during play (Hart et al., 1992). Brown, Mounts, Lamborn, and Steinberg (1993) report that "prosocial" parenting practices foster adolescents' prosocial peer relationships and that punitive parenting practices encourage children's involvement in deviant peer groups and deviant activities.

Youngblade and Belsky (1992) performed a longitudinal study of 73 families to see whether parent-child relationships measured when children were 1 and 3 years old were linked to the children's close friendships when they were 5 years old. Their most important finding was that children who share a warm, sensitive bond with their mothers and fathers are more likely to have positive friendships. Negative family relationships predicted more negative friendships. Thus, children apparently recreate in friendships the relationship patterns they practice with their parents (Strassberg et al., 1992).

How do they do this? It is likely that children develop expectations about "how relationships work" by participating in and observing family relationships and their parents' peer relationships (Miller, 1993; Sroufe & Fleeson, 1986). It is also likely that children acquire social and conflict resolution skills at home that they are able to generalize to non-family relationships (Kochanska, 1992).

Parents should not overreact when a child argues with friends. As with sibling conflict, arguments with friends provide opportunities for learning how to cope and how to resolve conflicts. Parents also should avoid premature interventions. Rather, they can acknowledge their children's strong feelings and ask helpful questions that will guide the child's efforts toward successful conflict resolution ("Why did she call you that name?" "How did it make you feel," "How can you make it better?"). Encouraging their child to see the other child's point of view also helps ("Was she angry when she said that?"). Fortunately, children usually do not hold grudges for long and the conflict may well be forgotten by the next day (Kutner, 1992b).

SUMMARY

1. The parenting goals cited in Chapter 1 are supported by skillful parental communication. Parents have difficulty communicating when they are upset, angry, or frustrated. Too many children receive more than their share of criticism, which erodes their self-esteem. Given children's emotional vulnerability and budding coping resources, it is important that parents adopt a supportive stance in communication and discipline.

2. To improve their communication skills, parents can tone down their lecturing, nagging, reminding, criticizing, demanding, and sarcasm. Good communication begins with careful attention to the child's verbal and nonverbal signals. Alert parents notice nonverbal cues that indicate that a child is upset. They inquire about and help clarify the child's feelings. Communication improves when parents listen sympathetically for the actual, often hidden meanings of children's behavior. When parents acknowledge and repeat the key feelings being expressed, children feel cared for and understood.

3. Descriptive praise and constructive feedback help parents to avoid the "criticism trap." Rather than solving children's problems by giving advice or telling them what to do (the "quick fix"), parents can help their children explore alternative solutions.

4. I messages allow parents to express their frustrations, annoyances, and disappointments in a constructive way. They give information about what the child did, how the parent feels about it, and why the parent feels that way. This form of expression is much more helpful than mere criticism or venting.

5. Occasional conflict between family members is common and, when handled properly, healthy. Since conflict between family members is inevitable, parents should model proper ways of disagreeing and resolving disputes sensitively. Punitive parents overreact when their children are defiant and risk modeling the very behaviors they criticize.

6. Children in large families benefit from the larger number of relationships they observe and participate in. Children in small families benefit from the greater amount of parental attention. Compared to other family variables, birth order and spacing between births have a minor influence on development.

7. The sibling relationship is distinctive in its complexity, intensity, and its duration. It encourages a closeness not often found in other types of relationships. The term "sibling rivalry" highlights only one part of sibling relationships. Sibling ambivalence is a more appropriate way of characterizing the "love-hate" pattern that both impresses and depresses parents.

8. Sibling conflict is normal and helpful to children's development of coping and conflict-resolution skills. Strategic nonintervention by parents allows children the opportunity to improve their social competence.

9. Children are very sensitive to differential parental treatment in affection, interest, and discipline, often interpreting it as favoritism. When children interpret their parent's interventions as being one-sided, the frequency of sibling conflict increases, particularly in distressed families. Children's judgments of favoritism (whether justifiable or not) have a significant impact on the sibling relationship and on children's self-esteem.

10. Friendships in childhood and adolescence are developmentally important. Much of what children learn about relationships at home will guide their efforts to form and maintain friendships with peers. Parents should be aware of who their children's friends are and the quality of the friendships they participate in.

GLOSSARY

attachment   The strong feelings that bind children to their caregivers and the behaviors that accompany these feelings

attachment theory   The premise that children's attachment to their parents reflects the quality of caregiving. A corollary of attachment theory is that the quality of attachment affects children's ability to form relationships with non-family members

brainstorming   Trying to come up with as many solutions to a problem as possible without judging or evaluating any particular solution

descriptive praise   Praise that specifies exactly what a child did that a parent appreciates

family meetings   Regularly scheduled meetings run in a democratic fashion during which family members discuss family issues, problems, and possible solutions

I messages   A communication that begins with the word "I" and that specifies how a parent feels about something specific that a child did

nonshared family influences   The observation that siblings have quite different family experiences that result in their becoming increasingly different from each other

sibling ambivalence   The combination of positive and negative feelings that siblings express toward each other

sympathetic (active) listening   Asking children good questions and listening carefully to hear the meaning behind what they say

THOUGHT QUESTIONS

1. What is the relationship between the quality of caregiving and children's feelings of security or insecurity?

2. Why is listening *the* crucial parental skill in parent-child communication?

3. How can parents encourage their children to be more emotionally expressive?

4. What effect might parental criticism have on children's ability to think for themselves?

5. How do some parents inadvertently encourage a "love-hate" relationship between siblings?

6. What do children learn about friendship from their family relationships?

8
CHAPTER

SELF-CONCEPT, SELF-ESTEEM, AND GENDER IDENTITY

OBJECTIVES 236
Mark #12 236
SELF-CONCEPT 237
Spotlight: Biracial Children's Self-Concept 238
SELF-ESTEEM 239
Box 8-1 The "Dark Side" of Self-Esteem 241
Erikson's Point of View 242
The Coopersmith Study 242
Carl Rogers's Point of View 244
    Unconditional Acceptance and Positive Regard 244
    Self-Esteem 245
    Feelings 245
    Evaluation 245
    Bandura's Model of Self-Efficacy 246
Spotlight: The Development of Empathy and Altruism 247
    Mark #13 247
    Empathy and Altruism 247
    Promoting Empathy and Altruism in Children 248
SEX DIFFERENCES AND PARENTING: "IS IT A BOY OR IS IT A GIRL?" 248
Parenting Sons and Daughters 250
Gender Identity and Gender Typing 254
Learning Models 255
Kohlberg's Cognitive-Developmental Model 256
Bandura's Social-Cognitive Model 256
Cross-Gender Behavior 257
Androgyny 257

Sexual Orientation 258
Spotlight: Children's Household Work 258
Promoting Cooperation in Household Work 259
SUMMARY 260
GLOSSARY 261
THOUGHT QUESTIONS 262

OBJECTIVES

After studying Chapter 8, students should be able to:

1. Describe how parents influence the development of children's self-concept
2. Describe how parents of biracial children can encourage pride in their ethnic heritage
3. Summarize the key findings of Coopersmith's study of self-esteem in preadolescent boys
4. Compare the following theorists' models of the development of self-esteem:
   a. Erikson
   b. Coopersmith
   c. Rogers
   d. Bandura
5. Describe Bandura's distinction between self-efficacy and self-esteem
6. Describe how self-efficacy is related to the following:
   a. The initiation of behavior
   b. The generalization of behavior to new situations
   c. Persistence
   d. Choice
   e. Emotional reactions
7. Discuss how parents can encourage the development of empathic and altruistic behavior in their children
8. Summarize the research findings concerning gender differences in children

9. Describe some of the ways parents might raise their daughters differently than their sons
10. Describe the development of sexual identity in young children, according to:
    a. Maccoby and Jacklin
    b. Kohlberg
    c. Bandura
11. Describe the issues concerning children's performance of household chores

Mark #12

"In the past, when Mark wanted to attempt something I thought he couldn't handle or possibly master, I'd tell him outright. Voicing my doubts and lack of confidence in him now seems inappropriate. Our parenting class has made me realize that I have encouraged my child to display inadequacy and end up self-critical, suffering from a lack of self-worth. Rather, I should practice encouraging him to approach situations more realistically. Ideally, he will look at them as challenges and be willing to 'take risks,' knowing he doesn't have to be perfect."

It would probably never occur to a young child to evaluate herself, to ask, "How am I doing with these blocks?" or even, "What am I doing with these blocks?" Young children have little reason to evaluate themselves or their own behavior. Rather, they accumulate a variety of evaluations and judgments from others: "What a good girl you are"; "What's wrong with you?"; "You are being so helpful today"; "You wimp." Self-evaluation probably begins when parents express conditional contingencies such as, "If you are good, then we can go to the toy store." A child might then monitor her own behavior, "Am I being good?"

Most preschool children receive enough positive feedback to balance the negative reactions that they may occasionally encounter (Stipek & Mac Iver, 1989). Some disapproval—for example from older siblings—is inevitable, and, of course, children must learn to cope with occasional negative feedback. However, some children, perhaps those who are less competent or who are poorly behaved, become overwhelmed by the harsh, persistent criticism that they receive in their daily encounters (Kernis, Cornell, Sun, Berry, & Harlow, 1993). These children may come to believe, "I can't do anything right."

Children whose behavior is overly criticized may place undue emphasis on their performance to the point of obsessive worry and anxiety. Many parents, like Mark's mother, eventually realize the impact that their criticisms are having on their children's self-esteem and become more encouraging. Underestimating children's ability to solve their own problems undermines their self-confidence and their willingness to take responsibility for their actions.

Parenting goal #4, self-esteem and self-confidence, emphasizes the role that socialization plays in the development of these desirable traits. What children come to *believe* about themselves will influence how they *feel* about themselves. Both depend heavily upon the feedback that they get from others. Generally lacking in self-evaluation skills and standards, young children see themselves through their parents' and teachers' eyes. Older children may compare their achievements to those of their peers and evaluate their own behavior according to standards that they have learned from their caregivers, teachers, and peers (Stipek & Mac Iver, 1989). Adolescents evaluate themselves more independently of adults' evaluations (Isberg et al., 1989), but still have internalized the standards of behavior learned at home and at school.

This chapter explores how parenting practices influence children's self-concept and self-esteem. An important part of one's self-concept is one's **gender identity**, that is, identifying oneself as male or female. We will consider, therefore, how parents treat their sons and daughters differently and how such differential treatment might influence children's gender identity and gender-role development.

SELF-CONCEPT

Among the most significant tasks of infancy are the formation of a concept of self and a corresponding concept of nonself, or others. There is "me" and there is "everyone else." Bandura (1986) defines **self-concept** as a "composite view of oneself that is formed through direct experience and evaluations adopted from significant others" (p. 409).

Newborns and very young infants probably experience the world as a stream of sensory impressions. By the middle of the first year, if not earlier, they have come to realize that they exist independently of the objects and people with which they interact. Speech and other social encounters during the second year broaden their awareness of self.

There are several indications during the latter part of the second year of life that infants have a self-concept. They can recognize themselves in a mirror (18–20 months), make self-descriptive sentences about age and gender (19–24 months), emit "mastery" smiles when they accomplish something (by 2 years), and recognize themselves in pictures (by 2 years) (Smolak, 1986).

Children use the word "my" to indicate possession ("my blanket") by the age of 3 or 4 years. School-age children are better able to see themselves as others see them. Their self-concepts incorporate the feedback they get from others. They also learn what attributes are valued by others (e.g., appearance, possessions, abilities) and assess themselves accordingly (see Spotlight: Biracial Children's Self-Concept).

Theorists disagree about the relative importance of social interaction and cognitive changes in the development of self-concept. Both appear to be crucial. Theorists do agree that the mother (or primary caregiver) plays a key role in shaping a child's self-concept. "It is surely clear that the mother's view of the infant will affect the way she treats the infant, which in turn will affect the way the infant views itself, its mother, and the other inhabitants of its social world" (T.B.R. Bower, 1982, p. 278).

Spotlight

Biracial Children's Self-Concept

An important component of the self-concept of minority children is their ethnic and racial identity (Tizard & Phoenix, 1995). It is not so much belonging to a minority group that introduces conflict into children's self-concept as it is the social message that equates being different with being not as good. Ambivalence about one's personal qualities usually is rooted in hostile and rejecting treatment. For white children in the United States, ethnic and racial heritage is invisible and therefore is not usually an issue.

About 1 percent, or 500,000 marriages in the United States are between African-Americans and whites. More Asians and Hispanics marry outside of their race than African-Americans. In 1990, the U.S. Census Bureau reported that almost 2 million children lived in households where the primary adults were of different races, twice as many as in 1980 (Holmes, 1996). While most biracial children result from these unions, some children "become" multiracial through adoption—for example, an African-American child who is adopted by a white family (McRoy, Zurcher, Lauderdale, & Anderson, 1984).

Biracial children have an extra "identity problem:" they belong to two (or more) different racial groups and usually are pressured to identify with only one of them (Mathews, 1996; Tizard & Phoenix, 1995). For example, a child of an African-American father and a caucasian mother might consider herself African-American, white, or multiracial. Many children born in one culture and raised in another consider themselves to be "marginal" people—associated with two or more ethnic or cultural groups, but feeling that they belong to none. Note that biracial children differ from even their own parents in their ethnic heritage and may experience rejection from grandparents, aunts, uncles, and cousins (Gibbs, 1987; LaFromboise, Coleman, & Gerton, 1993).

Many biracial children report that they feel torn between choosing one parent's racial identification over the other. When they choose one, they may feel like a traitor to the other (Winn & Priest, 1993). Their choice usually reflects society's acceptance of the parents' ethnic background, parental influence on the child's attitudes, and the child's physical appearance and cultural knowledge (Hall, 1980; Poston, 1990).

Some parents attempt to influence a child's identification. Choosing to identify with one parent's background and not with the other's elicits guilt in some biracial children (Sebring, 1985). "A biracial adolescent . . . may be ashamed and scared to have friends meet his or her parent whose racial background is different from the norm in the neighborhood or school; the adolescent may also feel guilty and angry about feeling this way. Eventually the child must resolve the anger and guilt and learn to appreciate both parental cultures . . ." (Poston, 1990, p. 154).

It is the family that provides the best pro-tection from bigotry (Overmier, 1990; Winn & Priest, 1993). Accomplishing this formidable task without being overprotective or under-mining a child's self-confidence is a chal-lenge to parents. McRoy and Freeman (1986) recommend that parents of biracial children encourage them to acknowledge and discuss their racial heritage with family members and peers. Biracial children should not learn to view the fact that they are differ-ent from either parent as bad. Living in an integrated or at least tolerant neighborhood and attending an integrated school encour-age self-acceptance. Participating in support groups that provide positive biracial role models also helps biracial children appreci-ate their unique qualities.

SELF-ESTEEM

Study Question *How can parents encourage the development of positive self-esteem in their children?*

If self-concept refers to "one's identity as dis-tinct from others," then **self-esteem** refers to "the value one places on that identity" (Berns, 1989, p. 431). In a sense, self-esteem reflects how we feel about our self-concept. Most of us like certain aspects of our "selves" and dis-like other aspects. In children, these mini-evaluations may change from day to day. After a victorious baseball game, an eight-year-old may think he's Babe Ruth. After a loss, he's convinced he "stinks" at baseball.

Self-esteem can also be defined in terms of satisfying one's expectations of oneself. Such expectations, for young children at least, are ultimately rooted in other people's expecta-tions (Smolak, 1986). If our parents, friends, and teachers are happy with us, then we can be happy with us.

Self-concept and self-esteem appear to be linked in middle childhood by the process of self-evaluation. Parents and teachers encour-age children to monitor and evaluate their own behavior ("Were you a good girl in school today?"). Eventually, children monitor their own behavior using their parent's standards. Many years ago, my son's friend Mike (8 years old at the time) said to me, looking at his re-port card, "I should have done better. I'm dis-appointed in myself." Self-esteem is deflated when children do not satisfy the standards that they have internalized from their parents.

Self-esteem and self-confidence also ap-pear to be related. Children who accumulate a "track record" of success in their early years learn to expect that, if they are persistent, they will continue to be successful. They become more likely to seek challenges that allow them to demonstrate their competence. A cycle is established in which further achievement leads to a greater sense of competence, or ef-ficacy. This, in turn, encourages them to seek further challenges. Children obviously enjoy their successes (evidenced by the "mastery

Close parent-child relationships appear to contribute to healthy self-esteem in children and adolescents.

smile") and the recognition that they receive for their efforts. Self-esteem appears to be relatively stable over childhood, adolescence, and young adulthood (O'Malley & Bachman, 1983), although for some individuals, self-worth fluctuates according to momentary self-evaluations (Kernis, Cornell, Sun, Berry, & Harlow, 1993).

"Earned self-esteem is based on success in meeting the tests of reality—measuring up to standards—at home and in school. It is necessarily hard won, and develops slowly, but it is stable and long-lasting, and provides a secure foundation for further growth and development. It is not a precondition of learning but a product of it" (Lerner, 1985, p. 13).

Low self-esteem and self-doubt are associated with social, emotional, and academic problems in childhood and adolescence (Harter, 1987; 1990; Klein, 1992; Phinney & Alipuria, 1990). "Children who lack self-confidence are not optimistic about the outcome of their efforts. They feel incapable, inferior, pessimistic, and easily discouraged. Things always seem to go wrong; these children give up easily and frequently feel intimidated . . . Frustration and anger are handled poorly, and often turn into vengeful behavior against others or themselves. Unfortunately, their behavior typically leads others to view them as negatively as they see themselves" (Schaefer & Millman, 1981, p. 99).

Schaefer and Millman associate children's low self-esteem with faulty child-rearing practices. Parents who are overprotective prevent their children from learning self-reliance. Instead, by protecting their children from "failure," they encourage vulnerability and timidity. Neglecting parents have children who feel unworthy of being cared for. Perfectionistic and punitive parents encourage their children to feel inadequate and incapable. Children of critical and disapproving parents are likely to accept their parent's low estimation of them, but may also resent it.

Good parent-child relationships contribute to healthy self-esteem in adolescent boys and girls (Isberg et al., 1989). Positive self-esteem

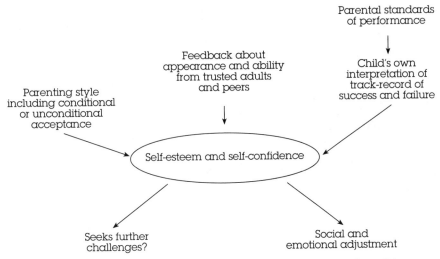

Figure 8.1   Factors influencing children's self-esteem and self-confidence.

in adolescent girls is also correlated with peer support and evaluating oneself as being popular. School and athletic performance are good predictors of self-esteem in boys (Boivin & Begin, 1989; Walker & Greene, 1986). Thus, whereas positive social relations seem to boost self-esteem in girls, accomplishment is a primary determinant of self-esteem in boys. Children who are physically attractive and who are popular with their peers see themselves more positively and like themselves more than do unpopular children (Harper & Marshall, 1991; Mullis, Mullis, & Normandin, 1992; Walker & Greene, 1986).

B o x   8 - 1

The "Dark Side" of Self-Esteem

Psychologist Roy Baumeister, one of the most accomplished researchers on the topic of self-esteem, is concerned that children in the United States think *too highly* of themselves (Baumeister, 1996). Baumeister cites the results of an international scholastic competition in which students from the United States achieved the lowest average scores among the participating nationalities but rated themselves and their performance the highest. "This is precisely what comes of focusing on self-esteem: poor performance accompanied by plenty of empty congratulation. Put another way, we get high self-esteem as inflated perceptions over a rather dismal reality" (p. 14).

Baumeister is critical of the common parental and educational practice of praising children and adolescents for achievements that are mediocre at best. Baumeister warns that undeserved praise undermines children's willingness to work hard and gain personal satisfaction from their efforts. Equating high self-esteem with egotism, Baumeister notes that people with inflated views of themselves are more prone to delinquent and violent behavior (Baumeister, Smart, & Boden, 1996). "Looking ahead, it is alarming to think what will happen when this generation of schoolchildren grows up into adults who may continue thinking they are smarter than the rest of the world—while actually being dumber. America will be a land of conceited fools" (Baumeister, 1996, p. 14).

While acknowledging some of the benefits of positive self-esteem and granting that high self-esteem helps people feel good, Baumeister reminds us that self-esteem is a perception of oneself, not a reality. He maintains that self-esteem makes little difference in children's performance or adjustment. "Self-esteem is not altogether useless, but its benefits are isolated and minor, except for the fact that it feels good. When I embarked on a career of research on self-esteem, I had hoped for a great deal more" (p. 16).

Erikson's Point of View

Erik Erikson (1963) proposed eight stages of psychosocial development that are manifested as conflicts or challenges that must be resolved for healthy personality development (see Appendix C for more detail). The resolution of the first two stages, *trust versus mistrust* during the first 18 months and *autonomy versus shame and self-doubt* during the second and third years, can have a profound impact on children's self-esteem. Parents play an important role during each of these stages by either supporting or hindering children's ability to feel worthy and competent.

Successful resolution of the first stage requires sensitive and consistent parenting. It results in infants' ability to trust themselves and to trust their caregivers to be there when needed. Successful resolution of the second stage allows infants to believe that they can satisfy their parents' expectations, an important element of self-confidence (Smolak, 1986).

Successful resolution of the third stage (*initiative versus guilt*) allows toddlers to take pride in and enjoy their emerging skills and abilities. During this stage, punitive and insensitive parenting fosters feelings of unworthiness and guilt. Successful resolution of the fourth stage (*industry versus inferiority*) during the elementary school years encourages feelings of mastery and competence in the academic domain. Children believe that they can satisfy their parents and teachers. Note that the development of a sense of industry or competence depends upon the prior emergence of trust, autonomy, and initiative.

The Coopersmith Study

In reviewing the theoretical and empirical literatures on the development of self-esteem, Coopersmith (1967) identified four factors as potentially significant. They are (1) the amount of respectful, accepting, and concerned treatment that children receive from their caregivers; (2) children's history of success and the resulting recognition they receive; (3) children's values and goals, which influence how they interpret the outcomes of their efforts; and (4) children's ability to protect their self-esteem when they are criticized.

In order to assess these factors, Coopersmith investigated the relationship between parenting practices and attitudes, as reported by mothers, and the self-esteem of preadolescent middle-class boys. Coopersmith studied

TABLE 8.1 Parenting Qualities and Behaviors Associated With Children's Self-Esteem

Positive Self-Esteem	Negative Self-Esteem
Sensitive, caring parenting	Overprotective
Recognizing and valuing achievement	Neglectful
Unconditional acceptance of child	Use punitive discipline practices
Positive regard (praise, affection)	Overly critical, rejecting
Clearly defining and enforcing limits	
Respect for child's desire for autonomy	
Modeling self-assurance	
Encourage and validate child's expression of feelings	

85 boys who were categorized as having high, medium, or low self-esteem. The assignment of boys to these three categories was based on self-esteem inventories that they completed and their teachers' ratings of their behaviors. Their mothers were interviewed for an average of 2½ hours and completed 80-item questionnaires on their child-rearing practices.

Coopersmith concluded that children's self-esteem is essentially determined by their rearing: "The most general statement about the antecedents of self-esteem can be given in terms of three conditions: total or nearly total *acceptance* of the children by their parents, clearly defined and enforced *limits*, and the *respect and latitude for individual action* that exist within the defined limits . . . In effect, we can conclude that the parents of children with high self-esteem are concerned and attentive toward their children, that they structure the worlds of their children along lines they believe to be proper and appropriate, and that they permit relatively great freedom within the structures they have established" (p. 236). Note that Coopersmith's description of mothers of boys with high self-esteem resembles Baumrind's depiction of the authoritative or democratic parenting style discussed in Chapter 5.

Coopersmith also reported that the parents

of children with high self-esteem "are themselves active, poised, and relatively self-assured individuals who recognize the significance of child rearing" (p. 237). They believe that they have the resources to parent well, they get along well with their spouses, and they establish clear boundaries regarding authority and responsibility. Parents with high self-esteem avoid punitive discipline strategies, according to Coopersmith. They "accept and tolerate dissent within the limits that they have established" (p. 237).

People with low self-esteem, "reared under conditions of rejection, uncertainty, and disrespect, have come to believe they are powerless and without resource or recourse. They feel isolated, unlovable, incapable of expressing and defending themselves, and too weak to confront, and overcome their deficiencies (p. 250) . . . By virtue of the treatment he receives and the self-attitudes he develops as a consequence, the child with low self-esteem is unlikely to believe that his personal actions can have a favorable outcome, that he can effectively cope with adversity, or that he is worthy of love and attention" (Coopersmith, 1967, p. 251).

Like Diane Baumrind, Coopersmith found that parents who are warm *and* firm and who encourage responsibility, have children who are self-reliant, competent, and happy. Coopersmith concluded that "definite and enforced limits" by parents are associated with children's high self-esteem. Both researchers maintain that parental firmness encourages the development of "inner controls" that allow children to behave successfully. C. C. Lewis (1981) questioned Coopersmith's (and Baumrind's) conclusion that firm parental control contributes positively to the development of self-esteem. Rather, he suggests, it is the child's opportunity "to shape and to alter rules" (p. 560), and not parental enforcement of rules, that is the active ingredient in the parental nurturance of self-esteem.

Carl Rogers's Point of View

Carl Rogers (1902-1987) and his colleagues have contributed what sometimes is called a "third force" model of personality development. Freudian psychology and behaviorism are the first two forces. Rogers's (1961) approach, known as *humanistic* or *existential psychology*, describes the conditions that allow the fulfillment of one's potential for growth, or what Rogers called **self-actualization**.

Actualizing tendencies represent an innate force inside all living things to become whatever we are capable of becoming. Most of us have experienced wanting to change, to expand, to excel at something. Rogers believed that children's self-concept largely reflects the feedback that they receive from other people. Children tend to get diverse reactions from adults, but they are not always positive or encouraging (e.g., the common parental retort, "What's wrong with you?"). Some children will fail to realize their full potential because of the "constricting and distorting influences of parental training, education, and other social pressures" (Hall & Lindzey, 1978, p. 279). For example, parents who frequently criticize or disapprove of their children encourage

feelings of inadequacy or unworthiness that stifle the actualizing tendency.

Unconditional Acceptance and Positive Regard

Rogers maintained that children require **unconditional acceptance** and **positive regard** from their caregivers. Parental acceptance and affection are often expressed conditionally. "Children learn when they are 'good' and when they are 'bad.' These values are incorporated by them as their 'conditions of worth.' They feel worthwhile only when engaging in certain activities and avoiding others. If these conditions of worth are few and reasonable, children can be open to a variety of experiences and learn from them. If there are many conditions of worth and if these conditions have to do with inevitable human feelings, such as sexual arousal and anger, children may deny or distort large portions of their lives to maintain a sense of worth. This denial and distortion, meant to gain parental and ultimately self-acceptance, actually deprives them of necessary information to guide their behavior. Self-actualization is thus impeded" (Christenson, 1983, pp. 426-427).

When parents convey that the child's expression of anger toward them is unacceptable, the child must adapt by suppressing or even denying such feelings when they occur. This prevents the child from learning how to handle such feelings and results, ultimately, in his or her being controlled by them. The supportive parental message is, "I love you, no matter what." This does not mean that parents accept or condone misbehavior. Rather, they distinguish between who the child is (which they love no matter what) and what the child does (which may or may not be acceptable).

According to Rogers, positive regard from others leads to positive self-esteem and the ability to care for others. In other words, children who feel accepted, valued, and loved by their caregivers can accept and love themselves. They can then learn how to accept and show love to other people including, eventually, their own children.

Self-Esteem

Like most clinicians, Rogers observed that clients who are anxious and depressed usually have low self-esteem and difficult relationships. According to Rogers, personality problems arise when individuals are given conditional regard. "If you are good (or smart, beautiful, rich, successful) then I will accept and love you." Because it is often difficult or impossible to satisfy other people's conditions, we become wrapped up in our own perceived inadequacies. We may suffer from crippling defenses and fail to thrive. We may try to become what we think other people want us to be instead of being and accepting ourselves as we are.

One therapist writes, "Most of my high-achieving clients share a background in which one or both of their parents was experienced as overly critical and unsupportive. As children my clients report that they often felt like they were a disappointment and a burden to their parents. They could not say or do the right thing" (Post, 1988, p. 196).

Feelings

Rogers advocated that parents encourage their children to have feelings and express them freely. Some parents find the expression of negative feelings threatening and may attempt to suppress such displays. As we discussed in Chapter 7, some parents find their children's negative feelings annoying and refuse to validate them. If little Jason says, "Mommy, I hate you," will Mom respond angrily? "How dare you!" Or will she react sensitively and help him clarify his strong feelings ("Jason, are you angry at me?"). In other words, will Mom show caring? Many, if not most, children eventually learn to keep their feelings to themselves. They have learned that it is not always safe to express them.

Rogers advocated a warm and emotionally permissive home environment, one in which children are encouraged to express themselves freely without fear of harsh judgment or ridicule. Parents of course may *disagree* with a child's point of view, but they should take it seriously anyway. Rogers's view is sensible. When children feel accepted and loved, when they feel "lovable," they accept, respect, and trust themselves, even when they "mess up." But if the prevailing message they receive is of the rejecting "bad boy/bad girl" variety, then they may come to doubt their worthiness and competence.

"Every word, facial expression, gesture, or action on the part of the parent gives the child some message about his worth. It is sad that so many parents don't realize the effect these messages have on the child, and often don't even realize what messages they are sending" (Satir, 1972, p.25).

Evaluation

Carl Rogers acknowledged our human disposition to grow, to feel, to love, and to fulfill our human potential. He described the relationship between the feedback we get from our caregivers, how we feel about ourselves, how we feel about others, and our willingness to be complete, loving, and feeling individuals. Personality problems, according to Rogers, reflect distortions of our true nature, rooted in critical, unsupportive family environments. There is much that Rogers's theory has in common with Erikson's, although Rogers's is neither a stage nor a conflict theory. Both theories relate nurturant parenting to the development of a healthy personality. Rogers presented an optimistic view of human personality and development. Critics point out that Rogers's model is somewhat vague and lacks scientific precision. To some extent, this reflects the subjective domain of personality and emotions that Rogers addressed.

Bandura's Model of Self-Efficacy

Study Question   What does Bandura mean by "self-efficacy," and what role does efficacy play in human personality?

According to Albert Bandura (1977a, 1982, 1986), a major ingredient of a healthy personality is confidence in one's ability to solve a given problem and to cope with a threatening situation. He refers to this ability as **self-efficacy**. Self-efficacy generally takes the form of judgments or expectations that one will perform well in a given situation.

Efficacy expectations play an important role in human personality (Bandura, 1986). They motivate the initiation of behavior ("I can handle this"); the generalization of behavior to new situations ("Since I have succeeded before, I will probably succeed again"); persistence ("If I continue to try, I will eventually succeed"), choice ("I will take on the task I am most likely to complete successfully"), and emotional reactions ("I'm proud of my achievements"). Individuals with low self-efficacy have learned to expect negative outcomes. Their behavior becomes excessively cautious or defensive. Self-doubters give up quickly or do not try at all ("I know I will fail, so what's the use of trying").

Bandura distinguishes between self-efficacy, a judgment of one's capabilities, and self-esteem, the evaluation of one's worth as a person. He suggests that they are not necessarily related. Nevertheless in children, competence, self-confidence (efficacy), and positive self-esteem usually go together (Chance, 1982; Nottelmann, 1987).

"Efficacy experiences in the exercise of personal control are central to the early development of social and cognitive competence. Parents who are responsive to their infants' communicative behavior, who provide an enriched physical environment, and who permit freedom of movement for exploration have infants who are relatively accelerated in their social and cognitive development" (Bandura, 1986, p. 415). Enhancing an individual's self-confidence is associated with the alleviation of a wide range of emotional and interpersonal problems (Grusec, 1992; McCleod, 1986).

Parents promote the development of children's feelings of efficacy by arranging situations in which children can perform successfully. "Successes raise efficacy appraisals; repeated failures lower them . . . After a strong sense of self-efficacy is developed through repeated successes, occasional failures are unlikely to have much effect on judgments of one's capabilities" (Bandura, 1986, p. 399).

Parents contribute to this process by teaching their children realistic standards of performance ("Try to do your best") rather than perfectionistic or unattainable standards ("Be the best"). Parents can also foster a child's self-esteem by valuing those abilities in which he or she excels ("I knew you could do it"), rather than emphasizing weaknesses or deficits ("What's wrong with you?"). Since occasional failure is inevitable, children must learn realistic ways of evaluating themselves ("I tried my hardest" or "Well, nobody's perfect"). They also must understand that their worth as a person and their parents' feelings about them do not depend upon any particular achievement or failure.

We should not overlook the role that parental modeling plays in the development of self-esteem. Re-read Coopersmith's description of parents with high self-esteem. Children of parents with low self-esteem, on the other hand, may learn that "not thinking much of yourself is natural . . . The children are not growing up in an atmosphere where positive things are felt about oneself. Parents who do not strive to do their best frequently have children who behave similarly" (Schaeffer & Millman, 1981, p. 100).

Spotlight

The Development of Empathy and Altruism

Mark #13

"Mark's camp counselor told me that Mark had been cruel by laughing when another child got hurt. He said Mark laughed while the boy cried. I told the counselor I was sorry and that I'd have a talk with my son. Mark rationalized away all the implications by saying that the boy was cruel to him, had scratched him under the eye, drawing blood (there was no evidence of blood) and by explaining that the child is regularly a 'crybaby.'

"I asked Mark how he would feel if it were him and he said it wouldn't matter to him. I tried a few times to gently prod him to admit his regret and/or guilt but when he would not, I resigned. I told him I was very displeased with his attitude."

Empathy and Altruism

Two types of social behavior that develop very gradually, from a parent's point of view, are empathy and altruism. **Empathy** refers to the ability to understand and care about people's feelings. **Altruism** refers to one's willingness to help someone in need, even if there is a personal cost to the helper. The learning of prosocial behavior depends heavily upon cognitive structures that allow children to understand that other people may feel differently from them (Roberts & Strayer, 1996). As they mature, children become better at interpreting other people's feelings.

A primitive form of "empathy" can be seen when a newborn cries in the presence of other crying infants. Some sensitivity to other people's feelings is present by the age of two years. Such acts as helping, comforting, sharing, and cooperating are commonly observed in 3- and 4-year-olds (Kohn, 1988). Preschool children display altruistic behavior, but their motives are not always clear.

Presumably, empathic feelings are elicited when a child identifies with a distressed sibling ("How would I feel if that were happening to me?"). It might occur to an older child that "I know how she feels." Understanding other people's feelings is probably rooted in our ability to imagine ourselves "in their shoes." However, an empathic response may not be sufficient to motivate helping. In fact, understanding how their actions can affect other people encourages young children, occasionally, to intentionally elicit distress, as when children tease and torment each other.

Most children eventually demonstrate concern in the presence of another child (or adult or animal) who is distressed. Whether or not they offer help partly depends upon their ability to interpret the situation. The major considerations are, "Am I responsible for your distress" and "Am I responsible for and capable of alleviating your distress, even though I didn't cause it?" When empathic responses are elicited, and a sense of responsibility is experienced, helping is likely, or at least feeling guilty for not helping (Chapman, Zahn-Waxler, Cooperman, & Iannotti, 1987). Dunn (1987) suggests that children as young as 24 months "show some grasp of the notion of responsibility and blame in relation to feelings and to social rules" (p. 107).

Parents like Mark's mom become frustrated when their children do not share, help, or offer comfort to someone in need. They are even more disturbed when their children make the "victim" feel worse ("You're a crybaby"). Parental disapproval is counterproductive when we're trying to teach empathic skills (Murray, 1996).

Promoting Empathy and Altruism in Children

Parents encourage the development of empathy and altruism by teaching young children sensitivity toward other people's feelings. Showing seems to work better than telling (Murray, 1996). Perhaps the best opportunity to display these interpersonal skills is when the child herself is upset or irritable. The parent can then demonstrate patience and caring rather than irritation. Parents also can model altruistic behavior for someone in distress (perhaps a sibling) in the child's presence and then give the child the opportunity to help too (Denham, Mason, & Couchoud, 1995).

When parents observe their child behaving in a non-caring or abusive manner, they should ask empathy-inducing questions based on the child's actual experiences. "Do you remember when Adrianne took your book without asking? How did you feel?. . . . Well how do you think Sarah felt when you took her pail without asking?" Children like Mark, who say defiantly that it wouldn't matter to them, are displaying a defensive attitude. Children become defensive when they feel that they are under attack.

Parents can calmly explain to their children how our actions influence other people's feelings, and why we should be more sensitive to how our actions make other people feel. While reading to children, parents can ask questions about how people in the story feel about and react to the circumstances being depicted. With older children, parents can discuss their own relevant life experiences or hypothetical situations with ethical or moral implications. Children also need instruction about how to help someone in need, according to the nature of the specific problem (Denham et al., 1995).

Coercing or shaming children into being "nice" is self-defeating. Complying with adult requests or demands to be kind is not as effective in developing empathic skills as long-term interactions with others (Eisenberg, Lundy, Shell, & Roth, 1985). In other words, if children perceive themselves as being kind because they want to be rather than because they're told to be, they are more likely to repeat the behavior. Nevertheless, by modeling and giving children reasons for helping, parents assist them in internalizing altruistic standards of conduct.

SEX DIFFERENCES AND PARENTING: "IS IT A BOY OR IS IT A GIRL?"

Study Question   *Is there such a thing as a male or female personality trait?*

One important component of self-concept is identification with either the male or female gender and sex role. Being classified as a boy or girl at birth has a major influence on a person's life. From birth "males and females will begin to have different kinds of experiences that to some extent will influence who and

Justin Jaffe

what they will become and the nature of their life courses" (Williams, 1987, p. 135).

Do parents raise sons and daughters differently? Do children identify with the same-gendered parent and adopt gender roles and personal styles accordingly? Do males and females, in fact, differ from each other? If so, how do they differ and what causes these differences? These are difficult, even controversial questions. Some wonder why we even care about gender differences in the first place.

Unger and Crawford (1992) note that male supremicists would love to have "scientific evidence" to justify women's unequal treatment by society. We pursue the issue because we want to know whether or not parents treat their sons and daughters somewhat differently. Material in the last section of Chapter 3

suggests that they do. If so, what are the consequences?

Everyday observation suggests that there are gender differences in behavior. For example, we perceive the average female as more expressive, warm, and sensitive to other people's feelings than the average male. We view the average male as more assertive and competitive than the average female. Psychologist Carol Gilligan (1982) contends that females have a greater need to connect emotionally with other people. This colors their relationships and their reasoning in ways that distinguish them from males.

Surprisingly, researchers have had a hard time confirming apparent differences. One reason is that girls are so different from each other, and boys are so different from each other. And girls, as a group, are not that different from boys. This makes it very difficult to identify any subtle psychological and behavioral differences that might exist (Unger & Crawford, 1992; Williams, 1987).

The most obvious sex differences are biological, with males, on the average, being larger and weighing more. Females mature faster and live longer. Because they mature faster, girls develop motor and other skills a little earlier than boys. The most clear-cut gender differences are related to reproduction and health. Mortality rates are higher for males than for females at virtually every stage of life. Females' lowered susceptibility to most diseases may reflect the genetic advantages of having two similar sex chromosomes, but there are other theories (Jacklin, 1989). Biological models of gender differences (for example, looking for differences in brain structure or functioning of males and females) so far have received little empirical confirmation (Unger & Crawford, 1992). As far as we know, males and females are far more alike biologically than they are different (hardly "opposite" sexes).

Of the hundreds of ways in which males and females could differ psychologically, few significant differences have been identified (e.g., Davis, 1995). In a somewhat controversial review of the psychology of gender differences, Maccoby and Jacklin (1974) concluded that girls have slightly greater verbal ability than boys (at least after age 11), that boys slightly excel in visual-spatial and mathematical abilities, and that boys are more physically aggressive (pp. 351–352).

Hyde and Linn (1988) performed a meta-analysis on 165 studies of gender difference in verbal abilities. They concluded that there is no such difference, at least at the present time, with the possible exception of the quality of speech production. Other reviews agree that if gender differences in intellectual and other abilities existed in the past, they have lessened

as social roles, career, and educational opportunities have become more equitable (Adler, 1989c; Jacklin, 1989). Cognitively, socially, and emotionally, males and females are much more similar than different.

Parenting Sons and Daughters

Study Question   *Do parents treat their sons and daughters differently?*

If we accept that there are slight to moderate gender differences in some aspects of personality such as emotional expressiveness and competitiveness, then what is their source? Are they rooted in biology, child-rearing practices, cultural beliefs, or in some combination of these factors? Low (1989) contends that "sons and daughters are trained differently in ways that relate to the evolutionary history of reproductive success of the two sexes" (p. 316).

According to Low, compared to girls, boys are encouraged to be more aggressive and self-reliant and to develop greater endurance. Girls are trained to be more responsible, obedient, and sexually-restrained than boys. Additionally, boys are socialized more intensely and consistently than girls. Low hypothesizes that these traits and rearing patterns maximize reproductive success in each gender. Sociobiological models like this one do not lend themselves easily to empirical tests.

There is evidence that mothers and fathers treat their sons and daughters differently, although many studies (reviewed by Lytton & Romney, 1991) report few, if any, differences. Inconsistent findings usually suggest that researchers are overlooking important moderator variables, such as children's age or personality. The nature of the subtle differences in how parents treat their sons and daughters varies from culture to culture. Within a given culture, we observe differences in parental treatment of sons and daughters from family to family. Within a given family, we observe differences in parental treatment from child to child (and for a given child from day to day or even moment to moment). This is the main reason why differences in parental treatment according to gender are so difficult to pin down.

Parents might attempt to raise their sons and daughters exactly the same way, and gender differences might still emerge due to factors such as genetics or imitation. It is also possible that parents might treat their sons and daughters differently, and we might still find minimal gender differences. Parental influence competes with so many other forces that could encourage behavioral similarities between boys and girls. Parental attributes, when they have any effect at all, seem to operate in the same direction of influence for boys and girls (Turner & Gervai, 1995).

Let's say we have a family with two sons and two daughters. Let's suppose that one daughter is outgoing, ambitious, and has positive self-esteem. The other daughter is shy, insecure, and moody. Let's also assume that one son is "easy" and the other son is "difficult." Will we find that the parents treat their sons and daughters differently? Or will the differences in personality between the two brothers and the differences between the two sisters evoke quite different rearing strategies from their parents?

In this hypothetical family, the differences among the siblings in their personalities may well overshadow the differences in their genders regarding the parenting strategies and styles we observe. This does not preclude, however, the parents giving the boys more educational opportunities than the girls or requiring the girls to help out more around the house than the boys. As noted in Chapter 7, differential parental treatment is inevitable, but its effects would be mild compared to the unique ways each parent treats each child.

Another way of saying this is that parental behavior is affected more by a child's behavior and temperament (and other situational factors such as parental mood) than by a child's gender.

As noted, Maccoby and Jacklin (1974) conducted an extensive review of the parenting literature. They tested four hypotheses regarding differential parental treatment of sons and daughters. Their first hypothesis asserted that parents "treat children of the two sexes so as to shape them toward the behavior deemed appropriate for their sex" (p. 305). The investigators, in 1974, found very little evidence to support this hypothesis. They could find no clear-cut differences in the amount of parental interaction with sons and daughters; no difference in the amount of vocalizations to both genders; no differences in the expression of parental warmth; no clear demonstration of greater reinforcement for dependency in either gender; and no differences in sexual information given to boys and girls.

Although they found no consistent differences in parental restrictiveness, there was a tendency toward greater restriction of boys' behavior, but also more positive feedback given to boys. They speculated that boys may receive more positive *and* negative feedback because their behavior is more attention-getting than girls'. Maccoby and Jacklin also concluded, surprisingly, that the research literature does not support the assumption of greater permissiveness toward boys' aggressive behavior, at least by mothers.

The greatest difference in socialization between boys and girls involves parental encouragement of gender-appropriate behavior (Beal, 1994). (Many studies of this topic assessed children's toy preferences. Boys and girls differ in their play and toy preferences (Lawson, 1989).) Both parents, but particularly fathers, encourage gender-appropriate behavior and discourage gender-inappropriate behavior in sons more than in daughters.

Maccoby and Jacklin acknowledged the scanty evidence in some areas of this literature and the flaws in many of the studies. They concluded that the "reinforcement contingencies for the two genders appear to be remarkably similar" (Maccoby & Jacklin, 1974, p. 342). Still, we must acknowledge that parents encourage different types of play activities in their children and, as we shall see later in the chapter, often assign household chores on the basis of gender (White & Brinkerhoff, 1981b). There is also evidence that parents respond more punitively to the moral transgressions of boys compared to those of girls (e.g., Smetana, 1989b).

Their second hypothesis was that, due to innate characteristics, "boys and girls stimulate their parents differently and hence elicit different treatment from them" (Maccoby & Jacklin, 1974, p. 305). For example, temperamental differences between boys and girls in their ability to be comforted may elicit different patterns of handling by their parents. These, in turn, could affect the child's behavior. Such "circular" patterns of interaction could have a profound effect on how boys and girls are raised. If boys are more noncompliant, parents may respond with less nurturance and greater restrictiveness, leading to more anger in their sons, and so on.

Maccoby and Jacklin concluded, based on their review of the literature, that "there are probably not very many initial biologically based behavioral differences, at least not many that are strong enough to elicit clear differential reactions from caregivers" (p. 343). Studies have indicated that male infants sleep less and cry more than female infants, and that mothers are more likely to respond to irritability in female infants. But overall, "mothers are equally warm, nurturing, and accepting of boy and girl babies" (Williams, 1987, p. 171).

Maccoby and Jacklin's third hypothesis was that parents "base their behavior toward a child on their conception of what a child of a given sex is likely to be like" (p. 305). Parents might compensate for "natural weaknesses," such as aggressive behavior in their sons. They might accept as inevitable such behaviors ("Boys will be boys"). Or they might overreact to behaviors that they believe are unusual for a boy or girl.

Maccoby and Jacklin concluded, based on the limited evidence available, that parents do not advocate different values for how boys and girls should behave. Parents do perceive their sons and daughters as different regarding how rough, noisy, competitive, defiant, and helpful they are. There are very few differences, however, in the values that guide their raising of their sons and daughters.

Parental expectations may influence socialization soon after birth if parents view their newborns in gender-typed ways (Sweeney & Bradbard, 1988). "Girls are rated as smaller, softer, and less alert than boys despite the absence of real physical differences.

TABLE 8.2 How Parents Treat Sons and Daughters Differently

Boys receive more intense socialization (more praise, more punishment)

More restrictions placed on boys, at least until adolescence

Greater encouragement of gender-appropriate behavior for boys

More self-reliance encouraged for boys

Parents view girls as more vulnerable

Parents more task-oriented with boys but give more feedback to girls

Fathers interact and play more with sons

Parents may treat children of their gender more harshly

Parental purchase of clothing and toys usually is gender-typed

Parents often assign household tasks according to gender

Fathers of newborns rate boys as stronger and hardier . . . Such differences in perceptions may result in differential treatment of boy and girl infants" (Smolak, 1986, p. 227). Keep in mind, however, that parents' treatment of their children does not necessarily reflect their gender-related beliefs (Turner & Gervai, 1995).

Maccoby and Jacklin's fourth hypothesis was that a "parent's behavior toward a child will depend, in some degree, upon whether the child is of the same sex as himself" (p. 306). This influence can be mediated by the parent's modeling behavior considered appropriate for his or her child, or by falling into stereotypical male-female roles (e.g., a mother acting submissively to her adolescent son). Parents may also identify with the same-gender child, with stronger empathic reactions to that child. Again, the investigators could not find support for this hypothesis, although "fathers appeared to be more tolerant of aggression from a daughter, mothers from a son (p. 347) . . . We cannot conclude that either sex is dealt with more leniently, on the whole" (p. 348).

Despite the many limitations of the studies they examined, Maccoby and Jacklin's review of the literature is remarkable in that so few differences were found in the ways parents socialize their sons and daughters. One theme that did emerge, unexpectedly, was that boys "seem to have more intense socialization experiences than girls. They receive more pressure against engaging in gender-inappropriate behavior, whereas the activities that girls are not supposed to engage in are much less clearly defined and less firmly enforced. Boys receive more punishment, but probably also more praise and encouragement. Adults respond as if they find boys more interesting and more attention-provoking, than girls" (p. 348).

Summarizing, there is little evidence of psychological or behavioral differences between boys and girls. The slight differences that exist may be due not to innate differences in ability

and not to differential rearing patterns but rather to powerful cultural and environmental forces, including sexual stereotypes and parental expectations.

Parents themselves may accept gender stereotypes, but usually do not apply them to their own children! People are more likely to stereotype those that they do not know well. Since parents are quite familiar with their children, they treat them as individuals rather than as members of a group. Others with less information may view children stereotypically (Turkington, 1984a).

In suggesting that parents sometimes treat their sons and daughters differently, we do not mean to imply that parents love their sons more or less than they love their daughters. However, we have noted that traditional fathers distance themselves more from their sons, at least regarding displays of emotion or affection. Fathers play more with their sons, but perhaps in ways that communicate the traditional message, "This is how men act—competently, with courage, and with minimal expression of tenderness."

"Fathers' higher level of physical activity in their play with sons may communicate to children that boys are better equipped to handle and enjoy the challenges of the physical world. Girls, for their own safety, had best be more cautious. And of course, as they are communicating different attitudes to and about girls and boys, fathers are differentially imparting skills in these areas, so that they may in fact be creating self-fulfilling prophecies" (Bronstein, 1988a, p. 119).

The different ways that parents interact with sons and daughters may convey traditional gender-based expectations about how males and females conduct themselves (Peters, 1994). This may reinforce aggressive tendencies in boys, "while providing them with less opportunity to learn cooperation and empathy. In treating sons more instrumentally and less sociably than daughters, fathers may be providing their sons with less opportunity to learn the interpersonal skills necessary for establishing and maintaining intimate relationships, while also providing an early model of a traditional male-male relationship—of *doing* things together, rather than verbally connecting in a more intimate way" (Bronstein, 1988a, p. 119).

Study Question *Do children identify with the parent of the same gender?*

One long-standing assumption in the developmental literature is that girls become like their mothers and boys become like their fathers. Psychoanalytic theorists assume that children unconsciously identify with the same-gender parent. This process would be more powerful for females, because "a young girl's identification with her mother continues throughout life, whereas a young boy's identification with his mother is broken and switched to his father . . . A daughter continues to identify with her caregiving mother, thereby maintaining the mother-daughter relationship while establishing her identity. A son, however, must begin to seek his identity with his more absent father, an emotional maneuver that disengages him from the intensity of the mother-child relationship. Because of their prolonged identification with their mothers, daughters often perceived themselves as more 'like' their mothers than sons are 'like' their fathers" (Boyd, 1989). Would we predict this outcome for daughters of mothers who work full-time?

Social-learning theories also predict that children will resemble the same-gender parent more than the opposite-gender parent, but for different reasons. They cite modeling and reinforcement for gender-appropriate behav-

ior as mechanisms of influence. It is assumed that parents, often in subtle ways, treat their sons and daughters differently.

Parents do treat children of their own gender more harshly. Williams (1987) suggests that the father-son interaction reflects a struggle for male dominance. "That is, the father is reacting to the son as a male who is challenging him, whereas a daughter is no such threat" (p. 194). This is supported by Barber and Thomas's (1986) observation that, unlike mothers, fathers express much less physical affection to their sons than daughters. Mothers' greater tolerance for their sons' behavior may reflect the fact that women "are accustomed to use moderation in their reactions to male threat, and perhaps this conditioning comes into play when they are confronted with boys' flouting of their authority" (Williams, 1987, p. 194).

If mothers and fathers treat their sons and daughters somewhat differently, why are clear-cut gender differences in children and adolescents so hard to find? To shed light on this question, current research is focusing on possible differences between all four parent-child gender combinations: mother-son, mother-daughter, father-son, and father-daughter (Boyd, 1989; Jacobvitz & Bush, 1996; Steinberg, 1987d).

Gender Identity and Gender Typing

Study Question *In what ways might parents encourage "gender-appropriate" behavior in their children?*

Gender identity refers to perceiving oneself as male or female. In fact, gender often is the first distinction that children make in classifying people (Turner & Gervai, 1995). Most children label themselves correctly as boy or girl by the age of 2½ to 3 years. They base their gender label on "superficial" characteristics such as clothes or hair length, rather than on sex organs (Beal & Lockhart, 1989). They also know that there are two genders and that they "belong" to one (Emmerich, Goldman, Kirsh, & Sharabany, 1977). Once children define themselves as a boy or girl, they use these labels to guide their behavior.

Gender typing refers to the psychosocial processes by which children acquire, value, and perform gender-typed behavior patterns—those considered appropriate for their gender. Even though gender behaviors and roles are learned, in some sense we are already "gendered" at birth. Some aspects of our masculinity and femininity are innate but what they are, how they manifest themselves, and how culture gives them form and meaning is not well-understood (Beal, 1994).

Gender-typed behaviors, such as toy and play activities, emerge during the preschool years, as do beliefs about what is considered masculine and what is considered feminine (Huston, 1983). Traditionally, males and females have been distinguished by their anatomy, clothes, roles, occupations, and behaviors. Gender typing is multidimensional in that many different behavior patterns and personality characteristics become gender-predictable, including preferred activities and interests, relationships, and language patterns (Turner & Gervai, 1995).

Learning Models

Different models of gender typing exist (Beal, 1994). A simple learning model based on rewards and punishments suggests that parents reward gender-appropriate traits and behaviors. They reward displays of bravery and independence in boys. They reward nurturance and warmth in girls. Parents do not encourage, and often punish, behavior that they consider to be gender-inappropriate, such as playing with dolls for boys and rough-and-tumble play for girls. Most parents strongly encourage gender-appropriate play, especially for boys (Snow, Jacklin, & Maccoby, 1983).

Parents, particularly fathers, are concerned about their sons' preferences in toys. "We can assume that this concern is communicated to children in indirect and subtle ways; even if specific rewards and punishments are not given, the children are reinforced by smiles, frowns, and other expressions of approval or disapproval that can be even more powerful" (Freedman et al., 1981, p. 494).

Learning models of gender typing cannot account for the rate, scope, and endurance of gender typing and gender-role acquisition. Even though parents treat boys and girls similarly in most domains, gender stereotyped toy preferences are observed prior to two years of age! Parental concern about sex-appropriate play may be expressed more through the room decor and selection of toys than through direct reward and punishment of gender-appropriate behavior (Fling & Manosevitz, 1972).

"The decor and objects in the rooms of boys are different from those typically found in girl's rooms . . . Boys are more likely to be given trucks, construction sets, and sports equipment. Girls' toys are more likely to include dolls and their accompanying paraphernalia" (Smolak, 1986, p. 227). An editor of *Ms. Magazine* recalled buying a basketball hoop for her infant son. "He was two years old. The girls were five, and very athletic. My husband said, 'Why are you putting this in *his* room?' It was a moment of truth for me. After that, I looked at everything in a whole new way" (Pogrebin, quoted by Lawson, 1989).

Additionally, masculine and feminine toys elicit different patterns of parent-child interaction. Parents play differently with their young children according to the child's gender-predictable toy choices. Parents (mothers and fathers) express greater enthusiasm for a toy that is stereotyped for the child's (and parent's) gender (Caldera, Huston, & O'Brien, 1989).

Kohlberg's Cognitive-Developmental Model

Kohlberg's (1966) cognitive-developmental model maintains that by about the age of 3 years, children learn to label their own gender identity as male (boy) or female (girl). Then they learn to recognize the gender of other people. Children evolve masculine and feminine stereotypes as oversimplified rules (e.g., men are doctors, women are nurses; all people with long hair are girls). These rules are learned through exposure to distinctive behavior patterns or traits associated with males or females.

With experience, their gender conceptions become more flexible. For example, "All married women are mothers" becomes "Not all married women have children."

Once they grasp the permanence of their own maleness or femaleness, by about the age of 5 or 6 years, they come to value and try to learn those behaviors that they perceive as consistent with their gender identity. According to Kohlberg, until they are about 5 years old, children lack the cognitive structures necessary for grasping the permanence and irreversibility of gender.

Kohlberg's model is contradicted by the fact that children much younger than 5 or 6 years show gender-related preferences and behavior patterns (Freedman et al., 1981; Ruble & Ruble, 1980). Bem (1989) confirmed that preschool children can show "gender constancy," that is, they can understand that one's gender does not change when one's appearance changes. The key is grasping that gender is defined by one's genitals, not one's appearance (Beal & Lockhart, 1989).

Bandura's Social-Cognitive Model

Maccoby and Jacklin (1974) and Kohlberg (1966) downplayed the role of social learning and modeling in the development of gender identity and gender roles in favor of biological dispositions or cognitive processing. Bandura (1986) and Bem (1981) advocate a "gender-schema" model of gender typing that incorporates both cognitive change and social learning.

Bandura suggests that children acquire a gender identity by cognitively processing their own experiences and by watching other people. They learn about gender roles by extracting rules about what behaviors are considered appropriate for males and females. Children of mothers who perform traditionally masculine role behaviors have less stereotyped views of adult professions (Serbin, Powlishta, & Gulko, 1993). Similarly, fathers who perform traditionally female household tasks have children who are less aware of gender role stereotypes (Turner & Gervai, 1995).

Children are subject to direct reinforcement of gender-appropriate behaviors by their caregivers. They also learn about gender roles vicariously, by observing same-gender models in their family, on TV, or in books and movies. We observe direct socialization of gender roles in children's play when parents select different toys or play equipment for their sons and daughters. We see vicarious socialization in educational materials and books that portray boys as more active and inventive and girls as more dependent and passive (Beal, 1994).

Bandura suggests that gender role learning is an "ongoing process" that is not confined to early childhood (p. 98). Socialization processes do begin at birth, with distinctions based on the gender of the child being made regarding clothing, color schemes of rooms, and children's names. Toward the end of infancy, many children can identify their gender. They have already acquired verbal labels for what is male or female, such as boys, girls, mommy, daddy, man, woman, and so on.

Gender identity broadens, according to Bandura, to include behavioral, social and vocational distinctions. Since men today are so different from each other, as are women, it is difficult for children to acquire consistent information about gender roles. They still are susceptible to stereotypical formulations. Valid distinctions are facilitated when large numbers of same-gender models exhibit similar behavior patterns. For example, on "Super Sunday," most of the men are watching football on TV and most of the women are conversing in another room. Children have many such opportunities to view the gender-predictable behaviors of their parents and peers and of characters on TV sitcoms and in movies.

It is likely that children learn about gender roles in several ways: observation of same-gender models, direct or subtle parental reinforcement of gender-appropriate behavior, and through the acquisition of rules based on observation (Beal, 1994). "It is probable that all these processes are involved in the emergence of [gender-related behavior], in different degrees of importance, depending on the situation and the age of the child" (Williams, 1987, p. 180).

Cross-Gender Behavior

None of the current models can account for people who adopt a gender identity inconsistent with their biological gender (Beal, 1994). There are people who "have an intense, apparently irreversible conviction of belonging to the other sex and who trace the onset of this cross-sex identity to early childhood" (Roberts, Green, Williams, & Goodman, 1987, p. 544). They usually report that as children, they role-played being of the opposite gender. They preferred dressing like the opposite gender, avoided same-gender playmates and toys and games typical of their gender, and wanted to be of the opposite gender.

Roberts et al. (1987) compared families of boys exhibiting cross-gender behaviors with families of boys displaying typically mascu-

line behaviors. They found that boys living without their fathers were more "feminine" than boys whose parents had intact marriages. Femininity in boys was associated with the mother's approval of cross-gender behavior at an early age and the father's desire for a girl when his partner was pregnant with her son. The dynamics of gender identity appear to be different in such families. These researchers suggest that the father's availability and possibly biological dispositions may determine whether boys' gender identity is typical or atypical.

Androgyny

Study Question *To what extent, if any, should we raise children according to their gender?*

Living in a time when gender roles are becoming more flexible, it is awkward maintaining stereotypical role distinctions based on gender or even to talk about "gender-appropriate behavior." Most mothers work and some men stay home to provide care for their children. More men are becoming nurses and secretaries, and more women are becoming doctors and lawyers.

Rejecting the idea that masculinity and femininity are at opposite ends of a continuum or that certain behaviors should be expected of children on the basis of their gender, Sandra Bem (1974) introduced the concept of **androgyny**. Androgynous traits represent the most desirable characteristics of both genders. According to Bem, parents should encourage attributes such as integrity, sensitivity, assertiveness, independence, and competence in all children, regardless of their gender. People should have the choice of pursuing the career or lifestyle that best suits their personal needs and preferences rather than one that conforms to their chromosomal and genital makeup.

Sexual Orientation

The origins of sexual orientation are not well understood. Some theorists contend that biological factors such as prenatal hormonal imbalances determine sexual orientation. Others have suggested that social learning experiences are the key (M. Hoffman, 1977a). Different types of homosexuality appear to have different causes. Both biological and social learning factors probably are involved, perhaps to a different degree for each type of sexual orientation (Bell, Weinberg, & Hammersmith, 1981).

Evidence does not support the common belief that homosexuality in men is created by ineffective fathers and domineering mothers. It is also unlikely that painful experiences with the opposite sex or seduction by a member of one's own gender precipitates homosexual preferences. Play activities and toy preferences of children certainly are not causally related to eventual sexual orientation. Some have suggested that a poor relationship with one's father is one of several factors for both male and female gays (Bell, Weinberg, & Hammersmith, 1981). Even though a poor father-child relationship is often mentioned by lesbians and gays, most people who feel distant from their fathers are heterosexual.

Spotlight

Children's Household Work

Parents raise many questions about children's participation in household work. What chores should children perform around the house? At what age should children be expected to participate in household work? Should children be paid for their contributions? Should boys and girls perform the same tasks, or should chores be differentiated by gender? And, do children benefit from engaging in household work?

Goodnow (1988b) explored these and other questions related to children's participation in work around the house. In the past, children's labor in and out of the home was a necessity. Changing conceptions of children and childhood, together with changes in family configurations, have generated new perspectives and issues regarding the potential benefits of children's housework.

Many parents believe that participating in household work is good for children. It builds character while promoting cooperation and responsibility. It encourages a sense of belonging to the family unit. Some parents, especially single parents, dual-career parents, and those in large families, report that they really depend on their children's help. More than a third of parents questioned in one study reported occasionally paying their children for their help.

Household tasks usually are differentiated by gender. Reviewing the findings of Thrall's (1978) study, Goodnow writes, "Mothers or children . . . set and cleared the table, but fathers did not. Fathers or children shoveled snow, but mothers did not. Mothers had fairly exclusive ties to ironing, cleaning the oven, and picking up the living room before company came. Fathers had fairly exclusive ties to fixing things around the house. Mothers or fathers might change light bulbs, but children did not" (p. 13).

Some parents believe that children should perform "tasks that teach." Others will assign any necessary task, regardless of its educational value. Many parents believe that children's participation in household chores promotes responsibility and cooperation. Others respond, "You're only young once," maintaining that children should be relatively free of adult responsibilities. Those who advocate "domestic democracy," would require that all family members share the labor.

The age and gender of a child are important variables influencing children's participation. Age "brings changes in how much is done, what is done, how much help is expected to be given, definitions of help, offers of help and reports of satisfaction" (Goodnow, 1988, p. 13). Parents also take into account children's abilities and the effort required to teach a child to perform a task successfully. Various tasks that might be assigned to younger children, such as "picking up after themselves," would not be considered as work for older children. It is expected of them.

One study found that over 90 percent of children, by the age of 9 or 10 years, are involved in regular chores. Younger children are considered responsible only for themselves (e.g., cleaning up after themselves). As they get older, there is an increase in family work. There also is a transition from assisting their parents to assuming full responsibility for certain chores (White & Brinkerhoff, 1981a).

Regarding gender, White and Brinkerhoff (1981b) found that girls are more likely than boys to be assigned domestic chores such as cooking and cleaning. Boys are more likely to do outside work including taking out garbage, shoveling snow and lawn-mowing. Out-of-doors work performed by boys was more likely to earn money. Girls, like their mothers, are apparently being socialized to work "for love" (Goodnow, 1988, p. 15). The implication is that females' housework, al-

though appreciated, does not merit economic compensation. Not all tasks are differentiated by gender, for example, feeding pets and cleaning one's room. Parental attitudes about the gender-typing of chores also reflect the number of sons and daughters available to perform these tasks (Brody & Steelman, 1985).

Parents report using a variety of techniques to motivate children to help, including rewards, punishment, social reinforcement, instruction, and 'moral exhortation.' Many prefer to use the principle of 'minimal justification.' They encourage a sense of responsibility rather than using external incentives (Goodnow, 1988b). Young children are more eager to help when there is an incentive. "I hate picking up because it's so boring, and you have to keep bending down and standing up. But I want my lollipop" (Yvette, 5 years old, quoted by Foderaro, 1987).

When conflict arises regarding chores, the issue typically is the choice of task and time limits set by parents for task completion. Children usually accept parental authority regarding the assignment of tasks, but they may argue about the details of their execution (Montemayor, 1983).

Promoting Cooperation in Household Work

It is not clear how, or even whether, children benefit from performing housework. Studies generally have not discovered impressive differences in responsibility or dependability between children who perform household chores and those who do not. However, children may benefit by learning skills with potentially educational or practical value.

It seems likely that children could benefit more from their participation if parents attend as much to the process of participation as they do to the outcome of the child's efforts. This includes helping children understand why they are being asked to help, how their efforts are contributing to the family, and that their efforts are appreciated.

With young children, parents can promote cooperation by selecting a particular domain to work on, such as "keeping your room neat." Parents of young children can promote the learning of basic "tidying" skills by arranging the child's room in such a way that cleaning up becomes a manageable task for a toddler with a lot of stuff. Providing them with safe open-top storage boxes, oversized colorful buckets, hangers with the likeness of a cartoon character, or wicker hampers in the shape of a duck motivate their participation.

"To entice a child to tidy up, storage items with cheerful associations may help. A wise parent sets up a child's room so that straightening it up is not only possible but almost pleasurable" (Louie, 1987). The natural consequences of not being able to find a favorite toy or a needed baseball glove also encourage neatness.

Young children may need specific instructions about how to perform a task that a parent takes for granted. "A 5-year-old might not know what to do if you say, 'clean your room.' Break the task down into specific actions like 'put your clothes in the dresser and your toys in the basket.' To a toddler, pushing all of his toys into a pile in the middle of the room seems an appropriate way to clean the room. It meets his needs, even if it doesn't meet those of his parents" (Kutner, 1987c). Rather than arbitrarily assigning tasks, parents also can arrange family meetings and assign chores democratically.

Some parents of gay teenagers suffer from "homosexual panic," engaging in denial, guilt, and self-blame, all of which leave them emotionally unavailable to their children. A mother of a gay child disclosed, "I found out my son was gay when he was 16. And when I did, I was very, very upset. I thought there were few things in the world that would happen to me that would be worse" (quoted by Tabor, 1992). She has since participated in Gay Pride marches and speaks about her experiences at local high schools.

Some parents verbally or physically abuse their gay or lesbian children or expel them from the family (Zera, 1992). A young woman from Brooklyn, New York, reports that she was driven out of her house when she told her mother that she is a lesbian. "Now she calls me a freak and says she wishes I was never born" (quoted by Tabor, 1992). It is a terrible feeling for most adolescents to so disappoint their parents or to feel that they are not living up to the religious or moral ideals that they were taught.

Parents should not feel responsible for their children's eventual sexual orientation. There seems to be little that parents can do to influence their children's sexuality one way or another. Like skin color and gender, people do not choose their sexuality. It's just there. As painful as it might be for some parents to discover that their children are not heterosexual, their love for their children can help them overcome the irrational prejudices that otherwise divide and destroy families.

SUMMARY

1. To a large extent, children's self-concept and self-esteem depend upon the feedback that they get from other people and the performance standards that they are encouraged to meet. Children who perceive themselves as different from the majority group or who receive negative feedback about their ethnic or racial characteristics may require special sup-

port. Their parents play an important role in helping them to accept the positive aspects of their ethnic heritage.

2. Self-esteem generally refers to how we feel about ourselves. Children with a track record of success in valued activities develop a sense of "self-efficacy" that allows them to seek new challenges and to take risks. Children who have overprotective, punitive, neglecting, perfectionistic, or disapproving parents may develop negative self-esteem or learn unrealistic standards of performance. They may learn to fear situations when their competence is being evaluated.

3. Coopersmith related children's self-esteem to a variety of parenting practices, including parental acceptance of the child, clearly defined and enforced limits, and flexibility. Baumrind, Rogers, and Erikson have described parenting practices for promoting self-esteem that are very similar to those advocated by Coopersmith. Bandura described the critical role that self-efficacy (self-confidence) plays in personality development.

4. Research on gender differences confirms that males and females are much more similar than different. Biological differences are related primarily to reproduction and health. The most clear-cut gender difference in behavior is that boys behave more aggressively and competitively than girls. If differences in abilities have existed in the past, they are lessening, possibly because males and females are being treated more equitably.

5. Although most parents raise their sons and daughters similarly, subtle differences in expectations, beliefs, and values may encourage the slight gender differences that seem to exist in achievement and self-esteem. Parents socialize their sons somewhat more intensely than their daughters, perhaps believing that boys require firmer limits to be set on their behavior.

6. Parents encourage what they consider to be gender-appropriate behaviors in their children, especially sons. Parents are more concerned about "effeminate" behavior in boys than about "masculine" behaviors in girls. Perhaps as a result, boys are more rigid in the distinctions they make about gender-role behavior. Household chores sometimes are assigned on the basis of a child's gender.

7. Theorists attribute gender-typing to some combination of biological dispositions, socialization, and cognitive development. Very early in life, children begin to learn about gender roles from their parents, their peers, and from the media. Television and movies often portray gender roles stereotypically.

8. Some parents, aware of the limitations that gender roles impose on their children, encourage desirable ("androgynous") characteristics such as independence and assertiveness in their children.

9. Although the determinants of sexual orientation are not known, parents should not feel responsible for their children's sexuality. Rogers's concept of unconditional acceptance reminds us that competent parenting requires accepting our children as they are (although not necessarily accepting their behavior).

GLOSSARY

androgyny A sex role orientation in which an individual adopts the most desirable characteristics of both genders

altruism Expressing concern for other people by offering help when it seems to be needed

empathy The ability and desire to understand people's experience and feelings from their point of view

gender identity Identifying oneself as male or female

gender typing   The ways in which children are raised to take on the roles and values traditionally associated with their gender

positive regard   The expression of unconditional acceptance of someone's basic worth as a person regardless of whether one approves of that person's behavior

self-actualization   The fulfillment of one's potential for personal growth

self-concept   A set of beliefs about one's unique characteristics, traits, and behaviors

self-efficacy   Judgments or expectations that one will perform successfully in a given situation

self-esteem   How we feel about who we think we are

unconditional acceptance   As Carl Rogers described, expressing acceptance of someone regardless of his/her achievements or behavior

THOUGHT QUESTIONS

1. In what sense do children see themselves through their parent's eyes?

2. How can parents of biracial children help them appreciate their special ethnic status?

3. On what key points concerning the development of self-esteem do theorists seem to agree?

4. If you were a parent of a son and a daughter, in what ways would you treat them differently (according to gender)?

5. Why are parents more concerned about "effeminate" behavior in sons than "masculine" behavior in daughters?

9
CHAPTER

ADJUSTMENT, STRESS, AND COPING

OBJECTIVES 264
HAPPINESS 265
Spotlight: Encouraging Honest Behavior 266
CHILDHOOD FEARS 268
The Development of Childhood Fears 269
Parental Handling of Children's Fears 269
SHYNESS 270
ANGER 271
JEALOUSY 273
SHAME, EMBARRASSMENT, AND PRIDE 274
LEARNED HELPLESSNESS 275
STRESS 276
Separation from Parents 277
Birth of a Sibling 278
Marital Tension 278
Spotlight: Stranger Anxiety and Separation Distress 278
Sources of Stress During Adolescence 279
COPING 279
Coping Ability 280
Humor and Coping 281
Resilient Children 282
UNDERSTANDING AND COPING WITH DEATH 283
Children's Limited Understanding of Death 284
When a Parent Dies 286
Helping Children Cope with Death 286

"In listening to children, it is difficult not to be touched by the profound sense of vulnerability among them. They are afraid of being left alone, apprehensive of what lies ahead, and uncertain of what they can do. They are so fundamentally dependent upon adults as to be almost powerless in the face of upsetting events and unpredictable developments. Often they wait—wait until something happens, wait until an adult intervenes . . . Too often they must persevere and persist alone in the face of the unknown and overwhelming" (Dibrell & Yamamoto, 1988, p. 22).

When a Child Dies 288
Adult's Loss of a Parent 290
Spotlight: Letter to a Dying Father 290
SUMMARY 292
GLOSSARY 292
THOUGHT QUESTIONS 293

OBJECTIVES

After studying Chapter 9, students should be able to:

1. Describe how parents can encourage honest behavior in their children
2. List several of the common stressors of childhood
3. Describe how parents can help their children cope with strong emotions
4. Describe the general characteristics of shy children, and how parents can help children overcome their social anxieties
5. Describe how children attempt to cope with parental displays of anger
6. Distinguish between jealousy and envy, and describe the conditions under which children might express each
7. Define "learned helplessness" and the conditions that foster its development
8. Describe the development of various coping styles in children and how they vary according to age
9. Identify the characteristics of "resilient" children and the factors that promote their ability to adjust to very stressful life events
10. Describe how can parents help children cope with the death of a loved one

June 14, 1989

To Whom It May Concern,

I began working with Rosa and her mother during the summer of 1987. I have had over 30 counseling sessions with them over the past two years, and I have observed Rosa in her classroom. I was originally consulted because Rosa was having difficulty getting along with the children in her special preschool class. Because of her aggressive behavior (screaming, biting, pinching, scratching, teasing), the other children were avoiding her.

Her teachers reported that Rosa was uncooperative, stubborn, and defiant. She was almost constantly testing their authority. Occasionally, she would have a tantrum or pinch or bite a teacher, and she would have to be physically restrained. Her teachers and the school's child study team reported that Rosa has a short attention span and is mildly hyperactive. She also has speech problems and poor listening skills. Her parents' troubled relationship and eventual separation has exposed her to additional stresses.

Rosa has good and bad days, good and bad weeks. Eventually, the director of her special program felt that they could not handle Rosa because her presence was too disruptive, and she had to leave the program. Her teachers tried various behavior modification strategies, including time out and daily report cards, with some degree of success. Teachers who were firm with Rosa usually had better results than teachers who were permissive.

As long as Rosa continues to be placed in settings where her special needs are addressed, I would expect to see progress both academically and in her social skills. At the present time, her adjustment to her parents' separation and her father's lessening involvement in her life are my greatest concerns. If I can be of further help, please let me know.

I wrote this letter to a judge to support Rosa's mother's request for additional financial support from her ex-husband. Rosa's mother, an elementary school teacher, was having difficulty finding proper day care because of Rosa's behavior problems and special needs. The letter describes some of the adjustment problems 5-year-old Rosa had been having in school.

As many as one in five children suffers from emotional or behavior problems that impair their lives (Achenbach & Howell, 1993). Many of these children are born to drug-addicted or teenage mothers, and many have been abused or neglected. Only a small percentage of children with adjustment or emotional problems ever receive treatment (Achenbach & Howell, 1993).

Like Rosa's mother, most parents try to protect their children from serious emotional distress. Rosa apparently was unaware of her parents' longstanding marital problems until her father left. Because of her age, she could not understand why her parents no longer loved each other and why they could no longer live together. Children like Rosa—in fact, all children—must develop skills and personal resources that will allow them to solve common life problems, as well as cope with those that cannot be quickly resolved. Rosa will have to cope with her father's lessening availability.

Rosa is not alone. Many children experience insoluble problems, such as parental divorce or sexual abuse, that overwhelm their ability to cope. These stressors may precipitate a wide range of maladaptive behaviors, ranging from nervous habits to suicide attempts. Children who experience chronic (long-term) stressors may develop fears, phobias, and depression. They often do poorly in school and have troubled relationships with their peers and family members. Many exhibit antisocial behaviors such as bullying and shoplifting. Childhood aggression like Rosa's, if untreated, may lead to continued adjustment problems during adolescence and adulthood (Lerner, Hertzog, Hooker, Hassibi, & Thomas, 1988).

HAPPINESS

Study Question   *How are children's negative emotional responses adaptive?*

Parents value their children's happiness. Children's sad faces and crying are disturbing. They motivate most parents to "correct" the circumstances that led to the distress. Children's smiles and happy behaviors reinforce sensitive, nurturant caregiving. In a very important sense, then, children's emotional reactions (positive and negative) gradually shape more effective parenting responses. Happy, affectionate children are a good sign that parents are doing something right. Children's expressions of joy also elicit pleasurable emotions in parents that probably strengthen the parent-child bond.

Negative emotions usually receive more attention than expressions of joy and happiness. It is more important for a child's survival that parents notice and alleviate distress than elicit joy. However, this may encourage children to express negative feelings manipulatively, for example, by crying to get something that they want. Giving children what they want simply because they are distressed encourages manipulative emotional expressions. The parental communication skills described in Chapter 7, especially active listening and acknowledging feelings, are excellent tools for handling children's distress.

Parents should notice and reinforce children's expressions of positive feelings by responding in kind. We can assume that children will learn to model parental expressions of happiness and satisfaction. I do not believe that happy parents necessarily have happy children, but I suspect that there is some correlation. The opposite also is probably true. As noted in Chapter 2, children of depressed mothers display fewer positive emotions than children of non-depressed mothers. Davies and Cummings (1995) report that negative parental emotions increase children's distress and positive emotions reduce their distress.

This is not to suggest that children, or anyone, can always feel happy. Responsive parents support whatever emotional state a child is expressing, whether it is positive or negative. Ginott (1965) and others have noted that some parents overreact when their children are upset. They try too hard to make everything all right. A mother I was seeing in family therapy could not bear to see her children quarrel or show distress. When they did, she felt compelled to find a "quick fix," even though that is not usually helpful or possible. Her older son, not surprisingly, is also overly sensitive during conflict.

Again, when children are upset or angry, the parental communication skills discussed in Chapter 7 can help them clarify their problem and find a possible solution. We all must learn how to accept and cope with negative feelings. Parents should be aware that they are models for expressing both positive and negative feelings. In this chapter, we concentrate more on negative than on positive emotions, mainly because there are far more negative than positive emotions. This entire book, however, is dedicated to promoting parenting skills that encourage cheerful, affectionate relationships between parents and children.

Spotlight

Encouraging Honest Behavior

Like most other aspects of development, children's perception of "reality" changes over time. What adults call "lies" for toddlers may be nothing more than a failure to distinguish between reality and fantasy. "At first, the lies children tell seem to be an effort to remake reality so that it conforms to a more desirable state of affairs. It appears that when children first tell lies they are trying as hard to deceive themselves as other people. By age four, however, children seem really to be trying to deceive their parents" (Stone & Church, 1984, p. 371).

Usually the false statements of toddlers are so preposterous that parents gently accept or question the assertions rather than criticize them. As children get older, many learn that lying and exaggerating are easy ways of gaining attention or admiration. Repeatedly lying to impress people is an indication of low self-esteem and insecurity. Lying is more commonly used to avoid blame and thus, punishment ("I didn't do it"). Adolescents lie about their activities when they feel that their parents are being too nosy or will "go nuts" if they find out the truth.

Lying is considered a serious problem for about 3 percent of all children, usually those who are getting in trouble for other reasons. Children who are chronic liars are at risk for committing criminal offenses later in life (Goleman, 1988a). Stouthamer-Loeber and Loeber (1986) found that chronic lying is significantly related to delinquency, theft, and fighting in boys. "Subjects who lied were more likely to come from families where mothers poorly supervised their children and rejected them and where parents did not get along well or did not live together" (p. 551).

Society generally condemns lies that are told for personal gain. So-called "white lies" that are told to avoid hurting someone's feelings are condoned, or at least tolerated, by most adults. The intention is to protect rather than deceive another person. Children who observe their parents telling lies of convenience may imitate this behavior. However, when asked, most children acknowledge that lying is wrong or bad.

When parents catch their children lying for personal gain, they may be quick to criticize or punish this behavior. This is unfortunate because parents, in effect, may be punishing the child for "getting caught," rather than for lying. If children successfully cover up their misbehavior and thereby avoid punishment, future deceptive behavior is encouraged (Blechman, 1985). For this reason, punishing lying may be counterproductive. It is clear that with proper parental "training," children can become very good liars. Those who learn that lying is "too risky" may invent excuses to lessen their responsibility in difficult situations.

Thoughtful parents discourage deceptive behavior by discussing rather than punishing misbehavior. Young children know that lying is bad, but they may not understand why. When my children were younger, I tried to help them appreciate the relationship between honesty and credibility by using a natural consequence. Children enjoy telling their parents about their accomplishments. If one of my sons lied to me and at a later time told me about an achievement, I would question the truthfulness of their account. I wanted to believe them, but how did I know that this was not just another lie? Distrust is a natural consequence of dishonest behavior and very frustrating to a child who is seeking credit for an actual achievement.

Honest behavior is promoted when parents reinforce children for telling the truth about their misbehavior. "Make sure that honesty has a bigger payoff than dishonesty. If your child is honest about misbehavior, praise your child's honesty, while still letting the child suffer the consequences of his behavior" (Blechman, 1985, pp. 186-187). Punishing truth-telling and ignoring honest behavior are common parental pitfalls. Demonstrating integrity and owning up to one's mistakes are effective ways of encouraging honest behavior in children.

CHILDHOOD FEARS

On May 20, 1988, in Winnetka, Illinois, an 8-year old boy was shot to death by a psychologically disturbed woman who had entered his school with a gun. In the weeks following the tragedy, many children in that town, some of whom attended the school where the boy was killed, exhibited their distress in a variety of ways. "Five- and six-year-olds are afraid to leave their homes or let their parents out of sight. A third-grade boy tells his mother he will take a bazooka to school to protect himself. A 10-year-old talks incessantly about blood splattering on the floor. Even teenagers have trouble sleeping" (Kutner, 1988r).

The random nature of the violence in a classroom setting taxed the coping abilities of many of the town's children. Unlike their parents, who have learned to cope with traumatic events through rationalization and denial, many of the children "coped" with their anxieties by developing psychosomatic symptoms that lasted for weeks or months (Kutner, 1988r; Swenson et al., 1996). Fortunately, most children do not have to cope with events as traumatic as random violence in a school setting. Fear, however, is very much a part of every child's existence.

Infants generally show little fear until they are about 6 or 7 months old. Then they begin to display the facial expressions that indicate fear when they are in the presence of strangers or when they are separated from their caregivers (Kagan, 1984). A fear of heights emerges by 6 months, when infants are beginning to explore their environments by crawling. As children learn more about the world, they develop fears of dangerous situations like fire, falling, and becoming separated from their parents. Because their interpretive abili-

Justin Jaffe

ties are limited, they are susceptible to irrational fears. These usually diminish as children's cognitive abilities expand.

The Development of Childhood Fears

Study Question *How do childhood fears develop?*

Fearfulness has moderate heritability (Marks, 1987), presumably because in a dangerous world, fear and caution are adaptive. Children are predisposed to fear unfamiliar people, settings, and situations. Childhood fears can also be learned. Children acquire fears in at least three ways: through (1) conditioning, (2) modeling, or (3) instruction. Children may learn to fear painful events and objects, such as injections and hot stoves, through conditioning. Children might experience painful bowel movements, and then become constipated. They have associated toileting with pain.

Many children who experienced northern California's "World Series" earthquake in 1989 lost their homes, saw neighbors who had been injured, and felt hundreds of aftershocks. Some said that they had never seen their parents so frightened (*The New York Times*, October 24, 1989). When parents exhibit fear of an event or object ("Eek . . . there's a spider on you"), children are likely to model their apprehension ("Get it off, get it off"). Through instruction or modeling, parents can teach children to fear dangerous situations such as being in an open field during a thunderstorm. Children can also be taught to fear harmless situations, such as using a public lavatory.

In two surveys of children in 6 countries, grades 2 through 9, children were asked to rate the stressfulness of common, everyday situations (Yamamoto et al., 1996; Yamamoto, Soliman, Parsons, & Davis, 1987). The survey results revealed commonalities across cultures in children's perception of what is stressful. The death of a parent and going blind were the two most threatening possibilities. Fear of being humiliated was ranked much higher than the birth of a sibling or having an operation.

Henker and her colleagues (Henker, Whalen, & O'Neil, 1995) solicited "worries" from 194 students in grades 4–8. The children reported worrying about personal matters such as grades and relationships and about death and global issues, including homelessness and the environment. Early adolescents report being concerned about school, friends, parents, and conflicts with peers (Stark, Spirito, Williams, & Guevremont, 1989).

Parental Handling of Children's Fears

One of the great frustrations of parenting is that we cannot guarantee our children's safety. However, by modeling thoughtfulness about social problems like crime, disease, and war, and by teaching children what people can do collectively or as individuals, we can help ease children's fears (Garbarino, 1995). Children are less distressed by serious problems like war and homelessness when they believe that people are doing something about them.

Steps that parents can take to lower the risk of harm to their children include not leaving young children alone and, when they are

Figure 9.1 Pathways to children's fears.

old enough, making sure that youngsters have telephone numbers to call in emergencies. It is important to discuss in advance with children and adolescents situations that might be hazardous.

Dibrell and Yamamoto (1988) suggest that parents provide their children with suitable explanations for anticipated events that upset them, such as doctor visits and hospitalization. Children of different ages show their distress differently, but they always should be encouraged to express their feelings.

Parents can use sympathetic listening to help children clarify their fear and also to convey parental acceptance of those feelings. Studies of children who are good copers find that their parents do not indulge or overprotect them. We can also help young children cope with their fears by using drawings, puppets, role-playing, and story-telling.

SHYNESS

Study Question *How can parents discourage shy behaviors in their children?*

About 42 percent of people in the United States consider themselves to be shy and about 80 percent report either being shy or having been shy at some point in their lives (Caspi, Elder, & Bem, 1988; Honig, 1987; Zimbardo & Radl, 1981). Children in grade school who characterize themselves as shy also consider themselves to be more fearful, passive, and introverted and less friendly and tolerant of others than their non-shy peers. They also like themselves less. Zimbardo notes that their intolerance reflects the tendency of shy people to be critical of others.

Asendorpf (1993) distinguishes three types of solitude in children: temperamental shyness, social-evaluative shyness, and unsociability. Although there are innate (temperamental) dispositions toward sociability or cautious-

TABLE 9.1 How to Help a Shy Child

Use authoritative parenting style (warm, accepting)

Don't pressure child to be assertive, don't embarrass or refer to his/her behavior as shy

Don't speak on the child's behalf

Model assertive, friendly behavior when with child

Practice social skills with children, including meeting someone, introducing oneself, speaking at appropriate loudness, maintaining eye contact, joining ongoing activities

Arrange play activities for child with friendly, accepting children

Monitor such activities and provide constructive feedback

ness, shyness appears to reflect experiential factors to a greater degree than inborn tendencies. This may not apply to the very inhibited children studied by Jerome Kagan and his colleagues (Azar, 1995d; Kagan, Reznick, & Gibbons, 1989). However, for most children, shyness probably reflects deficits in the very skills that enable "sociable" people to interact confidently and effectively.

At the root of shyness and other types of social anxiety is the fear of social evaluation, criticism, closeness, or rejection (Azar, 1995c). Parents who judge their children's worth on the basis of their behavior or accomplishments render what Carl Rogers called conditional acceptance. The child feels accepted only when he or she satisfies the parent's standards of acceptable performance, which may rarely occur.

Parents can discourage the development of bashful behavior by modeling appropriate social behaviors, giving timid children practice in a variety of social situations, providing constructive feedback to help refine the child's social skills, and by rewarding skillful social behavior (Azar, 1995d; Zimbardo & Radl,

1981). Rather than being critical, parents can help their children develop social skills and self-confidence by role-playing social interactions with them. Children can be taught what to say when meeting or greeting someone, how to speak in a loud voice while maintaining eye contact, and so on. When children successfully display these behaviors, parents should reinforce their efforts ("Nice job") (see table 9.1).

ANGER

Study Question *How do children cope when their parents quarrel?*

In this section, we examine how children cope with anger expressed by others and how parents can support children's healthy expression of anger. In Chapter 3, we discussed how parental expressions of emotions influence children. In Chapter 4, we noted that children are especially sensitive to displays of anger by adults and more likely to behave aggressively after witnessing an angry confrontation. Given the prevalence of emotional distress in families (Ross & van Willigen, 1996), it is important to assess its potential effects on children.

As described in Chapter 4, children of divorce suffer more from witnessing angry confrontations between their parents than from parental separation. Even young children are sensitive to displays of anger and may subsequently behave aggressively. E. M. Cummings (1987) refers to displays of anger observed by children in families as "background anger," which seems to emotionally arouse and distress them. "I know she doesn't like it when we argue, because she cries and gets extremely upset when I'm upset. The worst thing is when she pushes him [the father] away. She thinks he's upsetting me. She can't help it. She has to realize that people do fight. It doesn't mean that they don't love each other" (mother of a 3-year-old girl).

Intense hostility that is not openly expressed also takes its toll on children, but verbal and physical expressions of anger are perceived most negatively. Parental anger arouses more angry feelings in boys than in girls, and boys are more likely to react with hostility. Girls are more likely to propose solutions to the problem or to become involved in mediating the dispute (Amato & Keith, 1991b; Cummings, Vogel, Cummings, & El-Sheikh, 1989; Davies & Cummings, 1995; Shifflett-Simpson & Cummings, 1996).

Intense conflict between parents can frighten or upset children. Such distress is seen in children as young as one year of age. Some children, believing that they are responsible for parental anger, feel guilty and blame themselves. By the age of 5 or 6 years, many children try to intervene when parents fight, attempting to alleviate their parents' distress (Covell & Abramovitch, 1987; Covell & Miles, 1992).

In one study (Jenkins, Smith, & Graham, 1989), 71 percent of the children interviewed reported that they intervened when their parents quarreled. The researchers concluded that since intervention is so common, it should be considered normal behavior. "Children may feel that by intervening in a quarrel they gain some direct control over an event that otherwise would make them feel helpless" (p. 187). Children also dealt with their own distress by approaching their siblings or parents.

Most children can cope with occasional displays of parental anger, but when overt hostility persists, children may become either disposed to emotional outbursts themselves or fearful of expressing anger (Goleman, 1985a). "Angry confrontations between parents, which go on for many years, create a negative emotional climate that can undermine a child's psychological development. It can spill over into problems the child has with playmates, which can be among the early signs of trouble"

(Radke-Yarrow, quoted by Goleman, 1985a). Many studies report correlations between marital disharmony and behavioral, social, emotional, and even health problems in children (e.g., Gottman & Katz, 1989).

Study Question *What coping styles do children adopt after witnessing hostile interactions?*

E. M. Cummings (1987) and his colleagues (El-Sheikh, Cummings, & Goetsch, 1989) studied how 4- and 5-year-old children cope with background anger. They exposed pairs of children, with their mothers present, to adult strangers (trained actors) who engaged in positive or angry verbal interactions in a nearby room. This was followed by a "no emotion" period without the strangers. Children's immediate emotional responses to other people's anger and their subsequent aggression toward a friend were assessed.

Children demonstrated "greater distress, social sharing, preoccupation, and positive affect, congruent with exposure to background anger. Increased verbal aggressiveness in play occurred in the period following exposure" (E. M. Cummings, 1987, p. 976). Thus, children "coped" with their exposure to anger in a variety of ways, some more adaptive than others.

Witnessing angry interactions between adults clearly arouses and disturbs children, particularly when there is no resolution to the problem. Older children in particular are relieved when their parents apologize to each other after an angry confrontation (Cummings, Vogel, Cummings, & El-Sheikh, 1989).

Observing positive resolutions (e.g., compromise, apology) of heated arguments between their parents helps children cope with even frequent parental conflict in the home. Negative resolutions of parental conflict (e.g., continued fighting, the "silent treatment") upset young children and may be more distressing than the conflict itself. "Whether verbal conflicts are typically resolved may be more important than the frequency of verbal conflict in the home" (Cummings, Pellegrini, Notarius, & Cummings, 1989, p. 1042).

Children usually do not get to see their parents "making up" after a conflict. Seeing parents achieve resolution helps children feel secure (Cummings, Ballard, El-Sheikh, & Lake, 1991; Cummings, Pellegrini, Notarius, & Cummings, 1989; Cummings, Simpson, & Wilson, 1993; Shifflett-Simpson & Cummings, 1996).

Crockenberg (1987) found that angry and punitive adolescent mothers had children who were angry and noncompliant. These children also show diminished self-confidence regarding their ability to cope with challenging problems. Particularly, infants who were cranky to begin with, showed these characteristics. This highlights the potentially explosive combination of angry mother and irritable infant. Crockenberg (1985) also found that toddlers display more self-concern and angry defiance toward others and less concern for others who are distressed when their mothers express anger rather than other negative emotions.

It appears that children who witness chronic displays of anger in their families, or who are recipients of intense emotional outbursts, suffer and attempt to cope in a variety of ways. There is a tendency for children to attribute their anger, but not their happiness or sadness, to their family (Covell & Abramovitch, 1987)

Expressions of anger are inevitable, even in the most harmonious families. Children (and their parents) benefit when they can accept their angry feelings and express them assertively rather than aggressively (Schaefer & Millman, 1981). Anger that is not expressed may accumulate until it reveals itself explosively or self-destructively.

Children, to some extent, learn how to express their intense emotions by watching other people do so. If they observe their frustrated parents intentionally hurting each other, children may learn that this is an acceptable means of expressing strong feelings. If children observe parental expressions of anger that lead to violence, they might learn to associate the two.

Miller and Sperry (1987) studied the role that language plays in the early socialization of anger and aggression in an urban, working-class community. Mothers in the community witnessed many episodes of anger and violence and talked about them with their children. They taught their children that retaliation is justifiable when another person initiates a confrontation. Thus, mothers socialized their children's anger and aggression by exposing them to "narratives" about highly emotional events that the mothers experienced and by differentially reacting to the children's displays of anger and aggression.

"Anger was valued insofar as it supported the goal of self-protection, impelling the child to act quickly and decisively to defend herself" (p. 26). Children who failed to respond with anger and aggression when attacked were considered sissies. Children who initiated angry or aggressive acts were regarded as spoiled. Anger and aggression were deemed justifiable in self-defense, but not under other conditions.

Mothers' responses to their children's displays of anger were consistent with this philosophy. They tolerated such displays when they felt that their children were justified, as when a parent teased them. However, when unprovoked, the mothers disapproved of their children's expressions of anger. Thus, an important consideration in conflict becomes who is perceived to be at fault. This accounts for the predictable childhood defense, "He started it."

Even by age 2½ years, children were able to justify their anger in terms of another child's instigation. "The children also learned how to communicate anger and aggression.

They responded with verbal refusals, protests, threats, insults, and assertions . . ." (p. 28). Even though the children were becoming adept at justifying their actions, they generally lacked an emotional vocabulary. Miller and Sperry concluded that these children were learning that expressions of vulnerability and sadness are less acceptable than expressions of anger and aggressiveness.

Parental response to children's anger also appears to be an important determinant of their coping ability. Young children who tell their parents that they hate them are demonstrating their frustration in dramatic fashion (Kutner, 1988b). Parents who angrily respond, "Don't you dare talk to me that way," encourage this type of expression. In effect they are saying, "When you hurt me, I will hurt you back." Demonstrating concern and caring, particularly in the face of strong emotion, usually removes fuel from a child's emotional fire. It models a more sensitive approach to handling strong feelings ("You're angry at me. Do you want to talk about it?"). Apologizing and solving the problems that lead to angry exchanges are optimal ways of resolving discord.

JEALOUSY

Harry Stack Sullivan (1956/1973) characterized jealousy as a "horribly unpleasant mental state" (p. 138). It is evoked when an individual perceives intimacies between other people that he wishes he could experience. Jealousy, a stress reaction similar to anxiety (Brody, 1987g), is distinguished from envy. Sullivan defined envy as "an acute discomfort caused by discovering that somebody else has something that one feels one ought to have" (p. 129). Thus, jealousy occurs when an individual desires, or fears losing, intimacy with another person. Envy refers to one's desire for another's possession (Boris, 1994).

Many investigators, including Sullivan, suggest that both jealousy and envy reflect feelings of insecurity and inadequacy. Presumably, having desired relationships or possessions proves one's worthiness. Conversely, lacking these things proves one's unworthiness. Jealousy can be so intense that it drives some to violence. Most instances of wife battering apparently involve jealous husbands (Brody, 1987g; Parrott & Smith, 1993).

Young children are often jealous of their siblings. Perhaps the classic example is the proverbial reaction to the birth of a sibling, "Can't we send her back?" Not understanding that Mom and Dad have enough love and attention for two or more children, youngsters assume that sharing parental resources means less for them. Most children gradually learn how to share parental time and attention. They understand that they will not be "short changed" in the long run. Children do not like to share because it usually does mean less for them in the short run. Socialization teaches children that sharing is beneficial because their generosity will be reciprocated (usually).

Many preschool children attempt to interfere when their mothers are nursing or otherwise caring for younger siblings. They may demand immediate attention and even display tantrum behavior (Dunn, 1995). Parents should try to not overreact or become angry. This adds fuel to the resentful child's fire. Rather, the parent can explain, "This is the time I spend with the baby. If you leave us alone, I will spend time with you when I am finished."

Naturally, parents should not reinforce jealous behavior; the insecurity behind it should be addressed. "Parents who cannot stand to see the child even momentarily unhappy risk rearing a self-centered child. These 'spoiled' children dread any sense of deprivation and tend to become inordinately demanding of attention and affection" (Brody, 1987g).

Children also express jealousy when they perceive their parents showing favoritism. "No fair!" exclaim older children when their younger sibling receives a disproportionate amount of parental attention or patience. "No fair!" exclaim younger children when their older siblings enjoy the privileges of age.

Expressions of jealousy should be taken seriously by parents. They can practice sympathetic listening and other communication techniques described in Chapter 7. "You wish you were older, don't you, so that you could stay up late like your sister." Parents try to be fair, but it is not possible or appropriate to treat siblings identically.

SHAME, EMBARRASSMENT, AND PRIDE

Research suggests that shame emerges at about the age of 18 months, and pride by 2 years of age. "Feelings of shame begin to emerge in the second year of life, at the very formation of the infant's sense of self . . . As the infant realizes that he is a separate person, he is first able to understand that others are directing emotional messages to him. Pride and shame appear—pride at pleasing others and shame at displeasing them" (Goleman, 1987f).

Presumably, the specific cognitive constructs that underlie these emotions must be present. To experience these emotions, children must be able to interpret other people's reactions and understand that these reactions are directed toward them and related to something that they did. Children also have to learn the cultural guidelines that dictate how these feelings are labeled. Emotional labels play a major role in structuring emotional experience and behavior.

Parents facilitate the learning of these labels by using the context of a situation to infer the child's experience and then tentatively labeling it. "You must be so proud of yourself for getting such a good report card." Children also learn from their parents what level of achievement will be praised (Reissland, 1994). Ultimately, feelings of pride or embarrassment come to serve as powerful reinforcers for new learning. Young children may feel pride when they use the toilet successfully, or feel shame when they have an accident.

The experience of pride requires the ability to take responsibility for actions that one can control. One can take pride in an inherited characteristic such as ethnic group membership, but one cannot consider it an achievement. Older children may experience pride or embarrassment even in the absence of another person when they compare their performance to someone else's.

Personal responsibility is not required for feeling embarrassed. Simply having attention drawn to oneself for any reason may be sufficient to precipitate this uncomfortable feeling (Seidner, Stipek, & Feshbach, 1988). When my younger son was about 4 years old, I attended a program at his nursery school. He looked uncomfortable standing among the other children, and he showed little enthusiasm in his singing. Later, when I asked him about his apparent discomfort, he said being in front of all of those people was "embarrassing." This was the first time I had heard him use that word. It reminded me that children may be uncomfortable being the center of attention. Such discomfort is probably related to shyness and to social-evaluation anxiety.

Seidner, Stipek, and Feshbach (1988) interviewed adults and 5-, 7-, 9-, and 11-year-old children about what made them feel proud, embarrassed, happy, and sad. They found that most 5-year-olds "understood that feelings of pride and, to a lesser extent, embarrassment result primarily from outcomes controlled by and contingent on one's own behavior or characteristics" (p. 357). All age groups implied that the presence of an audience is important for experiencing both pride and embarrassment, but especially embarrassment.

LEARNED HELPLESSNESS

Martin Seligman (1975, 1990) and his colleagues have described a pattern of helpless behavior that is associated with a variety of psychological disorders, including depression. Humans (and members of many other species) who are initially exposed to uncontrollable events learn to avoid taking steps to improve their situation. In a sense, the individual learns, "No matter what I try, it makes no difference. I may as well not try at all." Bandura (see Chapter 8) would describe this attitude as revealing low self-efficacy.

Feelings of helplessness predict lower initiative and lower persistence in problem situations. Cognitive and emotional deficits, including sadness and lowered self-esteem, also characterize the **learned helplessness syndrome** (Nolen-Hoeksema, Girgus, & Seligman, 1986). Helplessness is associated with a faulty explanatory style that discourages an individual from believing that he or she can improve a bad situation (Seligman, 1990). Some students, for example, attribute academic failure to their own stupidity. Others attribute their success to good luck. Both attributions imply a lack of control over life problems and discourage efforts to improve a bad situation.

Children who explain positive and negative outcomes in ways that belittle their abilities usually are more depressed and are lower achievers than children who view their abilities realistically (Nolen-Hoeksema, Girgus, & Seligman, 1986). Children who take credit for their successful efforts, and who correctly assess the relationship between effort, ability, and outcome, typically are not depressed and do not have achievement problems (Seligman, 1990).

It is possible that children who experience unfortunate, uncontrollable life events, such as the death of a parent or sibling, might experience helplessness. They often show the motivational, cognitive, and emotional deficits mentioned above. A maladaptive explanatory style may emerge from such a pattern, leaving the child vulnerable to depressive episodes in the future (Nolen-Hoeksema, et al., 1986).

It is not clear whether faulty explanatory styles lead to depression, or whether depression encourages the development of faulty explanatory styles. Nevertheless, children who learn realistic ways of appraising their efforts, and who learn to put failure in perspective, are much less susceptible to depression (Seligman, 1990).

STRESS

Some adults express discomfort about bringing children into our unpredictable world. As protective as we try to be, there is no way to guarantee a child's safety or survival. As previously noted, the best that parents can do is minimize children's exposure to physical danger and sources of psychological distress. Second best, parents teach their children how to cope with potentially dangerous, threatening, and stressful life experiences (Gambarino, 1995).

Stress and coping are vague concepts. There is no consensus about their definitions or the processes that they refer to. Psychologists often define **stress** as the body's physiological response to a challenge or demand (Selye, 1976). When the brain perceives an emergency or a challenge, the body's energy resources are mobilized for immediate action. It is not helpful to perceive stress as being good or bad. It is an inevitable consequence of being alive. The emotional response to negative stressors is sometimes referred to as *distress*.

Despite the variety of stressful childhood experiences, there is surprisingly little research on this topic. "The degree of neglect is puzzling in the light of evidence that, in a world of heightened stress, children are fre-

quently among the most affected victims of a range of threatening events" (Garmezy, 1988, p. 51). In this section, we will examine some common stressors of childhood and how children cope with them. We will also discuss the characteristics of "resilient" children who adjust well despite extremely stressful life circumstances.

Study Question   *What types of life events are stressful for children?*

We have seen that, in infancy, the presence of strangers and the absence of one's caregivers can elicit marked distress (see Spotlight: Stranger Anxiety and Separation Distress). Infant responses that encourage the return of absent caregivers are among the earliest coping behaviors (Compas, 1987).

Depending upon a child's age, negative stressors may also include the following: the birth of a sibling; harsh toilet training; observing intense family disharmony or violence; living in poverty; homelessness; natural disasters; moving to a new neighborhood; visits to a doctor or dentist; disability; serious illness; prolonged hospitalization; pressure to perform well in school or school failure; parental divorce or death; racial or ethnic slurs; and rejection from peers.

Note that some of these stressors are chronic. That is, they persist over long periods. Chronic stressors usually change over time, and therefore require a variety of coping mechanisms. There is evidence that early exposure to negative stressors alters a child's sensitivity to future stressors and her general manner of coping with stress (Compas, 1987). Distress can be reciprocal in parent-child relations. Just as parental distress will affect children, a "distressed, disorganized child imposes additional stresses upon caretakers" (Maccoby, 1988, p. 220).

Children seem to be most vulnerable to either long-term, chronic stressors such as serious illness or accumulating short-term stressors like parental conflict. Sensitive parents are alert to changes in their children that indicate serious distress. They notice sadness; impulsive, acting out behaviors; sleep-related problems; problems in school; reports of bodily symptoms such as headaches and stomach problems; and talk about hurting themselves. The particular behavior problems and symptoms usually depend upon the type of stressor. For example, children respond differently to parental death than they do to parental divorce.

It is unlikely that mild stressors will alter the course of a child's development. In fact, everyday stressors provide opportunities for children to learn effective coping strategies. Drastic conditions, however, such as extreme abuse or neglect, increase the risk of serious disturbance in all but the most resilient children. Many children of parents who have suffered traumatic experiences, such as the holocaust or combat in Vietnam, develop emotional problems. The National Vietnam Veterans Readjustment Study reported that 15 percent of the 3.1 million Vietnam veterans suffered from posttraumatic stress disorder. They are irritable, easily startled, occasionally become violent, and may be overly protective of their families and suspicious of outsiders. Many have difficulty feeling close to their children, some of whom behave as if they had experienced the trauma of war. One 10-year-old son of a veteran feared that he and his father would be shot in combat. He had trouble paying attention in school, difficulty falling asleep, and frequently complained of headaches. It is not known why these children display some of their fathers' symptoms (Brooks, 1992).

Three additional examples of stressors that produce at least short-term difficulties for some children are separations from their parents, the birth of a sibling, and parental divorce. (Coping with the death of a close relative is discussed in a separate section.)

Separation from Parents

One of the most potentially frightening experiences for children is being separated unexpectedly from their parents. The popular *Home Alone* movie turns what would be an average child's nightmare into an entertaining family comedy. It does so by empowering the young boy left behind by his vacationing parents with incredible resourcefulness in his battles with bungling burglars. Most children lack the coping resources of the movie's clever young hero and would react with considerable distress to an unplanned separation.

The separation from parents that accompanies admission to a hospital usually can be a major stressor for young children. Hospital stays of longer than one week may produce disturbances that last for several months. This is particularly true of preschool children. They are the most threatened by interference with their parental attachments. It is not just separation that upsets hospitalized children. Their parents' attitudes and anxiety about the events related to the hospitalization and the medical and hospital routines are also possible sources of distress (Rutter, 1988).

Initial separations from parents are more stressful than repeated separations. Field (1991b) observed infants, toddlers, and preschoolers before, during, and after separations from their mothers. All of the mothers were attending conferences that were about four days long. Stress was measured by changes in the children's play, activity level, sleep, and other behaviors. Half of the children were separated only once and the other half experienced three separations over a 6-month period. Field reported that the separations were stressful for the children, although not as stressful as separations for the birth of a sibling. Separation from their mother was most stressful for the children in the single-separation group. Field concluded that children adapt to repeated separations from their mothers.

Birth of a Sibling

Most preschool children are both excited and disturbed by the birth of a sibling. They may develop sleep and toileting problems and show an increase in clinging and oppositional behavior. Some behavior problems seem to reflect changes in the patterns of family interaction (particularly the mother-child relationship) to which the older child had been accustomed. As previously discussed, parents can compensate for these changes, to some extent, by giving special attention to the older sibling. They also can point out the advantages of having a younger sibling and request the child's assistance in caring for the newborn (Rutter, 1988). There are even classes offered by hospitals that teach children how to be older siblings (Kutner, 1989b).

Marital Tension

As discussed in Chapter 4, much of the distress experienced by children of divorce reflects the long-standing and intense hostility expressed by their parents before, during, and following their separation. Their parent's

Spotlight

Stranger Anxiety and Separation Distress

Between the ages of 5 and 12 months, when infants are in the presence of strangers they display intense distress behaviors such as crying, clenching their fists, and quickly crawling to a parent (Sroufe, 1977). The infants' distress signals are adaptive in our potentially dangerous world. They bring immediate parental attention and protection if necessary. They are disturbing, however, to visiting grandparents and family friends who approach the infant for the first time during this period.

The intensity of an infant's distress response depends on the setting, whether a familiar caregiver is present, the stranger's appearance, how a stranger approaches the child, and how a caregiver responds to the stranger (Dickstein & Parke, 1988). Although it may be difficult for grandparents or family friends to delay holding the new arrival, gradual approach reduces the infant's distress. Wariness of strangers continues throughout the preschool years (Greenberg & Marvin, 1982). Under "secure" conditions, some children relate well to strangers.

Separation distress consists of an intense emotional reaction precipitated by separation from primary caregivers (Weinraub & Lewis, 1977). It peaks between the ages of 14 to 20 months and gradually lessens throughout the preschool years. When infants see their parents getting ready to leave home without them, they usually become distressed, creep or run to a parent, and cling for dear life. Although both types of distress reactions are disturbing to parents, keep in mind that they are adaptive. Infants generally are safer in the presence of familiar people than in their absence or in the presence of strangers.

When leaving an infant with a new babysitter, parents can ease the separation distress by having the babysitter spend some time with the infant while they are present. Optimally, this would be done before the first time the parents leave the infant alone with the sitter. Not surprisingly, parents also suffer from separation anxiety (Hock, McBride, & Gnezda, 1989; McBride & Belsky, 1988; McClelland, 1995).

TABLE 9.2 Common Stressors in Childhood and Adolescence

Infancy
Encountering strangers
Being separated from parent or other caregiver
Birth of a sibling

Childhood
Conflict between parents
Parental separation or divorce
Moving to a new neighborhood
Visiting a doctor or dentist
Aggressive peers
School failure
Loss of a family member

Adolescence
Rejection from peers
Peer pressure
School failure
Preparing for the future

marital conflict and the divorce process expose children to a wide range of potential stressors that may tax their ability to cope (Crockenberg & Forgays, 1996; Irion, Coon, & Blanchard-Fields, 1988; O'Brien, Margolin, & John, 1995).

Sources of Stress During Adolescence

The early years of adolescence are very stressful for most young people. Changes related to puberty, more challenging school work, and increased conflict with parents over autonomy issues, burden most young teenagers. At a time of heightened vulnerability, adolescents are expected to perform at a higher, more adult-like level. Exposure to drugs and sexual opportunities are additional potential hazards (Jessor, Van Den Bos, Vanderryn,

Costa, & Turbin, 1995). In Chapter 11, we will discuss the importance of the parent-adolescent relationship in helping adolescents become "their own person" while staying emotionally in touch with their families.

COPING

Parents do what they can to minimize their children's distress, but for almost everyone, daily living is at least mildly stressful. Children's sense of well-being seems to reflect, more than the type or amount of stress they experience, their ability to cope with everyday stressors (Hardy, Power, & Jaedicke, 1993). Kagan (1988) defines **coping** as "a reaction to a stressor that resolves, reduces, or replaces the affect state classified as stressful" (p. 196). Coping ability varies with many factors, including the child's history and temperament, the type of stressor, social support, beliefs about control over the stressor, and the number of concurrent stressors (Rossman & Rosenberg, 1992).

Childrens' coping resources and style are best understood in a family context (Dumas & LaFreniere, 1993). Patterson (1988) suggests that chronic stress threatens not just children, but the entire family system. Certain negative life events, such as temporary parental unemployment, do not directly affect a child. Rather, children are affected by the distressed reactions of family members. Children suffer when their distressed parents cannot provide them with adequate nurturance and support and expose them to stressful or punitive encounters (Dumas & LaFreniere, 1993; Elkind, 1994; Hardy et al., 1993).

"Fathers who respond to economic loss with increased irritability and pessimism are less nurturant and more punitive and arbitrary in their interventions with the child. These fathering behaviors increase the child's risk of socioemotional problems, deviant behavior, and reduced aspirations and expectations. The child may also model the somatic complaints of the father" (McLoyd, 1989, p. 293). It is not the economic problem but the father's response to it that harms the child. Children also suffer when family economic distress leads to marital friction or divorce.

Coping Ability

What we call coping ability refers to at least two separate skills: (1) **primary coping**, the ability to define a problem in a way that leads to constructive action, and (2) **secondary coping**, the ability to regulate the emotional distress caused by the problem or stressor (Rutter, 1988). Strong feelings can be regulated by avoiding stressors or by thinking about them constructively (Compas, 1987; Rossman & Rosenberg, 1992). Avoidant strategies make the most sense when a situation is uncontrollable.

How children react to events depends partly on their interpretation of the situation (Kopp, 1989). Children who are teased because of their nationality or race will be less angry if they can attribute the attack to the other child's prejudice rather than to their own characteristics (Kagan, 1988). A realistic appraisal of the stressor, combined with an understanding of what can be done about it, foretells successful coping. Parents can encourage such coping skills using the parenting and communication skills outlined in Chapters 6 and 7.

TABLE 9.3   Types of Coping

Primary coping: defining a problem in a way that leads to constructive action

Secondary coping: the ability to regulate emotional distress

Transitional objects: provide feelings of safety and security

People generally use several coping strategies when confronted with everyday stressors. Like adults, children differ in their "coping efficacy," the belief that they can cope successfully with a stressor. Children of emotionally supportive parents usually display a more varied coping repertoire (Hardy, Power, & Jaedicke, 1993; McIntyre & Dusek, 1996).

Highly aroused infants are soothed by swaddling and pacifiers (Campos, 1989). Older infants and toddlers, slightly less dependent on their parents for relief from distress, find security in a soft blanket, doll, or cloth (Lehman, Arnold, & Reeves, 1995). These so-called **transitional objects** provide feelings of safety and security. They are particularly handy at bedtime, although not all young children have the ability to comfort themselves with such objects.

Older children develop more sophisticated ways of coping with distress. Adolescents cope differently than younger children (Blanchard-Fields & Irion, 1988). "Young children are likely to become fearful of stressors, while older children are likely to become angry" (Kagan, 1988, p. 196).

Band and Weisz (1988) asked 6-, 9-, and 12-year old children to recall episodes involving 6 different types of stressful life situations, such as being separated from parents or school failure. They were asked to describe their reactions to each. Interestingly, only 3.5 percent of all episodes involved relinquished control. This suggests that even young children have accepted the cultural rule against "giving up" when they have a problem.

Styles of coping varied according to age and situation. As the investigators hypothesized, self-reports of primary coping (i.e., problem solving) decreased with age. Secondary coping strategies (i.e., handling distress) increased with age. This was especially true when there was little a child could do to improve the circumstances, as when they were getting vaccinated. Younger children

Children differ in their belief that they can cope successfully with a stressful event.

were as likely to use primary coping (e.g., screaming) to avoid getting an injection as they were to use secondary coping (e.g., distracting themselves). Older children accepted the inevitability of the medical procedure and attempted to cope with it.

Many children are sensitive to displays of violence witnessed on television dramas, news shows, and in movies. Seeing children or parents being harmed and violence in schools is very disturbing to them. Because it is almost impossible to prevent children from seeing violence, it is important that parents discuss such incidents with their children. Parents should explain that violence is almost never acceptable. For dramas, parents can point out the individuals are "playing" and not really hurting each other. For disturbing news stories, parents can explore the child's interpretation of and feelings about the events observed, express their own reactions (without preaching), and then explain what is being done to reduce violence (e.g., the role of the United Nations). Having a child draw a picture or tell a story that makes the situation better often helps.

For most of us, talking about our problems and concerns with someone who cares usually helps us feel better. Younger children need help verbalizing their feelings. Older children and adolescents also need help in finding ways to address their problems (Jessor, Van Den Bos, Vanderryn, Costa, & Turbin, 1995). It is possible that older children have learned something that younger children haven't. Improve the situation when possible. If you can't improve it, accept it. Cognitive strategies appear to work better in the latter case (Campos, 1987). Parents can encourage the use of both types of coping strategies by modeling them and by encouraging children to explore their alternatives when confronted with stressors ("What can you do to make it better?").

Humor and Coping

A sense of humor is an important coping resource. Most children enjoy playing with words and ideas. They quickly learn that saying or doing funny things brings them attention. Freud (1916) speculated that humor or wit is a socially acceptable way of relieving pent-up emotions, including sexual and aggressive impulses. Many top comedians report that during their childhoods, humor was a helpful way of coping with family conflict, isolation, and deprivation. Humor provided both an escape from suffering and a defense for handling anxiety (McGhee, 1979).

"Jokes told by children during therapy sessions offer support for the view that humor is often used to help cope with conflict. For example, many of the anxieties felt by children concern parent-child relationships in some way. When children are asked to tell their favorite jokes during therapy, the jokes often center on parent conflicts or other sources of family dissension" (McGhee, 1979, p. 230).

McGhee cautions that a preoccupation with jokes could prevent children from dealing with their strong feelings and life problems. "The possession of a good sense of humor increases the odds of a person's being well adjusted, but emotional difficulties may also develop that cannot be mastered by means of humor ... although humor may be effective in dealing with certain sources of anxiety and distress, there is no evidence that it is a cure-all for all emotional difficulties that children encounter" (p. 238). In other words, humor helps, but don't overdo it.

Resilient Children

Study Question *Some children manage to "survive" extreme conditions of deprivation and neglect during childhood. How do they do it?*

Children vary considerably in both their susceptibility to life stressors and in their resiliency or ability to cope. Most children raised by neglecting, addicted, impoverished, or mentally ill parents will have adjustment

TABLE 9.4 Protective Factors of Resilient Children

Personality and dispositions:
Adaptable, recover quickly from upsets
Positive thinkers
Easygoing temperament
Positive self-esteem
High frustration tolerance
Persistence

Family:
Good relationships with supportive parents
Seeking help from other caring adults
Positive coping model

Situational:
The fewer the risk factors, the better the adjustment
Supportive school environment
Recognition for some skill or achievement
Non-family support system

problems. And each additional stressor increases their risk.

Werner (1989a), for example, found that two-thirds of the Hawaiian children he studied who experienced four or more risk factors (such as poverty and parental divorce) by the age of 2 years, developed serious learning or behavior problems by the age of 10. Some resilient children, however, survived under the same awful conditions that emotionally devastated others. One out of three of the children in Werner's high risk sample "grew into competent young adults who loved well, worked well and played well" (p. 108).

Researchers wonder, "what the protective factors are in these children and in their caregiving environments that ameliorate, or buffer, their responses to stressful life events" (Warner, 1989b, p. 72). Are there innate fac-

Knapp interviewed 155 families who had recently lost a child through terminal illness, suicide, murder, or whose children died suddenly and unexpectedly. He found 6 significant similarities in how they reacted to the deaths: (1) the desire never to forget the child and a need to talk about their tragic experience and about their memories of the child; (2) a loss of hope, with no way to justify their lives, or continue to live without their child; (3) an attempt to find some reason or justification for the loss to make it meaningful; (4) a significant change in values, giving up worldly ambitions and searching for personal satisfaction; (5) a sense of vulnerability regarding life and death and greater tolerance of and sensitivity toward other people; and (6) the existence of "shadow grief," grief that is never totally resolved, an emotional dullness that prevents a person from responding fully and completely to outer stimulation. Knapp considers these reactions normal for parents who have lost a child.

Even parents who lose children after prolonged illness, which seemingly would give them time to prepare for the loss, often carry a burden of guilt for not preventing their child's death (Gaylin, 1985). Guilt is also a common reaction when a child dies suddenly and unexpectedly, as in Sudden Infant Death Syndrome (see Chapter 2). Parents wonder, or obsess about, whether they could have prevented the death. Common reactions following unbearable loss include shock; denial; loneliness; depression; loss of appetite; insomnia; feelings of guilt, anger, and hostility; lack of energy; perpetual grief; and an inability to resume a normal lifestyle (Gaylin, 1985). Life seems to have lost its meaning. Some of these reactions resemble the symptoms of posttraumatic stress disorder (Applebaum & Burns, 1991).

"Compounding the tragedy of losing a child are friends and relatives who say the wrong things or who try to avoid the issue altogether; death-denying medical professionals who remain aloof from the emotional turmoil or compound it with their callousness, and the parents themselves, whose different responses to a child's death may lead to misunderstanding, resentment, and distance at a time when mutual support is most crucial" (Brody, 1983).

Parental acceptance of a child's death is facilitated by social support and understanding from others, giving grieving parents the opportunity to share their strong feelings (when they're ready) and allowing them to express their grief totally (Thomas, 1995). People who seek solace from their religious beliefs find greater meaning in the loss and feel less distressed months later (McIntosh, Silver, & Wortman, 1993).

It would not be helpful to suggest to grieving parents that "you can always have another," to suppose "it's all for the best," or to criticize the child's medical care, if he died as the result of illness or accident. Being available, sorry, attentive, patient, and caring are important forms of support. Common pitfalls include staying away from the bereaved, changing the subject when a parent needs to discuss the death, and trying to find something positive to say about the loss (Blakeslee, 1988; Gaylin, 1985; Ostfeld, Ryan, Hiatt, & Hegyi, 1993).

Although most parents never fully recover from a loss of a child, even one who lived only for a few hours, they do eventually "learn to get on with life, to laugh again, take pleasure without guilt and remember without grief" (Brody, 1983). The most intense mourning occurs within a year or two of the loss, with recurring episodes on anniversaries, birthdays, or other special days that bring the child to mind.

Some marriages become unstable following a tragedy. Men and women cope differently with their sorrow: women grieve intensely; men return to work. Women may misperceive their husband's lack of visible grieving as a lack of caring (Smart, 1992). "Surviving brothers and sisters also suffer when a child dies, but parents in pain may overlook the siblings' anguish, anxiety and guilt. A surviving sister may think the same thing will happen to her. A child may think he somehow caused his brother's death" (Brody, 1983). Grieving siblings need good information, reassurance, understanding, attention, and security (Hindmarch, 1995). There are many support groups and family therapists that specialize in helping families grieve and accept the loss of a child.

Adult's Loss of a Parent

The loss of a parent can occur at any age and is, of course, more likely in adulthood than childhood. Each year, in the United States, about 12 million adults lose a parent. Parental loss is therefore the most common source of bereavement. Sometimes death comes gradually, and sometimes suddenly, without any opportunity to say those things that we would like or need to say to feel complete in our relationship (see *Spotlight*: Letter to a Dying Father). "No chance to say, 'Goodbye Daddy—I love you,' 'Thanks for all you have given me and my children,' 'I'm sorry for all the times I must have hurt you'" (Brody, 1987a). Some

people who have lost parents find that writing a letter or speaking to the deceased in one's mind can create a sense of completion.

When children grow up and perhaps become parents themselves, their relationships with *their* parents remain intense, unique, and irreplaceable. The loss can be devastating. "Even when parents are old and have lived fulfilling lives, or when death terminates a prolonged illness and might be a welcome relief, the pain felt by children can be surprisingly intense. And even when children had a hostile or ambivalent relationship with their parents they might grieve for might-have-beens, the rapport they never experienced" (Brody, 1987a).

Some adult children feel guilty for not having done enough for their parents. Many feel anger toward a wide range of targets, including the parent who died and abandoned them, doctors and siblings who didn't show enough caring, and toward life, for its harsh realities. Like most life experiences, losing a parent can serve as a vehicle for emotional growth. "Some learn not to postpone the frills of life—vacation trips, visits and other pleasures. Some are spurred to restore lost contacts with friends and relatives or establish a closer relationship with their own children. Some simply become more sensitive, more aware of the needs of others and more willing to give of themselves, even without being asked" (Brody, 1987a).

Spotlight

Letter To a Dying Father

Dear Daddy,
I lie in bed at night composing eloquent messages I wish to send you. Then, in the cold light of the morning I invariably dismiss

my nighttime thoughts as melodramatic, morbid, or at the very least, irrelevant. And yet, every night, I am flooded by pressing images and ideas that I feel I must convey. I am finally crying "uncle" and giving in to my nighttime self. Feel free to stop reading here...

First, I am astonished that you are dying. That probably comes as no big surprise since it's not exactly something you anticipated either. Nonetheless, I am talking about early shattering mind boggling astonishment that makes me feel constantly breathless. Life has caught me off-guard both because you have cancer and in the way it makes me feel.

Once, years ago when we lived in Hackensack, and you and mommy were in a rough time in your marriage, you admonished me to refrain from becoming overly involved in other peoples' lives and problems. You told me that my blessing and my curse was my ability to stand totally in someone else's shoes and to experience their emotions. Yes, that means that I suffer for more than just myself. Too often I stand in the shoes of your wife, grandsons, son-in-law, parents-in-law and other children. After all, why just wallow in my own misery when I can really indulge in someone else's! On the other hand, I walk around tallying all of the people I know who have lost a parent, or even more accurately a father, and survived. I see that some have survived better than others. I try to visualize myself "standing in the shoes" of the heartiest survivors... just in case.

I think that what awakens me at night (aside from Noah, Jonah, and Seth, of course) is something that Carol once told me about her father's sickness and death. She said that by the time her father had died, he had been dead for her for quite some time. As he underwent progressively more strenuous forms of chemotherapy, he was unable to maintain contact with her. All of his emotional and psychological strength was needed just to stay alive. I am so afraid that I will have left something unsaid.

You told me that you and I have nothing to say to one another. I took that as a sort of compliment. There is nothing left to say, we each are fully aware of and embraced by the extent of our love for one another. But, but, but the unspoken message haunts me (I told you there would be melodrama if you read this far). I think perhaps that the unspoken message is that you are more to me than you could possibly know. It is not our love that is unclear. You father, me daughter, I get that. It is our relationship that is so incredibly expansive as to defy definition. Never mind that you are my friend, advisor, confidant, and companion. That is apparent to mere strangers. There is something else, something special, even unique that I feel we share. There are parts of you that will remain with me and in me for the rest of my life. Will I ever find a job or career that I love? Will I ever abandon pacificism? Will I ever make TONS of money? (Will I ever learn to type?) It's not so much that I share your views as that knowing yours has permanently shaped mine. After all, I believe in God (sort of) and you don't.

Remember when Carol's father was dying and Cheryl wouldn't bring her kids to visit him anymore because she didn't want them to remember him like that? You told me that you understood her actions because to a young child there would be no difference between someone passing out of their lives at age 3 as compared with age $3\frac{1}{4}$. Actually, that should be more true of an adult since a few weeks or months represent a far smaller fraction of an entire adult lifetime. I have to confess that although that sounds good in theory, I have dug my heels in against the passing of time and grab at the minutes of each day as they slip from my grasp. (If you have read this far you're entitled to a little poetry!)

When I sit with you, or more accurately, doze next to you, I always feel that you know what is in my heart. But in the middle of the night when you are not around I am clenched by the fear that I assume too much. I do not know what the course of your illness will be. Whatever the future holds for us all, I want you to know that your life fills me with admiration for a man who is honest, courageous, loving, and above all, consistent. You are my hero and my role model. This would not be a good time to tell me the emperor is wearing no clothes.

I know that, especially now, I fulfill a certain function in your life and in mommy's. I will try not to let either of you or, I guess, myself, down. A very long time ago,

in a department store, mommy asked me to stop calling her "mommy" at the top of my lungs because it sounded so childish coming from a grown up of nineteen years old. For some reason, that request, which I hardly ever honored and which now she herself would probably deem nonsensical, comes to mind almost daily. I LOVE YOU DADDY (get the message?). [Jeri Wahrhaftig's father died about 3 weeks later. Her journal entries are found throughout this section.]

SUMMARY

1. Stress is a normal and inevitable part of life. All people benefit from having coping skills that allow us to identify and solve problems that can be solved and accept and adjust to problems that can't be solved.

2. It is important that parents learn how to validate the expression of both positive and negative emotions in their children. Positive adjustment is encouraged by parental support and understanding of children's strong feelings and concerns.

3. Mild stressors encourage the development of coping skills, but children can become overwhelmed by extreme circumstances, such as chronic parental conflict, abuse, or neglect. Some children develop maladaptive behaviors that persist throughout childhood, adolescence, and adulthood.

4. Most adults find their mortality intimidating. Children are no different. Children's understanding of death changes over time. Older children come to understand that death is inevitable and irreversible. Children initially deny these realities and then desperately search for a way to cope with them. The inevitable death of their parents and other loved ones intensifies children's natural fears of

being abandoned. Direct experiences with dying people and the death of loved ones, including pets, may facilitate their understanding of the process.

5. Parents can support their children's grieving by answering their questions truthfully at a level they can understand and by not hiding their own expressions of grief. Children should be given choices regarding participation in the rites and rituals for the deceased. Talking about the loss, asking children sensitive questions, and giving them thoughtful answers to their questions is good parenting. Parents who lose a child and adult children who lose parents also require special understanding and support.

GLOSSARY

coping   A reaction to a stressor that lessens arousal

learned helplessness syndrome   A pattern of helpless behavior that usually reflects prior exposure to uncontrollable events

primary coping   The ability to define a problem in a way that leads to constructive action

secondary coping   The ability to regulate emotional distress

stress The body's physiological response to a challenge or demand

transitional objects Objects like blankets that provide infants and toddlers with feelings of safety and security

THOUGHT QUESTIONS

1. How do some parents inadvertently teach deceptive behavior to their children?

2. Are happy parents likely to have happy children? Explain.

3. How can parents prepare their child for a visit to the dentist?

4. How does good family communication help children cope with everyday stressors?

5. How can parents support a preschool child through the death of a grandparent?

10
CHAPTER

PARENTING AND ACHIEVEMENT

OBJECTIVES 296
Mark #13 296
HOME AND FAMILY FACTORS IN ACHIEVEMENT 297
Verbal Interaction and Stimulation 299
Good Parent-Child Relationship 300
Parental Beliefs and Expectations about Achievement 301
Parental Style of Discipline 303
Summarizing Family Influences 304
TOO MUCH TOO SOON?: CREATING SUPERKIDS 305
EARLY SCHOOLING 307
THE PROCESS OF SCHOOLING 307
Mark #14: The Book Report 307
Spotlight: Asian-American Superachievers? 308
Cultural Perspective: The Japanese Mother 310
Reading and Writing 312
Parental Involvement in Schooling 313
Handling School-Related Problems 315
Achievement and Underachievement in Adolescents 316
The Case of Peter 316
Encouraging Creative Expression 317
PLAY 318
Parents as Playmates 320
Gender Differences in Play and Toy Preferences 320
TELEVISION 321
Effects on Children 322

"The failure to bridge the social and cultural gap between home and school may lie at the root of the poor academic performance of [poor minority] children . . . A child from a poor, marginal family is likely to enter school without adequate preparation. The child may arrive without ever having learned such social skills as negotiation and compromise. A child who is expected to read at school may come from a home where no one reads and may never have heard a parent read bedtime stories" (Comer, 1988, pp. 43, 45).

What's A Parent To Do? 323
SUMMARY 324
GLOSSARY 325
THOUGHT QUESTIONS 325

OBJECTIVES

After studying Chapter 10, students should be able to:

1. List several home and family factors that predict children's achievement
2. Describe how the following family factors encourage children's achievement:
   a. Verbal interaction between parent and child
   b. Good parent-child relationship
   c. Parental expectations and beliefs about achievement
   d. Parental style of discipline
3. Describe the issues involved in the "superkid" controversy.
4. Analyze the high achievement of Asian-American students.
5. Describe the special efforts made by Japanese mothers to promote their children's achievements.
6. Explain why reading and writing are considered fundamental skills and discuss how parents can promote their development
7. Describe how parental involvement in their children's schooling benefits children
8. Describe how parental pressure may inadvertently discourage achievement
9. Describe how parents can promote children's cognitive development and creativity through play and expressive activities

10. Describe how television may influence children's behavior and what parents can do to guide their children's viewing

Mark #13

"On Thursday, I had a conference with Mark's homeroom teacher, and I was given his grades. During the semester, parents were sent a progress report. On that he seemed to be doing OK but nothing I'd settle for happily. Purposely, I reserved my opinion and asked what he thought of his grades. He said, 'OK.' I asked did he feel he had done his best and when he said 'yes' what could I do? So I said 'OK' if he felt he was doing his best then how could I ask for more?

"When I spoke to Mr. B, I wasn't surprised that all the teachers felt Mark needed better class preparation (including homework), participation, and concentration. 'He's easily distracted' was a typical comment. In Math and English he got Bs, Social Studies a C, Science a D, Art 'outstanding,' Health Satisfactory, and Gym, Satisfactory. I reserved comment as long as I could and deeply pondered how to broach the subject. Finally, after I asked him the usual questions and got the usual answers, I told him that I know he's got to make more of an effort to pay attention in class and in doing his homework.

"I asked him to think of ways he can improve and ways that I can help. What we came up with was that he'd bring home his homework pad nightly for starters. On each page I wrote his subject names. I suggested that all

296

he had to do each day is write in the assignment page numbers and which books (notebook, textbook, workbook) to bring home. He agreed to try.

"So far he's brought the pad home both days. One day he wrote in both assignments but forgot the second subject's book. The next day he remembered the books but not to write the assignments down. Both times I tried to suggest how he could avoid these problems next time and I encouraged him to solve each problem."

Children's first schools are their homes, and their first teachers are their parents. Infants and toddlers typically display an intense curiosity and wonder about their environment ("What's this?"). We can also observe children's desire to manipulate objects and make interesting things happen ("Look what I can do"). These natural tendencies can be enhanced or diminished by the specific experiences they have at home, in school, and anywhere else.

Most parents, like Mark's mother, have had no training as educators. Though they may value achievement and competence, it is not obvious how they can enhance their children's abilities. Despite her frustration with Mark's performance in school, his mother is learning to be patient and understanding in helping him to become better organized.

Parenting goal #2, competence, encompasses not only teaching children problem-solving skills but also encouraging an appreciation of this remarkable world and children's ability to study and understand it. Many parents view competence and achievement as the school-related domain of their children's development. By the time most children begin formal schooling, however, they have already developed an orientation to learning that will influence their future academic and intellectual accomplishments. The preparation for learning that children receive at home is as important to their education as what happens in the classroom.

In this chapter, we explore the roots of competence. We focus on family resources that appear to promote achievement and the process of schooling. We consider how high-achieving children differ from low-achieving children, examine parenting styles that encourage competence and achievement, and note the influence of cognitive and affective variables on academic performance. We keep in mind the ecological perspective that children's achievement occurs mainly in the context of their family circumstances and relationships (Brooks-Gunn, Klebanov, & Duncan, 1996; Luster & McAdoo, 1996; Slaughter-Defoe, Nakagawa, Takanishi, & Johnson, 1990; Westerman & La Luz, 1995).

HOME AND FAMILY FACTORS IN ACHIEVEMENT

Study Question *How can parents promote in their children a love of learning?*

Traditional models of cognitive growth have assumed that high-achieving parents provide their children with an enriched and stimulating environment. R. White (1959) suggested that play and exploratory behavior produce feelings of efficacy (or mastery) in children which serve to intrinsically reinforce these behaviors. A motivational cycle results that fosters the development of competent behaviors. Parents support this cycle by providing their children with frequent opportunities to make interesting things happen (Hauser-Cram, 1996).

Children who are raised under economically and socially impoverished conditions, particularly if education is not highly valued by their parents, may not master basic literacy skills (Samuels, 1986). The greater the number of risk factors, such as poverty and family instability, the poorer children's academic performance (Gorman & Pollitt, 1996; Luster & McAdoo, 1994; Samuels, 1986). "Unable to achieve in school, these children begin to see academic success as unattainable, and so they protect themselves by deciding school is unimportant . . . Such children are at risk for dropping out, teen-age pregnancy, drug abuse and crime" (Comer, 1988a, p. 46).

Yet many of the children of poor and illiterate Jewish and Asian immigrants who settled in this country excelled academically. This may reflect the "reverence for education

which these groups had and which their children accepted and adopted . . . What seems important in the cognitive development of children, then, is not the social class or race of the family, but the lifestyle and culture in the home" (Samuels, 1986, p. 8). African-American children who enjoy supportive family environments and come from small families well above the poverty line score highly on tests of cognitive competence (Luster & McAdoo, 1994, 1996).

Few would deny that the home environment is a major factor in children's school

Justin Jaffe

performance. Many investigators have emphasized the importance of children's *early* home environment in promoting achievement. It is plausible that parenting style, language use, opportunities for problem solving, economic resources, and family stability, promote social and cognitive skills that encourage academic achievement (Amato, 1989; Ginsburg & Bronstein, 1993; Gottfried, Fleming, & Gottfried, 1994; Hinshaw, 1992; Landau & Weissler, 1993; Weissler & Landau, 1993). Kagan (1984), however, contends that the influence of early environment on achievement has been exaggerated. He suggests that it is a child's *contemporary* home environment that is the key to understanding achievement.

A problem in distinguishing between these two models is that children who were fortunate enough to have enjoyed a nurturant early home environment are also more than likely to have a stimulating contemporary home environment. A third model of achievement emphasizes the *cumulative* effects of a stable and nurturant home environment over childhood.

Bradley, Caldwell, and Rock (1988) compared these three models of family influence on children's school performance. They examined the home environments of 42 demographically diverse children when the children were infants and again during middle childhood. Although all three models received some support, the children's current environment was the best predictor of their classroom behavior and achievement. The researchers concluded that "all three models of environmental action seem useful in explaining parts of the results obtained. However, none of the three models is adequate to explain all of the data" (p. 865).

Rutter (1985b) hypothesized that stimulation by itself does not promote cognitive growth. Rather, growth is enhanced by "the reciprocity of the parent-child interactions,

the variety and meaningfulness of their content, and the active role taken by the child" (p. 686). Rutter suggested that when interacting with their children, parents should minimize background noise that might distract and confuse the child. Parents are encouraged to provide a variety of opportunities for active rather than passive participation in parent-child play and conversation.

Like other theorists, Rutter emphasized the importance of parental nurturance, sensitivity, and responsiveness to the child's verbal and non-verbal behaviors. In teaching children how to learn, parents should provide interesting and meaningful experiences and many opportunities for discovery and experimentation. The extent to which any one of these factors promotes a child's cognitive development partly depends on a child's age. For example, physical contact may be particularly important early in infancy, and responsiveness to non-verbal signals may increase in importance during the second year.

Hess and Holloway (1984) identified five family factors that predict school achievement: (1) verbal interaction between parent and child, (2) realistic parental expectations about achievement, (3) a good parent-child relationship, (4) parental beliefs and attributions concerning the child, and, especially, (5) parental style of discipline. Home background variables, including the parents' educational level, income, and number of books in the home, have been shown to be related to children's achievement.

Verbal Interaction and Stimulation

Q. Are clouds alive?

A. No.

Q. How do you know?

A. Because Timmy the Tooth on TV, now he's alive. And Frosty the Snowman, when he puts his hat on, he's alive.

Now, that Frosty's not real, he's pretend because he doesn't move.

Q. Are the trees alive?

A. No way.

Q. Why?

A. They're pretend life

Q. What would happen if the sun never came up again?

A. You would go to bed and sleep forever.

Q. Do you have a person you call grandma?

A. Yes, I call her bubble Grandma.

Q. Why?

A. Because I want to.

Q. Do you know why your grandma is your grandma?

A. Because she baby-sits me and reads me storybooks.

[Conversation with 4-year-old Kali].

As this conversation indicates, parents can create endless opportunities for verbal exchange and, in the process, stimulate children's curiosity and expressiveness. Children benefit from learning environments that "permit them to be verbally active while solving problems and completing tasks" (Berk, 1986, p. 42). Given the critical role that language plays in cognitive and social development, verbal interaction between parent and child can easily be appreciated as an influence on competence and achievement (Olson, Bates, & Kaskie, 1992; Weissler & Landau, 1993). Five- to fifteen-year-olds speak approximately 20,000 words a day, resulting in about 2 to 3 hours of pure speaking time (Wagner, 1985).

Rutter (1985b) attributes the slightly higher academic achievement and verbal intelligence levels observed in firstborn and only children to the fact that parents interact with and talk more to their firstborns. Many studies have related characteristics of mothers' speech to the rate of language acquisition in their children (e.g., Harris, Jones, Brookes, & Grant, 1986).

Children who frequently talk out loud to themselves usually are the most socially advanced and brightest preschoolers (Berk, 1986). Such private talk apparently fosters the development of internalized private speech. Children need learning environments that "permit them to be verbally active while solving problems and completing tasks" (Berk, 1986, p. 42).

Parents can promote children's intellectual development by serving as models for good language skills (Samuels, 1986). Parents can provide work spaces for children to read and to do their homework. They can provide children with stimulating reading materials, take them to museums and libraries, and "establish a model of the parent as one who reads and respects scholarship" (Samuels, 1986, p. 8).

Good Parent-Child Relationship

High-achieving children often come from homes that are more like learning laboratories. These homes are not cold and sterile but rather warm, inviting, interesting environments. They are safely arranged to encourage free exploration and equipped not with expensive toys, but with objects that teach. Such children have responsive parents to whom they are securely attached. These parents encourage stimulating interaction and share with their children the excitement of exploration and discovery.

B.L. White (1988) summarized the recommendations of the Harvard Preschool Project for promoting young children's intelligence as follows: "Newly crawling infants should be allowed to practice their climbing and other emerging motor skills. For most of their waking hours, they should have easy access to people who have a very special love for them. Those people should talk to them about what they are focusing on at the moment, using or-dinary language to expand ideas and intro-duce new ideas. They should lavish affection, encouragement, and enthusiasm on the ba-bies, thereby intensifying their interest and excitement in learning. They need not make use of elaborate educational toys or pro-grams" (pp. 18–19).

Estrada and her colleagues performed a longitudinal study of 67 mothers and their children. The children were observed twice—at the ages of 4 years and 12 years. The study revealed a significant correlation between the affective quality of the mother-child relation-ship and the child's mental age at 4 years, readiness for school at ages 5–6 years, I.Q. at age 6, and the child's school achievement at age 12 (Estrada et al., 1987).

The parent-child relationship thus provides an important medium for encouraging chil-dren's cognitive development (Bretherton, 1985). "Children who are securely attached as infants subsequently approach cognitive tasks in ways conducive to cognitive development. Their problem-solving style is characterized by more curiosity, persistence and enthusi-asm, and less frustration than less securely at-tached infants. Securely attached children also appear to use adult direction and atten-tion in ways that promote cognitive and social development. They are more able to benefit from maternal assistance during problem-solving tasks and to interact effectively with teachers" (Estrada et al., 1987, p. 210).

Parental Beliefs and Expectations about Achievement

Study Question   *Do parents expect too much or too little from their children regarding schoolwork and homework?*

As discussed in Chapter 3, parent's beliefs guide their child-rearing practices and thus indirectly, their children's academic achieve-ment (Chao, 1996; Hortaçsu, 1995). It really is a two-way street. Children's academic achievement partly determines their parent's expectations. When children excel, their par-ents see them as "smart." Ideally, parents will expect the most that their children are capa-ble of and their children's academic perfor-mance will confirm these expectations (Reynolds & Gill, 1994). Conversely, parents who expect very little from their children usu-ally are not disappointed. Parental expecta-tions also reflect cultural norms regarding achievement and parents' own education and aspirations (Johnson & Martin, 1985; Ladd & Price, 1986; S.A. Miller, 1988; Sameroff & Feil, 1985; Seginer, 1983).

Okagaki and Sternberg (1993) studied the relationship between parents' beliefs about child rearing and intelligence and children's school performance. They interviewed immi-grant parents from Cambodia, Mexico, the Philippines, Vietnam, and native-born Anglo-American and Mexican-American parents about what their children should be taught and what characterizes an intelligent child.

Hispanic and Asian parents held a view of intelligence that considered motivation and social skills to be as important as cognitive skills like creativity and verbal expression. Fil-ipino and Vietnamese parents emphasized the role of motivation in intelligence. Anglo-American parents rated cognitive abilities as more important factors in intelligence than noncognitive factors. This latter view allows for the phenomenon whereby a bright child does not do well in school because he or she is not sufficiently motivated.

Asian-American parents in the study dis-agreed—they viewed working hard as an im-portant component of intelligence. Regarding beliefs about child rearing, immigrant parents emphasized more than did parents born in the United States the importance of conform-ing to external standards. It is not hard to understand why immigrants, unfamiliar with customs in the United States, would encourage their children to copy or conform to what other children are doing. Most parents born in the United States value autonomy more than conformity.

Children's beliefs about their academic competence apparently are influenced by their parents' beliefs and practices (Hortaçsu, 1995). For example, children develop greater confidence in their abilities when their parents require them to solve problems on their own. Children's confidence may suffer when parents provide them with answers or tell them how to solve a problem (Wagner & Phillips, 1992). There is growing evidence that children view excessive parental involvement as intrusive and discouraging (e.g., Deci, Driver, Hotchkiss, Robbins, et al., 1993; Grolnick, Ryan, & Deci, 1991).

Parents of high-achieving children usually have high expectations about their children's abilities (Reynolds & Gill, 1994). More importantly, they set *realistic* standards that the child will not only be able to satisfy but also will find challenging. Parents of low-achieving children often do not model success-oriented behavior or teach achievement-related values (Luster & McAdoo, 1994). Parents who set standards that are too high or too low risk creating unnecessary obstacles to their children's achievement.

Parents who establish unrealistically high (or perfectionistic) standards may be setting up their children for failure (Seligman, 1990). Eventually, they may exhibit low self-efficacy—a fear of failure that discourages intellectual risk-taking. Many children give up prematurely and avoid taking on challenging tasks (see "Too Much Too Soon?: Creating Superkids"). Parent's whose standards are too low settle for mediocre performance. It helps when there is a "goodness of fit" between parental expectations about children's achievement and children's actual perfor-

TABLE 10.1 Three Types of Readiness to Learn, Using Bicycle Riding as an Example

Biological:	A child must be physically mature enough to acquire a skill, for example, having the ability to balance while riding a bicycle.
Prerequisite skills:	A child must have the prerequisite motor and cognitive skills, for example, mounting, pedaling, and steering the bike and knowing the rules for safe riding.
Motivational:	A child will learn more quickly if he or she wants to learn to ride, perhaps because a friend or sibling rides and it looks like fun.

mance in school (Feagans, Merriwether, & Haldane, 1991).

What constitutes a realistic expectation about achievement partly depends upon a child's *readiness* to address and master a problem-solving task. It is beneficial for parents to provide engaging, challenging tasks when their children are ready maturationally, behaviorally, and motivationally. For a child to perform successfully, whether it be toilet training or reading, she must be biologically mature enough to acquire the skill, have the prerequisite behavioral and cognitive abilities, and be willing to accept the challenge (see Table 10.1). While parents have little to say about biological readiness (other than by simply waiting), there is much that they can do regarding prerequisite skills and motivation (Gottfried, Fleming, & Gottfried, 1994).

Western culture is, for the most part, competitive and achievement-oriented. However, parents differ substantially in their achievement standards. Most middle-class parents cultivate a future orientation which encourages delay of gratification. Middle-class children eventually learn to be guided by the longer-term consequences of their behaviors, such as grades, diplomas, and jobs. Less advantaged parents may encourage an orientation toward the present. The meaning of an action lies in its immediate "payoff." Children who become "dependent" on immediate consequences or parental surveillance of school work may be less susceptible to the rewards inherent in achievement behavior and, as a result, may not do as well in school (Ginsburg & Bronstein, 1993; Santrock, 1988).

We still have much to learn about how parental expectations are communicated to children and how children come to interpret their parents' expectations. Research and clinical observation (e.g., Bandura, 1977b) confirm that children eventually adopt their parents' standards, whether or not the standards are realistic. During the early school years, children also will compare their performance to that of their peers (this is called **social comparison**). Thus, children's standards eventually reflect a combination of personal, parental, and peer influences.

Parental Style of Discipline

As discussed in Chapter 5, Diane Baumrind and others (Dornbusch, Ritter, Leiderman, Roberts, & Fraleigh, 1987) have noted a relationship between the authoritative parenting style and children's achievement. Children of parents who practice the authoritative parenting style usually receive higher grades than children of authoritarian or permissive parents. Children from "inconsistent" families that combine punitive and other parenting styles typically receive the worst grades (Dornbusch, Ritter, Leiderman, Roberts, & Fraleigh, 1987; Steinberg, Lamborn, Dornbusch, & Darling, 1992). These findings apply to males and females, children and adolescents, children living in different family configurations, and

to different levels of parental education (but not to all ethnic groups).

What might children be learning from authoritative parents that could enhance their achievement motivation and cognitive development? The authoritative approach apparently promotes the development of self-reliance, positive self-esteem, and realistic standards of performance. Parents who are accepting and encouraging, who avoid distressing children by equating their self-worth with achievement, and who model problem-solving skills seem to be providing their children with the essential ingredients of achievement motivation. In effect, authoritative parents are better teachers than punitive or neglecting parents (Pratt, Kerig, Cowan, & Cowan, 1988).

We recall from Chapter 5 that a parenting style really is a "package deal" in that it includes quality of communication, displays of affection, rearing strategies, a certain degree of involvement and control, and many other factors. This raises the question, what specific aspects of the authoritative parenting style contribute to children's academic success? What do children gain from their warm, but firm parents that allows them to excel academically? Steinberg, Elmen, and Mounts (1989) tested the hypothesis that specific elements of the authoritative parenting style *facilitate* rather than simply accompany academic success.

These investigators collected data on family relationships (by interviewing the adolescents) and adolescents' school grades and scores on standardized achievement tests. Data were collected for 120 white, middle-class families with a firstborn child between the ages of 11 and 16 years. They found that "adolescents who describe their parents as treating them warmly, democratically, and firmly are more likely than their peers to develop positive attitudes toward, and beliefs about, their achievement, and as a consequence, they are more likely to do well in school" (p. 1433). The researchers tentatively concluded that authoritative parents encourage a healthy sense of autonomy in their children, and a willingness to work hard. These attributes contribute to their school success. Similar findings were reported by other investigators (Amato, 1989; Grolnick & Ryan, 1989; Olson, Bates, & Kaskie, 1992).

As noted in Chapter 5, middle-class children of authoritative parents generally are receptive to their help and involvement in school-related matters. This is another crucial link between authoritative parenting and children's school success (Snodgrass, 1991; Steinberg, Lamborn, Dornbusch, & Darling, 1992).

Summarizing Family Influences

Parents can promote their children's cognitive development within the broad limits set by

TABLE 10.2 Home and Family Factors in Achievement

Arrange a safe and stimulating learning environment.

Set and convey realistic expectations regarding child's ability.

Present tasks in meaningful and challenging way.

Provide assistance and scaffolding as needed.

Encourage children to notice interesting features of their environment.

Teach children how to learn and how to think for themselves.

Engage in stimulating conversations and ask interesting questions.

Model achievement behaviors, including reading and writing.

Encourage intellectual risk taking and persistence.

Emphasize longer-term consequences of behavior rather than immediate gratification.

Use authoritative parenting style.

---

heredity. They do so by arranging a safe and interesting environment that encourages free exploration and the manipulation of objects. Parents of high-achieving children convey realistically high expectations regarding their child's cognitive development. They provide assistance with everyday problems and schoolwork as needed. They realize that as children mature, less supervision and control are required (Amato, 1989; Eccles, Buchanan, Flanagan, Fuligni, Midgley, & Yee, 1991).

These children are encouraged to use their senses to notice interesting features of their home and neighborhood settings. Musical instruments, records, and tapes encourage them to listen and to hear. Children who accompany their parents out of the home on walks, trips, or shopping excursions are exposed to rich combinations of meaningful experiences that contribute to their understanding of the world (Piaget, 1954).

Children who observe their parents performing household tasks and who participate in such chores as food preparation or caring for younger siblings or pets have the opportunity to develop a variety of competencies that serve their development. In the process of these ordinary, everyday experiences, children develop attentional skills, persistence, and enthusiasm for discovery—in effect, they learn how to learn.

The most promising sources of enriching experiences for young children are stimulating parent-child interactions that occurs in the context of a warm, emotionally supportive relationship (Wagner & Phillips, 1992). Examples of such interactions are conversations, story telling, and playing games that challenge a child's imagination while teaching basic skills (e.g., Freund, 1990).

Parents of high-achieving children provide a nurturant and supportive learning environment and establish their child's readiness and willingness to learn. They seek to present a task in a way that is optimally meaningful and

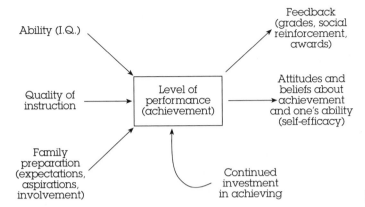

Figure 10.1 Achievement cycle.

challenging, taking advantage of the child's motivation to participate and to succeed.

Children have greater opportunity for such challenges and more frequent one-to-one interactions with adults in the home environment than they do in school, where teachers generally work in a group setting (Tizard & Hughes, 1985). Children have more frequent, more complex, and longer conversations at home than at school and are asked more interesting and more complex questions at home.

Parents of children who become high achievers generally model achievement behaviors, express lots of encouragement, reward accomplishment, and foster independence and creativity of thought. Positive self-esteem has the self-fulfilling effect of encouraging children to take intellectual and social risks.

The sequence becomes clear whereby achievement breeds more achievement (see Figure 10.1). Challenge leads to intellectual risk taking, which may lead to success. This encourages further risk taking and persistence. Occasional failure is seen in a positive light as the inevitable by-product of risk taking. Accepting new challenges becomes a sign of personal growth. The parental contributions to high achievement are not mysterious;

rather, they reflect nurturant and stimulating rearing styles that encourage children to appreciate and expand their abilities.

TOO MUCH TOO SOON?: CREATING SUPERKIDS

Study Question *Do children benefit from very early schooling?*

Western culture is very competitive. More, faster, and sooner are often equated with better. We are tempted to judge people by their material "success" rather than by their characters. In the past, parents hoped that their children would be normal. Many parents today expect their children to excel, to be "the best." They worry that their children will not get into the right preschool or kindergarten program. They seek a competitive advantage for their children academically.

Psychologist David Elkind (1984, 1987a) chides parents who either "hurry" or "miseducate" their children. Why would parents want to speed up their children's intellectual development? Hurrying children to grow up, Elkind surmises, alleviates some of the inconveniences and stresses parents face in raising dependent preschool children. Miseducating children, or exposing them to formal instruction during the "preschool" years, satisfies parents' need to provide their children with academic advantages while proving their own talent for parenting.

"Parents today believe they can make a difference in their children's lives, that they can give them an edge that will make them brighter and abler than the competition. Parents who started out in the seventies hurry their children; parents of the eighties are miseducating them. Parents who started in the seventies need mature children, while parents of the eighties want superkids" (Elkind, 1987a, p. xiii).

The so-called "superkid" syndrome is a middle-class phenomenon in the United States and Japan (Elkind, 1987b; WuDunn, 1996a). Parents who overly value achievement and equate it with success and happiness read books like *Give Your Child A Superior Mind*, *Raising Brighter Children*, and *How To Have A Smarter Baby*. They seek out special enrichment or accelerated learning environments for their children (Collins, 1985a).

Young children are instructed not only in academic subjects, but also foreign languages, music, dance, swimming, gymnastic activities, and competitive sports. As their youngsters are learning to walk, some parents have visions of Princeton, Stanford, or an Olympic gold medal. Elkind cautions that parents should examine their motives for placing children in high-pressure learning environments. Whose needs are being addressed?

To some extent, parental excitement about preschool enrichment programs may reflect the successes of early intervention programs like Head Start and the Brookline Early Education Project. These projects, however, were directed at culturally and economically disadvantaged children. They targeted families rather than individual children. It has not been demonstrated that middle-class children

benefit, in the long run, from such interventions. Most receive enough stimulation and encouragement during the course of their daily lives.

Research has not revealed clear-cut long-term benefits of early preschool or even full-day kindergarten. Early schooling clearly benefits economically disadvantaged children, but middle-class children gain little from exposure to early education (Bennett, 1985; Campbell & Ramey, 1994). "Certainly parents play a crucial role in the lives of individuals who are intellectually gifted or creatively talented. But this role is not one of active instruction . . . Rather it is the support and encouragement parents give children and the intellectual climate that they create in the home which seem to be the critical factors" (Elkind, 1987a, p. 21).

Educators and developmental specialists contend that young children benefit from participating in low-pressure, relaxed, interesting, and unstructured activities with their caregivers. Most preschool and nursery school programs provide a comfortable, nurturant setting for children, with activities that are appropriate for the children's age and interests.

Elkind refers to early, formal instruction as miseducation, not so much because such training is ineffective, but because it may be harmful. Placement in high-pressured, structured preschoool learning environments may create unnecessary stress for children (Elkind, 1987a). Other risks of exposing children to challenges that are beyond their current capabilities include achievement anxiety and fear of failure. The optimal formula is for parents to have realistic expectations and set appropriate goals for their children but to avoid being pushy and critical (K. Fisher, 1989).

"If we have reared a well-mannered, good and decent person, we should take pleasure and pride in that fact. More likely than not, if we have achieved those goals, the child's success will take care of itself. Each child has a unique pattern of qualities and abilities that makes him or her special. In this sense, every single child is a superkid" (Elkind, 1987b, p. 61).

EARLY SCHOOLING

Historically, preschool and day-care programs have had quite different origins. Until recently, the two have remained distinct entities (Scarr & Weinberg, 1986). Today, the two services are merging as working parents search for the most beneficial arrangements for their children.

It is not so much education as child care that concerns working parents. They must choose a preschool program for their child from the increasing variety of available day-care and early-schooling alternatives. "Today's parents want professionals to care for their young children because they do not have the time to do so themselves" (Elkind, 1988, p. 22).

Modern preschools reflect the influences of Maria Montessori, Jean Piaget, and John Dewey. They involve children in a variety of individual and group activities that encourage them to develop their motor, perceptual, and social skills through play rather than through instruction. Teachers read stories, and children sing songs, pile up blocks, paint pictures, and talk about their families and themselves. Teachers, aware of a given child's readiness to learn, provide materials and activities that will stimulate and challenge him or her. Aware of children's developing, but still limited social skills, teachers promote peer interactions in small groups and remind children to "keep your hands to yourself."

"Teachers at the preschool level must do more comforting, more limit setting, more crisis intervention than teachers at the higher grade levels. But they are also helping children acquire the fundamental concepts of space, time, number, causality, relations, and nature-concepts that form the essential data base for all later learning" (Elkind, 1988, p. 23). Teachers should give children freedom to decide when to pursue a particular activity, Elkind suggests, but much less freedom to decide what curricular areas to pursue.

Parents who are seeking a safe and healthy environment for their preschoolers should consider the student-teacher ratio, the qualifications of the teaching staff, and the physical layout of the school. Most important are the school director's child-care philosophy and the child's reactions to the school (Shell, 1989).

Should advantaged children attend preschool? Elkind (1988) suggests that "if parents do not have the commitment, the time, the energy, and the resources to provide young children with an environment that approaches that of the good early childhood program, then it *does* matter whether the child attends a preschool . . . The issue then is not whether preschool is important, but rather to what extent home schooling can duplicate what preschool has to offer" (p. 26).

THE PROCESS OF SCHOOLING

Mark # 14: The Book Report

"The weekend was a toughy. Mark had almost half of his library book to finish so he could write his book report for Wednesday. Saturday wasn't feasible because we had to spend it with the family for an early Thanksgiving. Sunday Mark procrastinated the whole day. As it began to drive me insane, I prayed, kept my cool, and offered my help.

"For example, as soon as he began to read, he squawked that he didn't have any idea what 'they' were talking about. (There were some new characters already involved in a conversation). So I had him read it aloud and I explained how the sentences should be read. I

Most Asian-American children work hard in and out of school to compensate for anticipated racial discrimination.

Spotlight

Asian-American Superachievers?

A **stereotype** is an overgeneralized belief about a group of people. It emphasizes one trait or characteristic that all members of a group presumably share. Stereotypes ignore the usually considerable differences among group members (Slaughter-Defoe et al., 1990). The image of Asian "whiz-kids," model students living trouble-free lives, has been popularly presented in national magazines and newspapers. The image ignores the real struggles of immigrant children trying to adapt to an alien culture (Fischer, 1988; TerLouw, 1994).

Some Asian children, particularly those who came to the United States in the late 1960s and early 1970s, and those who arrived after the Vietnam war in 1975, are exceptional achievers (Kim & Chun, 1994). We can see this in their grades, scores on achievement tests, success in scholarship competitions, and in rates of admissions to the best schools and colleges (Chen & Stevenson, 1995). Their parents are "mostly middle- to upper-income professional people who were fairly well-educated and who passed on to their children an abiding interest in education and a strong work ethic . . . While Asians make up just 2.1% of the U.S.

population, last fall's freshman class at Harvard was 14% Asian American; at the Massachusetts Institute of Technology, 20%; and at the University of California at Berkely, 25%. Of the 70 students who've won scholarships in the Westinghouse Science Talent Search since 1981, 20 have been of Asian descent. In 1986, Asians won all five top scholarship awards from Westinghouse . . . An Asian student's average math SAT score is 518 out of 800—43 points above the national average" (Fischer, 1988, pp. 14-15).

In 1986, all five Westinghouse Science Talent Search scholarships were awarded to Asian-Americans. In 1988, 11 of the 14 Westinghouse finalists in New York City were Asian, four of them female. Ironically, their successes have given rise to discriminatory attempts to limit the number of Asians in the best universities and to rejection from their non-Asian peers who resent their hard work and achievement. Part of the irony is that many Asian-American students work hard to compensate for anticipated racial discrimination.

These data arouse our curiosity—why do Asian children succeed, when so many of their native-born peers in the United States languish? High school teachers in Queens, New York were asked to rank their students according to ethnic or national group membership. The Asians students were "ranked highest for motivation and blacks the lowest, with blacks given highest marks for physical ability and Asians the lowest. 'Nature' did not dictate that this be so. If it had, there would be no explaining the great Asian successes in the Olympics. Nor did 'nature' intend blacks to be 'athletic.' Had that been the design, blacks from Africa would invariably beat the competition from other continents" (Graubard, 1988).

It is tempting to compare Asian school systems with ours to seek reasons for the high achievement of many Asian children. Most observers credit the Asian mother (native or Asian-American) more than the

school for encouraging her children to value high achievement (Choi, Bempechat, & Ginsburg, 1994; WuDunn, 1996a) (see Cultural Perspective: The Japanese Mother). "Japanese mothers play a prominent role in their children's education. And while opinion polls here show that American parents want their children to succeed in school, studies of family life suggest that most parents are too stressed, tired or self-absorbed to support and encourage their youngsters' academic endeavors during after-school hours . . . The strains of divorce and single parenthood, and the stress of juggling two wage earners' work schedules have made it all but impossible for American parents to keep up their end of the bargain" (Steinberg, 1987e).

Stevenson (1985) administered a battery of 10 cognitive tasks and achievement tests in reading and math to 1,440 Chinese, Japanese, and United States children in grades 1 and 5. Children in the 3 cultures were similar in their cognitive abilities. The Chinese children surpassed Japanese and United States children in reading scores, and both Chinese and Japanese children produced higher math scores than children in the United States. Stevenson concluded that the superior performance of the Asian children could not be attributed to higher intellectual abilities and, therefore, must reflect home and school experiences.

Asian youngsters provide each other with considerable peer support for achievement, compared to children in the United States who may value social and material gains more than academic success. Many high school students in the United States work part time, which is unheard of in Japan during the school year. "No one would argue that the intense do-or-die pressure to succeed felt by Japanese adolescents is a healthy state toward which our youngsters should be pushed. But there surely is an appropriate middle ground between being neurotically obsessed with an important exam and being riveted to MTV" (Steinberg, 1987e).

C u l t u r a l   P e r s p e c t i v e

The Japanese Mother

The best predictors of children's academic achievement are related to their mothers or primary caregivers (Shoho, 1994). They include maternal level of education, maternal involvement in child rearing, and most of all, the quality of the mother-child relationship. As previously noted, the outstanding success of Asian-American children is usually attributed to their mothers. Asian women typically stay home with their young children rather than pursue a career. They help their children do their schoolwork and create a home environment that fosters achievement.

"The Japanese mother spends hours reading stories to her children and playing what we would call educational games. She breaks each task into small steps, lavishes praise on the children as they master each one and seldom resorts to punishment . . . The mother forms an alliance with her child; they work together to conquer educational challenges" (Chance, 1987a, p. 80).

Most Asian mothers do not believe that achievement is rooted in innate ability. They value instead, a commitment to excellence, selflessness, and hard work (Chao, 1996; Kim & Chun, 1994). "Until her child goes to school, the Japanese mother devotes herself to the rearing of the child. In verbal and nonverbal ways, she reminds the child of her deep, deep, warm feelings and that the child is the most important thing in the world to her" (Kagan, quoted by Garfinkel, 1983, p. 56). Japanese mothers discipline their children gently, often by patiently expressing their displeasure.

Japanese and Chinese school children surpass their western counterparts virtually across the board academically, but particularly in science and mathematics (Chen & Stevenson, 1995). A recent study comparing fifth and eleventh grade students in Minneapolis (Minnesota), Taipei (Taiwan), and Sendai (Japan) reported that students in the United States significantly lagged behind students in the other two countries in math ability (*The New York Times*, January 1, 1993). The best students in Minneapolis were only as good as the average Japanese and Taiwanese students. A survey of the parents of the children in the United States found that despite the findings, the parents were satisfied with their children's achievements. Parents in the United States apparently have lower expectations regarding their children's achievement than parents in the other countries (Chao, 1996).

Asian children spend more time in school than children in the United States and spend more time after school in school-related activities, including homework. They also receive more help from family members (Chen & Stevenson, 1989, 1995; Stevenson, Lee, & Stigler, 1986). There is no reason to assume they are innately brighter or that they get an earlier start in their schooling (Stevenson, 1987). The size of their classes is larger, not smaller, than classes in the United States. Japanese teachers are more highly paid, more enthusiastic in the classroom, and much more respected than their counterparts in the United States.

Japanese students attend school 240 days a year, compared to 178 days for children in the United States. Japanese first-graders work on homework for an average of 233 minutes a week compared to 79 minutes for first-graders in the United States (Garfinkle, 1983). Importantly, Chinese and Japanese elementary school children are as happy and well-adjusted as their counterparts in this country (Stevenson, 1987; Chen & Stevenson, 1995). Some Japanese educators complain about the competitive pressures that motivate many Japanese students. "It's not healthy for kids to have so little free time. It is not healthy to become completely caught up in competition and status at such a young age" (Ikuo Amano, professor of sociology, quoted by Weisman, 1992). But one science teacher maintains that the kids don't mind. "Don't believe what the mass media say, that all we do is force kids to memorize and pass tests. We use experiments and we break the information down into more digestible bites. The kids enjoy it" (Weisman, 1992).

As noted previously, one critical difference between Asian and United States mothers is the level of expectations about their children's progress in school. "American children had to do less well than Japanese and Chinese children for their mothers to be satisfied and much worse before their mothers expressed dissatisfaction with their academic performance. Such high evaluations of ability and achievement by the American children and their mothers cannot be conducive to a child's diligent study" (Stevenson, 1987, p. 30). Parents with low expectations do not encourage their children to try their hardest. This is true of families in the United States, despite the fact that the curriculum in

the United States is less demanding than Asian curricula (Chen & Stevenson, 1995).

Cross-cultural comparisons help us put into perspective our own society's assumptions, expectations, and practices (Chao, 1996). We can appreciate that there are distinctive cultural values regarding dependency, harmony, obligation, conformity, and perseverance that influence how Asian and American children are viewed and treated by their parents and teachers. But American children have fallen behind their Asian peers academically, and we can identify several relevant factors. These include a less demanding curriculum, less time spent in class, low parent and teacher expectations about children's ability, the lack of a work ethic, and less stable domestic environments in the United States (Chen & Stevenson, 1995).

On a daily basis, Asian children seem to benefit, in terms of achievement and self-efficacy, from their mother's active involvement in their lives. It seems that the attitudes and behaviors inculcated at home during and following the preschool years prepare Asian children for levels of effort and achievement that are beyond the expectations of most parents in the United States (WuDunn, 1996a).

told him that books are like that at times, and we have to read on until we can figure out what's happening. He wouldn't settle for that and kept complaining and trying to get me involved. As I would not get perturbed or help any more, he eventually threw a tantrum (which I ignored) and then stormed to his room. Later when he decided to approach me again he was calmer. He did attempt to finish the chapter again and when he told me that he now understood, I told him, 'I knew you would.' "

The 10,000 or so hours that children spend in classrooms by the time they graduate from

high school account for a significant part of their socialization. School influence is probably second only to that of the family environment as a factor in personality and cognitive development. Teachers and schools can make a big difference in children's development (Good & Weinstein, 1986; Linney & Seidman, 1989), but there is widespread agreement that academic environments could and should be more effective.

In addition to time spent in classrooms, most children will devote thousands of hours to homework, special projects, and school-related activities. Perhaps the key factor determining how much value children will derive from schooling is their interest in learning. Achievement motivation is very susceptible to home influences (Hess & Holloway, 1984).

Parental encouragement and involvement can increase the value of a school's curriculum and of school assignments, particularly when children are frustrated by their lack of progress or understanding (Kay, Fitzgerald, Paradee, & Mellencamp, 1994; Patton, 1994). Unfortunately, many parents feel unprepared to help their children with schoolwork (Kay et al., 1994). Parents like Mark's mother must find the fine line of encouraging and helping without actually doing the assignment. Parents should avoid becoming overly controlling, which discourages children. Asking children, "Would you like some help?" avoids imposing unwanted assistance while showing interest and support.

Reading and Writing

Study Question *Should parents teach their children to read?*

A telephone poll of 1000 parents by the Roper organization (*The New York Times*, May 25, 1988) reported that only 44 percent of the parents polled said that their children read for pleasure every day. Girls were reported to read more than boys; younger schoolchildren read more than older. Children of well-educated parents read more than those of less-educated parents.

Ninety-one percent of the parents felt that reading is important to their child's success. One-third reported not being satisfied with how well their child read. Only a bare majority of the parents said that their children were very interested in reading, with a big drop in interest following the fifth grade.

Reading is a fundamental skill; so many other skills depend upon reading ability. Chil-

dren who can read by the time that they are four or five years old have an academic advantage in the first grade, when most of their peers are just beginning to master basic literacy skills. But more importantly, early readers begin to explore new worlds and appreciate the richness of written language. They can enjoy the classic children's literature and assimilate interesting information about their environment.

Since reading and writing emerge from more general language and communication skills, talking and reading to children are optimal ways of promoting these skills. Reading stories to children, asking them to tell the story in their own words, using the pictures as guides, and possibly drawing pictures based on the story all foster verbal and motivational skills that encourage early reading ability. Conversations that provide children with opportunities to describe their experiences and their feelings also sharpen language skills (Jackson, 1977).

Conventional wisdom suggests that children are not ready to learn how to read until they are at least 6 years old, but many educators disagree. Literacy-related skills, such as oral communication, begin to emerge during early childhood (W.S. Hall, 1989). Two-year-olds know what a story is, how to hold a book, and they understand that adults "get" a story from the pages of a book. At this age, children may believe that each letter stands for a word, that each page tells a whole story, or they may think that the parent is "reading" the picture.

We can view reading as a set of skills that gradually emerge during the preschool years. Children are ready to begin to learn these skills when they show interest in stories that are being read to them and when they show willingness to learn words that are associated with pictures. A good way to encourage the development of reading skills is to read interesting stories to children frequently. We can ask them questions about the story and answer their questions. When children are being read to, they are learning far more than just the story. Attentional, perceptual, memory, and other cognitive abilities are exercised (Beck & Carpenter, 1986; Hall, 1989).

When teaching children to read, they should have the background knowledge required to understand the story they will be reading. They should also be given frequent opportunities to read out loud. If they make many errors, the selection that they are reading is too difficult. Mistakes should generally be ignored, because correcting them detracts from the child's train of thought and comprehension.

"The emphasis during reading lessons should be on understanding and appreciating the content of the story. Lessons in which the children do little else but take turns reading the story, and the teacher does little else but correct reading errors, are ineffective" (R.C. Anderson, 1985, p. 29). Silent reading also is an important component of the more successful reading programs and should usually precede oral reading. In a classroom or home environment, a discussion following the child's reading motivates higher level thinking (Anderson, 1985).

Should parents teach their children to read? If a child is interested in learning to read, if he or she can recognize letters and identify their corresponding sounds, and if parents can make learning to read fun for the child, there is no reason not to try. "No roadblocks of any kind should be put in the way of children who want to read on their own . . . You can never miseducate children by responding appropriately to their demands for information" (Elkind, 1987a, pp. 184-185).

Because writing involves motor skills that require considerable practice, writing ability emerges later than reading. Initially, children may believe that each letter stands for a word, and may write sentences like URVRE NIS (you are very nice). Early writing involves the composition of sentences reflecting an understanding of the relationship between letters and words, between words and sentences (Wells, 1988).

Hayes and Flower (1986) analyzed three major writing processes: (1) planning (generating and organizing ideas), (2) sentence generation (producing formal sentences), and (3) revision (improving the first draft). Older models of reading and writing that stressed the importance of maturation denied the possibility that very young children could learn these skills. Newer models allow for the early emergence of these capabilities. They emphasize activities that parents can arrange to promote literacy skills.

Parental Involvement In Schooling

Schooling can make an enormous contribution to children's development, particularly when parents become involved in the educational process (Stevenson & Baker, 1987). Showing interest in schoolwork and homework lets children know that what they are doing is important. Attending school activities such as assembly programs and open houses emphasizes the importance of school and provides parents with useful information about helping their children succeed (Epstein, 1992). Do parents understand the potential value of their participation? And, what can school systems do to bring parents into the educational fold?

In 1987, 22,000 teachers from all 50 states participated in a survey (*The New York Times*, December 12, 1988). Ninety percent of the teachers reported that the lack of parental support at their schools was a problem. My home state, New Jersey, with the help of generous corporate contributions, promoted a large-scale, three-year public-relations campaign ("Partners in Learning") to increase parent's involvement in their children's education (*The New York Times*, November 15,

1987). Through the use of television and radio commercials, McDonald's place mats, Johanna Farms milk cartons, oil bills, and paychecks, parents were reminded of six ways to improve their children's performance in school.

It was suggested that parents check that homework is completed each day; make sure that their children get a good night's sleep; provide a quiet place and time for children to study; have children arrive at school on time; talk to children about their daily school experiences; and read with them, or encourage them to read, at least 15 minutes a day. Schools that made exemplary efforts to promote parental involvement received special recognition from the state. Grants were available for pilot projects that foster home-school partnerships.

TABLE 10.3   Parental Involvement in Schooling

Explain to a child why education is important (what role it plays in life) and that parent values effort and persistence.

Check each homework assignment and provide assistance when appropriate.

Provide a quiet place and time for study.

Discuss with children their daily school experiences.

Rather than ask "How did you do?," ask "What did you do?"

For younger students, reward achievement with praise and affection.

Participate in school-related activities and parent organizations.

Rather than punish poor school performance, find out what the problem is and come up with a specific plan to improve performance.

As children progress through elementary school, encourage self-reliance rather than allowing child to depend on parent to monitor assignments and study.

Parental support of children's efforts in school encourages both greater achievement and more positive attitudes toward school. It helps parental decision-making about school-related matters and improves communication between parents and teachers (*NJEA Review*, May, 1988; Wells, 1987). Stevenson and Baker (1987), for example, found that children of parents who are involved in school activities perform better in school than children of less-involved parents.

Children from low-income families benefit the most when parents become actively involved in their education (Wells, 1987). "The failure to bridge the social and cultural gap between home and school may lie at the root of the poor academic performance of [disadvantaged minority] children" (Comer, 1988a, p. 43). "A child from a poor marginal family . . . is likely to enter school without adequate preparation. The child may arrive without ever having learned such social skills as negotiation and compromise. A child who is expected to read at school may come from a home where no one reads and may never have heard a parent read bedtime stories" (p. 45).

Some adults feel uncomfortable in school settings, perhaps reflecting difficult times in their own educational history (McClelland, 1995). Other parents report that they just hear from school personnel when their children are in trouble. These parents often become suspicious or resentful of school staff. "And those individuals under great stress, with their own personal problems and failures, often view the school problems of their children as yet another failure. Thus, many parents stay away from schools or interact with school people in angry, defensive, and confrontational ways" (Comer, 1988a, pp. 37–38).

School personnel may react defensively and view such parents as part of the problem rather than seeing that they could be part of the solution. Many teachers complain that parents are uncooperative—they don't show

municate their desire to deal with such potentially dangerous behavior as chasing and escaping, attacking and defending. In play they can express these desires safely, because they give each other signals showing that they do not really mean what they are doing. Monkeys use a play face, dogs wag their tails and children say, 'I'm just pretending' " (Sutton-Smith, 1985, p. 64).

It has been said that "play is the work of the child" because play behavior serves virtually every domain of development. Physical play provides children with exercise and sharpens both gross and fine motor coordination. Pretend, dramatic, and creative play stimulate children's imaginations and help them distinguish between reality and fantasy. Play helps children appreciate the countless possibilities that exist in any situation. Children play for

fun but, in the process, develop competencies that prepare them for school.

Playing with other children sharpens communication and interpersonal abilities and dispositions, including conflict-resolution skills, sharing, empathy, and cooperation. Play also can be a form of coping, as when children act out fearful situations. Play can also serve as an outlet for frustration and anger. Observing children in play gives parents an excellent opportunity to assess their children's perceptions of the world and of themselves.

In the past, play was much more of a communal pastime than it is today. Modern children are more likely than their ancestors to spend their time in solitary play—perhaps alone in their bedrooms or playrooms—watching TV, playing a video game, or playing with an electronic toy or action figure. "The shift in play has been steady: a taming of most

Parents can structure play activities to increase their social and cognitive value to the young child.

violence; mechanization of toys, increasingly electronic in character; symbolization in games of language, information and strategy, which have largely replaced rough physical play; decreasing differentiation between the play of boys and girls; increasing remoteness from direct experience through fantasy; and most significantly, isolation" (Sutton-Smith, 1985, p. 64).

Parents as Playmates

Parents provide a structure to play interactions with very young children that would not be present when young siblings play with each other (Stevenson, Leavitt, Thompson, & Roach, 1988). Hence, if a parent is present, a preschooler might initiate play behavior that requires a partner. If a young sibling is present, the child would be more likely to play with a toy. Parents, not young children, determine the course of a play interaction.

Parents naturally simplify their play behaviors with very young children. Even infants enjoy bouts of "pat-a-cake" and "peek-a-boo." "These and other games introduce infants to the rules of social behavior. Being highly repetitive with simple roles for both parent and infant, these games help infants learn such things as the rules of give-and-take during conversations" (Trotter, 1987b, p. 31).

Parents naturally adjust their play behaviors according to a child's age and level of maturity. Power (1985) videotaped mothers and fathers playing with their boys and girls at ages 7, 10, and 13 months. He found that parents of the older children were more likely to "encourage pretend, turn-taking, and relational behavior and less likely to direct infant attention. Moreover, parents of older infants were more likely to use verbal techniques alone and less likely to physically perform behaviors for their children" (p. 1514).

Ross and Lollis (1987) had parents participate in a variety of "baby games" with their infants. The parents then were instructed to *not* take their turn and sit quietly for several seconds. When the adults ceased their participation, the infants displayed considerable independent understanding of the games they were playing. Through sounds and gestures, the infants appeared to be signaling their parents to take their turn. The older the infants, the more signals they displayed, encouraging their parents to continue.

Given the potential value of interactive play in children's development and the tendency of middle-class children to isolate themselves in their fully-equipped electronic bedrooms or playrooms, parents should consider making interactive play a priority when helping a child decide how to spend his or her day. Solitary play can be valuable, too, but a balance should be struck between both types of play.

Gender Differences in Play and Toy Preferences

Some parents, particularly fathers, assume that the toys children play with influence their sexual identity. Research, however, demonstrates that children's gender identities and eventual sexual orientation are in no way influenced by their toys. Mothers are more likely to give children of either gender the freedom to play with whatever toys they desire.

Bradbard (1985) asked the parents of 47 preschool children to list the toys their children received for Christmas. Although the children requested an average of 3 or 4 toys, they received an average of 11 to 12 toys. Boys ask for and receive vehicle toys (e.g., cars, airplanes) and "spatial-temporal" toys (e.g., building blocks) whereas girls are more likely to request and receive "domestic" toys (e.g., dolls, toy dishes). Other types of presents (e.g., books, stuffed animals) are given equally often to boys and girls. Ironically, it is the parent's attitude toward a child's choice of toys that is associated with later school adjustment and friendship patterns. In infancy, children are already demonstrating preferences for toys that are associated with their gender.

Generally, mothers play differently with children than do fathers. Mothers are more verbal with infants and preschoolers; fathers are more physical. Power (1985), in the study cited previously, reported that as children aged, mothers of girls became more directive in play and mothers of boys became less directive. In most other respects, mothers and fathers are similar in their play behavior. They adjust their reactions according to the situation and modify their play behavior according to their children's age.

TELEVISION

Study Question *How are children affected by what they see on television?*

For over 40 years, serious questions have been raised about television's impact on children. Parents and psychologists wonder whether televised violence and the portrayal of other antisocial behaviors "toughen" children or desensitize them to real-life violence. Do televised portrayals of women, the elderly, and minorities encourage unflattering stereotypes about these groups? What are the effects, if any, of exposing children to a steady diet of sexual innuendo and activity? Are children manipulated by misleading commercials that present distorted or exaggerated claims about products? (Liebert & Sprafkin, 1988; van der Voort & Valkenburg, 1994).

We also must ask whether children should be spending so much of their time so passively. Television watching has become the default activity for most people in the United States. It is what we do when there is "nothing else worth doing." Parents encourage this habitual pattern in children by using TV as a babysitter instead of encouraging more active and challenging pursuits.

A survey published by *Weekly Reader Magazine* in May, 1988, confirmed that watching television is children's favorite leisure activity. Reading has become the least popular, at least for children in grades 4-6. In addition to distracting children from more beneficial play and social experiences, television is a teacher. Children in the United States watch an average of 25 hours of TV a week, which accumulates to about 15,000 hours by the time they graduate from high school. Compare that figure to the 11,000 hours that they spend in classrooms. Lawrence (1986) reported that adolescents watch an average of 17 hours of TV a week.

Most children (and some adults) are not aware that the primary purpose of TV programming is to get viewers to watch the commercials. Young children do not understand that the purpose of a commercial is to get them to buy a product. In fact, young children may not distinguish between the program and the commercial! Further, many toy commercials are followed by disclaimers ("partial assembly required") that children do not understand. Food commercials directed at children offer heavily sugared, non-nutritious junk food (Liebert & Sprafkin, 1988).

"In the course of their viewing, they will see perhaps 350,000 commercial messages, many for unhealthful foods and other products that are not conducive to health. The social messages are often no better: sex without affection or regard to the risk of pregnancy or disease; frequent consumption of alcohol and drugs; misrepresentations of women, minorities, the elderly and the handicapped; unrealistically easy solutions to complex problems, and countless depictions of violence" (Brody, 1987e). Cable movies and video rentals increase children's possible exposure to sadistic violence and tasteless, sexually explicit material. Afternoon talk shows expose children to such topics as teenage prostitution, incest, violent sexual relationships, and to an endless procession of antisocial models (Strasburger, 1995).

A study conducted for the Planned Parenthood Federation of America concluded that there are 65,000 sexual references a year broadcast during prime afternoon and evening hours on the major networks. Each hour there are 9 kisses, 5 hugs, 10 sexual innuendoes, and 1 or 2 references each to sexual intercourse and "deviant" sexual practices. Comparable references to birth control, sexually transmitted diseases, and sex education are rare. The study estimated that people in the U.S. view almost 14,000 instances of sexual material a year in popular time slots (*The New York Times*, January 27, 1988).

When young children watch TV programs aimed at a general audience, they usually do so with their mothers. When they watch programs aimed solely at children, parents usually are not present. Children come to prefer the programs that their parents watch. Much of what critics would consider to be inappropriate content, children view in the company of their parents. As they get older, children continue to watch these programs, but unattended (St. Peters, Fitch, Huston, Wright, & Eakins, 1991).

Effects on Children

Television is an instrument of social learning, particularly as a provider of information (Huston, Watkins, & Kunkel, 1989; Strasburger, 1995). Young children, having difficulty distinguishing between fantasy and reality (Flavell, 1986), are particularly susceptible to the values, attitudes, and behaviors portrayed in the electronic media. Children as young as 14 months of age show deferred imitation of TV models, even after a 24-hour delay (Meltzoff, 1988).

It would be an oversimplification to conclude that children automatically believe everything that they see and hear, or that they will blindly imitate violent or other behaviors viewed on TV. Even young children are aware that the programs they watch on TV are not "real." Five-year-olds apparently have the impression that everything on television is pretend (Wright, Huston, Reitz, & Piemyat, 1994), but they are less aware that roles are played by actors who rehearse before they act. High levels of televised violence inhibit fantasy play (van der Voort & Valkenburg, 1994) and probably create in children an impression that their world is more dangerous than it really is.

Blaming television for children's misbehavior or underachievement is misguided. Japanese adolescents watch as much TV as adolescents in the United States, yet score higher on standardized tests. "Television is not the culprit behind low scores . . . a more likely culprit is the little time Americans give to intellectual tasks outside their classrooms" (Fischman, 1986).

Children who are already aggressive may be attracted to violent TV programming and behave more aggressively following such viewing (Josephson, 1987). Boys may imitate behaviors of appealing heroes (e.g., Mighty Morphin Power Rangers) who use violence and then are rewarded for it (Boyatzis, Matillo, & Nesbitt, 1995). Children are more likely to tolerate aggressive behavior in others after viewing televised or film violence (Molitor & Hirsch, 1994).

However, children who have incorporated many of their parents' values, and who have learned how to inhibit their antisocial impulses, are not likely to blindly copy behaviors viewed on TV (Abelman, 1985). Liebert and Sprafkin (1988) conclude, tentatively, that TV violence is one of many possible causes of aggressive behavior for children. When all possible causes are considered (especially family violence), televised violence may not be one of the most influential.

TABLE 10.5 Tips for Parents Regarding Children's TV Watching

Monitor and guide children's selections to avoid inappropriate programming.

Find programs that are both entertaining and educational.

Tape or rent special programs.

Watch stimulating programs with children and discuss their content.

Keep track of viewing time and negotiate reasonable limits.

Review TV listings at the beginning of the week to decide on programming ahead of time.

Direct children toward less passive activities such as reading and play.

Remind young children that what they are watching is not real, plots are made up and performed by actors and actresses in a studio using a script.

Remind children that the purpose of commercials is to sell products.

What's A Parent To Do?

Television is here to stay. Over 99 percent of homes in the United States have TV sets. A majority of homes have more than one set. Most parents are probably not aware of how much time their children spend watching TV. Keeping track of viewing time is probably a good first step. If you judge that your children spend too much time viewing low-quality programming, consider setting time limits on their viewing. Credit card type devices are becoming available that limit children's television watching to an amount of time previously negotiated by parent and child.

Attempts to keep offensive programming off the air conflict with our free speech tradition. Concerned parents, therefore, monitor and guide their children's selections of TV programs (Meyer, 1989; Singer, 1989). There is a considerable amount of programming, particularly on cable TV, that is just not ap-

propriate for children. New technologies such as a "V-chip" (V for violence) that allow parents to censor violent programs are becoming available (Andrews, 1993), although this doesn't address sexual content and commercials.

Families with VCRs can rent or tape quality programs of interest to children so that when they sit down to watch, children are not limited to programs currently being broadcast. Parents can establish rules about what children can watch, when, and how much. "Together, establish some reasonable rules, such as limits on viewing time or no television until homework assignments are completed or none during meals . . . Each week, review the television listings with your children, and write down which programs each child can watch" (Brody, 1987e).

Concerned parents help their children find programs that they view as beneficial (e.g., educational shows, specials for children) and are willing to watch some of these programs with their children. By asking good questions and pointing out the fantasy nature of most television content, parents can help their children become media literate (Strasburger, 1995). Many parents pay little or no attention to their children's choice of programming (St. Peters et al., 1991). They do not keep track of what their children are seeing. Apparently, they believe that their children are not adversely affected by what they view on TV, or they simply don't care.

Optimally, parents will steer their children away from compulsive TV watching and video game playing toward more beneficial activities such as reading and play. When children do watch TV, parents should set weekly limits on viewing, turn the TV on only for specific programs, watch with their children, make comments, put disturbing events in context, ask questions, challenge objectionable opinions and values expressed by TV characters, and explain content that may confuse children (deGroot, 1994).

Children can be taught to be television-literate. Dorr, Graves, and Phelps (1980) developed a curriculum to teach children how to watch television. Children are taught that what they are watching is not real. They learn that the plots are fabricated, and the characters are actors and actresses who are reading from scripts. The settings are constructed, they are told, and commercials are shown to make money. Children can gain insight about TV production methods by creating their own videotapes of original material.

SUMMARY

1. High-achieving parents typically raise high-achieving children. Children raised under economically deprived conditions are at risk for low achievement and even illiteracy. It is not poverty, per se, that inhibits intellectual development but rather a lack of stimulating and meaningful parent-child interactions during infancy and toddlerhood.

2. Parents can encourage the development of competent behavior in children by arranging safe and interesting environments and activities. They can stimulate verbal interaction and have realistic expectations about their children's achievements. They can also practice the authoritative parenting style, offering affection and support. Ultimately, the key factor in parental competence is the reciprocal patterns of parent-child interaction and parental involvement in learning. Japanese mothers are excellent examples of this phenomenon.

3. Some parents push their young children into activities for which the youngsters are not prepared. This can discourage them, damage their self-esteem, and encourage negative attitudes about the activity or even about learning in general. Young children seem to

benefit most from low-pressure, relaxed, interesting, unstructured activities.

4. Culturally disadvantaged children show clear gains from attending preschool programs such as Head Start. Such programs compensate for the inadequate stimulation they may receive at home. Advantaged children generally do not benefit academically from preschool programs, but they may benefit socially.

5. Many school systems are encouraging parents to become more involved in their children's schooling. Parental support of children's schooling is predictive of greater achievement and more positive attitudes toward school. Some parents feel uncomfortable in schools or believe that they don't belong there. Given the amount of time children work in and out of school, parental involvement and support can dramatically enhance their education.

6. The topic of early schooling is controversial. Most educators agree that 4- and 5-year-old children should not be exposed to formal education. Preschool programs should accommodate individual children's readiness to participate in particular activities. They should also provide appropriate play materials and activities that will stimulate and challenge but not overwhelm.

7. Parents, teachers, and students in the United States have lower expectations regarding achievement than their counterparts in Asian countries. Whereas Asian parents attribute achievement to hard work, parents and students in the United States tend to view achievement in terms of innate ability.

8. Underachieving students perform at an academic level that is below what we would expect based on their ability. Underachievers lack persistence in the face of challenge and

adversity. Many underachieving adolescents have family and other life problems. Youngsters who enjoy supportive family and peer relationships usually do well in school.

9. Through unstructured play, children gain in virtually every domain of development. Modern children play differently than children in the past. They prefer more solitary activities. Given the potential benefits of play behavior, parents should encourage children's exploration of the environment, manipulation of objects, and enjoyable interactions with other children. By playing with their children in thoughtful and challenging ways, parents can encourage a wide range of useful skills. Parents can also encourage creative expression in children by reinforcing creative risk-taking and original behaviors.

10. Children spend more time watching television than in any other waking activity. Television can be a powerful instrument of social learning and there are excellent programs available. Parents can limit the amount of children's viewing and help them avoid inappropriate or offensive programs. They can also establish rules about viewing and watch TV with their children, helping them put what they view into perspective.

GLOSSARY

social comparison   Comparing ourselves to someone else to see how we measure up

stereotype   An overgeneralized belief about a group of people that focuses on a trait or behavior that all group members supposedly share

THOUGHT QUESTIONS

1. How do high achieving parents cultivate a love of learning in their children?

2. Why is the parent-child relationship such a critical factor in children's achievement?

3. Why is exposing children to academic material prematurely harmful to their achievement motivation?

4. What family factors explain the superior academic performance of Asian children compared to children in the United States?

5. How does play contribute to children's cognitive development?

6. Should parents censor what their children watch on television?

11
CHAPTER

PARENTING ADOLESCENTS

OBJECTIVES 328
ADOLESCENCE AS A STAGE OF DEVELOPMENT 329
FAMILY RELATIONSHIPS AND CONFLICT 331
Puberty and Family Relationships 333
Parenting and Peer Group Influence 334
COGNITIVE DEVELOPMENT 335
Adolescent Adjustment 336
PREPARING FOR INDEPENDENCE 337
Older Adolescents' Goals and Values 338
RISK-TAKING BEHAVIOR 339
ADOLESCENT SEXUALITY 340
Adolescent Sexual Activity, Pregnancy, and Child Care 340
A Mixed Message for Teenage Fathers 342
Spotlight: Adolescents, Parents, and Birth Control 343
"Everyone Else Is Doing It": Guidelines for Parents Teaching
    Sexual Responsibility 344
ADOLESCENT DRUG USE 345
ADOLESCENT SUICIDE: A PERMANENT SOLUTION TO A
    TEMPORARY PROBLEM 347
Signs of Suicide: "I Might As Well Be Dead" 348
Spotlight: Empty Nests That Do Not Always Remain
    Empty 348
Return to the Nest 349
RESIDENTIAL SETTING DURING THE COLLEGE
    YEARS 350
SUMMARY 350
GLOSSARY 351
THOUGHT QUESTIONS 351

"Adolescents want more of a say in decisions that affect them and the family, yet may not know how to express that adult need in an adult manner. They may ask to come home at 2 a.m. on a school night, or mention that they admire another teenager's shaved head. Parents, who expect power struggles at this time, often react poorly" (Kutner, 1988s).

OBJECTIVES

After studying Chapter 11, students should be able to:

1. Describe the characteristics of adolescence as a stage of development
2. Describe some stereotypes of adolescence, such as the defiant, antisocial teenager, and explain why they are false
3. List the most common causes of conflict between adolescents and their parents
4. Describe the characteristics of formal operational thought and its role in adolescent development
5. List the most common worries and concerns of adolescents
6. Describe the ways in which adolescents display their need for independence
7. Identify the factors that promote "risk-taking" behaviors in adolescents
8. Describe what parents and schools can do to discourage adolescent pregnancy
9. Discuss the issues that surround teenage pregnancy, the availability of birth control devices, and abortion
10. Identify factors associated with drug use during adolescence
11. Describe personal and family factors associated with adolescent suicide

Sitting uneasily before me was Kenny, a bright 16-year-old, eleventh grader. His mother, Annie, was telling me that her relationship with her husband was being destroyed by their problems with Kenny. Kenny's father, Steve, no longer wanted Kenny in his house. He rarely spoke to him unless to criticize or argue.

Kenny's parents voiced the following complaints. He drove his parents' car without their permission. He had 11 cavities because of his candy-laden diet. He was extremely uncooperative. He never washed or put away his dirty clothes. He left his school books on the kitchen table despite his parents' repeated protests. Occasionally, he missed school because he woke up too late for the bus. He performed poorly in school. He talked back to his parents, cursed in their presence, and even had had fist fights with his father. As a result, Kenny was not allowed to use the family car, his television, or the family phone. These punishments, in turn, enraged Kenny and he responded with even greater defiance.

Kenny's father, Steve, confessed that he did not handle Kenny's defiance well. He claimed that he "goes crazy" when Kenny provokes him, and that he often hated his son. He yearned to have Kenny move out. He also reported feeling guilty about their terrible relationship. He was now struggling to show good faith and hoped that they could learn to get along. He also felt that his wife was too sympathetic to Kenny. His own "strategy," he realized, was to hurt Kenny as much as Kenny was hurting him. I was surprised when Kenny told me that his father was really a "good guy" but unable to overcome their years of perpetual antagonism.

Annie agreed that Kenny was trying harder than her husband to improve their relationship. With tears streaming down her face, she told me that she was being torn apart by their endless bickering. Steve, in his own frustration, was doing nothing to improve what was certainly his own greatest personal failure. Kenny's behavior was certainly "obnoxious," but not that unusual for someone his age. I was sure that this bit of information would not help Steve be more patient with his son.

Kenny and his father were caught in an escalating, sometimes violent, pattern of mutual distrust and animosity. They had reached a point where they could barely communicate with each other. Fortunately, in most families with adolescents, parent-child conflict does not reach this level of intensity.

In this chapter, we address the fascinating challenge of parenting adolescents. We will emphasize the family environment as the primary social context for adolescent growth and maturation. We also consider some of the potential hazards of adolescence, including unwanted pregnancy, drug abuse, impulsive risk-taking behavior, and suicide.

ADOLESCENCE AS A STAGE OF DEVELOPMENT

Study Question *What is adolescence?*

Prior to the late nineteenth century, those whom we today call adolescents were considered to be adults. Adolescence as a sheltered phase of development had not yet been "invented" (Fasick, 1994). Today, we view adolescence not only as a transition period between childhood and adulthood but also as a stage of development that is important in its own right. We consider teenagers too old to be treated like younger children, but too young to be given full adult responsibilities and privileges

Based on this so-called *moratorium* arrangement, adolescents enjoy the continuing financial support of their parents and the security of family life. Unlike their counterparts of previous centuries, young people are shielded from the demands of the adult work world. What adolescents give up in the moratorium arrangement are the adult freedoms and privileges enjoyed by youth in previous centuries (Lapsley & Rice, 1988).

Study Question *Are adolescents really "out-of-control" or do most live in relative harmony with their parents?*

Adolescence has been stereotyped as a time of stress, emotional turmoil, and intergenerational conflict. Freud, Erikson, and other theorists in the psychiatric tradition assumed that intense emotional reactions and maladjustment are inevitable (and therefore normal) during adolescence. The emotional strains we commonly observe in families with adolescents presumably reflect the challenges of the teenage years: becoming less dependent on one's parents, establishing one's personal identity, and, ultimately, trying to separate from one's family (Jaffe, 1998; Powers, Hauser, & Kilner, 1989).

Research has not supported the stereotype of adolescents as maladjusted or unstable (Adelson, 1979; Offer, 1987). Individual adolescents respond to the challenges of this stage in extremely varied ways. If there is any one theme that characterizes this formative stage of development that our ancestors called "youth," it is adjustment to change. "Changes that may challenge and stimulate some young people can become overwhelming and stressful to others. The outcome seems to depend on prior strengths and vulnerabilities—both of the individual adolescents and their families—as well as on the pattern, timing, and intensity of changes" (Peterson, 1987, p. 32).

Adolescence is a period of remarkable change, with relatively rapid physical growth, unparalleled sexual development, a substantial broadening of the peer network, and the expansion of cognitive abilities (Jaffe, 1998; Pestrak & Martin, 1985). The strained relationships that we observe in many families with adolescents reflect these dramatic changes. For the first time in their lives, adolescents find themselves making decisions that could have life-long consequences.

Study Question *What special challenges face parents of adolescent children?*

TABLE 11.1 Developmental Tasks of Adolescence

Accepting one's changing body

Creating an adult identity and taking on adult roles

Becoming more independent and self-regulating

Achieving emotional independence from one's parents

Accepting one's sexuality

Achieving mature relationships with peers of both genders

Preparing for marriage and family life

Preparing for a career

Acquiring a set of values that will guide one's behavior

Engaging in socially responsive behavior

Based on Havighurst (1972).

It would be unfortunate if parents adopted a stereotypical view of adolescence. Assuming that out-of-control behavior is normal during adolescence could foster in parents feelings of helplessness and despair. Naturally, parents become concerned when their children's physical and sexual maturity precedes the development of corresponding cognitive, judgmental, and emotional resources (Hamburg & Takanishi, 1989). It would be a serious mistake, however, to assume that today's adolescents experience severe identity crises or perpetual emotional distress. Most adolescents want and need adult guidance and support (Frey & Röthlisberger, 1996; Takanishi, 1993b). Parents should take comfort in knowing that the "vast majority of these teenagers function well, enjoy good relationships with their families and friends, and accept the values of the larger society" (Offer, 1987). Changes that occur in adolescents and their parents may temporarily destabilize families,

but this is "natural, expected and healthy" (Steinberg, 1987b, p. 77).

Raising adolescents evokes a variety of strong emotions in parents. Baldwin (1986) describes the following: (1) *fear* about what the secretive child will do next; (2) a deep sense of *helplessness* when their children are in emotional turmoil but refuse their parents' offers of help or comfort; (3) high levels of *frustration and anger* when adolescents confront their parents verbally, and when they violate rules and test limits; (4) *awareness of loss* as the adolescent withdraws from the family and the parents recognize that their teenage children will eventually leave the family unit; and (5) *personal hurt and rejection* when teenagers do not show appreciation and gratitude for parent's support and sacrifices.

Erikson (1968) viewed this stage of life as a time when adolescents create an adult identity. Parents are well aware of adolescents' attempts to assert or even demand their independence of adult authority. Today's adolescents are pressured to grow up quickly and to emulate adult values and practices (Elkind, 1981). Some compromise their health and safety in doing so. Middle and late adolescents know that they are fast approaching the time when they will live separately from their parents and take on demanding adult roles (Frank, Avery, & Laman, 1988).

At the same time that adolescent children are adjusting to their physical and social changes, their parents are approaching middle-age. For many of them, the middle years are a time of frustration, appraisal, and renewal. As their daughters become fertile, middle-aged women are about to lose their fertility. As their sons are creating an adult identity, some middle-aged men are questioning their own. The parallel challenges of adolescence and middle age increase the likelihood of conflict and misunderstanding in unwary families (Larson & Richards, 1994).

FAMILY RELATIONSHIPS AND CONFLICT

Communication between parents and young adolescents may become increasingly strained. Parents come to expect more "adult-like" behavior, and adolescents begin to question parental authority. Adolescent strivings for autonomy sometimes clash with parental attempts to regulate their behavior. This may set the stage for intergenerational conflict and occasional heated confrontation, as between Kenny and his father.

Before industrialization, many children were sent away from their families at the onset of puberty to work and live under the authority of adults who were not their parents. (Steve's wanting Kenny out of the house reminded me of this tradition). *"Placing out,"* as this practice is called, still exists in many non-industrialized societies. It also resembles emigration patterns observed in other primate species, such as monkeys and apes (Schlegel & Barry, 1991). In primate communities, male and female "adolescents" leave their natal group and seek mates elsewhere. In primates, this practice improves reproductive fitness by minimizing inbreeding and promoting genetic diversity (Steinberg, 1987a).

Many adolescents report feeling increasingly distant from both parents (Holmbeck & Hill, 1991; Steinberg, 1988a). Steinberg suggests that the conflict between parents and teenagers that is so common during early adolescence might be "a vestige of our evolutionary past, when prolonged proximity between parent and offspring threatened the species' genetic integrity" (p. 38).

Many studies confirm that the onset of puberty is correlated with strained family relationships, particularly between adolescents and their mothers. Mothers of adolescents report lower levels of life satisfaction and marital happiness and more distress than mothers of younger children (Steinberg, 1987a). Perhaps this is because mothers usually play a greater role in socialization. Adolescents with personal problems are more likely to seek assistance and comfort from mothers than from fathers.

Why do most adolescents approach their mothers when they are upset? Many young people report that their mothers are more sympathetic and nurturant than their fathers (LeCroy, 1988). Mothers spend more time with their teenage children, provide more support, and express more love. Thus, it is not surprising that adolescents report feeling more emotionally connected to their mothers. This is not to say that most adolescents report poor relationships with their fathers. However, relationships with mothers usually are deeper and more satisfying than relationships with fathers. Not surprisingly, mothers report greater peace of mind when they get along well with their teenaged children (LeCroy, 1988; Miller & Lane, 1991; Youniss & Ketterlinus, 1987). However, intimacy with fathers usually is a better predictor of adolescent adjustment than intimacy with mothers (LeCroy, 1988). Why do you think this is so?

Although biology may play a role in family conflict, adolescents and their parents also have differing views about what constitutes acceptable behavior. Smetana (1989a) refers to adolescents' "minor but persistent conflict with parents over the everyday details of family life" (p. 1052). These include "doing the chores, getting along with others, regulating activities and interpersonal relationships, appearances, and doing homework" (p. 1063). Other common issues in parent-adolescent conflict include personal possessions, family obligations, use of time, emotional support, dating, and ideology (Hall, 1987; Hill & Holmbeck, 1987; Smetana, Yau, Restrepo, & Braeges, 1991).

Conflict is most likely to occur when adolescents are noncompliant or when they violate their parents' expectations about what constitutes proper behavior. Alsaker (1995) acknowledges the difficulty that many parents have deciding what is appropriate behavior for their children. Most parents grew up in a time when adolescence was not given the same importance that it is today. Parents get varying and contradictory information from experts about what constitutes healthy development. Mothers and fathers often do not agree with each other about what constitutes appropriate behavior for adolescents.

Teenagers believe that they should have the right to privacy and the right to reach their own decisions about personal matters. Parents may agree, but differ on which decisions are considered personal. The larger conflict is between an adolescent's desire for greater freedom and parents' intention to maintain authority and an orderly family system. The important point is that adolescents view family and personal issues differently than do their parents (Smetana, 1989a).

In most families, negotiation replaces confrontation as adolescents and parents become more sensitive to each other's points of view. The principle that most parents apply is that greater freedom can be earned by displays of good judgment and responsible behavior. By late adolescence, parents and children usually treat each other as equals. Along the way, male and female adolescents adopt somewhat different conflict-resolution strategies. Males are generally more controlling, especially with their mothers. Both genders prefer to negotiate with their mothers rather than with their fathers. In the process, they develop a more diverse "arsenal of strategies" to use with mothers (White, Pearson, & Flint, 1989).

Over the course of adolescence, most parents gradually relinquish control over their children's behavior. Those who do not anticipate change, or who do not know how to ad-

TABLE 11.2 Some Causes of Parent-Adolescent Conflict

Parents have higher expectations of adolescents following puberty

Adolescents generally are more moody and less compliant than younger children

Reflecting cognitive advances, adolescents are more likely to question their parent's decisions

Adolescents want more say regarding decisions that they believe are personal

Inflexible, punitive parents provoke greater resistance from their adolescent children

Adolescents are trying to separate emotionally from their parents

Incomplete socialization results in adolescent behavior that adults may find obnoxious

just to change, become increasingly frustrated and punitive. Parents who are unwilling to relax their restrictions evoke considerable resistance from their young teenagers. Adolescent desire for self-regulation clashes with parental attempts to regulate their behavior.

Families with poor communication and conflict-resolution skills experience especially intense parent-adolescent conflict. In these families, parents encounter more physical and verbal aggression and have adolescents who are at greater risk for deviant peer influence, drug abuse, running away, school failure, and delinquency (Ge et al., 1996; Hall, 1987). Families that provide mutual support and a sense of belonging on the one hand, while allowing increased autonomy to the adolescent on the other, have the fewest intergenerational conflicts.

Some parents, like Kenny's father, are too easily provoked into verbal confrontations. One of the "secrets" of parenting adolescents is overlooking as much obnoxious behavior as possible. It's not easy, but criticism, sarcasm, and conflict almost never improve family relationships. Punitive parental control should not be confused with reasonable parental supervision and monitoring of adolescent behavior, which are predictive of positive adjustment (Kurdek & Fine, 1994).

Newman (1985) suggests that parents and teachers find adolescents exasperating because adults lack awareness of the "incompetencies of adolescents that lead to their obnoxious behavior" (p. 635). We think that they should know better but they really don't! Some adults expect adolescents to be defiant and hostile, and perhaps overreact to mild provocations (Hall, 1987).

Stefanko (1987) maintains that parents and adolescents see each other stereotypically. Both groups expect to be viewed in a distorted way by members of the other group and adopt a somewhat defensive posture. Youniss and Ketterlinus (1987) asked ninth and eleventh graders how well their parents knew them and how much they cared about what their parents thought about them. Sons and daughters felt that their mothers knew them fairly well. Daughters reported that their fathers did not know them so well. Importantly, sons and daughters were concerned about what both parents thought of them.

Puberty and Family Relationships

Study Question *How does puberty affect the parent-child relationship?*

Steinberg (1987c) investigated the relationship between the onset of puberty and family relations. He studied 204 families with a firstborn child between the ages of 10 and 15 years. He found that the onset of puberty is associated with increased emotional distance between parents and children, but also greater adolescent autonomy.

The onset of puberty, according to the study, is accompanied by increased adolescent-mother conflict, though the pattern differs for boys and girls. Early-maturing boys have increased conflict with their mothers, compared to later-maturing boys. For girls, the increase in conflict is not related to the timing of puberty. Steinberg suggests that adolescent-mother conflict may be more likely when puberty occurs before a certain chronological age. Since girls mature, on the average, about two years before boys, their "on-time" maturation may be early enough to provoke mother-daughter conflict.

An equivalent increase in conflict with fathers was not found. Steinberg suggests four possible reasons: (1) mothers are perceived as having a lower status than fathers; (2) adolescents have a greater need to separate from their mothers; (3) mothers are more active in disciplining their children; and (4) the emotional quality of adolescents' relationships with their mothers may be stronger than with their fathers. Overall, there are relatively few differences between male and female adolescents in their family interaction patterns (Steinberg, 1987d).

Steinberg (1988a) longitudinally studied 157 male and female firstborn adolescents and their parents. He confirmed that biological maturation increased adolescent autonomy but also increased conflict between parents and children and reduced parent-child closeness. Maturation thus accelerates the development of autonomy in adolescents. Perhaps this occurs by increasing parent-child distance and encouraging parent-child conflict. Studies suggest that less mature, and therefore younger, teenagers experience greater friction with their parents than more mature teenagers.

In late adolescence and young adulthood, males and females differ in the way that they relate to their parents. There is evidence that males move in the direction of greater autonomy, or increased separateness, from their parents. Females try to maintain higher levels of "connectedness" with their parents, particularly with their mothers (Frank, Avery, & Laman, 1988). "As adults, women develop a greater capacity for closeness and empathy than men, but they also remain more entangled in and preoccupied with their family relationships. In particular, the mother-daughter relationship continues to be especially close, but the daughter's unresolved, ambivalent struggle for greater separateness often tinges this relationship with strong emotional conflict" (Frank et al., p. 730).

Parents may be unaware of their reluctance to let go of their role as nurturer. One mother, gazing at her 14-year-old daughter in a strapless dress, expressed her mixed feelings this way: "She is beautiful and looks so grownup. I feel such bittersweetness. I see her future ahead of her and I see her past 14 years in a flash. I'm not ready to let her go, yet it is out of my hands." Another mother expressed similar sentiments: "I'm happy, but sad. I'm losing the little girl I once had" (from Jaffe, 1998).

Parenting and Peer Group Influence

Healthy families support their adolescents' striving for autonomy rather than resist or discourage it. Peer relationships give adolescents the opportunity to learn how to participate in adult-like relationships with non-family members. Adolescent friendships give parents the opportunity to observe their children's social behaviors outside of the family.

The peer group also provides adolescents with countless opportunities to distance themselves from their parents and become more independent ("their own person"). Peers often are better able (and more willing) than parents to satisfy some of the social needs of young adolescents, including autonomy and identity needs. Hunter (1985) found that peers generally are better listeners than parents.

Older adolescents prefer to discuss personal issues with friends rather than with parents. Whereas they prefer to discuss their current problems with their friends, they are likely to discuss decisions about education, vocation, money, and marriage with their parents (Wilks, 1986). "Adolescents will seek their parents' advice and opinions for longer-term, important, and difficult decisions, whereas friends' opinions and feelings will be more important for decisions in short-term, less important, and less difficult areas" (p. 333). When family ties are strained, adolescents become more susceptible to peer pressure and are at greater risk for peer-related adjustment problems, including drug use and delinquency (Ge et al., 1996). The more controlling their parents are, the more adolescents become oriented toward their peers (Fuligni & Eccles, 1993).

Study Question *Should parents try to influence their children's friendships?*

Fear of deviant peer pressure motivates some parents to attempt to restrict their children's choice of friends. Most children resist direct parental input regarding their friendships ("I don't tell you who your friends should be"). Nevertheless, parents influence their children's peer relationships indirectly. For example, children's choice of friends and friendship quality is influenced by their parents' child rearing style. In a study by Gold and Yanof (1985), girls who identified their mothers' parenting style as authoritative reported greater mutual influence in their friendships. Girls who had positive relationships with their mothers emulated their mother's relationship skills in their close peer relationships.

Brown and his colleagues (Brown, Mounts, Lamborn, & Steinberg, 1993) interviewed 3,781 high school students aged 15 to 19 years about their friendships and their parents' child rearing practices. They found that specific parenting behaviors, including monitoring, encouragement of achievement, and joint

about was not in evidence among the vast majority of subjects we studied" (p. 36).

Study Question *Do children automatically accept their parent's values?*

Clearly, children's values reflect the socialization patterns in their family of origin (Kilby, 1993). Children are more likely to internalize the values of a parent who is nurturant and respectful of the child's point of view (Maccoby, 1980). Cold and controlling parents often have children who are aggressive and antisocial (Kazdin, 1987).

Some theorists suggest that the materialistic and prosocial values that we teach young people in our culture are contradictory. The more that people value material possessions, the less they seem to be interested in pursuing close relationships (Kasser & Ryan, 1993; Richins & Dawson, 1992).

Kasser and his colleagues (Kasser, Ryan, Zax, & Sameroff, 1995) suggest a link between parenting style and teenagers' orientation to prosocial versus financial values. They hypothesized that mothers who are cold and controlling have offspring who are more money-oriented than people-oriented. They also hypothesized that teenagers from less-advantaged socioeconomic backgrounds would value financial success more than personal relationships. They interviewed a heterogeneous sample of 140 eighteen-year-olds and their mothers or other available family members. The study confirmed that nonnurturant mothers and economic disadvantage are associated with adolescents' valuing financial success more than relationships, self-acceptance, and community feeling.

Parental warmth seems to foster children's identification with their parent's prosocial values; parental control seems to have the opposite effect. "Thus, cold and controlling environments may make individuals feel relatively insecure regarding their personal worth, in that expressions of their own desires are unlikely to be accepted. Individuals who experience such environments may then concentrate on pursuing financial success as a means of obtaining security and a sense of worth" (p. 913).

RISK-TAKING BEHAVIOR

Study Question *In what ways are adolescents particularly vulnerable to life-threatening activities?*

Most of the parents I know who have adolescent children keep their fingers crossed. They hope that their children won't follow in their collective footsteps in the kind of risk-taking behaviors that became part of adolescent subculture in the 1960s. At the same time that they are thinking "I hope my children won't do what I did," they may also think "but I'm glad I had the experience." Do we detect a double-standard?

Under the guise of social protest or spiritual liberation, the counterculture of the 1960s advocated a hedonistic philosophy revolving around "drugs, sex, and rock n' roll" (known as "wine, women, and song" to previous generations). For the past three decades, adolescents have had to make hard choices about whether to experiment with the legal and illegal drugs that are so prevalent in our society. At the same time, they have had to balance their strong sexual drive against the constraints placed on sexual activity by the possibility of sexually-transmitted diseases and the risk of pregnancy. They must make these difficult decisions at a time when their judgment is someplace between that of a child's and that of an adult's.

Psychologists have come to refer to such behaviors as "risk-taking." These are potentially self-destructive behaviors that violate society's conventions and good judgment. In addition to the use of drugs, risk-taking behaviors include unsafe sexual practices, reckless use of vehicles and weapons, suicide, and violent behavior (Landers, 1988g).

Diana Baumrind (1987) contends that many of the characteristics associated with risk-proneness are actually normal, even healthy, factors in adolescent development. She distinguishes between growth-enhancing risk taking, which is desirable, and health-compromising risk taking, which is not. Baumrind suggests that prevention efforts should concentrate on problem drinking, a precursor for many other self-destructive acts.

As Baumrind notes, growth-enhancing risk taking is one way in which teenagers assert their independence. Unfortunately, they have not yet achieved a level of cognitive maturity that allows a realistic assessment of the risk involved. ". . . by age 10 or so, they enter a risky period when they do lots of exploring at a time when their cognitive development has not yet reached the point where they can make judgments that will keep them out of trouble. They cannot really comprehend laws of probability. And they also have ideas of invulnerability that persuade them that they can safely take a known risk" (Hamburg, quoted in Goleman, 1987g).

Parents can apply the communication skills described in Chapter 7 to help their children anticipate the possible consequences of risk-taking behaviors. Asking good questions is particularly helpful. "How can your teachers give you enthusiastic letters of recommendation for college if you show off in class?" "What do you think will happen if an officer pulls you over and finds that you have been drinking?" "How will your life and Jill's life be changed if she gets pregnant?"

ADOLESCENT SEXUALITY

Earlier puberty and later marriage mean that today's fertile adolescents have to wait consid-erably longer than our ancestors did before they can engage in socially sanctioned sexual behavior. Girls carry a heavier burden than boys do regarding their fertility. Traditionally, females, not males, have been expected to inhibit sexual encounters that could lead to unwanted pregnancies. Research confirms that girls are more sexually conservative than boys, less sexually impulsive, and more relationship-oriented. Nevertheless, despite social sanctions, about half of all teenage girls report having had intercourse (Brooks-Gunn, 1988).

Parents often have difficulty knowing how to respond to their children's emergent sexuality. Fearing that their daughters are ripe for sexual coercion, some parents become more restrictive rather than less controlling. Most teenage girls resist increased restrictions. Parents also fear that their sons' sexual interests will override their achievement needs and future planning.

Through thoughtful socialization practices, parents can play a big part in encouraging their children to have responsible romantic relationships (Barnett, Papini, & Gbur, 1991; Pick & Palos, 1995; Romig & Bakken, 1992). Adolescents who communicate well with their parents receive more sex education at home (Baldwin & Baranoski, 1990). Children (particularly daughters) in families with reasonable parental supervision and close relationships usually become sexually active later than those in unstable families (Inazu & Fox, 1980; Pick & Palos, 1995; Thornton, 1990). Family stability, economic security, religious affiliation, and sex education foretell sexually responsible behavior during the adolescent years (Forste & Heaton, 1988).

Adolescent Sexual Activity, Pregnancy, and Child Care

Sexual prohibitions have gradually weakened in our society over the course of this century, largely due to the availability of safe and effective birth control technologies. We still confront serious problems, including sexually transmitted diseases, such as AIDS, and adolescent pregnancies. Healthier attitudes about sexuality have been evolving, fostered by an increase in sexual knowledge, though not necessarily among adolescents.

At least 80 percent of boys and 70 percent of girls report having had sexual intercourse by age 20, with age of first intercourse averaging about 16 years (Murstein & Mercy, 1994). Half of those who are sexually active do not use contraceptives, and one in five report having four or more sex partners (Brooks-Gunn, 1988; Faulkenberry, Vincent, James, & Johnson, 1987; Lewin, 1988c). Each year, over one million teenage girls become pregnant. About 80 percent of these pregnancies are unwanted (Miller, Christopherson, & King, 1993).

About half a million girls continue their pregnancies to birth, about one-third have abortions, and about 14 percent of teenage pregnancies end in miscarriage. Only 4 percent of unwed teenage mothers give up their infants for adoption. Teenagers in the U.S. are not more sexually active than those in western Europe, yet the incidence of adolescent pregnancy is much higher in this country. A key factor is the failure to use contraceptives (Brooks-Gunn & Furstenberg, 1989; Zabin & Hayward, 1993).

It is not pregnancy itself so much as its timing that is problematical. Premature sexual activity and pregnancy outside of marriage violate what our society considers to be the normative progression of life events for adolescents. Pregnant teenage girls lead stressful lives at a time when their coping resources are still developing (Raeff, 1994). Adolescent mothers' development is out of synchrony with the developmental milestones of their peers. Those who delay their childrearing years until their twenties are more mature cognitively and emotionally and usually are better parents (Zabin & Hayward, 1993).

Why do so many teenage girls decide to keep their babies rather than give them up for adoption? Having conceived and born an infant, many feel that it is their responsibility to raise it. Girls' families typically oppose adoption as an alternative. The status of "unwed mother" also has become more acceptable over time (Folkenberg, 1985).

Premature sexual activity is more common among disadvantaged youth. Half of all African-American adolescent females conceive before marriage (Conger, 1988; Hayes, 1987) and opt to keep their babies. Perhaps they understand the difficulty in finding homes for minority infants and fear that their infants otherwise would be placed in orphanages or institutions. Additionally, parenthood is an easy path to adult life for those with few educational or vocational alternatives. Many of their families are tolerant of early sexual behavior and pregnancy (Conger, 1988; Hayes, 1987; Stark, 1986; Zabin & Hayward, 1993).

Most teenage girls are not aware of how drastically pregnancy and single motherhood will change their lives. Adolescent mothers are twice as likely to drop out of school and to become dependent on welfare. Lacking high school diplomas and job skills, they are likely to raise their child or children in poverty. One 18-year-old mother said, referring to pregnant adolescents, "I go to school, take care of my baby and go to sleep. If they understand that there is no time for parties or even going to a shopping mall, it might help them" (Sullivan, 1987).

Given the serious and occasionally tragic consequences of adolescent pregnancy, it is preferable that such pregnancies be prevented. Teenage girls underestimate their fertility and, like teenage boys, are poorly informed about conception and the timing of intercourse. They also highly value spontaneity rather than preparation in sexual activity (Stark, 1986). Pregnant teenagers often report that they did not think that they could get pregnant.

Some adolescents have sex to satisfy emotional needs that are essentially nonsexual. "Adolescents have sex when, in fact, they primarily want and need something else, such as affection, to ease loneliness, to confirm masculinity or femininity, to bolster self-esteem, to express anger or escape from boredom. In short, during adolescence, sex becomes a coping mechanism to express and satisfy nonsexual needs" (Hajcak & Garwood, 1988, p. 755).

Some want to become pregnant. "For those who feel isolated, the prospect of a baby offers the possibility of someone to love. Pregnancy also brings attention to a girl who feels neglected. The ploy of entrapping a reluctant suitor may motivate some teenagers. Others may see pregnancy as a way to assert their independence from their parents, to become their mothers' equal. Some may want to keep up with their pregnant girlfriends" (Stark, 1986, p. 30).

Study Question   *What quality of care do adolescent mothers provide for their children?*

Adolescent pregnancies are considered high-risk for both the mother and child. Being risk-takers, young mothers usually smoke, drink alcohol, and use other drugs. Early sexual onset also is associated with multiple sexual partners and an increased risk of genital infection. Children born to adolescent mothers typically have lower birth weights. They are more likely to suffer from a variety of neurological problems. They are more susceptible to childhood illnesses, partly due to the poor prenatal care received by their mothers. Many children of adolescent mothers have major delays in their intellectual, language, and socioemotional development and are at greater risk for child abuse (Miller, Miceli, Whitman, & Borkowski, 1996; Stark, 1986; Zabin & Hayward, 1993).

Children (especially boys) born to teenage mothers are more likely to show cognitive and psychosocial deficits that predict later academic and social problems (Furstenberg, Brooks-Gunn, & Chase-Lansdale, 1989). Adolescent mothers usually are caring parents (they want and love their babies), but are not as socially competent as pregnant adults. Compared to older mothers, teenage mothers speak less to their children, are less responsive and more punitive, and express more stress and negative emotions (Passino et al., 1993; Sommer, Whitman, Borkowski, Schellenbach, Maxwell, & Keogh, 1993).

Since so many children are raised by poor single mothers, it is difficult separating out the effects of early childbearing, poor prenatal care and nutrition, the mother's cognitive and emotional immaturity, and economic hardship (Garcia Coll, Hoffman, & Oh, 1987; Luster & Mittelstaedt, 1993; Reis & Herz, 1987; Sommer, Whitman, Borkowski, Schellenbach, Maxwell, & Keogh, 1993; Zabin & Hayward, 1993).

The prognosis for teenage mothers and their children is not necessarily negative (Baranowski, Schilmoeller, & Higgins, 1990; Buchholz & Korn-Bursztyn, 1993). Parenting education programs and enrichment programs like Head Start have been successful in improving teenagers' parenting practices and their children's development. Family support that allows teenage parents to complete their education and job-training benefits young parents and their children. Teenage mothers who return to school and who are supported by their families often "catch up" developmentally with their peers, although their children do not fare as well. In any case, the better the mother does, the better the child does (Baptiste, 1986; Black & DeBlassie, 1985; Buchholz & Gol, 1986; Furstenberg, Brooks-Gunn, & Chase-Lansdale, 1989; Luster & Mittelstaedt, 1993; Miller, 1992).

A Mixed Message for Teenage Fathers

Teenage males are often happy when their girlfriends become pregnant, even those who have no intention of caring for the infant (Stark, 1986). It is a blow to their masculinity when, due to family pressure, their girlfriends have abortions. Contrary to the popular stereotype of the opportunistic teenage boy looking only for sexual gratification, teenage fathers are often emotionally attached to their girlfriends and want to be involved in supporting and caring for the infant (Robinson & Barret, 1985).

They usually do not marry the mother, and face contempt from her family. Their feelings and opinions are almost never considered when the infant is aborted, born, or put up for adoption. A study done by the Bank Street College of Education of 395 teenage fathers showed that 82 percent maintained daily contact with their children and 72 percent pro-

vided financial support. Fewer than 10 percent married their child's mother.

Teenage fathers often want babies as much as teenage mothers do, for many of the same reasons. A child may be the first meaningful "possession" in their young lives that seems truly theirs. "For those performing poorly in school, caring for a baby may be their first tangible accomplishment. For those reared in troubled homes, the infant may be the first human from whom they can receive love" (Robinson & Barret, 1985, p. 68). A child can only benefit from the involvement of a concerned, responsible father. However, teenage fathers typically are poorly educated and dependent on their own families financially (Kiselica & Sturmer, 1993; Robinson & Barret, 1985). Like teenage mothers, they do not

Spotlight

Adolescents, Parents, and Birth Control

Study Question Should adolescents have the right to obtain birth control devices without their parents' permission or knowledge?

The controversial topic of adolescent sexuality raises many difficult questions, including whether adolescents should have rights to obtain birth control information, birth control devices, and even abortions, without their parents' knowledge or consent (Griffin-Carlson & Mackin, 1993). Some argue that parents have the right to be notified about any transaction that could affect their children's health. Others contend that adolescents should have the same rights to confidentiality that adults enjoy. If adolescents are not guaranteed confidentiality, it is maintained, they will avoid contraception but not sexual activity. This will lead to high rates of adolescent pregnancy. Those who simply advo-

cate abstinence ("Just say no") are not being realistic, given current statistics.

When these matters have been litigated, courts have generally supported adolescent rights to obtain birth control and abortion without parental approval (Brozan, 1982; Jorgensen, 1993). Nevertheless, about half the states have passed legislation requiring some notification of, or consent from, parents or a judge before a minor can obtain an abortion. These laws have been challenged by such groups as the American Civil Liberties Union (Bishop, 1987). The Supreme Court has been moving in the direction of greater restrictions on abortion and adolescents' rights. Girls who feel close to their parents and who are financially dependent on them are more likely to confide in their parents regarding the decision to have an abortion (Griffin-Carlson & Mackin, 1993).

have realistic expectations about the cost of supporting a child. When their meager funds are depleted, they are likely to terminate all involvement with the infant and its mother. Kiselica and Sturmer (1993) note that society gives teenage fathers a mixed message—We expect you to be a responsible parent but we won't provide you with the resources you need to become one.

"Everyone Else Is Doing It": Guidelines for Parents Teaching Sexual Responsibility

Most parents prefer that their children not be sexually active, at least until they are in a committed relationship. But many parents today are resigned to the fact that they can not dictate their adolescent children's sexual behavior. They believe that their children will do what they want whether the parent approves or not. Most parents prefer that their children abstain. But if adolescents are sexually active, their parents hope that they will be sexually responsible and take proper precautions (Furstenberg, Herceg-Baron, Shea, & Webb, 1986).

It is desirable for parents to provide sexual knowledge in an accepting and matter-of-fact way to their children. Most parents do not do so. Most children (about 60%) therefore acquire sexual information (and misinformation) from the friends. "Young people want to know about homosexuality, penis size, masturbation, female orgasm, and the answers to such questions as how can I tell if I'm really in love, what constitutes sexual desire, what is the best contraceptive, when are you most likely to get pregnant, and various questions about oral and anal sex" (Gordon, 1986, p. 24).

Effective sex education also includes discussions of dating and relationships, beliefs, life goals, and values (Stark, 1986). Being able to discuss sexuality with children without preaching is an important family resource.

And the earlier the better, because children are more comfortable talking to their parents about sex before they are sexually active.

"Keep in mind that children learn at least as much from context as they do from content; your child will learn and remember more from how you present things than from what you say. If you are upset and uncomfortable discussing sexual issues with your child, your child will feel uncomfortable discussing his own sexuality" (Kutner, 1988n).

Most parents have not had the benefit of sex education themselves and may be misin-

TABLE 11.4 Talking to Adolescents About Sex

Children usually are more willing to discuss sex and reproduction before puberty.

Ask sensitive questions to determine their knowledge of the consequences of careless sexual activity.

Let your children know what your values are and why you have them.

If you are comfortable doing so, provide accurate information about reproduction in an accepting and matter-of-fact way, but avoid preaching.

If you are not comfortable discussing sex and reproduction with your children, give them a book to read that is appropriate for their age.

Meaningful discussions include topics like dating, relationships, values, and the possible consequences of careless behavior.

Help children view sexual behavior as an expression of love and as a source of pleasure in an intimate relationship.

If it is consistent with your values, consider offering the following message: your (mother, father) and I urge you to not have sex until you are older, but if you do, it is important that you take proper precautions to avoid pregnancy or a sexually-transmitted disease like AIDS.

Teach your child assertiveness skills to avoid being pressured into doing something that he/she does not want to do

formed about sexual matters. Many parents are uncomfortable discussing sex and will shy away from any direct dialogue about sex with their children. Parents who are uncomfortable broaching the topic with their children can offer them reading materials that are appropriate for their age and perhaps volunteer to answer any questions that they might have after their reading. Parents who are uneasy about such matters should admit their discomfort rather than try to conceal it. "Children appreciate honesty and easily see through hypocrisy" (Brody, 1986b). Keep in mind that some children are more receptive to such discussions than others.

Giving children good information about sexuality and reproduction before they are sexually active is essential, even though they might learn more about their parents' values than about sex (Fisher, 1986; Moore, Peterson, & Furstenberg, 1986). During and after puberty, adolescents have strong sexual feelings that they may not be able to manage successfully without guidance. Helping them see that fantasy and masturbation are satisfying, low-risk alternatives to intercourse is an example of such support. Almost all people derive gratification from genital self-stimulation. Such behavior should be viewed as normal, but private. Many boys also worry about nocturnal emissions ("wet dreams") and spontaneous erections. They can be reassured that emissions are normal and diminish with age.

"Tell the boys not to worry about penis size. You can't tell the size of the penis by observing its detumescent state. (Freud got it wrong—men are the ones with penis envy.) Reassure girls about their vaginas—one size fits all . . . Sexual orientation is not a matter of choice. It's not OK to be antigay" (Gordon, 1986, p. 26).

Parents should also help children view sexuality as an expression of love and as a source of pleasure within an intimate relationship. "Instead of sitting a child down for an awk-ward 'heart to heart' talk, it is usually easier to let conversations about sex emerge naturally from shared events, such as a movie, television program, sexy advertisement, even a pop song with sexual messages" (Brody, 1986b).

Threatening children or otherwise inducing sexual fears are self-defeating strategies that communicate to children that they will have to act deceptively. Brody suggests the following appeal: "We hope that you won't have sex until you're much older, but if you do, we want you to know what it's all about and especially how to avoid unwanted consequences."

Many teenagers who would otherwise refuse sexual advances find that they lack the assertiveness skills to do so. They do not know what to say or do in the face of intense pressure from peers and romantic partners. "Teenagers should be urged to consider whether sexual intercourse is something they are ready for and want for themselves, not because their partners are pushing them into it" (Brody, 1986b). Girls and boys must learn that they can say no and learn how to recognize and avoid situations in which pressure might be applied to weaken their resolve. These skills are not easily learned, partly because it is almost impossible to anticipate all of the circumstances that can arise in an adolescent's social life.

ADOLESCENT DRUG USE

Study Question *How should parents respond if they discover that their child is using drugs?*

Drug abuse remains one of the most serious health problems in the United States. It is not surprising that adolescents are particularly susceptible. Drugs (the term includes alcohol) provide a convenient, fast, and relatively inexpensive way of altering one's mood, an appealing combination to risk-taking teenagers. The use of mood-altering drugs to relieve stress is so common that many teenagers view it as "no big deal."

Partly out of curiosity, many adolescents experiment with legal and illegal substances. Experimentation usually begins with wine and beer, followed by cigarettes, and occasionally, marijuana. A few move on to harder drugs (Tang, Wong, & Schwarzer, 1996). A national survey of eighth graders released in 1993 by the University of Michigan at Ann Arbor revealed that 70 percent of the students reported using alcohol and 27 percent acknowledged getting drunk. Forty-five percent said that they smoked cigarettes and 11 percent admitted using marijuana or hashish.

A nationwide survey of adults' and children's attitudes toward drugs conducted by the Partnership for a Drug-Free America and released in February, 1996, revealed that teenagers are becoming increasingly tolerant of marijuana use (Wren, 1996). Forty-five percent of the teenagers agreed with the statement, "Being high feels good." According to the survey, "Today's teens are less likely to consider drug use harmful and risky, more likely to believe that drug use is widespread and tolerated, and feel more pressure to try illegal drugs than teens did just two years ago" (Wren, 1996, p. A11). Resistance to hard drugs such as crack and cocaine remains fairly high. The survey revealed that parents underestimate their children's encounters with drugs. Whereas 14 percent of the parents reported believing that their children had experimented with marijuana, 38 percent of the teenagers reported having tried it.

Like cigarette smoking, drinking gives adolescents the impression that they are more adultlike. Peer pressure to consume alcohol or other drugs is irresistible to those who have not learned how to say no. TV advertising, movies, and popular culture heroes glamorize the drug experience (Wren, 1996). Although illicit drug use by teenagers gradually decreased from the late 1970s to the early 1990s, there has been a gradual increase since 1992.

It is difficult discouraging adolescents from being curious about cigarettes and alcohol when family members model or condone use of these substances (Andrews, Hops, Ary, Tildesley, & Harris, 1993). Parents and peers are a major influence on the initiation and persistence of young teenagers' substance use (Foxcroft & Lowe, 1995; Stephenson, Henry, & Robinson, 1996). Parents who use cigarettes, alcohol, and other drugs have more difficulty convincing their children that these substances are potentially dangerous.

Parental, sibling, and peer modeling of drug use is a potent factor in encouraging adolescent drug use (Anderson & Henry, 1994; Denton & Kampfe, 1994). Conversely, adolescent closeness to parents and peers who do not use drugs serve as a buffer against experimentation with legal and illegal drugs (Dinges & Oetting, 1993). Harsh discipline style and parent-child distance predict drug problems (Coombs & Landsverk, 1988). Once teenagers begin to use drugs, parental influence lessens and peer influence increases (Halebsky, 1987). "Most use of drugs occurs as a result of social influences, whereas abuse of drugs is more strongly tied to internal, psychological processes" (Newcomb & Bentler, 1989, p. 244).

Parents, of course, should advocate responsible use of alcohol, although it is not always easy to describe what constitutes responsible use. The need for drug education is as important as that for sex education so that children can learn how drugs affect the body and mind and can learn to view drug use cautiously (Treaster, 1993). Unfortunately, providing information to adolescents about drugs and drug abuse has not had impressive results. Adolescents like to experiment. Those who have never "tried" cigarettes or alcohol might be considered deviant by their peers. Fortunately, most teens who occasionally use drugs do not develop drug problems (Newcomb & Bentler, 1989).

ADOLESCENT SUICIDE: A PERMANENT SOLUTION TO A TEMPORARY PROBLEM

Jody White, age 17 years, shot himself in his bedroom on May 9, 1977. "In the year before his death he had been expelled from school for lying about his participation in minor vandalism in the library and transferred to a new school; he regularly used marijuana and told his mother he needed it to concentrate on his studies; he took unreasonable risks with his motorcycle and had gone through a turbulent romance. In fact, he had told his girl-friend that unless they repaired their relationship, he would kill himself. Two and a half years earlier, in November, 1974, his father, John O'-Donnell White, also killed himself at home. After several separations, the Whites had been divorced eight months earlier. Mr. White returned for one more attempt at reconciliation. When his wife refused, he kissed her goodbye and shot himself" (Brozan, 1986).

A survey by the U.S. Department of Health and Human Services of 11,419 eighth and tenth graders found that 42 percent of the girls and 25 percent of the boys reported that they had seriously considered ending their lives. Eighteen percent of the girls and 11 percent of the boys claimed that they had attempted suicide (Dismuke, 1988).

Suicide is the third major cause of death for adolescents, after accidents and murder, accounting for 14 percent of all deaths in the 15- to 19-year-old age group (National Center for Health Statistics, 1992). The estimates for suicide attempts in this age group vary from 50,000 to 500,000 a year, and the number of successful suicides averages about 5,000 a year. This number may be an underestimate,

as many suicides are not recognized as such. About 2,245 adolescents take their own lives each year in this country.

"The typical adolescent suicide victim is white, male, and from the middle class. Guns are the means often used, and the most common reason is depression over the loss of loved ones or status" (Santrock & Yussen, 1984, p. 398). About 90 percent of those who attempt suicide are females (who typically try to poison themselves with prescription drugs), but 75 percent of those who succeed are male (guns are more lethal than pills). Most successful attempts at suicide are preceded by several unsuccessful attempts.

Like Jody White, many adolescents who attempt suicide report serious family problems. These include parental divorce and conflict, poor parent-child communication (excessive criticism, arguing), unrealistic parental expectations, school pressures, and sexual abuse (Henry, Stephenson, Hanson, & Hargett, 1994; Neiger & Hopkins, 1988; Vannatta, 1996). Many young people report feeling unwanted or believing that they are a burden to their parents. Intense family conflict that involves the adolescent seems to generate self-denigrating feelings which encourage suicidal thinking (Campbell, Milling, Laughlin, & Bush, 1993; Shagle & Barber, 1993, 1995; Shaunesey, Cohen, Plummer, & Berman, 1993). Parental alcoholism may be a more potent factor than adolescent alcohol use (Allen, 1987). Children of parents who have committed suicide also are considered to be high risk. Like Jody, they are more likely to model this extreme way of coping with temporary problems

Personal factors associated with attempted suicide include low self-esteem, drug use, loss of boyfriend or girlfriend, poor academic performance, and recent loss of a confidant. "When friends kill themselves on different occasions in close order, loss of a confidant may be the important factor" (Allen, 1987, p. 273). Some psychologists believe that adolescents do not fully appreciate the irreversibility of death. "They see this as an easy way out of their troubles, a way to get even with people they have a grudge with, 'I'll die and you'll be sorry' " (Eron, quoted by Barron, 1987b).

Signs of Suicide: "I Might As Well Be Dead"

It is no surprise that suicidal adolescents usually are depressed. Garfinkel (cited by Swartz, 1987) found that only 12 percent of the suicidal adolescents he studied were not depressed. Depressed behaviors, such as crying and hopelessness, and statements about wanting to die, are considered "signs" of suicide, that is, "signals emitted by the person which 'telegraph' an impending act of self-destruction" (Allen, 1987).

Other signs include previous suicide attempts, drug use, recent suicide of a loved one, preoccupation with death, giving away personal belongings, changes in eating and sleeping patterns and school performance, and unusual personality changes. Families of suicidal adolescents often deny the reality of the problem, block out the threat, dissociate themselves from it, or are unsympathetic (Allen, 1987).

Jody White's mother explained that he "was screaming with problems, though he was not talking about them. His appearance was different, he stopped caring about his clothes or his hair, and he was no longer concerned about making plans for the future. He did once ask another boy what it was like to be in therapy, but he didn't want to worry me by asking me" (Brozan, 1986).

There is no simple way of protecting children from the stresses and pressures of life. We can, as parents, attempt to prepare them for life's inevitable problems and disappointments by teaching them problem-solving and coping skills. Parents can also provide children with the emotional support that we all require in difficult situations. Most problems have several possible solutions, but these may not occur to some adolescents or younger children. Fortunately, the vast majority of adolescents learn to deal effectively with their problems. The signs of suicide we have indicated are not subtle. Parents would have to exercise extreme denial to not notice them. It happens every day.

Spotlight

Empty Nests That Do Not Always Remain Empty

"In some ways I can't imagine the children not being here—in this house. It will seem like a totally useless place, except for them to come back to" (mother quoted by Galinsky [1981, p. 286]). If we review the reasons we desire children (see Chapter 1), it is not surprising that many parents dread the day their youngest child departs to live elsewhere.

I am not immune to these feelings. A major part of my identity is "father of two sons." I do not look forward to the time that I will have to redefine my identity as "father of two grown sons who live elsewhere." Of course, there are moments when I feel that they cannot leave soon enough. Like many parents, I am ambivalent about the profound, and probably inevitable, changes that will occur in my family when my children are grown. Separating from one's parents and from one's children is normal and healthy. It is also a little bit scary. I must reassure myself that the so-called empty nest will give me a freer lifestyle, fewer responsibilities, and more time (and money) to spend with my wife. Studies confirm that most parents, particularly primary caregivers, respond to the empty nest with relief, not depression (e.g., Rubin, 1979). But who will laugh at my corny jokes or tell me theirs? I guess that is why they invented grandchildren.

Parents who have careers, hobbies, and interests other than caregiving are in the best position to adjust to the empty nest. Women who have devoted their adult lives to child care are the most vulnerable to depression when their children leave. "What have their years of motherhood prepared them for? To start back at the beginning of the career ladder? That can be a painful thought, especially when their friends (men and women) who have stayed in the job market are rungs ahead, seemingly reaching the pinnacle of success" (Galinsky, 1981, p. 291).

Return To the Nest

In the past, most children, particularly daughters, lived at home until they married. Families today still discourage their daughters' premarital independence, at least compared to sons'. Nevertheless, delaying marriage to pursue educational and other goals has increased the likelihood that young adults will live away from home before marriage. Goldscheider and Goldscheider (1989) found that most adolescents expect to live independently before marriage, and most of their parents agree. The average age of first marriage for men is now 26, and for women is 24, higher for both genders than its been for almost a century (A.L. Cowan, 1989).

This delay in marriage, together with high divorce rates and the high cost of housing, has led to the "return to the nest" phenomenon. About half of single men in their early twenties, and about one-third of single women this age live with their parents. About half of them have never left home. The presence of "unlaunched" adult children is most likely in families with harmonious relationships (Aquilino, 1991). Ironically, adult children of affluent parents are more likely to return home, not being able to duplicate their parents' living standards. Middle class parents find coresidence more burdensome than do poorer parents, probably because they expect their children to be more self-sufficient.

Most parents are happy, or at least satisfied, with their children's return (especially if they lived harmoniously before their children's departure). They enjoy spending time with their adult children and get along well if workable agreements can be negotiated about sharing the household. Satisfaction turns to regret if there is conflict and disagreement, especially about money and employment (Aquilino & Supple, 1991; Thornton, Young-DeMarco, & Goldscheider, 1993; Ward & Spitze, 1992, 1996).

Parents vary in their response to living with adult children. It is not so much the presence or absence of adult children in the home or the age of the children that determines parental well-being as it is the specific living arrangements and the quality of the parent-child relationship (Aquilino, 1991). Most parents are willing to provide a "safety net" for their children during hard times. They hope that the stay is temporary, and they encourage their children to become more self-sufficient (A.L. Cowan, 1989). Some adult children who live with older parents in poor health provide care. However, coresidence usually reflects the needs of the child rather than those of the parent.

RESIDENTIAL SETTING DURING THE COLLEGE YEARS

Study Question *How does an adolescent's living away from home affect the parent-child relationship?*

Most children first leave home to attend college, get married, or just live on their own. However, many adolescents reside at home or return home after a temporary or prolonged separation. Flanagan, Schulenberg, and Fuligni (1993) wondered how parent-adolescent relationships differ depending upon whether college students live at home or away at school. Previous research suggested that college students living away from home become more independent, feel greater affection for their parents, and communicate better with them.

Flanagan and her colleagues surveyed 404 undergraduates at two midwestern universities, half living with their parents and half living away at college. Controlling for students' age and other demographic considerations, the researchers found that living at college was associated with greater independence, support, and mutual respect between parents and adolescents. Students who lived at home felt their parents underestimated their maturity. They reported more conflict and avoidance in their relationships with their parents.

The investigators concluded that it is harder for college students who live at home to redefine their relationships with their parents and become independent. College students living at home were a little more negative about their relationships with their parents, complaining that their parents treated them like high school students. This is not to say that living with parents during the college years harms the parent-adolescent relationship. The researchers note that there are

many relational paths open to adolescents during the transition to young adulthood. Residence is but one of many factors that color the parent-adolescent relationship.

SUMMARY

1. There are many stereotypes of adolescents, but few, if any, capture the diversity we observe in children during this distinctive stage of development. Adolescence is a time of change and adjustment. Some adolescents adjust better than others, and the same can be said of their parents.

2. Conflict between parents and teenagers is to be expected and is normal. Living with adolescent children is associated with diminished life satisfaction for middle-aged parents, particularly mothers. Families with poor communication skills are most likely to suffer through their children's changes.

3. As puberty takes its course, most adolescents strive to assert their independence. They attempt to create an adult identity separate from, but consistent with, their family associations and values. They are doing so in an era in which children are pressured to grow up quickly. They are expected to take on adult responsibilities while showing good judgment and consideration of others.

4. Most adolescents satisfy these expectations despite the challenges of physical and cognitive growth and sexual development. With physical maturity comes the long-anticipated lessening of parental control and increased susceptibility to peer influences. The latter can be helpful or harmful. Some parents find their teenager's desire for freedom threatening. Some do not know how to gradually lessen their involvement in their child's

daily lives. Most parents (especially mothers) are relieved when their young adult children leave home and are disappointed but supportive if they return home as dependents.

5. Even adolescents with good family relationships will occasionally argue with their parents about homework, schoolwork, personal grooming, family obligations, and many other issues. Parents who understand their adolescent's concerns and social deficits are more patient and caring in the face of inappropriate behavior. The more life stresses faced at a given time by a teenager, the greater the adjustment necessary to maintain normal functioning.

6. There is disagreement about the value of "risk-taking" behavior in adolescents, whether such behaviors are inherently destructive, or whether they are "growth enhancing." Many adolescents take unnecessary risks by being sexually active and not taking proper precautions.

7. Over one million adolescent girls become pregnant each year, and over half eventually deliver their infants. Being unmarried, unemployed, and poor is not conducive to a satisfying lifestyle or good parenting. Children born to adolescent mothers are at risk for a variety of problems, partly due to the immaturity of their mothers' reproductive systems and poor prenatal care. However, many adolescent mothers do a good job of providing care for their children, especially when they have the support of their families.

8. Teenage pregnancy usually is a painful experience for the mother, the father, and their families. Parents and schools can do more to prevent irresponsible sexual behavior in teenagers. Many parents are uncomfortable discussing sexuality with their children. Even school sex-education programs fall short of providing teenagers with the information and assertiveness skills they need to make good choices.

9. Drug and alcohol use among adolescents is a serious health problem. Adolescent drug use appears to be related to parental and peer attitudes about drugs and, to a lesser extent, parental drug use. While adolescents seem to be using fewer illicit drugs than their predecessors, alcohol use is still high.

10. Suicide is the third major cause of death among teenagers, after accidents and homicide. Most adolescents who attempt suicide have serious family problems, low self-esteem, and may be experiencing a crisis for which they can see no solution. Most suicidal teenagers communicate their desperation in many ways before attempting to take their lives, but they may not be heard in time.

11. About half of all individuals in their mid-twenties live with their parents. Parents usually have mixed feelings when their children leave home and, after living independently, return to the nest. Parents whose lives are overly invested in their children fare most poorly. It is important that parents support their children in the direction of greater self-sufficiency.

GLOSSARY

adolescent egocentrism Adolescents are less self-centered than younger children but they are considerably more self-conscious

formal operations Advanced reasoning abilities that usually emerge during early adolescence

imaginary audience Adolescents' belief that they are the focus of other people's attention and interest

personal fable   Dramatic fantasies created by adolescents in which they are the stars

---

THOUGHT QUESTIONS

1. Why is early adolescence a particularly stressful time of life?

2. Does puberty automatically increase parent-adolescent tensions?

3. How do authoritative parents respond to their children's requests for greater freedom? How do punitive parents respond?

4. What values would you want to teach your children about their sexuality?

5. How can parents get along better with their young adult children who live at home?

beliefs about what constitutes normality. Labels like "special" and "exceptional" are relative terms. They are usually defined on the basis of children's attributes or the circumstances of their life situation in comparison to those of more "typical" children (Lewis & Rosenblum, 1981).

Children considered special on the basis of psychological or biological characteristics might be labeled developmentally disabled, learning disabled, autistic, emotionally disturbed, antisocial, handicapped, or chronically ill. Children may also be considered special on the basis of characteristics that are

not considered impairments. Exceptionally bright and gifted children also are special, too, having distinctive needs and problems. (See "Parenting Gifted Children" later in this chapter).

Children who become special because of their life circumstances include abused and neglected children; children of addicted, depressed, or mentally ill parents; and children raised in nonconventional families. Similarly, parents may be considered "special" on the basis of their personal characteristics or their life circumstances (Lewis & Rosenblum, 1981).

Spotlight

What It Means to Have Juliet

"Juliet has brain damage," said the neurologist to us 3 months ago. It has been a lifetime. A hard and painful lifetime, mixed with a little joy and a sea of tears.

We have two older, wonderful boys (ages 6 and 3½), and I thought a third child would be a snap. No problem—parenting comes as easily as breathing to us. We are turning out such happy children, why shouldn't the third be just as easy? And a girl, which made it even better.

We did not receive a diagnosis of brain damage resulting in spastic quadriplegia until she was 6 months old. Until then, we though she was perfectly beautiful, happy, and healthy. A little fussy, perhaps, but fundamentally OK. She wasn't though. Much of her brain had atrophied in utero, and now we must deal with what is left.

We decided right away, in the darkest, blackest days, that we would work together to make her the best baby she could be. Whatever brain she had, we would make sure she used all of it. We loved her so much before we found out, and even more after.

The problem is, our good attitudes and enthusiasm alone don't make her all better right away. At first, seeing normal kids her age was devastating. They can do so much. They can reach for things. They can sit up. They can hold bottles. They can roll over. Juliet can't, but she can try, with our help.

Seeing normal babies now is getting easier, because I see where we are heading, even though we are on a different road. It is exhausting to undergo the daily therapies and the doctors' visits and to keep up with the research in the field. But we have no choice, and no desire to do anything else. I want her to be able to do everything. If she can't, I want to know I did everything I could do, every step of the way. She deserves it, and we owe it to her.

We believe she is fully aware of her surroundings, and she sees everything that goes on. She recognizes us and her brothers, and she laughs out loud at them. They roughhouse with her until she lets them know she's had enough. She may not have the words (yet), but she makes herself understood.

She seems to know she can wrap her dad (her favorite companion) around her little finger. When she wants to get his attention, she does what she does best; she smiles at him as "loudly" as she can. We feel like we have woken up to a new world. I was in a coma in my old world where nothing really bad ever happened. Now I live in my new world where my worst nightmare has come true, and I have to live with it every single day.

We are more awake, more appreciative of the good things, and more perceptive since we had Juliet. Our childhood is behind us for sure, but Juliet's is just beginning.

Lynne Federman
January 20, 1990

Juliet redux

It has been four years since I wrote the brief piece above. And it has not been a lifetime—just an extraordinary time of work, learning, and love. Juliet has taught us so much about life that it is hard to simply sum it up in just a few paragraphs. I definitely learned more during these years than I did in the same period of time at college.

Juliet is now five years old and she is happy and healthy and just as handicapped as we feared she would be. She is unable to do anything an able child can do. The hardest thing, I think, is not that she is physically handicapped but that she cannot speak. She appears to be so bright and alert, but there is almost no way for us to determine the extent or depth of her intelligence and understanding. At school she is working on a computer in the most elementary fashion. I hope technology will catch up to Juliet and she will be able to use a very advanced communication system. We still don't know what Juliet has to tell us.

We have learned so much about the world of children, especially handicapped children. I immersed myself in the medical, social, and educational aspects of cerebral palsy. I came into contact with some of the most dedicated professionals and parents of handicapped children. It is from them that I have learned the most about coping with Juliet. But it is Juliet herself who teaches us how to enjoy her and the rest of our lives. We work with her every day and she is an essential part of our family constellation. In fact, with all of her difficulties, she might be the brightest star.

Lynne Federman
January 12, 1994

[Juliet died quietly in her parents' arms in late November, 1995, at the age of 6½ years.]

PARENTING CHILDREN WITH SPECIAL PROBLEMS

Study Question *What obstacles confront parents raising special children?*

First-time parents have little basis for comparing their infant's development to that of other children. They suspect that something is not quite right, but they attribute this uneasy feeling to their lack of knowledge about normal development or to a lack of parenting experience. For example, they may view hyperactivity and a short attention span as disobedient or defiant behavior rather than as being symptomatic of a hidden organic or emotional problem.

"When Dylan was four months old, I sensed that something was wrong because I would talk to him or play with him or anything. He would not look at me. I would always ask questions like, 'Is this normal for a two year old...' Everyone told me that it was OK, that he was normal. I couldn't get anyone to agree with me. Even the pediatrician said that there was nothing wrong with Dylan. He developed fine. When he was three and a half we started having him tested. We found out that he was autistic, although high functioning. But the real moment I thought something was wrong was when he was four months old" (Dylan's mother).

For certain disabilities, the parent-infant bonding process may suffer. The infant may be very difficult to care for and may provide few social cues to family members. "Social interactions with disabled babies are often less spontaneous, less fun, require more effort, and even become less frequent than with 'easier' babies" (J. McCollum, 1985, p. 6).

Handicapped infants may not emit the sounds and gestures exhibited by nonhandicapped infants. They may not smile or greet a parent with anticipation. Blind and deaf infants are less likely to provide their parents with the kinds of pleasing interactions that foster the bonding process in other families. Some parents have to learn how to accept and care for children who have unusual appearances and behaviors (J. McCollum, 1985; Trout & Foley, 1989).

There is some commonality across families in initial reactions to a dreaded diagnosis, the disability's disorganizing effect on family functioning, and the ways in which family members cope with the disability. Denial and grief are common first reactions. "The doctor came in and told me that Paul had Down Syndrome. He also told me that I should consider putting him into an institution. He said that Paul will never be able to walk or talk. But I did not want to hear it" (Mother of 8-year-old diagnosed with Down Syndrome).

Another parent disclosed: "After the facts of

the disease became clear, Will and I went through a period of vacillating between grief and denial. We spent many nights crying and holding on to each other, feeling completely helpless. At other times we refused to acknowledge that Jesse had muscular dystrophy, hoping that if we did not give it a name, it might go away. Why think about it since nothing could be done anyway?" (Gamble, 1985, p. 16).

With less clear-cut disabilities, parents (usually mothers) seek diagnostic services to help resolve their apprehensions. This may be more of a coping response than an act of denial. "In reflecting over their initial reactions to the diagnosis [of learning disability] the majority of mothers described feeling relief on confirmation of their suspicions, not defensive reactions" (Faerstein, 1986, p. 9). Of course, the parents' reactions will reflect their understanding of the diagnosis and the prognosis they are given for their child's future development.

Handicapped children will confirm that other children's reactions to their disability can be as much a source of stress and pain as the disability itself. They have to learn to adjust not only to their disability but to its social and emotional consequences. Being "different" is one of the most difficult problems for disabled (or any) children. Many children with special needs are ashamed of their handicaps and have low self-esteem. Even adults can be insensitive, treating children with physical disabilities as though they were less than whole. Children adjust better when they can communicate to their parents their strong feelings about people's insensitivity (Gamble, 1985; Rousso, 1985).

Case History

Harris and Powers (1984) describe, in a case history, a couple's reaction when they discovered that their son is autistic.

"By the time the boy was 18 months old it was impossible to turn away from the problems; he was not developing as he should. There were no indications that he was going to talk, he seemed quite indifferent to other people, and appeared content to be left alone. At first, his parents wondered if he were deaf, but since he would respond to the soft rustling of a candy wrapper this hardly seemed likely. By 24 months of age, their anxiety was acute and they began to push their pediatrician for more information. It was at that point that they were referred for a complete assessment at a special child evaluation center of the local hospital. Shortly before their son was 30 months of age the parents received a definitive diagnosis: their boy was autistic.

"His parents recall vividly the sickening impact of that first conference in the pediatric neurologist's office. A feeling in the stomach of dread and fear that remained for weeks and still, after all these years, returns when they talk about that day.

"Abruptly, the woman and the man underwent a transformation in their view of themselves and their child. They were the parents of a defective child. This child, made of their body and their love, was irreversibly damaged. A child who would never be normal. A child whose future was radically different from all they had envisioned. Their sense of normalcy, of belonging in a snug niche in the community around them, was rudely shaken. They were different and life would never be the same for them. Their dreams were shattered and they hardly knew what to do."

Waisbren (1980) confirmed that many parents of developmentally delayed infants see themselves more negatively and express ambivalent or negative feelings about the child.

Family Life-Cycle Model

Study Question   *How does raising a child with special needs affect a parent's development and lifestyle?*

Harris and Powers (1984), applying the family life-cycle view described in Appendix A, view family adjustment as a series of tasks, conflicts, or challenges. All families face these challenges. Since families with special children are more similar to other families than different (Ievers, Drotar, Dahms, Doershuk, et al., 1994), they face similar challenges (Harris & Bruey, 1988). Nevertheless, the presence of a handicapped child magnifies the obstacles they must confront in each phase of the family's life cycle (Miller, Gordon, Daniele, & Diller, 1992).

For example, two young people enter into an intimate marital relationship and anticipate the birth of a healthy child. They are learning how to settle their problems through mutual accommodation. They look forward to seeing themselves as a threesome. They begin to consider how, with a child, they will protect the boundaries of their marital relationship. Their lives are going smoothly. They become comfortable viewing themselves as wife and husband. They are then stunned to find themselves raising a child diagnosed as autistic (Harris & Powers, 1984).

Many profound questions occur to these parents in their confusion and pain. Can they love this child? How will they cope? What do they have to offer the child as parents? How will his presence affect the family, their marital relationship, and other siblings? Will he be dependent upon them for the rest of their lives? If so, who will care for him when they cannot? Where can they find help? (Kraus-Mars & Lachman, 1994).

Strong feelings usually accompany these questions. Parents report sadness about their child's prospects and their own. They sometimes feel angry at the child or at his "problem." They feel disappointed that their anticipated normal child is not there to enrich their lives. Most report guilt about having these "awful" feelings. Some couples cannot adjust to this profound change in their lives and eventually separate. "At a time when mutual support may be vital, individuals may withdraw from one another or turn their pain outward and become hurtful to each other" (Harris & Powers, 1984). Worse, they may withdraw from the child.

Perhaps the main challenge facing parents in this phase is to accept the reality of their child's status and to not sacrifice their relationship to child care. Couples often report that marital and family tensions increase following the birth of a child with special needs (Dahlquist, Czyzewski, Copeland, Jones, et al., 1993). This is not surprising. In Chapter 2, we reviewed the research literature concerning the transition to parenting. Recall that marital satisfaction typically decreases following childbirth, particularly for women. The best predictor of marital satisfaction after birth is marital satisfaction before birth. Thus, the strength of the relationship, not the baby, is the critical factor in this well-documented phenomenon.

Becoming parents of a disabled or ill child not only lessens a couple's opportunities to engage in shared, pleasurable activities, it also provides many potential stressors that require coping and adjustment on the part of both new and experienced parents (Margalit, Raviv, & Ankonina, 1992; Sloper & Turner, 1993; Thompson, Gustafson, Hamlett, & Spock, 1992). "From the parent's point of view, it may be simply that it is not pleasant to go to Johnny's crib, that it is immensely frustrating to try to put on his snowsuit, to feed him, or to carry out the home assignment delivered by that well-meaning specialist from

the early intervention program" (Trout & Foley, 1989, p. 61).

The greater a child's physical limitations, the greater the blow to a couples' psychological well-being and marital satisfaction. Like that of a healthy child, the presence of a handicapped or ill child brings some couples closer together and separates others. The stability of the relationship before the birth predicts which of these outcomes is more likely (Byrne & Cunningham, 1985; Kazak, 1986; Klinnert, Gavin, Wamboldt, & Mrazek, 1992; Perry, Sarlo-McGarvey, & Factor, 1992; Waddington & Busch-Rossnagel, 1992).

As the child grows, the nature of the challenges facing the family changes. Even when reaching school age, the special child still requires an inordinate amount of attention and care. "Over the years a number of mothers have shared with us their sense of entrapment about their lives. They fear that they will never be free to define the space of their own existence. This sense of helplessness and burden can produce feelings of depression" (Harris & Powers, 1984).

Study Question   *How are siblings affected by the presence of a disabled sister or brother?*

"We don't have a normal family. Ronnie has a lot of respiratory problems. He will need intense medical care for at least one more year. The kids are resentful of him at times because he needs so much care. He's so prone to infections that they have to be isolated from him.

"He has changed our lives a lot. You love him so much because of all he's gone through. There's a special bond that I'll never have with the other two because of what he's gone through and what we've gone through with him. You can't give up on him because if it wasn't for us fighting for him he wouldn't be here.

"The hard part is helping his sisters understand that he will get better. They ask, 'Is he going to die?' They are resentful of him but they've learned a lot from having him as a brother. It's just hard to promote a bond between them when they've been separated so much. I find myself saying to them, 'You can't touch the baby until you've washed your hands.' The three of them need us in such different ways" (mother of three).

Siblings of handicapped children may develop behavior problems of their own. Like Ronnie's siblings, many report strong, ambivalent feelings about their disabled sibling (Trout & Foley, 1989). They know that their sibling requires more parental help and attention but perhaps because of limited parental attention, they feel left out or neglected. Sisters of disabled siblings in particular often become discouraged by the burdens of caring for and coping with their disabled brother or sister. They may have more conflict with their mothers (McHale & Gamble, 1989). Those who perceive themselves as receiving favorable treatment from their parents may feel guilty. Their guilt apparently motivates them to act more kindly toward their less advantaged brother or sister (Lavigne & Ryan, 1979; Martin & Cole, 1993; McHale & Pawletko, 1992).

Siblings also must adjust to other people's reactions, including those of their friends and family members. "In my family, we were not allowed to discuss our feelings about Bonnie. After all, she was retarded and if we said anything negative, we might hurt her feelings. Well, what about my feelings? Who was concerned about how I felt? I hated my sister for ruining my life . . . I lay awake at night praying that God would forgive me for having such thoughts about my sister. The range and intensity of emotions were too much for me to handle. My parents never sat me down and said, 'This is the problem. This is what's

wrong with her...' I remember several times trying to tell my Mom how I felt and she would say, 'Your feelings are wrong and you'd better change them' " (Ellifritt, 1985, p. 46).

Family Stressors

Lipsky (1985) described the unique stresses that befall parents of special children. As both a researcher and a parent of a teenager with spina bifida, she resents that our culture focuses "solely on the negative emotional aspects of raising children with handicapping conditions. [Professionals] give little attention to the resilience shown by the many parents and families who do well in spite of having experienced a form of stress often thought to carry a substantial risk of adverse outcome" (p. 614).

Many parents with special children occasionally report that inadequate professional support provides additional stress (Trout & Foley, 1989). Most families with special children have a high frequency of contact with service providers. Difficulty in obtaining needed information from professionals becomes one of many sources of life stress (Sloper & Turner, 1992). Lipsky criticizes the double messages that professionals sometimes give parents. On the one hand, they view parents as crucial to their child's growth and development. On the other hand, parents are told that they are ill-equipped to meet their children's emotional and other needs.

Some professionals treat parents of special children as obstacles to treatment or as the cause of the child's adjustment problems (see Spotlight: Blaming Mothers for Children's Problems, later in this chapter). Such attitudes increase parental distress. "It is essential that parents and professionals attempt to understand and make others aware that stress most often is not a factor of psychological dysfunction, but, rather, the absence of a sympathetic social or economic support system"

TABLE 12.2 Common Stressors in Families with Children with Disabilities

Adjusting to the child's special needs, including hospitalization

Financial pressures

Inadequate professional support

Difficulty in getting good information about the disorder and the child's prognosis

Parents' believing that they are not doing enough for the child and feeling guilty

Marital conflict regarding division of labor

(p. 617). The bitterness expressed at the beginning of this chapter by Charles's parents toward his unsupportive grandparents reinforces this point.

Parents of children with cystic fibrosis report coping successfully. However, during interviews, they expressed having difficulty in adjusting to their children's hospitalization. They also complained about strained marital relationships. Many found it hard to accept their child's illness. Some felt that they weren't doing enough for their child. Many parents were concerned that the siblings of the ill child were being neglected or deprived (Blankfeld & Holahan, 1996; Phillips, Bohannon, Gayton, & Friedman, 1985; Quittner, DiGirolamo, Michel, & Eigen, 1992; Thompson, Gustafson, Hamlett, & Spock, 1992).

Supportive social networks are associated with positive personal and family adjustment and positive child behavior outcomes (Dunst, Trivette, & Cross, 1986; Fagan & Schor, 1993; Pelletier, Godin, Lepage, & Dussault, 1994). To a large extent, a family's adjustment will reflect the support they receive from their relatives and from support services available in their community. "We found other parents who had children with muscular dystrophy and met with them on a regular basis. This told us more about the disease than any book, doctor, or social worker we had previously encountered" (Gamble, 1985, p. 17).

Parents who bear a developmentally disabled child generally have ambivalent feelings about the child, in addition to their sadness and disappointment. Most parents marshal their personal and family resources and do what must be done. Raising disabled or chronically ill children can be a challenging, but very rewarding, experience. After parents adjust to the initial shock, denial, anger, and guilt, they usually find they have a delightful child who is very difficult to care for. Most of these children will eventually participate fully in the adult world, especially those with parents who commit themselves to working with their children to fully realize their potential (Hauser-Cram, 1996).

"There are thousands of Americans with disabilities who are leading satisfying lives. Disabled people are husbands, wives, and stamp collectors. They are members of virtually every profession. Time and time again, disabled individuals have proven that anatomy is not destiny" (Blumberg, 1985, p. 129).

PARENTING CHILDREN WITH ACUTE AND CHRONIC ILLNESS

Study Question   What special problems face parents of chronically ill children?

About 2 percent of all children are chronically ill. They suffer from cancer, kidney problems, cystic fibrosis, spina bifida, sickle cell anemia, diabetes, or heart disease. They are "for the most part, normal children in different situations. Nevertheless, such children as a group have a higher rate of significant emotional and social difficulties. Separation from parents, missed days from school, painful medical procedures, complex medical regimens and changes in body appearance are just some of the stresses they may face" (Hurley, 1987, p. 34).

Since many chronically ill children died in the past, there were few services available to prepare those who lived for returning to a more normal daily existence. Today, most of these children survive. Together with their families, they require extensive medical and social support for their full recovery. Most children with debilitating illnesses have medical, social, and educational needs that are not likely to be met.

Children's reactions to their serious illness and to the separation from their parents that accompanies hospitalization depend upon many factors. These include the type and length of illness, their age, their ability to communicate about their distress, and the quality of their family relationships (Hurley, 1987; Thunberg, 1981).

Some chronically ill children must learn to cope with painful treatment procedures, such as spinal taps. Unlike adults, children have little influence over the course of these events. In addition to their confusion and distress, they may feel helpless and discouraged. Young children might interpret hospitalization and separation from their family as abandonment or punishment. Some regress to lower levels of functioning. "Thus an already verbal child may decide to stop speaking, or a toilet-trained child . . . may begin wetting or soiling himself. Initial protest of separation may be followed by withdrawal behavior with depressed affect" (Thunberg, 1981, p. 175).

Hospitalization intensifies children's fears. Parental expression of fear, dramatic hospital encounters, and painful diagnostic procedures carried out by insensitive personnel also contribute to a child's distress. If the hospitalization is brief, the impact on the child's development will probably be minor or nonexistent. Chronic or long-term hospitalization requires considerably greater coping from both children and parents.

Ruth Stein, founding director of the Pediatric Home Care program at Bronx Municipal Hospital Center, suggested that there are two levels of support for chronically ill children. The first is good medical care. "The second is help in living a complicated life under difficult circumstances, and that kind of help is the same for most illnesses. The parents have day-to-day problems like finding baby sitters who can understand the child's illness, explaining the illness to the child's schoolteacher, dealing with economic burdens and handling their own worries" (quoted by Hurley, 1987, p. 36). Social and psychological care not only benefit the children but also their parents and siblings. They are all profoundly affected by the illness and sometimes are more in need of support than the ill child (Pelletier, Godin, Lepage, & Dussault, 1994).

The impact on family life of having a chronically ill child depends upon several factors. These include the severity of the illness, the child's age, and medical complications. The parent's coping resources, particularly marital satisfaction and the quality of family life, are important predictors of adjustment (Atkinson, Scott, Chisholm, Blackwell, et al., 1995; Fagan & Schor, 1993; Margalit, Raviv, & Ankonina, 1992; Timko, Stovel, & Moos, 1992).

Mothers and fathers of chronically ill children are susceptible to depression (Quittner et al., 1992; Sloper & Turner, 1993; Timko et al., 1992; Trute, 1995). Sometimes fathers withdraw from child-care responsibilities. Some siblings of ill children may suffer adjustment problems, while others seem to benefit from the experience. Family stress appears to be related to the type of disability and is greater when children have multiple problems or handicaps. Educated parents, having higher aspirations for their child, report more child-related stress than parents who are less educated (Palfrey, Walker, Butler, & Singer, 1989).

Parents of chronically ill children may require more social support than their children.

Open and honest communication and expression of feelings among all parties appear to be crucial for successful adjustment. Many psychologists have noticed that these trying circumstances often bring family members closer together. "Resiliency is the rule rather than the exception. And if you talk with enough parents and children, they're likely to emphasize how the illness brought them in touch with each other. Facing common adversity forces some families to work together more effectively. It sounds horrible to say that there are benefits to chronic childhood illness. No one would choose to have the illness, but psychological benefits can happen as a result" (Drotar, quoted by Hurley, 1987, p. 43).

PARENTING DOWN SYNDROME CHILDREN

Approximately one in 800 infants is born with Down syndrome, a form of mental retardation caused by an extra chromosome. Down syndrome children have characteristic facial features that reinforce the stereotypes that they are all alike and that they cannot be educated. Isolating them in institutions where they experience unstimulating environments has led to self-fulfilling, tragic outcomes that mask their true potential.

Down syndrome children like Charles, whose parents' are interviewed at the beginning of this chapter, are typically multihandicapped, with heart and other organ abnormalities. They usually have problems with their motor coordination, hearing, and seeing. They do not seem to hear and recognize words normally and may speak in incomplete sentences. Most are mildly retarded, but they differ extensively in their intellectual potential (Kolata, 1987b; Turkington, 1987).

Developmentally delayed infants require extra stimulation from their caregivers. For some types of developmental disability, children's infrequent initiations of interactions may discourage parental responsiveness. How parents respond to their children's initiations may be the crucial factor in remedial play (Baker, Landen, & Kashima, 1991; Berlin & Critchley, 1989; Landry, Garner, Pirie, & Swank, 1994).

The development of social interaction usually depends upon infant-generated signals that stimulate reactions in the parent. Retarded infants, however, are less responsive and less verbal than normal infants. They also show fewer attentional and emotional responses. Parents may fail to notice or respond to the signals the infant is providing (McConachie & Mitchell, 1985).

Parents of developmentally disabled children can learn to compensate for their children's lowered responsiveness by using more commands (Hauser-Cram, 1996; Landry et al., 1994). They also can learn to become more active in general, prompting the child to behave more (Hanzlik & Stevenson, 1986).

Today there are effective intervention programs that teach parents how to encourage social behavior and intellectual development in their children (Baker, Landen, & Kashima, 1991; Breiner, 1989; Riley, Parrish, & Cataldo, 1989). Many programs appeared in the wake of the Education for All Handicapped Children Act of 1975 (see Box 12-1). This law requires that disabled children receive an education in the least restrictive environment possible, preferably classrooms. Most programs show parents of children like Charles how to provide their handicapped children with enriched and stimulating home environments. With intensive training, retarded children can acquire social skills that usually develop more naturally in children of average intelligence.

Educators and parents have discovered that many Down syndrome children can achieve after all (Turkington, 1987). Parent training programs are critical for these children's development. Child-rearing strategies exert a greater influence on mildly retarded children's conduct than do organic factors (Richardson, Koller, & Katz, 1985).

Parents of Down Syndrome children have been trained to help them acquire language skills. For example, a study called EDGE (Expanding Developmental Growth through Education) attempted to improve communication skills by teaching parents how to play with their children. About two-thirds of the study participants, when tested at the age of 5 years, scored in the educable range. Only half of those who did not receive special lessons accomplished this criterion.

Although mothers and fathers are similar in their interactions with their special children, a few differences have been noted (Barnett & Boyce, 1995). The differences correspond to those described previously between mothers and fathers of nondisabled children. Fathers of retarded children are more similar to their counterparts in families with ordinary children than are mothers. Fathers seem to be less distressed by the burdens of rearing a disabled child. Perhaps this is due to their lesser involvement in caregiving. As in families with nondisabled children, the stronger the marital relationship, the closer the father is to the disabled child (Bailey, Blasco, & Simeonsson, 1992; Hadadian & Merbler, 1995; Levy-Shiff, 1986; Martin & Cole, 1993).

Mothers usually react more effectively than fathers and show greater flexibility. Fathers

Box 12-1

The Americans With Disabilities Act

The Americans with Disabilities Act (ADA) became law in 1990. It is the first comprehensive federal law that prohibits local and state agencies from discriminating against disabled individuals in regard to employment, services, and facilities (Gostin & Beyer, 1993). The U.S. Justice Department defines a **disability** as "a physical or mental impairment that substantially limits one or more of [an individual's] major life activities." The ADA supplements other laws, especially the Education for all Handicapped Children Act and Section 504 of the Rehabilitation Act, in requiring quality educational services for disabled children (*NJEA Review*, November, 1995, p. 11).

may elicit more negative responses. Dominating fathers usually have less-compliant children. Most professionals who train parents work with mothers, but fathers also benefit from professional guidance (McConachie & Mitchell, 1985). Siblings sometimes are involved in training programs. They learn how to become more accepting and caring of their retarded brother or sister.

At least half of Down Syndrome children who are raised at home by middle- and upper-class parents are educable when they start school. They will read at or above the second grade level in elementary school (Turkington, 1987). Unfortunately, many school districts resist mainstreaming these children, and many parents remain unaware of their children's true potential.

PARENTING AUTISTIC CHILDREN

Autism, previously known as childhood schizophrenia, is a severely debilitating disorder, the causes of which remain unknown. Evidence suggests that autism has a variety of causes, including a genetic defect. Older theories attributing autism to inadequate parental care have been discarded (Plienis, Robbins, & Dunlap, 1988).

A rare disorder that occurs in about 5 out of 10,000 live births, autism usually emerges by the age of $2\frac{1}{2}$ years. It is far more common in males. In the film *Rain Man*, Dustin Hoffman movingly portrays an autistic adult with astonishing mathematical abilities. The portrayal is generally realistic. However, most autistic people are retarded; only some are of average or superior intelligence.

Virtually all autistic individuals are withdrawn and nonresponsive to other people, including their parents (Plienis, Robbins, & Dunlap, 1988). Most either do not speak or mechanically repeat whatever is said to them, a condition known as **echolalia**. Repetitive behaviors, such as rocking back and forth, and self-destructive behaviors are common. A 5- or 10 year-old autistic child might behave like a normal one-year-old, requiring constant, long-term supervision (Lovaas, 1987; Lovaas, Koegel, & Schreibman, 1979; Lovaas & Smith, 1989).

The demands of raising an autistic child can seriously strain a family's resources. Family relationships, the emotional well-being of the parents, family recreation, and finances are adversely affected. Mothers, in particular, report feeling guilty and inadequate. Parents of children with autism or Down syndrome report frequent use of wish-fulfilling fantasy and

Spotlight

Children's Reactions To Peers with Disabilities

The practice of **mainstreaming** has led to increased numbers of special children attending classes with those who are not handicapped. Today's public classrooms may include children with physical, emotional, and learning disabilities, or children with cancer or AIDS. All children seem to benefit from exposure to those who are different from them, even though many children take some time to adjust (Kutner, 1988i).

Mainstreamed children benefit from the opportunity to interact and compete with nonhandicapped children. The latter benefit from learning how to relate to and understand human disability. "Helping able-bodied children understand what has happened to someone who is sick, scarred or disabled can be complex. As children develop, they respond to different cues and have very different concerns from those of their parents" (Kutner, 1988i).

Toddlers tend to disregard physical differences, but preschoolers judge other children on the basis of their appearance and behavior. Older children may express their curiosity in ways that would embarrass adults. Teenagers appear to be the most uncomfortable with individual differences, perhaps reflecting their own heightened self-consciousness. Most people, children and adult, have not learned how to relate comfortably to handicapped or disabled people. Focusing on the disability prevents us from seeing the person "inside." This can be quite painful to the child who is struggling to accept, but not identify with, her disability.

When children make insensitive comments about disfigured individuals, parents should withhold judgment about the child's remark. They should ask questions that will help the child understand her own feelings about the individual. "Do the scars scare you? Are you frightened by how the other children might treat him? Do you worry that this might happen to you?" (Kutner, 1988i). Parents can help their children avoid the common pitfall of equating people with their appearance or behavior, and see instead that people are basically similar despite outward appearances.

---

information-seeking in addition to avoidant coping strategies (DeMyer, 1979; DeMyer & Goldberg, 1983; Margalit, Raviv, & Ankonina, 1992; Rodrigue, Morgan, & Geffken, 1992).

In *Rain Man*, the autistic man throws a tantrum that allows him to avoid having to fly on an airplane. Research with autistic children suggests that their bizarre behavior may be a learned way of expressing, "I don't want to do this. If you try to make me do this, I'll act crazy until you stop" (Carr & Durand, 1987, p. 63). Autistic children apparently learn to punch, bite, kick, or scratch themselves or others so that they can have their way.

The concept of bizarre behavior as a form of communication brings together interpretational approaches to abnormal behavior and behavior modification models that emphasize the powerful influence of consequences on behavior. Carr and Durand (1987) taught autistic children better ways of communicating their desires, for example, by saying "Help me" or "Look at what I've done." After training, the children had fewer severe behavior problems.

Unresponsive to traditional "talk" therapies, autistic children have shown remarkable progress from participation in behavior modification and parent-training programs (Harris & Bruey, 1988; Lovaas & Smith, 1989). Children treated in a program at U.C.L.A. received 40 hours of training a week from a behavior modification specialist. They were then treated at home by their parents and by teachers in special preschool programs.

"The therapy puts a huge demand on the child's family, as the parents must be alert to the child's behavior to be able to respond appropriately. The responses include praising appropriate speech or actions, ignoring bizarre behavior, putting a child who became aggressive in a room alone for a time-out period, or responding to undesirable behavior with a loud 'no' " (Goleman, 1987e).

Lovaas (1987) observed that autistic children who live with their parents after training continue to make progress whereas children who reside in institutions typically regress. Children receiving the most intensive treatment gained an average of 30 IQ points. "The training only really works if you get the parents involved" according to Lovaas (quoted by Goleman, 1987e). Some question the wisdom of exposing families to the burden of working with their autistic children, particularly when positive results are not guaranteed (B. Bower, 1989). Lovaas contends that mainstreaming autistic children is the optimal treatment. Parents must become part of the therapy team if their children are to progress.

As with other serious childhood disabilities, "unless parents push for change, they may never become free of their role as caretaker and the child may remain so dependent that when the parents die there is little choice but institutional care" (Harris & Powers, 1984).

PARENTING CHILDREN WITH LEARNING DISABILITIES

Some of us know children of normal intelligence and even bright children who learn to read, write, or do math only with great difficulty. Such children express intense frustration when trying to master certain basic skills. As a result of frequent failure, they misbehave in school, get along poorly with their peers, and suffer from low self-esteem. Some eventually develop an aversion to school, the scene of their embarrassing failures. Some drop out of school before completing high school.

It is estimated that 5 to 10 percent of all children have learning problems. Attention deficit disorder (ADD) and attention deficit hyperactivity disorder (ADHD), characterized by impulsive behavior, overactivity, and an inability to concentrate, occur three times more frequently in boys than in girls (Evans, Vallano, & Pelham, 1995). By 1987, almost 2 million children had been identified as learning disabled (LD), almost half of the nation's special education students (Bales, 1985; Landers, 1987b).

Who are the learning disabled? There is still considerable controversy about this designation (Gallagher, 1985). The label refers to children who show a significant deficit in some academic area but who score in the normal range on standardized intelligence tests. They show no major emotional or sensory impairments. In other words, children are classified as learning disabled if their achievement in some academic area is less than what would be expected based on their intelligence.

"Learning disabled children are often reported to be poorly coordinated in both gross and fine motor activities. They are likely to have trouble catching a ball, tying shoelaces, or writing with a pencil. Some learning disabled children have speech difficulties. Others may suffer from memory problems, difficulties in coordinating vision and action, or defective ability to process information and make sense of what they see or hear. They can be either overactive or lethargic" (Stone & Church, 1984, p. 554).

As with other disorders, parents of very

young LD children suspect that something is wrong. Years may elapse, however, between the onset of parental suspicions (at about age 2½ years) and an actual diagnosis of learning disability (at about age 6 years, on the average). This delay in diagnosis is unfortunate. The earlier LD is diagnosed and treated the better the child's eventual adjustment.

In Faerstein's (1986) study, a majority (58 percent) of the mothers reported feeling responsible in some way for the disability. Raising an LD child, particularly one that is hyperactive, can be extremely frustrating (Evans, Vallano, & Pelham, 1995; Waggoner & Wilgosh, 1990). LD children, like other children who are difficult to care for, are at greater risk for child abuse. "The mothers in this study found that society does not accept them or their child because they are unable to demonstrate that their child is ill. The children are not seen by the community as having a physical problem but rather as being bad or different and therefore undesirable" (Faerstein, 1986, p. 11).

Some parents, frustrated by their child's noncompliance or lack of achievement, become coercive and overly demanding. Buhrmester and his colleagues (1992) observed that mothers of hyperactive sons were more coercive than mothers of less active sons. In mother-father-son triads, fathers became coercive when trying to "rescue" their partners during parent-child confrontations.

Once parents understand the problem, there is much that they can do to help their children compensate for their disability (Cantwell, 1996). An article by the parents of an LD child and co-written by the child (McWhirter, McWhirter, & McWhirter, 1985) describes retrospectively how the family helped their son build his self-esteem and focus on his strengths rather than becoming overwhelmed by his disability.

"We used many strategies with Robert to build his self-esteem. These included educat-

ing him about his specific disability, the identification and emphasis on his strengths, the use of I-messages and ego-inflating terms, the minimization of criticism, and others" (p. 315). Having graduated from his college's Honors Program with a magna cum laude designation and being on the Dean's honor roll, Robert's achievements confirm his family's and his own efforts.

PARENTING GIFTED CHILDREN

No widely accepted definition of giftedness exists. It is not clear whether giftedness is simply high intelligence or something else. Gifted children have superior intelligence. They usually are highly motivated to learn and to achieve. They are more likely to fulfill their potential in special, supportive learning environments (Freeman, 1995; Sternberg & Davidson, 1986).

Intellectually gifted children are sometimes stereotyped as poorly adjusted, socially inept individuals who get lost in their scholarly pursuits. Research does not support this portrait (Freeman, 1995). Gifted children usually are not only very intelligent and high achieving, but also emotionally stable, popular, social leaders at school, and happy. Nevertheless, very bright individuals who are teased by their peers, unchallenged by ordinary schoolwork, or who feel that they don't fit in may experience stress and adjustment problems.

Some children's exceptional talents go unrecognized because of parental or societal indifference or due to lack of opportunity to develop their potential. They may be at risk for academic, social, and emotional maladjustment (Freeman, 1985; 1995). Etlin (1988) describes the "gifted underachiever" as having high intelligence but also as being insecure and having low self-esteem, poor social skills, and less persistence than other students. "Paradoxically, the students with the

S p o t l i g h t

Blaming Mothers For Children's Problems

Psychologists Paula Caplan and Ian Hall-McCorquodale observed a tendency in the clinical literature to blame mothers for their children's problems. A survey of 125 articles in major clinical journals revealed 72 kinds of psychopathology attributed to mothers. Examples include agorophobia, arson, bed-wetting, and hyperactivity.

Eighty-two percent of the articles attributed at least part of a child's pathology to the mother (Caplan & Hall-McCorquodale, 1985a; 1985b). In more than three-quarters of the articles, research or therapy addressed the mother-child relationship rather than the father-child relationship or just the child.

"In the articles we reviewed, not a single mother was ever described as emotionally healthy, although some fathers were, and no mother-child relationship was said to be healthy, although some father-child ones were described as ideal. Far more space was used in writing about mothers than about fathers. Furthermore, fathers were often described mostly or only in terms of their age and occupation, whereas mothers' emotional functioning was usually analyzed (and nearly always deemed essentially 'sick' ")(Caplan, 1986, p. 70).

Similarly, almost all studies of physical and sexual child abuse and neglect focus on mothers rather than fathers even though fathers tend to be more coercive than mothers, and less patient (Hooper, 1992). "Because of this selective attention, mothers are often seen as responsible for child abuse even when it is a male who commits the abusive acts. This is perhaps most apparent in the literature of incest, which regularly casts the mother in the role of the dysfunctional parent despite recognition of the father as the actual perpetrator" (Margolin, 1992, p. 412).

Phares and Compas (1992) reviewed the research literature on the role played by fathers in their children's psychopathology. They concluded that "fathers play a significant and substantial role in the occurrence of psychopathology in their children . . . Paternal behaviors, personality characteristics, and psychopathology are significant sources of risk for child and adolescent psychopathology" (p. 403).

Freud was perhaps the first psychologist to emphasize the mother's role in the development of neurosis. More recently, we hear about "overprotective mothers," "maternal deprivation," and "schizophrenogenic mothers" (Caplan, 1986). Mothers, more than fathers, are blamed for children's problems because they are more visible to therapists. "It's easier to blame the person in the waiting room than to explore arduously what—and who—else might contribute to the child's problems" (Caplan, 1986, p. 71).

Caplan contends that viewing mothers as the only or main cause of children's psychopathology is destructive to mothers, children, society, and to the discipline of psychology. It encourages mothers (including competent mothers) to feel guilty about their children's problems. It discourages researchers from searching for the many factors that contribute to children's disorders.

Mothers may indeed inadvertently encourage poor adjustment, but so do fathers, siblings, peers, and others. Some children may be so vulnerable that they adjust poorly despite competent parenting. "Mothers, despite their anxiety and guilt, manage to raise millions of reasonably well-adjusted kids. They deserve far more credit for this than they get" (Caplan, 1986, p. 71).

highest intelligence often suffer from the lowest self-image and the most severe emotional and behavioral problems."

Parents of gifted children sometimes have difficulty disciplining their precocious children, who are very adept at getting their way. It is important that parents of gifted children set limits and delegate responsibilities just as parents of less talented children do.

PREVENTION OF PSYCHOLOGICAL PROBLEMS

Study Question   *Why is treatment of psychological disorders given so much more attention than prevention?*

It is remarkable how many of society's resources are directed toward treatment and remediation and how few to preventing serious problems from occurring in the first place. Given the cost to society of treating mental and physical health problems and the human suffering involved, a greater allocation of resources to preventative practices makes sense (Azar, 1995b; Offord, 1987).

Primary prevention consists of reducing the frequency of new cases of a disorder by eliminating its cause (Offord, 1987). Good examples of effective primary prevention include good prenatal care for pregnant women, nutritional counseling, parent education, and vaccinating children. Immunizations have almost eliminated new cases of potentially devastating childhood illnesses (Bumpers, 1984). Parents who are mentally ill, retarded, very young, poor, or abusive often place their children in jeopardy through faulty rearing practices. Parents can prevent or at least reduce the severity of certain types of developmental disabilities by providing their children with a stimulating, language-rich environment (Azar, 1995b). Programs that identify special, partic-

TABLE 12.3   Prevention of Psychological problems

Primary prevention: Reducing the frequency of new cases of a disorder by eliminating its cause (e.g., good prenatal care)

Secondary prevention: Early detection and treatment of a disorder (e.g., early screening for speech problems before kindergarten and intervention)

Tertiary prevention: Rehabilitation or remediation of an established problem (e.g., physical therapy or psychological counseling)

ularly "hard-to-reach" parents, and provide effective early interventions, exemplify primary prevention (Finney & Edwards, 1989; Jaffe, 1990; Kessler, 1988).

Secondary prevention refers to the early detection and treatment of existing physical or psychological problems. Early intervention is more likely to be successful than remediating a problem after it has become firmly ingrained. Most children, prior to entering kindergarten, are routinely screened for speech, visual, and hearing problems. Those who are identified as having problems are treated. This allows them to benefit fully from their school attendance.

Recent successful interventions focus on the "mother-child system," rather than on just the child. Routine psychological screening of preschool children (and their parents) could be useful. Some infants who are at risk for developmental problems could be treated as early as infancy. Early treatment increases the likelihood that intervention will succeed (Turkington, 1984c).

So-called **tertiary prevention** involves intervention in the form of rehabilitation or remediation of established problems to limit their harmful effects (Offord, 1987). Such interventions emphasize a child's resources.

Their goal is to achieve as normal a life-style as possible. Most children needing such attention are not receiving it. Of the 7.5 to 9.5 million children needing mental health services, less than one-third are being helped. Many of these problems could be successfully treated or prevented (Fisher, 1987b).

Clearly, primary prevention is the most cost efficient and humane of the three prevention strategies. Early intervention programs, for example, have enormous potential that is, as yet, unfulfilled. Obstacles include identifying children or families who are at high risk for psychological or physical disorders and demonstrating the effectiveness of such programs (Marfo, 1991). Poor, young families are particularly vulnerable (Halpern, 1990). Sometimes, resistant parents have to be persuaded to participate in prevention programs (Greenspan, Wieder, Nover, Lieberman, Lourie, & Robinson, 1987). Programs will be more effective when parents and teachers coordinate their efforts in minimizing the effects of a child's disability.

SUMMARY

1. Families with disabled or chronically ill children are more similar to than different from ordinary families. Parenting ordinary children is not easy. Parents of children with special needs face a host of additional obstacles that sometimes seem insurmountable. The nature of the obstacles depends partly upon the specific disability and its severity. The child's age and family and personal resources are also important factors. As always, a critical family resource is a strong marital relationship or partnership.

2. Typical stressors in families with disabled children include frustrating interactions with professionals and inadequate professional support. Financial problems, finding appropriate educational resources and child care, and marital discord are additional challenges. Because of the added stressors, good communication and coping skills are particularly helpful. Parents adjust best when they have realistic expectations about their children's development and about their own ability to provide care for their children.

3. As disabled children mature, the nature of the challenges and tasks facing the family changes. The school-aged child may still require an inordinate amount of care. Mothers fear that they will never be free to pursue their own life goals. Brothers and sisters may have ambivalent feelings about their disabled sibling. Some develop behavior problems of their own.

4. Fortunately, there are intervention programs that teach parents how to provide their disabled children with enriched and stimulating home environments. Support groups help parents cope with their ambivalent feelings about their child. Mainstreaming helps disabled children learn to interact and compete with nondisabled children, who also benefit from this contact. They become more empathic and sensitive to individual differences.

5. Unfortunately, theorists and researchers sometimes hold mothers responsible for their children's disorders. Although some mothers may encourage poor adjustment, so may fathers and siblings.

6. The optimal approach to psychological and physical disorders is to prevent their occurrence when possible. Primary prevention, eliminating the causes of these disorders, is the most cost-effective and humane strategy. Although the effectiveness of most early intervention programs has not been demonstrated, parent-training programs help parents learn the skills that they need to create for their children an interesting, stimulating, and supportive home environment.

GLOSSARY

disability   A physical or mental impairment that substantially limits one or more of an individual's major life activities

echolalia   Typical of autistic individuals, repetition of heard speech without any sign of understanding

mainstreaming   Integrating students with disabilities into regular classrooms for part or all of a school day

primary prevention   Reducing the frequency of new cases of a disorder by eliminating its cause

secondary prevention   Early detection and treatment of existing physical and psychological problems

tertiary prevention   Remediation of established problems to limit their harmful effects

THOUGHT QUESTIONS

1. How do you think you would react if you discovered that your child were "less than perfect?"

2. In two-parent families, how would the presence of a disabled or chronically ill child test the parental relationship?

3. How do siblings of special children benefit from the sibling relationship?

4. How responsible are parents for their children's emotional and behavioral problems?

13 CHAPTER

FAMILY VIOLENCE, CHILD ABUSE, AND NEGLECT

OBJECTIVES 376
INTRODUCTION 376
FAMILY VIOLENCE 377
Families With Marital Violence 379
Spotlight: Bullies and Their Victims 380
Parental Discipline Style 382
CHILD ABUSE 382
Physical Abuse 384
Effects of Abuse on Children 386
Fathers and Abuse 387
Psychological Maltreatment (Emotional Abuse) 387
Breaking the Cycle of Abuse 388
SEXUAL ABUSE 389
Effects of Sexual Abuse 391
Causes of Sexual Abuse 393
Child Care and Sexual Abuse 393
Assessment of Sexual Abuse 394
Prevention of Sexual Abuse 394
CHILD NEGLECT 395
FAMILY, ANTISOCIAL BEHAVIOR, AND
    DELINQUENCY 396
Prevention and Treatment 397
Spotlight: Do Toy Guns Encourage Aggression? 398
SUMMARY 399
GLOSSARY 400
THOUGHT QUESTIONS 400

"Abuse appears to emerge . . . when a parent with a predisposition toward anxiety, depression, and hostility becomes irritated with a child, attempts to physically and instrumentally control the child, but becomes so aroused as to lose control of him or herself and overdoes what was initially intended to be an act of discipline" (Belsky, 1993, p. 421).

OBJECTIVES

After studying Chapter 13, students should be able to:

1. Describe the various forms of family violence and their prevalence in the United States
2. Describe the profiles of violent husbands, battered wives, and their children and the situational factors that are associated with family violence
3. Distinguish between physical abuse, psychological maltreatment (emotional abuse), sexual abuse, and neglect
4. Describe the "typical" abusive parent and the life circumstances that increase the risk of child abuse
5. Describe the effects of physical abuse on children's emotional and social development
6. Describe the various forms of psychological maltreatment (emotional abuse)
7. Describe the effects of sexual abuse on children
8. Discuss steps that parents can take to protect their children from being sexually abused
9. Describe the characteristics of neglecting parents and neglected children
10. Describe the distinctive psychological profiles of bullies and their victims

INTRODUCTION

The 36-year-old single, unemployed father was describing how he had tied the hands of his defiant 9-year-old stepdaughter and "kicked her butt." He told me that he had slapped her face and body several times and hit her with a belt. His attack left visible bruises on her body. Her 10-year-old sister, the father's biological daughter, observed the beating. (The girls' mother, never married to the father, had long ago fled to California).

The day following the incident, the abused girl, in considerable pain, visited the school nurse. The nurse reported the incident to New Jersey's Division of Youth and Family Services. The father subsequently was arrested for child endangerment and abuse. He plead guilty. The two girls were placed in the temporary custody of their aunt and uncle. The agency referred the father to me for counseling.

The father told me that he had beaten the girl because she had misbehaved in school. She had been bouncing a ball in the school building and had talked back to a teacher. He believed that the only alternative to beating her was to "give her away." In other words, he felt that unless he beat her, she would not take him seriously and he couldn't continue to raise her. He told me that he wanted to regain custody of his biological daughter. He said that he had learned his lesson. In his mind, that meant not getting arrested again.

Almost every day, in newspapers and on TV, we hear startling accounts of parents turning on their children. We hear reports of neglect, sexual abuse, beatings, stabbings, shootings, and worse. Family violence and brutality take many forms. Husbands batter their wives or children; children attack their parents or grandparents; parents sell their children for drugs.

There are about three million episodes of child abuse and neglect reported each year in the United States (Children's Defense Fund, 1994). Experts suggest that most incidents are not reported. Thus, the number of actual incidents of abuse is probably much higher. Almost 2 million women are battered by their husbands each year. The FBI reports that about 20 percent of all murders are committed by family members. Emotional abuse and neglect leave scars as deep and enduring as battering.

It is risky to make general statements about those who commit family violence; they are a varied lot. Nevertheless, the situational and psychological factors related to family violence are becoming clearer. In this chapter, we consider these factors and review what is known about the psychological impact of family violence on children.

As we shall see, the same parents who practice violence within their marital relationship are likely to be abusive when "disciplining" their children. Children who are victims of abuse may subsequently display violent behaviors during conflict with siblings or peers. In this chapter, we examine the darker side of family life. We attempt to understand the irrational, destructive behavior that is all too common in families.

FAMILY VIOLENCE

Study Question *What factors predict violent behavior in children?*

We observe violence and conflict at all levels of society and in all social classes. Children are exposed daily to violence in movies, on TV news programs and dramas, and, for some children, on the streets where they live and in their own homes (Landers, 1990).

Theorists have suggested many models of aggressive behavior (Kashani, Daniel, Dandoy, & Holcomb, 1992). Some contend that aggressive behavior is instinctive; others suggest that it is learned. Some view aggression as a response to frustration; others appeal to the arousing effects of group pressure or aggressive models. Many studies confirm that aggressive behavior sometimes results from the temporary weakening of an individual's ability to control his or her aggressive impulses. The truth probably encompasses all these factors and others. Profiles of violent parents suggest a combination of personality dispositions and stressful life and situational factors. These lead to a loss of control, violent behavior, and, usually, feelings of remorse (Patterson, DeBaryshe, & Ramsey, 1989).

Many children witness the brutal domestic disputes of their parents. Some are victims of violence themselves (McCloskey, Figuerdo, & Koss, 1995). Children, particularly boys, who observe repeated domestic violence may suffer from emotional disturbance, behavior problems, and social maladjustment. Children who run away from home often report that physical violence and verbal abuse were common occurrences between parents or between parent and child (Ek & Steelman, 1988).

Boys who are not abused but who are exposed to repeated family violence resemble abused boys in their pattern of adjustment problems (Jaffe, Wolfe, Wilson, & Zak, 1986). Thus, exposure to family violence can be as harmful as abuse itself. Both groups of children, however, may have other situational factors in common that could account for their adjustment problems. These include family stress, inadequate child management, and parental strife. About 40 percent of the boys in this study witnessed family violence and were abused themselves. Children who are both victims and observers of family violence are most prone to psychological problems (Kalmuss, 1984).

Over 200 incarcerated juvenile offenders from New Jersey were interviewed during a federal study of child abuse and neglect (Geller, 1984). Investigators found that about 70 percent of these children had been beaten with a belt or extension cord. About half were beaten with a stick, 12 percent were attacked with a weapon, and a third were beaten so severely that bruises resulted. A quarter were beaten until they bled. A quarter saw their mothers punched by their fathers. Almost 10

Psychological and sexual abuse may leave emotional scars that are deeper than those caused by battering.

percent saw their mothers beaten so severely that they had to be hospitalized.

Most of these juvenile offenders "had a history of violent behavior, of offenses like assault and rape and even murder. But in general, the more violent their homes, the more violent were the offenders themselves" (Geller, 1984). This is the first lesson in family violence. Children who witness brutality at home often imitate their violent parents or siblings when they leave their homes (Loeber & Dishion, 1983) (see *Spotlight*: Bullies and Their Victims). Domestic violence, often a prelude to juvenile delinquency, is associated with many situational factors. These include poor discipline of children, less family cohe-

TABLE 13.1 Profile of Violent Parents

Violent husbands usually are impulsive, punitive, irritable, jealous, and abuse alcohol

Elevated levels of depression and anxiety

Lower levels of assertiveness and problem-solving skills

Lower levels of marital satisfaction

Verbal abuse and poor communication skills

sion, parental conflict, financial problems, job stress, unemployment, poor money management, illness, and poor communication (Gorman-Smith, Tolan, Zelli, & Huesmann, 1996; Loeber & Dishion, 1983; McCord, 1991; Patterson, 1982, 1986).

Families with Marital Violence

Violent husbands are usually impulsive, excessively dependent upon their wives, and irrationally jealous. Their most common emotional expression is anger. Battered women are typically submissive and quiet. Perhaps this reflects their "learned helplessness" (discussed in Chapter 9). They report that they are highly stressed; stress seems to interfere with their parenting behavior (Holden & Ritchie, 1991).

Children from maritally violent homes often exhibit a range of behavior problems. In families where battering is extreme, boys are more often victims of aggression than girls (by mothers and fathers) and exhibit more externalizing behaviors (Jouriles & Norwood, 1995; Jouriles et al., 1996). Many have low self-esteem, psychosomatic and sleep disorders, and exhibit antisocial behavior. Battered women frequently report that their children are physically aggressive, even toward them (Emery, 1989; Gullette, 1987; Holden & Ritchie, 1991). Perhaps this is because children of battered women often are abused

themselves (McCloskey, Figuerdo, & Koss, 1995). Battered women report that their partners often hit them for failing to control their children to their partner's satisfaction (Jouriles & Norwood, 1995).

Gullette (1987) interviewed and observed parents and children from maritally violent families and interviewed professionals who work with such families. She identified two types of violent families, labelled Type 1 and Type 2. In *Type 1* families, marital violence "served as a method of establishing hierarchy and maintaining control of family members" (p. 122). Violence was inflicted by the father, whose role it was to keep order in the family. Fathers stated rules, and mothers enforced them. In *Type 2* families, anyone could be violent when expressing anger or reacting to stress. Mothers and fathers competed for the role of "decision maker." Children felt helpless, not knowing with which parent to side. They risked harsh treatment when they made the wrong decision.

Children from Type 1 families became violent when the controls were absent. They used violence as a means to an end or to accomplish a goal. Imitating their father's behavior, they frequently directed violence against their mothers. Children in Type 2 families used violence to express anger, as a response to stress, or when they lost control. Their goal was to intimidate. "Teenagers frequently directed their violence against their fathers, as an escalation of a disagreement with the father or to protect the mother from the father's violence" (p. 127).

The effects on children of parent's marital violence were mediated by the quality of the parent-child relationships. Many fathers in the study reported not knowing how to get close to their children. Like the abusive father described at the beginning of this chapter, they believe that force is the only way to get their children to take them seriously (Jouriles & Norwood, 1995).

Bullies often have parents who are punitive, critical, and hostile.

Spotlight

Bullies and Their Victims

"I can still remember him in vivid detail: the edge in his voice as he taunted his victims, the delight in his face, even his name, though I won't say it here. I always gave him a wide berth and so avoided his aggression, but other kids, not so lucky, were his constant victims. You probably remember him, too, by a different name. He's the schoolyard bully" (Roberts, 1988, p. 52).

Most children at one time or another will find themselves, reluctantly, confronted by a bully (Brody, 1996a). It has been estimated that about 20 percent of school-age boys become involved in on-going aggressive confrontations. Half are bullies and half are victims. A survey by the National Association of Secondary School Principals revealed that 25 percent of the students polled consid-

ered the possibility of being bullied a major worry. Most children have not been taught how to handle such threatening situations. They are therefore susceptible to intimidation, fear, embarrassment, and guilt (Olweus, 1993).

Recently, researchers have addressed the psychology of the bully and of his victim. Although some models of bullying behavior support psychologist Alfred Adler's (1927) contention that their aggressive, controlling behavior is an attempt to compensate for feelings of inferiority and inadequacy (Boulton & Smith, 1994; Olweus, 1993), newer models suggest that bullies are not lonely, insecure children who make themselves feel better by abusing others. Recent studies found that bullies "learn their aggressive, intimidating tactics from others, especially from parents or caretakers who rely on severe and often capricious physical discipline to get their way" (Brody, 1996a, p. C11).

As we have seen, aggressive children often come from aggressive families. Parents of bullies are typically punitive, critical, and sarcastic with their children (and each other). They model aggressive and confrontational behavior for their children (Brody, 1996a; Kutner, 1988j). They respond in unpredictable ways and appear to have little interest in their children. Their children learn that "being aggressive and physically coercive is a way to get what they want and to increase their status and self-esteem. They learn this long before school age, from television as well as from parents" (Psychologist Leonard Eron, quoted by Brody, 1996a, p. C11).

Lacking opportunities to develop empathic and prosocial skills at home, bullies often have distorted, even paranoid, perceptions of other children's behavior. They might interpret a harmless encounter, such as an ambiguous facial expression, as an intentional provocation and feel justified in striking back (Goleman, 1987h; Kutner, 1993). They cannot tolerate teasing or harmless comments from other children. They overreact and eventually alienate their peers and teachers. Such antisocial behavior patterns elicit reactions from other people, especially social avoidance, that perpetuate the self-defeating pattern and prevent the learning of more adaptive social skills (Boulton & Smith, 1994).

Eron has profiled the "typical" bully. By the age of 8, he repeatedly initiates fights for no obvious reason. He has a quick temper and takes other people's possessions. He is a poor student and, because of his brutality, he becomes a social outcast. His parents punish him harshly for his behavior but otherwise show little interest in him. He is defiant with his teachers and therefore disliked. As adults, "they have more arrests for felonies and more convictions for serious crimes, are more abusive toward their spouses and are more likely to have highly aggressive kids" (Eron, cited by Brody, 1996a, p. C11).

Females rarely are bullies but those who are, bully other girls. They harass them verbally rather than physically. Very aggressive girls may become mothers of bullying sons. About half of all victims of bullying are girls (Perry, Kusel, & Perry, 1988).

The Victims of Bullies

Researchers also have discovered that the victims of bullies have their own distinctive profile. Like some rape victims, they blame themselves. Because of their shame they are reluctant to seek the counsel of their teachers or parents. "The child who is bullied often will hide his predicament out of shame. He will mention it to his parents only obliquely, testing the home waters for an emotional chill. It is better to pay the money and go without lunch than to risk being called a coward or a failure" (Kutner, 1988j).

School, a place where children are supposed to feel safe, becomes marred by taunting, threats, and fighting (Brody, 1996b). Some children may feign illness to avoid having to be "picked on" at school. Many become truants, or even commit suicide or kill their tormentors (Roberts, 1988). Some victims provoke aggression; some passively submit to it. "A dance goes on. It is as if they court each other, and often it seems as if neither can leave the other alone. Bullies seem to need a victim, and may work hard to create a victim, even if there isn't one there . . . When these bullies see kids they perceive as vulnerable, they are threatened because it reminds them of the shame and humiliation of their own victimization. In the bully's constant teasing and aggression, it is as if he is desperately trying to get the victim to say no, so that the bully himself will feel less threatened" (Floyd, quoted by Collins, 1986e). Both bullies and victims often are rejected by their peer groups (Boulton & Smith, 1994). They may be "stuck" with each other because of this exclusion. Some bullies develop a model of relationships that is based on power and a lack of warmth (Perry, Kusel, & Perry, 1988; Smith, Bowers, Binney, & Cowie, 1993).

Intervention programs teach aggressive children social skills. They reduce the incidence of bullying by 50 percent (Olweus, 1993, 1994). Such programs also teach potential victims how to handle aggressive confrontations. There is some agreement among experts that children should be encouraged to approach an authority figure and report the harassment. If no adults are available, the child can attempt to ignore the bully's taunts. Victims can be taught to act assertively by demanding that the bully cease his harassment ("Don't do that. I don't like it") and then walking away to avoid escalating the conflict. Engaging bullies in power struggles usually makes things worse for victims (Brody, 1996b; Kutner, 1993).

Children also can learn various strategies of "disarming" the bully, including walking away (Seppa, 1996c). Whether children should be encouraged to meet violence with violence depends upon their parents' values. Some parents teach their children to hit back; other parents discourage such behavior. Children can be offered the option of fighting back, acting assertively, ignoring the bully, or seeking help from an adult. It is important that schools identify victims and reassure them that adults care about their problem and will keep them safe (Brody, 1996b).

The optimal strategy for handling bullying is prevention. This strategy requires working with the parents of bullies, teaching them parenting skills that will promote prosocial behavior in their children. Bullies can learn social skills, non-aggressive conflict-resolution skills, and other prosocial behaviors. They learn these skills through group discussion, role-playing, watching videotapes of confrontational encounters, and assertiveness training (Brody, 1996b; Olweus, 1994).

Parental Discipline Style

Aggressive behavior in children is associated with various features of the punitive (authoritarian) parenting style. These include parental rejection, ineffective discipline, and the use of harsh methods (Chilamkurti & Milner, 1993; Weiss, Dodge, Bates, & Pettit, 1992). Through coercive discipline encounters children can become either instigators or victims of aggressive behavior.

Aggressive children are training and being trained by their parents to use power in a mutually escalating pattern of violence (Patterson, 1982; Vuchinich, Bank, & Patterson, 1992). Harsh physical punishment and inconsistent discipline strategies predict a range of antisocial behaviors. Children raised in violent families often display delinquent behav-

ior, criminality, drug abuse, depression, and alcoholism (Holmes & Robins, 1988). Coercive parents are teaching their children that violence is appropriate and socially acceptable (McCord, 1988b; McCord, 1991).

CHILD ABUSE

Study Question   *Are parents ever justified in hitting or beating their children?*

In early 1996, an 8-year-old boy received a 5-day suspension from school for carrying a razor blade. At home, his father whacked him several times across his chest and back with a three-foot rubber hose, leaving several welts on the boy's body. Someone reported the father, who happens to be the superintendent of the local school system, to New York State's Child Abuse Hot Line. The father was arrested on charges of third-degree assault and endangering the welfare of a child. The boy was worried that his actions had jeopardized his father's job and career. Did this father go too far? Is he fit to be a superintendent of schools? Or was this father simply exercising his right to discipline his child as he sees fit? (Berger, 1996).

Most parents probably have experienced "dark urges" to strike out at their children (Ungar, 1988). "I'm going to kill them" is not an unusual parental aside. As we have seen, raising children can be extremely frustrating. If one is having a bad day, has no support from one's partner, or has had too much to drink, aggressive impulses may spill over into violent behavior. In a statement to the police, the father who beat his son admitted that his actions were excessive.

Most parents have dark urges but do not act on them for a variety of reasons. Perhaps our enduring love of our child is stronger than our momentary anger. Maybe we anticipate the terrible guilt or remorse we would be feeling a few moments later. Certainly we know it's wrong for a big person to hurt a little person. Some parents, however, cannot always inhibit their aggressive impulses, and they lash out at a helpless, frightened child.

Even more horrifying, parents who suffer from a disorder known as **Munchausen's Syndrome by Proxy** fabricate or induce illnesses or death in their children to gain sympathy or attention from others (Levin & Sheridan, 1995). Hundreds of cases have been reported since 1977. The primary indication is a child with a history of unexplainable, prolonged, and extraordinary illnesses or injuries. Parents (usually mothers) displaying this syndrome charm doctors and staff, welcome medical attention and tests (even painful ones) for their children, and exaggerate their children's symptoms. The connec-

tion between this disorder and "ordinary" child abuse is not known (Balleza, 1992; Schreier, 1992).

It is helpful to distinguish between physical abuse, psychological maltreatment (emotional abuse), sexual abuse, and neglect. Definitions of these terms vary according to the nature of the abusive act, its effects on the victim, the intentions of the perpetrator, relevant situational factors, and community standards (Emery, 1989).

Physical abuse is said to occur when children are intentionally injured, leaving bruises, wounds, or burns. Physical abuse usually occurs when parents are angry. As long as spanking is considered acceptable, however, it will be difficult to tell when parents have exceeded the limits set by society on the use of corporal punishment. **Psychological maltreatment (emotional abuse)** occurs when parents continually berate, ridicule, or ignore their children, when "parents are inconsistent in their talk, rules or actions, when they have unrealistic expectations of their children, when they belittle and blame their children, when they do not take an interest in any of their activities, or when they do not ever praise them" (Berns, 1993, p. 518).

Sexual abuse occurs when children are inappropriately held or fondled or encouraged

---

TABLE 13.2 Types of Abuse

Physical abuse: children are intentionally injured by adults leaving bruises, wounds, or burns

Psychological maltreatment (emotional abuse): children are rejected, exploited, berated, ridiculed, or ignored

Sexual abuse: children are inappropriately held, fondled, or encouraged or forced to engage in sexual activities; any kind of sexual contact between an adult and child

Neglect: children's basic physical and emotional needs are not met

or forced to engage in sexual activities. Sexual contact between parents and their children is called **incest**. **Neglect** occurs when children are "abandoned, lack supervision, are not fed properly, need medical or dental care, are frequently absent or late for school, do not have appropriate or sufficient clothing, are unclean, or live in unsafe or filthy homes" (Berns, 1993, p. 518). Most abused children experience two or more of these forms of abuse simultaneously.

Physical Abuse

"I became terrified that when I started hitting my son, I couldn't seem to stop. I kept hitting and hitting him without ever thinking about how hard I was slapping him. Actually, it was my bottled rage that was coming out on him, but I didn't know what to do or who to talk to about it" (mother, quoted by Zigler & Rubin, 1985, p. 102).

A poll on child discipline conducted by the Gallup Organization during the summer of 1995 suggests that more than 3 million children are physically abused by their parents each year in the United States (Lewin, 1995b). A representative nationwide sample of 1000 parents was questioned about how they disciplined a child who misbehaves. About 5 percent of the parents admitted to punishing their children by kicking them or throwing them down, or hitting them with a hard object. The study did not consider as abusive punishments such as spanking, slapping, cursing, or shouting.

The National Center on Child Abuse and Neglect reported in 1993 that there were 200,000 confirmed instances of child abuse that year, a number much smaller than that suggested by the Gallup Poll. It is widely accepted that most cases of abuse are never reported or confirmed. Because it is based on self-reporting, even the Gallup Poll probably underestimates the actual incidence of physical abuse (Lewin, 1995b).

These statistics raise many questions about the identification, causes, prevention, and treatment of physical abuse. Should abused children be taken away from their parents? Can abusive parents be trained to become more understanding and patient with their children? How reliable is young children's testimony about abuse? Are therapists who work with families obligated to report incidents of abuse, voiding their obligation of confidentiality, and possibly discouraging abusive parents from seeking help?

Accusations of child abuse create tremendous strains on courts and agencies. These institutions must respond quickly to possibly life-threatening situations. They also must respect the rights of all parties involved, including the accused adult. In 1974, the United States federal government enacted the Child Abuse Prevention and Treatment Act. This law led to the establishment of the National Center on Child Abuse and Neglect. Before this time, the ancient practice of battering children received very little research and clinical attention. In the nineteenth century, battered children were rescued by the Society for the Prevention of Cruelty to Animals! (Kessler, 1988).

Although abusive parents now are the focus of research and treatment, the primary victims of physical abuse are, of course, children. Being so dependent upon their parents leaves children vulnerable to the vagaries of human emotion and parental fallibility. Infants who are the "wrong" gender, disabled, mentally retarded, have minor physical problems, or who are born prematurely are at an increased risk for abuse (Martin, 1995a, 1995b). In other words, children who are unwanted or generally difficult to care for are more likely to evoke aggressive behaviors from or be neglected by their frustrated caregivers (National Center on Child Abuse and Neglect, 1993).

TABLE 13.3 Profile of the Abusive Parent

Emotionally troubled and insecure

Easily frustrated

Undereducated

Socially isolated

Poor coping skills

In troubled relationships

Limited social support and financial resources

Low self-esteem

Unrealistic expectations about children

Drug and alcohol problems

Difficulty interpreting children's moods and emotions

Were abused themselves as children

Although no "abusive personality syndrome" has been identified, correlates of abuse are known (Emery, 1989). The profile of abusive parents depicts them as emotionally troubled, easily frustrated, undereducated, and socially isolated. Their lives usually are very stressful. They have limited child-rearing skills. They often are in unsatisfying relationships and have limited social support and financial resources. The Gallup study mentioned above identified a high correlation between family income and abuse. The physical abuse rate was three times higher in families earning $20,000 a year than in those earning $50,000 a year. The rate of abuse also was three times higher in single-parent families (Lewin, 1995b).

Abusive parents typically suffer from low self-esteem and have unrealistic expectations about their infants or children. They do not understand why their young children misbehave. With their low tolerance for frustration, abusive parents have difficulty inhibiting their angry, violent impulses. When in pain or under stress, they strike out. Kropp and Haynes (1987) report that abusive parents do not know how to interpret their children's

emotions correctly. They may even believe that they are not capable of exerting a positive influence on their children (Bugental, Blue, and Cruzcosa, 1989). Therefore, they respond coercively when their children are "annoying" or distressed.

Many abusive parents have been abused or witnessed abuse as children (Belsky, 1993). In the 1995 Gallup Poll, parents who reported being abused as children were overrepresented among those who admitted severely abusing their own children, beating, burning, and choking them (Lewin, 1995b). Abusive parents, like the mother quoted at the beginning of this section, are "troubled, isolated individuals, often as much a victim as the child" (Zigler & Rubin, 1985). The role of alcoholism and drugs such as cocaine and crack in the maltreatment of children should not be overlooked (Famularo, Stone, Barnum, & Wharton, 1986; Kerr, 1988).

Trickett and Susman (1988) found that compared to nonabusive families, abusive parents enjoyed their children less, found child rearing more difficult, and were generally isolated. They observed a suppression of positive emotions, such as affection and satisfaction, but frequent expression of conflict, anger, and anxiety. Abusive mothers believed more strongly in the value of spanking than did abusive fathers or nonabusive parents and reported more frequent verbal and material punishment.

They were more likely to report using such harsh punishments as striking the child's face, hitting them with objects, and pulling their hair. They do not believe that reasoning is an effective discipline strategy (Trickett & Kuczynski, 1986). Trickett and Susman (1988) emphasize the importance of broadening the social and educational supports of abusive parents. They need good information about child rearing. They must be encouraged to adopt more nurturant and realistic discipline strategies.

Clearly, most of these young (and often impoverished) parents love their children. However, they have difficulty caring for and nurturing them, and some are weakly bonded. Most incidents of abuse follow ineffective attempts to discipline or control crying or defiance. Let's not forget that even nonabusive parents experience frustration and occasional aggressive feelings when their children are misbehaving.

A popular, although somewhat simplistic, model of abuse suggests that to the insecure, abusive parent, the child's crying or defiance signifies rejection. This enrages the frustrated parent, who, rather than comforting the infant, provokes additional crying, perhaps by shouting at or threatening him. When the child continues to cry, the parent's frustration builds. This cycle escalates until the parent loses control.

Clearly, any plausible model of child abuse must take into account the *interaction* between parent characteristics, child characteristics (including temperament), situational factors, and cultural attitudes that support parents' rights to raise their children as they see fit. As Belsky (1993) notes, there is no single cause of child abuse. When parents' life stressors outweigh their social supports, the risk of child abuse increases. Another cultural norm, family privacy, reduces the likelihood of swift intervention for family violence (Lloyd & Emery, 1993).

Effects of Abuse on Children

Study Question *What does abuse teach children about family relationships?*

In his review of the child-abuse literature, Emery (1989) emphasized two important points: "First, there is no single behavioral or emotional reaction that has been found to characterize abused children. Second, the experience of being a victim of violence may not be the principal factor responsible for many of the psychological difficulties that have been found among abused children. Other aspects of the child's psychological environment that often accompany physical abuse may be more psychologically damaging" (p. 324). For example, abused children often witness violent fights between their parents (Jouriles, Barling, & O'Leary, 1987). The combination of being abused and witnessing abuse is more destructive emotionally than simply witnessing abuse (Hughes, 1988).

Compared to nonabused children, abused children are more aggressive, less compliant, and less empathic (Knutson, 1995; Main & George, 1985). They are less competent, have lower self-esteem, and have more difficulty getting along with their peers than nonabused children (Kaufman & Cicchetti, 1989; Salzinger, Feldman, & Hammer, 1993). "Classmates view abused children as meaner and more likely to start fights, and as showing less cooperation and leadership, than their other classmates" (Salzinger et al., 1993, p. 182).

Their language and cognitive development may suffer (Coster, Gersten, Beeghly, & Cicchetti, 1989). The greater the abuse, the more extreme its effects. We still do not know whether these differences between abused and nonabused children are partly dispositional or reflect their history of abuse or their parents' deficient child-rearing practices (Emery, 1989; Trickett & Susman, 1988).

TABLE 13.4 Effects of abuse on child

Insecure attachment

Wariness of relationships, poor relationship skills

More aggressive, less compliant and empathic

Less competent

Lower self-esteem

Anger and depression

Not surprisingly, many abused infants and toddlers are insecurely attached to their caregivers (Aber & Allen, 1987; Carlson, Cicchetti, Barnett, & Braunwald, 1989). Growing up in an emotionally unpredictable and sometimes violent environment leaves children fearful and inhibited. They are wary of relationships in and out of the family.

Other studies have found that abused children exhibit more frustration, aggression, and negative emotions in problem-solving situations. A few abused children develop multiple personalities, with only one or two sub-personalities being aware of previously abusive encounters. Perhaps this is their way of protecting themselves from remembering their physical and emotional pain (Coons & Milstein, 1986).

As adults, violent individuals, spouse abusers, substance abusers, and alcoholics report higher rates of physical abuse during childhood than does the general population (Malinosky-Rummell & Hansen, 1993).

Not all abused children are infants or toddlers. Almost half of abused children are between the ages of 12 and 17 years. Most of these are white females whose parents do not conform to the profile described above. Their parents are better educated and financially secure (Cappelleri, Eckenrode, & Powers, 1993; Moore, Nord, & Peterson, 1989).

Fathers and Abuse

Most research on child abuse has focused on mothers, despite the fact that paternal neglect may be the most common form of child maltreatment. Mother abuse is more common than father abuse only because mothers usually are primary caregivers and have more opportunities to maltreat their children (Belsky, 1993). Historically, fathers have been more physically and sexually abusive and neglectful of children than mothers. Fathers have also been more likely to "abandon" their children following marital separation or divorce. Addi-

tionally, lack of partner support is one of the prime risk factors for abusive mothers. Biller and Solomon (1986) include as instances of father neglect paternal unavailability, rejection, disinterest, and verbal criticism.

Psychological Maltreatment (Emotional Abuse)

Study Question   In what ways might parents emotionally abuse their children?

Many psychologists contend that psychological maltreatment or emotional abuse is at least as destructive to children's development as physical abuse (Hart & Brassard, 1987). Emotional abuse probably is more common, although harder to identify (Knutson, 1995). It often precedes or accompanies physical abuse (Garrison, 1987).

It is estimated that there are at least 200,000 cases of maltreatment a year. The absence of precise definitions of what constitutes maltreatment makes such estimates tentative. Child welfare advocates maintain that parental drug use, parental neglect, and children's observing domestic violence are forms of psychological maltreatment (Gabel & Shindledecker, 1992; Rosenberg, 1987).

Children differ in their sensitivity to harsh parental communications. Some children cry when their parents raise their voices. Other, more resilient children become accustomed to daily criticism and disapproval. Some children are threatened with parental abandonment. "If you do that again, I'll leave you here and you'll never see me again." Insensitive parents reject, terrorize, ridicule, and otherwise intimidate their children in countless ways (e.g., "I wish you were never born"). Emotional abuse also appears to be a precursor to childhood depression and suicide (Becker-Lausen, Sanders, & Chinsky, 1995; Stone, 1993).

A national media campaign on emotional abuse in the 1980s expressed the following message: "Words hit as hard as a fist. Next time, stop and listen to what you're saying. You might not believe your ears" (Denton, 1987). Assessing emotional abuse is a problem. Physical abuse leaves visible scars, but verbal attacks and emotionally unavailable parents do not. Some children are emotionally or physically abused by their teachers (Anyon, 1995; Denton, 1988; Forero, 1996).

Breaking the Cycle of Abuse

Although it is popularly believed that abused children inevitably become abusive parents, Kaufman and Zigler (1987) refuted this notion. They reported that two-thirds of the people who are physically or sexually abused or neglected as children do not abuse their own children but provide them with adequate care. "Although it is true that most parents who abuse their children were themselves maltreated, this group of parents are a minority of all individuals who were maltreated as children" (Kaufman, 1987). Thus, most abused children do not become abusive parents, but most abusive parents were abused as children. Belsky (1993) contends that this conclusion is premature.

Kaufman acknowledged that the likelihood that abuse will be transmitted across generations depends upon many factors. These include the parents' social support system, the quality of the marital relationship, the number of stressful life events, and whether the individual was abused by one or both parents. A third of those who have been abused become abusive parents themselves. It is important, however, that those who have been victims not believe that they must inevitably continue the cycle.

Women who were abused as children but who did not abuse their own children were more likely as children to have received emotional support from a caring adult in childhood (Egeland, Jacobvitz, & Sroufe, 1988). They were more likely to have been in therapy at some point in their lives and have an emotionally supportive, satisfying relationship with a mate. Most mothers who were abused as children declare that they would not abuse their own children, but a substantial number do. These women report considerable life stress, and are more anxious, dependent, immature, and depressed (Egeland, Jacobvitz, & Sroufe, 1988).

Many of the mothers who broke the cycle of abuse had a relationship with a supportive, nonabusive adult during their childhood or with a therapist. Such a relationship "may have enhanced the abused parent's self-esteem and helped them realize that others can be emotionally available in time of need . . . Emotional support from a partner may help provide parents with the emotional resources necessary to give adequate care to their children" (Egeland, Jacobvitz, & Sroufe, 1988, p. 1087).

Prosecuting or punishing parents who abuse their children or separating children from their abusive parents may not always be in the best interests of a child. It certainly does not rehabilitate the parent (Melton & Davidson, 1987). Children may end up in foster homes, group homes, or institutions that do not provide adequate rearing conditions.

Punitive actions discourage some abusive parents from seeking help (Denton, 1987). However, children should never be left in the custody of parents when they are in danger of being sexually or physically abused or neglected. We still have difficulty determining when removing children from abusive households is ultimately in their best interest (Emery, 1989).

Should citizens report suspected incidents of abuse to local social service agencies? Definitely! An official investigation will be conducted and all involved parties will be interviewed. Not getting involved may condemn an innocent child to years of terror. In many states, bystanders are required by law to report suspected cases of abuse.

The Child Abuse Prevention Act provided funds for research programs aimed at preventing future cases of abuse. This is best accomplished by training parents to use effective, positive forms of discipline. Parents can also learn to control their aggressive impulses through stress management procedures. Parents Anonymous was founded in 1970 as a support group for abusive parents. This organization gives parents the opportunity to share their frustrations with other parents and to learn healthier ways of relating to their children (Berns, 1993).

Studies show that abusive parents can be helped by home visits by carefully trained counselors and by parent training programs (Belsky, 1993; Wolfe, Edwards, Manion, & Koverola, 1988). More effective interventions are needed. When necessary, foster care and crisis nursery placements are available to provide temporary shelter. Providing parent training for high-risk families probably is the best preventive measure. Unfortunately, poverty and drug abuse increase the risk of child abuse, and there are few, if any, simple solutions to these problems.

SEXUAL ABUSE

Sexual Abuse *How common is sexual abuse in the United States today?*

Incest is not a new phenomenon. Parents and relatives have sexually exploited children over the ages. Incest taboos, universal across human cultures, evolved to protect both the vulnerable child and the community from inappropriate sexual expression. Despite the severity of the act and the trauma involved for child victims, researchers and the public paid little attention to the sexual exploitation of children until recently. One problem is that there are marked differences among cultures and even within cultures regarding what is considered proper sexual conduct. Adult-child sexual interactions that are considered criminal in some societies may be considered desirable or necessary in others (Konker, 1992).

Many of Freud's female patients reported painful sexual trauma suffered during early childhood. Their accounts led Freud to suggest his "seduction theory." He contended that the neurotic syndrome known as hysteria is precipitated by incestuous advances by patients' fathers. Partly based on his clinical observations, he soon began to question his theory. He eventually abandoned it. Instead, he interpreted his patients' reports as unconscious incestual *fantasies* (Rosenfeld, 1987). In other words, he no longer took their reports literally. In what has since been called "blaming the victim," Freud interpreted their accounts as Oedipal wish-fulfillments. He believed that these women unconsciously longed to have sexual relations with their fathers.

"In the period in which the main interest was directed to discovering infantile sexual traumas, almost all my women patients told me that they had been seduced by their father. I was driven to recognize in the end that these reports were untrue and so came to understand that hysterical symptoms are derived from phantasies and not from real occurrences. It was only later that I was able to recognize in this phantasy of being seduced by the father the expression of the typical Oedipus complex in women" (S. Freud, 1933/1965, p. 120).

Note that Freud discloses that he felt "driven to recognize" that his female patients' reports of abuse were false. Rather than pursue the possibility that father-daughter incest was common, he devised the concept of the female Oedipal complex, partly to explain his patients' disturbing accounts. Given his influence, if Freud had accepted the fact of widespread incest within families, child sexual abuse might have been taken seriously as a serious societal problem much earlier.

Today we encounter sensational news headlines about incest, reports of day-care center scandals, and TV dramas and talk-shows focusing on child sexual abuse. They all attest both to the scope of the phenomenon and society's willingness, finally, to acknowledge that some families sexually exploit their children. Sexual molestation includes exhibitionism, pornography, fondling, and sexual intercourse. Fondling and exhibitionism are the most common forms. Since the research in this area is relatively new, the statistics cited in this section should be treated cautiously.

In 1984, there were more than 123,000 reports of sexual abuse of children, believed to be the tip of the iceberg (*The New York Times*, February 17, 1985). A study published by *The Los Angeles Times* in August, 1985, based on a national telephone poll of 2,627 randomly selected adults, stated that 22 percent of those interviewed (27 percent of the women and 16 percent of the men), reported being sexually abused. A 1984 Gallup poll of 2,000 Canadians confirmed the 22 percent figure. The number almost doubles when sexual advances not reaching sexual contact are included (Kohn, 1987b). Results of the 1995 Gallup Poll cited earlier suggest that 1.3 million children a year are sexually abused. Government estimates, based on confirmed cases, are much lower, at 130,000 a year (National Center on Child Abuse and Neglect, 1993).

David Finkelhor, associate director of the Family Violence Research Program at the University of New Hampshire, studied 521 Boston families as part of a study on the prevalence of child sexual abuse (Finkelhor,

1984). This study was conducted for the National Center for the Prevention and Control of Rape. Nine percent of the parents reported that their children had been victims of abuse or attempted abuse. Forty-seven percent of the parents reported knowing of a child who had been sexually abused. Dr. Finkelhor estimated that the actual number of sexually abused children might be double the 9 percent reported. Many, perhaps most abused children do not report the incident. They fear being blamed, punished, or not being believed.

Over one million women in the United States have had incestuous relations with their fathers. There are about 16,000 new incidents reported each year. In Finkelhor's (1984) study, 94 percent of the sexual abusers were men, usually relatives. Father-daughter abuse is the most common variation, estimated at 75 percent of sexual abuse incidents that take place at home (Menard & Johnson, 1992; Trotter, 1985).

Watkins and Bentovim (1992) offer as their "best guess" that 2 to 5 percent of the male population has been sexually abused, 1 boy for every 4 girls. Others suggest that the incidence is higher than suspected (Black & DeBlassie, 1993). Older boys may be reluctant to admit being abused because they fear being branded "homosexual."

Paternal stress, social isolation, and mother absence are risk factors for sexual abuse. The latter two factors decrease the likelihood of detection. Abusers sometimes justify their actions by claiming that they are educating the child about sex or protecting her from other males. Stepfamilies, families where the mother has a live-in male companion, and families with marital problems, are at greater risk for experiencing child sexual abuse. Uncles are occasionally reported as perpetrators. With adolescent children, parents must concern themselves with the possibility of sexual abuse during courtship,

SUMMARY

1. It is difficult for those who have been raised by supportive, caring parents to appreciate the daily terror facing children living in violent families. Even nonviolent parents, when frustrated, occasionally experience "dark urges" to hurt their children. Many adults with violent family histories, drug problems, or extraordinary life stresses, are unable to control their destructive impulses and attack their children. Most adults, fortunately, have acquired strong inhibitions against hurting children.

2. Children suffer when they witness violence between their parents or are victims of such violence themselves. Family violence appears to be intergenerational, that is, passed on from one generation to the next. Life stresses that tax the coping resources of vulnerable parents include financial problems, job stress, drug abuse and alcoholism, unemployment, and marital conflict. Unwanted children and those who are difficult to care for are at greater risk for abuse.

3. Violent husbands are impulsive and jealous. Their battered wives usually are submissive and passive. Their children often end up being aggressive and underachievers. Some are at risk for becoming delinquents. Violent husbands usually are violent fathers. Using coercive discipline methods, misguided parents train their children to use threats or violence to get what they want.

4. Abusive parents are typically emotionally immature, poorly educated, socially isolated, and insecure. They lack effective parenting skills and adopt punitive discipline methods. Most love their children, but have difficulty providing care for them. When frustrated, they lack the controls necessary to inhibit violent behavior. Adults who have been able to break the cycle of abuse usually have had a supportive, caring relationship with an adult when they were children.

5. As many as 22 percent of the population have been sexually abused as children. Apparently, most instances of sexual abuse are never reported. Children are unwilling or unable to implicate the family members involved. Incest usually persists over a period of years. It may only be discovered through the occurrence of pregnancy or venereal disease.

6. Sexually abused children show many symptoms, including sexual preoccupation, physical complaints, and fears. As adults, they have difficulty forming trusting relationships and may suffer from sexual dysfunctions. It is important that children be told that they are not to blame for the encounters. Parental support of the abused child plays a major role in adjustment. Fathers who are weakly attached to their daughters are at higher risk for committing incest.

7. It is not clear that preschool children can protect themselves from sexual abuse. Parents and teachers therefore play a particularly important role in ensuring their safety and welfare. Older children can benefit from instruction and rehearsal in recognizing and refusing inappropriate sexual advances from others.

8. Child neglect is more common and potentially more destructive than abuse. It is difficult and painful to imagine children growing up with little or no adult support and nurturance. Children raised under social and emotional deprivation are at very high risk for a wide range of psychological disorders. By adolescence, a disproportionate number are mentally ill or emotionally handicapped. Whereas abusive parents love their children, neglecting parents usually are indifferent and unavailable. Attempts to help neglecting parents usually fail. Working with neglected children can overwhelm social service agencies,

which must take over parental responsibilities.

9. Juvenile delinquents typically come from unstable homes where they may repeatedly observe parental violence, criminality, and drug abuse. Parents of delinquent children usually lack effective parenting and discipline skills. They use coercive methods that provoke violent interactions. Traditional prevention and treatment programs have not been successful in helping such children. Behavioral techniques that emphasize positive outcomes for prosocial behavior have been more promising.

GLOSSARY

acquaintance (date) rape Rape and sexual assault perpetrated by someone who is known by the victim, most typically a boyfriend

antisocial behavior Repeated behavior that is annoying, offensive, or hurtful to another person

incest Inappropriate sexual contact between family members

juvenile delinquency A term applied to individuals 18 years old or younger who commit illegal acts

Munchausen's Syndrome by Proxy Said to occur when parents fabricate or induce illnesses or death in their children to gain sympathy and attention

neglect Said to occur when parents do not provide adequate care for their children

physical abuse Term used when children are intentionally battered or otherwise injured by an adult

posttraumatic stress disorder A disorder involving impaired functioning that develops in response to an extremely stressful experience such as physical assault or natural disaster

psychological maltreatment (emotional abuse) Said to occur when parents insult, ridicule, reject, or ignore their children

sexual abuse Any sexual contact between an adult and a child

sexualization A preoccupation with sexual thoughts and behaviors

THOUGHT QUESTIONS

1. In what sense are bullies and their victims "in the same boat?"

2. How can we understand the relationship between poverty, parental stress, and child abuse?

3. What child characteristics make abuse more likely?

4. Are young children capable of protecting themselves from being sexually abused by family members? Explain.

5. Why is child neglect more damaging than physical abuse?

14
CHAPTER

SELECTED TOPICS

TOPIC #1 PARENT-SUPPORT AND TRAINING
   PROGRAMS 402
TOPIC #2 HAVING IT ALL?: DUAL-CAREER
   PARENTING 404
Maternal Employment 404
Children In Dual-Career Families 407
Evaluation 408
TOPIC #3 DAY-CARE PROGRAMS 410
Day Care for Infants 412
Evaluation 413
TOPIC #4 CHILDREN IN SELF-CARE 414
Effects on Children 415
Alternatives to Self-Care 415
SUMMARY 416
GLOSSARY 416
THOUGHT QUESTIONS 417

SELECTED TOPIC #1 PARENT-SUPPORT AND TRAINING PROGRAMS

Study Question *How do most parents learn to parent?*

Given the importance of parenting, it is remarkable that mothers and fathers receive so little preparation for this role. Most learn to parent "on the job," an inefficient and often discouraging process. As we have seen in earlier chapters, when trying to gain compliance from their children, many parents resort too quickly to punitive, coercive methods when positive, supportive techniques would be more effective.

Although most parents manage to get the job done, those referred to as **high-risk** or **multiproblem parents** struggle to provide even minimal care for their offspring. We know little about multiproblem fathers. Multiproblem mothers have "inadequate social skills, little social support, and emotional problems (such as depression), conditions that interfere with their ability to focus on the infant or to assimilate new information" (Booth, Mitchell, Barnard, & Spieker, 1989, p. 403).

Whereas **parent education programs** such as Parent Effectiveness Training (Gordon, 1970) help parents prevent the development of behavior problems, **parent training programs** help parents resolve existing troublesome behaviors. "Both the parent training and parent education approaches are aimed at assisting parents at helping their children by providing the parents with practical information by teaching them principles of learning and behavior modification, building parenting and communication skills, and the development of problem-solving skills" (Schaefer & Briesmeister, 1989, p. 2).

Although most parents benefit from parent training, they differ in the particular deficits

TABLE 14.1 Key Components of Parent Training Programs

Educate parents about prenatal care, immunizations, and day care.

Teach parents how to communicate with their children.

Teach a variety of positive discipline strategies.

Discourage punitive and coercive parenting.

Teach parents how to recognize the causes of misbehavior.

Allow parents to share their experiences with other parents.

they bring to the parenting role. In order to be successful, training programs have to identify and then remediate specific skill deficits. Parents must learn how to validate feelings, motivate compliance, be consistent, and set limits on behavior, as well as identify faulty parental perspectives, such as blaming children for their misbehaviors (Booth, Mitchell, Barnard, & Spieker, 1989; Frankel & Simmons, 1992; Stern, 1996).

One of the best ways to help children is to support their families. Almost any serious family problem, such as chronic illness, unemployment, divorce, or drug abuse, will directly or indirectly affect its children. Fortunately, family-support, education, and training programs are becoming more available (Cunningham, Bremner, & Boyle, 1995; Williams, 1989). Centers have been established across the country that provide needed support to parents and children. Most programs provide assistance in such areas as prenatal care, immunizations, parenting skills, and day care (Baker, Landen, & Kashima, 1991; Benasich, Brooks-Gunn, & Clewell, 1992; Cowan & Cowan, 1995; Williams, 1989).

Cowan and Cowan (1995) recommend that parent education programs help new parents adjust to the transition to parenthood (discussed in Chapter 2). Even couples who are

Parent training programs that change caregiver attitudes about child rearing during the first years of life appear to be most effective.

considering starting a family can benefit from the opportunity to discuss child rearing and parenting issues. Low-risk couples, the researchers suggest, might benefit from participation in couples groups led by mental health professionals. High-risk parents, including those who are young, troubled, or poor and those with disabled children, would benefit from more comprehensive interventions that include hospital and home visits that begin during pregnancy and continue through the early months or years of parenthood.

Programs that change the family environment and caregiver attitudes about childrearing during the first years of life are most promising (Benasich, et al., 1992; van den Boom, 1995). Family-support programs usually are open to everyone who applies, but they often are located in poor neighborhoods (Lewin, 1988b). Research supports the efficacy of well-run programs in reducing child abuse, academic problems, delinquency, and teenage pregnancies (Schaefer & Briesmeister, 1989).

A model parent training program instituted in Missouri in 1982, the New Parents as Teachers Project, began by studying parents who displayed impressive parenting skills. They found that these parents provided their infants and toddlers with easy access to interesting environments that they could explore. Rather than restrict their movements, parents of competent children redesigned their homes to encourage their youngsters to have interesting, educational experiences (Meyerhoff & White, 1986).

Between 1982 and 1985, 380 families located in four very different socioeconomic communities in Missouri received a variety of services. The cost of $800 per family each year was publicly and privately funded. Groups of 10 to 20 parents met with parent educators once a month for $1\frac{1}{2}$ hour sessions. Assistance began during the last three months of pregnancy and continued until the child's third birthday. Fathers, grandparents, and even babysitters were encouraged to attend.

Trainers visited each home once a month. Children were evaluated for social, language, and intellectual progress. If problems were identified, prompt assistance was offered. Parents watched videotaped demonstrations of typical behavior of infants and toddlers.

Age-appropriate activities were suggested and books, magazines, and advice were available (Meyerhoff & White, 1986).

Parents were encouraged to speak to their children. They learned how to use simple language and respond to the child's current motivational state. Parents were taught how to set realistic but firm limits and how to enforce them. They were encouraged to display unconditional love and to use discipline techniques appropriate to a child's level of development. These were the patterns identified in the rearing techniques of the parents of competent children. An evaluation team reported, "Children of parents participating in the New Parents as Teachers Project consistently scored significantly higher on all measures of intelligence, achievement, auditory comprehension, verbal ability, and language ability than did comparison children" (Maeroff, 1985).

The Addison County Parent-Child Center in Middlebury, Vermont, trains and pays 12 parents for 6-month periods. The center seeks out new parents who are at high risk for raising children with developmental problems. Such parents often are young high school dropouts. They are socially isolated, many have drug problems, and most were abused as children. This multifaceted program provides assertiveness training, practical experience with child care, home visitation, and basic parenting skills.

The director, Susan Harding, explained that "We have some clear rules. It's not O.K. to hit children or yell at them or call them names. A lot of young women come here with no idea that there is an alternative to hitting children" (S. Johnson, 1988a). The Vermont Department of Health compiled data indicating that Addison County had the lowest teenage pregnancy rate in the state. A federal report indicated a drop in welfare dependency in the families served by the center. Incidents of child abuse were significantly reduced and employment significantly increased in the county.

The best parent-training programs do not present parents with rigid sets of procedures but rather encourage them to provide their own solutions to everyday problems. Parents need to learn how to recognize the causes of misbehavior and take corrective actions. Programs that allow groups of parents to share their observations and experiences help them to see that their child-rearing problems are not unique.

Parent-training programs have helped parents become more confident in their parenting abilities (Pehrson & Robinson, 1990; Seitz & Apfel, 1994). Parents need to understand that their discipline strategy should be guided partly by their child's age and temperament. The crucial lesson for parents is that to change their children's behavior, the parents must first change their own behaviors (Jaffe, 1990).

SELECTED TOPIC #2 HAVING IT ALL?: DUAL-CAREER PARENTING

Is it possible for two adults to have a strong, supportive relationship, pursue satisfying full-time careers, and still be good parents? Absolutely, if they have the patience of a saint, boundless energy, team spirit, a sense of humor, and plenty of money. It also helps if they have a full-time, preferably live-in sitter-housekeeper (or at least high-quality day care). In other words, it is possible, but far from easy to achieve. I think most of the 13 million two-worker families with children would agree.

Maternal Employment

Study Question *Does having a full-time job and a family enhance a woman's emotional well-being or threaten it?*

"I knew I would never stay home full-time with a child. There are times I have regretted it. I've missed a lot. Sometimes I think, 'Wouldn't this be great to spend more time and be here?' But you can't have both" (mother of 5-year-old boy) (quoted by Richardson, 1992). "I guess something happened from the time that I was pregnant and he was born that changed my thinking. I couldn't leave this baby full-time. It was too important to me. I couldn't leave him with a stranger" (mother of 3-year-old boy) (quoted by Richardson, 1992).

Two women who have made two different choices regarding employment, one succumbing to the tug of the marketplace, the other to the tug of a dependent child. United States Bureau of Labor statistics indicate that about three-quarters of mothers of school-age children and sixty percent of the mothers of infants and pre-school children are employed. Not all employed women work because they want to. Today, many mothers seek employment out of financial necessity (Volling & Belsky, 1993). Single mothers, those living in poverty, and those having husbands who earn less than $15,000 a year, comprise two-thirds of all working mothers.

Some contend that most employed mothers would continue to work even if they were not financially pressed (Cotton, Antill, & Cunningham, 1989; DeChick, 1988; Hiller & Dyehouse, 1987). For married women, being employed is a form of protection—it lessens the financial blows that are associated with divorce or the death of one's spouse. This is a realistic consideration in a society with close to a 50 percent divorce rate. Women who temporarily leave employment for family reasons worry that they will never match the earning power of those who remain at work. They also are seen by some employers as less committed to their jobs (Rowland, 1992).

Working women fear that even occasional absenteeism due to pregnancy, birth, or child care will bring disapproval from unsympathetic employers. There is evidence that this may be as true for professional women as it is for women who work at low-paying jobs (Painton, 1993). On the positive side, some male employers whose wives never worked are becoming more supportive of working mothers as they see their daughters struggle to manage job and family.

Many women report that they work because they no longer find the housewife-mother role to be as fulfilling as their employment (Volling & Belsky, 1993). Although some working mothers have higher aspirations than others, almost all have come to expect paid employment as part of their lives. "They have developed committed, permanent ties to the workplace that resemble the pattern once reserved for men alone. When they have had children, they have tried to combine careers with motherhood. In short, they have rejected the domestic path that places children, family, and home above all else" (Gerson, 1986, p. 32).

Some women may choose a domestic lifestyle because of their unsatisfactory work experiences, or they may reject the double burden of career and home responsibilities. Of course, many women affirm that the opportunity to stay home with their children more than compensates for financial and career sacrifices. Ironically, some nonworking mothers view working mothers as selfish despite the sacrifices that almost always accompany maternal employment. Penelope Leach, for example, author of Children First (Knopf) and other child care books, condemns substitute care on the grounds that children need the individual attention of a devoted mother or father.

Are dual-employed parents less committed to raising their children? Do they raise their children differently than parents in preceding generations? Greenberger and Goldberg (1989) questioned 94 employed mothers and 104 employed fathers about how they raise

TABLE 14.2 Issues Faced by Working Mothers

Balancing demands of employment with family life

Division of labor with partner

Little time for social life or leisure time activities

Feelings of conflict and guilt about dual role

and their perceptions of their children. Each parent questioned had an employed spouse and a young child. According to the parents' responses, their employment did not detract from their commitment to child rearing. Nevertheless, mothers who work part-time or not at all are more likely to breastfeed (and for longer durations) than women who work full-time (Lindberg, 1996).

The cost to parents of the dual-career lifestyle is considerable (Warren & Johnson, 1995). Hertz (1987) interviewed successful dual-career couples. Most couples depended upon other, less privileged individuals, usually women, to provide the housekeeping and child-care services that they were too busy to perform themselves. After satisfying their professional responsibilities, most had little time left for their partners. Their decisions about having children were based primarily on professional considerations. Childrearing was seen as a professional handicap. Many of these women returned to work within months of childbirth.

Even when working parents share the domestic responsibilities or hire housekeeping help, they have minimal leisure time and limited social lives. This outcome is accepted as part of the compromise they made for the economic and professional satisfactions of their dual-career lifestyle (Apostal & Helland, 1993; Williams, 1987).

Partners of employed women often express more child-related frustrations. Many husbands are not entirely comfortable in their role

of house-father, although they still support their wife's employment (Russell & Radin, 1983). Husbands in dual-earner families help out more than husbands in single-earner families, especially when their wives work full-time. Their increased involvement provides children (especially boys) with a positive role model and lessens mothers' role strain. Some fathers feel good about their assistance, but pressure on fathers to help out sometimes leads to decreased marital intimacy and increased marital discord (Hoffman, 1989; Olds, Schwartz, Eisen, Betcher, et al., 1993).

The findings are inconsistent regarding whether men and women have different expectations about how household labor should be shared (Benin & Agostinelli, 1988; Sanchez & Kane, 1996) or whether they are in agreement about who should do what in the home (Apostal & Helland, 1993; Greenstein, 1996). Equitable division of family labor comes more naturally to couples who are latecomers to parenting. As noted in Chapter 2, those who delay marriage and childbearing usually are better prepared emotionally and financially to accept the responsibilities and chores of family life. Latecomer fathers become more attached to the father role and latecomer mothers expect and elicit more involvement from their partners (Coltrane, 1990).

Working mothers spend more time than working fathers providing child care and performing household chores. The more hours that mothers spend at their jobs, the less time that they have for housework, but the level of child care doesn't seem to be related to time spent at work (Bryant & Zick, 1996). Women who work long hours typically have helpful husbands and children. Yet they generally spend as much time in child care as mothers who work part-time. Working mothers place a higher priority on their children than on housework. Some chores apparently never get done (Almeida, Maggs, & Galambos, 1993).

Parental division of labor in dual-employed

grams receive little more than custodial care, or "babysitting"

Parents who must pay for day care generally have three options: leaving their child in a sitter's home (**family day care**), having a sitter come to their home (**in-home care**), or leaving their child in a **day-care center** (Johansen, Leibowitz, & Waite, 1996). There are over 60,000 licensed day-care centers in the United States, and over 161,000 licensed day-care homes. Family day care usually is less expensive than in-home care and it involves smaller groups of children than day-care centers. Most children, however, are placed in unlicensed (though legal) family day-care homes where the staff and facilities are not regulated. Even licensing may mean little in states where an application and fee are sufficient to register a family day-care home. Licensing reflects health and safety standards, not quality of care. It is important that parents interview sitters carefully. In-home sites should be visited to ensure that they are safe and well-equipped with appropriate toys and materials. Parents must have the right to visit at any time and should check references carefully (Bogat & Gensheimer, 1986; Kutner, 1988p; Rubenstein, 1993).

Parents considering enrolling their children in a day-care center should start looking early, since some centers have long waiting lists. Kutner suggests that if the center director does not invite parents to visit the center or if they do not feel welcome when visiting, they should look elsewhere. Parents should visit for at least one hour, preferably in the morning, when the children are most active. Parents should observe whether the facilities are safe (capped electrical outlets, bars on first floor windows, gates at stairways, fire exits). They should notice whether the rooms are nicely decorated for children. The most important factors are the training, qualifications, sensitivity, and responsiveness of the caregivers.

Parents also should ask many questions about the quality of care. What is the staff-to-

TABLE 14.3 Characteristics of High Quality Day Care

Licensed or registered by the state
Safe, clean, nicely decorated environment
Trained staff who are warm and responsive
Low staff-to-child ratio
Low-pressure activities that stimulate curiosity and creativity
Responsive to individual needs of each child
Encourages parents to observe or participate in activities

child ratio? What precautions are taken to prevent sexual abuse? Parents gain important information by watching how the staff handle conflicts among the children, episodes of crying, or toileting accidents. Parents should consider interviewing the parents of children who have previously attended the center (Kutner, 1988p).

Bogat and Gensheimer (1986) administered structured telephone interviews to a predominantly white group of 167 married females in their late twenties who were employed part- or full-time and who had called a day care referral agency for information. They found that these parents valued most of the positive qualities of day-care facilities cited above. Sadly, most parents did not follow through in their actual search behaviors to locate the optimal facility. Even though parents can only evaluate facilities through direct observation, these parents "rarely acted in ways to evaluate these characteristics within facilities and to make discriminative comparisons between alternatives. During their child care search, these parents called an average of three providers, over one-fourth did not visit any facilities, and of those who did visit, most only visited one facility... This points to a striking discrepancy between the attitudes of parents regarding quality day care and the behavior they use to secure such care" (p. 167).

Bradbard and her colleagues report that parents depend mainly on friend's recommendations when choosing a day-care center (Bradbard, Brown, Endsley, & Readdick, 1994). Their most important considerations in selecting a particular center were health and safety, caregiver quality, and the child's social and educational development. Cost was the least important consideration.

Researchers have attempted to isolate those factors in the day-care environment that predict positive social and cognitive outcomes. Phillips, McCartney, and Scarr (1987) studied 166 children attending representative child-care centers of varying quality. They found that the overall quality of the center, the caregiver-child verbal interactions, and the director's experience were good predictors of the children's social development in child care.

C. Peterson and R. Peterson (1986) compared groups of 3- to 5- year-old children from high- and low-quality day-care centers to same-aged children receiving home care. They observed the children interacting with their mothers in a laboratory setting. The children attending the low-quality facilities were less likely to follow task instructions and were less verbal. The home-care children were the most verbal. Children attending high-quality centers were intermediate on this measure. The researchers concluded that children attending day-care facilities learn ways of behaving that guide their interactions with their mothers. We need better understanding of how day care and family care exert their joint influence on children and how they influence each other (Zaslow, 1991). This is particularly important because children from stressed families typically receive the lowest-quality day care.

Day Care for Infants

Half of the mothers of children 12 months or younger are working. Researchers, who generally accept the benefits of high-quality child care for older children, are debating the possible long-term effects of day care on young infants. Several investigators report less secure attachment in infants who receive extensive nonmaternal care during their first year of life (e.g., Lamb, Sternberg, & Prodromidis, 1992).

Belsky and Rovine (1988) found evidence of less-secure attachment in infants who were placed in day care during their first year of life. Their research revealed that 12- and 13-month-old infants exposed to 20 or more hours of day care a week exhibited more avoidance when reuniting with their mothers in the Strange Situation test than children with less than 20 hours of day care a week. They also were more likely to be classified as insecurely attached. Sons receiving more than 20 hours a week of nonmaternal care were more likely to be insecurely attached to both parents. Boys appear to be more vulnerable than girls to psychosocial stress.

Some studies have found that children who as infants had been in day care may be more aggressive with their peers and less compliant to their parents' instructions. Other studies have not confirmed these findings. The age of entry into care, the amount of time spent in day care, and the quality of care appear to be mediating factors (Field, 1991a; Howes, 1990).

In a longitudinal study of Swedish children, Andersson (1989) observed that children entering day care before their first birthday "were generally rated more favorably and performed better than children with late entrance or home care" cognitively and in their emotional development (p. 857). Andersson notes that Swedish day care is of exceptionally high quality.

We should not hastily conclude that infant day care is harmful (McGurk, Caplan, Hennessy, & Moss, 1993). In Belsky and Rovine's study, a majority of the infants exposed to extensive day care displayed secure attachments to their mothers. Half of the sons with extensive day care experiences showed secure relationships with their fathers and almost two-thirds of the boys receiving extensive nonmaternal care showed secure attachment to at least one parent. Characteristics of the mother, of the child, the quality of the day-care arrangements, and the father's involvement all appear to mediate the effects of extensive nonmaternal care on infants (Azar, 1996). Early-entry children in low-quality care seem to be the most vulnerable to social and academic problems (Howes, 1990).

One potential hazard of day care, particularly for infants and toddlers in diapers, is increased risk of infection for the children and, eventually, their families (Feagans & Manlove, 1994). "Centers that care for children still in diapers account for the vast majority of day care related illnesses which are often easily transmitted through saliva or stool. Toddlers tend to crowd together, making it easy to spread infections; their hygiene usually leaves much to be desired; their immune systems are not fully developed, and they have not yet had the opportunity to acquire immunity to common infectious organisms" (Brody, 1986a).

Evaluation

Most studies find few if any differences in parent-child relationships for infants in high-quality day care and infants cared for by their parents at home (Lamb & Sternberg, 1990). Most child care experts contend that high-quality, parental home care is preferable to day care. Not all parents have this option; affordable high-quality day care becomes a necessity.

In terms of children's social and intellectual development, high-quality day care is preferable to ordinary or low-quality parental home care (Burchinal, Roberts, Nabors, & Bryant, 1996; Clarke-Stewart, Gruber, & Fitzgerald, 1994). Some parents who stay home with their children spend little time with them or have too many poor-quality in-

teractions. Ironically, high-quality day care can compensate to some extent for low quality home care (Caughy, DiPietro, & Strobino, 1994; Clarke-Stewart, 1991; Clarke-Stewart et al., 1994; Zaslow, 1991). The two main points are that quality of care is more important than its setting and that family influence is greater than child care effects.

SELECTED TOPIC # 4 CHILDREN IN SELF CARE

Study Question *When is a child old enough to remain home alone?*

Every now and then we read or hear about parents who abandon their young children for days or weeks, sometimes with teenage babysitters and sometimes alone or with siblings. Such abandonment is a clear example of child endangerment and is illegal. Yet, questions remain about what constitutes adequate child supervision and about how old children need to be before they are left home alone (Chira, 1994b).

Rodman, Pratto, and Nelson (1988) suggest the following definition of **self-care**: "A self-care child is one between the ages of approximately 6 and 13 years who spends time at home alone or with a younger sibling on a periodic basis" (p. 294). Self-care children spend their before-school, after-school, or evening hours alone at home without adult supervision. Many spend their self-care time away from home, in a friend's home or in a public place. Some are responsible for the after-school care of their younger siblings. Many do chores; some prepare dinner for themselves or their families (Landers, 1988f).

About a quarter of a million 5- to 7-year-olds are in self- or sibling-care after school (Cain & Hofferth, 1989). The United States Department of Labor and the National P.T.A. estimate that 5 to 7 million children, a fourth of the elemen-

It seems likely that some children benefit, some children suffer, and some children are not affected by the lack of adult supervision.

tary school population, are left alone at least two hours a day. Cain and Hofferth (1989) report that 2½ million children either care for themselves after school or are cared for by a child (usually a sibling) under age 14.

Very little is known about child care arrangements in dual-employment families over the summer months when children are not in school (Crouter & McHale, 1993b). Families that cannot afford full-time day or overnight camp may provide piecemeal arrangements for children, including lots of TV watching and time at the park or at the homes of friends or relatives.

Cain and Hofferth (1989) and a 1987 Federal study by the National Institute of Child Health and Human Development concluded that most so-called "latch-key" children are white and middle class, 10 to 13 years old, and live in suburban or rural communities. Others contend that self-care children are not predominantly white or middle class (Collins, 1987b).

Another issue is whether adolescents need after-school supervision (Steinberg, 1988b). Many teenagers play the role of parent-surrogate. Others are susceptible to peer pressure and get into trouble. Studies of inner-city children report that delinquent males and females usually have inadequate supervision after school (Galambos & Dixon, 1984).

How do self-care children feel about their time spent alone? Does a lack of supervision increase the risk of accidents or fire? Do these children feel isolated? Or do they benefit by becoming more independent, self-reliant, and responsible? The answers to these questions depend upon many factors. These include children's attitudes about being alone or caring for siblings, available activities, their age, sex, socioeconomic level, neighborhood, the length of time spent alone each day, whether the arrangement is voluntary or not, and the quality of the parent-child relationship (Galambos & Dixon, 1984; Lovko & Ullman, 1989).

Effects on Children

The research addressing self-care children is inconclusive. Family circumstances are so varied. A Louis Harris survey of 2,000 parents and 1,000 teachers conducted in 1987 reported that 51 percent of the teachers polled cited lack of after-school supervision as the major cause of children's difficulty in school. Forty-one percent of the parents said their children were often alone between the end of school and 5:30 P.M. Most parents said they would enroll their children in after-school programs if such programs were available.

Rodman, Pratto, and Nelson (1985) and Howie (1996) found no significant differences in self-esteem or social competence between matched samples of self-care and adult-care children. Galambos and Maggs (1991) compared sixth-graders in self-care with those in adult care. They found no differences between the two groups in how the children perceived themselves, although self-care girls who were very removed from adult supervision reported more problem behaviors.

Vandell and Corasaniti (1988) found no difference between self-care third-graders and those returning home on a variety of academic, self-esteem, and interpersonal variables. In fact, self-care children did better than children in after-school day care programs on most measures. Many third graders attending the after-school program (designed for preschoolers) reported feeling embarrassed that they had to attend day care.

Long and Long (cited by Landers, 1986b) surveyed 362 parochial school children in Washington, D.C. Self-care children were more likely to suffer from mild depression, engage in solitary drinking, and be sexually active. These researchers suggest that the presumed benefits of self-care, such as increased independence and responsibility, could be achieved with less risk.

All investigators in this area agree that

TABLE 14.4 Tips for Parents of Children in Self-Care

Only leave child alone or with siblings if child is comfortable with situation

Make sure child is responsible enough to follow instructions and rules

Be available to child by telephone

Provide child with phone numbers of adults to consult in emergency

Have clear-cut rules about conduct

Teach children self-help and safety skills

When parents arrive home, converse with child about the day's events

much more research is needed. It is safe to assume that some children suffer, that some children benefit, and that some children are not affected by the lack of adult supervision (Freiberg, 1996). Given the scope of the phenomenon, it is important to identify the factors that predict these outcomes.

Alternatives to Self-Care

Many parents report that they would have greater peace of mind regarding their children's safety and well-being (and experience fewer interruptions at work), if their children were receiving competent adult supervision. Most self-care children seem to prefer spending their before- or after-school hours with other people, rather than with a TV set. Having parents be "psychologically" available via phone calls appears to alleviate feelings of isolation or loneliness. There are hundreds of Phone Friend programs available nationwide allowing children to communicate with adults who can support them through a minor crisis.

In Virginia, the Family Day Care Check-In Program for 10 to 14-year-olds provides children with a neighbor who is designated as their check-in person. After checking-in, children can go out and play or stay in the neighbor's home. Other communities have telephone "hot lines" that self-care children can call when lonely, bored, or afraid (Landers, 1986b). Teenagers occasionally call with school- or sex-related problems. Other programs have volunteers who call children at home to check up and chat briefly.

In the absence of such programs, there is still much that parents can do to prepare their children for the self-care experience (see Table 14.4). Cain and Hofferth (1989) suggest that parents decide whether to allow their children to remain unsupervised on the basis of their children's maturity and independence. It seems unwise to leave any child under the age of 10 home alone or to use babysitters who are younger than 15-years-old. Children should only be left alone if they are comfortable with the arrangement and know what to do in emergency situations. Parents should know where their children are at all times and have clear-cut rules about their conduct. They should maintain telephone contact and teach their children self-help and safety skills, including cooking and how to use a phone cautiously (Peterson, 1989). It is also important that when they arrive home, parents convey interest about the child's day.

SUMMARY

1. Families require considerable support from the larger community. Parent support and training programs are becoming more available. Parent education programs help parents prevent the development of child behavior problems. Parent training programs help parents resolve existing problems by teaching them how to communicate with their children and understand and address children's misbehavior.

2. A majority of mothers work part-time or full-time. Some work because they want to and some work because they have to. Even when working parents share domestic responsibilities, there are other stresses and strains on the family unit. Many working mothers who have infants at home experience guilt, conflict, and separation anxiety regarding their dual roles.

3. When both parents work, other caregivers must be found. High-quality home care usually is the optimal arrangement; high-quality day care is preferred to low-quality home care. Many children of school age care for themselves or for younger siblings after school when their parents are working. It is not yet clear how self-care, day care, and other arrangements affect young children's development. We do know that the quality of care is more important than its setting.

GLOSSARY

day-care center   A community setting with facilities and a trained staff that provides child care

family day care   Parents leave their children in a sitter's home

high-risk (multiproblem) parents   Parents who are ill-prepared to provide competent child care due to emotional problems and minimal social support

in-home day care   Having a babysitter come to a child's home

parent education programs   Programs that help parents prevent child behavior problems from developing

parent training programs   Programs that help parents resolve existing behavior problems

children in self-care   Children between the ages of 6 and 13 years who spend time at home alone or with a younger sibling on a regular basis

THOUGHT QUESTIONS

1. Should all parents be compelled to receive formal instruction in parenting?

2. Do preschool children necessarily suffer when both of their parents work? Explain.

3. Should parents have children if they cannot stay home to raise them?

4. What personal qualities of children should parents take into account before allowing a child to remain home unsupervised?

ple who had attended a parenting workshop of mine came in with various complaints about their 3-year-old son. They portrayed him as a difficult only child who was quiet and withdrawn with unfamiliar people. He behaved very aggressively with his parents and their full-time housekeeper. He had temper tantrums, was defiant, did what he wanted to do, and occasionally hit them. He would not let his parents speak to each other in his presence. They could only speak to him. They had to wait until he was asleep to communicate with each other. The parents were particularly eager to toilet train him and dispense with diapers. The housekeeper was resisting such training because she would have to clean up his "accidents."

In describing their problems with their son, both parents seemed somewhat bewildered by their ineffective parenting. The mother believed that it was a mistake for them to have a child, given their personal inadequacies. She expressed intense guilt about her poor mothering. She very much resented her husband's criticisms of her yelling and of her displays of anger toward him and their son.

Over the first few sessions, it became clear that their marriage was not succeeding. The wife described her husband as totally unsupportive, a liar, undependable, unambitious, and antisocial. He characterized her as loud, occasionally physically abusive, very negative, and critical; and he felt unappreciated. Both were overweight and implied that their partner was partly responsible. Both reported coming from dysfunctional families that encouraged extreme dependency in both of them.

Despite their problems, they felt that they were "lucky" to find each other; they felt that no one else would want them. Most of their conflict centered around their handling of their son's misbehavior. In a typical situation, the child would behave defiantly. The mother

would threaten and yell at him. The father would then "protect" the child from the mother by yelling at her for yelling at the boy. No wonder the 3-year-old didn't want them to speak to each other!

In family systems terms, the father was overly engaged in his son's life, and the mother was disengaged from both her husband and son. The father's closeness with his son was at the expense of his closeness to his wife. The mother felt left out and actually threatened to leave several times. The live-in housekeeper was a very powerful figure in this family. Both parents lacked the assertiveness to guide the caregiving behaviors of their employee ("What would she think?" or "She would never agree to that").

As marital therapy progressed, both learned how to support each other's parenting efforts. They realized that their son would benefit more from a "unified parental front" than from the divide-and-conquer strategy he was learning. They learned how to avoid conflict by using effective communication and problem-solving skills. They discussed effective ways of handling their son's misbehavior. It was also important that they learn to treat each other well and spend time with each other away from their son. The main point is that their son's problems were rooted in their dysfunctional relationship.

Evaluation

Family systems theory is a powerful model because it views conflict in terms of family relationships rather than as individual maladjustment. It treats the family system rather than its individual members. A major problem confronting this model is the enormous complexity of the family system, particularly when several generations are included in the analysis. (see Figure A.1)

FREUD'S PSYCHODYNAMIC MODEL

It would be difficult to exaggerate the contributions of Sigmund Freud (1856–1939) to our understanding of human personality and development. In so many different areas of human functioning, Freud boldly went where no man or woman had gone before. Freud was trained as a physician in Vienna in the late nineteenth century. Based on his analysis of himself and many of his "neurotic" patients, Freud originated a very biological theory of human personality and psychopathology. His influential theory emphasizes our animal nature and, therefore, our primitive, irrational impulses.

Because of the radical nature of many of his ideas, particularly about children's sexuality, Freud's views were ridiculed in Europe. In the United States, the more open-minded people of the 1920s considered his views with interest. From a contemporary perspective, Freud's interpretational methods and some of his conclusions are flawed. However, by investigating such topics as sexuality, dreams, conflict, and unconscious motivation, Freud stimulated considerable interest and research in these areas and furthered our understanding of them.

We will concentrate on those aspects of Freudian theory that contribute to our understanding of children. In essence, Freud contended that a child's unconscious conflicts and defenses reflect child-parent interactions. Parents contribute immensely to children's psychological makeup, according to Freud, by gratifying or frustrating their needs and desires (Christenson, 1983).

The Id: Our "Animal" Nature

Philosophers and theologians have had difficulty coming to terms with our irrational nature. Freud, like Charles Darwin, appreciated or, at least, accepted our animal nature because, well, we *are* animals! An objective view of human history must encompass not only our wondrous achievements but also our species' history of war, brutality, intolerance, and oppression. After reading a daily newspaper, defending rationality and altruism as definitive human traits becomes difficult. It sometimes seems as though there are two vastly different sides to our human nature—our rational intellect and our irrational desires—both competing for control of our personality and behavior.

Freud portrayed our impulsive, demanding nature as the **id**. This primitive basis of personality is an irrational, survival-oriented "energy source." The id supplies all motivational energy and is the driving force of personality. It is the biological component of our personality, one that we share with other species. Throughout life, it remains the embodiment of our psychological needs, drives, impulses, urges, and desires.

The id operates according to the **pleasure principle**, which Freud considered to be the "primary process" of human motivation. Anything that provides gratification is good, and anything that is painful or annoying is bad. When an infant's needs or appetites are not satisfied, it becomes irritable and demands immediate gratification.

Is Freud telling us that humans (and other animals) are basically selfish, irrational, and driven by primitive impulses? In effect, he is.

We see this aspect of human nature most clearly in the infant's impulsive, demanding temperament. The id consists of many powerful drives, including sexual and aggressive impulses. Freud contended that these two drives become frustrated when society attempts to place constraints on their expression (e.g., "Keep your hands to yourself").

Enlightened Self-Interest: The Ego

Obviously, human personality is not all id; if it were, society as we know it could not exist. The **ego**, representing enlightened self-interest, gradually emerges from the id during the school years, using logical and realistic thinking to solve practical problems. However, its primary function is to satisfy the id's urges and desires. The ego obeys the **reality principle**, which Freud considered the "secondary process" of human motivation. Unlike the id, the ego considers the consequences of its actions. The ego, in effect, admonishes the id, "I know what you want, and I'll get it for you, but we have to do it my way."

In other words, the ego serves the id by seeking approved means of satisfying needs and desires. Marriage, for example, becomes the socially sanctioned convention for satisfying our sexual desires. Sports and humor may provide an acceptable outlet for aggressive impulses. Those who impulsively satisfy their desires at another person's expense risk serious consequences that the ego tries to avoid. The ego "understands" that there is little gratification to be obtained if one becomes a social outcast. We can see that the ego has its hands full dealing with the irrational, impulsive id and its primitive pleasure principle. All it needs now is a third component of personality to deal with.

Guilt and Shame: The Superego

Yes, you guessed it. Along comes the **superego**, the internalization of our parent's standards of acceptable behavior. "The part which is later taken on by the superego is played to begin with by an external power, by parental authority. Parental influence governs the child by offering proofs of love and by threatening punishments which are signs to the child of loss of love and are bound to be feared on their own account . . . subsequently the superego takes the place of the parental agency and observes, directs, and threatens the ego in exactly the same way as earlier the parents did with the child" (Freud, 1933/1965, p. 62).

The superego, then, is essentially a built-in parent/judge that attempts to guide our conduct through guilt and shame. Because morality is relative (people often disagree about what is right and wrong), the superego, like the id, is said to be irrational. (The term "irrational" is not derogatory. It simply implies that reason or logic are not necessarily involved in the "judgments" of the id and superego). As you may have assumed, the id and the superego are in perpetual conflict, and yes, the ego must mediate between them to arrive at an acceptable compromise. Hence, Freud is suggesting a conflict model of human personality that is brilliantly illustrated by Shakespeare's play *Hamlet*.

Unconscious Motivation

In addition, these forces usually operate outside of our awareness. To Freud, the conscious mind is a tiny part of the psyche because it consists only of material in our immediate awareness. The preconscious mind contains our normal, everyday thoughts, feelings, and memories when they are not in consciousness. The unconscious, however, is the enormous repository of repressed urges, desires, wishes, needs, and fantasies. Why are they repressed? Because, according to Freud, they are threatening to us (or at least to "society"). If we were aware of them, they would elicit considerable discomfort.

For example, Freud observed that infants

TABLE A.1   Erikson's Eight Stages of Psychosocial Development

Phases of the life cycle

	1	2	3	4	5	6	7	8
Late adulthood								Integrity vs. despair
Middle adulthood							Generativity vs. stagnation	
Young adulthood						Intimacy vs. isolation		
Adolescence					Identify vs. identify confusion			
Middle and late childhood				Industry vs. inferiority				
Early childhood			Initiative vs. guilt					
Toddlerhood		Autonomy vs. shame, doubt						
Infancy	Trust vs. mistrust							

From John W. Santrock, *Life-Span Development*, 3d ed. Copyright © 1989 Wm. C. Brown Publishers, Dubuque, Iowa. All Rights Reserved. Reprinted by permission.

quate, insensitive parenting promotes the negative outcomes of mistrust, shame, guilt, and inferiority. Nurturant, supportive parenting encourages the positive outcomes of trust, autonomy, achievement, and self-esteem.

Erikson's theory, unlike Freud's, also acknowledges the special challenges of adolescence and adulthood. Each stage of life, from infancy through old age, presents opportunities for growth or stagnation. The nurturance we receive from our parents disposes us to nurture our children. Although Erikson does not present a formal theory of parenting, the implications of his life-cycle theory for parenting are considerable. To a considerable extent, how we evaluate our lives in late adulthood will reflect the satisfaction we have derived from raising our own children.

GLOSSARY

alliances Some family members join forces in opposition to other family members

anal stage Freud's second psychosexual stage; during the toddler years, children derive gratification from bowel movements and by pleasing (or frustrating) their parents during toilet training

autonomy versus shame and doubt Second stage in Erikson's model; will children have pride or shame in their abilities?

basic trust versus mistrust First stage in Erikson's model of development; will an infant trust or mistrust its caregivers?

boundaries Rules or patterns of interaction establishing the physical and emotional barriers within a family and, thereby, regulating family interaction

clear boundaries Patterns of interaction that allow family members to maintain a healthy balance of adaptation and change

defense mechanism Unconscious "strategies" that protect us from anxiety by distorting reality

denial Pretending that a problem does not exist

diffuse boundaries Patterns of interaction that encourage family members to be overly invested in each others' lives

disengage To avoid meaningful contact among family members

ego Freud's term for the part of personality that solves practical life problems

Electra complex Girls' feelings of longing for their father

enmesh To establish a pattern of emotional overinvolvement in families that stifles each family member's emotional development

erogenous zones Parts of the body that are sources of pleasure

exclusions One or more family members are excluded from the family system, for example, the "bad child"

fixation Being "stuck" at a particular stage of development

generativity versus stagnation Erikson's seventh stage; will the middle-aged adult contribute to the next generation or be preoccupied with his/her own needs?

genital stage According to Freud, the last stage of psychosexual development, comprised of heterosexual interest and activity

id Freud's term for the component of personality that is comprised of instinctual urges and desires

identity versus role confusion Erikson's fifth stage; will an adolescent be able to construct a meaningful adult identity or will he/she lack direction?

industry versus inferiority Erikson's fourth stage; will children feel self-assured about their abilities or feel that they do not measure up?

initiative versus guilt Erikson's third stage; can a child take initiative without offending others?

integrity versus despair Erikson's eighth stage; will the older adult look back on life as a valuable experience or will he/she think, "I blew it"?

432

strain and well-being. *Journal of Personality and Social Psychology, 51*(5), 983–992.

Baruch, G.K., & Barnett, R.C. (1986b). Father's participation in family work. *Child Development, 57,* 1210–1223.

Baskett, L.M. (1985). Sibling status effects: Adult expectations. *Developmental Psychology, 21*(3), 441–445.

Bates, J.E., Lounsbury, M.L., & Klein, A. (1976). *Mother-infant interaction in the supermarket.* Unpublished manuscript, Indiana University.

Baumeister, R.F. (1996, Summer). Should schools try to boost self-esteem? *American Educator,* pp. 14–19, 41.

Baumeister, R.F., Smart, L., & Boden, J.M. (1996). Relation of threatened egotism to violence and aggression: The dark side of high self-esteem. *Psychological Review, 103*(1), 5–33.

Baumrind, D. (1966). Effects of authoritative parental control on child behavior. *Child Development, 37,* 887–906.

Baumrind, D. (1967). Child care practices anteceding three patterns of preschool behavior. *Genetic Psychology Monographs, 75,* 43–88.

Baumrind, D. (1968). Authoritarian vs. authoritative parental control. *Adolescence, 3,* 255–272.

Baumrind, D. (1971). Current patterns of parental authority. *Developmental Psychology Monographs, 4*(1, Pt. 2), 1–103.

Baumrind, D. (1975). *Early socialization and the discipline controversy.* Morristown, NJ: General Learning Press.

Baumrind, D. (1978). Reciprocal rights and responsibilities in parent-child relations. *Journal of Social Issues, 34*(2), 179-196.

Baumrind, D. (1987). Developmental perspective on adolescent risk taking in contemporary America. *New Directions in Child Development, 37,* 93–125.

Baumrind, D. (1991). Parenting styles and adolescent development. In J. Brooks-Gunn, R. Lerner, and A.C. Petersen (Eds.). *The encyclopedia of adolescence.* NY: Garland.

Baumrind, D. (1993). The average expectable environment is not good enough: A response to Scarr. *Child Development, 64,* 1299–1317.

Baydar, N., & Brooks-Gunn, J. (1991). Effects of maternal employment and child-care arrangements on preschoolers' cognitive and behavioral outcomes: Evidence from the children of the National Longitudinal Survey of Youth. *Developmental Psychology, 27*(6), 932–945.

Beal, C.R. (1994). *Boys and girls: The development of gender roles.* NY: McGraw-Hill.

Beal, C.R., & Lockhart, M.E. (1989). The effects of proper name and appearance changes on children's reasoning about gender constancy. *International Journal of Behavioral Development, 12*(2), 195–205.

Beaty, L.A. (1995). Effects of paternal absence on male adolescents' peer relations and self-image. *Adolescence, 30*(120), 873–880.

Beck, I.L., & Carpenter, P.A. (1986). Cognitive approaches to understanding reading: Implications for instructional practice. *American Psychologist, 41*(10), 1098–1105.

Becker, W.C. (1964). Consequences of different kinds of parental discipline. In M.L. Hoffman and L.W. Hoffman (Eds.), *Review of child development* (Vol. 1). NY: Sage Foundation.

Becker-Lausen, E., Sanders, B., & Chinsky, J.M. (1995). Mediation of abusive childhood experiences: Depression, dissociation, and negative life outcomes. *American Journal of Orthopsychiatry, 65*(4), 560–573.

Behrman, R.E. (1992). *Nelson textbook of pediatrics* (13th ed.). Philadelphia: Saunders.

Bell, R.Q. (1968). A reinterpretation of the direction of effects in socialization. *Psychological Review, 75,* 81–95.

Bell, R.Q. (1979). Parent, child, and reciprocal influences. *American Psychologist, 34,* 821–827.

Bell, R.Q., & Harper, L.V. (1977). *Child effects on adults.* Hillsdale, NJ: Erlbaum.

Bell, R.Q., Weinberg, M.S., & Hammersmith, S.K. (1981). *Sexual preference: Its development in men and women.* Bloomington: Indiana University Press.

Belsky, J. (1981). Early human experience: A family perspective. *Developmental Psychology, 17*(1), 3–23.

Belsky, J. (1984). The determinants of parenting: A process model. *Child Development, 55,* 83–96.

Belsky, J. (1990). Children and marriage. In F.D. Fincham and T.N. Bradbury (Eds.), *The psychology of marriage: Basic issues & applications.* NY: Guilford Press.

Belsky, J. (1993). Etiology of child maltreatment: A developmental-ecological analysis. *Psychological Bulletin, 114*(3), 413–434.

Belsky, J. (1996). Parent, infant, and social-contextual antecedents of father-son attachment security. *Developmental Psychology, 32*(5), 905–913.

Belsky, J., Crnic, K., & Gable, S. (1995). The determinants of coparenting in families with toddler boys: Spousal differences and daily hassles. *Child Development, 66*(3), 629–642.

Belsky, J., Lang, M., & Huston, T.L. (1986). Sex typing and division of labor as determinants of marital change across the transition to parenthood. *Journal of Personality and Social Psychology, 50*(3), 517–522.

Belsky, J., Lerner, R.M., & Spanier, G.B. (1984). *The child in the family.* Reading, MA: Addison- Wesley.

Belsky, J., & Pensky, E. (1988). Marital change across the transition to parenthood. *Marriage and Family Review, 12,* 133–156.

Belsky, J., Rosenberger, K., & Crnic, K. (1995). The origins of attachment security: "Classical" and contextual determinants. In S. Goldberg, R. Muir, and J. Kerr (Eds.). *Attachment theory: Social, developmental, and clinical perspectives*. Hillsdale, NJ: The Analytic Press.

Belsky, J., & Rovine, M.J. (1988). Nonmaternal care in the first year of life and the security of infant-parent attachment. *Child Development*, *59*, 157–167.

Belsky, J., & Rovine, M.J. (1990). Patterns of marital change across the transition to parenthood: Pregnancy to three years postpartum. *Journal of Marriage and the Family*, *52*, 5–20.

Belsky, J.B., & Volling, B.L. (1987). Mothering, fathering, and marital interaction in the family triad during infancy: Exploring family system's processes. In P.W. Berman and F.A. Pedersen (Eds.), *Men's transitions to parenthood: Longitudinal studies of early family experience*. Hillsdale, NJ: Erlbaum.

Belsky, J.B., Youngblade, L., Rovine, M., & Volling, B. (1991). Patterns of marital change and parent-child interaction. *Journal of Marriage and the Family*, *53*, 487–498.

Belsky, J., Woodworth, S., & Crnic, K. (1996). Trouble in the second year: Three questions about family interaction. *Child Development*, *67*, 556–578.

Bem, S.L. (1974). The measurement of psychological androgyny. *Journal of Consulting and Clinical Psychology*, *42*, 155–162.

Bem, S.L. (1981). Gender schema theory: A cognitive account of sex-typing. *Psychological Review*, *88*, 354–364.

Bem, S.L. (1989). Genital knowledge and gender constancy in preschool children. *Child Development*, *60*, 649–662.

Benasich, A.A., & Brooks-Gunn, J. (1996). Maternal attitudes and knowledge of child-rearing: Associations with family and child outcomes. *Child Development*, *67*, 1186–1205.

Benasich, A.A., Brooks-Gunn, J., & Clewell, B.C. (1992). How do mothers benefit from early intervention programs? *Journal of Applied Developmental Psychology*, *13*(3), 311–362.

Bengston, V., & Robertson, J.F. (Eds.). (1985). *Grandparenthood*. Beverly Hills, CA: Sage.

Benin, M.H., & Agostinelli, J. (1988). Husbands' and wives' satisfaction with the division of labor. *Journal of Marriage and the Family*, *50*, 349–361.

Benn, R.K. (1986). Factors promoting secure attachment relationships between employed mothers and their sons. *Child Development*, *57*, 1224–1231.

Bennett, D. (1985, November). Early preschool benefits are few. *APA Monitor*, p. 3.

Benson, M.J., Arditti, J., De Atiles, J.T.R., & Smith, S. (1992). Intergenerational transmission: Attributions in relationships with parents and intimate others. *Journal of Family Issues*, *13*(4), 450–464.

Benson, S. (1981). *Ambiguous ethnicity*. London: Cambridge University Press.

Berger, J. (1996, January 30). Discipline or abuse? Arrest renews a debate. *The New York Times*, pp. A1, B6.

Berk, L.E. (1986, May). Private speech: Learning out loud. *Psychology Today*, pp. 34–42.

Berk, R.A., & Berk, S.F. (1979). *Labor and leisure at home*. Beverly Hills, CA: Sage Publications.

Berlin, I.N., & Critchley, D.L. (1989). The therapeutic use of play for mentally ill children and their parents. In C.E. Schaefer and J.M. Briesmeister (Eds.). *Handbook of parent training*. NY: John Wiley.

Berns, R.M. (1985). *Child, family, community*. NY: Holt, Rinehart, & Winston.

Berns, R.M. (1989). *Child, family, community* (2nd ed.). NY: Holt, Rinehart, & Winston.

Berns, R.M. (1993). *Child, family, community* (3rd ed.). NY: Holt, Rinehart, and Winston.

Bernstein, R. (1988, February 29). Twenty years after the Kerner Report: Three societies, all separate. *The New York Times*.

Berzonsky, M.D. (1987). A preliminary investigation of children's conceptions of life and death. *Merrill-Palmer Quarterly*, *33*(4), 505–513.

Beschner, G. (1985). The problem of adolescent drug abuse: An introduction to intervention strategies. In A.S. Friedman and G. Beschern (Eds.), *Treatment services for adolescent substance abusers* (pp. 1-12). Washington, DC: U.S. Government Printing Office.

Bettelheim, B. (1987). *A good enough parent*. NY: Knopf.

Bierman, K.L., & Furman, W. (1984). The effects of social skills training and peer involvement on the social adjustment of preadolescents. *Child Development*, *55*, 151–162.

Biller, H.B., & Solomon, R.S. (1986). *Child maltreatment and paternal deprivation: A manifesto for research, prevention, and treatment*. Lexington, MA: Lexington Books.

Biringen, Z. (1990). Direct observation of maternal sensitivity and dyadic interactions in the home: Relations to maternal thinking. *Developmental Psychology*, *26*(2), 278–284.

Birnbrauer, J.S. (1994). Should only positive methods be used by professionals who work with children and adolescents? No. In M.A. Mason and E. Gambrill (Eds.). *Debating children's lives: Current controversies on children and adolescents*. Thousand Oaks, CA: Sage.

Bischof, G.P., Stith, S.M., & Whitney, M.L. (1995). Family environments of adolescent sex offenders and other juvenile delinquents. *Adolescence*, *30*(117), 157–170.

(1993). The psychosocial climate of families with suicidal pre-adolescent children. *American Journal of Orthopsychiatry, 63*(1), 142–145.

Campbell, S.B. (1995). Behavior problems in preschool children: A review of recent research. *Journal of Child Psychology & Psychiatry & Allied Disciplines, 36*(1), 113–149.

Campbell, S.B., Cohn, J.F., & Meyers, T. (1995). Depression in first-time mothers: Mother-infant interactions and depression chronicity. *Developmental Psychology, 31*(3), 349–357.

Campos, R.G. (1987). *Soothing pain-elicited distress in infants with swaddling and pacifiers.* Unpublished doctoral dissertation, University of Denver.

Campos, R.G. (1989). Soothing pain-elicited distress in infants with swaddling and pacifiers. *Child Development,* 1989, *60*, 781–792.

Camras, L.A., Oster, H., Campos, J.J., Miyake, K., & Bradshaw, D. (1992). Japanese and American infants' responses to arm restraint. *Developmental Psychology, 28*(4), 578–583.

Camras, L.A., Ribordy, S., Hill, J., Martino, S., Sachs, V., Spaccarelli, S., & Stefani, R. (1990). Maternal facial behavior and the recognition and production of emotional expression by maltreated and nonmaltreated children. *Developmental Psychology, 26*(2), 304–312.

Cantor, C. (1988, March 13). SIDS: We don't know why your baby died. *The New York Times.*

Cantwell, D.P. (1996). Attention deficit disorder: A review of the past 10 years. *Journal of the Academy of Child and Adolescent Psychiatry, 35*(8), 978–987.

Caplan, P.J., (1986, October). Take the blame off mother. *Psychology Today,* pp. 70–71.

Caplan, P.J., & Hall-McCorquodale, I. (1985a). Mother-blaming in major clinical journals. *American Journal of Orthopsychiatry, 55*(3), 345–353.

Caplan, P.J., & Hall-McCorquodale, I. (1985b). The scapegoating of mothers: A call for change. *American Journal of Orthopsychiatry, 55*(4), 610–613.

Cappelleri, J., Eckenrode, J., & Powers, J. (1993). The epidemiology of child abuse: Findings from the Second National Incidence and Prevalence Study of Child Abuse and Neglect. *American Journal of Public Health, 83,* 1622–1624.

Carlson, V., Cicchetti, D., Barnett, D., & Braunwald, K. (1989). Disorganized/disoriented attachment relations in maltreated infants. *Developmental Psychology, 25*(4), 525–531.

Carr, E.G., & Durand, V.M. (1987, November). See me, help me. *Psychology Today,* pp. 62–64.

Carter, B., & McGoldrick, M. (Eds.). (1988). *The changing family life cycle: A framework for family therapy.* (2nd ed.). NY: Gardner Press.

Cashion, B.G. (1982). Female-headed families: Effects on children and clinical implications. *Journal of Marital and Family Therapy, 8*(2), 77–86.

Caspi, A., Elder, G.H., & Bem, D.J. (1988). Moving away from the world: Life-course patterns of shy children. *Developmental Psychology, 24,* 824–831.

Catron, T.F., & Masters, J.C. (1993). Mothers' and childrens' conceptualizations of corporal punishment. *Child Development, 64,* 1815–1828.

Caughy, M.O., DiPietro, J.A., & Strobino, D.M. (1994). Day-care participation as a protective factor in the cognitive development of low-income children. *Child Development, 65*(2), 457–471.

Cavaliere, F. (1995a, July). Society appears more open to gay parenting. *APA Monitor,* p. 51

Cavaliere, F. (1995b, November). How to discuss sex without blushing. *APA Monitor,* p. 38.

Chadez, L.H., & Nurius, P.S. (1987). Stopping bedtime crying: Treating the child and the parents. *Journal of Clinical Child Psychology, 16*(3), 212–217.

Chaffin, R., & Winston, M. (1991). Conceptions of parenthood. *Journal of Applied Social Psychology, 21,* 1726–1757.

Chance, P. (1982, January). Your child's self-esteem. *Parents Magazine.*

Chance, P. (1987a, July). Asian studies. *Psychology Today,* p. 80.

Chance, P. (1987b, May). A touching story. *Psychology Today,* p. 14.

Chao, R.K. (1994). Beyond parental control and authoritarian parenting style: Understanding Chinese parenting through the cultural notion of training. *Child Development, 65,* 1111–1119.

Chao, R.K. (1996). Chinese and European American mothers' beliefs about the role of parenting in children's school success. *Journal of Cross-Cultural Psychology, 27*(4), 403–423.

Chapman, M., Zahn-Waxler, C., Cooperman, G., & Iannotti, R. (1987). Empathy and responsibility in the motivation of children's helping. *Developmental Psychology, 23*(1), 140-145.

Chase-Lansdale, P.L., Brooks-Gunn, J., & Zamsky, E.S. (1994). Young African-American multigenerational families in poverty: Quality of mothering and grandmothering. *Child Development, 65,* 373–393.

Chase-Lansdale, P.L., & Owen, M.T. (1987). Maternal employment in a family context: Effects on infant-mother and infant-father attachments. *Child Development, 58,* 1505–1512.

Chen, C., & Stevenson, H.W. (1989). Homework: A cross-cultural examination. *Child Development, 60,* 551–561.

Chen, C., & Stevenson, H.W. (1995). Motivation and mathematics achievement: A comparative study of Asian-American, Caucasian-American, and East Asian high school students. *Child Development, 66,* 1215–1234.

Cherlin, A.J. (1981). *Marriage, divorce and remarriage.* Cambridge, MA: Harvard University Press.

Cherlin, A.J., & Furstenberg, F., Jr. (1986). *The new American grandparent: A place in the family, a life apart.* NY: Basic Books.

Cherlin, A.J., & Furstenberg, F. (1989, March 19). Divorce doesn't always hurt the kids. *The Washington Post*, p. C1.

Chilamkurti, C., & Milner, J.S. (1993). Perceptions and evaluations of child transgressions and disciplinary techniques in high- and low-risk mothers and their children. *Child Development, 64*, 1801–1814.

Chin, A.(1988). *Children of china.* NY: Knopf.

Chipuer, H.M., Plomin, R., Pedersen, N.L., McClearn, G.E., et al. (1993). Children from divorced and intact homes: Similarities and differences in perceptions of family. *Developmental Psychology, 29*(1), 110–118.

Chira, S. (1994a, May 8). Images of the perfect mother: Put them all together in a multitude of ways. *The New York Times*, p. 26.

Chira, S. (1994b, October 6). Left alone at home: O.K. or a danger? *The New York Times*, pp. C1, C8.

Choi, S. (1993). Mothers' and older siblings' scaffolding of preschool children's pretend play. *Dissertation Abstracts International, 53*(7-A), 2234–2235.

Choi, Y.E., Bempechat, J., & Ginsburg, H.P. (1994). Educational socialization in Korean American children: A longitudinal study. *Journal of Applied Developmental Psychology, 15*(3), 313–318.

Christenson, A. (1983). Intervention. In H.H. Kelley, E. Bersheid, A. Christenson, J.H. Harvey, T.L. Huston, G. Levinger, E. McClintock, L.A. Peplau, and D.R. Peterson, (Eds.). *Close relationships.* NY: Freeman.

Cifrese, L. (1993, March). Fathers and daughters. *Carrier Foundation Medical Education Letter.*

Clarke-Stewart, K. A. (1989a). Infant day care: Maligned or malignant? *American Psychologist, 44*(2), 266–273.

Clarke-Stewart, K.A. (1989b, January). Single-parent families: How bad for the children? *NEA Today*, pp. 60–64.

Clarke-Stewart, K.A. (1991). A home is not a school: The effects of child care on children's development. *Journal of Social Issues, 47*(2), 105–123.

Clarke-Stewart, K.A., Gruber, C.P., & Fitzgerald, L.M. (1994). *Children at home and in day care.* Hillsdale, NJ: Erlbaum.

Claxton-Oldfield, S. (1992). Perception of stepfathers: Disciplinary and affectionate behavior. *Journal of Family Issues, 13*(3), 378–389.

Clay, R.A. (1995a, November). Working mothers: happy or haggard? *APA Monitor*, pp. 1, 37.

Clay, R.A. (1995b, December). Courts reshape image of 'the good mother.' *APA Monitor*, p. 31.

Clay, R.A. (1996a, February). Beating the 'biological clock' with zest. *APA Monitor*, p. 37.

Clay, R.A. (1996b, February). Older men are more involved fathers, studies show. *APA Monitor*, p. 37.

Cleverley, J., & Phillips, D.C. (1986). *Visions of childhood: Influential models from Locke to Spock* (Revised ed.). NY: Teachers College Press.

Clingempeel, W.G., Colyar, J.J., Brand, E., & Hetherington, E.M. (1992). Children's relationships with maternal grandparents: A longitudinal study of family structure and pubertal status effects. *Child Development, 63*, 1404–1422.

Clingempeel, W.G., & Segal, S. (1986). Stepparent-stepchild relationships and the psychological adjustment of children in stepmother and stepfather families. *Child Development, 57*, 474–484.

Cochran, M. (1993). Parenting and personal social networks. In T. Luster and L. Okagaki (Eds.), *Parenting: An ecological perspective.* Hillsdale, NJ: Erlbaum.

Cohen, L.H., Burt, C.E., & Bjorck, J.P. (1987). Life stress and adjustment: Effects of life events experienced by young adolescents and their parents. *Developmental Psychology, 23*(4), 583–592.

Cohen, N.J., Coyne, J., & Duvall, J. (1993). Adopted and biological children in the clinic: Family, parental and child characteristics. *Journal of Child Psychology & Psychiatry & Allied Disciplines, 34*(4), 545–562.

Cohn, D.A. (1990). Child-mother attachment of six-year-olds and social competence at school. *Child Development, 61*, 152-162.

Cohn, J.F., Campbell, S.B., Matias, R., & Hopkins, J. (1990). Face-to-face interactions of postpartum depressed and nondepressed mother-infant pairs at 2 months. *Developmental Psychology, 26*(1), 15–23.

Cohn, J.F., & Tronick, E. (1989). Specificity of infants' response to mothers' affective behavior. *Journal of the American Academy of Child and Adolescent Psychiatry, 28*(2), 242–248.

Coleman, M., & Ganong, L. (1987). Marital conflict in stepfamilies. *Youth and Society, 19*(2), 151–172.

Coleman, M. & Ganong, L.H. (1992). Financial responsibility for children following divorce and remarriage. *Journal of Family and Economic Issues, 13*(4), 445–455.

Coleman, M. & Ganong, L. (1993). Families and marital disruption. In T.H. Brubaker (Ed.), *Family relations: Challenges for the future.* Newbury Park, CA: Sage.

Coller, D.R. (1988). Joint custody: Research, theory and policy. *Family Process, 27*, 459–469.

Collins, C. (1995, May 11). Spanking is becoming the new don't. *The New York Times*, p. C8.

Collins, G. (1983, February 2). Child sexual abuse prevalent, study finds. *The New York Times.*

Collins, G. (1984b, August 13). Dispelling myths about the only child. *The New York Times.*

Collins, G. (1985a, November 4). Children: Teaching too much, too soon? *The New York Times.*

Collins, G. (1986a, September 26). A survey of parents' views. *The New York Times*.

Collins, G. (1986c, March 3). Parents' reactions to bad marks. *The New York Times*.

Collins, G. (1986e, May 12). Studying the behavior of bully and victim. *The New York Times*.

Collins, G. (1987b, October 14). Latchkey children: A new profile emerges. *The New York Times*.

Collins, G. (1988, May 19). The fears of children: Is the world scarier? *The New York Times*.

Collins, W.A., & Russell, G. (1991). Mother-child and father-child relationships in middle childhood and adolescence: A developmental analysis. *Developmental Review*, *11*, 99–136.

Collins, W.E., Newman, B.M., & McKenry, P.C. (1995). Intrapsychic and interpersonal factors related to adolescent psychological well-being in stepmother and stepfather families. *Journal of Family Psychology*, *9*(4), 433–445.

Colman, L.L., & Colman, A.D. (1991). *Pregnancy: The psychological experience*. NY: Noonday Press.

Colpin, H., Demyttenaere, K., & Vandemeulebroecke, L. (1995). New reproductive technology and the family: The parent-child relationship following in vitro fertilization. *Journal of Child Psychology and Psychiatry*, *36*(8), 1429–1441.

Coltrane, S. (1990). Birth timing and the division of labor in dual-earner families. *Journal of Family Issues*, *11*(2), 157–181.

Coltrane, S. (1995). The future of fatherhood: Social, demographic, and economic influences on men's family involvement. In W. Marsiglio (Ed.). *Fatherhood: Contemporary theory, research, and social policy*. Thousand Oaks, CA: Sage.

Comer, J.P. (1988a, January). Is "parenting" essential to good teaching? *NEA Today*, pp. 34–40.

Comer, J.P. (1988b, November). Educating poor minority children. *Scientific American*, pp. 42–48.

Compas, B.E. (1987). Coping with stress during childhood and adolescence. *Psychological Bulletin*, *101*(3), 393–403.

Conger, J.J. (1988). Hostages to fortune: Youth, values, and the public interest. *American Psychologist*, *43*(4), 291–300.

Conger, K.J., & Conger, R.D. (1994). Differential parenting and change in sibling differences in delinquency. *Journal of Family Psychology*, *8*(3), 287–302.

Conger, R.D., Conger, K.J., Elder, Jr., G.H., Lorenz, F.O., Simons, R.L., & Whitbeck, L.B. (1993). Family economic stress and adjustment of early adolescent girls. *Developmental Psychology*, *29*(2), 206–219.

Cook, R., Golombok, S., Bish, A., & Murray, C. (1995). Disclosure of donor insemination: Parental attitudes. *American Journal of Orthopsychiatry*, *65*(4), 549–559.

Cook, W.L., & Goldstein, M.J. (1993). Multiple perspectives on family relationships: A latent variables model. *Child Development*, *64*, 1377–1388.

Cooksey, E.C., & Fondell, M.M. (1996). Spending time with his kids: Effect of family structure on fathers' and children's lives. *Journal of Marriage and the Family*, *58*, 693–707.

Coombs, R.H., & Landsverk, J. (1988). Parenting styles and substance use during childhood and adolescence. *Journal of Marriage and the Family*, *50*, 473–482.

Cooney, T.M., Hutchinson, M.K., & Leather, D.M. (1995). Surviving the breakup? Predictors of parent-adult child relations after parental divorce. *Family Relations*, *44*, 153–161.

Cooney, T.M., Pedersen, F.A., Indelicato, S., & Palkovitz, R. (1993). Timing of fatherhood: Is "on-time" optimal? *Journal of Marriage and the Family*, *55*, 205–215.

Cooney, T.M., Smyer, M.A., Hagestad, G.O., & Klock, R. (1986). Parental divorce in young adulthood: Some preliminary findings. *American Journal of Orthopsychiatry*, *56*(3), 470-477.

Coons, P.M., & Milstein, V. (1986). Psychosexual disturbances in multiple personality: Characteristics, etiology, and treatment. *Journal of Clinical Psychology*, *47*, 106–110.

Coopersmith, S. (1967). *The antecedents of self esteem*. San Francisco: Freeman.

Cordes, C. (1985, November). Type A children anxious, insecure. *APA Monitor*.

Costanzo, P.R., & Woody, E.Z. (1985). Domain-specific parenting styles and their impact on the child's development of particular deviance: The example of obesity proneness. *Journal of Social and Clinical Psychology*, *3*(4), 425–445.

Coster, W.J., Gersten, M.S., Beeghly, M., & Cicchetti, D. (1989). Communicative functioning in maltreated toddlers. *Developmental Psychology*, *25*(6), 1020–1029.

Cotton, S., Antill, J.K., & Cunningham, J.D. (1989). The work motivations of mothers with preschool children. *Journal of Family Issues*, *10*, 189–210.

Covell, K., & Abramovitch, R. (1987). Understanding emotions in the family: Children's and parent's attributions of happiness, sadness, and anger. *Child Development*, *58*, 985–991.

Covell, K. & Miles, B. (1992). Children's beliefs about strategies to reduce parental anger. *Child Development*, *63*, 381–390.

Cowan, A.L. (1989, March 12). 'Parenthood II': The nest won't stay empty. *The New York Times*.

Cowan, C.P., & Cowan, P.A. (1992). *When partners become parents: The big life change for couples*. NY: Basic Books.

Cowan, C.P., & Cowan, P.A. (1995). Interventions to ease the transition to parenthood: Why they are needed and what they can do. *Family Relations, 44,* 412–423.

Cowan, G., & Avants, S.K. (1988). Children's influence strategies: Structure, sex differences, and bilateral mother-child influence. *Child Development, 59,* 1303–1313.

Cowan, P.A. (1988). Becoming a father. In P. Bronstein and C.P. Cowan (Eds.). *Fatherhood today.* NY: John Wiley.

Cowan, C.P., Cowan, P.A., Heming, G., & Miller, N.B. (1991). Becoming a family: Marriage, parenting, and child development. In P.A. Cowan and E.M. Hetherington (Eds.), *Family transitions: Advances in family research* (Vol. 2). Hillsdale, NJ: Lawrence Erlbaum Associates.

Cowen, E.L., Pedro-Carroll, J.L., & Alpert-Gillis, L.J. (1990). Relationships between support and adjustment among children of divorce. *Journal of Child Psychology and Psychiatry, 31*(5), 727–735.

Cox, M.J., Owen, M.T., Henderson, V.K., & Margand, N.A. (1992). Prediction of infant-father and infant-mother attachment. *Developmental Psychology, 28*(3), 474–483.

Cox, M.J., Owen, M.T., Lewis, J.M., & Henderson, V.K. (1989). Marriage, adult adjustment, and early parenting. *Child Development, 60,* 1015–1024.

Crain, W. (1992). *Theories of development: Concepts and applications* (3rd. edition). Englewood Cliffs, NJ: Prentice-Hall.

Cranley, M.S., Hadahl, K.J. & Pegg, R.J. (1983). Women's perspectives of giving birth: A comparison of vaginal and cesarean deliveries. *Nursing Research, 32,* 10–15.

Creasey, G.L., & Koblewski, P.J. (1991). Adolescent grandchildren's relationships with maternal and paternal grandmothers and grandfathers. *Journal of Adolescence, 14,* 373–387.

Crittenden, P.M., & DiLalla, D.L. (1988). Compulsive compliance: The development of an inhibitory coping strategy in infancy. *Journal of Abnormal Child Psychology, 16,* 585–599.

Crnic, K.A., & Greenberg, M.T. (1990). Minor parenting stresses with young children. *Child Development, 61,* 1628–1637.

Crockenberg, S. (1981). Infant irritability, mother responsiveness, and social support influences on the security of infant-mother attachment. *Child Development, 52,* 857–865.

Crockenberg, S. (1985). Toddlers' reactions to maternal anger. *Merrill-Palmer Quarterly, 31*(4), 361–373.

Crockenberg, S. (1987). Predictors and correlates of anger toward and punitive control of toddlers by adolescent mothers. *Child Development, 1987, 58*(4), 964–975.

Crockenberg, S., & Forgays, D.K. (1996). The role of emotion in children's understanding and emotional

reactions to marital conflict. *Merrill-Palmer Quarterly, 42*(1), 22–47.

Crockenberg, S., & Litman, C. (1991). Effects of maternal employment on maternal and two-year-old child behavior. *Child Development, 62,* 930–953.

Crockenberg, S., & Litman, C. (1992). Autonomy as competence in 2-year-olds: Maternal correlates of child defiance, compliance, and self-assertion. *Developmental Psychology, 26,* 961–971.

Crockenberg, S., & McCluskey, K. (1986). Change in maternal behavior during the baby's first year of life. *Child Development, 57*(3), 746–753.

Crosbie-Burnett, M., & Helmbrecht, L. (1993). A descriptive empirical study of gay male stepfamilies. *Family Relations, 42,* 256–262.

Crossette, B. (1996, June 11). Toll of childbearing: 585,000 women die per year. *The New York Times,* p. A12.

Crouter, A.C., & McHale, S.M. (1993). The long arm of the job: Influences of parental work on childrearing. In T. Luster and L. Okagaki (Eds.). *Parenting: An ecological perspective.* Hillsdale, NJ: Erlbaum.

Csikszentmihalyi, M., & Larson, R. (1984). *Being adolescent: Conflict and growth in the teen-age years.* NY: Basic Books.

Cummings, E.M. (1987). Coping with background anger in early childhood. *Child Development, 58,* 976–984.

Cummings, E.M., Ballard, M., El-Sheikh, M., & Lake, M. (1991). Resolution and children's responses to interadult anger. *Developmental Psychology, 27*(3), 462–470.

Cummings, E.M., & Davies, P. (Eds.). (1994). *Children and marital conflict: The impact of family dispute and resolution.* NY: Guilford Press.

Cummings, E.M., Davies, P., & Simpson, K.S. (1994). Marital conflict, gender, and children's appraisals and coping efficacy as mediators of child adjustment. *Journal of Family Psychology, 8*(2), 141–149.

Cummings, E.M., Pellegrini, D.S., Notarius, C.I., & Cummings, E.M. (1989). Children's responses to angry adult behavior as a function of marital distress and history of interparent hostility. *Child Development, 60,* 1035–1043.

Cummings, E.M., Simpson, K.S., & Wilson, A. (1993). Children's responses to interadult anger as a function of information about resolution. *Developmental Psychology, 29*(6), 978–985.

Cummings, E.M., Vogel, D., Cummings, J.S., & El-Sheikh, M. (1989). Children's responses to different forms of expression of anger between adults. *Child Development, 60*(6), 1392–1404.

Cunningham, C.E., Bremner, R., & Boyle, M. (1995). Large group community-based parenting programs for families of preschoolers at risk for disruptive behaviour disorders: Utilization, cost effectiveness, and outcome. *Journal of Child Psychology & Psychiatry & Allied Disciplines, 36*(7), 1141–1159.

Cutrona, C.E., & Troutman, B.R. (1986). Social support, infant temperament, and parenting self-efficacy: A mediational model of postpartum depression. *Child Development, 57,* 1507–1518.

Dadds, M.R. (1987). Families and the origins of child behavior problems. *Family Process, 26,* 341–357.

Dahlquist, L.M., Czyzewski, D.I., Copeland, K.G., Jones, C.L., et al. (1993). Parents of children newly diagnosed with cancer: Anxiety, coping, and marital distress. *Journal of Pediatric Psychology, 18*(3), 365–376.

Daly, K.J. (1995). Reshaping fatherhood: Finding the models. In W. Marsiglio (Ed.). *Fatherhood: Contemporary theory, research, and social policy.* Thousand Oaks, CA: Sage.

Damon, L., Todd, J., & Macfarlane, K. (1987). Treatment issues with sexually abused young children. *Child Welfare, 66*(2), 125–137.

Dangel, R.F., & Polster, R.A. (1988). *Teaching child management skills.* Elmsford, NY: Pergamon Press.

Daniels, D. (1986). Differential experiences of siblings in the same family as predictors of adolescent sibling personality differences. *Journal of Personality and Social Psychology, 51*(2), 339–346.

Daniels, D., Dunn, J., Furstenberg, F.F., & Plomin, R. (1985). Environmental differences within the family and adjustment differences within pairs of adolescent siblings. *Child Development, 56*(3), 764–774.

Daniels, P., & Weingarten, K. (1988). The fatherhood click: The timing of parenthood in men's lives. In P. Bronstein and C.P. Cowan (Eds.). *Fatherhood Today.* NY: John Wiley.

Darling, N., & Steinberg, L. (1993). Parenting style as context: An integrative model. *Psychological Bulletin, 113*(3), 487–496.

Davies, P.T., & Cummings, E.M. (1995). Children's emotions as organizers of their reactions to interadult anger: A functionalist perspective. *Developmental Psychology, 31*(4), 677–684.

Davis, T.L. (1995). Gender differences in masking negative emotions: Ability or motivation? *Developmental Psychology, 31*(4), 660–667.

Deal, J.E., Halverson, Jr., C.F., & Wampler, K.S. (1989). Parental agreement on childrearing orientations: Relations to parental, marital, family and child characteristics. *Child Development, 60,* 1025–1034.

Deal, J.E., Wampler, K.S., & Halverson, C.F. (1992). The importance of similarity in the marital relationship. *Family Process, 31,* 369–382.

DeAngelis, T. (1989, November). Men's interactional style can be tough on women. *APA Monitor,* p. 12.

DeAngelis, T. (1993, February). Juggler's nightmare: Job and family responsibility. *APA Monitor,* p. 29.

DeAngelis, T. (1995, January). Custody battles challenging for parents with disabilities. *APA Monitor,* p. 39.

DeAngelis, T. (1996a, April). Fathers strongly influenced by culture. *APA Monitor,* pp. 1, 39.

DeAngelis, T. (1996b, April). Men learn the craft of being a good dad. *APA Monitor,* p. 38.

Deater-Deckard, K., & Scarr, S. (1996). Parenting stress among dual-earner mothers and fathers: Are there gender differences? *Journal of Family Psychology, 10*(1), 45–59.

DeBaryshe, B.D. (1995). Maternal belief systems: Linchpin in the home reading process. *Journal of Applied Developmental Psychology, 16*(1), 1–20.

DeChick, J. (1988, July 19). Most mothers want a job, too. *USA Today.*

Deci, E.L. (1985, March). The well-tempered classroom. *Psychology Today,* pp. 52–53.

Deci, E.L., Driver, R.E., Hotchkiss, L., & Robbins, R.J., et al. (1993). The relation of mothers' controlling vocalizations to children's intrinsic motivation. *Journal of Experimental Child Psychology, 55*(2), 151–162.

deGroot, G. (1994, June). Psychologists examine what makes TV 'good.' *APA Monitor,* p. 5.

Dekovic, M., Gerris, J.R.M., & Janssens, J.M.A.M. (1991). Parental cognitions, parental behavior, and the child's understanding of the parent-child relationship. *Merrill-Palmer Quarterly, 37*(4), 523–541.

de Luccie, M.F. (1995). Mothers as gatekeepers: A model of maternal mediators of father involvement. *Journal of Genetic Psychology, 156*(1), 115–131.

de Luccie, M.F., & Davis, A.J. (1991). Father-child relationships from the preschool years through mid-adolescence. *Journal of Genetic Psychology, 152*(2), 225–238.

Demo, D.H., & Acock, A.C. (1988). The impact of divorce on children. *Journal of Marriage and the Family, 50,* 619–648.

Demo, D.H., & Acock, A.C. (1996). Singlehood, marriage, and remarriage: The effects of family structure and family relationships on mothers' well-being. *Journal of Family Issues, 17*(3), 388–407.

DeMyer, M.K. (1979). *Parents and children in autism.* NY: John Wiley.

DeMyer, M.K., & Goldberg, P. (1983). Family needs of the autistic adolescent. In E. Schopler and G.B. Mesibov (Eds.). *Autism in adolescents and adults.* NY: Plenum.

Denham, S.A., Mason, T., & Couchoud, E. (1995). Scaffolding young children's prosocial responsiveness: Preschoolers' responses to adult sadness, anger, and pain. *International Journal of Behavioral Development, 18*(3), 489–504.

Denton, L. (1987, June). Emotional abuse hardest to evaluate. *APA Monitor,* p. 22.

Denton, L. (1988, January). School- cause or cure for abuse? *APA Monitor,* p. 29.

Denton, R.E., & Kampfe, C.M. (1994). The relationship between family variables and adolescent substance abuse: A literature review. *Adolescence*, *29*(114), 475–495.

Denton, R.T., & Denton, M.J. (1992). Therapists' ratings of fundamentalist and nonfundamentalist families in therapy: An empirical comparison. *Family Process*, *31*, 175–185.

de Toledo, S., & Brown, D.E. (1995). *Grandparents as parents: A survival guide for raising a second family*. NY: Guilford Press.

Deveaux, F. (1995). Intergenerational transmission of cultural family patterns. *Family Therapy*, *22*(1), 17–23.

deYoung, M. (1988). The good touch/bad touch dilemma. *Child Welfare*, 1988, *67*(1), 60–70.

Deyoung, Y., & Zigler, E.F. (1994). Machismo in two cultures: Relation to punitive child-rearing practices. *American Journal of Orthopsychiatry*,*64*, 386–395.

Dibrell, L.L., & Yamamoto, K. (1988). In their own words: Concerns of young children. *Child Psychiatry and Human Development*, *19*(1), 14–25.

Dick-Read, G. (1933). *Childbirth without fear: The principles and practices of natural childbirth*. NY: Harper & Row.

Dickson, L.R., Heffron, W.M., & Parker, C. (1990). Children from disrupted and adoptive homes on an inpatient unit. *American Journal of Orthopsychiatry*, *60*(4), 594–597.

Dickstein, S., & Parke, R.D. (1988). Social referencing in infancy: A glance at fathers and marriage. *Child Development*, *59*, 506–511.

DiLalla, L.F., Mitchell, C.M., Arthur, M.W., & Pagliocca, P.M. (1988). Aggression and delinquency: Family and environmental factors. *Journal of Youth and Adolescence*, *17*(3), 233–237.

Dinges, M.M., & Oetting, E.R. (1993). Similarity in drug use patterns between adolescents and their friends. *Adolescence*, *28*(110), 253–266.

Dinkmeyer, D., & McKay, G.D. (1982). *The parent's handbook-STEP- Systematic training for effective parenting*. Circle Pines, MN: American Guidance Service.

Dinkmeyer, D., McKay, G.D., & McKay, J.L. (1987). *New beginnings: Skills for single parents and stepfamily parents*. Champaign, IL: Research Press.

Dion, K.K. (1995). Delayed parenthood and women's expectations about the transmission to parenthood. *International Journal of Behavioral Development*, *18*(2), 315–333.

Dismuke, D. (1988, November). Reducing suicides. *NEA Today*.

Dix, T. (1991). The affective organization of parenting: Adaptive and maladaptive processes. *Psychological Bulletin*, *110*(1), 3–25.

Dix, T., & Grusec, J.E. (1985). Parental attribution processes in the socialization of children. In I.E. Sigel (Ed.). *Parental belief systems* (pp. 201–233). Hillside, NJ: Erlbaum.

Dix, T., & Reinhold, D.P. (1991). Chronic and temporary influences on mothers' attributions for children's disobedience. *Merrill-Palmer Quarterly*, *37*(2), 251–271.

Dix, T., Reinhold, D.P., & Zambarano, R.J. (1990). Mothers' judgment in moments of anger. *Merrill-Palmer Quarterly*, *36*(4), 465–486.

Dix, T., Ruble, D.N., Grusec, J.E., & Nixon, S. (1986). Social cognition in parents: Inferential and affective reactions to children of three age levels. *Child Development*, *57*(4), 879–894.

Dix, T., Ruble, D.N., & Zambarano, R.J. (1989). Mothers' implicit theories of discipline: Child effects, parent effects, and the attribution process. *Child Development*, *60*(6), 1373–1391.

Dodge, K.A. (1983). Behavioral antecedents of peer social status. *Child Development*, *54*, 1386–1399.

Dodge, K.A. (1990). Developmental psychopathology in children of depressed mothers. *Developmental Psychology*, *26*(1), 3–6.

Dodge, K.A., Pettit, G.S., & Bates, J.E. (1994). Socialization mediators of the relation between socioeconomic status and child conduct problems. *Child Development*, *65*, 649–665.

Doelling, J.L., & Johnson, J.H. (1990). Predicting success in foster placement: The contribution of parent-child temperament characteristics. *American Journal of Orthopsychiatry*, *60*(4), 585–593.

Doerner, W.G. (1987). Child maltreatment seriousness and juvenile delinquency. *Youth & Society*, *19*(2), 197–224.

Doherty, W.J. (1991). Beyond reactivity and deficit model of manhood: A commentary on articles by Napier, Pittman, and Gottman. *Journal of Marital and Family Therapy*, *17*, 29–32.

Doka, K.J., & Mertz, M.E. (1988). The meaning and significance of great-grandparenthood. *The Gerontologist*, *28*(2), 192–197.

Donate-Bartfield, E., & Passman, R.H. (1985). Attentiveness of mothers and fathers to the baby's cries. *Infant Behavior and Development*, *8*(4), 385–393.

Donovan, W.L., Leavitt, L.A., & Walsh, R.O. (1990). Maternal self-efficacy: Illusory control and its effect on susceptibility to learned helplessness. *Child Development*, *61*, 1638–1647.

Dornbusch, S.M., Ritter, P.L., Leiderman, H., Roberts, D.F., & Fraleigh, M.J. (1987). The relation of parenting style to adolescent school performance. *Child Development*, *58*, 1244–1257.

Dorr, A., Graves, S.B., & Phelps, E. (1980). Television literacy for young children. *Journal of Communication*, *30*(3), 71–83.

Dowdney, L., & Pickles, A.R. (1991). Expression of negative affect within disciplinary encounters: Is there dyadic reciprocity? *Developmental Psychology*, 27(4), 606–617.

Downey, D.B., & Powell, B. (1993). Do children in single-parent households fare better living with same-sex parents? *Journal of Marriage and the Family*, 55, 55–71.

Dreikurs, R. (1964). *Children: The challenge*. NY: Hawthorne Books.

Dreikurs, R., & Grey, L. (1970). *Guide to child discipline*. NY: Hawthorne Books.

Dryfoos, J.G. (1990). *Adolescents at risk: Prevalence and prevention*. NY: Oxford University Press.

Dubrow, N., & Garbarino, J. (1989). Living in the war zone: Mothers and children in public housing developments. *Child Welfare*, 68(1).

Dumas, J.E., & LaFreniere, P.J. (1993). Mother-child relationships as sources of support or stress: A comparison of competent, average, aggressive, and anxious dyads. *Child Development*, 64, 1732–1754.

Duncan, G.J., Brooks-Gunn, J., & Klebanov, P.K. (1994). Economic deprivation and early childhood development. *Child Development*, 65(2), 296–318.

Dunn, J. (1983). Sibling relationships in early childhood. *Child Development*, 54, 787–811.

Dunn, J. (1985). *Sisters and brothers*. Cambridge, MA: Harvard University Press.

Dunn, J. (1987). The beginnings of moral understanding: Development in the second year. In J. Kagan and S. Lamb (Eds.). *The emergence of morality in young children*. Chicago, IL: University of Chicago Press.

Dunn, J. (1988). Sibling influences on childhood development. *Journal of Child Psychology and Psychiatry*, 29(2), 119–127.

Dunn, J. (1993). *Young children's close relationships: Beyond attachment*. Newbury Park, CA: Sage.

Dunn, J. (1995). *From one child to two*. NY: Ballantine Books.

Dunn, J., Bretherton, I., & Munn, P. (1987). Conversations about feeling states between mothers and their young children. *Developmental Psychology*, 23(1), 132–139.

Dunn, J., & Kendrick, C. (1980). The arrival of a sibling: Changes in patterns of interaction between mother and first-born child. *Journal of Child Psychology and Psychiatry*, 21, 119–132.

Dunn, J., & McGuire, S. (1992). Sibling and peer relationships in childhood. *Journal of Child Psychology and Psychiatry*, 33(1), 67–105.

Dunn, J., & Munn, P. (1985). Becoming a family member: Family conflict and the development of social understanding. *Child Development*, 56, 480–492.

Dunn, J., & Munn, P. (1986). Sibling quarrels and maternal intervention: Individual differences in understanding and aggression. *Journal of Child Psychology and Psychiatry*, 27(5), 583–595.

Dunn, J., & Munn, P. (1987). The development of justification in disputes. *Developmental Psychology*, 23, 791–798.

Dunn, J., & Plomin, R. (1990). *Separate lives: Why siblings are so different*. NY: Basic Books.

Dunn, J., & Plomin, R. (1991). Why are siblings so different? The significance of differences in sibling experiences within the family. *Family Process*, 30, 271–283.

Dunn, J., Slomkowski, C., Beardsall, L., & Rende, R. (1994). Adjustment in middle childhood and early adolescence: Links with earlier and contemporary sibling relationships. *Journal of Child Psychology & Psychiatry & Allied Disciplines*, 35(3), 491–504.

Dunst, C.J., Trivette, C.M. & Cross, A.H. (1986). Mediating influences of social support: Personal, family, and child outcomes. *American Journal of Mental Deficiency*, 90(4), 403–417.

Dworetzky, J.P. (1984). *Introduction to child development*. St. Paul, MN: West Publishers.

East, P.L. (1991). The parent-child relationships of withdrawn, aggressive, and sociable children: Child and parent perspectives. *Merrill-Palmer Quarterly*, 37(3), 425–444.

Easterbrooks, M.A., Cummings, E.M., & Emde, R.N. (1994). Young children's responses to constructive marital disputes. *Journal of Family Psychology*, 8(2), 160–169.

Easterbrooks, M.A., & Goldberg, W.A. (1984). Toddler development in the family: Impact of father involvement and parenting characteristics. *Child Development*, 55, 740–752.

Eccles, J.S., Buchanan, C.M., Flanagan, C., Fuligni, A., Midgley, C., & Yee, D. (1991). Control versus autonomy during early adolescence. *Journal of Social Issues*, 47(4), 53–68.

Edwards, K.J., & Christopherson, E.R. (1994). Treating common sleep problems of young children. *Journal of Developmental & Behavioral Pediatrics*, 15(3), 207–213.

Egan, T. (1995, May 31). When young break the law, a town charges the parents. *The New York Times*, pp. 1, B7.

Egeland, B., Jacobvitz, D., & Sroufe, L.A. (1988). Breaking the cycle of abuse. *Child Development*, 59, 1080–1088.

Egeland, B., & Sroufe, L.A. (1981). Attachment and early maltreatment. *Child Development*, 52, 44–52.

Eggebeen, D.J., Snyder, A.R., & Manning, W.D. (1996). Children in single-father families in demographic perspective. *Journal of Family Issues*, 17(4), 441–465.

Eiger, M.S., & Olds, S.W. (1987). *The complete book of breastfeeding* (2nd ed.). NY: Bantam.

Eisenberg, A.R. (1992). Conflicts between mothers and

their young children. *Merrill-Palmer Quarterly*, *38*(1), 21–43.

Eisenberg, N., Fabes, R.A., Carlo, G., Troyer, D., Speer, A.L., Karbon, M., & Switzer, G. (1992). The relations of maternal practices and characteristics to children's vicarious emotional responsiveness. *Child Development*, *63*, 583–602.

Eisenberg, N., Fabes, R.A., Schaller, M., Gustavo, C., & Miller, P.A. (1991). The relations of parental characteristics and practices to children's vicarious emotional responding. *Child Development*, *62*, 1393–1408.

Eisenberg, N., Lundy, T., Shell, R., & Roth, K. (1985). Children's justifications for their adult and peer-directed compliant (prosocial and nonprosocial) behaviors. *Developmental Psychology*, *21*(2), 325–331.

Ek, C.A., & Steelman, L.C. (1988). Becoming a runaway: From the accounts of youthful runners. *Youth and Society*, *19*(3), 334–358.

Elder, G.H., Conger, R.D., Foster, E.M., & Ardelt, M. (1992). Families under economic pressure. *Journal of Family Issues*, *13*(1), 5–37.

Elder, Jr., G.H., Eccles, J.S., Ardelt, M., & Lord, S. (1995). Inner-city parents under economic pressure: Perspectives on the strategies of parenting. *Journal of Marriage and the Family*, *57*, 771–784.

Elkind, D. (1978). Understanding the young adolescent. *Adolescence*, *13*, 127-134.

Elkind, D. (1981). *The hurried child*. Reading, MA: Addison-Wesley.

Elkind, D. (1984). *All grown up and no place to go*. Reading, MA: Addison-Wesley.

Elkind, D. (1987a). *Miseducation: Preschoolers at risk*. NY: Knopf

Elkind, D. (1987b, May). Superkids and super problems. *Psychology Today*, 60–61.

Elkind, D. (1988, January). Educating the very young: A call for clear thinking. *NEA Today*, pp. 22–27.

Elkind, D. (1994). *Ties that stress: The new family imbalance*. Cambridge, MA: Harvard University Press.

Ellifritt, J. (1985). Life with my sister- Guilty no more. *The disabled child and the family: An exceptional parent reader*. Boston, MA: The Exceptional Parent Press.

El-Sheikh, M., Cummings, E.M., & Goetsch, V.L. (1989). Coping with adults' angry behavior: Behavioral, physiological, and verbal responses in preschoolers. *Developmental Psychology*, *25*(4), 490–498.

Eltgroth, M.B. (1989, January). Starting them young. *PC/Computing*, pp. 257-259.

Emery, R.E. (1982). Interparental conflict and the children of discord and divorce. *Psychological Bulletin*, *92*, 310–330.

Emery, R.E. (1988). *Marriage, divorce, and children's adjustment*. Beverly Hills: Sage.

Emery, R.E. (1989). Family violence. *American Psychologist*, *44*(2), 321–328.

Emery, R.E., & O'Leary, K.D. (1984). Marital discord and child behavior problems in a nonclinic sample. *Journal of Abnormal Child Psychology*, *12*, 411–420.

Emery, R.E., & Tuer, M. (1993). Parenting and the marital relationship. In T. Luster and L. Okagaki (Eds.), *Parenting: An ecological perspective*. Hillsdale, NJ: Erlbaum.

Emmerich, W., Goldman, K.S., Kirsh, B., & Sharabany, R. (1977). Evidence for a transitional phase in the development of gender constancy. *Child Development*, *48*, 930–936.

Entwisle, D.R., & Doering, S.G. (1981). *The first birth: A family turning point*. Baltimore, MD: Johns Hopkins University Press.

Epstein, J.L. (1992). School and family partnerships. In M. Alkin (Ed.). *Encyclopedia of educational research* (6th. ed.). NY: Macmillan.

Erel, O., & Burman, B. (1995). Interrelatedness of marital relations and parent-child relations: A meta-analytic review. *Psychological Bulletin*, *118*(1), 108–132.

Erikson, E. (1963). *Childhood and society* (2nd. ed.). NY: Norton.

Erikson, E. (1964). *Insight and responsibility*. NY: Norton.

Erikson, E. (1968). *Identity: Youth and crisis*. NY: Norton.

Erikson, E. (1982). *Identity and the life cycle*. NY: Norton.

Eskilson, A., Wiley, M.G., Muehlbauer, G., & Dodder, L. (1986). Parental pressure, self-esteem and adolescent reported deviance: Bending the twig too far. *Adolescence*, *21*(83), 501–515.

Estrada, P., Arsenia, W.F., Hess, R.D., & Holloway, S. (1987). Affective quality of the mother-child relationship: Longitudinal consequences for children's school-relevant cognitive functioning. *Developmental Psychology*, *23*(2), 210–215.

Etlin, M. (1988, April). Is there a gifted underachiever? *NEA Today*, pp. 10–11.

Evans, O. (1989, February 16). For infants, quiet and a warm bath. *The New York Times*.

Evans, S.W., Vallano, G., & Pelham, W. (1995). Attention-deficit hyperactivity disorder. In V.B. Van Hasselt and M. Hersen (Eds.). *Handbook of adolescent psychopathology: A guide to diagnosis and treatment*. NY: Lexington Books.

Everson, M.D., Hunter, W.M., Runyon, D.K., Edelsohn, G.A., & Coulter, M.L. (1989). Maternal support following disclosure of incest. *American Journal of Orthopsychiatry*, *59*(2), 197–207.

Faber, A., & Mazlish, E. (1987). *Siblings without rivalry*. NY: W.W. Norton.

Faber, A., & Mazlish, E. (1995, Summer). Praise that

doesn't demean, criticism that doesn't wound. *American Educator*, pp. 33–38.

Fabes, R.A., Eisenberg, N., Karbon, M., Bernzweig, J., Speer, A.L., & Carlo, G. (1994). Socialization of children's vicarious emotional responding and prosocial behavior: Relations with mothers' perceptions of children's emotional reactivity. *Developmental Psychology*, 30(1), 44–55.

Fabes, R.A., Eisenberg, N., & Miller, P.A. (1990). Maternal correlates of children's vicarious emotional responsiveness. *Developmental Psychology*, 26(4), 639–648.

Fabes, R.A., Fultz, J., Eisenberg, N., May-Plumlee, T., & Christopher, F.S. (1989). Effects of rewards on children's prosocial motivation: A socialization study. *Developmental Psychology*, 25(4), 509–515.

Fackelmann, K.A. (1990, August 11). Sweeter slumber for tots who sleep solo. *Science News, 138*, p. 87.

Faerstein, L.M. (1986). Coping and defense mechanisms of mothers of learning disabled children. *Journal of Learning Disabilities, 19*(1), 8–11.

Fagan, J., & Schor, D. (1993). Mothers of children with spina bifida: Factors related to maternal psychosocial functioning. *American Journal of Orthopsychiatry, 63*(1), 146–152.

Fagot, B.I., & Hagan, R. (1991). Observations of parent reactions to sex-stereotyped behaviors: Age and sex effects. *Child Development, 62,* 617–628

Falbo, T. (1984). *The single-child family.* NY: Guilford Press.

Falbo, T. & Polit, D.F. (1986). Quantitative review of the only child literature: Research evidence and theory development. *Psychological Bulletin, 100*(2), 176–189.

Faller, K.C. (1988). Criteria for judging the credibility of children's statements about their sexual abuse. *Child Welfare, 67*(5), 389–400.

Famularo, R., Stone, K., Barnum, R., & Sharton, R. (1986). Alcoholism and severe child maltreatment. *American Journal of Orthopsychiatry, 56*(3), 481–485.

Farber, E., & Egeland, B. (1987). *The invulnerable child.* NY: Guilford Press.

Farrell, L.T. (1988). Factors that affect a victim's self-disclosure in father-daughter incest. *Child Welfare, 67*(5), 462–470.

Fasick, F.A. (1994). On the 'invention of adolescence.' *Journal of Early Adolescence, 14*(1), 6–23.

Fauber, R.L., & Long, N. (1991). Children in context: The role of the family in child psychotherapy. *Journal of Consulting and Clinical Psychology, 59,* 813–820.

Faulkenberry, J.R., Vincent, M., James, A., & Johnson, W. (1987). Coital behaviors, attitudes, and knowledge of students who experience early coitus. *Adolescence, 22*(86), 321–325.

Feagans, L.V., & Manlove, E.E. (1994). Parents, infants, and day-care teachers: Interrelations and implications for better child care. *Journal of Applied Developmental Psychology, 15*(4), 585–602.

Feagans, L.V., Merriwether, A.M., & Haldane, D. (1991). Goodness of fit in the home: Its relationship to school behavior and achievement in children with learning disabilities. *Journal of Learning Disabilities, 24*(7), 413–420.

Fein, E. (1991). Issues in foster care: Where do we stand? *American Journal of Orthopsychiatry, 61*(4), 578–583.

Fein, E., Maluccio, A.N., & Kluger, M. (1990). *No more partings: An examination of foster family care.* Washington, D.C.: Child Welfare League of America.

Feingold, A. (1992). Gender differences in mate selection preferences: A test of the parental investment model. *Psychological Bulletin, 112*(1), 125–139.

Felmlee, D.H. (1994). Who's on top? Power in romantic relationships. *Sex Roles, 31*(5/6), pp. 275–295.

Felner, R. (1985). Child custody: Practices and perspectives of legal professionals. *Journal of Clinical Child Psychology, 14*(1), 27–34.

Ferber, R. (1985). *Solve your child's sleep problems.* NY: Fireside.

Fergusson, D.M., Horwood, L.J., & Lynskey, M.T. (1992). Family change, parental discord and early offending. *Journal of Child Psychology and Psychiatry, 33*(6), 1059–1075.

Fergusson, D.M., Lynskey, M., & Horwood, L.J. (1995). The adolescent outcomes of adoption: A 16-year longitudinal study. *Journal of Child Psychology & Psychiatry & Allied Disciplines, 36*(4), 597–615.

Fernald, A., & Kuhl, P.K. (1987). Acoustic determinants of infant preference for motherese speech. *Infant Behavior and Development, 10,* 279–293.

Fernald, A., & Morikawa, H. (1993). Common themes and cultural variations in Japanese and American mothers' speech to infants. *Child Development, 64,* 637–656.

Field, T. (1991a). Quality infant day-care and grade school behavior and performance. *Child Development, 62,* 863–870.

Field, T. (1991b). Young children's adaptations to repeated separations from their mothers. *Child Development, 62,* 539–547.

Field, T. (1995). Infants of depressed mothers. *Infant Behavior & Development, 18*(1), 1–13.

Fiese, B.H. (1990). Playful relationships: A contextual analysis of mother-toddler interaction and symbolic play. *Child Development, 61,* 1648–1656.

Fiese, B.H., Hooker, K.A., Kotary, L., Schwagler, J., & Rimmer, M. (1995). Family stories in the early stages of parenthood. *Journal of Marriage and the Family, 57,* 763–770.

Fincham, F.D. (1994). Understanding the association between marital conflict and child adjustment:

Overview. *Journal of Family Psychology*, 8(2), 123–127.

Fincham, F.D., Grych, J.H., & Osborne, L.N. (1994). Does marital conflict cause child maladjustment? Directions and challenges for longitudinal research. *Journal of Family Psychology*, 8(2), 128–140.

Fine, M.A. (1993). Current approaches to understanding family diversity: An overview of the special issue. *Family Relations*, 42, 235–237.

Fine, M.A., & Kurdek, L.A. (1995). Relation between marital quality and (step)parent-child relationship quality for parents and stepparents in stepfamilies. *Journal of Family Psychology*, 9(2), 216–223.

Fine, M.A., Voydanoff, P., & Donnelly, B.W. (1993). Relations between parental control and warmth and child well-being in stepfamilies. *Journal of Family Psychology*, 7(2), 222–232.

Finkelhor, D. (1984). *Child sexual abuse: New theory and research*. NY: Free Press.

Finkelhor, D., Araji, S., Baron, L., Browne, A., Peters, S.D., & Wyatt, G.E. (1986). *A sourcebook on child sexual abuse*. Beverly Hills, CA: Sage.

Finkelhor, D., & Dziuba-Leatherman, J. (1994). Victimization of children. *American Psychologist*, 49, 173–183.

Finney, J.W., & Edwards, M.C. (1989). Prevention of children's behavior problems. *The Behavior Therapist*, 12(8), 183–186.

Fischer, A. (1985, November). Should parents assume a child's duty? *The New York Times*.

Fischer, B. (1988, March). 'Whiz Kid' image masks problems of Asian Americans. *NEA Today*, pp. 14–15.

Fischman, J. (1986, October). The children's hours. *Psychology Today*, pp. 16–18.

Fischman, J. (1988, November). Stepdaughter wars. *Psychology Today*, pp. 38–45.

Fish, L.S., New, R.S., & Van Cleave, N.J. (1992). Shared parenting in dual-income families. *American Journal of Orthopsychiatry*, 62(1), 83–93.

Fish, M., & Stifter, C.A. (1993). Mother parity as a main and moderating influence on early mother-infant interaction. *Journal of Applied Developmental Psychology*, 14(4), 557–572.

Fishel, A.H. (1987). Children's adjustment in divorced families. *Youth and Society*, 19(2), 173–196.

Fisher, K. (1985, November). Parental support vital in coping with abuse. *APA Monitor*, p. 12.

Fisher, K. (1987a, March). Kids' services work; too few receive them. *APA Monitor*, p. 26.

Fisher, K. (1987b, June). Sexual abuse victims suffer into adulthood. *APA Monitor*, p. 25.

Fisher, K. (1989, July). Pushing preschoolers doesn't help, may hurt. *APA Monitor*, p. 9.

Fisher, P.A., & Fagot, B.I. (1993). Negative discipline in families: A multidimensional risk model. *Journal of Family Psychology*, 7(2), 250–254.

Fisher, S., & Greenberg, R.P. (1977). *The scientific credibility of Freud's theories and therapy*. NY: Basic Books.

Fisher, T.D. (1986). Parent-child communication about sex and young adolescents' sexual knowledge and attitudes. *Adolescence*, 21(83), 517–527.

Flanagan, C., Schulenberg, J., & Fuligni, A. (1993). Residential setting and parent-adolescent relationships during the college years. *Journal of Youth and Adolescence*, 22(2), 171–187.

Flavell, J.H. (1986, January). Really and truly. *Psychology Today*, pp. 38–44.

Fleming, A.S., Klein, E., & Corter, C. (1992). The effects of a social support group on depression, maternal attitudes and behavior in new mothers. *Journal of Child Psychology & Psychiatry & Allied Disciplines*, 33(4), 685–698.

Fleming, A.S., Ruble, D.N., Flett, G.L., & Van Wagner, V. (1990). Adjustment in first-time mothers: Changes in mood and mood content during the early postpartum months. *Developmental Psychology*, 26(1), 137–143.

Fling, S., & Manosevitz, M. (1972). Sex typing in nursery school children's play interests. *Developmental Psychology*, 7, 146–152.

Flynn, C.P. (1994). Regional differences in attitudes toward corporal punishment. *Journal of Marriage and the Family*, 56, 314–323.

Foderaro, L.W. (1987, November 19). Voices of the counterculture. *The New York Times*.

Folkenberg, J. (1985, May). Teen pregnancy: Who opts for adoption? *Psychology Today*, p. 16.

Forehand, R. (1977). Child noncompliance to parental requests: Behavioral analysis and treatment. In M. Hersen, R.M. Eisler, and P.M. Miller (Eds.). *Progress in behavior modification* (Vol. 5). NY: Academic Press.

Forehand, R. (1992). Parental divorce and adolescent maladjustment: Scientific inquiry vs. public information. *Behavior Research and Therapy*, 30(4), 319–327.

Forehand, R., & Nousiainen, S. (1993). Maternal and paternal parenting: Critical dimensions in adolescent functioning. *Journal of Family Psychology*, 7(2), 213–221.

Forero, J. (1996, February 19). Mom charges teacher told class to beat son. *The Star-Ledger*, p. 21.

Forgatch, M.S. (1989). Patterns and outcome in family problem solving: The disrupting effect of negative emotion. *Journal of Marriage and the Family*, 51, 115–124.

Forste, R.T., & Heaton, T.B. (1988). Initiation of sexual activity among female adolescents. *Youth and Society*, 19(3), 250–268.

Fowers, B.J., & Richardson, F.C. (1996). Why is multiculturalism good? *American Psychologist*, *51*(6), 609–621.

Fox, R.A., Platz, D.L., & Bentley, K.S. (1995). Maternal factors related to parenting practices, developmental expectations, and perceptions of child behavior problems. *The Journal of Genetic Psychology*, *156*(4), 431–441.

Foxcroft, D.R., & Lowe, G. (1995). Adolescent drinking, smoking and other substance use involvement: Links with perceived family life. *Journal of Adolescence*, *18*, 159–177.

Framo, J. (1975). Personal reflections of a family therapist. *Journal of Marriage and Family Counseling*, *1*, 1–22.

Framo, J. (1976). Family of origin as a therapeutic resource for adults in marital and family therapy: You can and should go home again. *Family Process*, *15*, 193–210.

Frank, S.J., Avery, C.B., & Laman, M.S. (1988). Young adults' perceptions of their relationships with their parents: Individual differences in connectedness, competence, and emotional autonomy. *Developmental Psychology*, *24*(5), 729–737.

Frank, S.J., Olmstead, C.L., Wagner, A.E., Lamb, C.C., et al. (1991). Child illness, the parenting alliance, and parenting stress. *Journal of Pediatric Psychology*, *16*(3), 361–371.

Frankel, F., & Simmons, J. Q. (1992). Parent behavior training: Why and when some parents drop out. *Journal of Clinical Child Psychology*, *21*(4), 322–330.

Frankel, M.T., & Rollins, Jr., H.A. (1983). Does mother know best? Mothers and fathers interacting with preschool sons and daughters. *Developmental Psychology*, *19*(5), 694–702.

Franz, C.E., McClelland, D.C., & Weinberger, J. (1991). Childhood antecedents of conventional social accomplishment in midlife adults: A 36-year prospective study. *Journal of Personality and Social Psychology*, *60*(4), 586–595.

Fraser, B.C. (1986). Child impairment and parent/infant communication. *Child Care, Health and Development*, *12*(3), 141–150.

Freedman, J.L., Sears, D.O., & Carlsmith, J.M. (1981). *Social psychology* (4th ed.). Englewood Cliffs, NJ: Prentice-Hall.

Freeman, J. (Ed.). (1985). *The psychology of gifted children: Perspectives on development and education*. NY: John Wiley.

Freeman, J. (1995). Recent studies of giftedness in children. *Journal of Child Psychology & Psychiatry & Allied Disciplines*, *36*(4), 531–547.

Freiberg, P. (1996, September). Latchkey kids not always trouble-prone. *APA Monitor*, p. 48.

Frenkiel, N. (1993, November 11). 'Family planning': Baby boy or girl? *The New York Times*, pp. 1, C6.

Frerking, B. (1992, April 9). Millions of parents wage uphill fights to collect child support. *New Jersey Star-Ledger*, p. 21.

Freud, S. (1916). *Wit and its relation to the unconscious*. NY: Moffat Ward.

Freud, S. (1933/1965). *New introductory lectures on psychoanalysis*. NY: Norton. (Original work published 1933).

Freund, L.S. (1990). Maternal regulation of children's problem-solving behavior and its impact on children's performance. *Child Development*, *61*, 113–126.

Frey, C.U., & Röthlisberger, C. (1996). Social support in healthy adolescents. *Journal of Youth and Adolescence*, *25*(1), 17–31.

Friedland, S. (1993, August 8). Workshops required for parents in divorce. *The New York Times*, New Jersey Weekly, pp. 1, 4.

Friedrich, W.N., & Schafer, L.C. (1995). Somatic symptoms in sexually abused children. *Journal of Pediatric Psychology*, *20*(5), 661–670.

Friedrich, W.N., Urquiza, A.J., & Beilke, R.L. (1986). Behavior problems in sexually abused young children. *Journal of Pediatric Psychology*, *11*(1), 47–57.

Friedrich, W.N., Wilturner, L.T., & Cohen, D.S. (1985). Coping resources and parenting mentally retarded children. *American Journal of Mental Deficiency*, *90*(2), 130–139.

Frost, A.K., & Pakiz, B. (1990). The effects of marital disruption on adolescents: Time as a dynamic. *American Journal of Orthopsychiatry*, *60*(4), 544–554.

Fuligni, A.J., & Eccles, J.S. (1993). Perceived parent-child relationships and early adolescents' orientation toward peers. *Developmental Psychology*, *29*(4), 622–632.

Furman, W. (1982). Children's friendships. In T.M. Field, A. Huston, H.C. Quay, L. Troll, and G.E. Finley (Eds.). *Review of human development*. NY: John Wiley.

Furstenberg, F.F., Jr. (1995). Fathering in the inner city: Paternal participation and public policy. In W. Marsiglio (Ed.), *Fatherhood: Contemporary theory, research, and social policy*. Thousand Oaks, CA: Sage.

Furstenberg, F.F., Jr., Brooks-Gunn, J., & Chase-Lansdale, L. (1989). Teenaged pregnancy and childbearing. *American Psychologist*, *44*(2), 313–320.

Furstenberg, F.F., Jr., Herceg-Baron, R., Shea, J., & Webb, D. (1986). Family communication and contraceptive use among sexually active adolescents. In B.A. Hamburg and J.B. Lancaster (Eds.). *School age pregnancy and parenthood*. NY: Aldine De Gruyter.

Furstenberg, F.F., Jr., & Nord, C.W. (1985). Parenting apart: Patterns of childrearing after marital disruption. *Journal of Marriage and the Family*, *47*, 893–905.

Gable, S., Belsky, J., & Crnic, K. (1995). Coparenting during the child's 2nd year: A descriptive account. *Journal of Marriage and the Family*, *57*, 609–616.

Gabel, S., & Shindledecker, R. (1992). Behavior problems in sons and daughters of substance abusing parents. *Child Psychiatry & Human Development*, 23(2), 99–115.

Gabriel, T. (1996, January 7). The fertility market: High-tech pregnancies test hope's limit. *The New York Times*, pp. 1, 18.

Galambos, N.L., & Dixon, R.A. (1984). Toward understanding and caring for latchkey children. *Child Care Quarterly*, 13(2), 116–125.

Galambos, N.L., & Maggs, J.L. (1991). Out-of-school care of young adolescents and self-reported behavior. *Developmental Psychology*, 27(4), 644–655.

Galinsky, E. (1981). *Between generations: The six stages of parenthood*. NY: Times Books.

Gallagher, J.J. (1985). Unthinkable thoughts- Reexamining the concept of learning disability. *The disabled child and the family: An exceptional parent reader*. Boston, MA: The Exceptional Parent Press.

Galston, W.A. (1995, December 27). Needed: A not-so-fast divorce law. *The New York Times*.

Gamble, M. (1985). Helping our children accept themselves. *The disabled child and the family: An exceptional parent reader*. Boston, MA: The Exceptional Parent Press.

Ganong, L.H., & Coleman, M.M. (1987). Stepchildren's perceptions of their parents. *Journal of Genetic Psychology*, 148(1), 5–17.

Ganong, L.H., & Coleman, M. (1988). Do mutual children cement bonds in stepfamilies? *Journal of Marriage and the Family*, 50, 687–698.

Garbarino, J. (1995). The American war zone: What children can tell us about living with violence. *Journal of Developmental & Behavioral Pediatrics*, 16(6), 431–435.

Garbarino, J., & Kostelny, K. (1993). Neighborhood and community influences on parenting. In T. Luster and L. Okagaki (Eds.). *Parenting: An ecological perspective*. Hillsdale, NJ: Erlbaum.

Garcia Coll, C.T., Hoffman, J., & Oh, W. (1987). The social ecology and early parenting of Caucasian adolescent mothers. *Child Development*, 58, 955–963.

Garfinkel, P. (1983, September). The best "Jewish Mother" in the world. *Psychology Today*, pp. 56–60.

Garmezy, N. (1988). Stressors of childhood. In N. Garmezy and M. Rutter (Eds.). *Stress, coping, and development in children*. Baltimore, Md: Johns Hopkins University Press.

Garrison, E.G. (1987). Psychological maltreatment of children: An emerging focus for inquiry and concern. *American Psychologist*, 42(2), 157–159.

Gaylin, J. (1985, February). When a child dies. *Parents*, pp. 80–83.

Ge, X., Best, K.M., Conger, R.D., & Simons, R.L. (1996). Parenting behaviors and the occurrence and co-occurrence of adolescent depressive symptoms and conduct problems. *Developmental Psychology*, 32(4), 717–731.

Ge, X., Conger, R.D., Cadoret, R.J., Neiderhiser, J.M., Yates, W., Troughton, E., & Stewart, M.A. (1996). The developmental interface between nature and nurture: A mutual influence model of child antisocial behavior and parent behaviors. *Developmental Psychology*, 32(4), 574–589.

Gelfand, D.M., Teti, D.M., & Fox, C.R. (1992). Sources of parenting stress for depressed and nondepressed mothers of infants. *Journal of Clinical Child Psychology*, 21(3), 262–272.

Geller, M. (1984, May 20). Family violence: The price we pay is dear. *Newark Star Ledger*.

Gelles, R.J. (1989). Child abuse and violence in single-parent families: Parent absence and economic deprivation. *American Journal of Orthopsychiatry*, 59(4), 492–501.

Gelles, R.J., & Straus, M.A. (1987). Is violence toward children increasing? A comparison of 1975 and 1985 national survey rates. *Journal of Interpersonal Violence*, 2, 212–222.

Gerson, K. (1986, November). Briefcase, baby or both? *Psychology Today*, pp. 30–36.

Gerson, M., Berman, L.S., & Morris, A.M. (1991). The value of having children as an aspect of adult development. *The Journal of Genetic Psychology*, 152(3), 327–339.

Gesell, A.L. (1928). *Infancy and human growth*. NY: Macmillan.

Gibbs, J.T. (1987). Identity and marginality: Issues in the treatment of biracial adolescents. *American Journal of Orthopsychiatry*, 57(2), 265–278.

Giles-Sims, J. (1987). Parental role sharing between remarrieds and ex-spouses. *Youth and Society*, 19(2), 134–150.

Giles-Sims, J., Straus, M.A., & Sugarman, D.B. (1995). Child, maternal, and family characteristics associated with spanking. *Family Relations*, 44, 170–176.

Gilligan, C. (1982). *In a different voice*. Cambridge, MA: Harvard University Press.

Gilman, L. (1992). *The adoption resource book* (3rd ed.). NY: HarperCollins.

Ginott, H.G. (1965). *Between parent and child*. NY: Macmillan.

Ginsburg, G.S., & Bronstein, P. (1993). Family factors related to children's intrinsic/extrinsic motivational orientation and academic performance. *Child Development*, 64, 1461–1474.

Gjerde, P.F. (1986). The interpersonal structure of family interaction settings: Parent-adolescent relations in dyads and triads. *Developmental Psychology*, 22(3), 297–304.

Glasser, W. (1990). *The quality school*. NY: Harper & Row.

Gleick, J. (1987). *Chaos: Making a new science.* NY: Penguin.

Glenn, N. D. (1991). The recent trend in marital success in the United States. *Journal of Marriage and the Family, 53,* 261–270.

Glenn, N.D. (1993, May). What's happening to American marriage? *USA Today Magazine,* pp. 26–28.

Gold, M., & Yanof, D.S. (1985). Mothers, daughters, and girlfriends. *Journal of Personality and Social Psychology, 49*(3), 654–659.

Goldberg, S. (1983). Parent-infant bonding: Another look. *Child Development, 54,* 1355–1382.

Goldberg, S., Muir, R., & Kerr, J. (1995). (Eds.). *Attachment theory: Social, developmental, and clinical perspectives.* Hillsdale, NJ: The Analytic Press.

Goldscheider, F.K., & Goldscheider, C. (1989). Family structure and conflict: Nest-leaving expectations of young adults and their parents. *Journal of Marriage and the Family, 51,* 87–97.

Goldsmith, H.H. (1983). Genetic influences on personality from infancy to adulthood. *Child Development, 54,* 331–355.

Goldstein, L.H., Diener, M.L., & Mangelsdorf, S.C. (1996). Maternal characteristics and social support across the transition to motherhood: Associations with maternal behavior. *Journal of Family Psychology, 10*(1), 60–71.

Goleman, D. (1985a, June 25). Chronic arguing between parents found harmful to some children. *The New York Times.*

Goleman, D. (1985b, May 28). Spacing of siblings strongly linked to success in life. *The New York Times.*

Goleman, D. (1986a, October 21). Child development theory stresses small moments. *The New York Times.*

Goleman, D. (1986b, April 1). Two views of marriage explored: His and hers. *The New York Times.*

Goleman, D. (1987b, July 28). Each sibling experiences different family. *The New York Times.*

Goleman, D. (1987e, March 10). Research reports progress against autism. *The New York Times.*

Goleman, D. (1987f, September 15). Shame steps out of hiding and into sharper focus. *The New York Times.*

Goleman, D. (1987g, November 24). Teen-age risk taking: Rise in deaths prompts new research effort. *The New York Times.*

Goleman, D. (1987h, April 7). The bully: New research depicts a paranoid, lifelong loser. *The New York Times.*

Goleman, D. (1987i, October 13). Thriving despite hardship: Key childhood traits identified. *The New York Times.*

Goleman, D. (1988a, May 17). Lies can point to mental disorders or signal normal growth. *The New York Times.*

Goleman, D. (1988c, December 1). Nurturing can offset the trauma of loss in childhood, study says. *The New York Times.*

Goleman, D. (1988f, April 14). When a baby cries: Researchers seek clues to potential problems. *The New York Times.*

Goleman, D. (1989a, March 23). Infants in need of psychotherapy? A fledgling field is growing fast. *The New York Times.*

Goleman, D. (1989b, January 10). Pioneering studies find surprisingly high rate of mental ills in young. *The New York Times.*

Golombok, S., Cook, R., Bish, A., & Murray, C. (1995). Families created by the new reproductive technologies: Quality of parenting and social and emotional development of the children. *Child Development, 66,* 285–298.

Golombok, S., & Tasker, F. (1996). Do parents influence the sexual orientation of their children? Findings from a longitudinal study of lesbian families. *Developmental Psychology, 32*(1), 3–11.

Good, T.L., & Weinstein, R.S. (1986). Schools make a difference: Evidence, criticisms, and new directions. *American Psychologist, 41,* 1090–1097.

Goodman, S.H., Brogan, D., Lynch, M.E., & Fielding, B. (1993). Social and emotional competence in children of depressed mothers. *Child Development, 64,* 516–531.

Goodnow, J.J. (1988a). Parents' ideas, actions, and feelings: Models and methods from developmental and social psychology. *Child Development, 59,* 286–320.

Goodnow, J.J. (1988b). Children's household work: Its nature and functions. *Psychological Bulletin, 103*(1), 5–26.

Goodnow, J.J., Knight, R., & Cashmore, J. (1983). Adult social cognition: Implications of parents' ideas for approaches to development. In M. Perlmutter (Chair), *Minnesota Symposium on Child Development,* Minneapolis.

Goodyer, I.M. (1990). Family relationships, life events and childhood psychopathology. *Journal of Child Psychology and Psychiatry, 31*(1), 161–192.

Gordon, M., & Creighton, S.J. (1988). Natal and non-natal fathers as sexual abusers in the United Kingdom: A comparative analysis. *Journal of Marriage and the Family, 50,* 99–105.

Gordon, S. (1986, October). What kids need to know. *Psychology Today,* pp. 22–26.

Gordon, T. (1970). *Parent effectiveness training.* NY: Peter H. Wyden.

Gorman, K.S., & Pollitt, E. (1996). Does schooling buffer the effects of early risk? *Child Development, 67,* 314–326.

Gorman-Smith, D., Tolan, P.H., Zelli, A., & Huesmann, L.R. (1996). The relation of family functioning to violence among inner-city minority youths. *Journal of Family Psychology, 10*(2), 115–129.

Gostin, L.O., & Beyer, H.A. (Eds.). (1993). *Implementing the Americans with Disabilities Act: Rights and responsibilities of all Americans*. Baltimore: Brookes.

Gottfried, A.E., Fleming, J.S., & Gottfried, A.W. (1994). Role of parental motivational practices in children's academic intrinsic motivation and achievement. *Journal of Educational Psychology, 86*(1), 104–113.

Gottman, J.M., & Katz, L.F. (1989). Effects of marital discord on young children's peer interaction and health. *Developmental Psychology, 25*(3), 373–381.

Gottman, J.M., Katz, L.F., & Hooven, C. (1996). Parental meta-emotion philosophy and the emotional life of families: Theoretical models and preliminary data. *Journal of Family Psychology, 10*(3), 243–268.

Gralinski, J.H., & Kopp, C.B. (1993). Everyday rules for behavior: Mothers' requests to young children. *Developmental Psychology, 29*(3), 573–584.

Graubard, S.G. (1988, January 29). Why do Asian pupils win those prizes? The New York Times.

Gray, M.M., & Coleman, M. (1985). Separation through divorce: Supportive professional practices. *Child Care Quarterly, 14*(4), 248–261.

Gray, R.E. (1987). Adolescent response to the death of a parent. *Journal of Youth and Adolescence, 16*(6), 511–525.

Greenberg, M.T., & Marvin, R.S. (1982). Reactions of preschool children to an adult stranger: A behavioral systems approach. *Child Development, 53*, 481–490.

Greenberger, E., & Goldberg, W.A. (1989). Work, parenting, and the socialization of children. *Developmental Psychology, 25*, 22–35.

Greenberger, E., & O'Neil, R. (1992). Maternal employment and perceptions of young children: Bronfenbrenner et al. revisited. *Child Development, 63*, 431–448.

Greenberger, E., & O'Neil, R. (1993). Spouse, parent, worker: Role commitments and role-related experiences in the construction of adults' well-being. *Developmental Psychology, 29*(2), 181–197.

Greenspan, S.I., Wieder, S., Nover, R.A., Lieberman, A.F., Lourie, R.S., & Robinson, M.E. (Eds.). (1987). *Infants in multirisk families: Case studies in preventive intervention*. Madison, CT: International Universities Press.

Greenstein, T.N. (1995). Are the "most advantaged" children truly disadvantaged by early maternal employment? Effects on child cognitive outcomes. *Journal of Family Issues, 16*(2), 149–169.

Greenstein, T.N. (1996). Husbands' participation in domestic labor: Interactive effects of wives' and husbands' gender ideologies. *Journal of Marriage and the Family, 58*, 585–595.

Greif, G.L. (1985). Single fathers rearing children. *Journal of Marriage and the Family, 47*, 185–191.

Gretarsson, S.J., & Gelfand, D.M. (1988). Mothers' attributions regarding their children's social behavior and personality characteristics. *Developmental Psychology, 24*(2), 264–269.

Griffin-Carlson, M.S., & Mackin, K.J. (1993). Parental consent: Factors influencing adolescent disclosure regarding abortion. *Adolescence, 28*(109), 1–12.

Gringlas, M., & Weinraub, M. (1995). The more things change . . . Single parenting revisited. *Journal of Family Issues, 16*(1), 29–52.

Griswold, R.L. (1993). *Fatherhood in America: A history*. NY: Basic Books.

Grolnick, W.S., & Ryan, R.M. (1989). Parent styles associated with children's self-regulation and competence in school. *Journal of Educational Psychology, 81*(2), 143–154.

Grolnick, W.S., Ryan, R.M., & Deci, E.L. (1991). Inner resources for school achievement: Motivational mediators of children's perceptions of their parents. *Journal of Educational Psychology, 83*(4), 508–517.

Gross, J. (1993, November 24). To help girls keep up: Math class without boys. *The New York Times*, p. 1.

Grossman, F.K., Pollack, W.S., & Golding, E. (1988). Fathers and children: Predicting the quality and quantity of fathering. *Developmental Psychology, 24*(1), 82–91.

Grusec, J.E. (1992). Social learning theory and developmental psychology: The legacies of Robert Sears and Albert Bandura. *Developmental Psychology, 28*, 776–786.

Grusec, J.E., & Goodnow, J.J. (1994). Impact of parental discipline methods on the child's internalization of values: A reconceptualization of current points of view. *Developmental Psychology, 30*(1), 4–19.

Grych, J.H., & Fincham, F.D. (1990). Marital conflict and children's adustment: A cognitive-contextual framework. *Psychological Bulletin, 108*, 267–290.

Grych, J.H., & Fincham, F.D. (1992). Interventions for children of divorce: Toward greater integration of research and action. *Psychological Bulletin, 111*(3), 434–454.

Grych, J.H., & Fincham, F.D. (1993). Children's appraisals of marital conflict: Initial investigations of the cognitive-contextual framework. *Child Development, 64*, 215–230.

Grych, J.H., Seid, M., & Fincham, F.D. (1992). Assessing marital conflict from the child's perspective: The children's perception of interparental conflict scale. *Child Development, 63*, 558–572.

Guidubaldi, J., & Nastasi, B.K. (1987). *Home environment factors as predictors of child adjustment in mother-employed households: Results of a nationwide study*. Paper presented at the biennial meeting of the Society of Research in *Child Development*, Baltimore, MD.

Guillette, L.C. (1987). Children in maritally violent families: A look at family dynamics. *Youth & Society, 19*(2), 119–133.

Gustafson, G.E., & Harris, K.L. (1990). Women's responses to young children's cries. *Developmental Psychology, 26*(1), 144–152.

Hackel, L.S., & Ruble, D.N. (1992). Changes in the marital relationship after the first baby is born: Predicting the impact of expectancy disconfirmation. *Journal of Personality and Social Psychology, 62*(6), 944–957.

Hadadian, A., & Merbler, J. (1995). Fathers of young children with disabilities: How do they want to be involved? *Child & Youth Care Forum, 24*(5), 327–338.

Hajal, F., & Rosenberg, E.B. (1991). The family life cycle in adoptive families. *American Journal of Orthopsychiatry, 61*(1), 78–85.

Hajcak, F., & Garwood, P. (1988). Quick-fix sex: Pseudosexuality in adolescents. *Adolescence, 23*(92), 755–760.

Halebsky, M.A. (1987). Adolescent alcohol and substance abuse: Parent and peer effects. *Adolescence, 22*(88), 961–968.

Haley, J. (1976). *Problem solving therapy.* San Francisco: Jossey-Bass.

Hall, C.C.I. (1980). *The ethnic identity of racially mixed people: A study of Black-Japanese.* Unpublished doctoral dissertation, University of California, Los Angeles.

Hall, C.S., & Lindzey, G. (1978). *Theories of personality* (3rd edition). NY: John Wiley.

Hall, E. (1987, July). China's only child. *Psychology Today,* pp. 45–47.

Hall, G.S. (1904). *Adolescence.* NY: Appleton.

Hall, J.A. (1987). Parent-adolescent conflict: An empirical review. *Adolescence, 22*(88), 767–789.

Hall, W.S. (1989). Reading comprehension. *American Psychologist, 44*(2), 157–161.

Halpern, R. (1990). Poverty and early childhood parenting: Toward a framework for intervention. *American Journal of Orthopsychiatry, 60*(1), 6–16.

Hamburg, D.A., & Takanishi, R. (1989). Preparing for life: The critical transition of adolescence. *American Psychologist, 44*(5), 825–827.

Hanson, S.M.H. (1988). Divorced fathers with custody. In P. Bronstein and C.P. Cowan (Eds.). *Fatherhood today: Men's changing role in the family.* NY: John Wiley.

Hanson, T.L., McLanahan, S.S., & Thomson, E. (1996). Double jeopardy: Parental conflict and stepfamily outcomes for children. *Journal of Marriage and the Family, 58,* 141–154.

Hanzlik M., & Stevenson, M.B. (1986). Interactions of mothers with their infants who are mentally retarded, retarded with cerebral palsy, or nonretarded. *American Journal of Mental Deficiency, 90*(5), 513–520.

Hardy, D.F., Power, T.G., & Jaedicke, S. (1993). Examining the relation of parenting to children's coping with everyday stress. *Child Development, 64,* 1829–1841.

Hare, J., & Richards, L. (1993). Children raised by lesbian couples: Does context of birth affect father and partner involvement? *Family Relations, 42,* 249–255.

Harkness, S. (1992). Cross-cultural research in child development: A sample of the state of the art. *Developmental Psychology, 28*(4), 622–625.

Harper, J.F., & Marshall, E. (1991). Adolescents' problems and their relationship to self-esteem. *Adolescence, 26*(104), 799–808.

Harris, I.D., & Howard, K.I. (1985). Correlates of perceived parental favoritism. *Journal of Genetic Psychology, 146*(1), 45–56.

Harris, J.R. (1995). Where is the child's environment? A group socialization theory of development. *Psychological Review, 102*(3), 458–489.

Harris, K.M., & Morgan, S.P. (1991). Fathers, sons, and daughters: Differential paternal involvement in parenting. *Journal of Marriage and the Family, 53,* 531–544.

Harris, M., Jones, D., Brookes, S., & Grant, J. (1986). Relations between the non-verbal context of maternal speech and rate of language development. *British Journal of Developmental Psychology, 4*(3), 261–268.

Harris, S.L., & Bruey, C.T. (1988). Families of the developmentally disabled. In I.R.H. Falloon (Ed.). *Handbook of behavioral family therapy.* NY: Guilford Press.

Harris, S.L., & Powers, M.D. (1984). Behavior therapists look at the impact of an autistic child on the family system. In E. Schopler and G. Mesibov (Eds.). *The effects of autism on the family.* NY: Plenum.

Harrison, A.O., Wilson, M.N., Pine, C.J., Chan, S.Q., & Buriel, R. (1990). Family ecologies of ethnic minority children. *Child Development, 61,* 347–362.

Hart, B., & Risley, T.R. (1992). American parenting of language-learning children: Persisting differences in family-child interactions observed in natural home environments. *Developmental Psychology, 28*(6), 1096–1105.

Hart, C.H., DeWolf, D.M., Wozniak, P. & Burts, D.C. (1992). Maternal and paternal disciplinary styles: Relations with preschoolers' playground behavioral orientations and peer status. *Child Development, 63,* 879-892.

Hart, S.N., & Brassard, M.R. (1987). A major threat to children's mental health: Psychological maltreatment. *American Psychologist, 42*(2), 160–165.

Harter, S. (1987). The determinants and mediational role of global self-worth in children. In N. Eisenberg (Ed.), *Contemporary issues in developmental psychology.* NY: John Wiley.

Harter, S. (1990). Self and identity development. In S.S.

Feldman and G.R. Elliot (Eds.), *At the threshold: The developing adolescent*. Cambridge, MA: Harvard University Press.

Hartup, W.W. (1986). On relationships and development. In W.W. Hartup and Z. Rubin (Eds.), *Relationships and development*. Hillsdale, NJ: Erlbaum.

Hartup, W.W. (1989). Social relationships and their developmental significance. *American Psychologist, 44*(2), 120–126.

Hartup, W.W. (1996). The company they keep: Friendships and their developmental significance. *Child Development, 67*, 1–13.

Harvey, P., Forehand, R., Brown, C., & Holmes, T. (1988). The prevention of sexual abuse: Examination of the effectiveness of a program with kindergarten-age children. *Behavior Therapy, 19*(3), 429–436.

Hashima, P.Y., & Amato, P.R. (1994). Poverty, social support, and parental behavior. *Child Development, 65*(2), 394–403.

Hauenstein, E. (1990). The experience of distress in parents of chronically ill children: Potential or likely outcome. *Journal of Clinical Child Psychology, 19*, 356–364.

Hauser, R.M., & Sewell, W.H. (1985). Birth order and educational attainment in full sibships. *American Journal of Educational Research, 22*, 1–23.

Hauser-Cram, P. (1996). Mastery motivation in toddlers with developmental disabilities. *Child Development, 67*, 236–248.

Hausman, B., & Hammen, C. (1993). Parenting in homeless families: The double crisis. *American Journal of Orthopsychiatry, 63*(3), 358–369.

Haveman, R., Wolfe, B.L., & Spaulding, J. (1991). Educational achievement and childhood events and circumstances. *Demography, 28*, 133–157.

Havighurst, R.J. (1972). *Developmental tasks and education*. 3rd ed. NY: David McKay Co.

Hawkins, A.J., Christiansen, S.L., Sargent, K.P., & Hill, E.J. (1995). Rethinking fathers' involvement in child care: A developmental perspective. In W. Marsiglio (Ed.), *Fatherhood: Contemporary theory, research, and social policy*. Thousand Oaks, CA: Sage.

Hawkins, A.J., Marshall, C.M., & Meiners, K.M. (1995). Exploring wives' sense of fairness about family work. *Journal of Family Issues, 16*(6), 693–721.

Hay, D.F., & Kumar, R. (1995). Interpreting the effects of mothers' postnatal depression on children's intelligence: A critique and re-analysis. *Child Psychiatry & Human Development, 25*(3), 165–181.

Hayes, D. (Ed.) (1987). *Risking the future: Adolescent sexuality, pregnancy, and childbearing* (Vol. 1). Washington D.C.: National Academy Press.

Hayes, J.R., & Flower, L.S. (1986). Writing research and the writer. *American Psychologist, 41*(10), 1106–1113.

Haynes-Seman, C., & Krugman, R.D. (1989). Sexual-

ized attention: Normal interaction or precursor to sexual abuse? *American Journal of Orthopsychiatry, 59*(2), 238–245.

Hazan, C., & Shaver, P.R. (1987). Conceptualizing romantic love as an attachment process. *Journal of Personality and Social Psychology, 52*, 511–524.

Hazzard, A., Weston, J., & Gutterres, C. (1992). After a child's death: Factors related to parental bereavement. *Journal of Developmental & Behavioral Pediatrics, 13*(1), 24–30.

Healy, J.M., Malley, J.E., & Stewart, A.J. (1990). Children and their fathers after parental separation. *American Journal of Orthopsychiatry, 60*(4), 531–543.

Heath, D.T. (1994). The impact of delayed fatherhood on the father-child relationship. *Journal of Genetic Psychology, 155*(4), 511–530.

Heaton, T.B., & Albrecht, S.L. (1991). Stable unhappy marriages. *Journal of Marriage and the Family, 53*, 747–758.

Heiman, M.L. (1992). Putting the puzzle together: Validating allegations of child sexual abuse. *Journal of Child Psychology & Psychiatry & Allied Disciplines, 33*(2), 311–329.

Henker, B., Whalen, C.K., & O'Neil, R. (1995). Worldly and workaday worries: Contemporary concerns of children and young adolescents. *Journal of Abnormal Child Psychology, 23*(6), 685–702.

Henry, B., Caspi, A., Moffitt, T.E., & Silva, P.A. (1996). Temperamental and familial predictors of violent and nonviolent criminal convictions: Age 3 to age 18. *Developmental Psychology, 32*(4), 614–623.

Henry, C.S., & Lovelace, S.G. (1995). Family resources and adolescent family life satisfaction in remarried family households. *Journal of Family Issues, 16*(6), 765–786.

Henry, C.S., Stephenson, A.L., Hanson, M.F., & Hargett, W. (1994). Adolescent suicide and families: An ecological approach. *Family Therapy, 21*(1), 63-80.

Henshaw, C.V. (1988, July 10). The baby has arrived. Now what? *The New York Times*.

Hergenhahn, B.R., & Olson, M. (1993). *An introduction to theories of learning* (4th edition). Englewood Cliffs, NJ: Prentice Hall.

Herman, M.A., & McHale, S.M. (1993). Coping with parental negativity: Links with parental warmth and child adjustment. *Journal of Applied Developmental Psychology, 14*(1), 121–136.

Hersov, L. (1990). The Seventh Jack Tizard Memorial Lecture: Aspects of adoption. *Journal of Child Psychology and Psychiatry, 31*(4), 493–510.

Hertz, R. (1987). *More equal than others: Women and men in dual-career marriages*. University of California Press.

Hess, R.D., & Holloway, S.D. (1984). Family and school as educational institutions. In R.D. Parke (Ed.), *Re-

view of child development research. Chicago: University of Chicago Press. (Vol. 7, pp. 179–222).

Hetherington, E.M. (1989). Coping with family transitions: Winners, losers, and survivors. *Child Development*, *60*, 1–14.

Hetherington, E.M. (1993). An overview of the Virginia Longitudinal Study of Divorce and Remarriage with a focus on early adolescence. *Journal of Family Psychology*, *7*(1), 39-56.

Hetherington, E.M. (1994). Siblings, family relationships, and child development: Introduction. *Journal of Family Psychology*, *8*(3), 251–253.

Hetherington, E.M., Stanley-Hagan, M., & Anderson, E.R. (1989). Marital transitions: A child's perspectives. *American Psychologist*, *44*(2), 303–312.

Hieshima, J.A., & Schneider, B. (1994). Intergenerational effects on the cultural and cognitive socialization of third- and fourth-generation Japanese Americans. *Journal of Applied Developmental Psychology*, *15*(3), 319–327.

Hill, J.P. (1985). Family relations in adolescence: Myths, realities and new directions. *Genetic, Social and General Psychology Monographs*, *111*(2), 233–248.

Hill, J.P., & Holmbeck, G.N. (1987). Disagreements about rules in families with seventh-grade girls and boys. *Journal of Youth and Adolescence*, *16*(3), 221–246.

Hiller, D.V., & Dyehouse, J. (1987). A case for banishing "dual-career marriages" from the research literature. *Journal of Marriage and the Family*, *49*, 787–795.

Hilton, J.M., & Haldeman, V.A. (1991). Gender differences in the performance of household tasks by adults and children in single-parent and two-parent, two-earner families. *Journal of Family Issues*, *12*(1), 114–130.

Himelstein, S., Graham, S., & Weiner, B. (1991). An attributional analysis of maternal beliefs about the importance of child-rearing practices. *Child Development*, *62*, 301–310.

Hindmarch, C. (1995). Secondary losses for siblings. *Child: Care, Health & Development*, *21*(6), 425–431.

Hinshaw, S.P. (1992). Externalizing behavior problems and academic underachievement in childhood and adolescence: Causal relationships and underlying mechanisms. *Psychological Bulletin*, *111*(1), 127–155.

Hirshberg, L.M., & Svejda, M. (1990). When infants look at their parents: I. Infants' social referencing of mothers compared to fathers. *Child Development*, *61*, 1175–1186.

Hock, E., & DeMeis, D.K. (1990). Depression in mothers of infants: The role of maternal employment. *Developmental Psychology*, *26*(2), 285–291.

Hock, E., McBride, S., & Gnezda, M.T. (1989). Maternal separation anxiety: Mother-infant separation from the maternal perspective. *Child Development*, *60*, 793–802.

Hock, E., Shirtzinger, B., Lutz, W.J., & Widaman, K., (1995). Maternal depressive symptomatology over the transition to parenthood: Assessing the influence of marital satisfaction and marital sex role traditionalism. *Journal of Family Psychology*, *9*(1), 79–88.

Hodges, J., & Tizard, B. (1989). Social and family relationships of ex-institutional adolescents. *Journal of Child Psychology and Psychiatry*, *30*, 77–97.

Hoeffer, B. (1981). Children's acquisition of sex-role behavior in lesbian-mother families. *American Journal of Orthopsychiatry*, *51*, 536–544.

Hoff-Ginsberg, E. (1991). Mother-child conversation in different social classes and communicative settings. *Child Development*, *62*, 782–796.

Hoffman, J. (1995, April 26). Divorced fathers make gains in battles to increase rights. *The New York Times*, pp. 1, B5.

Hoffman, L. W. (1974). Effects of maternal employment on the child- A review of the research. *Developmental Psychology*, *10*(2), 204–228.

Hoffman, L.W. (1989). Effects of maternal employment in the two-parent family. *American Psychologist*, *44*(2), 283–292.

Hoffman, L.W., & Manis, J.D. (1979). The value of children in the United States: A new approach to the study of fertility. *Journal of Marriage and the Family*, *41*, 583–591.

Hoffman, M. (1977). Homosexuality. In F.A. Beach (Ed.). *Human sexuality in four perspectives*. Baltimore: Johns Hopkins University Press.

Hoffman, M.L. (1967). Power assertion by the parent and its impact on the child. In G. Medinnus (Ed.). *Readings in the psychology of parent-child relationships*. NY: John Wiley.

Hoffman, M.L. (1970). Moral development. In P.H. Mussen (Ed.), *Carmichael's manual of child psychology* (Vol. 2). NY: John Wiley.

Hoffman, M.L. (1994). Discipline and internalization. *Developmental Psychology*, *30*(1), 26–28.

Hoffnung, M. (1989). Motherhood: Contemporary conflict for women. In J. Freeman (Ed.). *Women: A feminist perspective* (4th Ed.). Mountain View, CA: Mayfield.

Holden, G.W. (1983). Avoiding conflict: Mothers as tacticians in the supermarket. *Child Development*, *54*, 233–244.

Holden, G.W. (1988). Adults' thinking about a child-rearing problem: Effects of experience, parental status, and gender. *Child Development*, *59*, 1623–1632.

Holden, G.W., Coleman, S.M., & Schmidt, K.L. (1995). Why 3-year-old children get spanked: Parent and child determinants as reported by college-educated mothers. *Merrill-Palmer Quarterly*, *41*(4), 431–452.

Holden, G.W., & Ritchie, K.L. (1991). Linking extreme

marital discord, child rearing, and child behavior problems: Evidence from battered women. *Child Development, 62*, 311–327.

Holden, G.W., & West, M.J. (1989). Proximate regulation by mothers: A demonstration of how differing styles affect young children's behavior. *Child Development, 60*, 64-69.

Holmbeck, G.N., & Hill, J.P. (1991). Conflictive engagement, positive affect, and menarche in families with seventh-grade girls. *Child Development, 62*, 1030–1048.

Holmes, S.A. (1996, June 20). Income disparity between poorest and richest rises. *The New York Times*, pp. A1, A18.

Holmes, S.J., & Robins, L.N. (1988). The role of parental disciplinary practices in the development of depression and alcoholism. *Psychiatry, 51*, 24–32.

Holt, R.R. (1989). *Freud reappraised*. NY: Guilford Press.

Honig, A.S. (1987). The shy child. *Young Children, 17*, 34–64.

Hooker, K., Fiese, B.H., Jenkins, L., Morfei, M.Z., & Schwagler, J. (1996). Possible selves among parents of infants and preschoolers. *Developmental Psychology, 32*(3), 542–550.

Hooper, C. (1992). *Mothers surviving child sexual abuse*. London: Tavistock/Routledge.

Hopkins, J., Marcus, M., & Campbell, S.B. (1984). Postpartum depression: A critical review. *Psychological Bulletin, 95*, 498–515.

Hopper, J. (1993). The rhetoric of motives in divorce. *Journal of Marriage and the Family, 55*, 801–813.

Hortaçsu, N. (1995). Parents' education levels, parents' beliefs, and child outcomes. *Journal of Genetic Psychology, 156*(3), 373–383.

Hossain, Z., & Roopnarine, J.L. (1994). African-American fathers' involvement with infants: Relationship to their functioning style, support, education, and income. *Infant Behavior and Development, 17*(2), 175–184.

Hostetler, A.J. (1988, July). Why baby cries: Data may shush skeptics. *APA Monitor*, p. 14.

Houseknecht, S.K. (1979). Timing of the decision to remain voluntarily childless: Evidence for continuous socialization. *Psychology of Women Quarterly, 4*, 81–96.

Howe, N., & Ross, H.S. (1990). Socialization, perspective taking, and the sibling relationship. *Developmental Psychology, 26*(1), 160–165.

Howes, C. (1990). Can the age of entry into child care and the quality of child care predict adjustment in kindergarten? *Developmental Psychology, 26*(2), 292–303.

Howes, C., & Stewart, P. (1987). Child's play with adults, toys, and peers: An examination of family and child-care influences. *Developmental Psychology, 23*, 423–430.

Howes, P., & Markman, H.J. (1989). Marital quality and child functioning: A longitudinal investigation. *Child Development, 60*, 1044–1051.

Howie, P.M. (1996). After-school care arrangements and maternal employment: A study of the effects on third and fourth grade children. *Child & Youth Care Forum, 25*(1), 29–48.

Hughes, H.M. (1988). Psychological and behavioral correlates of family violence in child witnesses and victims. *American Journal of Orthopsychiatry, 58*(1), 77–90.

Hunter, F.T. (1985). Adolescent's perception of discussions with parents and friends. *Developmental Psychology, 21*(3), 433–440.

Hurley, D. (1985, March). Arresting delinquency. *Psychology Today*, pp. 63–68.

Hurley, D. (1987, August). A sound mind in an unsound body. *Psychology Today*, pp. 34–43.

Huston, A. Sex-typing. (1983). In P. Mussen (Ed.), *Handbook of child psychology* (4th ed.) (Vol.4). NY: John Wiley.

Huston, A.C., McLoyd, V.C., & Garcia Coll, C. (1994). Children and poverty: Issues in contemporary research. *Child Development, 65*, 275–282.

Huston, A.C., Watkins, B.A. and Kunkel, D. (1989). Public policy and children's television. *American Psychologist, 44*(2), 424–433.

Hyde, J.S. & Linn, M.C. (1988). Gender differences in verbal ability: A meta-analysis. *Psychological Bulletin, 104*(1), 53–69.

Hyson, M.C., Hirsh-Pasek, K., Rescorla, L., Cone, J., et al. (1991). Ingredients of parental "pressure" in early childhood. *Journal of Applied Developmental Psychology, 12*(3), 347–365.

Ievers, C.E., Drotar, D., Dahms, W.T., Doershuk, C.F., et al. (1994). Maternal child-rearing behavior in three groups: Cystic fibrosis, insulin-dependent diabetes mellitus, and healthy children. *Journal of Pediatric Psychology, 19*(6), 681–687.

Inazu, J.K., & Fox, G.L. (1980). Maternal influence on the sexual behavior of teenage daughters. *Journal of Family Issues, 1*, 81–102.

Irion, J.C., Coon, R.C., & Blanchard-Fields, F. (1988). The influence of divorce on coping in adolescence. *Journal of Youth and Adolescence, 17*(2), 135–145.

Isaacs, M.B., Leon, G.H., & Kline, M. (1987). When is a parent out of the picture? Different custody, different perceptions. *Family Processes, 26*, 101–110.

Isabella, R.A., & Belsky, J. (1991). Interactional synchrony and the origins of infant-mother attachment: A replication study. *Child Development, 62*, 373–384.

Isabella, R.A., Belsky, J., & von Eye, A. (1989). Origins of infant-mother attachment: An examination of interactional synchrony during the infant's first year. *Developmental Psychology, 25*(1), 12–21.

Isberg, R.S., Hauser, S.T., Jacobson, A.M., Powers, S.I., Noam, G., Weiss-Perry, B., & Follansbee, D. (1989). Parental contexts of adolescent self-esteem: A developmental perspective. *Journal of Youth and Adolescence, 18*(1), 1–23.

Ishii-Kuntz, M., & Ihinger-Tallman, M. (1991). The subjective well-being of parents. *Journal of Family Issues, 12*(1), 58–68.

Izard, C.E., Haynes, O.M., Chisholm, G., & Baak, K. (1991). Emotional determinants of infant-mother attachment. *Child Development, 62*, 906–917.

Jacklin, C.N. (1989). Female and male: Issues of gender. *American Psychologist, 44*(2), 127–133.

Jackson, S.A. (1977, October). Should you teach your child to read? *American Education.*

Jacobson, A.L., & Owen, S.S. (1987). Infant-caregiver interactions in day care. *Child Study Journal, 17*(3), 197–209.

Jacobson, J.L., & Willie, D.R. (1986). The influence of attachment pattern on developmental changes in peer interaction from the toddler to the preschool period. *Child Development, 57*, 338–347.

Jacobson, N.S. (1989). The politics of intimacy. *The Behavior Therapist, 12*(2), 29–32.

Jacobson, S.W., & Frye, K.F. (1991). Effect of maternal social support on attachment: Experimental evidence. *Child Development, 62*, 572–582.

Jacobvitz, D.B., & Bush, N.F. (1996). Reconstructions of family relationships: Parent-child alliances, personal distress, and self-esteem. *Developmental Psychology, 32*(4), 732–743.

Jaffe, M.L. (1990). Counseling parents in child management skills. *New Jersey Psychologist, 40*(1), 15–16.

Jaffe, M.L. (1997). *Adolescence.* NY: John Wiley.

Jaffe, P., Wolfe, D., Wilson, S., & Zak, L. (1986). Similarities in behavioral and social maladjustment among child victims and witnesses to family violence. *American Journal of Orthopsychiatry, 56*(1), 142–146.

Javaid, G.A. (1993). The children of homosexual and heterosexual single mothers. *Child Psychiatry & Human Development, 23*(4), 235–248.

Jaycox, L.H., & Repetti, R.L. (1993). Conflict in families and the psychological adjustment of preadolescent children. *Journal of Family Psychology, 7*(3), 344–355.

Jendrek, M.P. (1993a). Grandparents who parent their grandchildren: Effects on lifestyle. *Journal of Marriage and the Family, 55*, 609–621.

Jendrek, M.P. (1993b). Grandparents who parent their grandchildren. *The Gerontologist, 34*(2), 206–216.

Jenkins, J.M., & Smith, M.A. (1991). Marital disharmony and children's behavior problems: Aspects of poor marriage that affect children adversely. *Journal of Child Psychology and Psychiatry, 32*, 793–810.

Jenkins, J.M., Smith, M.A., & Graham, P.J. (1989). Coping with parental quarrels. *Journal of the American Academy of Child and Adolescent Psychiatry, 28*(2), 182–189.

Jenson, W.R., Sloane, H.N., & Young, K.R. (1988). *Applied behavior analysis in education.* Englewood Cliffs, NJ: Prentice-Hall.

Jessor, R., & Jessor, S.L. (1977). *Problem behavior and psychosocial development.* NY: Academic Press.

Jessor, R., Van Den Bos, J., Vanderryn, J., Costa, F.M., & Turbin, M.S. (1995). Protective factors in adolescent problem behavior: Moderator effects and developmental change. *Developmental Psychology, 6*, 923–933.

Johansen, A.S., Leibowitz, A., & Waite, L.J. (1996). The importance of child-care characteristics to choice of care. *Journal of Marriage and the Family, 58*, 759–772.

Johnson, J.E., & Martin, C. (1985). Parents' beliefs and home learning environments: Effects on cognitive development. In I.E. Sigel (Ed.), *Parental belief systems: The psychological consequences for children.* Hillsdale, NJ: Erlbaum.

Johnson, S. (1988, April 3). Learning the art of bringing up baby. *The New York Times.*

Johnston, J.R., Kline, M., & Tschann, J.M. (1989). Ongoing postdivorce conflict: Effects on children of joint custody and frequent access. *American Journal of Orthopsychiatry, 59*(4), 576–592.

Johnston, L.D., Bachman, J.G., & O'Malley, P.M. (1985, January 4). News and Information Services Release, Institute of Social Research, University of Michigan, Ann Arbor.

Jones, D.A. (1987). The choice to breast feed or bottle feed and influences upon that choice: A survey of 1,525 mothers. *Child: Care, Health, and Development, 13*(2), 75–85.

Jorgensen, S.R. (1993). Adolescent pregnancy and parenting. In T.P. Gullotta, G.R. Adams, and R. Montemayor, (Eds.), *Adolescent sexuality.* Newbury Park, CA: Sage.

Josephson, W.L. (1987). Television violence and children's aggression: Testing the priming, social script, and disinhibition predictions. *Journal of Personality and Social Psychology, 53*(5), 882–890.

Jouriles, E.N., Barling, J., & O'Leary, K.D. (1987). Predicting child behavior problems in maritally violent families. *Journal of Abnormal Child Psychology, 15*(2), 165–173.

Jouriles, E.N., Murphy, C.M., Farris, A.M., Smith, D.A., Richters, J.E., & Waters, E. (1991). Marital adjustment, parental disagreements about child rearing, and behavior problems in boys: Increasing the specificity of the marital assessment. *Child Development, 62*, 1424–1433.

Jouriles, E.N., Murphy, C.M., & O'Leary, K.D. (1989). Interspousal aggression, marital discord, and child problems. *Journal of Consulting and Clinical Psychology, 57,* 453–455.

Jouriles, E.N., & Norwood, W.D. (1995). Physical aggression toward boys and girls in families characterized by the battering of women. *Journal of Family Psychology, 9*(1), 69–78.

Jouriles, E.N., Norwood, W.D., McDonald, R., Vincent, J.P., & Mahoney, A. (1996). Physical violence and other forms of marital aggression: Links with children's behavior problems. *Journal of Family Psychology, 10*(2), 223–234.

Jouriles, E.N., & Thompson, S.M. (1993). Effects of mood on mothers' evaluations of children's behavior. *Journal of Family Psychology, 6*(3), 300–307.

Julian, T.W., McKenry, P.C., & McKelvey, M.W. (1994). Cultural variations in parenting: Perceptions of Caucasian, African-American, Hispanic, and Asian-American parents. *Family Relations, 43,* 30–37.

Kagan, J. (1978, August). The parental love trap. *Psychology Today,* pp. 54–91.

Kagan, J. (1981). *The second year.* Cambridge, MA: Harvard University Press.

Kagan, J. (1984). *The nature of the child.* NY: Basic Books.

Kagan, J. (1994). *The nature of the child.* NY: Basic Books.

Kagan, J. (1988). Stress and coping in early development. In N. Garmezy and M. Rutter (Eds.). *Stress, Coping, and Development in Children.* Baltimore, Md: Johns Hopkins University Press.

Kagan, J., Reznick, J.S., & Gibbons, J. (1989). Inhibited and uninhibited types of children. *Child Development, 60,* 838–845.

Kaitz, M., Lapidot, P., Bronner, R., & Eidelman, A.I. (1992). Parturient women can recognize their infants by touch. *Developmental Psychology, 28*(1), 35–39.

Kaitz, M., Meirov, H., Landman, I., & Eidelman, A.I. (1993). Infant recognition by tactile cues. *Infant Behavior and Development, 16*(3), 333–341.

Kaitz, M., Shiri, S., Danziger, S., Hershko, Z., et al., (1994). Fathers can also recognize their newborns by touch. *Infant Behavior and Development, 17*(2), 205–207.

Kalmuss, D. (1984). The intergenerational transmission of marital aggression. *Journal of Marriage and the Family, 47,* 11–19.

Kalter, N. (1987). Long-term effects of divorce on children: A developmental vulnerability model. *American Journal of Orthopsychiatry, 57*(4), 587–600.

Kalter, N., Kloner, A., Schreier, S., & Okla, K. (1989). Predictors of children's postdivorce adjustment. *American Journal of Orthopsychiatry, 59*(4), 605–618.

Kanfer, F.H., & Schefft, B.K. (1988). *Guiding the process of therapeutic change.* Champaign, Il: Research Press.

Kaplan, P.S. (1988). *The human odyssey.* St. Paul, MN: West.

Kashani, J.H., Daniel, A.E., Dandoy, A.C., & Holcomb, W.R. (1992). Family violence: Impact on children. *Journal of the American Academy of Child and Adolescent Psychiatry, 31*(2), 181–189.

Kaslow, F.W., & Schwartz, L.L. (1987). *The dynamics of divorce: A life cycle perspective.* NY: Brunner/Mazel

Kasser, T. & Ryan, R.M. (1993). A dark side of the American dream: Correlates of financial success as a central life aspiration. *Journal of Personality and Social Psychology, 65,* 410–422.

Kasser, T., Ryan, R.M., Zax, M., & Sameroff, A.J. (1995). The relations of maternal and social environments to late adolescents' materialistic and prosocial values. *Developmental Psychology, 31*(6), 907–914.

Kates, W.G., Johnson, R.L., Rader, M.W., & Strieder, F.H. (1991). Whose child is this? Assessment and treatment of children in foster care. *American Journal of Orthopsychiatry, 61*(4), 584–591.

Katz, L.F., & Gottman, J.M. (1993). Patterns of marital conflict predict children's internalizing and externalizing behaviors. *Developmental Psychology, 29*(6), 940–950.

Katzev, A.R., Warner, R.L., & Acock, A.C. (1994). Girls or boys? Relationship of child gender to marital stability. *Journal of Marriage and the Family, 56,* 89–100.

Kaufman, J. (1987, June 23). From abused child to good parent. Letter to Editor, *The New York Times.*

Kaufman, J., & Cicchetti, D. (1989). Effects of maltreatment on school-age children's socioemotional development: Assessments in a day-camp setting. *Developmental Psychology, 25*(4), 516–524.

Kaufman, J., & Zigler, E. (1987). Do abused children become abusive parents? *American Journal of Orthopsychiatry, 57*(2), 186–196.

Kay, P.J., Fitzgerald, M., Paradee, C., & Mellencamp, A. (1994). Making homework work at home: The parent's perspective. *Journal of Learning Disabilities, 27*(9), 550–561.

Kaye, K. (1982). *The mental and social life of babies.* Chicago: University of Chicago Press.

Kazak, A.E. (1986). Families with physically handicapped children: Social ecology and family systems. *Family Process, 25,* 265-281.

Kazdin, A.E. (1984). *Behavior modification in applied settings* (3rd ed.). Homewood, Il:Dorsey Press.

Kazdin, A.E. (1987). Treatment of antisocial behavior in children: Current status and future directions. *Psychological Bulletin, 102,* 187–203.

Kazdin, A.E. (1993). Adolescent mental health: Prevention and treatment programs. *American Psychologist, 48*(2), 127–141.

Keller, W.D., Hildebrandt, K.A., & Richards, M.E. (1985). Effects of extended father-infant contact during the newborn period. *Infant Behavior and Development*, 8(3), 337–350.

Kelley, M.L., Power, T.G., & Wimbush, D.D. (1992). Determinants of disciplinary practices in low-income black mothers. *Child Development, 63*, 573–582.

Kelley, M.L., Sanchez-Hucles, J. & Walker, R.R. (1993). Correlates of disciplinary practices in working- to middle-class African-American mothers. *Merrill-Palmer Quarterly, 39*(2), 252–264.

Kendall-Tackett, K.A., Williams, L.M., & Finkelhor, D. (1993). Impact of sexual abuse on children: A review and synthesis of recent empirical studies. *Psychological Bulletin, 113*(1), 164–180.

Kendrick, C., & Dunn, J. (1983). Sibling quarrels and maternal responses. *Developmental Psychology, 19*(1), 62–70.

Kennedy, J.F., & Keeney, V.T. (1988). The extended family revisited: Grandparents rearing grandchildren. *Child Psychiatry and Human Development, 19*(1), 26–35.

Kerig, P.K. (1995). Triangles in the family circle: Effects of family structure on marriage, parenting, and child adjustment. *Journal of Family Psychology, 9*(1), 28–43.

Kerig, P.K., Cowan, P.A., & Cowan, C.P. (1993). Marital quality and gender differences in parent-child interaction. *Developmental Psychology, 29*(6), 931–939.

Kernis, M.H., Cornell, D.P., Sun, C., Berry, A., & Harlow, T. (1993). There's more to self-esteem than whether it is high or low: The importance of stability of self-esteem. *Journal of Personality and Social Psychology, 65*(6), 1190–1204.

Kerns, K.A., Klepac, L., & Cole, A. (1996). Peer relationships and preadolescents' perceptions of security in the child-mother relationship. *Developmental Psychology, 32*(3), 457–466.

Kerr, P. (1988, June 23). Addiction's hidden toll: Poor families in turmoil. *The New York Times*.

Kerr, S., & Jowett, S. (1994). Sleep problems in preschool children: A review of the literature. *Child: Care, Health, & Development, 20*(6), 379–391.

Kessen, W. (1975). *Children in China*. New Haven: Yale University Press.

Kessler, J.W. (1988). *Psychopathology of childhood* (2nd ed.). Englewood Cliffs, NJ: Prentice-Hall.

Keyes, R. (February 7, 1993). "If only I could say, 'I love you, Dad.'" *Parade Magazine*.

Kilby, R.W. (1993). *The study of human values*. Lanham, MD: University Press of America.

Kim, U. & Chun, M.B.J. (1994). Educational "success" of Asian Americans: An indigenous perspective. *Journal of Applied Developmental Psychology, 15*(3), 329–339.

Kirchner, D.M. (1991). Using verbal scaffolding to facilitate conversational participation and language acquisition in children with pervasive developmental disorders. *Journal of Childhood Communication Disorders, 14*, 81–98.

Kirkpatrick, M., Roy, R., & Smith, C. (1978). A new look at lesbian mothers. *Human Behavior*, pp. 60–61.

Kirkpatrick, M., Smith, C., & Roy, R. (1981). Lesbian mothers and their children: A comparative survey. *American Journal of Orthopsychiatry, 51*, 545–551.

Kiselica, M.S., & Sturmer, P. (1993). Is society giving teenage fathers a mixed message? *Youth & Society, 24*(4), 487–501.

Kissman, K., & Allen, J.A. (1993). *Single-parent families*. Newbury Park, CA: Sage.

Kitzmann, K.M., & Emery, R.E. (1994). Child and family coping one year after mediated and litigated child custody disputes. *Journal of Family Psychology, 8*(2), 150–159.

Kivett, V.R. (1993). Racial comparisons of the grandmother role: Implications for strengthening the family support system of older Black women. *Family Relations, 42*, 165–172.

Klass, P. (1988, October 23). Survival odds. *The New York Times Magazine*.

Klaus, M., & Kennell, J.H. (1976). *Maternal-infant bonding*. St. Louis: Mosby.

Klein, H.A. (1992). Temperament and self-esteem in late adolescence. *Adolescence, 27*(107), 689–695.

Kline, M., Johnston, J.R., & Tschann, J.M. (1991). The long shadow of marital conflict: A model of children's postdivorce adjustment. *Journal of Marriage and the Family, 53*, 297–309.

Kline, M., Tschann, J.M., Johnston, J.R., & Wallerstein, J.S. (1989). Children's adjustment in joint and sole physical custody families. *Developmental Psychology, 25*(3), 430–438.

Kline, P. (1972). *Fact and fantasy in Freudian theory*. London: Methuen.

Klinge, V., & Piggott, L.R. (1986). Substance use by adolescent psychiatric inpatients and their parents. *Adolescence, 21*(82), 323–331.

Klinnert, M.D., Gavin, L.A., Wamboldt, F.S., & Mrazek, D.A. (1992). Marriages with children at medical risk: The transition to parenthood. *Journal of the American Academy of Child and Adolescent Psychiatry, 31*(2), 334–342.

Knapp, R.J. (1987, July). When a child dies. *Psychology Today*, pp. 60–67.

Knutson, J.F. (1995). Psychological characteristics of maltreated children: Putative risk factors and consequences. *Annual Review of Psychology, 46*, 401–431.

Kochanska, G. (1990). Maternal beliefs as long-term predictors of mother-child interaction and report. *Child Development, 61*, 1934–1943.

Kochanska, G. (1992). Children's interpersonal influence with mothers and peers. *Developmental Psychology, 28*(3), 491–499.

Kochanska, G. (1994). Beyond cognition: Expanding

the search for the early roots of internalization and conscience. *Developmental Psychology*, *30*(1), 20–22.

Kochanska, G., & Aksan, N. (1995). Mother-child mutually positive affect, the quality of child compliance to requests and prohibitions, and maternal control as correlates of early internalization. *Child Development*, *66*, 236–254.

Kochanska, G., Kuczynski, L., & Radke-Yarrow, M. (1989). Correspondence between mothers' self-reported and observed child-rearing practices. *Child Development*, *60*, 56–63.

Koeske, G.F., & Koeske, R.D. (1990). The buffering effect of social support on parental stress. *American Journal of Orthopsychiatry*, *60*(3), 440–450.

Kohlberg, L. (1966). A cognitive-developmental analysis of children's sex-role concepts and attitudes. In E.E. Maccoby (Ed.), *The development of sex differences*. Stanford, CA: Stanford University Press.

Kohn, A. (1987a, September). Art for art's sake. *Psychology Today*, pp. 52–57.

Kohn, A. (1987b, February). Shattered innocence. *Psychology Today*, pp. 54–58.

Kohn, A. (1988, October). Beyond selfishness. *Psychology Today*, pp 34–38.

Kohn, A. (1993). *Punished by rewards: The trouble with gold stars, incentive plans, A's, praise, and other bribes*. Boston: Houghton Mifflin.

Kojima, H. (1986). Japanese concepts of child development from the mid-17th to mid-19th century. *International Journal of Behavioral Development*, *9*(3), 315–329.

Kolata, G. (1987, December 22). The poignant thoughts of Down's children are given voice. *The New York Times*.

Kolata, G. (1988a, May 12). Confident obstetricians discovering new frontiers of prenatal diagnosis. *The New York Times*.

Kolata, G. (1988b, May 10). When the baby is late: Obstetricians search for the safest approach. *The New York Times*.

Konker, C. (1992). Rethinking child sexual abuse: An anthropological perspective. *American Journal of Orthopsychiatry*, *62*(1), 147-153.

Kopp, C.B. (1989). Regulation of distress and negative emotions: A developmental view. *Developmental Psychology*, *25*(3), 343–354.

Kornhaber, A. (1996). *Contemporary grandparenting*. Thousand Oaks, CA: Sage.

Kornhaber, A., & Woodward, K.L. (1981). *Grandparents/grandchildren: The vital connection*. Garden City, NY: Doubleday.

Kovacs, L. (1983). A conceptualization of marital development. *Family Therapy*, *10*, 183–210.

Kramer, L., & Baron, L.A. (1995). Parental perceptions of children's sibling relationships. *Family Relations*, *44*, 95-103.

Kraus-Mars, A.H., & Lachman, P. (1994). Breaking bad news to parents with disabled children: A cross-cultural study. *Child: Care, Health & Development*, *20*(2), 101–113.

Kropp, J.P., & Haynes, O.M. (1987). Abusive and nonabusive mother's ability to identify general and specific emotion signals to infants. *Child Development*, *58*, 187–190.

Kuczynski, L., & Kochanska, G. (1990). Development of children's noncompliance strategies from toddlerhood to age 5. *Developmental Psychology*, *26*(3), 398–408.

Kuczynski, L., & Kochanska, G. (1995). Function and content of maternal demands: Developmental significance of early demands for competent action. *Child Development*, *66*, 616–628.

Kuczynski, L., Kochanska, G., Radke-Yarrow, M., & Girnius-Brown, O. (1987). A developmental interpretation of young children's noncompliance. *Developmental Psychology*, *23*(6), 799–806.

Kurdek, L.A. (1993a). Predicting marital dissolution: A 5-year prospective longitudinal study of newlywed couples. *Journal of Personality and Social Psychology*, *64*(2), 221–242.

Kurdek, L.A. (1993b). Nature and prediction of changes in marital quality for first-time parent and nonparent husbands and wives. *Journal of Family Psychology*, *6*(3), 255–265.

Kurdek, L.A. (1993c). Issues in proposing a general model of the effects of divorce on children. *Journal of Marriage and the Family*, *55*, 39–41.

Kurdek, L.A. (1996). Parenting satisfaction and marital satisfaction in mothers and fathers with young children. *Journal of Family Psychology*, *10*(3), 331–342.

Kurdek, L.A., & Fine, M.A. (1993). Parent and nonparent residential family members as providers of warmth and supervision to young adolescents. *Journal of Family Psychology*, *7*(2), 245–249.

Kurdek, L.A., & Fine, M.A. (1994). Family acceptance and family control as predictors of adjustment in young adolescents: Linear, curvilinear, or interactive effects? *Child Development*, *65*, 1137–1146.

Kurdek, L.A., & Fine, M.A. (1995). Mothers, fathers, stepfathers, and siblings as providers of supervision, acceptance, and autonomy to young adolescents. *Journal of Family Psychology*, *9*(1), 95–99.

Kurdek, L.A., Fine, M.A., & Sinclair, R.J. (1994). The relation between parenting transitions and adjustment in young adolescents: A multisample investigation. *Journal of Early Adolescence*, *14*(4), 412–431.

Kutner, L. (1987a, December 30). Preparing a child for independence must begin early. *The New York Times*.

Kutner, L. (1987b, December 3). Temper tantrums: It helps to realize they're just a stage. *The New York Times*.

Kutner, L. (1987c, November 19). What's really impor-

ma: Motivation for search and reunion. *Journal of Marriage and the Family, 57,* 653–660.

Marfo, K. (Ed.). (1991). *Early intervention in transition: Current perspectives on programs for handicapped children.* NY: Praeger.

Margalit, M., Raviv, A., & Ankonina, D.B. (1992). Coping and coherence among parents with disabled children. *Journal of Clinical Child Psychology, 21*(3), 202–209.

Margolin, L. (1992). Beyond maternal blame: Physical child abuse as a phenomenon of gender. *Journal of Family Issues, 13*(3), 410–423.

Margolis, M. (1984). *Mothers and such: Views of American women and why they changed.* Berkeley, CA: University of California Press.

Marks, I. (1987). The development of normal fear: A review. *Journal of Child Psychology and Psychiatry, 28*(5), 667–697.

Marks, N. F. (1995). Midlife marital status differences in social support relationships with adult children and psychological well-being. *Journal of Family Issues, 16*(1), 5–28.

Marshall, S. (1995). Ethnic socialization of African-American children: Implications for parenting, identity development, and academic achievement. *Journal of Youth & Adolescence, 24*(4), 377–396.

Marsiglio, W. (1991). Paternal engagement activities with minor children. *Journal of Marriage and the Family, 53,* 973–986.

Marsiglio, W. (1992). Stepfathers with minor children living at home. *Journal of Family Issues, 13*(2), 195–214.

Marsiglio, W. (1995). Fathers' diverse life course patterns and roles: Theory and social interventions. In W. Marsiglio (Ed.), *Fatherhood: Contemporary theory, research, and social policy.* Thousand Oaks, CA: Sage.

Martin, A. (1996, February 8). Multiple births: A wake-up call. *The New York Times,* pp. C1, C4

Martin, B. (1990). The transmission of relationship difficulties from one generation to the next. *Journal of Youth & Adolescence, 19*(3), 181–199.

Martin, J.M., & Cole, D.A. (1993). Adaptability and cohesion of dyadic relationships in families with developmentally disabled children. *Journal of Family Psychology, 7*(2), 186–196.

Martin, P., Halverson, C.F., Wampler, K.S., & Hollett-Wright, N. (1991). Intergenerational differences in parenting styles and goals. *International Journal of Behavioral Development, 14*(2), 195–207.

Martin, S. (1994, October). Parenting roles less reliant on gender. *APA Monitor,* p. 20

Martin, S. (1995a, October). Children increase risk of spousal abuse. *APA Monitor,* p. 48.

Martin, S. (1995b, October). Are children with disabilities more likely to be abused? *APA Monitor,* p. 48.

Martinez, G.A., & Krieger, F.W. (1985). The 1984 milk-feeding patterns in the United States. *Pediatrics, 76,* 1004–1008.

Martinson, B.C., & Wu, L.L. (1992). Parent histories: Patterns of change in early life. *Journal of Family Issues, 13*(3), 351–377.

Masselam, V.S., Marcus, R.F., & Stunkard, C.L. (1990). Parent-adolescent communication, family functioning, and school performance. *Adolescence, 25*(99), 725–737.

Mathews, L. (1996, July 6). More than identity rides on a new racial category. *The New York Times,* pp. 1, 7.

Mathews, S.H., & Sprey, J. (1984). The impact of divorce on grandparenthood: An exploratory study. *The Gerontologist, 24,* 41–47.

Mboya, M.M. (1995). Variations in parenting practices: Gender- and age-related differences in African adolescents. *Adolescence, 30*(120), 955–962.

McBride, B.A. (1989). Stress and father's parental competence: Implications for family life and parent educators. *Family Relations, 38,* 385–389.

McBride, S., & Belsky, J. (1988). Characteristics, determinants, and consequences of maternal separation anxiety. *Developmental Psychology, 24*(3), 407–414.

McCall, R.B., Evahn, C., & Kratzer, L. (1992). *High school underachievers: What do they achieve as adults?* Newbury Park, CA: Sage.

McCartney, K., & Galanopoulos, A. (1988). Child care and attachment: A new frontier the second time around. *American Journal of Orthopsychiatry, 58*(1), 16–24.

McClelland, J. (1995). Sending children to kindergarten: A phenomenological study of mothers' experiences. *Family Relations, 44,* 177–183.

McCleod, B. (1986, October). Rx for health: A dose of self-confidence. *Psychology Today,* pp. 46–50.

McCloskey, L.A., Figueredo, A.J., & Koss, M.P. (1995). The effects of systemic family violence on children's mental health. *Child Development, 66,* 1239–1261.

McCollum, A.T. (1985). Grieving over the lost dream. In M.J. Schleifer and S.D. Klein (Eds.). *The disabled child and the family: An exceptional parent reader.* Boston, MA: The Exceptional Parent Press.

McCollum, J. (1985). Parenting an infant with a disability—A practical guide for interaction. In M.J. Schleifer and S.D. Klein (Eds.). *The disabled child and the family: An exceptional parent reader.* Boston, MA: The Exceptional Parent Press.

McCombs, A., & Forehand, R. (1989). Adolescent school performance following parental divorce: Are there family factors that can enhance success? *Adolescence, 24*(96), 871–880.

McConachie, H., & Mitchell, D.R. (1985). Parents teaching their young mentally handicapped children. *Journal of Child Psychology and Psychiatry, 26*(3), 389–405.

McCord, J. (1988a). Alcoholism: Toward understanding genetic and social factors. *Psychiatry*, *51*, 131–141.

McCord, J. (1988b). Parental behavior in the cycle of aggression. *Psychiatry*, *51*, 14–23.

McCord, J. (1991). Family relationships, juvenile delinquency, and adult criminality. *Criminology*, *29*, 397–417.

McCormick, N., Izzo, A., & Folcik, J. (1985). Adolescents' values, sexuality, and contraception in a rural New York County. *Adolescence*, *20*(78), 385–395.

McCoy, C.L., & Masters, J.C. (1985). Children's strategies for the social control of emotion. *Child Development*, *56*, 1214-1222.

McCoy, E. (1984, November). Kids and divorce. *Parents*.

McDevitt, T.M., Ewers, C.A., & Oreskovich, M. (1991). Mothers' beliefs about listening: Implications for children's comprehension and conceptions of listening. *Journal of Applied Developmental Psychology*, *12*(4), 467–489.

McGhee, P.E. (1979). *Humor: Its origin and development*. San Francisco: W.H. Freeman.

McGuire, S., Neiderhiser, J.M., Reiss, D., Hetherington, E.M., & Plomin, R. (1994). Genetic and environmental influences on perceptions of self-worth and competence in adolescence: A study of twins, full siblings, and step-siblings. *Child Development*, *65*, 785–799.

McGurk, H., Caplan, M., Hennessy, E., & Moss, P. (1993). Controversy, theory and social context in contemporary day care research. *Journal of Child Psychology & Psychiatry & Allied Disciplines*, *34*(1), 3–23.

McHale, J.P. (1995). Coparenting and triadic interactions during infancy: The roles of marital distress and child gender. *Developmental Psychology*, *31*(6), 985–996.

McHale, S.M., Bartko, W.T., Crouter, A.C., & Perry-Jenkins, M. (1990). Children's housework and psychosocial functioning: The mediating effects of parents' sex-role behaviors and attitudes. *Child Development*, *61*, 1413–1426.

McHale, S.M., Crouter, A.C., McGuire, S.A., & Updegraff, K.A. (1995). Congruence between mothers' and fathers' differential treatment of siblings: Links with family relations and children's well-being. *Child Development*, *66*(1), 116–128.

McHale, S.M., & Gamble, W.C. (1989). Sibling relationships of children with disabled and nondisabled brothers and sisters. *Developmental Psychology*, *25*(3), 421–429.

McHale, S.M., & Pawletko, T.M. (1992). Differential treatment of siblings in two family contexts. *Child Development*, *63*, 68–81.

McIntosh, D.N., Silver, R.C., & Wortman, C.B. (1993). Religion's role in adjustment to a negative life event: Coping with the loss of a child. *Journal of Personality and Social Psychology*, *65*(4), 812–821.

McIntyre, J.G., & Dusek, J.B. (1995). Perceived parental rearing practices and styles of coping. *Journal of Youth & Adolescence*, *24*(4), 499–509.

McLaughlin, B. (1983). Child compliance to parental control techniques. *Developmental Psychology*, *19*(5), 667–673.

McLoyd, V.C. (1989). Socialization and development in a changing economy: The effects of paternal job and income loss on children. *American Psychologist*, *44*(2), 293–302.

McLoyd, V.C. (1990). The impact of economic hardship on Black families and children: Psychological distress, parenting, and socioemotional development. *Child Development*, *61*, 311–346.

McNally, S., Eisenberg, N., & Harris, J.D. (1991). Consistency and change in maternal child-rearing practices and values: A longitudinal study. *Child Development*, *62*, 190–198.

McQuarrie, H.G. (1980). Home delivery controversy. *Journal of the American Medical Association*, *243*, 1747–1748.

McRoy, R., & Freeman, E. (1986). Racial identity issues among mixed-race children. *Social Work in Education*, 164–175.

McRoy, R.G., Zurcher, L.A., Lauderdale, M.L., & Anderson, R.E. (1984). The identity of transracial adoptees. *Social Casework: The Journal of Contemporary Social Work*, *65*, 34–39.

McWhirter, J.J., McWhirter, R.J., & McWhirter, M.C. (1985). The learning disabled child: A retrospective review. *Journal of Learning Disabilities*, *18*(6), 315–318.

Meier, B. (1993, February 14). Effective? Maybe. Profitable? Clearly. *The New York Times*.

Melton, G.B., & Davidson, H.A. (1987). Child protection and society: When should the state intervene? *American Psychologist*, *42*(2), 172–175.

Meltzoff, A.N. (1988). Imitation of televised models by infants. *Child Development*, *59*, 1221–1229.

Menard, J.L., & Johnson, G.M. (1992). Incest: Family dysfunction or sexual preference? *Family Therapy*, *19*(2), 115–122.

Meredith, D. (1985, June). Mom, dad and the kids. *Psychology Today*, pp. 60–67.

Meredith, R. (1996, May 10). Parents convicted for a youth's misconduct. *The New York Times*, p. A14.

Metcalf, K., & Gaier, E.L. (1987). Patterns of middle-class parenting and adolescent underachievement. *Adolescence*, *22*(88), 919–929.

Meyer, D.R., & Garasky, S. (1993). Custodial fathers: Myths, realities, and child support policy. *Journal of Marriage and the Family*, *55*, 73–89.

Meyer, M. (1989, April). Locking out sex and violence on cable. *Video Magazine*, pp. 61–62.

and children's school performance. *Child Development, 64*, 36–56.

Oldershaw, L., Walters, G.C., & Hall, D.K. (1986). Control strategies and noncompliance in abusive mother-child dyads: An observational study. *Child Development, 57*(3), 722–732.

Olds, J., Schwartz, R.S., Eisen, S.V., Betcher, R.W., et al. (1993). Part-time employment and marital well-being: A hypothesis and pilot study. *Family Therapy, 20*(1), 1–16.

Olson, S.L., Bates, J.E., & Kaskie, B. (1992). Caregiver-infant interaction antecedents of children's school-age cognitive ability. *Merrill-Palmer Quarterly, 38*(3), 309–330.

Olweus, D. (1993). *Bullying at school: What we know and what we can do.* Oxford, England: Blackwell.

Olweus, D. (1994). Annotation: Bullying at school: Basic facts and effects of a school based intervention program. *Journal of Child Psychology & Psychiatry & Allied Disciplines, 35*(7), 1171–1190.

O'Malley, P.M., & Bachman, J.G. (1983). Self-esteem: Change and stability between ages 13 and 23. *Developmental Psychology, 19*(2), 257–268.

Onyehalu, A.S. (1983). Inadequacy of sex knowledge of adolescents: Implications for counselling and sex education. *Adolescence, 18*, 627–630.

O'Reilly, E., & Morrison, M.L. (1993). Grandparent-headed families: New therapeutic challenges. *Child Psychiatry & Human Development, 23*(3), 147–159.

Ostfeld, B.M., Ryan, T., Hiatt, M., & Hegyi, T. (1993). Maternal grief after Sudden Infant Death Syndrome. *Journal of Developmental & Behavioral Pediatrics, 14*(3), 156–162.

Overmier, K. (1990). Biracial adolescents: Areas of conflict in identity formation. *The Journal of Applied Social Sciences, 14*(2), 157–176.

Painton, P. (May 10, 1993). The maternal wall. *Time Magazine*, pp. 44–45.

Palfrey, J.S., Walker, D.K., Butler, J.A., & Singer, J.D. (1989). Patterns of response in families of chronically disabled children: An assessment of five metropolitan school districts. *American Journal of Orthopsychiatry, 59*(1), 94–105.

Palkovitz, R. (1984). Parental attitudes and fathers' interaction with their 5-month-old infants. *Developmental Psychology, 20*, 1054–1060.

Palkovitz, R. (1985). Fathers' birth attendance, early contact, and extended contact with their newborns: A critical review. *Child Development, 56*(2), 392–406.

Parish, T.S., & Necessary, J.R. (1994). Parents' actions: Are they related to children's self-concepts, evaluations of parents, and to each other? *Adolescence, 29*(116), 943–948.

Parke, R.D. (1969). Effectiveness of punishment as an interaction of intensity, timing, agent nurturance and cognitive-structuring. *Child Development, 40*, 213–235.

Parke, R.D. (1973). Explorations in punishment, discipline and self-control. In P. Elich (Ed.), *Social learning.* Bellingham: Western Washington State Press.

Parke, R.D. (1995). Fathers and families. In M.H. Bornstein (Ed.), *Handbook of parenting*, (Vol. 3). Hillsdale, NJ: Erlbaum.

Parke, R.D., & Suomi, S. (1983). Adult male-infant relationships: Human and nonhuman primate evidence. In K. Immelmann, G. Barlow, M. Main, and L. Petrinovitch (Eds), *Behavioral development: The Bielefeld Interdisciplinary Project.* NY: Cambridge University Press.

Parker, H., & Parker, S. (1986). Father-daughter sexual abuse: An emerging perspective. *American Journal of Orthopsychiatry, 56*(4), 531–549.

Parker, J.G., & Asher, S.R. (1987). Peer relations and later personal adjustment: Are low-accepted children at risk? *Psychological Bulletin, 102*(3), 357–389.

Parks, P.L., Lenz, E.R., & Jenkins, L.S. (1992). The role of social support and stressors for mothers and infants. *Child: Care, Health & Development, 18*(3), 151–171.

Parrott, W.G., & Smith, R.H. (1993). Distinguishing the experiences of envy and jealousy. *Journal of Personality & Social Psychology, 64*(6), 906–920.

Paschall, M.J., Ennett, S.T., & Flewelling, R.L. (1996). Relationships among family characteristics and violent behavior by Black and White male adolescents. *Journal of Youth and Adolescence, 25*(2), 177–198.

Passino, A.W., Whitman, T.L., Borkowski, J.G., Schellenbach, C.J., Maxwell, S.E., Keogh, D., & Rellinger, E. (1993). Personal adjustment during pregnancy and adolescent parenting. *Adolescence, 28*(109), 97–122.

Patel, N., Power, T.G., & Bhavnagri, N.P. (1996). Socialization values and practices of Indian immigrant parents: Correlates of modernity and acculturation. *Child Development, 67*, 302–313.

Patterson, C.J. (1992). Children of lesbian and gay parents. *Child Development, 63*, 1025–1042.

Patterson, C.J. (1995). Families of the baby boom: Parents' division of labor and children's adjustment. *Developmental Psychology, 31*(1), 115–123.

Patterson, G.R. (1982). *Coercive family process.* Eugene, OR: Castalia.

Patterson, G.R. (1986). Performance models for antisocial boys. *American Psychologist, 41*, 432–444.

Patterson, G.R. (1988). Stress: A change agent for family process. In N. Garmezy and M. Rutter (Eds.), *Stress, coping and development in children.* Baltimore, MD: Johns Hopkins Press.

Patterson, G.R., DeBaryshe, B.D., & Ramsey, E. (1989). A developmental perspective on antisocial behavior. *American Psychologist, 44*(2), 329–335.

Patton, J.R. (1994). Practical recommendations for using homework with students with learning disabilities. *Journal of Learning Disabilities*, 27(9), 570–578.

Paulson, S.E., & Sputa, C.L. (1996). Patterns of parenting during adolescence: Perceptions of adolescents and parents. *Adolescence*, 31(122), pp. 369–381.

Peek, C.W., Fischer, J.L., & Kidwell, J.S. (1985). Teenage violence toward parents: A neglected dimension of family violence. *Journal of Marriage and the Family*, 47, 1051–1060.

Pehrson, K.L., & Robinson, C.C. (1990). Parent education: Does it make a difference? *Child Study Journal*, 20(4), 221–236.

Pelletier, L., Godin, G., Lepage, L., & Dussault, G. (1994). Social support received by mothers of chronically ill children. *Child: Care, Health & Development*, 20(2), 115–131.

Perry, A., Sarlo-McGarvey, N., & Factor, D.C. (1992). Stress and family functioning in parents of girls with Rett syndrome. *Journal of Autism & Developmental Disorders*, 22(2), 235–248.

Perry, D.G., Kusel, S.J., & Perry, L.C. (1988). Victims of peer aggression. *Developmental Psychology*, 24(6), 807–814.

Pestrak, V.A., & Martin, D. (1985). Cognitive development and aspects of adolescent sexuality. *Adolescence*, 20(80), 981–987.

Peters, J.F. (1994). Gender socialization of adolescents in the home: Research and discussion. *Adolescence*, 29(116), 913–934.

Peterson, A.C. (1987, September). Those gangly years. *Psychology Today*, pp. 28–34.

Peterson, C., & Peterson, R. (1986). Parent-child interaction and daycare: Does quality of daycare matter? *Journal of Applied Developmental Psychology*, 7(1), 1–15.

Peterson, G.W., & Rollins, B.C. (1987). Parent-child socialization. In M.B. Sussman and S.K. Steinmetz (Eds.), *Handbook of marriage and the family*. NY: Plenum.

Peterson, L. (1989). Latchkey children's preparation for self-care: Overestimated, underrehearsed, and unsafe. *Journal of Clinical Child Psychology*, 18(1), 36–43.

Pettit, G.S., & Bates, J.E. (1989). Family interaction patterns and children's behavior problems from infancy to 4 years. *Developmental Psychology*, 25(3), 413–420.

Pettit, G.S., & Mize, J. (1993). Substance and style: Understanding the ways in which parents teach children about social relationships. In S. Duck (Ed.), *Learning about relationships*. Newbury Park, CA: Sage.

Pettle, S.A., & Britten, C.M. (1995). Talking with children about death and dying. *Child: Care, Health & Development*, 21(6), 395–404.

Phares, V. (1993). Father absence, mother love, and other family issues that need to be questioned: Comment on Silverstein (1993). *Journal of Family Psychology*, 7(3), 293–300.

Phares, V. (1995). Fathers' and mothers' participation in research. *Adolescence*, 30(119), 593–602.

Phares, V., & Compas, B.E. (1992). The role of fathers in child and adolescent psychopathology: Make room for daddy. *Psychological Bulletin*, 111(3), 387–412.

Phillips, D., McCartney, K., & Scarr, S. (1987). Child-care quality and children's social development. *Developmental Psychology*, 23(4), 537–543.

Phillips, D.A., Voran, M., Kisker, E., Howes, C., et al. (1994). Child care for children in poverty: Opportunity or inequity? *Child Development*, 65(2), 472–492.

Phillips, S., Bohannon, W.E., Gayton, W.F., & Friedman, S.B. (1985). Parent interview findings regarding the impact of cystic fibrosis on families. *Journal of Developmental and Behavioral Pediatrics*, 6(3), 122–127.

Phinney, J.S., & Alipuria, L.L. (1990). Ethnic identity in college students from four ethnic groups. *Journal of Adolescence*, 13, 171–183.

Piaget, J. (1954). *The construction of reality in the child*. NY: Basic Books.

Piaget, J. (1972). Intellectual evolution from adolescence to adulthood. *Human Relations*, 15, 1–12.

Pick, S., & Palos, P.A. (1995). Impact of the family on the sex lives of adolescents. *Adolescence*, 30(119), 667–676.

Pina, D.L., & Bengston, V.L. (1993). The division of household labor and wives' happiness: Ideology, employment, and perceptions of support. *Journal of Marriage and the Family*, 55, 901–912.

Pitt, D.E. (1988, March 15). New program to combat child abuse. *The New York Times*.

Pleck, J.H. (1993). Are "family-supportive" employer policies relevant to men? In J.C. Hood (Ed.), *Men, work, and family*. Newbury Park, CA: Sage.

Plienis, A.J., Robbins, F.R., & Dunlap, G. (1988). Parent adjustment and family stress as factors in behavioral parent training for young autistic children. *Journal of the Multihandicapped Person*, 1(1), 31–52.

Plomin, R. (1989). Environment and genes: Determinants of behavior. *American Psychologist*, 44(2), 105–111.

Plomin, R., Reiss, D., Hetherington, E.M., & Howe, G.W. (1994). Nature and nurture: Genetic contributions to measures of the family environment. *Developmental Psychology*, 30(1), 32–43.

Plumert, J.M., & Nichols-Whitehead, P. (1996). Parental scaffolding of young children's spatial communication. *Developmental Psychology*, *32*(3), 523–532.

Polansky, N.A., Chalmers, M.A., Buttenwieser, E., & Williams, D.P. (1981). *Damaged parents: An anatomy of child neglect*. Chicago: University of Chicago.

Post, R.D. (1988). Self-sabotage among successful women. *Psychotherapy in Private Practice*, *6*(3), 191–205.

Poston, W.S.C. (1990). The biracial identity development model: A needed addition. *Journal of Counseling & Development*, *69*, 152–155.

Powell, D.R. (1993). Supporting parent-child relationships in the early years: Lessons learned and yet to be learned. In T.H. Brubaker (Ed.), *Family relations: Challenges for the future*. Newbury Park, CA: Sage.

Powell, L. (1977). The empty nest, employment, and psychiatric symptoms in college-educated women. *Psychology of Women Quarterly*, *2*, 253–265.

Power, T.G. (1984). Life with father: New directions for family policy. Review of M.E. Lamb and A. Sagi (Eds.). *Fatherhood and family policy*. Hillsdale, NJ: Erlbaum, 1983. In *Contemporary psychology*, *29*(4), 324–325.

Power, T.G. (1985). Mother- and father-infant play: A developmental analysis. *Child Development*, *56*(6), 1514–1524.

Power, T.G., & Chapieski, M.L. (1986). Childrearing and impulse control in toddlers: A naturalistic investigation. *Developmental Psychology*, *22*(2), 271–275.

Power, T.G., Kobayashi-Winata, H., & Kelley, M.L. (1992). Childrearing patterns in Japan and the United States: A cluster analytic study. *International Journal of Behavioral Development*, *15*(2), 185–205.

Power, T.G., McGrath, M.P., Hughes, S.O., & Manire, S.H. (1994). Compliance versus self-assertion: Young children's responses to mothers versus fathers. *Developmental Psychology*, *30*(6), 980–989.

Power, T.G., & Parke, R.D. (1986). Patterns of early socialization: Mother- and father-infant interaction in the home. *International Journal of Behavioral Development*, *9*(3), 331–341.

Powers, S.I., Hauser, S.T., & Kilner, L.A. (1989). Adolescent mental health. *American Psychologist*, *44*(2), 200–208.

Pratt, M.W., Hunsberger, B., Pancer, S.M., Roth, D., & Santolupo, S. (1993). Thinking about parenting: Reasoning about developmental issues across the life span. *Developmental Psychology*, *29*(3), 585–595.

Pratt, M.W., Kerig, P., Cowan, P.A., & Cowan, C.P. (1988). Mothers and fathers teaching 3-year-olds: Authoritative parenting and adult scaffolding of young children's learning. *Developmental Psychology*, *24*(6), 832–839.

Pratt, M.W., Kerig, P.K., Cowan, P.A., & Cowan, C.P. (1992). Family worlds: Couple satisfaction, parenting

style, and mothers' and fathers' speech to young children. *Merrill-Palmer Quarterly*, *38*(2), 245–262.

Pridham, K., Denney, N., Pascoe, J., Chiu, Y., & Creasey, D. (1995). Mothers' solutions to childrearing problems: Conditions and processes. *Journal of Marriage and the Family*, *57*, 785–799.

Putallaz, M. (1987). Maternal behavior and children's sociometric status. *Child Development*, *58*, 324–340.

Quittner, A.L., DiGirolamo, A.M., Michel, M., & Eigen, H. (1992). Parental response to cystic fibrosis: A contextual analysis of the diagnosis phase. *Journal of Pediatric Psychology*, *17*(6), 683–704.

Quittner, A.L., & Opipari, L.C. (1994). Differential treatment of siblings: Interview and diary analyses comparing two family contexts. *Child Development*, *65*, 800–814.

Rabow, J., Radcliffe-Vasile, S., Newcomb, M.D., & Hernandez, A.C.R. (1992). Teachers', students', and others' contributions to educational outcomes. *Youth & Society*, *24*(1), 71–91.

Radin, N. (1988). Primary caregiving fathers of long duration. In P. Bronstein and C.P. Cowan (Eds.)., *Fatherhood today: Men's changing role in the family*. NY: John Wiley.

Radin, N., & Goldsmith, R. (1985). Caregiving fathers of preschoolers: Four years later. *Merrill-Palmer Quarterly*, *31*(4), 375–383.

Radin, N., & Harold-Goldsmith, R. (1989). The involvement of selected unemployed and employed men with their children. *Child Development*, *60*, 454–459.

Raeff, C. (1994). Viewing adolescent mothers on their own terms: Linking self-conceptualization and adolescent motherhood. *Developmental Review*, *14*(3), 215–244.

Ragozin, A.S., Basham, R.B., Crnic, K.A., Greenberg, M.T., & Robinson, N.M. (1982). Effects of maternal age on parenting role. *Developmental Psychology*, *18*(4), 627–634.

Rath, F.H., & Okum, M.E. (1995). Parents and children sleeping together: Cosleeping prevalence and concerns. *American Journal of Orthopsychiatry*, *65*(3), 411–418.

Raver, C.C. (1996). Relations between social contingency in mother-child interaction and 2-year-olds' social competence. *Developmental Psychology*, *32*(5), 850–859.

Reese, E., & Fivush, R. (1993). Parental styles of talking about the past. *Developmental Psychology*, *29*(3), 596–606.

Reid, J.B., Kavanagh, K., & Baldwin, D.V. (1987). Abusive parents' perceptions of child problem behaviors: An example of parental bias. *Journal of Abnormal Child Psychology*, *15*(3), 457–466.

Reid, W.J., & Crisafulli, A. (1990). Marital discord and

child behavior problems: A meta-analysis. *Journal of Abnormal Child Psychology, 18,* 105–117.

Reinhold, R. (1987, October 4). California tries caring for its growing ranks of latchkey children. *The New York Times.*

Reis, J.S., & Herz, E.J. (1987). Correlates of adolescent parenting. *Adolescence, 22*(87), 599–610.

Reissland, N. (1994). The socialisation of pride in young children. *International Journal of Behavioral Development, 17*(3), 541–552.

Rende, R.D., Slomkowski, C.L., Stocker, C., Fulker, D.W., & Plomin, R. (1992). Genetic and environmental influences on maternal and sibling interaction in middle childhood: A sibling adoption study. *Developmental Psychology, 28*(3), 484–490.

Reynolds, A.J., & Gill, S. (1994). The role of parental perspectives in the school adjustment of inner-city Black children. *Journal of Youth & Adolescence, 23*(6), 671–694.

Richards, M.H., & Duckett, E. (1994). The relationship of maternal employment to early adolescent daily experience with and without parents. *Child Development, 65,* 225–236.

Richardson, L. (September 2, 1992). No cookie-cutter answers in 'mommy wars.' *The New York Times.*

Richardson, L. (May 2, 1993). Nannygate for the poor. *The New York Times.*

Richardson, S.A., Koller, H., & Katz, M. (1985). Relationship of upbringing to later behavior disturbance of mildly mentally retarded young people. *American Journal of Mental Deficiency, 90*(1), 1–8.

Richins, M.L., & Dawson, S. (1992). A consumer values orientation for materialism and its measurement: Scale development and validation. *Journal of Consumer Research, 19,* 303–316.

Richman, A.L., Miller, P.M., & LeVine, R.A. (1992). Cultural and educational variations in maternal responsiveness. *Developmental Psychology, 28*(4), 614–621.

Richters, J.E. (1992). Depressed mothers as informants about their children: A critical review of the evidence for distortion. *Psychological Bulletin, 112*(3), 485–499.

Riley, A.W., Parrish, J.M., & Cataldo, M.F. (1989). Training parents to meet the needs of children with medical or physical handicaps. In C.E. Schaefer and J.M. Briesmeister (Eds.), *Handbook of parent training.* NY: John Wiley.

Riley, D. (1990). Network influences on father involvement in childrearing. In M. Cochran, M. Larner, D. Riley, L. Gunnarsson, and C. Henderson, Jr. (Eds.), *Extending families: The social networks of parents and their children.* London/New York: Cambridge Unversity Press.

Risman, B.J. (1989). Can men "mother?" Life as a single father. In B.J. Risman and P. Schwartz (Eds.), *Gender in intimate relationships: A microstructural approach.* Belmont, CA: Wadsworth.

Roberts, C.W., Green, R., Williams, K., & Goodman, M. (1987). Boyhood gender identity development: A statistical contrast of two family groups. *Developmental Psychology, 23*(4), 544–557.

Roberts, M. (1988, February). Schoolyard menace. *Psychology Today,* pp. 52–56.

Roberts, R.N., & Barnes, M.L. (1992). "Let momma show you how": Maternal-child interactions and their effects on children's cognitive performance. *Journal of Applied Developmental Psychology, 13*(3), 363–376.

Roberts, W., & Strayer, J. (1996). Empathy, emotional expressiveness, and prosocial behavior. *Child Development, 67,* 449–470.

Robertson, J.F., & Simons, R.L. (1989). Family factors, self-esteem, and adolescent depression. *Journal of Marriage and the Family, 51,* 125–138.

Robinson, B.E., & Barret, R.L. (1985, December). Teenage fathers. *Psychology Today,* pp. 66–70.

Robinson, J.P. (1977). *How Americans use time: A social-psychological analysis of everyday behavior.* NY: Praeger.

Robinson, L.C., & Blanton, P.W. (1993). Marital strengths in enduring marriages. *Family Relations, 42,* 38–45.

Rodman, H., Pratto, D.J., & Nelson, R.S. (1985). Child care arrangements and children's functioning: A comparison of self-care and adult-care children. *Developmental Psychology, 21,* 413–418.

Rodman, H., Pratto, D.J. & Nelson, R.S. (1988). Toward a definition of self-care children: A commentary on Steinberg (1986). *Developmental Psychology, 24*(2), 292–294.

Rodrigue, J.R., Morgan, S.B., & Geffken, G.R. (1992). Psychosocial adaptation of fathers of children with autism, Down syndrome, and normal development. *Journal of Autism & Developmental Disorders, 22*(2), 249–263.

Rogers, C. (1961). *On becoming a person.* Boston: Houghton Mifflin.

Rogoff, B. (1990). *Apprenticeship in thinking: Cognitive development in social context.* NY: Oxford University Press.

Rohner, R.P. (1994). Patterns of parenting: The warmth dimension in worldwide perspective. In W.J. Lonner and R. Malpass (Eds.), *Psychology and culture.* Needham Heights, MA: Allyn and Bacon.

Romig, C., & Bakken, L. (1992). Intimacy development in middle adolescence: Its relationship to gender and family cohesion and adaptability. *Journal of Youth and Adolescence, 21*(3), 325–338.

Roopnarine, J.L., Talukder, E., Jain, D., Joshi, P. & Srivastav, P. (1990). Characteristics of holding, patterns of play, and social behaviors between parents and infants in New Delhi, India. *Developmental Psychology*, *26*(4), 667–673.

Rosenberg, B.G., & Hyde, J.S. (1993). The only child: Is there only one kind of only? *Journal of Genetic Psychology*, *154*(2), 269–282.

Rosenberg, M. S. (1987). New directions for research on the psychological maltreatment of children. *American Psychologist*, *42*(2), 166–171.

Rosenfeld, A. (1987). Freud, psychodynamics, and incest. *Child Welfare*, *66*(6), 485–496.

Rosenheim, E., & Reicher, R. (1985). Informing children about a parent's terminal illness. *Journal of Child Psychology & Psychiatry & Allied Disciplines*, *26*(6), 995–998.

Rosenthal, E. (1996, January 10). The fertility market: From lives begun in a lab, brave new joy. *The New York Times*, pp. 1, C6.

Rosenthal, P., & Rosenthal, S. (1984). Suicidal behavior by preschool children. *American Journal of Psychiatry*, *141*, 4.

Ross, C.E., & Willigen, M.V. (1996). Gender, parenthood, and anger. *Journal of Marriage and the Family*, *58*, 572–584.

Ross, H.S., Filyer, R.E., Lollis, S.P., Perlman, M., & Martin, J.L. (1994). Administering justice in the family. *Journal of Family Psychology*, *8*(3), 254–273.

Ross, H.S., & Lollis, S.P. (1987). Communication within infant social games. *Developmental Psychology*, *23*(2), 241–248.

Rossman, B.B.R., & Rosenberg, M.S. (1992). Family stress and functioning in children: The moderating effects of children's beliefs about their control over parental conduct. *Journal of Child Psychology and Psychiatry*, *33*(4), 699–715.

Ross Products Division of Abbott Laboratories. (1994). Ross mothers' survey. Columbus, OH: Author.

Rousseau, J.J. 1911 [1762]. *Emile*. NY: E.P. Dutton.

Rousso, H. (1985). Fostering healthy self esteem. *The disabled child and the family: An exceptional parent reader*. Boston, MA: The Exceptional Parent Press.

Rowe, D.C., & Plomin, R. (1981). The importance of nonshared (E1) environmental influences in behavioral development. *Developmental Psychology*, *17*(5), 517–531.

Rowland, M. (1992, August 23). Strategies for stay-at-home moms. *The New York Times*.

Rubenstein, C. (1988, May 12). The struggle to keep family time quality time. *The New York Times*.

Rubenstein, C. (1989, October 8). The baby boom. *The New York Times Magazine*, pp. 34–41.

Rubenstein, C. (1993, April 1). Child-care choices: At home in someone else's house. *The New York Times*, p. C2.

Rubin, L. (1979). *Women of a certain age*. NY: Harper and Row.

Rubinstein, J., & Slife, B.D. (1984). *Taking sides: Clashing views on controversial psychological issues* (3rd. ed.). Guilford, CT: Dushkin.

Ruble, D.N., & Ruble, T.L. (1980). Sex stereotypes. In A.G. Miller (Ed.), *In the eye of the beholder: Contemporary issues in stereotyping*. NY: Holt, Rinehart, and Winston.

Russell, A., Russell, G., & Midwinter, D. (1992). Observer influences on mothers and fathers: Self-reported influence during a home observation. *Merrill-Palmer Quarterly*, *38*(2), 263–283.

Russell, G., & Radin, N. (1983). Increased paternal participation: The fathers' perspective. In M. Lamb and A. Sagi (Eds.) *Fatherhood and social policy*. Hillsdale, NJ: Erlbaum.

Russell, G., & Russell, A. (1987). Mother-child and father-child relationships in middle childhood. *Child Development*, *58*, 1573–1585.

Russo, N.F. (1979). Overview: Sex roles, fertility, and the motherhood mandate. *Psychology of Women Quarterly*, *4*, 7–15.

Rutter, M. (1985). Family and school influences on cognitive development. *Journal of Child Psychology and Psychiatry*, *26*(5), 683–704.

Rutter, M. (1988). Stress, coping, and development. In N. Garmezy and M. Rutter (Eds.). *Stress, coping, and development in children*. Baltimore, Md: Johns Hopkins University Press.

Rutter, M. (1990). Commentary: Some focus and process considerations regarding effects of parental depression on children. *Developmental Psychology*, *26*(1), 60–67.

Rutter, M. (1994). Family discord and conduct disorder: Cause, consequence, or correlate? *Journal of Family Psychology*, *8*(2), 170–186.

Rutter, M. (1995). Clinical implications of attachment concepts: Retrospect and prospect. *Journal of Child Psychology & Psychiatry & Allied Disciplines*, *36*(4), 549–571.

Ryan, R.M., & Lynch, J.H. (1989). Emotional autonomy versus detachment: Revisiting the vicissitudes of adolescence and young adulthood. *Child Development*, *60*, 340–356.

Sachdev, P. (1991). Achieving openness in adoption: Some critical issues in policy formulation. *American Journal of Orthopsychiatry*, *61*(2), 241–249.

St. James-Roberts, I. (1989). Persistent crying in infancy. *Journal of Child Psychology & Psychiatry & Allied Disciplines*, *30*(2), 189–195.

St. Peters, M., Fitch, M., Huston, A.C., Wright, J.C., & Eakins, D.J. (1991). Television and families: What do young children watch with their parents? *Child Development*, *62*, 1409–1423.

Salt, R.E. (1991). Affectionate touch between fathers and preadolescent sons. *Journal of Marriage and the Family*, *53*, 545–554.

Saltzman, G.A. (1992). Grandparents raising grandchildren. *Creative Grandparenting*, 2(4), 2–3.

Salzinger, S., Feldman, R.S., & Hammer, M. (1993). The effects of physical abuse on children's social relationships. *Child Development*, 64, 169–187.

Sameroff, A.J. & Emde, R.N. (Eds.). (1989). *Relationship disturbances in early childhood: A developmental approach*. NY: Basic Books.

Sameroff, A.J., & Feil, L.A. (1985). Parental concepts of development. In I.E. Sigel (Ed.), *Parental belief systems: The psychological consequences for children*. Hillsdale, NJ: Erlbaum.

Sampson, R.J., & Laub, J.H. (1994). Urban poverty and the family context of delinquency: A new look at structure and process in a classic study. *Child Development*, 65, 523–540.

Samuels, S.J. (1986). Why children fail to learn and what to do about it. *Exceptional Children*, 53(1), 7–16.

Sanchez, L., & Kane, E.W. (1996). Women's and men's constructions of perceptions of housework fairness. *Journal of Family Issues*, 17(3), 358–387.

Sanders-Phillips, K., Strauss, M.E., & Gutberlet, R.L. (1988). The effect of obstetric medication on newborn infant feeding behavior. *Infant Behavior and Development*, 11(3), 251–263.

Sansbury, L.L., & Wahler, R.G. (1992). Pathways to maladaptive parenting with mothers and their conduct disordered children. *Behavior Modification*, 16(4), 574–592.

Santrock, J.W. (1988). *Children*. Dubuque, IA: Wm. C. Brown.

Santrock, J.W., Sitterle, K.A., & Warshak, R.A. (1988). Parent-child relationships in stepfather families. In P. Bronstein and C.P. Cowan (Eds.), *Fatherhood today: Men's changing role in the family*. NY: John Wiley.

Santrock, J.W., & Warshak, R.A. (1986). Development, relationships, and legal/clinical considerations in father-custody families. In M.E. Lamb (Ed.), *The father's role: Applied perspectives*. NY: John Wiley.

Santrock, J.W., & Yussen, S.R. (1984). *Children and adolescence: A developmental perspective*. Dubuque, IA: Wm. C. Brown.

Satir, V. (1972). *Peoplemaking*. Palo Alto, CA.: Science and Behavior Books.

Scarr, S. (1985). Constructing psychology. *American Psychologist*, 40, 499–512.

Scarr, S. (1992). Developmental theories for the 1990s: Development and individual differences. *Child Development*, 63, 1–19.

Scarr, S. (1993). Biological and cultural diversity: The legacy of Darwin for development. *Child Development*, 64, 1333–1353.

Scarr, S., & Grajek, S. (1982). Similarities and differences among siblings. In M.E. Lamb and B. Sutton-Smith (Eds.), *Sibling relationships: Their nature and significance across the lifespan*. Hillsdale, NJ: Erlbaum.

Scarr, S., Phillips, D., & McCartney, K. (1989). Working mothers and their families. *American Psychologist*, 44(11), 1402–1409.

Scarr, S., & Weinberg, R.A. (1986). The early childhood enterprise: Care and education of the young. *American Psychologist*, 41(10), 1140–1146.

Schachere, K. (1990). Attachment between working mothers and their infants: The influence of family process. *American Journal of Orthopsychiatry*, 60(1), 19–34.

Schaefer, C.E., & Briesmeister, J.M. (1989). *Handbook of parent training*. NY: John Wiley.

Schaefer C.E., & Millman, H.L. (1981). *How to help children with common problems*. NY: Van Nostrand Reinhold.

Schaffer, H.R., & Crook, C.K. (1980). Child compliance and maternal control techniques. *Developmental Psychology*, 16(1), 54–61.

Schlegel, A., & Barry, H. (1991). *Adolescence: An anthropological inquiry*. NY: Free Press.

Schmidt, W.E. (1993, December 29). Birth to 59-year-old Briton raises ethical storm. *The New York Times*, pp. A1, A6.

Schneider-Rosen, K.S., & Rothbaum, F. (1993). Quality of parental caregiving and security of attachment. *Developmental Psychology*, 29(2), 358–367.

Schreier, S. (1992). The perversion of 'mothering:' Munchausen Syndrome by Proxy. *Bulletin of the Meninger Clinic*, 56(4), 421-437.

Schultz, D.P., & Schultz, S.E. (1996). *A history of modern psychology* (6th edition). Orlando, FL: Harcourt Brace & Company.

Schwartz, B. (1986). *The battle for human nature: Science, morality, and modern life*. NY: Norton.

Schwartz, P. (1995a, April 20). When staying is worth the pain. *The New York Times*, pp. C1, C4.

Schwartz, P. (1995b, November 9). New bonds: Para-Dads, para-Moms. *The New York Times*, pp. C1, C10.

Scott, M. (1988, August 21). 'How adults could have helped me.' *Parade Magazine*.

Sears, R.R., Maccoby, E.E., & Levin, H. (1957). *Patterns of childrearing*. Evanston, IL: Row Peterson.

Sears, W. (1995). *SIDS: A parent's guide to understanding and preventing Sudden Infant Death Syndrome*. Boston: Little Brown and Company.

Sebring, D.L. (1985). Considerations in counseling interracial children. *The Personnel and Guidance Journal*, 13, 3–9.

Seginer, R. (1983). Parents' educational expectations and children's academic achievements: A literature review. *Merrill-Palmer Quarterly*, 29(1), 1–23.

Seidner, L.B., Stipek, D.J., & Feshbach, N.D. (1988). A developmental analysis of elementary school-aged children's concepts of pride and embarrassment. *Child Development*, 59, 367–377.

Seitz, V., & Apfel, N.H. (1994). Parent-focused intervention: Diffusion effects on siblings. *Child Development*, 65(2), 677–683.

Seligman, M.E.P. (1975). *Helplessness: On depression, development and death*. San Francisco: Freeman.

Seligman, M.E.P. (1990). *Learned optimism: How to change your mind and your life*. NY: Simon and Schuster.

Seltzer, J.A, & Bianchi, S.M. (1988). Children's contact with absent parents. *Journal of Marriage and the Family*, 50, 663–677.

Seltzer, J.A., Schaeffer, N.C., & Charng, H. (1989). Family ties after divorce: The relationship between visiting and paying child support. *Journal of Marriage and the Family*, 51, 1013–1032.

Selye, H. (1976). *The stress of life* (rev. ed.). NY: McGraw Hill.

Seppa, N. (1996a, May). A multicultural guide to less spanking and yelling. *APA Monitor*, p. 37.

Seppa, N. (1996b, June). Should states keep families tied together? *APA Monitor*, p. 4.

Seppa, N. (1996c, October). Keeping schoolyards safe from bullies. *APA Monitor*, p. 41.

Serbin, L.A., Powlishta, K.K., & Gulko, J. (1993). The development of sex typing in middle childhood. *Monographs of the society for Research in Child Development*, 58(2), Serial No. 232, 1–73.

Seydlitz, R. (1991). The effects of age and gender on parental control and delinquency. *Youth & Society*, 23(2), 175–201.

Shagle, S.C., & Barber, B.K. (1993). Effects of family, marital, and parent-child conflict on adolescent self-derogation and suicidal ideation. *Journal of Marriage and the Family*, 55, 964–974.

Shagle, S.C., & Barber, B.K. (1995). A social-ecological analysis of adolescent suicide ideation. *American Journal of Orthopsychiatry*, 65(1), 114–124.

Shapiro, J.L. (1987a, January). The expectant father. *Psychology Today*, pp. 36–42.

Shapiro, J.L. (1987b). *When men are pregnant*. San Luis Obispo, CA: Impact.

Shaunesey, K., Cohen, J.L., Plummer, B., & Berman, A. (1993). Suicidality in hospitalized adolescents: Relationship to prior abuse. *American Journal of Orthopsychiatry*, 63(1), 113–119.

Shaw, D.S., Emery, R.E., & Tuer, M.D. (1993). Parental functioning and children's adjustment in families of divorce: A prospective study. *Journal of Abnormal Child Psychology*, 21(1), 119–134.

Sheeber, L.B., & Johnson, J.H. (1992). Child temperament, maternal adjustment, and changes in family lifestyle. *American Journal of Orthopsychiatry*, 62(2), 178–185.

Shek, D.T.L. (1995). Chinese adolescents' perceptions of parenting styles of fathers and mothers. *Journal of Genetic Psychology*, 156(2), 175–190.

Shell, E.R. (1989, December). Now, which kind of preschool? *Psychology Today*, pp. 52–57.

Shifflett-Simpson, K., & Cummings, E.M. (1996). Mixed message resolution and children's responses to interadult conflict. *Child Development*, 67, 437–448.

Shoho, A.R. (1994). A historical comparison of parental involvement of three generations of Japanese Americans (Isseis, Niseis, Sanseis) in the education of their children. *Journal of Applied Developmental Psychology*, 15(3), 305–311.

Shore, B. (1986, May 28-31). NASW preliminary report: Single heads of household. Paper presented at the National Association of Social Workers National Conference on Women's Issues, Atlanta, GA.

Shucksmith, J., Hendry, L.B., & Glendinning, A. (1995). Models of parenting: Implications for adolescent well-being within different types of family contexts. *Journal of Adolescence*, 18, 253–270.

Siegel, J.M. (1995). Looking for Mr. Right? Older single women who become mothers. *Journal of Family Issues*, 16(2), 194–211.

Silberman, M.L., & Wheelan, S.A. (1980). *How to discipline without feeling guilty: Assertive relationships with children*. Champaign, Il: Research Press.

Silverman, I.W., & Dubow, E.F. (1991). Looking ahead to parenthood: Nonparents' expectations of themselves and their future children. *Merrill-Palmer Quarterly*, 37(2), 231–250.

Silverman, P.R., Nickman, S., & Worden, J.W. (1992). Detachment revisited: The child's reconstruction of a dead parent. *American Journal of Orthopsychiatry*, 62(4), 494–503.

Silverman, P.R., & Worden, J.W. (1992). Children's reactions in the early months after the death of a parent. *American Journal of Orthopsychiatry*, 62(1), 93–104.

Silverman-Watkins, L. T., & Sprafkin, J.N. (1983). Adolescents' comprehension of televised sexual innuendoes. *Journal of Applied Developmental Psychology*, 4(4), 359–369.

Silverstein, L.B. (1993). Primate research, family politics, and social policy: Transforming "Cads" into "Dads." *Journal of Family Psychology*, 7(3), 267–282.

Sim, H., & Vuchinich, S. (1996). The declining effects of family stressors on antisocial behavior from childhood to adolescence and early adulthood. *Journal of Family Issues*, 17(3), 408–427.

Simkin, P., Whalley, J., & Keppler, A. (1991). *Pregnancy, childbirth, and the newborn: The complete guide*. NY: Simon and Schuster.

Simmons, R.G., Burgeson, R., & Carlton-Ford, S. (1987). The impact of cumulative change in early adolescence. *Child Development*, 58, 1220–1234.

Simons, R.L., Beaman, J., Conger, R.D., & Chao, W. (1993a). Childhood experience, conceptions of parenting, and attitudes of spouse as determinants of parental behavior. *Journal of Marriage and the Family, 55,* 91–106.

Simons, R.L., Beaman, J., Conger, R.D., & Chao, W. (1993b). Stress, support, and antisocial behavior trait as determinants of emotional well-being and parenting practices among single mothers. *Journal of Marriage and the Family, 55,* 385–398.

Simons, R.L., Johnson, C., & Conger, R.D. (1994). Harsh corporal punishment versus quality of parental involvement as an explanation of adolescent maladjustment. *Journal of Marriage and the Family, 56,* 591–607.

Simons, R.L., Lorenz, F.O., Conger, R.D., & Wu, C. (1992). Support from spouse as mediator and moderator of the disruptive influence of economic strain on parenting. *Child Development, 63*(5), 1282–1301.

Simons, R.L., Lorenz, F.O., Wu, C., & Conger, R.D. (1993). Social network and marital support as mediators and moderators of the impact of stress and depression on parental behavior. *Developmental Psychology, 29*(2), 368–381.

Simons, R.L., Whitback, L.B., Conger, R.D., & Wu, C. (1991). Intergenerational transmission of harsh parenting. *Developmental Psychology, 27*(1), 159–171.

Singer, J.L. (1989, April 9). Why Johnny's watching needs watching. *The New York Times.*

Singh, D. (1993). Adaptive significance of female physical attractiveness: Role of waist-to-hip ratio. *Journal of Personality & Social Psychology, 65*(2), 293–307.

Sirignano, S.W., & Lachman, M.E. (1985). Personality change during the transition to parenthood: The role of perceived infant temperament. *Developmental Psychology, 21*(3), 558–567.

Skinner, B.F. (1953). *Science and human behavior.* NY: Macmillan.

Skinner, B.F. (1971). *Beyond freedom and dignity.* NY: Knopf.

Skinner, B.F. (1987). *Upon further reflection.* Englewood Cliffs, NJ: Prentice-Hall.

Slater, M.A. (1986). Modification of mother-child interaction processes in families with children at-risk for mental retardation. *American Journal of Mental Deficiency, 1986, 91*(3), 257–267.

Slaughter-Defoe, D.T., Nakagawa, K., Takanishi, R., & Johnson, D.J. (1990). Toward cultural/ecological perspectives on schooling and achievement in African- and Asian-American children. *Child Development, 61,* 363–383.

Sloper, P., & Turner, S. (1992). Service needs of families of children with severe physical disability. *Child: Care, Health & Development, 18*(5), 259–282.

Sloper, P., & Turner, S. (1993). Risk and resistance in the adaptation of parents of children with severe physical disability. *Journal of Child Psychology & Psychiatry & Allied Disciplines, 34*(2), 167–188.

Smart, L.S. (1992). The marital helping relationship following pregnancy loss and infant death. *Journal of Family Issues, 13*(1), 81–98.

Smetana, J.G. (1988). Adolescents' and parents' conceptions of parental authority. *Child Development, 59,* 321–335.

Smetana, J.G. (1989a). Adolescents' and parents' reasoning about actual family conflict. *Child Development, 60,* 1052–1067.

Smetana, J.G., (1989b). Toddlers' social interactions in the context of moral and conventional transgressions in the home. *Developmental Psychology, 25*(4), 499–508.

Smetana, J.G., & Asquith, P. (1994). Adolescents' and parents' conceptions of parental authority and personal autonomy. *Child Development, 65,* 1147–1162.

Smetana, J.B., Yau, J., Restrepo, A., & Braeges, J.L. (1991). Adolescent-parent conflict in married and divorced families. *Developmental Psychology, 27*(6), 1000–1010.

Smith, D.W., & Brodzinsky, D.M. (1994). Stress and coping in adopted children: A developmental study. *Journal of Clinical Child Psychology, 23*(1), 91–99.

Smith, M.A., & Jenkins, J.M. (1991). The effects of marital disharmony on prepubertal children. *Journal of Abnormal Child Psychology, 19*(6), 625–644.

Smith, P.K., Bowers, L., Binney, V., & Cowie, H. (1993). Relationships of children involved in bully/victim problems at school. In S. Duck (Ed.), *Learning about relationships.* Newbury Park, CA: Sage.

Smolak, L. (1986). *Infancy.* Englewood Cliffs, NJ: Prentice-Hall.

Snodgrass, D.M. (1991). The parent connection. *Adolescence, 26*(101), 83–87.

Snow, M.E., Jacklin, C.N., & Maccoby, E.E. (1983). Sex-of-child differences in father-child interactions at one year of age. *Child Development, 54,* 227–232.

Snowden, L.R., Schott, T.L., Awalt, S.J., & Gillis-Knox, J. (1988). Marital satisfaction in pregnancy: Stability and change. *Journal of Marriage and the Family, 50,* 325–333.

Sollie, D.L, & Miller, B.C. (1980). The transition to parenthood as a critical time for building family strengths. In N. Stinnett, B. Chesser, J. Defain, and P. Kraul (Eds.), *Family strengths: Positive models of family life.* Lincoln: University of Nebraska Press.

Sommer, K., Whitman, T.L., Borkowski, J.G., Schellenbach, C., Maxwell, S., & Keogh, D. (1993). Cognitive readiness and adolescent parenting. *Developmental Psychology, 29*(2), 389–398.

Sosa, R., Kennell, J., Klaus, M., Robertson, S., & Urrutia, J. (1980). The effect of a supportive companion on perinatal problems, length of labor, and mother-infant interaction. *New England Journal of Medicine*, *303*, 597–600.

Sperling, S. (1993). Evolutionary biology and human paternal behavior: Comment on Silverstein. *Journal of Family Psychology*, 7(3), 283–286.

Spitz, R.A. (1946). In R.S. Eissler (Ed.), *Psychoanalytic study of the child* (Vol. 2). NY: International Universities Press.

Spock, B., & Rothenberg, M.B. (1985). *Baby and child care*. NY: Pocket Books.

Sroufe, L.A. (1977). Wariness of strangers and the study of infant development. *Child Development*, *48*, 731–746.

Sroufe, L.A., & Fleeson, J. (1986). Attachment and the construction of relationships. In W.W. Hartup and Z. Rubin, (Eds.). *Relationships and development*. Hillsdale, NJ: Lawrence Erlbaum Associates.

Sroufe, L.A., Jacobvitz, D., Mangelsdorf, S., DeAngelo, E., & Ward, M. (1985). Generational boundary dissolution between mothers and their preschool children: A relationship systems approach. *Child Development*, *56*, 317–325.

Sroufe, L.A., & Ward, M. (1980). Seductive behavior of mothers of toddlers: Occurrence, correlates and family origins. *Child Development*, *51*, 1222–1229.

Stafford, L., & Bayer, C.L. (1993). *Interaction between parents and children*. Newbury Park, CA: Sage.

Stambrook, M., & Parker, K.C.H. (1987). The development of the concept of death in childhood: A review of the literature. *Merrill-Palmer Quarterly*, *33*(2), 133–157.

Stark, E. (1986, October). Young, innocent and pregnant. *Psychology Today*, pp. 28-35.

Stark, L.J., Spirito, A., Williams, C.A., & Guevremont, D.C. (1989). Common problems and coping strategies: I. Findings with normal adolescents. *Journal of Abnormal Child Psychology*, *17*(2), 203–212.

Starrels, M.E. (1994a). Gender differences in parent-child relations. *Journal of Family Issues*, *15*, 148–165.

Starrels, M.E. (1994b). Husbands' involvement in female gender-type household chores. *Sex Roles*, *31*(7/8), 473–492.

Stattin, H., & Klackenberg-Larsson, I. (1991). The short- and long-term implications for parent-child relations of parents' prenatal preferences for their child's gender. *Developmental Psychology*, *27*(1), 141–147.

Steelman, L.C., & Powell, B. (1985). The social and academic consequences of birth order: Real, artifact, or both? *Journal of Marriage and the Family*, *47*, 117–125.

Stefanko, M. (1987). Adolescents and adults: Ratings and expected ratings of themselves and each other. *Adolescence*, *22*(85), 208–221.

Steinberg, L. (1987a, September). Bound to bicker. *Psychology Today*.

Steinberg, L. (1987b). Family processes at adolescence: A developmental perspective. *Family Therapy*, *14*(2), 77–86.

Steinberg, L. (1987c). Impact of puberty on family relations: Effects of pubertal status and pubertal timing. *Developmental Psychology*, *23*(3), 451–460.

Steinberg, L. (1987d). Recent research on the family at adolescence: The extent and nature of sex differences. *Journal of Youth and Adolescence*, *16*(3), 191–197.

Steinberg, L. (1987e, April 25). Why Japan's students outdo ours. *The New York Times*.

Steinberg, L.D. (1988a). Reciprocal relation between parent-child distance and pubertal maturation. *Developmental Psychology*, *24*(1), 122–128.

Steinberg, L. (1988b). Simple solutions to a complex problem: A response to Rodman, Pratto, and Nelson (1988). *Developmental Psychology*, *24*(2), 295–296.

Steinberg, L. (1990). Autonomy, conflict, and harmony in the family relationship. In S.S. Feldman and G.R. Elliot (Eds.), *At the threshold: The developing adolescent*. Cambridge, MA: Harvard University Press.

Steinberg, L. (1992). Impact of parenting practices on adolescent achievement: Authoritative parenting, school involvement, and encouragement to succeed. *Child Development*, *63*, 1266–1281.

Steinberg, L., Elmen, J.D., & Mounts, N.S. (1989). Authoritative parenting, psychosocial maturity and academic success among adolescents. *Child Development*, *60*(6), 1424–1436.

Steinberg, L., Lamborn, S.D., Darling, N., Mounts, N.S., & Dornbusch, S.M. (1994). Over-time changes in adjustment and competence among adolescents from authoritative, authoritarian, indulgent, and neglectful families. *Child Development*, *65*, 754–770.

Steinberg, L., Lamborn, S., Dornbusch, S., & Darling, N. (1992). Impact of parenting practices on adolescent achievement: Authoritative parenting, school involvement, and encouragement to succeed. *Child Development*, *63*, 1266–1281.

Stemp, P.S., Turner, R.J., & Noh, S. (1986). Psychological distress in the postpartum period: The significance of social support. *Journal of Marriage and the Family*, *48*, 271–277.

Stephens, L.S. (1996). Will Johnny see Daddy this week? An empirical test of three theoretical perspectives on postdivorce contact. *Journal of Family Issues*, *17*(4), 466–494.

Stephenson, A.L., Henry, C.S., & Robinson, L.C. (1996). Family characteristics and adolescent substance abuse. *Adolescence*, *31*(121), 59–77.

Stern, J. (1996). A cognitive appraisal approach to parent training with affect-driven parents. *Psychotherapy*, *33*(1).

Stern, M., & Karraker, K.H. (1988). Prematurity stereotyping by mothers of premature infants. *Journal of Pediatric Psychology, 13*(2), 255–263.

Sternberg, R.J., & Davidson, J.E. (Eds.). (1986). *Conceptions of giftedness*. NY: Cambridge University Press.

Stevenson, D.L., & Baker, D.P. (1987). The family-school relation and the child's school performance. *Child Development, 58*(5), 1348–1357.

Stevenson, H.W. (1985). Cognitive performance and academic achievement of Japanese, Chinese, and American children. *Child Development, 56*(3), 718–734.

Stevenson, H.W. (1987, Summer). The Asian advantage: The case of mathematics. *American Educator*, pp. 26–48.

Stevenson, H.W., Lee, S.Y., & Stigler, J.W. (1986). Mathematics achievement of Chinese, Japanese and American children. *Science, 231*, 693–699.

Stevenson, M.B., Leavitt, L.A., Thompson, R.H., & Roach, M.A. (1988). A social relations model analysis of parent and child play. *Developmental Psychology, 24*(1), 101–107

Stevenson, M.R., & Black, K.N. (1995). *How divorce affects offspring: A research approach*. Dubuque, IA: Brown & Benchmark.

Stewart, B. (1995, August 20). Who will watch the baby? *The New York Times*, New Jersey Section, pp. 1, 10.

Stewart, R.B., Mobley, L.A., Van Tuyl, S.S., & Salvador, M.A. (1987). The firstborn's adjustment to the birth of a sibling: A longitudinal assessment. *Child Development, 58*, 341–355.

Stifter, C.A., Coulehan, C.M., & Fish, M. (1993). Linking employment to attachment: The mediating effects of maternal separation anxiety and interactive behavior. *Child Development, 64*, 1451–1460.

Stipek, D., & Mac Iver, D. (1989). Developmental change in children's assessment of intellectual competence. *Child Development, 60*, 521–538.

Stocker, C., Dunn, J., & Plomin, R. (1989). Sibling relationships: Links with child temperaments, maternal behavior, and family structure. *Child Development, 60*, 715–727.

Stone, L.J., & Church, J. (1984). *Childhood and adolescence* (5th ed.). NY: Random House.

Stone, N.M. (1993). Parental abuse as a precursor to childhood onset depression and suicidality. *Child Psychiatry & Human Development, 24*(1), 13–24.

Stoneman, Z., Brody, G.H., & Burke, M. (1989). Marital quality, depression, and inconsistent parenting: Relationship with observed mother-child conflict. *American Journal of Orthopsychiatry, 59*(1), 105–115.

Stouthamer-Loeber, M., & Loeber, R. (1986). Boys who lie. *Journal of Abnormal Child Psychology, 14*(4), 551–564.

Strasburger, V.C. (1995). *Adolescents and the media:*

Medical and psychological impact. Thousand Oaks, CA: Sage.

Strassberg, Z. (1995). Social information processing in compliance situations by mothers of behavior-problem boys. *Child Development, 66*, 376–389.

Strassberg, Z., Dodge, K.A., Bates, J.E., & Pettit, G.S. (1992). The longitudinal relation between parental conflict strategies and children's sociometric standing in kindergarten. *Merrill-Palmer Quarterly, 38*(4), 477–493.

Straus, M.A. (1991). Discipline and deviance: Physical punishment of children and violence and other crime in adulthood. *Social Problems, 38*, 133–154.

Straus, M.A. (1994a). *Beating the devil out of them: Corporal punishment in American families*. NY: Lexington Books/Macmillan.

Straus, M.A. (1994b). *Violence in the lives of adolescents*. NY: Norton.

Straus, M.A., & Donnelly, D.A. (1993). Corporal punishment of adolescents by American parents. *Youth & Society, 24*(4), 419–441.

Stringer, S.A., & la Greca, A.M. (1985). Correlates of child abuse potential. *Journal of Abnormal Child Psychology, 13*(2), 217–226.

Sullivan, H.S. (1973). *Clinical studies in psychiatry*. NY: Norton and Co., (Original work published 1956).

Sullivan, J.F. (1987, October 29). Pregnancy task force hears from teen-agers. *The New York Times*

Sutton-Smith, B. (1985, October). The child at play. *Psychology Today*, pp. 64–65.

Swartz, J. (1984, June). Behavior clue to child abuse. *APA Monitor*, p. 23.

Swartz, J. (1987, December). Depression often missed in teens. *APA Monitor*.

Sweeney, J., & Bradbard, M.R. (1988). Mothers' and fathers' changing perceptions of their male and female infants over the course of pregnancy. *Journal of Genetic Psychology, 149*(3), 393- 404.

Swenson, C.C., Saylor, C.F., Powell, M.P., Stokes, S.J., et al. (1996). Impact of a natural disaster on preschool children: Adjustment 14 months after a hurricane. *American Journal of Orthopsychiatry, 66*(1), 122–130.

Symons, D.K., & Moran, G. (1987). The behavioral dynamics of mutual responsiveness in early face-to-face mother-infant interactions. *Child Development, 58*, 1488–1495.

Synnott, A. (1988). Little angels, little devils: A sociology of children. In G. Handel (Ed.), *Childhood socialization*. NY: Aldine De Gruyter.

Tabor, M.B.W. (1992, June 14). For gay high school seniors, nightmare is almost over. *The New York Times*.

Takanishi, R. (1993a). The opportunities of adolescence- Research, interventions, and policy. *American Psychologist, 48*(2), 85-87.

Takanishi, R. (1993b). (Ed.). *Adolescence in the 1990s: Risk and opportunity*. NY: Teachers College Press.

Tamura, T., & Lau, A. (1992). Connectedness versus separateness: Applicability of family therapy to Japanese families. *Family Process, 31*, 319–340.

Tang, C.S.K., Wong, C.S.Y, & Schwarzer, R. (1996). Psychosocial differences between occasional and regular adolescent users of marijuana and heroin. *Journal of Youth and Adolescence, 25*(2), 219–240.

Tasker, F., & Golombok, S. (1995). Adults raised as children in lesbian families. *American Journal of Orthopsychiatry, 65*(2), 203–215.

Taylor, S.E., & Langer, E.J. (1977). Pregnancy: A social stigma? *Sex Roles, 3*, 25–35.

Teare, J.F., Garrett, C.R., Coughlin, D.G., Shanahan, D.L., et al., (1995). America's children in crisis: Adolescents' requests for support from a national telephone hotline. *Journal of Applied Developmental Psychology, 16*(1), 21–33.

Tein, J., Roosa, M.W., & Michaels, M. (1994). Agreement between parent and child reports on parental behavior. *Journal of Marriage and the Family, 56*, 341–355.

TerLouw, J. (1994, January). Understanding Asian students. *NJEA Review*, pp. 16–19.

Tessier, R., Piché, C., Tarabulsy, G.M., & Muckle, G. (1992). Mothers' experience of stress following the birth of a first child: Identification of stressors and coping resources. *Journal of Applied Social Psychology, 22*(17), 1319–1339.

Teti, D.M., & Abbard, K.E. (1989). Security of attachment and infant-sibling relationships: A laboratory study. *Child Development, 60*, 1519–1528.

Teti, D.M., & Gelfand, D.M. (1991). Behavioral competence among mothers of infants in the first year: The mediational role of maternal self-efficacy. *Child Development, 62*, 918–929.

Teti, D.M., Gelfand, D.M., Messinger, D.S., & Isabella, R. (1995). Maternal depression and the quality of early attachment: An examination of infants, preschoolers, and their mothers. *Developmental Psychology, 31*(3), 364–376.

Teti, D.M., Sakin, J.W., Kucera, E., & Corns, K.M. (1996). And baby makes four: Predictors of attachment security among preschool-age firstborns during the transition to siblinghood. *Child Development, 67*, 579–596.

Teyber, E., & Hoffman, C.D. (1987, April). Missing fathers. *Psychology Today*, pp. 36–39.

Thomas, A. M., & Forehand, R. (1993). The role of paternal variables in divorced and married families. *American Journal of Orthopsychiatry, 63*(1), 126–135.

Thomas, J. (1995). The effects on the family of miscarriage, termination for abnormality, stillbirth and neonatal death. *Child: Care, Health & Development, 21*(6), 413–424.

Thompson, L. (1991). Family work: Women's sense of fairness. *Journal of Family Issues, 12*, 181–196.

Thompson, R.J., Gustafson, K.E., Hamlett, K.W., & Spock, A. (1992). Stress, coping, and family functioning in the psychological adjustment of mothers of children and adolescents with cystic fibrosis. *Journal of Pediatric Psychology, 17*(5), 573–585.

Thornton, A. (1990). The courtship process and adolescent sexuality. *Journal of Family Issues, 11*, 239–273.

Thornton, A., Orbuch, T.L., & Axinn, W.G. (1995). Parent-child relationships during the transition to adulthood. *Journal of Family Issues, 16*(5), 538–564.

Thornton, A., Young-DeMarco, L., & Goldscheider, F. (1993). Leaving the parental nest: The experience of a young white cohort in the 1980s. *Journal of Marriage and the Family, 55*, 216–229.

Thrall, C.A. (1978). Who does what? Role stereotyping, children's work, and continuity between generations in the household division of labor. *Human Relations, 31*, 249–265.

Thunberg, U. (1981). Clinical perspectives on the sick and dying child. In M. Lewis and L.A. Rosenblum (Eds.). *The uncommon child*. NY: Plenum Press.

Tiger, L., & Fox, R. (1989). *The imperial animal*. NY: Henry Holt and Company.

Timko, C., Stovel, K.W., & Moos, R.H. (1992). Functioning among mothers and fathers of children with juvenile rheumatic disease: A longitudinal study. *Journal of Pediatric Psychology, 17*(6), 705–724.

Tisak, M.S. (1986). Children's conceptions of parental authority. *Child Development, 57*, 166–176.

Tizard, B., & Hughes, M. (1985). *Young children learning*. Cambridge, MA: Harvard University Press.

Tizard, B., & Phoenix, A. (1995). The identity of mixed parentage adolescents. *Journal of Child Psychology and Psychiatry, 36*(8), 1399–1410.

Tolan, P.H. & Loeber, R. (1993). Antisocial behavior. In P.H. Tolan and B.J. Cohler (Eds.), *Handbook of clinical research and practice with adolescents*. NY: John Wiley.

Toner, I.J. (1986). Punitive and non-punitive discipline and subsequent rule-following in young children. *Child Care Quarterly, 15*(1), 27–37.

Toner, I.J., Moore, L.P., & Ashley, P.K. (1978). The effect of serving as a model of self-control on subsequent resistance to deviation in children. *Journal of Experimental Child Psychology, 26*, 85–91.

Toner, I.J., & Potts, R. (1981). Effect of modeled rationales on moral behavior, moral choice, and level of moral judgment in children. *Journal of Psychology, 107*, 153–162.

Treaster, J.B. (1993, April 14). Drug use by younger teen-agers appears to rise, counter to trend. *The New York Times*, p. 1.

Trickett, P.K, & Kuczynski, L. (1986). Children's misbehaviors and parental discipline strategies in abusive and nonabusive families. *Developmental Psychology*, 22, 115–123.

Trickett, P.K., & Susman, E.J. (1988). Parental perceptions of child-rearing practices in physically abusive and nonabusive families. *Developmental Psychology*, 24(2), 270–276.

Tronick, E.Z. (1989). Emotions and emotional communication in infants. *American Psychologist*, 44(2), 112–119.

Tronick, E.Z., Morelli, G.A., & Ivey, P.K (1992). The Efe forager infant and toddler's pattern of social relationships: Multiple and simultaneous. *Developmental Psychology*, 28(4), 568–577.

Trotter, R.J. (1985, March). Fathers and daughters: The broken bond. *Psychology Today*, p. 10.

Trotter, R.J. (1987a, December). Project day-care. *Psychology Today*, pp. 32–38.

Trotter, R.J. (1987b, January). The play's the thing. *Psychology Today*, pp. 27–34.

Trotter, R.J. (1987c, May). You've come a long way, baby. *Psychology Today*, pp. 35–44.

Trout, M. & Foley, G. (1989). Working with families of handicapped infants and toddlers. *Topics in Language Disorders*, 10(1), 57–67.

Trute, B. (1995). Gender differences in the psychological adjustment of parents of young, developmentally disabled children. *Journal of Child Psychology & Psychiatry & Allied Disciplines*, 36(7), 1225–1242.

Tucker, L.A. (1985). Television's role regarding alcohol use among teenagers. *Adolescence*, 20(79), 593–598.

Turkington, C. (1984a, April). Parents found to ignore sex stereotypes. *APA Monitor*, p. 12.

Turkington, C. (1984b, December). Psychologists help spot danger in crib. *APA Monitor*.

Turkington, C. (1984c, October). Stepfamilies: Changes in the family tree can be for better or for worse. *APA Monitor*, pp. 8–9.

Turkington, C. (1984d, December). Support urged for children in mourning. *APA Monitor*, pp. 16–17.

Turkington, C. (1987, September). Special talents. *Psychology Today*, pp. 42–46.

Turner, H.A., & Finkelhor, D. (1996). Corporal punishment as a stressor among youth. *Journal of Marriage and the Family*, 58, 155–166.

Turner, P.J., & Gervai, J. (1995). A multidimensional study of gender typing in preschool children and their parents: Personality, attitudes, preferences, behavior, and cultural differences. *Developmental Psychology*, 31(5), 759–772.

Ubell, E. (1992, October 25). When is a cesarean really necessary? *Parade Magazine*, pp. 26–28.

Ubell, E. (1993, February 7). Are births as safe as they could be? *Parade Magazine*, pp. 9–11.

Umberson, D. (1989). Relationships with children: Explaining parents' psychological well-being. *Journal of Marriage and the Family*, 51, 999–1012.

Umberson, D., & Gove, W.R. (1989). Parenthood and psychological well-being: Theory, measurement, and stage in the family life course. *Journal of Family Issues*, 10(4), 440–462.

Ungar, J. (1988, May 10). 'Good' mothers feel dark urges. *The New York Times*.

Unger, R. & Crawford, M. (1992). *Women and gender: A feminist psychology*. NY: McGraw-Hill.

U.S. Bureau of the Census. Department of Commerce. (1989). *Statistical Abstract of the United States, 1989*. Washington, DC: U.S. Government Printing Office.

U.S. Bureau of the Census. Department of Commerce. (1991). *Statistical Abstract of the United States, 1991*. Washington, DC: U.S. Government Printing Office.

U.S. Bureau of the Census. Department of Commerce. (1992). *Statistical Abstract of the United States, 1992*. Washington, DC: U.S. Government Printing Office.

U.S. Bureau of the Census. Department of Commerce. (1993). *Statistical Abstract of the United States, 1993*. Washington, DC: U.S. Government Printing Office.

U.S. Bureau of the Census. Department of Commerce. (1994). *Statistical Abstract of the United States, 1994*. Washington, DC: U.S. Government Printing Office.

U.S. Bureau of the Census. Department of Commerce. (1995). *Statistical Abstract of the United States, 1995*. Washington, DC: U.S. Government Printing Office.

van den Boom, D.C. (1994). The influence of temperament and mothering on attachment and exploration: An experimental manipulation of sensitive responsiveness among lower-class mothers with irritable infants. *Child Development*, 65(5), 1457–1477.

van den Boom, D.C. (1995). Do first-year interventions endure? Follow-up during toddlerhood of a sample of Dutch irritable infants. *Child Development*, 66(6), 1798–1816.

Van der Voort, T.H.A., & Valkenburg, P.M. (1994). Television's impact on fantasy play: A review of research. *Developmental Review*, 14(1), 227–251.

van Ijzendoorn, M.H., & van Vliet-Visser, S. (1988). The relationship between quality of attachment in infancy and IQ in kindergarten. *Journal of Genetic Psychology*, 149(1), 23–28.

Vandell, D.L., & Corasaniti, M.A. (1988). The relation between third graders' after-school care and social, academic, and emotional functioning. *Child Development*, 59, 868–875.

Vandell, D.L. & Ramanan, J. (1992). Effects of early and recent maternal employment on children from low-income families. *Child Development*, 63, 938-949.

Vannatta, R.A. (1996). Risk factors related to suicidal behavior among male and female adolescents. *Journal of Youth and Adolescence*, 25(2), 149-160.

Vaughn, B.E., Block, J.H., & Block, J. (1988). Parental agreement on child rearing during early childhood and the psychological characteristics of adolescents. *Child Development, 59,* 1020–1033.

Ventura, J.N. (1987). The stresses of parenthood reexamined. *Family Relations, 36,* 26–29.

Verhulst, F.C., & van der Ende, J. (1992). Agreement between parents' reports and adolescents' self-reports of problem behavior. *Journal of Child Psychology and Psychiatry, 33*(6), 1011–1023.

Vianello, R., & Lucamante, M. (1988). Children's understanding of death according to parents and pediatricians. *Journal of Genetic Psychology, 149*(3), 305–316.

Visher, E.B., & Visher, J.S. (1988). *Old loyalties, new ties: Therapeutic strategies with stepfamilies.* NY: Brunner/Mazel.

Volling, B.L., & Belsky, J. (1991). Multiple determinants of father involvement during infancy in dual-earner and single-earner families. *Journal of Marriage and the Family, 53,* 461–474.

Volling, B.L., & Belsky, J. (1992). The contribution of mother-child and father-child relationships to the quality of sibling interactions: A longitudinal study. *Child Development, 63*(5), 1209–1222.

Volling, B.L., & Belsky, J. (1993). Parent, infant, and contextual characteristics related to maternal employment decisions in the first year of infancy. *Family Relations, 42,* 4–12.

Vondra, J., & Belksy, J. (1993). Developmental origins of parenting: Personality and relationship factors. In T. Luster and L. Okagaki (Eds.), *Parenting: An ecological perspective.* Hillsdale, NJ: Erlbaum.

Voydanoff, P. (1993). Work and family relationships. In T.H. Brubaker (Ed.), *Family relations: Challenges for the future.* Newbury Park, CA: Sage.

Vuchinich, S. (1985, October). Arguments, family style. *Psychology Today,* pp. 40–46.

Vuchinich, S., Bank, L., & Patterson, G.R. (1992). Parenting, peers, and the stability of antisocial behavior in preadolescent boys. *Developmental Psychology, 28*(3), 510–521.

Vuchinich, S., Emery, R.E., & Cassidy, J. (1988). Family members as third parties in dyadic family conflict: Strategies, alliances, and outcomes. *Child Development, 59,* 1293–1302.

Vuchinich, S., Hetherington, E.M., Vuchinich, R.A., & Clingempeel, W.G. (1991). Parent-child interaction and gender differences in early adolescents' adaptation to stepfamilies. *Developmental Psychology, 27*(4), 618–626.

Vuchinich, S., Vuchinich, R., & Coughlin, C. (1992). Family talk and parent-child relationships: Toward integrating deductive and inductive paradigms. *Merrill-Palmer Quarterly, 38*(1), 69–93.

Vuchinich, S., Vuchinich, R., & Wood, B. (1993). The interparental relationship and family problem solving with preadolescent males. *Child Development, 64,* 1389–1400.

Vuillemot, L. (1988, September 25). The fate of baby Amy. *The New York Times Magazine Section,* p. 39.

Wachs, T.D. (1996). Known and potential processes underlying developmental trajectories in childhood and adolescence. *Developmental Psychology, 32*(4), 796–801.

Waddington, S.R., & Busch-Rossnagel, N.A. (1992). The influence of child's disability on mother's role functioning and psychological well-being. *Genetic, Social, & General Psychology Monographs, 118*(3), 293–311.

Wadsworth, J., Burnell, I., Taylor, B., & Butler, N. (1985). The influence of family type on children's behavior and development at five years. *Journal of Child Psychology & Psychiatry & Allied Disciplines, 26*(2), 245–254.

Waggoner, K., & Wilgosh, L. (1990). Concerns of families of children with learning disabilities. *Journal of Learning Disabilities, 23*(2), pp. 97–98, 113.

Wagner, B.M., & Phillips, D.A. (1992). Beyond beliefs: Parent and child behaviors and children's perceived academic competence. *Child Development, 63,* 1380–1391.

Wagner, M.E., Schubert, H.J., & Schubert, D.S. (1985). Family size effects: A review. *Journal of Genetic Psychology, 146*(1), 65–78.

Wagonseller, B.R., & McDowell, R.L. (1979). *You and your child: A commonsense approach to successful parenting.* Champaign, Il: Research Press.

Wahler, R.G., & Dumas, J.E. (1989). Attentional problems in dysfunctional mother-child interactions: An interbehavioral model. *Psychological Bulletin, 105*(1), 116–130.

Waisbren, S. E. (1980). Parents' reactions after the birth of a developmentally disabled child. *American Journal of Mental Deficiency, 84*(4), 345-351.

Waite, L.J., Leibowitz, A., & Witsberger, C. (1991). What parents pay for: Child care characteristics, quality, and costs. *Journal of Social Issues, 47*(2), 33-48.

Walker, K., & Armstrong, L. (1995). Do mothers and fathers interact differently with their child or is it the situation that matters? *Child: Care, Health & Development, 21*(3), 161–181.

Walker, L.S., & Green, J.W. (1986). The social context of adolescent self-esteem. *Journal of Youth and Adolescence, 15,* 315–322.

Wallerstein, J.S. (1987). Children of divorce: Report of a ten-year follow-up of early latency children. *American Journal of Orthopsychiatry, 57*(2), 199–211.

Wallerstein, J.S. (1988). Children of divorce: Stress and developmental tasks. In N. Garmezy and M. Rutter (Eds.), *Stress, coping, and development in children.* Baltimore, MD: Johns Hopkins University Press.

Wallerstein, J.S. (1989, January 22). Children after divorce: Wounds that don't heal. *The New York Times Magazine*, pp. 19–44.

Wallerstein, J.S. (1991). The long-term effects of divorce on children: A review. *Journal of the Academy of Child Adolescent Psychiatry*, *30*(3), 349–360.

Wallerstein, J.S. (1994). The early psychological tasks of marriage: I. *American Journal of Orthopsychiatry*, *64*(4), 640–650.

Wallerstein, J.S., & Blakeslee, S. (1989). *Second chances*. NY: Ticknor and Fields.

Wallerstein, J.S. & Corbin, S.B. (1989). Daughters of divorce: Report from a ten-year follow-up. *American Journal of Orthopsychiatry*, *59*(4), 593-604.

Walters, G.C., & Grusec, J.F. (1977). *Punishment*. San Francisco: Freeman.

Wang, A.Y. (1994). Pride and prejudice in high school gang members. *Adolescence*, *29*(114), 279–291.

Ward, R.A. (1993). Marital happiness and household equity in later life. *Journal of Marriage and the Family*, *55*, 427–438.

Ward, R.A., & Spitze, G. (1992). Consequences of parent-adult child coresidence. *Journal of Family Issues*, *13*(4), 553–572.

Ward, R.A., & Spitze, G. (1996). Gender differences in parent-child coresidence experiences. *Journal of Marriage and the Family*, *58*, 718–725.

Warren, J.A., & Johnson, P.J. (1995). The impact of workplace support on work-family strain. *Family Relations*, *44*, 163–169.

Warshak, R.A. (1992). *The custody revolution: The father factor and the motherhood mystique*. NY: Poseidon Press.

Watkins, B., & Bentovim, A. (1992). The sexual abuse of male children and adolescents: A review of current research. *Journal of Child Psychology and Psychiatry*, *33*(1), 197–248.

Watson, J.B. (1924). *Behaviorism*. NY: People's Institute.

Watson, J.B. (1928). *Psychological care of infant and child*. NY: Norton.

Watson, J. S. (1981). Contingency experience in behavioral development. *Behavioral Development*, *18*, 83–89.

Ward, R.A. (1993). Marital happiness and household equity in later life. *Journal of Marriage and the Family*, *55*,

Weatherly, J. (1985). Meeting parental needs: A never-ending dilemma. In M.J. Schleifer and S.D. Klein (Eds.), *The disabled child and the family: An exceptional parent reader*. Boston, MA: The Exceptional Parent Press.

Webster-Stratton, C. (1989). The relationship of marital support, conflict, and divorce to parent perceptions, behaviors, and childhood conduct problems. *Journal of Marriage and the Family*, *51*, 417–430.

Weinraub, M., & Lewis, M. (1977). The determinants of children's responses to separation. *Monographs of the Society for Research in Child Development*, *48*, 1240–1249.

Weisman, S.R. (1992, April 27). How do Japan's students do it? They cram. *The New York Times*.

Weiss, B., Dodge, K.A., Bates, J.E., & Pettit, G.S. (1992). Some consequences of early harsh discipline: Child aggression and a maladaptive social information processing style. *Child Development*, *63*, 1321–1335.

Weiss, R.L. & Heyman, R.E. (1990). Observation of marital interaction. In F.D. Fincham and T.N. Bradbury (Eds.), *The psychology of marriage: Basic issues and applications*. NY: Guilford.

Weiss, R.S. (1990). *Staying the course: The emotional and social lives of men who do well at work*. NY: Free Press.

Weissler, K., & Landau, E. (1993). Characteristics of families with no, one, or more than one gifted child. *The Journal of Psychology*, *127*(2), 143–152.

Weisz, J.R. (1980). Autonomy, control, and other reasons why "Mom is the greatest": A content analysis of children's Mother's Day letters. *Child Development*, *51*, 801–807.

Weller, E.B., Weller, R.A., Fristad, M.A., Cain, S.E., & Bowes, J.M. (1988). Should children attend their parent's funeral? *Journal of the American Academy of Child and Adolescent Psychiatry*, *27*, 559–562.

Wells, A.S. (1987, Summer). The parent's place: Right in the school. *The New York Times*, Education Section.

Wells, M. (1988, June). The roots of literacy. *Psychology Today*, pp. 20–22.

Werner, E.E. (1989a, April). Children of the garden island. *Scientific American*, 106–111.

Werner, E.E. (1989b). High-risk children in young adulthood: A longitudinal study from birth to 32 years. *American Journal of Orthopsychiatry*, *59*(1), 72–81.

Westerman, M.A. (1990). Coordination of maternal directives with preschoolers' behavior in compliance-problem and healthy dyads. *Developmental Psychology*, *26*(4), 621–630.

Westerman, M.A., & La Luz, E.J. (1995). Marital adjustment and children's academic achievement. *Merrill-Palmer Quarterly*, *41*, 453–470.

Westerman, M.A., & Schonholtz, J. (1993). Marital adjustment, joint parental support in a triadic problem-solving task, and child behavior problems. *Journal of Clinical Child Psychology*, *22*(1), 97–106.

Whitbeck, L.B., Hoyt, D.R., & Huck, S.M. (1993). Family relationship history, contemporary parent-grandparent relationship quality, and the grandparent-grandchild relationship. *Journal of Marriage and the Family*, *55*, 1025–1035.

White, B.L. (1971, October 21-22). Fundamental early

environmental influences on the development of competence. Paper presented at Third Western Symposium on Learning: Cognitive Learning, Western Washington State College, Bellingham, WA.

White, B.L. (1988). *Educating the infant and toddler.* Lexington, MA: D.C. Heath.

White, K.D., Pearson, J.C., & Flint, L. (1989). Adolescents' compliance-resistance: Effects of parents' compliance strategy and gender. *Adolescence, 24*(95), 595–621.

White, L. (1992). The effects of parental divorce and remarriage on parental support for adult children. *Journal of Family Issues, 13*(2), 234–250.

White, L.K., & Brinkerhoff, D.B. (1981a). Children's work in the family: Its significance and meaning. *Journal of Marriage and the Family, 43*, 789–798.

White, L.K., & Brinkerhoff, D.B. (1981b). The sexual division of labor: Evidence from childhood. *Social Forces, 60*, 171–181.

White, R. (1959). Motivation reconsidered: The concept of competence. *Psychological Review, 66*, 297–333.

Wilks, J. (1986). The relative importance of parents and friends in adolescent decision making. *Journal of Youth and Adolescence, 15*(4), 323–335.

Williams, E., & Radin, N. (1993). Paternal involvement, maternal employment, and adolescents' academic achievement: An 11-year follow-up. *American Journal of Orthopsychiatry, 63*(2), 306–312.

Williams, J.A., & Campbell, L.P. (1985). Parents and their children comment on adolescence. *Adolescence, 20*(79), 745–748.

Williams, J.H. (1987). *Psychology of women* (3rd ed.). NY: Norton.

Williams, L. (1989, May 25). New rallying cry: Parents unite. *The New York Times.*

Willoughby, J.C., & Glidden, L.M. (1995). Fathers helping out: Shared child care and marital satisfaction of parents of children with disabilities. *American Journal on Mental Retardation, 99*(4), 399–406.

Wilson, B.F., & Clarke, S.C. (1992). Remarriages: A demographic profile. *Journal of Family Issues, 13*(2), 123–141.

Winn, M. (1989, April 16). New fights over spoiling your baby. *The New York Times Magazine,* pp. 27–68.

Winn, N.N., & Priest, R. (1993). Counseling biracial children: A forgotten component of multicultural counseling. *Family Therapy, 20*(1), 29–36.

Winner, E. (1986, August). Where pelicans kiss seals. *Psychology Today,* pp. 25–35.

Wolchik, S.A., Braver, S.L., & Sandler, I.N. (1985). Maternal versus joint custody: Children's postseparation experiences and adjustment. *Journal of Clinical Child Psychology, 14*(1), 5–10.

Wolfe, D.A., Edwards, B., Manion, I., & Koverola, C. (1988). Early intervention for parents at risk of child abuse and neglect: A preliminary investigation. *Journal of Consulting and Clinical Psychology, 56*(1), 40–47.

Wolff, P.D. (1966). The causes, controls, and organization of behavior in the neonate. *Psychological Issues, 5*(1, Serial No. 17).

Woodworth, S., Belsky, J., & Crnic, K. (1996). The determinants of fathering during the child's second and third years of life: A developmental analysis. *Journal of Marriage and the Family, 58*, 679–692.

Wren, C.S. (1996, February 20). Marijuana use by youths continues to rise. *The New York Times,* p. A11.

Wright, J.C., Huston, A.C., Reitz, A.L., & Piemyat, S. (1994). Young children's perceptions of television reality: Determinants and developmental differences. *Developmental Psychology, 30*(2), 229–239.

Wu, A. (1995). Premarital cohabitation and postmarital cohabiting union formation. *Journal of Family Issues, 16*(2), 212–232.

WuDunn, S. (1996a, January 23). In Japan, even toddlers feel the pressure to excel. *The New York Times,* p. A3.

WuDunn, S. (1996b, March 13). Stigma curtails single motherhood in Japan. *The New York Times,* pp. A1, A11.

Wurtele, S.K. (1990). Teaching personal safety skills to four-year-old children: A behavioral approach. *Behavior Therapy, 21*, 25–32.

Wurtele, S.K., & Miller, C.L. (1987). Children's conceptions of sexual abuse. *Journal of Clinical Child Psychology, 16*(3), 184–191.

Yamamoto, K., Davis, O.L. Jr., Dylak, S., Whittaker, J., et al. (1996). Across six nations: Stressful events in the lives of children. *Child Psychiatry & Human Development, 26*(3), 139–150.

Yamamoto, K., Soliman, A., Parsons, J., & Davis, O.L. (1987). Voices in unison: Stressful events in the lives of children in six countries. *Journal of Child Psychology and Psychiatry, 28*, 855–864.

Yarrow, A.L. (1991). *Latecomers: Children of parents over 35.* NY: Free Press.

Yogman, M.W., Cooley, J., & Kindlon, D. (1988). Fathers, infants, and toddlers. In P. Bronstein and C.P. Cowan (Eds.), *Fatherhood today: Men's changing role in the family.* NY: John Wiley.

Young, K.T. (1990). American conceptions of infant development from 1955 to 1984: What the experts are telling parents. *Child Development, 61*, 17–28.

Youngblade, L.M. & Belsky, J. (1992). Parent-child antecedents of 5-year-olds' close friendships: A longitudinal analysis. *Developmental Psychology, 28*(4), 700–713.

Youniss, J., & Ketterlinus, R.D. (1987). Communication and connectedness in mother- and father-adolescent relationships. *Journal of Youth and Adolescence, 16*(3), 265–280.

Youniss, J., & Smollar, J. (1985). *Adolescent relations with mothers, fathers, and friends*. Chicago: University of Chicago Press.

Zabin, L.S., & Hayward, S.C. (1993). *Adolescent sexual behavior and childbearing*. Newbury Park, CA: Sage.

Zahn-Waxler, C., Radke-Yarrow, M., & King, R. (1979). Child-rearing and children's prosocial initiation toward victims of distress. *Child Development, 50*, 319–330.

Zajonc, R.B., & Markus, G.B. (1975). Birth order and intellectual development. *Psychological Review, 82*, 74–88.

Zaslow, M.J. (1991). Variation in child care quality and its implications for children. *Journal of Social Issues, 47*(2), 125–138.

Zeman, J., & Shipman, K. (1996). Children's expression of negative affect: Reasons and methods. *Developmental Psychology, 32*(5), 842–849.

Zera, D. (1992). Coming of age in a heterosexist world: The development of gay and lesbian adolescents. *Adolescence, 27*(108), 849–854.

Zern, D.S. (1991). The nature and extent of obedience in elementary school classrooms. *The Journal of Genetic Psychology, 152*(3), 311–325.

Zervas, L.J., & Sherman, M.F. (1994). The relationship between perceived parental favoritism and self-esteem. *Journal of Genetic Psychology, 155*(1), 25–33.

Zeskind, P.S. (1980). Adult responses to cries of low- and high-risk infants. *Infant Behavior and Development, 3*, 167–177.

Zigler, E. F., & Rubin, N. (1985, November). Why child abuse occurs. *Parents*, pp. 102–218.

Zill, N., Morrison, D.R., & Coiro, M.J. (1993). Long-term effects of parental divorce on parent-child relationships, adjustments, and achievements in young adulthood. *Journal of Family Psychology, 7*(1), 91–103.

Zimbardo, P., & Radl, S. (1981). *Shyness*. NY: McGraw-Hill.

SUBJECT INDEX

Abortion, 343
Achievement, 296–324
  adolescent, 316–317
  creative expression and, 317–318
  ethnicity and, 308–311
  and gifted children, 370–372
  home and family factors in, 297–305
  play and, 297, 318–321
  schooling and, 306–318
  and "superkid" syndrome, 305–307, 308–309
  television and, 321–324
Active partnership, 78
Activity reinforcers, 188
Adjustment, 264–292
  adolescent, 336–337
  anger and, 271–273
  coping and, 265, 279–292
  to death, 283–292
  embarrassment and, 274–275
  fears and, 268–270
  happiness and, 265–266
  honest behavior and, 266–267
  jealousy and, 273–274
  learned helplessness and, 275–276
  pride and, 275
  shame and, 274–275
  shyness and, 270–271
  stress and, 276–279
Adolescence, 328–350
  achievement and underachievement in, 316–317
  adjustment to death in, 288
  adoption and, 62
  autonomy and, 331, 333, 337–339, 348–350
  cognitive development in, 335–337, 340
  as developmental stage, 14, 329–330, 430
  divorce of parents and, 119, 124
  dropping out in, 16–18
  drug use in, 339–340, 345–347
  family relationships in, 331–337
  fathering and, 90–91, 95
  mothering and, 93, 95
  parental authority and, 154–155
  peer group in, 334–335
  pregnancy in, 16, 340–344

relationship with grandparents in, 133
  risk-taking behavior in, 339–347
  self care in, 414–416
  sexuality in, 340–345
  stepfamilies and, 129, 130
  stress in, 279
  suicide in, 347–348
Adolescent egocentrism, 336
Adoption, 50, 59–63
Adulthood, psychosocial stages of, 37, 430
Affectionate touch, 22, 90, 217
Aggression
  in child abuse and neglect, 382–396
  in family violence, 376–382
  frustration and, 166
  of parents, 20–23, 76–77, 85, 125, 376–382
  toys and, 398
  See also Violence
AIDS, 18, 341, 344
Alcohol use, 346, 347
Alliances, 422
Altruism, 246–247
Americans with Disabilities Act (ADA), 367
Anal stage, 428
Androgyny, 256–257
Anger, 271–273
  parental, 76–77, 104, 271–272
  and sexual abuse, 392
Antisocial behavior, 396–398
Apologizing, 215–216
Artificial (donor) insemination, 39–40, 41
Assertiveness, 345
Attachment, 204–206
  achievement and, 301
  autonomy and, 337–339
  fathers and, 93
Attention, 210
Attention deficit disorder (ADD), 369
Attention deficit hyperactivity disorder (ADHD), 369
Attribution theory, 152
Authoritarian parenting, 158–160, 162, 164, 216, 219

Authoritative parenting, 158–160, 163, 164, 303, 398
Authority, 153–154, 158
Authority stage, 38, 39
Autism, 359, 367–369
Autonomy, adolescent, 331, 333, 337–339, 348–350
Autonomy versus shame and self-doubt (Erikson), 241, 429, 431

Bargaining, 147
Behaviorism, 72
Behavior modification, 180
Bidirectional models, 23–27
Binuclear family, 122–125. See also Single parents
Biracial children, 238–239
Birth control, 343
Birth order, 220–221, 223
Boundaries, 422
Brain damage, 357–358
Brainstorming, 215
Breast-feeding, 52–53
Bullies, 380–382

Chaos theory, 73
Child abuse, 382–389
Childbirth, 31, 46–47, 53
Childhood
  history of, 11–15
  psychosocial stages of, 241, 429–430
  See also Children; Infancy; Toddlers
Childlessness, 4–5
Child neglect, 160, 384, 395–396
Child rearing practices. See Parenthood
Children
  current status of, 15–18
  death of, 288–290
  divorce and, 108, 114–121, 271, 278–279
  in dual-career families, 407–410
  expectations of parents for, 252, 301–303, 304, 305–307
  reasons for having, 4–8
  in self care, 414–416
  See also Daughters; Sons; Special children
China, 41, 150–151, 178

489

Cognitive development
adolescent, 335–337, 340
and child abuse, 386
and gender identity, 255–256
See also Schooling
Cohabitation, 102
College, 350
Communication skills, 202–204, 209–219
and families with special children, 365
friendship and, 230–231
nonverbal, 213–214, 244
and parent-adolescent conflict, 332–333
Competence, 10, 74–87, 111. *See also* Achievement
Conditional acceptance, 244, 270
Conflict
in adolescence, 332–333
family meetings, 218–219
marital and family, 103–107, 116–117, 271–272, 278–279, 379
in parent-child relations, 105, 144–150, 153–154
sibling, 144, 223–228, 274, 278, 290, 362
See also Divorce
Consistency, parental, 82–83
Contextual factors, 26
Coparenting, 110–111
Coping behavior, 265, 279–292
of resilient children, 74, 116, 282–283, 387
Corporal punishment, 164–167, 198
Cosleeping, 176
Couvade syndrome, 46
Creativity, 317–318
Critical period, 50
Criticism, 214, 216–218
Cross-gender behavior, 256
Crying, infant, 176, 177–178
Custody arrangements, 109–111, 112–114, 122–127
Cystic fibrosis, 363

Daughters
divorce and, 119, 121, 124
fathers and, 91, 92, 105, 217, 253
mothers and, 217, 253
parenting sons versus, 249–253
Day-care programs, 410–414
Death, 283–292
mortality rates, 13, 14, 17, 249
sudden infant death syndrome (SIDS), 55–58, 289
Defense mechanisms, 427
Defiance, 22, 147

Delinquency, juvenile, 15, 396–398
Denial, 268, 427
Departure stage, 38, 39
Depression
adolescent, 337, 347–348
parental, 53–55, 75, 84, 207, 266, 364
Differential reinforcement of other behavior (DRO), 182–183
Disability, defined, 367
Discipline, 79–80, 140, 155–158, 303–304, 382
divorce and, 111, 114–115
fathers and, 95–96
grandparents and, 134–135
for infants and toddlers, 174–175
noncompliance and, 145–148
team approach to, 161
Disengagement, 422
Divorce, 15–16, 25, 35, 36, 104, 107–122
children and, 108, 114–121, 271, 278–279
custody arrangements, 109–111, 112–114, 122–127
Down Syndrome, 354–356, 359, 365–367
Drug use, 339–340, 345–347
Dual-career families, 258, 404–410

Early schooling, 306, 307
Echolalia, 367
Ecological model
of development, 25–27, 32–33
of parenting, 84–87, 105–107
Economic disadvantage hypothesis, 116
EDGE (Expanding Developmental Growth through Education), 366
Education, parental, 86, 125. *See also* Schooling
Education for All Handicapped Children Act, 366, 367
Ego, 426
Electra complex, 427
Embarrassment, 274–275
Emotional abuse (psychological maltreatment), 383, 387–388
Emotional and social adjustment. *See* Adjustment
Empathy, 246–247, 334
Employment, of mothers, 116, 123, 125, 258, 404–410
Empty nests, 348–349
Enculturation, 24
Enlightened self-interest, 426
Enmeshment, 422
Erikson's psychosocial theory,

36–37, 145, 156–157, 241–242, 429–431
Ethnicity
and achievement, 308–311
and biracial children, 238–249
and fathering, 88
and poverty, 17
and research on parenting, 22, 24, 301–303
and single parents, 16, 102, 123, 124
Ethnocentric bias, 24
Exclusions, 422
Existential psychology, 243–245
Expectations
about parenting, 42–44
of parents for children, 252, 301–303, 304, 305–307
Extinction, 179–180, 181
Extrinsic reinforcers, 186

Family, 219–231
achievement and, 297–305
adolescence and, 331–337
attitudes toward, 3–4
bidirectional influence in, 23–27
conflict and, 103–107, 116–117, 271–272, 278–279, 379
defined, 102
dual-career, 258, 404–410
foster, 63, 134
friendships outside, 228–231, 334–335
household tasks in, 91–92, 255, 257–259, 406–407
nuclear, 101, 108, 114, 126, 127, 129
sibling ambivalence/conflict in, 144, 223–228, 274, 278, 290, 362
step-, 108, 127–131
traditional, 100–101
violence in, 376–382
See also Children; Daughters; Fathers and fathering; Mothers and mothering; Sons
Family cohesiveness, 36
Family configuration, 100–101
Family conflict hypothesis, 117
Family day care, 411, 415–416
Family deficit model, 123, 127
Family life-cycle model, 360–362
Family meetings, 218–219
Family of origin, 20–23, 85
Family systems model, 30–31, 95, 103, 421–423
Fathers and fathering, 87–92
adolescent, 342–344
bad, 105

child abuse and, 387
comparison of mothering and, 92–96
daughters and, 91, 92, 105, 217, 253
divorce and, 112–114
expectant fathers, 45–46
father-infant bonding, 51
reasons for, 9
sibling ambivalence and, 225
single custodial fathers, 126–127
sons and, 90, 95, 217, 253
of special children, 364, 366, 371
in stepfamilies, 127–129
transition to, 31–32
See also Parenthood
Favoritism, 227–228, 274
Fears, childhood, 268–270
Feedback, 214
Feelings, 76–77, 211–213, 244–245
Fixation, 428
Flexibility, parental, 82–83
Formal operations, 336
Foster families, 63, 134
Freud's psychodynamic model, 144, 425–428
Friends, 228–231, 334–335

Gender constancy, 255
Gender differences
in household tasks, 255, 258–259
parenting and, 248–259
in play, 320–321
in socialization process, 249–253
See also Daughters; Sons
Gender identity, 237, 254–257, 320
Gender roles, 34–36, 88, 254–255, 320–321
Gender selection, 41
Gender typing, 255
Generativity versus stagnation, 37, 430, 431
Genital stage, 428
Ghetto environment, 283
Gifted children, 370–372
Grandparenting, 21, 131–135, 410
Grieving, 286–288, 289
Guilt, 44, 111, 426

Happiness, 265–266
Helpless behavior, 275–276, 379
High-risk parents, 402–404
Homosexuality, 135–137, 257
Honest behavior, 266–267
Hospitalization, 364
Household, defined, 102
Household tasks, 91–92, 255, 257–259, 406–407
Humanistic psychology, 243–245

Humor, 281–282

Id, 185, 425–426
Identification, 88, 253
Identity versus role confusion, 430, 431
Image-making stage, 37, 39
Imaginary audience, 336
I messages, 215
Incest, 389–395
Indulgent parenting, 159, 160
Industry versus inferiority (Erikson), 241, 429–430, 431
Infancy
abuse in, 387
attachment in, 205
day care in, 412–413
death in, 55–58, 289
disability in, 359
distress in, 171–172, 276, 280
newborn infants, 22, 48–53, 175–176, 223
oral stage in, 428
and parental authority, 153
parenting in, 175–179
and self-concept, 237–238
separation distress in, 278
setting limits in, 172–175
stranger anxiety in, 278
Infanticide, 12
Infertility, 39–40
In-home care, 411
Initiative versus guilt (Erikson), 241, 429, 431
Integrity versus despair, 430, 431
Interaction style, 77–79, 94–95
Interdependent stage, 38, 39
Internalization, 152–153
Interpretive stage, 38, 39
Intimacy, 102, 106, 107, 331
Intimacy versus isolation, 430, 431
Intrinsic reinforcers, 186
In vitro fertilization, 40, 41

Japan, 14, 23, 151, 309, 310–311
Jealousy, 227–228, 273–274
Joint custody, 110–111
Juvenile delinquency, 15, 396–398

Labor, child, 6, 13, 14, 15
Language
and creative expression, 318
reading and writing, 312–313
speech with infants, 23
Latency stage, 428
Law of effect, 148–149
Learned helplessness syndrome, 275–276, 379
Learning disabled (LD), 369–370

Learning models, and gender identity, 254–255
Legal issues
child abuse, 384, 389
child labor laws, 15
custody arrangements, 109–111
divorce, 109
gay and lesbian parents, 135–137
responsibilities of parents, 5, 6, 15
special children, 366–368
Listening skills, 210–211, 266
Logical consequences, 189–191
Lying, 266–267

Mainstreaming, 368
Male bonding, 90
Manipulative behavior, 266
Marriage
conflict and, 103–107, 278–279, 379
impact of death on, 290
male versus female style and, 106–107
remarriage, 15–16, 102, 106, 116
risks of, 102
and transition to parenting, 32–36
See also Divorce
Misbehavior, 143–144, 148–149, 180
Modeling, 88, 89, 212–213, 305, 346
Mortality rates, 13, 14, 17, 249. *See also* Death
Mother-infant bonding, 12, 14, 19, 22, 48–53
Mothers and mothering
and achievement of children, 310–311
adolescent, 340–342
breast-feeding in, 52–53
and child abuse, 388
comparison of fathering and, 92–96
daughters and, 217, 253
depression and, 53–55, 75, 84, 207, 266, 364
in dual-career families, 258, 405–410
employment of mothers, 116, 123, 125, 258, 404–410
as key role of women, 14, 32, 34, 88
single, 5, 114–116, 122–125, 405
sons and, 95, 217, 253
of special children, 364, 366, 371
in stepfamilies, 129
transition to, 31–32
See also Parenthood; Pregnancy
Multiproblem parents, 402–404

Munchausen's Syndrome by Proxy, 383
Muscular dystrophy, 359

Natural consequences, 188, 189–191
Negative punishment, 194
Negative reinforcement, 180–181.
    See also Punishment
Neglect, 160, 384, 395–396
Negotiation, 147
Newborn infants, 22, 48–53, 175–176, 223
New Parents as Teachers project, 403–404
NON (National Organization of Nonparents), 5
Noncompliance, 145–148
Nonshared family influences, 229
Nonverbal communication, 213–214, 244
Nuclear family, 101, 108, 114, 126, 127, 129
Nurturing stage, 38, 39

Objective observation, 22
Observational learning, 191–193
Oedipus complex, 427
Operant conditioning, 179–189
Oral stage, 428
Overcorrection, 196–198
Overprotectiveness, 43

Parental investment model, 69–70
Parent-child relationships, 11, 25, 40–42
    and achievement of children, 300–301
    adolescence and, 331–337
    communication in, 202–204, 209–219, 332–333
    conflict in, 105, 144–150, 153–154
    emotions in, 76–77
    and friendships of children, 228–231
    and nonshared family influences, 229
Parent education programs, 402–404
Parenthood
    authority in, 153–155, 158
    custody after divorce and, 109–111, 112–114, 122–127
    decision to parent and, 2–3, 4–8
    expectations about, 42–44
    gender differences and, 248–259
    parenting, defined, 39
    perceptions of children, 140–144
    process of parenting, 68–70
    research on, 18–23

single. *See* Single parents
    stages of, 36–42
    transition to, 29–63
Parent-infant bonding, 12, 14, 19, 22, 48–53, 359
Parenting alliance, 33
Parenting practices, 163–164
Parenting styles, 158–164
    achievement and, 303–304
    aggressive, 20–23, 76–77, 85, 125, 376–382
    Baumrind's model of, 158–164, 303–304
    discipline and, 382
    of fathers versus mothers, 92–96
    parenting practices and, 163–164, 303–304
    and security of attachment, 205–209
    and values, 339
    See also Discipline
Peer group, 228–231, 334–335
Perfectionism, 43
Permissive parenting, 159, 160, 162, 164
Personal fables, 336
Personality, 229
Persuasion, 147
Phallic stage, 428
Physical abuse, 383, 384–386
Placing out, 331
Play
    achievement and, 297, 318–321
    fathers and, 92, 93–94, 96
    gender identity and, 254–255, 320
Pleasure principle, 144, 425–426
Popularity, 230–231
Positive punishment, 194
Positive regard, 243–244
Positive reinforcers, 194
Postpartum adjustment, 53–55
Posttraumatic stress, 277, 391
Poverty, 16, 17
Power assertion, 162, 165–166, 196
Praise, 214
Pregnancy, 31, 37, 44–47
    adolescent, 16, 340–344
    age of mother and, 57–58
    loss of, 55
    postpartum adjustment, 53–55
Premack Principle, 188
Pride, 275
Primary coping, 280
Primary prevention, 372
Primary (unconditioned) reinforcers, 186, 187
Problem-solving skills, 214–215
Projection, 427
Psychoanalysis, 152

Psychohistory, 73
Psychological maltreatment (emotional abuse), 383, 387–388
Psychological problems
    in adolescence, 337, 347–348
    blaming parents for, 371
    of parents, 53–55, 75, 84, 124, 207, 266, 364
    prevention of, 372
Psychosexual stages of development, 427–428
Puberty, 333–334
Punishers, 193–194, 195
Punishment, 166–167, 193–198
    corporal, 164–167, 198
    as long-term discipline strategy, 175
    in operant conditioning, 179
    See also Discipline

Rationalization, 268, 427
Reaction formation, 427
Reading, 312–313, 321
Reality principle, 426
Reciprocal response patterns, 207
Refusal, 147
Reinforcement principle, 148–149
Reinforcers, 179
    differential reinforcement of other behavior (DRO), 182–183
    judicious use of, 188–189
    negative, 180–181. *See also* Punishment
    positive, 194
    strategic use of, 181–182
    time out from, 197
    types of, 186–188
Religion, attitudes toward death and, 285
Remarriage, 15–16, 102, 106, 116.
    See also Stepfamilies
Repression, 427
Reproduction technologies, 39–42
Resilient children, 74, 116, 282–283, 387
Risk-taking behavior, 339–347
Role models, 88, 89
Rule-following behavior, 173–174

Scaffolding, 79, 115
Schooling
    dropping out, 16–18
    early, 306, 307
    family factors and achievement in, 299–305
    mainstreaming and, 368
    parental involvement and, 93, 299–304, 312, 313–315
    problems related to, 315–316

reading and writing in, 312–313
and "superkid" syndrome, 305–307, 308–309
See also Teachers
Secondary coping, 280
Secondary prevention, 372
Secondary (conditioned) reinforcers, 186
Self-actualization, 243–245
Self-awareness, 212
Self care, 414–416
Self-concept, 237–239
Self-confidence, 11, 43, 180, 272, 283
Self-control, 160
Self-efficacy, 83–84, 245–246
Self-esteem, 11, 43, 91, 119, 239–247
adolescent, 316, 336
and birth order, 221
and child abuse, 386, 388
and conditional regard, 244
and criticism, 216
and parental support, 217
self-efficacy versus, 245–246
Self-regulation, 149
Self-reliance, 160, 178–179, 190–191
Sensitive period, 50
Separation, 107–122, 277, 278
Separation distress, 278
Sexual abuse, 85–86, 129, 383–384, 389–395
Sexuality, 106, 340–345
Sexualization, 391
Sexual orientation, 257
Shame, 274–275, 426
Shyness, 230–231, 270–271
Sibling ambivalence/conflict, 144, 223–228, 274, 278, 290, 362
Single-child families, 221–223
Single parents, 16, 101–103, 108
fathers, 126–127
grandparents and, 133
and household tasks, 258
mothers, 5, 114–116, 122–125, 405
Situational context, 148–149
Sleep, infants and, 175–177
Sleep-resistant children, 176
Small moments model of development, 71, 72–74, 78
Social cognition models, 152–153, 255–256

Socialization, 42, 71, 72, 152–153
adolescent, 338–339
of anger and aggression, 272–273
and birth order, 220–221
gender differences in, 249–253
gender identity and, 254–257
initial, 207
schooling in, 311
sharing and, 274
social skills and, 228–231, 270–271
Social referencing, 25
Social reinforcement, 186–188
Sons
divorce and, 118–119, 121, 124
fathers and, 90, 95, 217, 253
mothers and, 95, 217, 253
parenting daughters versus, 249–253
Special children, 353–373
with acute and chronic illness, 363–365
with autism, 359, 367–369
with brain damage, 357–358
described, 356–358
with Down Syndrome, 354–356, 359, 365–367
gifted, 370–372
with learning disabilities, 369–370
parenting, 358–372
preventing psychological problems of, 372–373
Spina bifida, 362
Split custody, 110
Spoiling children, 13, 15, 172
Sports, 94
Stage theories of development, 71, 73–74
of Erikson, 36–37, 145, 156–157, 241–242, 429–431
of Freud, 144, 425–428
Stepfamilies, 108, 127–131
Stereotypes
of adolescents, 329–330, 338
gender, 252–255, 320–321
and "superkid" syndrome, 308–311
Stranger anxiety, 278
Stress, 265, 276–279
of divorce, 117–118, 278–279
infant distress, 171–172, 276, 280

of parenthood, 5, 86–87
of pregnancy, 44–45
and special children, 361, 362–363
Sudden infant death syndrome (SIDS), 55–58, 289
Suicide, 347–348
Superego, 426
"Superkid" syndrome, 305–307, 308–309
Surrogate motherhood, 40
Sympathetic listening, 215

Tangible (token) reinforcers, 188
Tantrums, 182, 185
Tattling, 226
Teachers
and parental involvement in schooling, 313–315
and research on parenting, 19–20
and self-esteem of children, 239
See also Schooling
Television, 281, 321–324
Tertiary prevention, 372–373
Time out from reinforcement, 197
Toddlers
abuse of, 387
anal stage in, 428
false statements of, 267
and parental authority, 153
setting limits on, 172–175
Toilet training, 178–179, 413
Touch, affectionate, 22, 90, 217
Toys, 254–255, 320–321, 398
Transitional objects, 280
Trust versus mistrust (Erikson), 241, 429, 431

Unconditional acceptance, 243–244
Unconscious, 426–427
Unidirectional models, 23–25

Values, 266–267, 338–339
Verbal interaction, 299–300
Violence, 15, 281
in child abuse and neglect, 382–396
family, 376–382
television, 322, 323
Visitation, 113–114

AUTHOR INDEX

Abbard, K. E., 205
Abbott D. A., 38
Abelman, R., 322
Abelsohn, D., 108
Aber, J. L., 387
Abramovitch, R., 212, 271, 272
Achenbach, T. M., 265
Acock, A. C., 90, 120
Adams, J. W., 167
Adelson, J., 329
Adler, A., 220–221, 380
Adler, T., 249, 408, 409
Agostinelli, J., 406
Ahrons, C. R., 112, 115, 122
Ainsworth, M. D. S., 93, 205–207
Aksan, N., 145–147
Albrecht, S. L., 109
Aldous, J., 132, 133
Alessandri, S. M., 408
Alipuria, L. L., 240
Allen, B. P., 347, 348
Allen, J. A., 114, 122–126
Allen, J. P., 387
Allison, P. D., 115, 118, 121
Almeida, D. M., 406
Alpert-Gillis, L. J., 118
Alsaker, F. D., 332
Alvarez, L., 112
Alvarez, W. F., 86
Amabile, T. M., 317–318
Amano, I., 311
Amato, P. R., 17, 86, 115–117, 131, 229, 271, 299, 304
Ambert, A., 12, 14–16, 24, 126
Anderson, A. R., 346
Anderson, E. R., 114, 117, 121, 229
Anderson, K. E., 156, 162–163
Anderson, R. C., 313

Anderson, R. E., 238
Andersson, B., 412
Andrews, E. L., 323
Andrews, J. A., 346
Ankonina, D. B., 361, 364, 368
Antill, J. K., 405
Antonucci, T. C., 31
Apfel, N. H., 404
Apostal, R. A., 406
Applebaum, D. R., 289
Applebome, P., 6
Aquilino, W. S., 349
Ardelt, M., 17
Arditti, J. A., 85, 110
Aries, P., 12, 13, 15
Aristotle, 12
Armstrong, L., 92
Arnold, B. E., 280
Arsenia, W. F., 158
Arthur, M. W., 396
Ary, D., 346
Asendorpf, J. B., 270
Asher, S. R., 230
Ashley, P. K., 193
Asquith, P., 154–155
Atkinson, L., 364
Atkinson, M. P., 20, 88
Averill, P. M., 92
Avery, C. B., 330, 333–334
Awalt, S. J., 34
Axinn, W. G., 217
Azar, B., 63, 78, 270, 372, 413
Azmitia, M., 224
Azrin, N. H., 178

Baak, K., 76
Bachman, J. G., 240
Bachrach, C. A., 60, 61
Baden, A. D., 80–82
Bailey, D. B., 366
Baird, Z., 410
Baker, B. L., 366, 402
Baker, D. P., 313, 314
Baker, J. E., 286

Bakken, L., 340
Baldwin, B. A., 330
Baldwin, J. D., 173, 180
Baldwin, J. I., 173, 180
Baldwin, S. E., 340
Bales, J., 369, 395
Balka, E. B., 75, 206
Ballard, M., 272
Balleza, M., 383
Band, E. B., 280
Bandura, A., 83, 157, 191–192, 237, 245–246, 255–256, 275, 303
Bank, L., 125, 382
Baptiste, D. A., 342
Bar, O., 60, 61
Baranoski, M. V., 340
Baranowsi, M. D., 342
Barber, B. K., 217, 253, 347
Barglow, P., 407
Barich, R. R., 106
Barling, J., 386, 408
Barnard, K. E., 402
Barnes, M. L., 78, 79
Barnett, D., 387
Barnett, J. K., 340
Barnett, R. C., 88–90, 92, 93
Barnett, W. S., 366
Barnum, R., 385
Baron, L. A., 227
Barr, R. G., 171, 177, 178
Barratt, M. S., 79
Barret, R. L., 343
Barron, J., 348
Barry, H., 331
Baruch, G. K., 89, 90, 92
Basham, R. B., 58
Baskett, L. M., 222, 227
Bates, J. E., 17, 79, 80, 149, 165, 167, 231, 300, 304, 382
Baumrind, D., 70–72, 79, 82, 146, 152, 158,

160, 162, 231, 243, 303, 340
Bay, R. C., 112
Baydar, N., 407
Bayer, C. L., 25
Beach, L. R., 5, 7
Beal, C. R., 251, 254–256
Beaman, J., 77, 85–87, 125
Bearsdall, L., 225, 226
Beaty, L. A., 116
Beck, I. L., 313
Becker, W. C., 156
Becker-Lausen, E., 387
Beeghly, M., 386
Begin, G., 241
Behrman, R. E., 53
Beilke, R. L., 392
Bell, R. Q., 25, 167, 257
Belsky, J. B., 5, 25, 31, 33–36, 72, 74, 75, 78, 79, 84–86, 88, 91, 92, 94, 103, 105, 107, 109, 145, 158, 161, 204, 206, 207, 226, 227, 231, 278, 375, 385–389, 395, 405, 412–413
Bem, D. J., 185, 270
Bem, S. L., 255, 257
Bempechat, J., 309
Benasich, A. A., 402, 403
Bengston, V., 131
Benin, M. H., 406
Benn, R. K., 75
Bennett, D., 306
Benson, M. J., 85
Bentler, P. M., 346, 347
Bentley, K. S., 77, 86, 125, 163
Bentovim, A., 390, 392
Berger, J., 6, 383
Berger, S. H., 128, 131
Berk, L. E., 300
Berk, R. A., 93
Berk, S. F., 93

494